Lecture Notes in Computer Science 12555

Founding Editors

Gerhard Goos
  Karlsruhe Institute of Technology, Karlsruhe, Germany
Juris Hartmanis
  Cornell University, Ithaca, NY, USA

Editorial Board Members

Elisa Bertino
  Purdue University, West Lafayette, IN, USA
Wen Gao
  Peking University, Beijing, China
Bernhard Steffen
  TU Dortmund University, Dortmund, Germany
Gerhard Woeginger
  RWTH Aachen, Aachen, Germany
Moti Yung
  Columbia University, New York, NY, USA

More information about this subseries at http://www.springer.com/series/7409

Tien-Chi Huang · Ting-Ting Wu ·
João Barroso · Frode Eika Sandnes ·
Paulo Martins · Yueh-Min Huang (Eds.)

Innovative Technologies and Learning

Third International Conference, ICITL 2020
Porto, Portugal, November 23–25, 2020
Proceedings

Editors
Tien-Chi Huang
National Taichung University of Science
and Technology
Taichung City, Taiwan

João Barroso
University of Trás-os-Montes
and Alto Douro
Vila Real, Portugal

Paulo Martins
University of Trás-os-Montes
and Alto Douro
Vila Real, Portugal

Ting-Ting Wu
National Yunlin University of Science
and Technology
Douliou, Taiwan

Frode Eika Sandnes
Oslo Metropolitan University
Oslo, Norway

Yueh-Min Huang
National Cheng Kung University
Tainan City, Taiwan

ISSN 0302-9743   ISSN 1611-3349 (electronic)
Lecture Notes in Computer Science
ISBN 978-3-030-63884-9   ISBN 978-3-030-63885-6 (eBook)
https://doi.org/10.1007/978-3-030-63885-6

LNCS Sublibrary: SL3 – Information Systems and Applications, incl. Internet/Web, and HCI

© Springer Nature Switzerland AG 2020
This work is subject to copyright. All rights are reserved by the Publisher, whether the whole or part of the material is concerned, specifically the rights of translation, reprinting, reuse of illustrations, recitation, broadcasting, reproduction on microfilms or in any other physical way, and transmission or information storage and retrieval, electronic adaptation, computer software, or by similar or dissimilar methodology now known or hereafter developed.
The use of general descriptive names, registered names, trademarks, service marks, etc. in this publication does not imply, even in the absence of a specific statement, that such names are exempt from the relevant protective laws and regulations and therefore free for general use.
The publisher, the authors and the editors are safe to assume that the advice and information in this book are believed to be true and accurate at the date of publication. Neither the publisher nor the authors or the editors give a warranty, expressed or implied, with respect to the material contained herein or for any errors or omissions that may have been made. The publisher remains neutral with regard to jurisdictional claims in published maps and institutional affiliations.

This Springer imprint is published by the registered company Springer Nature Switzerland AG
The registered company address is: Gewerbestrasse 11, 6330 Cham, Switzerland

Preface

The International Conference of Innovative Technologies and Learning (ICITL 2020), is a platform provided for those who are working on educational technology to get together and exchange experience. Benefiting from using a variety of emerging innovative technologies, the e-learning environment has become highly diversified along the way. Diversified innovative technologies have fueled the creation of advanced learning environments by adopting appropriate pedagogies. Moreover, those technologies not only facilitate learning but also actively help students reach maximized learning performances. However, due to the rapid evolution of new technologies, how to make use of those technologies by complying with effective pedagogies to create adaptive or smart learning environments has always been in demand. Therefore, this conference intends to provide a platform for researchers in education, computer science, and educational technology to share experiences of effectively applying cutting-edge technologies to learning and to further spark brightening prospects. It is hoped that the findings of each work presented at the conference can enlighten relevant researchers and education practitioners to create more effective learning environments. ICITL is always ready to the public to share their works.

Due to the unfolding COVID-19 outbreak and travel restrictions, this year's conference was held virtually and interactively. Therefore, all accepted papers in each session were presented interactively in a virtual meeting room. This year, we received 127 submissions from 24 countries worldwide. After a rigorous double-blind review process, 65 papers were selected as full papers and 2 paper were selected as short papers, yielding an acceptance rate of 53%. These contributions cover the latest findings in the areas, including: 1) Application and Design of Innovative Learning Software; 2) Science, Technology, Engineering, Arts & Design, and Mathematics; 3) Augmented and Virtual Reality in Education; 4) Augmented and Virtual Reality in Education; 5) Educational Data Mining and Learning Analytics; 6) Emerging Issues and Trends in Education; 7) Innovative Learning in Education; 8) Online Course and Web-Based Environment; and 9) Technology-enhanced Learning. Moreover, ICITL 2020 featured two keynote presentations by renowned expert and scholars: Prof. Yi-Shun Wang and Prof. Carlos Fiolhais. They brought insight into Educational Technology Systems Success Models as well as Prophecies and Fulfilments in Computer-aided Education.

We would like to thank the Organizing Committee for their efforts and time spent to ensure the success of the conference. We would also like to express our gratitude to the Program Committee members for their timely and helpful reviews. And last but not least, we would like to thank all the authors for their contribution in maintaining a high-quality conference – we count on your continued support in playing a significant role in the Innovative Technologies and Learning community in the future.

November 2020

Yueh-Min Huang
João Barroso
Frode Eika Sandnes
Tien-Chi Huang
Paulo Martins
Ting-Ting Wu

Organization

Honorary Chairs

Yueh-Min Huang — National Cheng Kung University, Taiwan

Conference Co-chairs

João Barroso — University of Trás-os-Montes and Alto Douro, Portugal
Frode Eika Sandnes — Oslo Metropolitan University, Norway

Program Co-chairs

Tien-Chi Huang — National Taichung University of Science and Technology, Taiwan
Paulo Martins — University of Trás-os-Montes and Alto Douro, Portugal
Ting-Ting Wu — National Yunlin University of Science and Technology, Taiwan

Program Committee

Ana Balula — University of Aveiro, Portugal
Andreja Istenic Starcic — University of Ljubljana, Slovenia
António Coelho — University of Porto, Portugal
Arsênio Reis — University of Trás-os-Montes and Alto Douro, Portugal
Chantana Viriyavejakul — King Mongkut's Institute of Technology Ladkrabang, Thailand
Chi-Cheng Chang — National Taiwan Normal University, Taiwan
Claudia Motta — Federal University of Rio de Janeiro, Brazil
Constantino Martins — Polytechnic Institute of Porto, Portugal
Danial Hooshyar — University of Tartu, Estonia
Daniela Pedrosa — University of Aveiro, Portugal
Grace Qi — Massey University, New Zealand
Gwo-Dong Chen — National Central University, Taiwan
Hana Mohelska — University of Hradec Kralove, Czech Republic
Hanlie Smuts — University of Pretoria, South Africa
Hugo Paredes — University of Trás-os-Montes and Alto Douro, Portugal
João Pedro Gomes Moreira Pêgo — University of Porto, Portugal
José Cravino — University of Trás-os-Montes and Alto Douro, Portugal
José Alberto Lencastre — University of Minho, Portugal
Jun-Ming Su — National University of Tainan, Taiwan
Leonel Morgado — Universidade Aberta, Portugal

Lisbet Ronningsbakk — UiT The Arctic University of Norway, Norway
Manuel Cabral — University of Trás-os-Montes and Alto Douro, Portugal
Margus Pedaste — University of Tartu, Estonia
Paula Catarino — University of Trás-os-Montes and Alto Douro, Portugal
Paulo Martins — University of Trás-os-Montes and Alto Douro, Portugal
Qing Tan — Athabasca University, Canada
Rustam Shadiev — Nanjing Normal University, China
Satu-Maarit Frangou — University of Lapland, Finland
Shelley Shwu-Ching Young — National Tsing Hua University, Taiwan
Synnøve Thomassen Andersen — UiT The Arctic University of Norway, Norway
Tânia Rocha — University of Trás-os-Montes and Alto Douro, Portugal
Ting-Sheng Weng — National Chiayi University, Taiwan
Wu-Yuin Hwang — National Central University, Taiwan
Yi-Shun Wang — National Changhua University of Education, Taiwan
Yuping Wang — Griffith University, Australia

Technology Support

Yu-Cheng Chien — National Cheng Kung University, Taiwan
Pei-Yu Cheng — National Yunlin University of Science and Technology, Taiwan
Shih-Cheng Wang — National Cheng Kung University, Taiwan
Hsin-Yu Lee — National Cheng Kung University, Taiwan

Main Organizers

Co-organizers

Contents

Application and Design of Innovative Learning Software

A Model of a Cooperative Learning Technique in a Flipped International
Marketing Management Classroom 3
   Noviati Aning Rizki Mustika Sari and Ting-Ting Wu

Combining EEG Feedback on Student Performance and Self-efficacy 13
   Astrid Tiara Murti, Ting-Ting Wu, and Yueh-Min Huang

Design of Reciprocal Teaching-Collaborative Learning Approach
in Enhancing Students' Reading Comprehension Skill 23
   Olivia de H. Basoeki, Ting-Ting Wu, and Yueh-Min Huang

Mathematic Learning Efficiency Analysis of Story-Based Situated Learning
in Low-Achieving Elementary School Students 33
   *Chih-Wei Huang, Hong-Ren Chen, Sen-Chi Yu, Yi-Lun Su,
and Chia-Chen Chen*

Implementation of an Individual English Oral Training Robot System 40
   *Chen-Yu Lin, Wei-Wei Shen, Ming-Hsiu Michelle Tsai, Jim-Min Lin,
and Wai Khuen Cheng*

Pilot Study of Information Literacy Competency of the Elderly:
A Case Study of Multimedia Instant Messaging Applications 50
   Yi-Chen Lu and Ting-Ting Wu

Study on Development of Mobile App Design as Learning Media
in Student Internship Support: Toward Strengthening Tie and Realistic
Feedback in University-Industry Cooperation 59
   Andik Asmara and Ting-Ting Wu

Science, Technology, Engineering, Arts and Design, and Mathematics

3D Digital Design to Support Elementary School Students' Spatial
Visualization Skills: A Preliminary Analysis 71
   Pao-Nan Chou and Ru-Chu Shih

Developing the Scale of Technology Product Imagination Disposition 77
   Yi-Jin Wang, Hui-Min Lai, Tien-Chi Huang, and Pei-ling Chien

Development of a VR STEAM Welding Project Course 84
   Chih-Chao Chung, Chun-Chun Tung, Yuh-Ming Cheng, and Shi-Jer Lou

Enhancing Students' Learning Outcomes of a STEAM Permutations
Course Through a Game Based Visual Programming Environment
with Qualifying Rank Strategy 93
   Yu-Che Huang, Yueh-Ming Huang, and Andreja Istenic Starcic

A LUPDA Assessment Model for Activities in STEAM Education 100
   *Yu-Cheng Chien, Pei-Yu Chang, Hsin-Yu Lee, Tai-Yi Huang,
and Yueh-Min Huang*

Augmented and Virtual Reality in Education

A Testing Case of Simulation Learning in Nursing by Virtual Reality -
Subcutaneous Injection Training 109
   ChinLun Lai and Yu-mei Chang

Experiential Learning Through Controlling and Monitoring a Real-Time 3D
House Using LabVIEW in a Virtual Laboratory 119
   Bogdan M. Mîndruț and Claudiu A. Oprea

Students' Attitude Toward Learning and Practicing English in a VR
Environment 128
   Ying Ling Chen

The Impact of Applying Virtual Reality Technology to Spatial Ability
Learning in Elementary School Students 137
   Wen-Hung Chao and Rong-Chi Chang

Educational Data Mining and Learning Analytics

Competence Mining to Improve Training Programs 147
   Ildikó Szabó, Katalin Ternai, and Szabina Fodor

Personnel Learning Behavior in the Workplace: A Study of Workplace
Habits 158
   Waristha Saengrith, Chantana Viriyavejakul, and Paitoon Pimdee

Required English Communication Skill Levels of Mechanical Engineers
at the Workplace in Taiwan 167
   Judy F. Chen and Clyde A. Warden

Research on the Implementation Status and Learning Satisfaction
of Off-campus Internship Courses in the Department of Mechanical
Engineering of the University of Technology 172
   *Dyi-Cheng Chen, Hsi-Chi Hsiao, Jen-Chia Chang, Su-Chang Chen,
Kuo-Cheng Wen, Jia-Yue Guo, and Yu-Chen Gao*

Reviewing the Changes in Core Competencies for Undergraduates
in Technological Universities 182
    Jen-Chia Chang, Hsiao-Fang Shih, and Kuang-Ling Chang

Theoretical and Designing Framework of Constructivist Learning
Environment Model that Enhance Creative Thinking and Creative
Expression of Science for Medical Illustration Students 189
    Kan Komany and Sumalee Chaijaroen

Tracking At-Risk Student Groups from Teaching and Learning Activities
in Engineering Education...................................... 196
    Christopher Chung Lim Kwan

Where Are the Students? A Study of Norwegian Technology Students'
Perceptions of Emerging Trends in Higher Education 206
    Frode Eika Sandnes

Emerging Issues and Trends in Education

A Study of Learner's Computational Thinking Using Constructivist
Universal Design Learning Package for Kindergarten Education 219
    Chinnaphat Junruang and Issara Kanjug

Constructing an Information Search Platform Using Data Mining
to Improve Student Learning 227
    *Shu-Chen Cheng, Yu-Ping Cheng, Yueh-Min Huang,
    and I. Robert Chiang*

Digitalization of a Systematic Literature Review Process – Lean Startup
and Data Analytics Solution for Scholars........................... 236
    Zornitsa Yordanova

Effect of Facebook Use on Social Comparison Perceptions 245
    Fu-Rung Yang, Chih-Fen Wei, and Jih-Hsin Tang

Hands-on Statistical Methods: A Case Study with Hidden Markov Models
Using Simulations and Experiments............................... 255
    Steinar Thorvaldsen

Integrating Big Data in Introductory Statistics Education - Challenges
for Instructors and Students 263
    Jane Lu Hsu and You-Ren Chen

Integration of LUPDA Theory and STEAM with Computational Thinking
Concepts to Develop Assessment Principles for an AI Based STEAM
Activity 268
    Chih-Hung Wu and Yueh-Min Huang

Project Management for Innovation Projects – State of Art.............. 277
   Zornitsa Yordanova

Innovative Learning in Education

A Comparative Study on Ethics Guidelines for Artificial Intelligence Across Nations... 289
   Tony Szu-Hsien Lee, Shiang-Yao Liu, Yin-Ling Wei, and Li-Yun Chang

Analysis on the Application of AI Technology in Online Education Under the Public Epidemic Crisis...................................... 296
   Shuijing Li, Ming Yan, Xin Zhang, and Zhe Li

Design Aspects of a Virtual Reality Learning Environment to Assess Knowledge Transfer in Science...................................... 306
   Johanna Steynberg, Judy van Biljon, and Colin Pilkington

Research on Evaluation of Smart Learning Environment in Universities Based on AHP-FCE: A Case Study of Central China Normal University.... 317
   Zhicheng Dai, Mengting Wang, and Feng Liu

The Development of Simulation Web-Based Learning Environment to Enhance Ill-Structured Problem Solving for Engineering Students......... 328
   Thawach Thammabut, Sumalee Chaijaroen, and Suchat Wattanachai

The Study of Learner Context for the Development of Constructivist Learning Environment Model Combined with Mixed Reality Flipped Classroom to Enhance Creative Thinking in Product Design for the High School Students... 338
   Sathaporn Wongchiranuwat, Charuni Samat, Issara Kanjug, and Suchat Wattanachai

Transparent Player Model: Adaptive Visualization of Learner Model in Educational Games... 349
   Danial Hooshyar, Emanuele Bardone, Nour El Mawas, and Yeongwook Yang

Online Course and Web-Based Environment

A Study of Learner's Mental Model and Motivation Using Constructivism Online Learning Environment to Promote Programming in Rural School.... 361
   Poramin Attane and Issara Kanjug

Building an Online Learning Question Map Through Mining Discussion Content.. 367
   Hei Chia Wang and Ya Lan Zhao

Creating Interactive Non-formal Learning Opportunities
in Resource-Deprived Distant Learning Institutions 373
  Petra le Roux and Corné van Staden

Designing Framework of Constructivist Web-Based Learning Environment
Model to Enhance Creative Thinking in Engineering Design Process
for Grade 8th 385
  Pasatorn Puratep and Sumalee Chaijaroen

Designing Framework of Constructivist Web-Based Learning
Environments Model to Enhance Scientific Thinking for Secondary
Students. 391
  Autsanee Seenonlee Maneeratana and Sumalee Chaijaroen

Development of Constructivist Web-Based Learning Environment Model
to Enhance Problem-Solving and Transfer of Learning on Student
in Industrial: Integration Between Pedagogy and Neuroscience 399
  Chan Singkaew and Sumalee Chaijaroen

Digital Accessibility of Online Educational Platforms: Identifying Barriers
for Blind Student's Interaction 409
  Isolda Lisboa, João Barroso, and Tânia Rocha

Effect Analysis and Method Suggestions of Online Learning Under
the Public Epidemic Crisis 419
  Huimin Yuan, Ming Yan, and Zhe Li

Effective Blended Learning – A Taxonomy of Key Factors Impacting
Design Decisions 428
  Hanlie Smuts and Corlia Smuts

Effective Utilization of the Constructivist Web-Based Learning
Environment Model to Enhance Human Learning Efficiency Based
on Brain-Based Learning 442
  Wanwisa Wannapipat and Sumalee Chaijaroen

Effects of AI Scaffolding on ZPD in MOOC Instructional RPGs. 453
  Clyde A. Warden and Judy F. Chen

Survey Results of Learner Context in the Development of Constructivist
Learning Environment Model to Enhance Creative Thinking with Massive
Open Online Course (MOOCS) for Higher Education 465
  Benjaporn Sathanarugsawait, Charuni Samat, and Suchat Wattanachai

The Development of Constructivist Web-Based Learning Environments
to Enhance Learner's Information Processing and Reduce Cognitive Load . . . 475
  Nat Chaijaroen, Sarawut Jackpeng, and Sumalee Chaijaroen

Theoretical and Designing Framework of Constructivist Web-Based
Learning Environment Model to Problem Solving.................... 483
   Pitchaya Pimsook and Sumalee Chaijaroen

Technology-Enhanced Learning

A Study of Students' Context-Aware to Be Used as a Basis for Designing
and Developing a Model of Mobile-Based Learning Environment to
Enhance Computational Problem Solving in Programming for the High
School Students 493
   Kanyarat Sirimathep, Issara Kanjug, Charuni Samat,
   and Suchat Wattanachai

Assistive Technologies for Students with Dyslexia: A Systematic Literature
Review 504
   C. Smith and M. J. Hattingh

Assistive Technology for ADHD: A Systematic Literature Review 514
   Emily Black and Marie Hattingh

Chinese Students' Motivations to Adopt E-Learning 524
   James O. Stanworth

Designing Freirean-Inspired Community Relevant STEAM Curriculum
for Underserved Students in Pakistan Using Action Research Process 536
   Midhat Noor Kiyani, Imran Haider, and Fahad Javed

Digital Natives and Educational Traditions. What Changes When
Exchanging Textbook Content with Internet Search?................... 547
   Lisbet Rønningsbakk

Experiences Using Three App Prototyping Tools with Different Levels
of Fidelity from a Product Design Student's Perspective 557
   Amanda Coelho Figliolia, Frode Eika Sandnes, and Fausto Orsi Medola

How Engineering Design Ability Improve via Project-Based Truss Tower
STEM Course?... 567
   Wan-Hsuan Yen and Chi-Cheng Chang

Improving Student Learning Satisfaction in Lectures in English
as a Medium of Instruction with Speech-Enabled Language
Translation Application 576
   Rustam Shadiev, Narzikul Shadiev, Mirzaali Fayziev,
   and Yuliya Halubitskaya

Model of Technology Enhanced Affective Learning 582
   Satu-Maarit Frangou and Minna Körkkö

Outcomes of Problem-Solving Using Constructivist Learning Environment
to Enhance Learners' Problem Solving 591
   Sumalee Chaijaroen, Issara Kanjug, Charuni Samat,
   and Piyaporn Wonganu

Removing Digital Natives from Technological Illiteracy with the Weblog ... 598
   Michele Della Ventura

The Use of E-learning Tools and Log Data in a Course on Basic Logic..... 610
   Peter Øhrstrøm, Steinar Thorvaldsen, Ulrik Sandborg-Petersen,
   Thomas Ploug, and David Jakobsen

Towards a Knowledge Conversion Platform to Support Information
Systems Analysis and Design Industry Ready Graduates 621
   Marie Hattingh and Lizette Weilbach

Author Index 633

Application and Design of Innovative Learning Software

A Model of a Cooperative Learning Technique in a Flipped International Marketing Management Classroom

Noviati Aning Rizki Mustika Sari and Ting-Ting Wu[✉]

National Yunlin University of Science and Technology,
Yunlin 64002, Taiwan, R.O.C.
ttwu@yuntech.edu.tw

Abstract. The great changes in education have shifted the use of the traditional pedagogical approach to the techno-pedagogical approach. However, business or management education merely postulates the traditional one by the teacher-centered method. The techno-pedagogical approach will be designed to emphasize the use of flipped classroom and Jigsaw II cooperative learning approaches to optimize the learning process. Therefore, this research proposes a design of an innovative pedagogical model of teaching methodology with the Flipped-Jigsaw II Cooperative Learning approach in order to promote an effective learning environment of the International Marketing Management course which is later expected to activate the important skills as the element of the projected outcomes of the course. A deep interview has conducted to three interviewees in verifying the proposed model from the teachers' perspective. The result shows that the proposed model is projected to facilitate the learning process in order to attain the course's outcome better than the traditional ones.

Keywords: Jigsaw II cooperative learning · Flipped classroom · Design model of pedagogical approaches · International marketing management

1 Introduction

Business or management education merely postulates the traditional pedagogical approach by the teacher-centered method. Accordingly, the great changes in education are mainly caused by the use of technology [1] that has encouraged educational action improvement, increasing the motivation and availability of an extensive list of new pedagogical approaches [2, 3]. In order to stimulate students' autonomy, motivation, and interaction in the learning process, a new pedagogical approach should be applied, such as a techno-pedagogical approach [4–6].

The techno-pedagogical approach will be designed to emphasize the use of flipped classroom learning focusing on the use of time when students are outside the classroom to interact the content through digital platforms and tools generated by teachers [4] as it enables students and teacher to engage in both synchronous and asynchronous communication [7]. Jigsaw II cooperative learning approach as one of the cooperative learning techniques will be used to optimize the learning process throughout in-class activities as a part of the flipped classroom learning.

This research aims to propose a design of an innovative pedagogical model of teaching methodology with Flipped-Jigsaw II Cooperative Learning approach in order to promote an effective learning environment of International Marketing Management course which is later expected to activate the important skills as the element of the projected outcomes of International Marketing Management course.

These general suggestions lead to several specific questions to be discussed in this study on regard to the importance of the proposed pedagogical approaches.

RQ1. How is the design of the Flipped-Jigsaw II Cooperative Learning approach in promoting a better learning environment compared to the traditional pedagogical approach in the International Marketing Management course?

RQ2. How is the design of the Flipped-Jigsaw II Cooperative Learning approach likely to be implemented in an actual class?

RQ3. How do the teachers value the design of the Flipped-Jigsaw II Cooperative Learning approach?

2 Literature Review

2.1 Flipped Classroom

An approach called flipped classroom is considered as a form of blended learning combining two learning environments that are an in-class environment where the communication between teachers and students is face-to-face, and an out-of-class environment, an online environment [8]. It reflects a set of pedagogical approaches that (1) move most information-transmission in the teaching process out-of-class, (2) use class time on active and social learning activities, and (3) require students to complete pre and post-class activities to benefit from in-class activity [9, 10].

In the flipped classroom, teachers intend to transform the sequence of learning arrangements to be literally flipped, learners begin with a self-study phase before class that is normally supported by multimedia material in which they acquire knowledge at their own pace [11, 12]. It is able to free up valuable class time to promote more active learning and higher-level cognitive tasks [13–15].

Teachers will have pre-class materials prepared, such as online videos, online presentations, digital textbooks, etc. Switching up homework assignments and class time is aimed at providing more assistance to the students who demonstrate a lack of understanding and practice the setup skills from the course objectives. Teachers will be able to incorporate activities whose learning strategies promote higher-order thinking, social learning, and 21st-century skills [15, 16].

To conclude, flipped classroom learning involves the lower levels of learning in Bloom's taxonomy, in which remembering and understanding will occur outside the classroom at the student's own pace. While the higher levels of learning in Bloom's taxonomy, such as applying, analyzing, evaluating, and creating will occur inside the classroom.

2.2 Jigsaw II Cooperative Learning

Cooperative learning is able to optimize the cognitive, social, and affective outcomes of education [17, 18]. By learning cooperatively, it leads to the importance of support and mutual concern over the task within the group, which later enhance motivation on learning and increase students' academic achievement.

Jigsaw, one of the cooperative learning techniques, is based on group dynamics and social interaction. It is considered as one of the pure cooperative learning techniques [19]. The jigsaw technique allows students to actively participate in the learning process in which they are expected to feel more comfortable about their roles.

Jigsaw II was developed by Robert Slavin in 1980 as a variation of Jigsaw techniques in which home group members are assigned by the same materials but focus on different chunks of the materials. Besides increasing students' performance, it is projected to promote students' communication abilities and interpersonal relationships. Additionally, it allows students to focus on peer interaction and the cultivation of important abilities, for instance, critical thinking, problem-solving, and communication, independent thought, active exploration and research, clear expression, and teamwork [7].

2.3 International Marketing Management

Marketing turns out to be an integral aspect of modern society all over the world. Entire systems and social institutions that include culture, politics, entertainment, education, health care, religion, and others are affected by marketing processes, principles, and tactics. Since marketing extensiveness in modern international society is considered as an important practical and applied business subject, it is worthy of study as a pure scholarly subject as well [20].

Marketing educators tailor curriculum offerings to enhance students' knowledge and skills as required in the course outcomes. At the end of the learning process, students are expected to master the formation of abstract concepts, appreciation of cultural experiences, critical thinking, analytical skills, social and emotional judgment, independent thinking, leadership skills, and oral/written communication [21].

As discussed earlier, Jigsaw II cooperative learning combined with a flipped classroom are the proposed model of the pedagogical approaches designed to provide support and contribution to the International Marketing Management course.

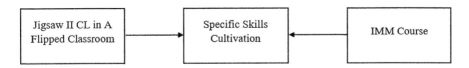

Fig. 1. The proposed pedagogical approaches and course outcomes linkage.

The overall course design is projected to facilitate the learning process in order to attain the goals or outcomes of the course. As illustrated in Fig. 1, there is a linkage between the benefits of the proposed pedagogical approaches and the goals or outcomes of the International Marketing Management course that contributes to the cultivation of specific skills, namely interpersonal relationship, communication abilities, critical thinking, problem-solving analytical skills, independent thought, and teamwork-leadership skills to be mastered by the learners.

3 Conceptual Model

3.1 A Conceptual Model Using a Flipped Classroom

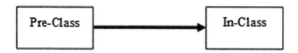

Fig. 2. Flipped classroom model.

Figure 2 adapted from a model proposed by [15] shows that flipped learning focuses on dividing its learning process into two different learning environments; home-based and school-based learning environments. Normally, teaching materials in the basic flipped classroom will be categorized by using online videos, online presentations, digital textbooks, and any other forms of media in order to enact them to be way more accessible to a home-based environment.

The process that takes place at home is called the pre-class. The pre-class session will begin with chunking and separating teaching materials by teachers into shorter online videos, shorter online presentations, split parts of a topic in digital textbooks, and any other divided forms of media. Online platforms will be used as the course management system in which teachers can distribute the materials to the students. Then, students will be requested to learn the provided teaching materials on their own, which means students will have a self-paced learning environment. Students are allowed to keep track of questions and concerns on which they need clarification [15].

The pre-class will be followed by an in-class session which will take place at school or later called a school-based environment. In-class session facilitates face-to-face class time in which students can use it to complete follow-up assignments as they come to the class by having the pre-class materials prepared. In this session, the old term of teacher-centered learning has shifted to student-centered learning as well as changing teachers' roles from "sage on the stage" to "guide on the side". Face-to-face instruction incorporates activities promoting higher-order thinking, social learning, and 21st-century skills cultivation [15, 16]. Moreover, the implementation of learning activities in-class encourages students' responsibility for operating both group and individual tasks.

3.2 A Conceptual Model Using Jigsaw II Cooperative Learning Approach

The Jigsaw II cooperative learning approach involves regular instructional stages of activities. There are six instructional stages of activities that should be conducted in the implementation [19], as shown in Fig. 3.

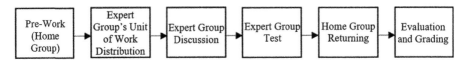

Fig. 3. Jigsaw II CL instructional stages of activities.

In this approach, each student needs to prepare a part of assignments outside the classroom or later described as pre-work. Students organize pre-work as they already assigned to groups. Each group represents a number of students that is called a home group and has an obligation to cover the assigned subject provided by teachers. The provided subject will be chunked into parts; thus, each member of the group will have a responsibility to learn and understand the assigned part given to him or her. Then, in the face-to-face class time, students will be split up from their original home group to gather up in a new form of the group with other students from different groups who are responsible for preparing the same parts of the assigned subject.

The new form of the group is called the expert group, in which students will have a discussion on regard to the parts of the assigned subject to make it way more understandable for each other. Also, they prepare a plan on how they teach the subject to their home group as well as preparing a report. Before going back to their home group, each student will be assigned in a test which aimed at verifying their knowledge and understanding the subject. The test can be performed in any kind of assessment format. Afterward, they turn back to their home group to teach their subject and contribute to preparing the report. In the last stage, teachers will facilitate learning activities by evaluating and grading.

3.3 Roles of the Proposed Pedagogical Approaches in International Marketing Management Course

The roles of the proposed pedagogical approaches with Jigsaw II cooperative learning and flipped classroom in the International Marketing Management course are analyzed through the proposed model, which is previously adjusted with referenced literature. The roles of both pedagogical approaches [7, 19, 22, 23] are explained in Table 1.

Table 1. Roles of the proposed pedagogical approaches.

No.	Flipped classroom	Jigsaw II cooperative learning
1	Students move at their own pace	Raise the interdependence of students and joint learning
2	Teachers have better insight into students' difficulties and learning styles in class	Enhance interaction, competition, cooperation, and research in the classroom
3	A more customize and update curriculum and a more effective and creative classroom time	Promote students' active participation and cooperation on their own roles
4	Increase the level of students achievement, interest, and engagement	Promote a sense of responsibility for students group performance
5	Learning theory supports the new approaches	Enhance the level of engagement and empathy
6	Appropriate technology usage for "21st-century learning", and so forth	Promote specific skills cultivation

4 Course Design with Jigsaw II Cooperative Learning Approach in a Flipped Classroom

4.1 Proposed Participants

This model of the Jigsaw II cooperative learning approach in a flipped classroom is designed to be implemented in the actual class of the International Marketing Management course. The proposed participant will be one to two one-semester period classes in a business or management department at a university, which includes one or more teachers and a number of students. In these two classes, new pedagogical approaches will be performed to support the learning activities in which teachers deliver the International Marketing Management course.

4.2 Overall Design Procedure

Figure 4 exhibits the overall design procedure of the proposed model using two pedagogical approaches; Jigsaw II cooperative learning and the flipped classroom. Since the course will be taught in the one-semester period, there are approximately eighteen meetings in which different topics of materials have been prepared by the teachers. This scenario of the proposed model will be applied in a week out of eighteen weeks with a selected topic to be discussed. The major concern of this proposed model is the learning environment offered; a self-paced at home and a student-centered at school.

Jigsaw II cooperative learning and flipped classroom will be combined together into a harmonized pedagogical approaches in supporting learning activities. In the implementation, the very first process is the pre-class session. Students who already assigned into groups are requested to perform an individual pre-work through a self-facilitated trajectory of teaching materials in the form of online videos prepared by teachers,

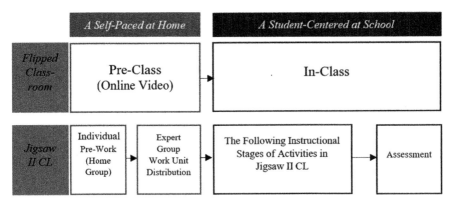

Fig. 4. Overall design procedure.

which are distributed over online platforms. Each group, later called home group, will divide the responsibility to cover a part of the chunked subject to each group member.

The following process is the in-class session. Students will have face-to-face class time at school with a student-centered learning environment. Students from original home groups will gather up in a new group called the expert group. In the expert group, students will perform discussions in order to make the assigned subject more understandable. Then, they will have a test before leaving the expert group aiming at verifying their knowledge and understanding over the subject. Students back to their original home group to teach other group members and help to prepare the report. In the end, teachers will facilitate the learning process to unify the class through evaluation and grading supported by designed assessment tools. Score as the result of the assessment will be given once to an individual student, then all group members' scores are averaged to generate a group score.

4.3 Teaching Materials and Assessment Design

Basically, the flipped classroom requires teachers to prepare teaching materials in advance. Teachers organize class management through online platforms to distribute teaching materials to the students outside the class. This proposed model adopts a design of flipped classroom by using online videos. One-week topic out of the one-semester course period will be chunked and separated into a much shorter video.

Since the proposed model will be conducted in a one-week topic out of the one-semester course period, formative assessment will be used as a proper assessment tool. Two stages in the Jigsaw II cooperative learning approach conducted in class require suitable assessment tools to perform an appropriate evaluation by using peer assessment and feedback to the team for expert group test stage and final report or presentation for evaluation and grading stage.

5 Result and Discussion

A deep interview has conducted to verify the proposed model of the Jigsaw II cooperative learning approach in a flipped International Marketing Management course. There are three interviewees who participated in the interview, as described in Table 2.

Table 2. General information of the interviewee.

No.	Participant	Teaching institution	Teaching period	Current teaching strategy
1	A	Jendral Soedirman University	4 yrs	Case study and discussion
2	B	Jakarta Global University	2 yrs	21st-century learning
3	C	Semarang State Polytechnic	29 yrs	Teamwork, discussion, and PBL

Three interviewees teach the International Marketing Management course in their institutions. They would be explained the overall design model using the Jigsaw II cooperative learning approach and the flipped classroom prior to the interview. Then, they would be questioned in the interview, which is divided into three sessions with fourteen questions in total. The first session of the interview is used to collect the interviewees' general information. While, the second and third sessions collect the interviewees' point of view toward the flipped classroom, Jigsaw II cooperative learning, and the proposed design of pedagogical approaches.

The results of the interview show that three interviewees agreed that flipping the learning process and using video lectures combined with Jigsaw II cooperative learning are excellent approaches to be implemented. They believe that it will benefit both teachers and students in accommodating learning activities and promoting higher-order thinking, students' autonomy, and learning effectiveness. Furthermore, they have the intention to apply these fascinating approaches since students will have variation in the learning process. However, they highlight the extra works teachers need to perform in order to prepare materials for the pre-class session, and the effectiveness of this approach may depend on the learning eagerness and readiness of both teachers and students.

6 Conclusions

The overall course design with the Jigsaw II cooperative learning approach in a flipped classroom is projected to facilitate the learning process in order to attain the goals or outcomes of the course better compared to the traditional pedagogical approaches. There is a linkage between the benefits of the proposed pedagogical approaches and the goals or outcomes of the International Marketing Management course that contributes to the cultivation of specific skills, namely interpersonal relationship, communication abilities, critical thinking, problem-solving analytical skills, independent thought, and teamwork-leadership skills to be mastered by the learners.

It is projected that the combination of both pedagogical approaches will work in harmony together and contribute to performing better learning activities in the International Marketing Management course from the teachers' perspectives. The overall course design promotes higher-order thinking. Moreover, this model is a prospect to be implemented for its roles in accommodating learning activities as well as optimizing cooperative learning. By these approaches, both teachers and students will be enriched with knowledge and skills. Also, this approach promotes students' engagement, creativity, activeness, self-efficacy, and autonomous learning.

Nonetheless, the learning eagerness and readiness of both teachers and students, as well as the teaching facilities, would contribute to the successful accomplishment of the proposed model. Teachers are advocated to perform extra works to have pre-class materials prepared and to concern about technology and computer literacy issues. However, it is projected that they will experience the benefit offered by this model as their critical roles in the classroom will be shifted to be a facilitator and won't be the ones who deliver the teaching materials to the students any longer. Moreover, this model plays an important role in optimizing cooperative learning and reducing the gap in students' knowledge and skills acquisition.

References

1. Hinojo Lucena, F.J., López Belmonte, J., Fuentes Cabrera, A., Trujillo Torres, J.M., Pozo Sánchez, S.: Academic effects of the use of flipped learning in physical education. Int. J. Environ. Res. Publ. Health (2019)
2. Álvarez-Rodríguez, M.D., Bellido-Márquez, M.d.C., Atencia-Barrero, P.: Teaching though ICT in obligatory secondary education. Analysis of Online Teaching Tools. Rev. Educ. a Distancia (2019)
3. Khine, M.S., Ali, N., Afari, E.: Exploring relationships among TPACK constructs and ICT achievement among trainee teachers. Educ. Inf. Technol. (2017)
4. Reidsema, C., Kavanagh, L., Hadgraft, R., Smith, N.: The Flipped Classroom Practice and Practices in Higher Education. Springer, Singapore (2017). https://doi.org/10.1007/978-981-10-3413-8
5. Ahmed, H.O.K.: Flipped learning as a new educational paradigm: an analytical critical study. Eur. Sci. J. (ESJ) (2016)
6. Zainuddin, Z., Halili, S.H.: Flipped classroom research and trends from different fields of study. Int. Rev. Res. Open Distance Learn (2016). https://doi.org/10.19173/irrodl.v17i3.2274
7. Huang, Y.-M., Liao, Y.-W., Huang, S.-H., Chen, H.-C.: A Jigsaw-based cooperative learning approach to improve learning outcomes for mobile situated learning. Educ. Technol. Soc. **17**, 128–140 (2014)
8. Almasseri, M., AlHojailan, M.I.: How flipped learning based on the cognitive theory of multimedia learning affects students' academic achievements. J. Comput. Assist. Learn. (2019)

9. Abeysekera, L., Dawson, P.: Motivation and cognitive load in the flipped classroom: definition, rationale, and a call for research. High. Educ. Res. Dev. (2015)
10. Strelan, P., Osborn, A., Palmer, E.: The flipped classroom: a meta-analysis of effects on student performance across disciplines and education levels (2020)
11. Lage, M.J., Platt, G.J., Treglia, M.: Inverting the classroom: a gateway to creating an inclusive learning environment. J. Econ. Educ. **31**, 30–43 (2000)
12. Sailer, M., Sailer, M.: Gamification of in-class activities in flipped classroom lectures. Br. J. Educ. Technol. (2020)
13. Kennedy, M.: Left to their own devices for education technology. Am. Sch. Univ. **84**, n9 (2012)
14. Roehl, A., Reddy, S.L., Shannon, G.J.: The flipped classroom: an opportunity to engage millennial students through active learning strategies. J. Fam. Consum. Sci. (2013)
15. Huang, C.K., Lin, C.Y.: Flipping business education: transformative use of team-based learning in human resource management classrooms. Educ. Technol. Soc. (2017)
16. Galway, L.P., Corbett, K.K., Takaro, T.K., Tairyan, K., Frank, E.: A novel integration of online and flipped classroom instructional models in public health higher education. BMC Med. Educ. (2014)
17. Slavin Robert, E.: Cooperative Learning: Theory, Research, and Practice. A Simon Schuster Co., Massachusetts (1995)
18. Ghaith, G.M., Bouzeineddine, A.R.: Relationship between reading attitudes, achievement, and learners' perceptions of their Jigsaw II cooperative learning experience. Read. Psychol. (2003)
19. Şahin, A.: Effects of Jigsaw II technique on academic achievement and attitudes to written expression course. Educ. Res. Rev. (2010)
20. Petkus Jr., E.: Enhancing the relevance and value of marketing curriculum outcomes to a liberal arts education. J. Mark. Educ. (2007)
21. Winter, D.G.: A new case for the liberal arts. Assessing Institutional Goals and Student Development. ERIC (1981)
22. Slavin, R.E.: Cooperative learning and student achievement: six theoretical perspectives. Adv. Motiv. Achiev. **6**, 161–177 (1989)
23. Herreid, C.F., Schiller, N.A.: Case studies and the flipped classroom. J. Coll. Sci. Teach. **42**, 62–66 (2013)

Combining EEG Feedback on Student Performance and Self-efficacy

Astrid Tiara Murti[1], Ting-Ting Wu[1], and Yueh-Min Huang[2(✉)]

[1] National Yunlin University of Science and Technology,
Yunlin 64002, Taiwan, R.O.C.
[2] Department of Engineering Science, National Cheng Kung University,
Tainan, Taiwan
huang@mail.ncku.edu.tw

Abstract. This study aims to investigate whether the feedback designed based on EEG (electroencephalography) signals and mind-mapping contributes to student attention, performance, and self-efficacy. The EEG headset was used to collect and measure the participant's attention levels. This study uses a mixed-methods of quasi-experimental design. The participants were 30 graduate students that randomly assigned to the control (non-feedback) group and experimental (with-feedback) group. A random grouping was used to divide the participants into two groups, control and experimental. The participants in experimental group will receive both negative and positive audio feedback. The research finding shows that the participants who receive the feedback had higher attention state and significant influence of self-efficacy compared to those in the groups without feedback. And the feedback does not influence the participant's performance. Meanwhile, participant's mind-maps score and performance between the two groups showed no significant influence. This study suggest for future studies, to explore the effect of different types of feedback on students attention.

Keywords: Electroencephalography · Feedback · Attention · Mind-maps · Performance · Self-efficacy · Plagiarism

1 Introduction

In the past, attention was measured using the attention scale and answered by participants to measure their concentrations. Nowadays, researchers use a physiological signal device named electroencephalography (EEG) to monitor and measure the changes in the participant's attention state [1, 2]. Depends on their states, different types feedback signals were given [2, 3]. The feedback can help the participants to be more conscious of the changes in their physiological states during the reading process, and help them to improve the conditions. Previous studies have shown that EEG feedback that is given according to participant's levels of attention can improve the attention in the reading process, which help them to achieve better reading performance [1, 3–5]. Besides paying attention during the reading task, the participants also need to organize the knowledge to generate ideas [6, 7]. Mind mapping is a note-taking method proposed by Tony Buzan in early 1970 that helps to distinguish words or ideas into a hierarchical tree format [8]. The mind mapping approach could be useful in developing cohesive and organized writing texts. The visual illustrations of mind maps assist with managing, though, directing learning, and making connections.

Plagiarism is a controversial problem among higher education students. It can be described as presenting someone else's work or ideas as your own, without their consent and full knowledge. The main concern is to acknowledge others' work or ideas not only to text but also to computer code, illustrations, graphs, etc. To avoid plagiarism, students demanded to learn the principles of good academic practice from the beginning of the study.

The purpose of the study is to investigate whether the feedback designed based on EEG (electroencephalography) signals and mind-mapping contributes to student attention, performance, and self-efficacy. This study aims to solve the following questions:

1. Does the feedback mechanism cause different brainwaves states in participants' attention?
2. Does the feedback mechanism contribute to student performance and self-efficacy?
3. Does mind-mapping contribute to student performance?

2 Literature Review

2.1 Sustained Attention and EEG Feedback

Maintaining attention among students during learning activity for an extended period of time is a challenging task [1]. The difficulty of concentrating is a significant cause of ineffective processes of learning, which include frequent inattentiveness and the inability to employ sustained attention [2]. Sustained attention is the ability to focus on specific stimuli in order to complete a task over a period of time [9]. If the students are inattentive while reading, they were likely to be impatient and distracted, as well as weaken their comprehension of the content.

EEG is a type of psychophysiological measurement used to examine the relationship between the physical and physiological processes. It was widely used in health and medical research, especially in epileptic seizures, sleep disorders, and attention-deficit/hyperactivity disorder (ADHD) [10]. In recent years, EEG has been put into other fields, including computer interfaces, computer game development, neuro-marketing research, and more rarely educational research.

In a study conducted by [4] and [2], the researchers used EEG feedback to help monitoring the participants while completing the reading task. Research related to the reading task often involves monitoring and measuring the attention level to achieve better learning outcomes. The feedback can be in the form of audio, visual, or a combination. Mostly the feedback were given in the form of audio voice, which is a less intrusive form of feedback, especially during learning activities. This study also uses audio feedback, which is a more appropriate choice for a reading task.

The feedback mechanism can be divided into two categories according to their purpose. Encouraging positive feedback is to inform participants that their current performances have reached or above the standard; studies shown that this type of feedback promote longer attention during tasks. Whereas the reminding negative feedback is to inform participants that their performance has not reached or lower than the standard, reminder feedback was used to promote higher level of attention and improve the reading performance [1–3]. This study attempted to explore whether providing audio feedback that give both reminding and encouraging the participants simultaneously would effectively improve their attention during reading process.

2.2 Mind-Mapping

A mind map is a non-linear visual tool for expressing ideas and the association between the ideas [8], which help students explicate their mental models [11]. It is a graphic organizer in which the major categories expand from a central point and lesser categories portrayed as tree branches. Mind mapping is a visual technique that presents the knowledge, ideas, concepts, and the relationship between them in an individual's mental construction [12]. A simple and brief process of structure knowledge presentation [13].

The mind map is a kind of divergent thinking tool. It could be applied in brainstorming and create an association with something. In a study conducted by [6] the mind map strategy can help the participants identify the main ideas of reading texts, visualize and externalize their understanding, and develop summaries. [7] used mind map tools to help students grabs the concept of reading tasks more effectively, especially within a gaming environment. Past research shown that mind-mapping has an impact on student learning performance [7, 14].

2.3 Feedback, Performance, and Self-efficacy

Self-efficacy refers to the confidence level of oneself to successfully complete a particular task [15]. [16] commented that the confidence in doing the task and the expectation of success will directly influence the willingness to make an effort, and the motivation to endure when faced on learning difficulties. Most research that explore the relationship between EEG biofeedback and self-efficacy commonly in the domains of medical research [10]. A study conducted by [17] found that applying a feedback of electrodermal activities can promote additional feeling of self-efficacy during work-out. In contrary, the research done by [2] shows a different result, where participants' self-efficacy and achievement between the two groups show no significant differences.

The majority of studies on feedback indicates that a timely and appropriate type of feedback during the learning process can significantly improve the learning performance. Moreover, feedback can aid the participants in maintaining a better self-regulating behavior, thus leading to higher learning performance [2, 18]. This study was expected that the feedback mechanism will promote the self-regulating behavior in participants, so they can readily adjust their learning states and improving their performance and self-efficacy.

2.4 Plagiarism Education

Research was conducted to produce knowledge that able to improve human situations. Unfortunately, during the creation of knowledge, there happens to be scientific misconduct. Most of the academic scholars agree that plagiarism is a serious violation of research ethics. Oxford English Dictionary defines the word "plagiarize" as an act of fraud that involves copying or incorporating someone else's work or ideas without acknowledging the sources [19]. Plagiarism is a controversial issue in higher education and its increasingly widespread among students [20]. No doubt, the challenges in academic activities are due to the increasing number of students and the progress of information technology.

In order to prevent plagiarism among students and young researchers, training, and education on how to detect and avoid plagiarism are needed. The students must take the initiative to search for internet information to acquire knowledge. Fortunately, some universities provided a free access website and courses to learn about plagiarism and how to avoid it, although the use of it is yet to be maximized. The instructional materials of plagiarism were a collection of information from various resources that can aids in developing a more comprehensive ideas of plagiarism. Combining the reading material and feedback mechanism can facilitate the students' depth understanding of the reading topic. [1] mention that the sustained attention can be enhance using negative feedback mechanism that also enhance the self-efficacy [21].

3 Methods

3.1 Instruments

The instrument used in this research can be categorized into 3 types, such as experimental, quantitative, and qualitative tools. The experimental tools included portable EEG headsets that was developed by NeuroSky Inc, a feedback mechanism, plagiarism instructional materials, and mind mapping tool. The portable EEG headsets is a type of non-invasive brainwave sensor that can accurately reads the mindwave [10]. The EEG headsets then connected to the computers, where a specific computer program has been prepared to translate the signal into attention values [3]. The range of attention is between 0 to 100; the higher the value, the more concentrated the participant.

The plagiarism instructional materials used in this study was a compilation and summary of plagiarism information from various websites. The plagiarism instructional material content includes the definition of plagiarism, and why it is unethical; the types of plagiarism; how to avoid it; the importance of citations, references, and acknowledging other's work. This study used a mind-mapping mobile software named SimpleMind Lite installed in a tablet device for more easy use. The scoring system of mind-maps developed by [12] was used to calculate the score of mind-maps.

The quantitative tools consist of self-efficacy scale and plagiarism test, and an open-ended questionnaire for qualitative tool. The self-efficacy sub-scale of Motivated Strategies for Learning Questionnaire (MSLQ), developed by [22] was used. There was a total of 8 questions, and a 5-point Likert Scale was applied. The plagiarism test was compiled by the researcher to assess how well the participants understand the material.

A total of 5 items were asked. The open-ended questionnaire content for the experimental group, asking their feeling about the equipment, the experimental mechanism, and the state of their mind when receiving the feedback. While the questionnaire content for control group only asking about their feelings toward the equipment and experimental mechanism.

3.2 Experiment Procedure

As per the purpose of this study, to explore the impacts of the feedback and performance, the Indonesian graduate students in Yuntech were invited to partake in the experimental study. The students took turns in determining the sequence of participating. If the first student participates in a non-feedback condition, the next one will participate in feedback condition, and continue to take turns.

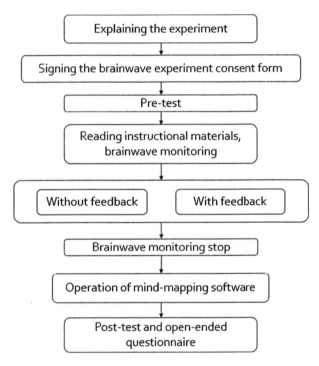

Fig. 1. The experimental procedure.

The experimental procedure process, as shown in Fig. 1, was similar to the experiment done by [2]. First, the researcher give an explanation about the procedure and the content of experiment to the participants. Continued by signing the con-sent form and perform the pre-test task. Followed by the experiment activity where participants required to wear the EEG headsets. The activity involve reading the plagiarism instructional materials. The audio feedback would be given only to the experimental group, and not for the control group. The experimental group would receive both the encouraging and reminding feedback, the audio feedback of "Please pay attention!" provided when an individual brainwave indicated low concentration (attention < 40, and lasted for 5 s), while the audio feedback of "You are doing great!" will be provided when the brainwaves showed a very high concentration (attention > 60 and lasted for 5 s). When the reading task was completed, the participants were requested to make a mind-map according to the reading materials. Afterwards, the post-test, performance test, and open-ended questionnaire were filled out.

4 Result

4.1 Analysis of Attention Measured by EEG

ANOVA analysis was used to measure whether the feedback mechanism cause different brainwaves states in participants. The results of attention are shown in Table 1.

Table 1. ANOVA result of attention.

Group	N	Mean	SD	F	P
Control	15	46.30	5.50	5.341	.028
Experiment	15	59.93	11.54		

The ANOVA result of attention when reading the instructional materials ($F = 5.341, p = 0.028$), showed that there were significant differences between the two groups of participants. It means that providing a timely audio feedback when there were changes in the attention state during the reading process can significantly improve the attention.

4.2 Analysis of Mind-Maps

The mind-maps was assessed using the scoring system developed by [12]. The score then was analyze using ANOVA analysis to measure there is a differences of mind-maps score between two groups (Table 2).

Table 2. ANOVA result of mind-maps score.

Group	N	Mean	SD	F	P
Control	15	126.53	69.98	.517	.478
Experiment	15	110.53	50.33		

The ANOVA result for mind-maps score ($F = 0.517, p = 0.478$) shows that there were no significant differences between the two groups of participants. Which can be seen from the mean result that the control group has better performance than the experiment group.

4.3 Analysis of Self-efficacy and Performance

ANCOVA analysis was used to measures the differences of self-efficacy between two groups, while ANOVA analysis was applied to measure the differences in performance scores.

The pre-test mean scores for the control group were 3.95, with the standard deviation was 0.523, while the post-test mean scores were 4.03, and with the standard deviation was 0.424. Furthermore, the pre-test mean scores for the experimental group were 3.8, with the standard deviation was 0.406, while the post-test mean scores were 4.21, and with the standard deviation was 0.333. The ANCOVA analysis was performed for comparing the self-efficacy between-groups. The result disclose that the post-test score between the two groups showed a significant difference ($F = 4.4913$, $p = 0.35$). It implies that the self-efficacy for learning about plagiarism can be influenced by the feedback. Table 3 exhibit the ANOVA result of performance test ($F = 0.160$, $p = .692$), that shows no significant differences between two groups. Its mean that the feedback given to the participants did not able to influence their performance.

Table 3. ANOVA result of performance test

Group	N	Mean	SD	F	p
Control	15	81.33	17.67	.160	.692
Experiment	15	84.00	18.82		

4.4 Analysis of Open-Ended Questionnaire

The open-ended questionnaire was used to explore the participant's feelings regarding this study. The questions for the two groups can be categorized as "the feeling about the experimental mechanism", "the feeling about the equipment", and "the feeling about the reading materials"; while the experimental group receive an additional question of "what are they doing when receiving the feedback."

The result of "the feeling about the experimental mechanism", both the experimental and control groups, participant believe that the experiment had an effect on their attention states. It makes them more focused when reading. Most participants were enthusiastic about participating as this is their first time being part of the experiment, and the first time using EEG headsets. When asked about their "feeling about the equipment", whether it is using the EEG headsets and the mind-maps tool, the participants from both groups give a similar answer. They thought that wearing the EEG headsets was uncomfortable, especially for women, as they need to adjust their hijab constantly. Meanwhile, for the mind-map tool, the participants are not accustomed to using the mobile version and need to take time to be more accustomed. Regarding the "feeling about the reading materials", the participants believe that the reading material will help them avoid plagiarism. The additional questions to the experimental group of "what are they doing when receiving the feedback" were answered as absentmindedly thinking unrelated things to the instructional materials (reminder feedback) and paid more attention to their reading (encouraging feedback).

5 Discussion

The aim of this study was to explore the effects of providing an audio feedback on participant's attention, mind-maps, self-efficacy, and performance. The results reveal that (1) the feedback cause a higher attention value and significant influence of self-efficacy compared to the group with no feedback; (2) the feedback does not have a significant influence on the performance and the mind-maps score; and (3) using mind-maps does not necessarily influence student performance.

The findings showed that the average attention states of the experimental group were adhere with previous research that providing feedback to the students during inattentiveness can help maintain better attention [1–3, 23]. The study also found that the self-efficacy between two groups were significant different. This probably due to the types of adopted feedback is both encouraging and reminding. When they receive the encouraging feedback, the participants get a sense of pleasure. While the moment they receive the reminding feedback, the participants will tried to maintain better concentration.

Other than that, the exclusiveness of plagiarism topic, resulting in the similar result for participant's performance and mind-maps scores. Plagiarism is very important topic for the graduate students, who become the participants in this study. Thus the novel feeling for the special topic of plagiarism can arise. The answer to the open-ended questionnaire was indistinguishable between the two groups. The participants from both groups feel that wearing the EEG was uncomfortable and need longer time to be accustomed of using one. The researcher expected that a novel feeling of participating in this study plays a significant role in their response.

6 Conclusion

From this study we can conclude that, the participants who receive the feedback have higher attention value and significant influence of self-efficacy compared to those in the groups without feedback. And the feedback does not influence participants' performance and mind-maps score. Furthermore, the researcher believes that a novel feeling of participating in this study plays significant role in their performance, seeing that this is their first time participating in experiment study and wearing EEG Mindset. This study focused on the graduate university student, and the topic of plagiarism. The topic of plagiarism was very special and indispensable in academic practice; thus it also plays significant role for the participants. It is suggested that for future research to use greater number of participants; use different subject learning; and comparing how different types of feedback can influence the attention.

References

1. Chen, C.M., Huang, S.H.: Web-based reading annotation system with an attention-based self-regulated learning mechanism for promoting reading performance. Br. J. Educ. Technol. (2014). https://doi.org/10.1111/bjet.12119
2. Sun, J.C.Y., Yeh, K.P.C.: The effects of attention monitoring with EEG biofeedback on university students' attention and self-efficacy: the case of anti-phishing instructional materials. Comput. Educ. (2017). https://doi.org/10.1016/j.compedu.2016.12.003
3. Yang, X., Lin, L., Cheng, P.Y., Yang, X., Ren, Y.: Which EEG feedback works better for creativity performance in immersive virtual reality: the reminder or encouraging feedback? Comput. Hum. Behav. (2019). https://doi.org/10.1016/j.chb.2019.06.002
4. Lin, C.S., Lai, Y.C., Lin, J.C., Wu, P.Y., Chang, H.C.: A novel method for concentration evaluation of reading behaviors with electrical activity recorded on the scalp. Comput. Methods Prog. Biomed. (2014). https://doi.org/10.1016/j.cmpb.2014.02.005
5. Kuo, Y.C., Chu, H.C., Tsai, M.C.: Effects of an integrated physiological signal-based attention-promoting and English listening system on students' learning performance and behavioral patterns. Comput. Hum. Behav. (2017). https://doi.org/10.1016/j.chb.2017.05.017
6. Yang, Y.F.: Automatic scaffolding and measurement of concept mapping for EFL students to write summaries. Educ. Technol. Soc. (2015)
7. Fu, Q.K., Lin, C.J., Hwang, G.J., Zhang, L.: Impacts of a mind mapping-based contextual gaming approach on EFL students' writing performance, learning perceptions and generative uses in an English course. Comput. Educ. (2019). https://doi.org/10.1016/j.compedu.2019.04.005
8. Chang, J.H., Chiu, P.S., Huang, Y.M.: A sharing mind map-oriented approach to enhance collaborative mobile learning with digital archiving systems. Int. Rev. Res. Open Distance Learn. (2018). https://doi.org/10.19173/irrodl.v19i1.3168
9. Ko, L.W., Komarov, O., Hairston, W.D., Jung, T.P., Lin, C.T.: Sustained attention in real classroom settings: an EEG study. Front. Hum. Neurosci. (2017). https://doi.org/10.3389/fnhum.2017.00388
10. Xu, J., Zhong, B.: Review on portable EEG technology in educational research. Comput. Hum. Behav. (2018). https://doi.org/10.1016/j.chb.2017.12.037
11. Malycha, C.P., Maier, G.W.: The random-map technique: enhancing mind-mapping with a conceptual combination technique to foster creative potential. Creat. Res. J. (2017). https://doi.org/10.1080/10400419.2017.1302763
12. Evrekli, E., Inel, D., Balim, A.G.: Development of a scoring system to assess mind maps. In: Procedia - Social and Behavioral Sciences (2010)
13. Wu, T.T., Chen, A.C.: Combining e-books with mind mapping in a reciprocal teaching strategy for a classical Chinese course. Comput. Educ. (2018). https://doi.org/10.1016/j.compedu.2017.08.012
14. Hwang, G.J., Yang, L.H., Wang, S.Y.: A concept map-embedded educational computer game for improving students' learning performance in natural science courses. Comput. Educ. (2013). https://doi.org/10.1016/j.compedu.2013.07.008
15. Bandura, A.: Self-efficacy: toward a unifying theory of behavioral change. Psychol. Rev. (1977). https://doi.org/10.1037/0033-295X.84.2.191
16. Bandura, A.: Self-efficacy mechanism in human agency. Am. Psychol. (1982). https://doi.org/10.1037/0003-066X.37.2.122

17. Teufel, M., et al.: Impact of biofeedback on self-efficacy and stress reduction in obesity: a randomized controlled pilot study. Appl. Psychophysiol. Biofeedback. (2013). https://doi.org/10.1007/s10484-013-9223-8
18. Zimmerman, B.J.: A social cognitive view of self-regulated academic learning. J. Educ. Psychol. (1989). https://doi.org/10.1037/0022-0663.81.3.329
19. Plagiarism | University of Oxford. https://www.ox.ac.uk/students/academic/guidance/skills/plagiarism
20. Awasthi, S.: Plagiarism and academic misconduct: a systematic review. J. Libr. Inf. Technol. (2019). https://doi.org/10.14429/djlit.39.2.13622
21. Schunk, D.H., Swartz, C.W.: Goals and progress feedback: effects on self-efficacy and writing achievement. Contemp. Educ. Psychol. (1993). https://doi.org/10.1006/ceps.1993.1024
22. Pintrich, P.R.R., Smith, D., Garcia, T., McKeachie, W.: A manual for the use of the Motivated Strategies for Learning Questionnaire (MSLQ). Ann Arbor. Michigan. (1991). https://doi.org/ED338122
23. Chen, C.M., Wang, J.Y., Yu, C.M.: Assessing the attention levels of students by using a novel attention aware system based on brainwave signals. Br. J. Educ. Technol. (2017). https://doi.org/10.1111/bjet.12359

Design of Reciprocal Teaching-Collaborative Learning Approach in Enhancing Students' Reading Comprehension Skill

Olivia de H. Basoeki[1], Ting-Ting Wu[1], and Yueh-Min Huang[2(✉)]

[1] Graduate School of Technological and Vocational Education,
National Yunlin University of Science and Technology, Douliu, Taiwan
d10843012@gemail.yuntech.edu.tw, ttwu@yuntech.edu.tw
[2] Department of Engineering Science, National Cheng Kung University,
Tainan, Taiwan
huang@mail.ncku.edu.tw

Abstract. Reading comprehension is one of the English language abilities for academic learning and as a crucial component of lifelong learning. Through reading, students will develop themselves and achieve progress in every aspect of their life. Referring to the importance of reading, appear the question of how to improve students' reading comprehension skills. Therefore, teachers should develop their method effectively and use appropriate learning strategies independently to improve students' reading comprehension skills. One best strategic method to develop reading comprehension skills is the reciprocal teaching. Therefore, this study was preliminary research to obtain perceptions about the design of reciprocal teaching combine with collaborative learning in large classes. This study conducted a qualitative approach to collect some perceptions from the English expert. The participants were English teachers of Polytechnic in Indonesia. Then, the result of the study was students predicted more interactive, communicative, active group discussion, critical thinking, motivation, leadership, and cooperation.

Keywords: Reciprocal teaching (RT) · Collaborative learning (CL) · Reading comprehension

1 Introduction

Generally, there are four abilities that should be mastered by language learners in learning a language, namely reading, listening, speaking, and writing. Reading comprehension is one of the English language skills for academic learning and a crucial component of lifelong learning [1]. It became necessary for students' personal development as an individual to improve their value of life. That is why reading taught at every level of education, from elementary to university. Through reading, students will develop themselves and achieve progress in every aspect of their life. As the saying goes, that book is a window of science; by reading, people know any various information throughout the entire world, both about history, science, and other essential things.

The primary goals of the reading process are to gain understanding, or comprehension, counterbalance knowledge related to the textual information, and its interpretation [2–4]. Students cannot escape from reading in their daily activities. They are surrounded by so many reading materials every day. By reading activities, students get benefits for themselves, such as build a better vocabulary, lights up new ideas, improve language skills, get new knowledge, think critically, and better writing skills. Referring to the importance of reading, appear the question of how to improve students' reading comprehension skills. Teachers must use reading strategies effectively to help students learn to apply reading comprehension strategies independently.

Therefore, teachers should develop their method and use appropriate learning strategies to improve students' reading comprehension skills. The excellent learning strategy is the teacher's role in shaping students into quality figures of science, independence, democracy, and responsibility. It is related to the learning strategy according to Oxford [5] that through the specific actions, the learner can create learning more accessible, faster, enjoyable, self-directed, effective, and move transferrable to new situations. Experts introduce the various strategy of developing reading comprehension skills. One type of them is the reciprocal teaching strategy [6]. This teaching strategy is in the form of multiple comprehension strategy usages that combine four thinking techniques: predicting, clarifying, questioning, and summarizing. Reciprocal teaching becomes one of the best strategic methods in teaching reading [7]. Many different studies have been carried out to show the effectiveness of using its strategies [8–10].

One of the theories states that the positive results of reciprocal teaching more useful while applied it with a small sample size [11]. This statement encourages the researcher to try to use reciprocal teaching to combine with collaborative learning in large classes. Since the English subject at universities is taught in large classes so that to reduce the potential of some students not being active in learning reading, reciprocal teaching-collaborative learning be used to know its effectiveness in large classes.

Moreover, the reason for using the collaborative learning strategy is to form groups so that intertwined teamwork among the students to comprehend English text in a short duration of time. Yet, this research has not been carried out. It is still in the form of a design or preliminary investigation. The purpose of this study was to examine the model by giving the leads in advance in order to make the students easier to comprehend the basic ideas of the text, developing questions about the passage, and also summarizing the primary information of the reading text as the project outcome. Specifically, the research question was how the design of reciprocal teaching-collaborative learning approach in enhancing students' reading comprehension skills based on the experts' point of view is?

2 Literature Review

2.1 Reading Comprehension

The definition of reading is a particular way by which the meaning of written text understood [12], the process of receiving and interpreting information through the print media, and a powerful means of sharing information with others through understanding written texts [13]. Reading becomes part of people's activity. People read newspapers, reports, books, notes, journals, and many other writings to increase their knowledge.

Reading comprehension is the competence to understand text, purpose, and to integrate with what the reader already knows [7], or connection of previous knowledge [14]. Deep comprehension needs more than mere interpretation of single words, phrases, sentences, and entails aware attempts from the readers to collect related information from the text and produce them into the meaning of the whole text.

2.2 Reciprocal Teaching (RT)

Reciprocal teaching is known as the instructional method in enhancing reading comprehension skills [15] designed by Palinscar and Brown [6] to meet the needs of learners who were robust decoders but with weak comprehension skills. It is the approach that teachers and students exchange the role in leading a dialogue of the text. According to Palincsar and Brown's study in 1984, reciprocal teaching has four major approaches: predicting, clarifying, questioning, and summarizing [6]. This method can help students to increase their ability in reading comprehension.

Reciprocal teaching provides students with four specific reading strategies. In the predicting, students must activate the relevant background knowledge they already possess to the text they are working on. Questioning gives a student the opportunity to identify their understanding of the text by making questions as a self-testing [6]. Clarifying has a purpose to train students to identify and analyze the unclear, complicated, or unfamiliar words, phrases of a text. Then, summarizing is the process of distinguishing between important and unimportant information in the text.

2.3 Collaborative Learning (CL)

Collaborative learning is an approach in teaching strategy that involving a small group of learners work together to figure out a problem, or fill out the task [16]. In the collaborative learning atmosphere, students are challenged to listen to different perspectives, begin to develop their idea, and not depend on an expert's or a text's scheme.

Students have the chance to discuss with their classmates, develop information exchange, asking other ideas, giving feedback, and be actively involved. In collaborative classrooms, teacher-centered or lecture-centered is the shift away. The process of learning concentrates on students' discussion about the subject material. Teachers become a coach or instructor in the learning atmosphere than an expert to the learners [17].

3 Research Design

This paper was conducting a qualitative research approach. The characteristic of qualitative research involves collecting and analyzing data in order to understand theories, assumptions, or experiences [18]. The most common qualitative methods are observation, interview, focus group, survey, and secondary research.

3.1 Participants

The six English teachers from several Polytechnics in Indonesia were involved in the interview (Table 1).

Table 1. List of participants.

No.	Participants	Position	Polytechnic
1.	P (1)	Head of the Language Centre	Shipping State Polytechnic of Surabaya
2.	P (2)	Secretary of English Dept.	State Polytechnic of Sriwijaya Palembang
3.	P (3)	Head of the Language Centre	State Polytechnic of Banjarmasin
4.	P (4)	English teacher	State Polytechnic of Ujung Pandang
5.	P (5)	Head of the Language Centre	State Polytechnic of Jakarta
6.	P (6)	English teacher	Kupang State Polytechnic

3.2 Data Collection

Interviews were conducted from several participants of English teachers to obtain data or respondent information related to the recent study of the research questions. The interview was conducted by a question and answer to get information or opinions on a specific matter [19]. The interview guideline includes participants' views on the weaknesses, strengths, and suggestions in the implementation of reciprocal teaching-collaborative learning design.

3.3 Data Analysis

The grounded theory is used to analyze the researcher's findings. Grounded theory research design is a set of procedures used to arrange a theory that explains the process of an important topic [20]. Data in grounded theory can be collected through interviews, observation, recording, or a combination of these methods [21].

4 Findings

4.1 Proposed Design

The method used in this research, quasi-experimental design study. It is aimed to examine the amalgamation effectiveness of reciprocal teaching-collaborative learning in enhancing students' reading comprehension skills. The detailed of reciprocal teaching-collaborative learning implementation procedure is shown in Fig. 1. The design will be conducted in the academic year of 2020/2021 at Kupang State Polytechnic (PNK), East Nusa Tenggara-Indonesia. The class will be held for eight meetings, including pre-test and post-test sessions.

The subject will be the third semester of the Electrical Engineering Department of PNK. Since the students have already got two semesters in English subjects, and they can be assumed to have the same level. Then, the design will be applied in two classes.

Each class will consist of 35 students, so the total is 70 students with the same English subject, and the students have a homogeneous English proficiency level. These two classes will assist by the same English teacher. The reason is there are no differences in the assessment and teacher treatment of the two groups.

Two instruments are existing in this design, the pre-test, and the post-test. The pre-test is used to measure students' performance before reciprocal teaching treatments to both groups. Then, the post-test will be conducted after reciprocal teaching treatments to both groups. The reading comprehension pre-and post-test are consisting of the reading passage in the ESP field, which is composed of multiple-choice, true-false, and matching. The reading comprehension text of the post-test will different from the pre-test.

4.2 Proposed Experimental Procedure

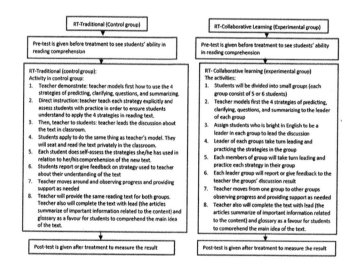

Fig. 1. Experimental procedure.

Each class will be treated about the four thinking strategies of reciprocal teaching. The detail of four procedures:

Predicting. It helps students to link new ideas to prior knowledge by using cues from the text, such as the title, illustrations, subtitles, and diagrams, to find a purpose for reading. Students learn to guess what the author will discuss and then confirm or disprove it.

Clarifying. When students are asked to clarify, they are taught to focus on unfamiliar or new words, new or difficult ideas, unusual passages or paragraphs, and loss of meaning. In clarifying, the students are encouraged to take necessary steps such as rereading, using a dictionary, atlas, or other resources asking for help, or asking if others need anything clarified.

Questioning. It gives students' opportunity to identify kind of information that provides the basis of a good question, develop a question, find the facts that will enable them to answer their questions, and help other students to answer questions. It also a self-testing and encourage students being active in the reading activity.

Summarizing. Students try to identify the most crucial content of the paragraph or section of the text, then combine relevant information in the whole passage. Summarizing is a useful skill for remembering, studying, and self-review (Table 2).

Table 2. Example of reciprocal activity.

Procedure	Activities example
Teacher:	Could you please read to …
Predicting:	I **predict** that … will occur next; I assume that the next section will be about …
Clarifying:	Does anybody need anything **clarified**? Is there something you would like to share? I'd love to find out about … Means; What is this word?
Questioning:	My **question** is …; What, Where, When, Which, Why, Who, How
Summarizing:	The paragraph is about …; Could you please **summary** is …
Can you be the next 'teacher' please …	

5 Discussion

This research is preliminary research before the actual research is carried out. Evaluating whether the design is useful and can be implemented it takes participants' opinions. The perception of participants about reciprocal-collaborative learning design in enhancing students' reading comprehension skills will be described. Generally, there are some strengths and weakness from the participants' point of view. They also give suggestions to make the design more acceptable.

Based on the participants' perception, the reciprocal teaching-collaborative learning design will effective in helping students comprehend reading. In a group, students help each other to learn. The members of the group have to achieve the goal of a course. The evidence from participants that say:

> … *"In-group, the student, searching for understanding, solution, or meanings (P1), they work as a team to solve the problem (P2), there is mutual cooperation (P3), work together to complete the assignment (P4), they talk to each and through the talk that learning occurs (P5), and togetherness to learn something (P6) …"*

The perception above supported by many previous studies on reciprocal teaching that show the effectiveness in reading comprehension [8, 9] as well as many studies also indicate that collaborative learning in the past two decades is effective in promoting the quality of ES/FL learning [22]. Besides that, reciprocal teaching-collaborative learning is useful for students who have an average ability in reading comprehension [7]. The next strength is it trains the students to have critical thinking skills. One of the participants stated that:

> ..."Students exchange their ideas or opinion among them can increase interest and also can promote critical thinking (P5) ..."

The students can learn to make a good question through the question section as one of these four strategies of reciprocal teaching [24].

Other benefits of reciprocal teaching-collaborative learning design are establishing interaction, communication, group discussion, and collaboration among students [25]. This testimony state by all of the participant as below:

> ..."Automatically in the group's communication established (P1), discussions formed (P2), certainly, cooperation exists because the sense of togetherness will arise between them (P3), members of group encourage each other to learn (P4, P5), and interactions occur (P6) ..."

It is emphasized by Carter that when students involved as the teacher and interacted with their peers. It is enhanced their comprehension [26]. Then, leadership is also one of its strengths. Leadership formed when students take turns leading groups discussion about implementing four strategies. It can be stated that the sequence of reciprocal teaching reflects learning from shared group tasks, interaction, scaffolding, shared leadership, and also the responsibility.

The next strength is grouping makes students active. According to Pressley [27], the essential point in reading comprehension strategies is that students should be active during the process. It also states that collaboration becomes a trend in the twenty-first-century. The requirement in community works together on several issues of serious concern, changing an individual attempt to group work, from self-governing to togetherness [28].

The engagement of students in the group is more reliable. In other words, the students support each other in share knowledge, work together to solve problems, complete a task [29]. Bright students can help unsuccessful students, or vice versa sometimes causes weaker students can disclose some unexpected insights in a collaborative surrounding [25]. The witness from the participant that says:

> ..."Everyone is supposed to learn from everyone else (P5); every student has abilities, achievements, and interests that sometimes have not been developed (P6) ..."

The same thought came from Vygotsky [30] that group various knowledge and experience make a positive contribution to the learning process. The group presence minimizes students to be passive so that learning becomes more productive and positive. It is the same as [31] emphasized that collaborative learning provides an energetic and more effective alternative to competitive ethnic, which influences much educational thinking today. Another strength is motivation. The evidence from the participant that says:

> ..."Motivation to learn will be formed (P2); if students feel not smart, they overcome it by study hard (P3), weaker students as possible to do their assigned part (P4) ..."

Westera [32] stated that metacognitive instruction, as used in reciprocal teaching, had a positive effect on both reading and dialogue while improving the skill of content and motivation to learn. Another significant benefit gained is that students not only have an understanding of reading, but students also simultaneously learn other language skills such as listening, speaking, and writing. The evidence from participants that say:

> ..."Under the big umbrella of learning reading, other abilities occur (P1), without being aware students can speak when delivery opinion (P2), discussing to each other (P3), ability to listen when they have to do clarification (P4), and writing skills when they have to make a summary or paraphrase (P6) ..."

From the various benefits obtained by students, there is also a value for the teacher. The participant emphasizes teacher who works with reciprocal teaching is a good one. It pointed as a pedagogical practice that more natural caring, inclusive, and cohesive learning groups that teachers work smarter, not harder [6, 32].

In the reciprocal teaching-collaborative learning design, there must be weaknesses that will address in future implementation. The gap noted is that not all students are willing to be taught by their peers. The teachers must consider this situation. The evidence from the participant says:

> ..."Not all children want to be taught by their peers. This case must receive special attention from the teacher how to deal with students in this type (P2) ..."

Another weakness is that teachers have to pay attention to class management. Class noise is unavoidable in the groups of students. These two weaknesses are the major concern in this model, so they need to be addressed and overcome when implementing the design of reciprocal teaching-collaborative learning.

The suggestion also is given for the improvement of design implementation in the future. The opinion is the teacher who will carry out the design have to understand the application of reciprocal teaching-collaborative learning correctly. The workshop needs to give to the teachers for 3–5 days, so they know this design well. Another opinion is the three strategies implemented in the class, and one approach summarizing be a student's independent assignment at home. The reason is students can repeat learning by sum up an essential part of reading text. Then, the last suggestion is the reciprocal teaching-collaborative learning design in its implementation must consider the local context or adapted to regional culture. The application does not have to follow the original form of the origin country of reciprocal teaching.

6 Conclusion

The participants support this reciprocal teaching-collaborative learning approach design to be implemented. The participants, who are English teachers at several polytechnics in Indonesia, argue that this is a breakthrough in teaching reading and also useful. Mostly the noticeable answer of participants shows that reciprocal-collaborative learning helps enhance students' reading comprehension skills. According to them, there is some crucial benefit through this design, namely interactive, communicative, active group discussion, critical thinking, motivation, leadership, and cooperation.

Then, the goal of the reciprocal-collaborative learning approach is students comprehend English reading text with a short duration of time but have an enormous impact. It means that at the time student learn reading, they also get another essential skill, namely listening, speaking, and writing that integrated into its design. Besides that, the teaching style in polytechnics is a collaboration where students have formed collaborate in completing projects or assignments. As a result, the formation of groups will be useful and also shorten the duration time of reading learning, especially reading English text. Generally, good learning has to be positive and avoiding stressful learning environments for students.

References

1. Dreyer, C., Nel, C.: Teaching reading strategies and reading comprehension within a technology-enhanced learning environment. System **31**, 349–365 (2003). https://doi.org/10.1016/S0346-251X(03)00047-2
2. Adams, T.L., Lowery, R.M.K.: An analysis of children's strategies for reading mathematics. Read Writ. Q. **23**, 161–177 (2007). https://doi.org/10.1080/10573560601158479
3. Pang, E.S, Muaka, A.B., Kamil, M.: Teaching reading. Brussels: Int. Acad. Educ. Teach. Mindful Writ. (2003). https://doi.org/10.7330/9781607329374.c017
4. Rahimi, M., Sadeghi, N.: Impact of reciprocal teaching on EFL learners' reading comprehension. Res. Appl. Linguist. **6**, 64–86 (2014)
5. Oxford, R.L.: Language learning styles and strategies: an overview. In: Learn Styles Strateg GALA 2003 (2003)
6. Palinscar, A.S., Brown, A.L.: Reciprocal teaching of comprehension-fostering and comprehension monitoring activities. Cogn. Instr. **1**, 117–175 (1984)
7. Grabe, W.: Teaching and testing reading. In: M.H. Long, C.J. Doughty (eds.) The Handbook of Language Teaching, pp. 441–462. Wiley, Hoboken. (2009). Handb. Lang. Teach. 412–440
8. Anjomshoaa, L., Golestan, S., Anjomshoaa, A.: The influences of metacognitive awareness on reading comprehension in Iranian English undergraduate students in Kerman. Iran. Int. J. Appl. Linguist. English Lit. **1**, 193–198 (2012). https://doi.org/10.7575/ijalel.v.1n.6p.193
9. Yousefvand, Z., Lotfi, A.R.: The effect of strategy-based reading instruction on Iranian EFL Graduate students reading comprehension and their attitudes toward reading strategies instruction. **1**, 39–55 (2011)
10. Okkinga, M.: Effects of reciprocal teaching on reading comprehension of low-achieving adolescents. The Importance of Specific Teacher Skills, pp. 1–22 (2016). https://doi.org/10.1111/1467-9817.12082
11. Rosenshine, B., Meister, C.: Reciprocal teaching: a review of the research. Rev. Educ. Res. **64**, 479–530 (1994)
12. Richards, J.C., Schmidt, R.: Longman: Dictionary of Language Teaching & Applied Linguistics, 4th edn (2010)
13. Alfassi, M.: Reading to learn: effects of combined strategy instruction on high school students. J. Educ. Res. **97**, 171–185 (2004). https://doi.org/10.3200/JOER.97.4.171-185
14. Gibbons, P.: Scaffolding Language, Scaffolding Learning: Teaching Second Language in Mainstream Classroom. Heinemann, Portsmounth (2002)
15. McAllum, R.: Reciprocal teaching: critical reflection on practice. Kairaranga **15**, 26–35 (2014)

16. Dillenbourg, P.: What do you mean by collaborative learning? In: Dillenbourg, P. (ed.) Collaborative-Learning: Cognitive and Computational Approaches, pp. 1–19. Elsevier, Oxford (1999)
17. Smith, L., Macgregor, J.T.: What is collaborative learning? Assessment **117**, 10–30 (1992)
18. Haradhan, M.: Qualitative research methodology in social sciences and related subjects. J. Econ. Dev. Environ. People **7**, 23–48 (2018)
19. Moleong, L.J.: Metodologi Penelitian Kualitatif. Remaja Rosda Karya, Bandung (2012)
20. Charmaz, K.: Constructing Grounded Theory. Sage, London (2014)
21. Kosasih, A.: Grounded theory approach. In: Proceedings of the Seminar on Lecturer Research Results (UNINDRA), pp. 122–132 (2018)
22. Roskams, T.: Chinese EFL students' attitudes to peer feedback and peer assessment in an extended pairwork setting. RELC J. **30**, 79–123 (2018). https://doi.org/10.1177/003368829903000105
23. Spörer, N., Brunstein, J.C., Kieschke, U.: Improving students' reading comprehension skills: effects of strategy instruction and reciprocal teaching. Learn. Instr. **19**, 272–286 (2009). https://doi.org/10.1016/j.learninstruc.2008.05.003
24. Todd, R.B., Tracey, D.H.: Reciprocal teaching and comprehension: a single subject research study. **11**, 1–113 (2006)
25. Momtaz, E., Garner, M.: Does collaborative learning improve EFL students' reading comprehension? In: IRAL - International Review of Applied Linguistics in Language Teaching, pp. 15–36 (2010)
26. Carter, C.: Reciprocal Teaching: The Application of a Reading Improvement Strategy on Urban Students in Highland Park, Michigan. Cambridge University Press, Cambridge (2001)
27. Pressley, M.: Comprehension instruction: what makes sense now, what might make sense soon. Comput. Sci. **5** (2001)
28. Leonard, P.E., Leonard, L.J.: The collaborative prescription: remedy or reverie? Int. J. Leadersh. Educ. **4**, 383–399 (2001). https://doi.org/10.1080/13603120110078016
29. Johnson, D.W., Johnson, R.T., Stanne, M.B., Garibaldi, A.: Impact of group processing on achievement in cooperative groups. J. Soc. Psychol. **130**, 507–516 (1990). https://doi.org/10.1080/00224545.1990.9924613
30. Vygotsky, L.S.: Mind in Society. The Development of Higher Psychological Processes, 1st edn, Harvard University Press, Cambridge (1980)
31. Nunan D.: Collaborative Language Learning and Teaching, 1st edn (1992)
32. Westera, J.: Reciprocal teaching as a schoolwide inclusive strategy. Unpublished Doctoral thesis, University of Auckland, Auckland (2002)

Mathematic Learning Efficiency Analysis of Story-Based Situated Learning in Low-Achieving Elementary School Students

Chih-Wei Huang[1], Hong-Ren Chen[1(✉)], Sen-Chi Yu[2], Yi-Lun Su[3], and Chia-Chen Chen[3]

[1] Department of Digital Content and Technology, National Taichung University of Education, Taichung 403, Taiwan
hrchen@mail.ntcu.edu.tw
[2] Department of Counseling and Applied Psychology, National Taichung University of Education, Taichung 403, Taiwan
[3] Department of Management Information Systems, National Chung Hsing University, Taichung 402, Taiwan

Abstract. The objective of this study is to understand how story-based situated learning affect low-achieving students' learning performances and discuss their impact on learning efficiency, math anxiety and differences in attitudes toward mathematics. The subjects of this study were low-achieving 5–6th grade students of an unnamed elementary school in Taichung of Taiwan. Experimental group used story-based situated learning, while the control group used traditional lecture method. The study found the following: (1) Experimental group's post test scores regarding mathematic achievement exhibited significant difference in comparison with the control group. (2) Experimental group's math anxiety scale results had significant difference comparing to the control group. Experimental group students were also found to be less anxious than those of the control group. (3) Experimental group's math attitude scale results exhibited significant difference when compared to the control group. Experimental groups were also found to have better attitude scores than the control group.

Keywords: Low-achieving students · Story-based learning · Math anxiety · Math attitude

1 Introduction

Remedial teaching programs is already a common concept in Taiwan. Both the central and local government have been promoting various after class remedial programs, providing low-achieving students with a diversified and adaptive learning opportunity. The students are then screened with a standardized exam system to determine which low-achieving students should be admitted to the remedial program. However, despite the programs were already in use for almost a decade, the results of remedial teaching are still under heavy discussion between parents, there are also some researchers that suggested remedial teaching programs should be held during summer and winter vacations. Not only can students continue studying without having their study motivation being interrupted by the long breaks, but also it would be much easier to recruit teachers suitable for the program [1].

Ministry of Education's PRIORI (Project for Implementation of Remedial Instruction) website is the most widely-used platform for remedial programs in Taiwan. The quality of its teaching materials and learning efficiency are also recognized by many teachers. Thus, the study will mainly be using the materials available on said website while making adjustment to incorporate narrative elements and applying them to context-based teaching methods. Many students across the world face problems when learning math. One of the most common phenomenon is that students are more likely to achieve lower learning efficiency in learning math, which causes students to drop out of majors that concern math or science. Many female students are also discouraged from entering fields of science due to the difficulties they face in studying math [2]. Thus, the study will be exploring the differences between how genders react to math anxiety and their attitudes towards math.

The study will discuss the three following questions:

1. Discuss the learning efficiency differences of students taught using story-based situated learning and traditional lecture methods in remedial teaching programs.
2. Understand the attitude differences of students taught using story-based situated learning and traditional lecture methods in remedial programs.
3. Understand the change in math anxiety of students taught using story-based situated learning as opposed to students taught utilizing traditional lecture methods in remedial programs.

2 Literature Review

An effective context-based learning method can guide the learners to actively participate in the learning process. Combining environmental stimuli and technological applications, the learning content can be further enhanced to inspire curiosity and interest in the learners. In the age of the Internet, our lives are nigh inseparable from the web; hence learning materials should be able to connect with the students' experiences in life in order to increase learning interest and effectiveness while also making students able to apply the knowledge learned in class to real life [3]. Learners can actively explore the value of knowledge in the web of information on their own, not just passively receiving information from external influences. Learners are in charge of whichever knowledge they choose to receive, giving learning a purpose [4]. Thus, while students are learning 5th/6th grade math over the internet, they should be placed in a familiar environment where they could explore and learn on their own.

Math anxiety is one of the key elements to the success of a student's math learning, hence math teachers are very aware of how it affects learning. Richardson and Suinn [5] first developed the concept of math anxiety, which meant the emotional state in which one processes or applying mathematic concepts. The Wei [6] stated that math anxiety is a state anxiety which generates unease and nervousness during the processing of numbers or utilization of mathematic concepts. Many researches also found that the math anxiety of females are significantly higher than males. However, Frary and Ling [7] proposed a different finding which suggested students of different genders did not exhibit significant differences in their math anxiety scale scores. Although most research found females exhibiting significantly higher math anxiety than males, some studies still oppose this conclusion; hence the study will not explore the anxiety differences in genders.

In terms of the correlation between math learning efficiency and math anxiety, it can be broadly categorized into examining the existence of a negative correlation between learning efficiency and math anxiety or finding no correlation between the two. Wu and Su [8]'s study found that in 4th, 5th and 6th grade students, totaling at 990 subjects, the higher the math anxiety in students, the more passive their attitudes and the lower their achievements were. The Williams [9] focused his studies on high school students and discovered that female students had a generally higher math anxiety. Students' learning achievements and MAQ negative emotional responses were significantly negatively correlated, which showed the lower the learning achievement, the more fearful or negative the emotions were. The Meece [10] illustrated that out of the 250 grade 7 to grade 9 students, math anxiety had no significant influence on the students' math scores.

3 Research Method

The test subjects of the present study were 38 students of an unnamed elementary school in Taichung. The subjects included 18 fifth grade students and 19 sixth grade students, of whom 21 were male 16 were female. The students were randomly assigned to experimental group and control group, which contained 17 and 20 students respectively. Experimental group utilized story-based situated learning method while the control group were taught using traditional lecture. The math anxiety & attitude scale was adapted from [6, 11 and 12] 's designs. The scales were given to students along with math achievement tests after being edited and put through factor analysis.

The story-based situated learning model of the study used a map akin to the board game Monopoly. The map combined tourist attractions with math problems that inspired active participation. Teaching in a Monopoly game-like fashion, the study hoped to reduce anxiety and increase positive learning attitude and learning efficiency in the students. Before each lesson, class instructors will spend 10 min explaining the key points while the remaining 30 min will be group activities based on the narrative-based learning model. The present study will be introducing the game background, course content, game rules and schedules in the following paragraph. Game background: Shih and Gang are local students, they are troubled by how they should introduce their homes to the class. Come on kids, do you know what sort of tourist attractions are near their homes? Do you also know how you could introduce them? Let's help Shih and Gang and start exploring nearby! Course content: The game consisted of question cards, chance cards, community chest cards, game board and a die as shown in Fig. 1. Question cards contained fraction multiplication; chance and community chest cards contained events that happened around the students. The game board was designed with four different type of grids, including street grids, chance card grids, community chest card grids and tourist attraction grids. The die used in the game was a traditional six-sided die with numbers from 1 to 6.

Fig. 1. Board game Monopoly of story-based situated learning.

The board game rules are as follows and shown in Fig. 2. Every player should choose a token to represent themselves and a grid as their residence before beginning the game. Starting from the school grid, everybody will take turns to roll the die and advance the number of grids in accordance with the die. Depending on which grid the player arrives in, the following scenarios can happen: If the player reaches street grid, they shall turn over a question card and answer, which they will get to keep after answering it correctly; If the player reaches a chance card grid, they should turn over a chance card do as the card requests; if the player reaches a community chest card grid, they should turn over a community chest card and do as the card requests; Finally, If the player reaches a tourist attraction grid, they will go into timeout for one round. Every time a question is answered, the players can check with the instructor to see whether the answer is correct. If the answer is correct, then the player can continue playing; if the answer is incorrect, then the player should recalculate under the teacher's supervision. The player is allowed to receive an additional card after reaching their residence on the game board and having answered the question correctly. In solo play, each player will compete against one another to see who answers the most questions correctly in a limited time; In team play, players will compete in groups to see which team answered the most questions; If all questions are answered, the team who answered the quickest wins. The teaching model is expected to last a total of 320 min across 8 lessons, including pre-test (40 min), post test (40 min) and math anxiety & attitude test (40 min).

4 Experimental Analysis and Results

4.1 Analysis of Learning Effect

According to ANCOVA summary Table 1, the independent variables (the two teaching methods) had a significant treatment effect on the dependent variable (post-test scores) after excluding the influence of the covariate variable (pre-test scores) had on the

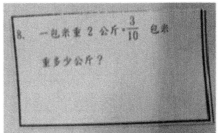

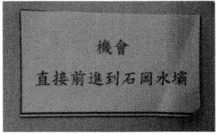

Fig. 2. Question and chance card.

dependent variable, $F = 6.720^*$, which meant post-test scores will have significant differences. The average test scores of the experimental group was 83.901, while the control group averaged at 71.184. The results indicated that students of the remedial programs had better math learning efficiency employing story-based situated learning method as opposed to traditional lecture method.

Table 1. Summary of covariate analysis of math achievement test.

Source	Sum of squares	df	Mean square	F	Sig.	Partial eta squared
Pre-test	5329.967	1	5329.967	24.326	.000	.417
Group	1472.381	1	1472.381	6.720	.014*	.165
Error	7449.665	34	219.108			
Corrected Total	13772.973	36				

$^*p < 0.05$

4.2 Analysis of Mathematics Anxiety

Results on Table 2 showed different groups of students perceived mathematics anxiety differently ($t = -3.193$, $p < 0.5$). Students taught using traditional lecture method had significantly higher anxiety ($M = 77.35$) than those who utilized narrative-based learning method ($M = 58.177$). $\eta^2 = .226$, which indicated that the 22.6% variance in general anxiety can be explained by the use of different teaching models. Judging from the amount, a strong correlation exists between the different teaching models and the general anxiety variable, with the statistical power indicating an 87.4% probability of the foregoing hypothesis. Summarizing the statements above, the experimental group exhibited lower math anxiety than the control group.

Table 2. Summary of t test of mathematics anxiety scale.

Variable	N	Mean	S.D.	t
Experiment group	17	58.177	18.211	−3.193*
Control group	20	77.350	18.196	

*$p < 0.05$

4.3 Analysis of Mathematics Attitude

Results on Table 3 showed different groups of students exhibited different "general attitude" ($t = 4.307$, $p < 0.5$). Students taught using traditional lecture method were significantly more negative ($M = 49.700$) than those who utilized narrative-based teaching method ($M = 61.824$). $\eta^2 = .346$, which indicated that the 34.6% variance in general attitude can be explained by the use of different teaching models. Judging from the amount, a strong correlation exists between the different teaching models and the general attitude variable, with the statistical power indicating a 98.7% probability of the foregoing hypothesis. This part of the results indicated that the experimental group exhibited a more positive math attitude than the control group.

Table 3. Summary of the statistical test the mathematical attitude.

Variable	N	Mean	S.D.	t
Experiment group	17	61.824	8.164	4.307*
Control group	20	49.700	8.832	

5 Conclusions

The study found that students using story-based situated learning method fared better in learning achievement than their peers taught traditionally. Students using story-based situated learning also had both a lower math anxiety and a much positive attitude than those who were taught using traditional lecture method. The study also advises future research could understand individual learning differences while giving each equal room for development. In the philosophy of teaching, taking initiative, engaging the public and seeking for the common good are the three tenets of the future trend of education. More and more experiments have proven that traditional lectures are no longer applicable to all students, especially to those who lagged behind. Only through designing a more suitable learning method and increasing the interaction between students can it change how students view studying, lower their anxiety and increase their learning efficiency.

References

1. Chang, Y.-C.: The analysis of new immigrant families between the degree of perception to teach, acceptance and digital online learning by remedial teaching policy. Sch. Adm. **108**, 119–136 (2017)
2. Wei, L.-M.: The effects of self-regulated learning and affective factors on mathematics achievement of primary students. Natl. Taichung Univ. Educ. Learn. Newsp. **11**, 39–63 (1997)
3. Chen, Y.-C., OuYang, Y.: The design, development and evaluation of applying situated learning in a netiquette education website. Curriculum Instr. Q. **18**(1), 59–92 (2015)
4. Black, R.S., Schell, J.W.: Learning within a situated cognition on framework: implications for adult learning. Retrieved from ERIC database (ED389939) (1995)
5. Richardson, F.C., Suinn, R.M.: The mathematics anxiety rating scale: psychometric data. J. Counsel. Psychol. **19**(6), 551–554 (1972)
6. Wei, L.-M.: The effects of self-regulated learning and affective factors on mathematics achievement of primary students and the effectiveness of strategies training. Unpublished doctoral dissertation. National Taiwan Normal University, Taipei, Taiwan (1988)
7. Frary, R.B., Ling, J.L.: A factor-analytic study of mathematics anxiety. Educ. Psychol. Meas. **43**(4), 985–993 (1983). https://doi.org/10.1177/001316448304300406
8. Wu, M.-L., Su, G.-Y.: The study of the relationship between belief, attitude perception of important others and mathematical attitude and mathematical achievement among the students of national primary school control. J. Elementary Educ. **4**, 181–200 (1995)
9. Williams, J.E.: The relation between efficacy for self-regulated learning and domain-specific academic performance, controlling for test anxiety. J. Res. Dev. Educ. **29**(2), 77–80 (1996)
10. Meece, J.L., Wigfield, A., Eccles, J.S.: Predictors of math anxiety and its influence on young adolescents' course enrollment intentions and performance in mathematics. J. Educ. Psychol. **82**(1), 60–70 (1990). https://doi.org/10.1037/0022-0663.82.1.60
11. Wu, M.-L.: A study of the relationship between the socio-psychological factors of primary and junior high school students and their belief and anxiety in math. Educ. Rev. **12**, 287–327 (1996)
12. Shie, B.-H.: Construction of mathematics anxiety scale for younger pupils: verification of theoretical models. National Taipei University of Education (2006)

Implementation of an Individual English Oral Training Robot System

Chen-Yu Lin[1], Wei-Wei Shen[2], Ming-Hsiu Michelle Tsai[2], Jim-Min Lin[1(✉)], and Wai Khuen Cheng[3]

[1] Department of Information Engineering and Computer Science, Feng Chia University, Taichung City 40724, Taiwan
qwell1845@gmail.com, jimmy@fcu.edu.tw
[2] Department of Foreign Languages and Literature, Feng Chia University, Taichung City 40724, Taiwan
{wwshen,mhtsai}@fcu.edu.tw
[3] Faculty of Information and Communication Technology, Universiti Tunku Abdul Rahman, Kampar, Malaysia
chengwk@utar.edu.my

Abstract. To improve oral English ability, in addition to learners' willingness to practice more, the learning effect will be more obvious if tutor assistance is provided and can involve one-on-one individual tutoring. However, due to the scarcity of English teacher manpower, teachers cannot take care of every student in class, nor can they teach students one by one after class. Robot-Assisted English Speaking may provide a feasible solution. Therefore, this research has developed an educational robot system that can support individual tutoring of English speaking after class. It is called "English Oral Training Robot Tutor System (EOTRTS)", which can actively lead students to learn through robots, and help students improve their oral English practice through individual tutoring and interactive methods. The implementation of this system is to use the social robot NAO's voice recognition, QR code scanning, humanized limbs, and various sensor functions as well as the ability to interact with people and other features to help students learn oral English after class. The experimental results show that, in addition to a slightly lower satisfaction with the robot's gesture performance, the students' acceptance of the EOTRTS system is promising.

Keywords: Educational robot · Robot assisted language learning · English Oral Training Robot Tutor System (EOTRTS) · Google Cloud Automatic Speech Recognizer (ASR) · NAO

1 Introduction

With the development of technology, many robots have been used in real life today, and the existence of social robots allows us to interact with them through dialogue or touch. The interaction with the robot has a positive impact on the body and mind [1]. Mubin et al. [2] also enumerate the various advantages of using robots in a teaching environment, such as dull and boring tasks without fatigue and remote teaching. Kang et al. [3] assumes that the robot is humanized and has the proper appearance to interact directly with the person. Extending these ideas, robots are an attractive tool that is brought into the second language learning arena and used to meet different teaching needs. Kanda et al. [4] and others placed robots in the primary school classroom for two weeks and compared the frequency of interactions between students and their English test scores. Although the two-week robot-assisted learning did not have any significant impact on students' oral English and listening test scores, students who showed great interest at the initial stage had significantly improved English scores.

In the previous research, most of the robots were used in the classroom. The purpose of using robots in the classroom was to attract students' attention and enhance the interest of learning. An ETAR system [4] was implemented to be a teaching assistant in class. It can help to improve the motivation of English learning in class and bring convenience to classroom teaching for English teachers. Research [5] was also proved to be effective. However, the robot cannot take care of every student in the classroom; likewise, after the class, the teacher cannot teach each student individually. Therefore, a robot system for after-school tutoring, called English Oral Training Robot Tutor System (EOTRTS) [6] is proposed. This paper presents how the system is implemented. In this system, the educational robot leads the students to learn in a one-to-one manner, using a social robot NAO with interactive functions such as voice function and touch as a personal lecturer for the learner to conduct after-school tutoring for oral English training. Different from the past research, the robot instructor can actively guide the learner to learn. It does not need to be triggered by the helper to guide the coaching process. Instead, the robot instructor NAO actively guides the students according to the progress of the student's curriculum to practice single words, recitation of texts, recording exercises, and evaluate the student's speech rate and correct reading rate through Google Cloud Voice to Text and Word Error Rate Calculation Formula.

The structure of this article is as follows. Section 2 explains how the system is designed, and describes the design of the student's interaction with the robot. The details of the experimental procedures is described in Sect. 3. Next, the analysis and discussion of the result are then explained in Sect. 4. Finally, a brief conclusion is made and the future research direction is explored in Sect. 5.

2 System Design

2.1 System Structure

Figure 1 shows the system structure of the educational robot (called EOTRTS) proposed in this study. This article uses NAO robots to conduct after-school tutoring and lead students to learn text materials. EOTRTS is mainly divided into three parts: cloud services, servers, and robots. The system software functions are implemented in Python language, and Socket is used as a network communication mechanism to connect various system components. Cloud services use Google Cloud services.

Server. The server is responsible for accessing the database and the cloud, obtaining course data to send to the robot, recording the session test data returned by the robot, etc., and respectively storing each student's recording files after reading the text. After

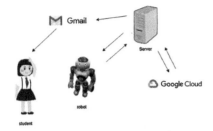
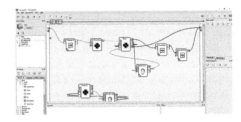

Fig. 1. System structure of EOTRTS.   **Fig. 2.** Choregraphe operational interface.

the server uploads the data and the data reaches the cloud, it uses Google Cloud Speech to Text (STT) and Word Error Rate (WER) formulas to calculate the accuracy of reading aloud and speaking rate of the text recording, and sends the recognition results of the text and the recognition results of the conversation test through SMTP (Simple Mail Transfer Protocol) after the session test of the unit is over.

Robot. The robot end mainly designs the functional process of the robot, including scanning the QR code to log in to the account, requesting the server to confirm the account, and returning the course progress and course data. The TTS technology of the Nao robot itself is used for the pronunciation of the words, and the storage of audio files, playback, and recording are implemented using the NAOqi SDK. Google Cloud STT is used for the real-time recognition function of the conversation test. After the result is recognized, the recording file is read to calculate the reading speed, and the result is finally returned to the server.

- Hardware – NAO robot

The NAO robot has enough sensors, so it is quite helpful for this research. This research uses sensors such as head and hand to enhance the interaction of tactile sense. It is also possible to use touch to continue the course to enhance the motivation of students to learn. There are 6 touch points (Head-front, Head-middle, Head-rear, Left hand, Right-hand, Right foot) provided for users to interact with EOTRTS.

- Software development – Choregraphe

EOTRTS uses the Choregraphe development platform because Choregraphe can directly use local calls to create modules for the use of various methods. The program in Choregraphe is coded in a way that each functional module has a block, and then it controls the process by connecting various modules. Therefore, it is relatively easy to know how each function is performed in terms of the program structure, and the process of after-school tutoring can also be simply modified according to the needs of the tutor. Choregraphe can visualize each function using the Python programming language. Figure 2 shows the operational interface of Choregraphe platform.

Implementation of an Individual EOTRS 43

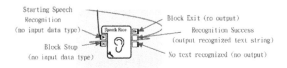

Fig. 3. Speech recognition block in choregraphe.

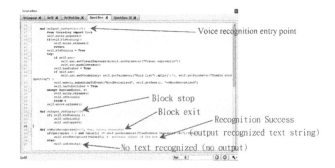

Fig. 4. Corresponding program python codes of Fig. 3

As shown in Fig. 2, there are many boxes, each of which is a module with the specified functions. By connecting each box to integrate the system, the box is normally the code, but it can also be Block flow chart as in the middle of Fig. 3. The advantage of developing on Choregraphe is that you can see which module is currently actively running, which is convenient for programmers to control the process of the system. However, the design of each module is not as simple as in writing usual programs. It is necessary to set the input data type and output format with a specific code-writing method for each module. Figure 3 and Fig. 4 illustrate the functional design examples of the block. Figure 3 is the speech recognition block, and Fig. 4 is the compiled version of the corresponding Python codes.

The entry point and exit point of each recognition box have their own input and output to be set, which have different colors according to different output data types. For example, the output string is blue; the type and length of the output data needs to be properly set in advance, otherwise the program will have an error occurred or fail to receive the data that should be obtained. For example, the voice recognition entry point in Fig. 4 will go to *def onInput_onStart(self)*: The method in this line will start to operate. If one want to get data, he must set the data input in the box and set the data type of the team, and then change the Python code part to *def onInput_onStart(self, data)*: to get the transferred data.

The above is briefly the preliminary process of designing each block. There are requirements to use the microphone and so on. The *ALSpeechRecognition* and the *ALMemory* modules can be used through the above mentioned NAOqi methods. Then the voice recognition function can be turned on through the methods inside.

Cloud Services. An important function of this system–"voice recognition"–is provided through cloud services. The robot saves the recording file of each student on the server after the text is read aloud, and then uploads it to the cloud service from the server. We use Google Cloud Speech-to-Text (STT) service to recognize the text recording and then convert it into a corresponding text file. Finally, we use the Word Error Rate (WER) formula to calculate the accuracy and speed of the student's reading aloud. After the end of the session test of a unit, the recognition result of the text read aloud and the session test will be sent to the student via SMTP (Simple Mail Transfer Protocol) by email.

- Google Cloud Platform Speech-To-Text (STT) Service

Google Cloud Platform has a forward-looking infrastructure, powerful data analysis services. EOTRTS uses Google Cloud Automatic Speech Recognizer (ASR) for speech recognition and its STT API for speech to text translation, in which a powerful neural network is added to the Cloud STT API. This model is convenient for developers to convert their audio messages into text. Additionally, because it is a voice recognition model, to have a higher recognition rate, it requires a complete and clear pronunciation for single words to be read. Therefore, it is very suitable for students to practice reading aloud. As a result, students would be able to read English clearly and completely, thereby improving their reading ability. This API mainly has two functions, namely:

– Synchronous voice recognition: For short voice message (less than 1 min), the recognized text will be recognized by a built-in STT function in NAO, and returned in the response immediately. EOTRTS uses this part in the robot conversation test. This function is particularly suitable for the conversation test as a conversation has fewer sentences and needs to be quickly identified and then sent back.
– Asynchronous voice recognition: Performing voice recognition on batches of long audio files will start long-running audio processing operations. Asynchronous voice recognition is used to recognize an audio message that is longer than 1 min and stored in Google Cloud Storage. The system then uses this API to identify the part of the text to be practiced in the system.

The recognition rate can be obtained by comparing the original text with its recording of student's read aloud voice. The ASR recognition rate is more than 80%, even up to as high as 92%, which is an acceptable recognition rate.

When using asynchronous voice recognition, only the audio files stored in Google Cloud Storage. The system creates a *bucket* named *speech_to_text_class* on the cloud platform to store the student audio files to be processed. Then we can upload audio files to this bucket from the server. In order for the data to be reusable, we use the *Regional* level storage space and grant permissions through Cloud Storage ID, so that project members can access Cloud Storage data based on their project roles. Server-end account access rights are also granted through Cloud Storage ID.

- Correct rate of reading aloud and calculation of speaking speed

WER is a common measurement of speech recognition or machine translation system performance. It was proposed by Levenshtein [7]. The calculation formula is as Eq. (1). The calculation method is as follows:

S is the number of different words in the original sentence, D is the number of missing words, I is the number of inserted words, and N is the number of correct words. The spaces, commas, and other symbols are removed in the calculation of correct rate.

$$WER = 100 * \frac{S+D+I}{N}\% \qquad (1)$$

The formula for calculating the speed of reading aloud is as Eq. (2), and Eq. (3).

$$Speaking\ Speed = \frac{text\ length\ (words)}{recording\ time(min)}, \ if \geq 1\ minute \qquad (2)$$

$$Speaking\ Speed = 60 * \frac{text\ length(words)}{recording\ time(min)}, \ if < 1\ minute \qquad (3)$$

2.2 English Oral Educational Functions in EOTRTS

EOTRTS has 4 main oral English education functions: single-word pronunciation exercises, text reading exercises, text recordings, and conversation tests. The robots in the process have operation tips to prevent students from forgetting how to operate them.

- Single-word pronunciation exercises

After entering the course practice, students begin to learn the vocabulary in the new course. The robot reads the words first, and the students follow along. Students learn the meaning of the words, so that the students will not have difficulty to read the new words in the text reading practice afterwards. After reading a word, there is a waiting interval of 3 s for students to practice the pronunciation of the word, and then NAO will read the next word. Vocabulary practice is about two and a half minutes, and students can follow their own abilities to choose whether to practice again.

- Text read-aloud exercises

The student touches NAO's head to enter the text reading exercise. The NAO robot will play the text audio files (real-person English pronunciation) of the practice unit, and can make some actions to attract the students' attention. It will stop at the appropriate semantic paragraph. After students listen to the audio file and practice reading the passage, they can listen to the audio file of the next passage by touching NAO's right hand or right foot. If they don't understand this passage, they can repeat this audio file by touching NAO's head (front). Then NAO will play the text audio file of the whole unit. If students want to practice again, they can touch NAO's head (middle) to listen to the entire audio file again. The estimated practice time for this process is around 10 min.

- Text read-aloud recordings

When the text reading exercise is over, the NAO robot prompts, "Touch my front head to start recording." After that, NAO will not take any action and wait. When a student thinks that he/she can start the next process, he/she will touch NAO's front head to start recording. After recording, the student can touch NAO's middle head to stop recording. Students choose whether to re-record the read-aloud again orally by saying "YES" or "NO". If students do not choose to re-record, the robot will upload the audio recording file to the server.

- Conversation tests

EOTRTS will firstly read the questions of the conversation test in the textbook. In order to train the student's listening ability, the test paper we give will only have the answer part, and the question will be read by the robot. The robot reads the question twice with 2 s apart each time. Student will first answer which choice (A-D) it is, and the robot will ask the student to read the complete sentence of that answer choice next. For example, if the student says, "A", the robot will ask the student to read the sentence of his answer choice. Students touch NAO's forehead to activate its short speech recognition function, and touch the middle of NAO's head to end the function after finishing reading. After that, an email with the text recognition content of the unit and the recognition content of the conversation test will be sent immediately to the student.

3 EOTRTS Experiment

3.1 Participants

The experiment is aimed at students in the science-related departments of a university in central Taiwan. The total number of students is 19, including 17 boys and 2 girls, with an average age of 21.65 years and a standard deviation of 1.06. A total of 19 people in the experimental group and the control group participated in the experiment.

3.2 Teaching Material

The textbook used in this study is 4000 Essential English Words 1. It's an English textbook selected for freshmen. It has a certain correlation with the participating students. Students have certain familiarity with the teaching materials, and the difficulty of the teaching materials is relatively low. It is suitable for students of science and engineering background for the purpose of improving their insufficient oral English ability.

3.3 Procedure

The experiment lasted a total of 6 weeks. In the first week, the overall experimental process and the pre-test group were introduced and the English learning motivation and English learning anxiety questionnaire were filled out. In the 2nd to 5th weeks, the experimental group and the control group were arranged in a quiet and undisturbed room space. The experimental group used EOTRTS for learning, while the control group learned English in a self-study manner. Participants spent half an hour per unit, and 1 h for two units per week. There were four main learning steps for each unit: single-word pronunciation practice, text reading practice, text reading-aloud practice and conversation test. In addition, the two groups of students recorded their text reading-aloud practices, and the session tests were recorded afterwards as well. The experimental group used the robot to record, and the control group used the mobile phone to record. In the sixth week, the two groups of students engaged in post-testing, and filled out the English learning motivation and English learning anxiety questionnaires, while the experimental group also filled out the technology acceptance questionnaire, and the control group filled out the learning satisfaction questionnaire.

4 Results: Analysis of Technology Acceptance Questionnaire

Limited by the paper length, this paper will only report the analysis of the Technology Acceptance Questionnaire. More results will be presented in our future papers. This questionnaire is designed based on the five-point Likert scale. All questionnaires have been evaluated by two English teachers to ensure that the questions are clear and structured. The technology acceptance questionnaire was conducted in the experimental group to understand students' satisfaction and acceptance of EOTRTS. The average of the item classification is shown in Table 1. Table 2 shows the questions with answers of lower mean.

Table 1. Technology acceptance questionnaire topic classification.

Evaluation items	Ease of use	Usefulness
Sound	4.3	4.2
Action	3.4	3.9
Procedure	4.4	4.3
Interaction	4.1	4.1

In terms of ease of use, except for the part of the gesture "action", the rest of the evaluation items receive all 4.0 or more, which means that the usability in sound, process, interaction, results and other items is acceptable. However, the action items got the lowest point at 3.4. After asking most students in the experimental group, the reason is that they think the robot had too many actions and big moves in its gestures. As shown in Table 2, it is indeed as low as 3.6 and 3.3 points.

In terms of usefulness, except for the part of gesture action, the other evaluation items all receive points above 4.0, which means that the usefulness of items such as sound, procedure, interaction, and results also has a good effect. Although the robot's action can attract the attention of students, its excessive movements can also distract students. The lowest-rated item in the questionnaire is the STT ability to recognize speech. This is partly because EOTRTS is recognized through the STT function of

Table 2. Technology acceptance questionnaire with answers of lower mean.

No	Questions	1	2	3	4	5	Mean
3	I think the speed of the Educational robot is appropriate	11.1%	11.1%	22.2%	22.2%	33.3%	3.6
4	I think that the display of Educational robot movements with spoken content is appropriate	11.1%	11.1%	22.2%	44.4%	11.1%	3.3
14	I am satisfied with the system ability to identify the voice recognition function of the server (the identification result sent back by email)	0%	22.2%	33.3%	11.1%	33.3%	3.6
15	I am satisfied with the Educational robot's ability to read English in real time	0%	22.2%	44.4%	22.2%	11.1%	3.2

strongly disagree (1) → strongly agree (5)

Google Cloud. It would have a great impact on the recognition of short speech, including the speech sound level, environmental noise, and even the name of the person, etc. Because the conversation test answer is a sentence, up to a dozen words, as long as one or two words are not recognized, it would have a very big impact on the scoring. Therefore, it would also affect the real-time STT recognition greatly, as shown in Table 2 in which the average score is only 3.2. On the contrary, the impact of that on the server's text reading-aloud recording recognition ability is relatively lowered. Because each text is more than 300 words, the impact on names or small number of errors is not very large, and the average recognition rate is 0.4 higher than that of real-time recognition.

5 Conclusion

This article proposes an educational robot system EOTRTS to provide individual tutoring to students to improve their oral English ability. It also proposes to use Google Cloud-STT and WER calculation formulas to evaluate the accuracy of students' reading aloud, so as to improve the accuracy of their English reading and reading rate. After six weeks of experiments, EOTRTS can indeed play the role of a tutor, helping students learn English in a one-on-one manner. The results of questionnaires show that, regardless of ease-of-use and usefulness, this system has good system acceptance for users, except for the robot action factor. It signifies that using robots as a language learning tool is a new way of oral English learning that can be accepted by students.

Future Works. EOTRTS can incorporate more robots with different functions, appearances, and operating types in the future to support language learning on different robots. In addition, EOTRTS can also be used for different foreign languages in the future, such as Japanese and Korean, etc. because NAO robots can support multiple languages. Furthermore, in the learning process, many people are attracted by the vivid and interesting appearance and actions of the robot and the lively and delicate nature of the interaction between the robot and the human. Therefore, EOTRTS can also be combined with the previous research results of [8–10] in the future to design more lively and vivid robot programs.

Acknowledgement. This study is partly supported in finance by the Ministry of Science and Technology, TAIWAN under the contract numbers MOST106-2511-S-035-003-MY2, MOST107-2511-H-035-004-MY2, and MOST108-2511-H-035-002-MY2.

References

1. Grewen, K.M., Anderson, B.J., Girdler, S.S., Light, K.C.: Warm partner contact is related to lower cardiovascular reactivity. Behav. Med. **29**(3), 123–130 (2003)
2. Mubin, O., Shahid, S., Bartneck, C.: Robot assisted language learning through games: a comparison of two case studies. Aust. J. Intell. Inform. Process. Syst. **13**, 9–14 (2013)
3. Kang, S.C., Chang, W.T., Gu, K.Y., Chi., H.L.: Robot Development Using Microsoft Robotics Developer Studio. CRC Press, Boca Raton (2016)
4. Kanda, T., Hirano, T., Eaton, D., Ishiguro, H.: Interactive robots as social partners and peer tutors for children: a field trial. Hum.-Comput. Interact. **19**, 61–84 (2004)
5. Shen, W.W., Tsai, M.M., Wei, G.C., Lin, C.Y., Lin, J.M.: ETAR: an english assistant robot and its effects on college freshmen's in-class learning motivation. In: L. Rønningsbakk et al. (eds.): ICITL 2019, LNCS 11937, pp. 77–86 (2019)
6. Lin, C.Y.: EOTRTS: Research into an English Oral Training Robot Tutor System to Support After-Class Individual Learning. Master Thesis, Feng Chia University, Taiwan (2019)
7. Levenshtein, V.I.: Binary codes capable of correcting deletions, insertions, and reversals. Sov. Phys. Dokl. **10**(8), 707–710 (1966)
8. Li, Y.H., Lin, J.M., Lee, K.Y., Chiou, C.W.: A robot motion control mechanism using robot drama markup language. J. Comput. Appl. Sci. Educ. **5**(2), 17–35 (2018)
9. Luo, B., Shen, W.W.: Repeated reading: a practical approach when using an ESL textbook? Feng Chia J. Hum. Soc. Sci. **30**, 77–103 (2015)
10. Wei, G.C., Shen, W.W., Tsai, M.H.M., Lin, J.M.: An education robot supporting adaptive learning for english as a foreign language. In: Lin, J.M., Chang, C.-C, Hwang, Y.M. (eds.) The 9th Conference on Engineering, Technological and Technology Education CETTE 2020, pp. 44–55 (2020)

Pilot Study of Information Literacy Competency of the Elderly: A Case Study of Multimedia Instant Messaging Applications

Yi-Chen Lu and Ting-Ting Wu[✉]

Graduate School of Technological and Vocational Education,
National Yunlin University of Science and Technology, Douliou, Taiwan
ttwu@yuntech.edu.tw

Abstract. The aging of the population and the rapid development of digital technology have brought many shocks to our world and changed the way of life we take for grant-ed. The development of mobile technology provides many opportunities for the elderly to improve their quality of life. A total of 20 subjects were enrolled in this study, with an average age of 71.5 years old. Through this course, we summarized the factors affecting information literacy as "learning motivation and attitude", "whether the application is close to needs in their lives", and "whether the family and friends can help the study" through observation and interviews. During the experiment we observed the information literacy performance of the elderly in the use of multimedia instant messaging applications. It is found that when learning digital technology and using multimedia instant messaging applications, information literacy is not directly related to age, education, or gender. It is mainly the acceptance attitude towards technology and the link degree between applications and life that affect the development of information literacy among the elderly.

Keywords: Information literacy · Elder education · Instant messaging · Multimedia · Application

1 Introduction

The two main challenges facing the world today are the socio-economic and cultural challenges brought about by the rapid population aging and the development of digital technology [1]. The aging of the population in most countries has entered an accelerated stage and has become a worldwide concern.

The rapid development of technology is accompanied by the rapid spread of information. The development of mobile technology provides many opportunities for the elderly to improve their quality of life [2]. The emergence of advanced Information and Communications Technology (ICT) in all areas of our lives has increased the importance of individuals' ability to make full use of ICT [3]. ICT is a generic term for any communication device or application, such as a mobile phone, computer, network hardware or software, and the various services and applications associated with it [4]. With the widespread use of smart phones, the age distribution of users has become more and more extensive, and APPs have become a trend [1]. With the evolution of technology carriers, the form of communication between people has changed from the traditional "face-to-face communication" to communication through the Internet and then mobile APPs. Due to its functionality and convenience, various instant messaging software has become an indispensable way of communication in people's daily life. With the development of touch screen technology, smart phones and tablets, the problem of complex computer operation has been solved, and a variety of practical and convenient applications can be run on smart phones through touch screens [1].

The proportion of mobile phone users over the age of 60 increased from 16.1% in 2016 to 20.2% in 2018 [5]. More and more elderly people are becoming technology users. The constant development of technology means that individuals need to constantly improve their digital literacy in order to maintain inclusiveness [6]. Despite a growing understanding of older people's acceptance and limitations of the Internet, older people in areas with low Internet usage rates lag behind in their acceptance and learning needs for touch-screen applications [1].

However, when thinking about the benefits of digital technology in increasing social inclusion and social connectivity of the elderly, it is necessary to understand the older people's ability to accomplish tasks rather than their knowledge of specific tasks [6]. Many older people are unable to use social media, which can affect their social support and intergenerational relationships and lead to depression [4]. Information literacy is an important concept for the elderly [7]. Therefore, the purpose of this study is to explore the information literacy of the elderly in terms of their ability to learn and use technology through their use of multimedia instant messaging applications.

2 Literatures

2.1 Information Literacy

Information literacy is also the foundation of lifelong learning, including the following aspects [8]:

1. Traditional literacy: it refers to the ability to read, write and calculate. In terms of library utilization, it means that people need to be able to understand library functions, book data types and shelving catalogs, and write research reports using literature.
2. Media literacy: it refers to the ability to use the non-print media to interpret, evaluate, analyze, and produce.
3. Computer literacy: it refers to the ability to use computer hardware and software, such as word processing, spreadsheet and other tools, to process data.
4. Network literacy: It refers to the ability to understand network functions, apply, retrieve, process, utilize and evaluate network resources.

2.2 Senior Citizen Education and Lifelong Learning

Elder education refers to a systematic and continuous teaching program for people over the age of 65, with the aim of promoting changes in knowledge, attitudes, values, and skills. Early studies mostly started from the perspective of "education", so many scholars and experts have published works on the theme of "elder education". However, recent studies have turned to the perspective of learners, taking elderly learning and the third age learning as the mainstream [8].

Cropley pointed out that lifelong learning consists of four aspects [9]: (1) time: lifelong learning lasts from birth to death; (2) pattern: lifelong learning occurs in formal and informal educational situations; (3) result: lifelong learning can lead to the acquisition or updating of knowledge, skills and attitudes; (4) goal: the ultimate goal of lifelong learning is to promote personal self-realization.

2.3 Instant Messaging

Instant Messaging (IM) is a real-time communication system through the network, which allows two or more people to use the network to transmit real-time text messages, files, voice, and video communication. It usually provides services in the form of websites, computer software or mobile applications.

Some popular instant messaging software include Line, What, WeChat, Telegram.

3 Method

3.1 Setting and Participants

The subjects of this study were 20 senior citizens over 65 years old (including 65 years old) in Taiwan. Free courses are available to people of all ages in the Senior Citizens Learning Center. The Senior Citizens Learning Center provides free learning services for middle-aged and elderly people to expand their lives after retirement for the new life.

The course aims to enable the elderly to learn about mobile applications through smart phones, connect with the information age, and further enhance their media literacy through multimedia instant messaging applications. During the experiment, a group was set up to observe the interaction of the elders in the process of information release and transmission and to examine their sensitivity to information.

Through the elderly learning to use smart phones, this paper discusses their development of information literacy when using multimedia instant messaging software.

3.2 Research Instrument

In this study, Line was used as multimedia instant messaging software for experiments. Users can transmit information and watch videos and movies on the Internet at no additional cost. They can also make purchases, mobile payments and obtain news and information through other functions.

Its main features are as follows:

1. Ubiquitous free messaging: in addition to one-on-one chat, you can also set up a group chat, or temporary chat room window.
2. Application accessibility: various carriers can be used, such as iPhone, Android, Windows Phone, BlackBerry, and Nokia Asha. Computer versions and network versions are also used.
3. Visual communication/voice calls: currently available for iOS, Android, Windows Phone, BlackBerry (voice call), and computer (Windows/Mac operating system). Visual communication features not only filters, but also special effects and interactive games to enhance the fun of the dialogue.
4. Sticker/emoticon: apart from the basic built-in functions, users can choose and purchase stickers and illustrations through Line online store to enrich text messages.
5. Easy information sharing: photos, videos, voice messages can be forwarded and shared, and phone number, location and other information can be transmitted to friends.
6. Dynamic messages: users can share updates with their friends via text, photos, videos, and stickers, or keep up with their friends' latest news.

3.3 Experimental Design

Before the experiment was carried out, the ability of the subjects to use smart phone applications was ensured. There were 8 courses, 2 courses per week for 4 weeks, and each course lasted 2 h.

In the first week, the subjects mainly learned and understood the application of smart phones. In the second week, they got to know the multimedia instant messaging software: the basic functions of Line include official account, service, stickers, themes, news, wallet, etc. In the third and fourth weeks, practical exercises were carried out and advanced applications were learned, including group creation, voting, location sharing, game interaction, production of pictures, and album and notepad setting.

At the end of the experiment, participants were asked to share their experiences for us to learn their feedback on the multimedia instant messaging software. The experimental design is shown in Fig. 1.

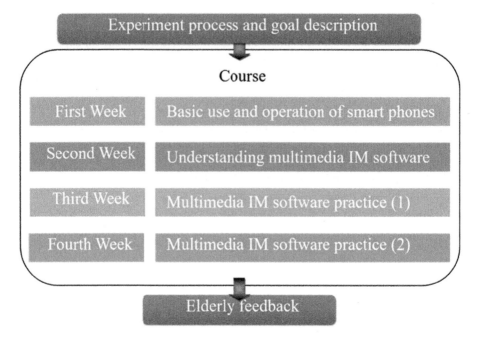

Fig. 1. Experimental design.

4 Results and Discussion

4.1 Participants' Characteristics at the Baseline

Table 1 shows the demographic characteristics and baseline of the participants in this study. 20 elderly people (average age: 71.5 years old; aged 66 to 83 years old) participated in the experiment and completed the course. The proportion of male and female participants was 50%. 75% of the participants had a high school education or equivalent. The more information is shown in Table 1.

Table 1. Demographic characteristics and baseline.

Sex	n
Male	10
Female	10
Age	
65-70	11
70-75	4
75-80	4
80-85	1
Arrangement Age	71.5 years
Education	
University/College	4
High School Vocational/College	11
Secondary	3

All 20 participants had experience in using smart phones, and all of them had basic knowledge of using multimedia social communication software. Only one of them had experience in using other advanced functions of the software, such as the production of pictures and voice input.

4.2 Participants' Feedback

Several elderly people said they had long wanted to learn the advanced features of multimedia instant messaging applications so that they could interact with family and friends and enhance their relationships. In class, many elderly people carefully recorded each step (E9, E10, E12–E20) with paper and pens, and asked questions after class or in groups. It was found that the elderly people aged about 60 (E11–E20) had a particularly high learning motivation and asked questions when they had problems (E13, E20).

During the experiment, the researchers summarized the factors affecting information literacy as "learning motivation and attitude", "whether the application is close to needs in their lives", and "whether the family and friends can help the study" through observation and interviews.

4.2.1 Learning Motivation and Attitude

Participants showed a strong interest in technology and applications that helped them learn and improve. E5, E6 and E7 expressed that they wanted to learn other functions of the mobile phone, but they don't know how to use it. They were afraid of damaging their phones, but they were confident in the knowledge learned in the course. Participants with positive attitudes used the Internet and applications more frequently and were constantly learning new applications [2]. These patients have gained a better understanding of the course and become more proficient in the application, which is consistent with previous studies.

E1 said he could keep up with the times and learn the latest technology through his mobile phone. However, researchers found that E1's mobile phone was not connected to the Internet, and he needed to rely on the shared network, so he could not focus on learning in class, and it was not easy to enjoy the participation process. While the Internet may have a positive psychological impact on older people, there is still a lag in technology adoption among older people [2]. Despite this, E1 has Wi-Fi at home, and he is very positive in communication and feedback in the group.

One of the elders wanted to give up the course because it was too difficult and his mobile phone was not good enough to keep up with his progress, but he persevered with the encouragement of his peers. E18 felt that he could not use the knowledge he had learned, and it was a little difficult. His mobile phone crashed frequently, but he was very happy to study with his classmates. It can be seen that friendship is also one of the driving forces affecting the learning of the elderly.

4.2.2 Applications Close to the Needs of Life

If the applications are relevant to their daily lives, the participants will be more motivated to learn and use them. E4 said that he learned how to make a video recording. Giving and receiving support through digital means can enhance people's sense of connection and happiness [11]. E3 had always wanted to learn the video function on his phone and was happy to chat face to face with friends he hadn't seen for a long time.

E11, E12, E14, E15, E16, and E17 said that in addition to application learning, other added values such as finding data, asking questions in groups, sharing information, and video-calling with grandchildren have benefited them a lot. As the younger generation is keen to use technology, older people are also looking to strengthen their connection with their children through social networking apps [2].

Participants with positive perceptions of the Internet and applications used them more frequently and actively and learned new applications continuously [2]. In the group observation, the researchers found that participants would forward information about entertainment or health, while the same type of information would be repeated, but this kind of situation gradually improved over time. At the same time, participants asked questions to the group member and discuss with each other, thus promoting the development of information literacy. If they could apply the application to their daily life, such as communicating with people, getting the information they are interested in, and keeping up to date, they would be motivated to use the application [2].

E2 has been recognized by its peers for its "daily sentence". The self-expression of the sender has its over-attribution of similarity, while the async use and self-fulfilling feedback prediction enhance the sense of intimacy [6].

4.2.3 Study with Family and Friends

Participants were assisted by family and friends to overcome learning disabilities and communicate with each other through communication applications [2].

E2 said his children could him how to operate, so he learned it more easily. E4, E13, and E20 said that when they had problems in class, they would ask for the help of a partner sitting next to them, so they didn't feel stressed. If they didn't understand, they would ask the teacher. They also shared with each other and learned about new technological tools.

Other studies have shown that older people's motivation to learn improves when they seek help or advice if they encounter problems [2].

Some participants said that they were worried about information security and fraud, or were too afraid to use their phones for fear of breaking them. E6 said he was afraid of being cheated and having his money stolen. E20 said he was worried about breaking the phone. These fears are real for older people and discourage them. In these situations, they feel helpless in protecting, identifying, and solving problems. However, once they overcome their fears and doubts about the safety of technology, they can concentrate on learning and using it [6].

5 Conclusions and Recommendations for Future Work

We live in the age of information and technology [7]. With the rapid development of technology, more and more have used communication software. Whether people are familiar with each other or not, we can communicate and interact with each other through the Internet media to shorten the distance between us. When the elderly encounter difficulties in learning to use multimedia instant messaging software, they need more technical support from family and friends. In addition, the elderly and their families and friends can interact with each other through multimedia instant messaging software, effectively enhancing their application of multimedia instant messaging software and other additional information.

The results show that in highly interactive classes (such as courses on asking questions and discussing ideas), learning from peers and working in groups were both effective ways for the elderly to learn new things [2]. Walther [12] provided an explanation of the hyperpersonal model. This model suggests that due to the communication characteristics of the elderly, it is possible for them to have social relationships characterized by high intimate relationships through computer-mediated communication. In addition, older people often have self-directed learning needs that require more time and practice and technical assistance [2].

Promoting social inclusion, network linkage and social participation are key to designing social resilience [6]. Older people don't care whether the information is correct or not. They only care about the popularity of the information. They are more skilled in using technology, but their media literacy needs to improve. It is found that as they get older, older people, aware of their limited time, tend to prioritize spending time with close people and focus on the meaningful things in their lives, rather than broadening their horizons and learning new information [13].

While identifying many positive aspects of technology, older people also recognize that technology can also disempower people [2]. The mastery of information and technology enables people to take more control over themselves, such as searching for problems, solving problems, or seeking help in real time through the Internet.

Multimedia instant messaging software is a guiding software, and information and communication technology (ICT) is not the only way to promote knowledge-related goals. The use of ICT to achieve socially meaningful goals should be linked to well-being [13].

5.1 Research Limitations

This is a pilot study with a small sample size and no control group. Training courses with sufficient practice time and supportive environment are required to gain an in-depth understanding of the differences and information literacy of the elderly before and after use. However, assessing the information literacy of the elderly using multimedia instant messaging software has not been explored in depth in other emerging technologies, so this study can be shown as an important first step in this field.

5.2 Future Work

In this study, we found that the content of training and the psychological factors of participants caused the learning difference of the elderly, so we will take a larger sample number in the future, compare the results between the experimental group and the control group, and consider the psychology of the elderly to understand the impact of the implementation process on the elderly.

In addition, basic personal data, including gender, life history, occupation, physical and cognitive status, as well as experience of using 3C products should be thoroughly investigated. These are likely to be important influencing factors and should be studied experimentally.

References

1. He, T., Huang, C., Li, M., Zhou, Y., Li, S.: Social participation of the elderly in China: The roles of conventional media, digital access and social media engagement. Telematics Inform. **48**, 101347 (2020)
2. Chiu, C.J., Hu, Y.H., Lin, D.C., Chang, F.Y., Chang, C.S., Lai, C.F.: The attitudes, impact, and learning needs of older adults using apps on touchscreen mobile devices: results from a pilot study. Comput. Hum. Behav. **63**, 189–197 (2016)
3. Choi, J.R., Straubhaar, J., Skouras, M., Park, S., Santillana, M., Strover, S.: Techno-capital: theorizing media and information literacy through information technology capabilities. New Med. Soc. 1461444820925800 (2020)
4. Wu, H.Y., Chiou, A.F.: Social media usage, social support, intergenerational relationships, and depressive symptoms among older adults. Geriat. Nurs. **41**(5), 615–621 (2020)
5. Vroman, K.G., Arthanat, S., Lysack, C.: "Who over 65 is online?" Older adults' dispositions toward information communication technology. Comput. Hum. Behav. **43**, 156–166 (2015)
6. Hill, R., Betts, L.R., Gardner, S.E.: Older adults' experiences and perceptions of digital technology:(Dis) empowerment, wellbeing, and inclusion. Comput. Hum. Behav. **48**, 415–423 (2015)
7. Linares-Soler, G.: Understanding how ageing australians experience information literacy using mobile devices. J. Aust. Libr. Inform. Assoc. **66**(2), 174–175 (2017)
8. McClure, C.R.: Network literacy: a role for libraries. Inform. Technol. Libr. **13**(2), 115–125 (1994)
9. Deng-Yuan, W.: Study of the constitutional foundations of the right to senior education in Taiwan: a lifelong-learning-right perspective. Jiaoyu Kexue Yanjiu Qikan **63**(2), 1 (2018)
10. Cropley, A.J. (ed.).: Towards a System of Lifelong Education: Some Practical Considerations, vol. 7. Elsevier (2014)
11. Thomas, P.A.: Is it better to give or to receive? Social support and the well-being of older adults. J. Gerontol. B Psychol. Sci. Soc. Sci. **65**(3), 351–357 (2010)
12. Walther, J.B.: Computer-mediated communication: impersonal, interpersonal, and hyperpersonal interaction. Commun. Res. **23**(1), 3–43 (1996)
13. Sims, T., Reed, A.E., Carr, D.C.: Information and communication technology use is related to higher well-being among the oldest-old. J. Gerontol.: Ser. B **72**(5), 761–770 (2017)

Study on Development of Mobile App Design as Learning Media in Student Internship Support: Toward Strengthening Tie and Realistic Feedback in University-Industry Cooperation

Andik Asmara and Ting-Ting Wu[(✉)]

National Yunlin University of Science and Technology, Douliu 64002, Yunlin, Taiwan, R. O. C.
{d10743015, ttwu}@yuntech.edu.tw

Abstract. The development of technology was rapidly especially in the mobile phone that equipped with various mobile apps. A mobile app was developed on the purpose to help humans toward an easier and efficient ways. Education was received resonance effect from mobile apps influencing to various fields. Therefore, this study was a mixed-method research approach, were had a purpose to obtain user responds on the engagement of mobile app into the student internship program toward successfully of cooperation between university-industry. The sample of this study was fifty-five students on engineering faculty, two teacher, and four industry supervisors. Questionnaires and interviews were used to collect the data as the mobile app user response which will be implemented on an internship program. The result was realistic feedback will be achieved through pictures and videos reporting that represent industry technology implementation, and through industry feedback that represents observation result on students' performance during the internship.

Keywords: Mobile apps · Student internships · University-industry cooperation

1 Introduction

As human life in the current era must feel rapid technology development particularly in communication technologies, and common development and wear the majority worldwide that is mobile phones [1, 2]. Rapid development from many sides, such as electronic devices, software operating systems, and mobile applications (apps) bring technology and usability changes. The development of mobile apps on a basis considers usability (user needs) and benefits that want to achieve [3, 4]. In current development, mobile apps can be implemented in various filed to reach more benefits, such as health care [5, 6], education [7], and transportation or services. Particularly digital era today had big roles such as mobile apps that offering user tools, helpers, and the solver in education that free or purchase to wears.

A mobile phone is one of device that proposed in past research's as most suitable device to promote learning media [7, 8]. The development of mobile app entrances to the education field, such as e-book, e-learning, ubiquitous learning [9], and video conference and learning [10]. Mobile apps as learning media have the flexibility and innovatively unlimited based on user or designer purpose development. In [8] described those mobile apps in the mobile phone which development by the user has been innovatively designed to enhance the value of e-learning. The value just does not come from the application itself; however, it is also usable, easy to use [11], ubiquitous reliable [1] and everyone has (common wearable). Based on these, mobile apps bringing education more flexible [2] and efficient to reach the goal and achieve the purpose. In addition, mostly mobile apps development bringing new ideas into education to enhance learning achievement and flexibility to merge with education program.

One of the activities that giving meaningful experience [12], enhancing knowledge and skills [13] to the student is the internship program. The internship facilitates students to balance theoretical and practical knowledge and should be encouraged to learn from classroom and real-life or work situations [14]. The benefit not just received by students, however, schools also receive potential positive impacts through adjusting the curriculum and programs accordingly [15] then had an alignment. The alignment between industries' needs and education outcome common importance [16], and could be facilitated or touched by technology to optimize and more simplify the process. Involved technology in education was begun to happen digital technologies be discovered.

The fundamental functions touched by technologies are to improve internship outcomes to more realistic or represent the industry's needs. The innovations needed to facilitate university and industry cooperation using touched by kinds of technology. Technology bringing easy and simple steps to put feedback or communication with each other members of cooperation. Possibly prior innovation involving mobile phones into a collaboration between university and industry especially in the internship program wasn't been happening. What university needs and another side what industry needs to be important consider notice in developing technology. Based on this introduction this study had proposed to offer mobile app design and identify a university-industry needs in the internship program. Furthermore, this study was conducted in-depth to interview both parties to learn and understand what they need. This study had a research question as follow:

1. What are students responding to in the mobile apps involvement to organize internship programs?
2. What are University-Industry needs to improve the quality of cooperation through mobile apps as an organizer of an internship program?

2 Literature Review

2.1 Student Internships Program as One of Activities in University-Industry Cooperation (UIC)

One of activities the cooperation program between university and industry is student internship programs. This is positive strategies for the university to promote their comprehensive curriculum [17] and in the future has an impact on outcome quality and student's intake. In addition, this is as a student learning and then applying knowledge and skill from academic settings to real workplace settings [13]. Chen and Shen in 2012 describe the purpose of an internship, that is: expand cooperation between university and enterprise; implementation of student knowledge into practice; and giving students first experience in the real job [18]. Research by Kim and Park in 2013 mentions that the internships program become one of the most prominent indicators in determining the quality of students [19]. Students have received knowledge and how much their fluence use knowledge can be seen from applying to a real job or workplace.

Cooperation between University and Industry not only on student internships program, however development technology, research collaboration, human development, patent and generation new products [20]. In order to create strong cooperation and high potential bring in mutual benefit into student internships program, university and industry constructing a mechanism to facilitate this program. The mechanism had existed was constructed to utilize the website base technology information [12]. Definitely, this mechanism need supported from internet access and computer device, included personal computer, laptop, and tablet.

2.2 The Role Mobile Apps on Education

Website platform was familiar mostly people around the world, in education viewpoint this become world's largest lesson [21]. The contains on the website has a lot of types and brings advantages or disadvantages to the education field. The most students access destination on web address is google and YouTube [22]. YouTube is a famous platform where students can learn anything about knowledge, skills, and entertainment from various fields. Students are able to upload, download, and streaming pictures or videos based on they want and needs, particularly as related to learning media that support the learning. YouTube is a video sharing provider and was integrated into the mobile phone applications currently [21]. Further, mobile phone though the development of mobile application (Mobile Apps) had prominent role to easier access and effectively times.

The term of mobile learning rises in line with an increment of usability of mobile phones for learning media. Through mobile learning user would be equip with easy access on learning content by the tips of their finger. In fact that increasingly recognize mobile learning in education institution was happening, due to the ubiquitous feature on mobile device which distinguish them from other learning tools [7]. In addition, several researchers previously had been proposing mobile phone is handle device that most suitable to promote mobile learning [7, 23, 24]. Hence, mobile phones equip with mobile apps benefitable if engagement in developing of facility that has a tie with education, for instance, propose into student internships program.

3 Methodology

The mixed-method approach was used in this study, consist of a quantitative approach using a Likert scale to collect data and a qualitative approach using the interview to collect data.

3.1 Research Framework

The mobile application become a solution to manage student achievements on internship program. This App facilitating user especially students to reporting many achievements, such as; daily activities, final report, take photo of activity, record and then upload video activity (see Fig. 2). The students as one of user who using mobile apps to report their activity industries. Another else as users are teachers/lecturers and supervisor in industries. Teacher as user have role to monitoring students' activities and maintain communication relationship with industries. Whereas supervisor of industry has role to validation of student activities and give feedback to universities related to knowledge, skills, and behaviors of students during the internship (Fig. 1).

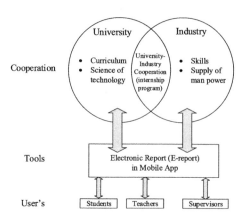

Fig. 1. Research framework of mobile app facilitate student internships.

3.2 Population and Samples

The population of this study consist of three categories; they are university students, university teachers or faculty members, and supervisors in industries. In order to collect the data, selection of samples and participants use random sampling. Students category were selected who has took internships program before, and got 55 students has return the questionnaires. Further, participant from teachers are two persons who has experience as internships advisor and supervisors of industry are four persons who has experiences as student's internships advisor. The sequence coding of interviewee details as follow, (Participant codes = position – duration (years) as advisor): $P1$ = Faculty internship coordinator – 5; $P2$ = Electrical department internship coordinator – 1; P3 = Production manager – 5; $P4$ = Director of PT. PMCT – 6; $P5$ = Marketing Manager – 5; $P6$ = R&D manager – 5.

3.3 Data Collection

The data collection consists to two ways; first is questionnaire to collect the data from student's interpretation about this mobile app will be implement. The question consists of 17 point and using five Likert-scale, included three-dimension measure that is components, content to reported and adequate of facilities. Second is interview to collect and record the data from participant, included teachers and supervisors of industries. The interview question consists of 12 point, and based on two-perspective viewpoint.

3.4 Data Analysis

The type of questionnaire data is the Likert-scale; therefore, data were analyzed used descriptive statistics using SPSS-22. In addition, the transcription of interviewee answer was used verbatim technique, had mean the whole conversation were transcript Indonesia language become English text. A Grounded theory were used to analyzing, in order to obtained generating a theory through systematic data collection and analysis [25].

4 Finding

4.1 User Interface on Mobile App

Figure 2 is user interface was design to propose facilitate the student during internship activities in industries. The interface that offered provide for student level, teacher level, and supervisor level in industries. The facilitate in application that include; student such as daily activity, final report, video learning, picture learning, and note; teacher and supervisor has similarity such as approval daily activity, approval final report, and feedback.

Fig. 2. User interface on mobile app.

4.2 Validity and Reliability Test

The first step was the validity test, and the result got a score of Pearson Correlation start .393 till .716 with $n = 54$. The result had meant more than r-table .279 ($n = 50$) and can be explain that each point question was valid. Second, reliability test had checked using Alpha Cronbach test to each category of the variable. The result was: purpose .763; readiness .663; contribute in learning .789; components of facilitate .807; and total .867. Based on the reliability test result the instrument used to collect the data can be explain that questionnaire was reliable, had significant result more than .6.

4.3 Finding of Students, Teachers, and Supervisors

The questionnaire data was collected and continually analyzed to obtain the mean and standard deviation. The result was (variable (mean), std. deviation): purpose (4.09), .493; readiness (4.31), .586; contribution in learning (4.19), .462; and component that facilitate (4.13), .476. This data has meant that majority answer from student got score more than 4 point. Whereas the interview data was analyzed and found saturation several statement question that raised. Another answer from participant would be evidences of user responds, especially from teachers and industry supervisors.

5 Discussion

Based on the research finding, design mobile app that has provided in this research could be fulfilled user needs. The evidence from a student's viewpoint; the result of the questionnaire had shown that purpose, contribute to learning, and component to facilitate user (students) needs have mean score is more than 4 Likert scale. What students need could be facilitated with all the menus that provide in the mobile app were design and developing this research. What teachers and industry supervisors need such as controlling, reporting, scoring and feedback was facilitation in this mobile app. Moreover, teachers had given a good response to several menus (pictures and videos attachment) as a breakthrough in education via a mobile app for reporting internships program. This aligns with P2 argument that says;

> "If using this mobile app, he/she can take pictures or video what they do and be updated every day. It's awesome and really-reporting and complete with evidence. And video could be shown on class learning activities, automatically student know what skills and knowledge that industry's needs." (P2)

This argues explaining and supporting that curriculums and technology in school/university should be updated as represent industries need [26, 27]. So that using pictures or videos that are attached to the mobile app as reporting internships, could support educational needs and eliminate the lacks of knowledge between education and industries, or between theory and practical reality [13, 17]. Through those media, the schools/universities get updated knowledge and technology.

In order to give optimum advantages from constructing a mobile app on the internship program needed responses from three group users, including students, teachers, and industry supervisors. The responses here have meant to gathering what the user needs to facilitate, how to make an internship program running well, and how-to bring effect on each party so can receive the benefits. Therefore, this study had collected responses data from three group users to create strengthen tie with each other.

The group firstly, students respond on mobile apps to facilitate their reporting activities. As long as, common reporting use paper-based and take longtime on administration. The innovation in mobile app, and focus on electronic reporting could be adjuster and trimer the situation previously, to be effectively and efficiently. It was welcomed positively on students; they give high expectations that evident from high score was gotten from questionnaire. The prominent interpretation from students' answers are emphasis on the meaning of each part. Begin from purpose of this mobile app has in line with student need to facilitate their activities on internship programs. Further, this study was collected data about student readiness to used mobile app, and brief conclusions is student have high readiness due to familiar with mobile phone [7]. Whereas, this mobile app could be contributing to education learning based on the student's viewpoint. Besides in order to facilitate students to submit administration affairs, this application also has a facility to attach pictures and videos that purpose to learning media in the class. Lastly, students had argued that components on the mobile app was complete and fulfill what student wants.

The second group is teacher, have role to bridge between school/university and industries [18], could be called as facilitator. Teacher every year will be touching with this mobile app, so quite important to get a response from this user. A teacher has familiar before with similar reporting into online system way, and system that offered useful to help teacher effectively and efficiently. Efficiently meant the teacher has reason to trim time on documents submission of internship to be shorter. Whereas, effectively come from eliminate distance (construct digital bridge) industry locations with school/university [28]. These got answer from teacher as a respondent said like as below;

> *"I believe they ready, because all the faculty members have familiar with mobile phone and Apps, and easy to access. ... In addition, administration, communication, and controlling student more efficient time, just use this app. ... For instance, location on far in Jakarta, Bali, or Lombok to direct monitoring come to in place considering the expensive cost. So, this mobile app giving solution to this issue." (P1)*

The last user's group is industry supervisor, and become consider to school/university party to giving the best cooperation and services. Hence, this study took participants from industries party more, more than teachers. The reason is to obtain what industries need particularly in student internship programs. Based on data results, showing that industries felt ready to implement mobile apps if begun used. Due to the majority industry currently in industrial 4.0 was implements information technology in each part of the enterprise [29]. For instance, communication each other employee and reporting were use mobile phone or online system. These had evidence from respondent say as below;

> *"Previously, we use mobile phone technology to communicate, coordination and reporting, such as WhatsApp group (P3, P5). Because this system simpler and effectively (P5)."*

Further, related to facilitation provided on a mobile app that offered in this research, industries were attracted. They are sure engagement mobile app in student internships program bringing a lot of benefits. This system will be simplifying reporting, easily on scoring, and make more students discipline. However, industries mention that socializes still needed to familiarize before widely implementations. It's important, due to several industries just follow what schools provided and unfamiliar with new technology. These concerns were gotten from participants answer as follow;

> "I am agreeing this implemented. Scoring easier (P3, P4, P5, P6), more student discipline (P4), and simplify reporting with paperless (P5, P6). ... And we need to pay attention to do socializing to industries and employees (P5)."

Another concern was pointed on taking pictures and videos to complete reporting. It's becoming students and teachers worries, due to industry prohibits to doing these activities. However, it's declined and industry is open, just several parts, the file needs to keep secret. Students in their activity want to take pictures and videos should get permits first.

Based on fact were gotten from samples on this research, engagement mobile app on student internships program bringing more advantages. In addition, to achieve realistic feedback in this mobile app was put several facilitations, such as picture and video learning, final e-report, and suggestion from industry supervisors. Feedback menu on this mobile app is quite important, due to giving personal suggestions from supervisors (observer) to school/university related to students' capabilities. It's become an improvement or evaluation for the school curriculum to improve or change with real knowledge and skill needs [18]. So, in the future curriculum of schools/universities up-to-date based on industries or workplaces needs [30]. In addition, the points are curriculum, learning activities, technology insight in education represent of industries situation currently.

6 Conclusion

The term of realistic feedback has meant included industry suggestions, the picture of a technology that implements on the industry, and the knowledge from industry could become an input to schools/universities improvement the curriculum quality. Through mobile app creating new value on student internships program and all aspect become effectively and efficiently. The students believed, and got good respond that implement mobile app technology aligns with the purpose of the internship program, and could facilitation on internship activities. Whereas two parties that have interests which are school/university and industry felt welcome open to the implementation of a mobile app in an internship program. It's could be a breakthrough in quality improvement, strengthen collaboration ties, and simplify-effectively process on internships.

References

1. Rashid, A.T.: Mobile phones and development: an analysis of IDRC-supported projects. EJISDC **36**, 1–16 (2009)
2. Aitkenhead, M.J., Donnelly, D., Coull, M.C., Hastings, E.: Innovations in environmental monitoring using mobile phone technology – a review. Int. J. Interact. Mob. Technol. **8**(2), 42–50 (2014). https://doi.org/10.3991/ijim.v8i2.3645
3. Bhatheja, S., et al.: Developing a mobile application for global cardiovascular education. J. Am. Coll. Cardiol. **72**(20), 2518–2527 (2018). https://doi.org/10.1016/j.jacc.2018.08.2183
4. Chávez, A., Borrego, G., Gutierrez-Garcia, J.O., Rodríguez, L.F.: Design and evaluation of a mobile application for monitoring patients with Alzheimer's disease: a day center case study. Int. J. Med. Informatics **131**, 103972 (2019). https://doi.org/10.1016/j.ijmedinf.2019.103972
5. Anderson, K., Burford, O., Emmerton, L.: Mobile health apps to facilitate self-care: a qualitative study of user experiences. PLoS ONE **11**(5), 1–21 (2016). https://doi.org/10.1371/journal.pone.0156164
6. Dute, D.J., Bemelmans, W.J.E., Breda, J.: Using mobile apps to promote a healthy lifestyle among adolescents and students: a review of the theoretical basis and lessons learned. JMIR mHealth uHealth **4**(2), e39 (2016). https://doi.org/10.2196/mhealth.3559
7. Ismail, I., Azizan, S.N., Azman, N.: Mobile phone as pedagogical tools: are teachers ready? Int. Educ. Stud. **6**(3), 36–47 (2013). https://doi.org/10.5539/ies.v6n3p36
8. Cahyana, U., Paristiowati, M., Savitri, D.A., Hasyrin, S.N.: Developing and application of mobile game based learning (M-GBL) for high school students performance in chemistry. Eurasia J. Math. Sci. Technol. Educ. **13**(10), 7037–7047 (2017). https://doi.org/10.12973/ejmste/78728
9. Pishtari, G., et al.: Learning design and learning analytics in mobile and ubiquitous learning: a systematic review. Br. J. Educ. Technol., 1–23 (2020). https://doi.org/10.1111/bjet.12944
10. Ting, Y.L., Tai, Y., Tseng, T.H., Tsai, S.P.: Innovative use of mobile video conferencing in face-to-face collaborative science learning: the case of reflection in optics. Educ. Technol. Soc. **21**(3), 74–85 (2018)
11. Pauljuinnbing Tan, P., Chihsuan Lin, C., Weichuan Wang, W.: Understanding college students' desire for internships in the information technology industry, pp. 202–211 (2016). https://doi.org/10.2991/mse-15.2016.36
12. Ashton, W.S., Hurtado-Martin, M., Anid, N.M., Khalili, N.R., Panero, M.A., McPherson, S.: Pathways to cleaner production in the Americas I: bridging industry-academia gaps in the transition to sustainability. J. Clean. Prod. **142**, 432–444 (2017). https://doi.org/10.1016/j.jclepro.2016.03.116
13. Bukaliya, R.: The potential benefits and challenges of internship programmes in an ODL Institution: a case for the Zimbabwe Open University. Int. J. New Trends Educ. Implic. **3**(1), 13–1309 (2012)
14. Kounlaxay, K., Kyun Kim, S.: Design of learning media in mixed reality for Lao Education. Comput. Mater. Continu. **64**(1), 161–180 (2020). https://doi.org/10.32604/cmc.2020.09930
15. Haag, S., Guilbeau, E., Goble, W.: Assessing engineering internship efficacy: industry's perception of student performance. Int. J. Eng. Educ. **22**(2), 257–263 (2006)
16. D'Este, P., Patel, P.: University-industry linkages in the UK: what are the factors underlying the variety of interactions with industry? Res. Policy **36**(9), 1295–1313 (2007). https://doi.org/10.1016/j.respol.2007.05.002
17. Lam, T., Ching, L.: An exploratory study of an internship program: the case of Hong Kong students. Int. J. Hosp. Manag. **26**(2), 336–351 (2007). https://doi.org/10.1016/j.ijhm.2006.01.001

18. Chen, T.L., Shen, C.C.: Today's intern, tomorrow's practitioner? - The influence of internship programmes on students' career development in the Hospitality Industry. J. Hosp. Leis. Sport Tour. Educ. **11**(1), 29–40 (2012). https://doi.org/10.1016/j.jhlste.2012.02.008
19. Kim, H.B., Park, E.J.: The role of social experience in undergraduates' career perceptions through internships. J. Hosp. Leis. Sport Tour. Educ. **12**(1), 70–78 (2013). https://doi.org/10.1016/j.jhlste.2012.11.003
20. Eom, B.Y., Lee, K.: Determinants of industry-academy linkages and their impact on firm performance: the case of Korea as a latecomer in knowledge industrialization. Res. Policy **39**(5), 625–639 (2010). https://doi.org/10.1016/j.respol.2010.01.015
21. Çimşir, B.T., Uzunboylu, H.: Awareness training for sustainable development: development, implementation and evaluation of a mobile application. Sustainability **11**(3) (2019). https://doi.org/10.3390/su11030611
22. Ngampornchai, A., Adams, J.: Students' acceptance and readiness for E-learning in Northeastern Thailand. Int. J. Educ. Technol. High. Educ. **13**(1), 1–13 (2016). https://doi.org/10.1186/s41239-016-0034-x
23. Suki, N.M., Suki, N.M.: Are lecturers- ready for usage of mobile technology for teaching? World Acad. Sci. Eng. Technol. **3**(6), 748–751 (2009). https://doi.org/10.5281/zenodo.1085490
24. Prensky, M.: What can you learn from a cell phone? Almost anything! In: From Digital Natives to Digital Wisdom: Hopeful Essays for 21st Century Learning, vol. 2002, no. 2001, pp. 179–191 (2005). https://doi.org/10.4135/9781483387765.n23
25. Reyes, A.T., Kearney, C.A., Bombard, J.N., Boni, R.L., Senette, C.L., Acupan, A.R.: Student veterans' coping with posttraumatic stress symptoms: a glaserian grounded theory study. Issues Ment. Health Nurs. **40**(8), 655–664 (2019). https://doi.org/10.1080/01612840.2019.1591545
26. Joós, G., Marceau, R.J., Scott, G., Péloquin, D.: An innovative industry-university partnership to enhance university training and industry recruiting in power engineering. IEEE Trans. Power Syst. **19**(1), 24–30 (2004). https://doi.org/10.1109/TPWRS.2003.821015
27. Rikap, C., Harari-Kermadec, H.: Motivations for collaborating with industry: has public policy influenced new academics in Argentina? Stud. High. Educ., 1–12 (2019). https://doi.org/10.1080/03075079.2019.1659764
28. Crescenzi, R., Filippetti, A., Iammarino, S.: Academic inventors: collaboration and proximity with industry. J. Technol. Transfer **42**(4), 730–762 (2017). https://doi.org/10.1007/s10961-016-9550-z
29. Oztemel, E., Gursev, S.: Literature review of Industry 4.0 and related technologies. J. Intell. Manuf. **31**(1), 127–182 (2018). https://doi.org/10.1007/s10845-018-1433-8
30. Valdez, A.P., et al.: The six-month internship training program for medical laboratory science education: an initial evaluation. JPAIR Multidiscip. Res. **9**(1), 269–283 (2012). https://doi.org/10.7719/jpair.v9i1.3

Science, Technology, Engineering, Arts and Design, and Mathematics

3D Digital Design to Support Elementary School Students' Spatial Visualization Skills: A Preliminary Analysis

Pao-Nan Chou(✉) and Ru-Chu Shih

Graduate Institute of Technological and Vocational Education,
National Pingtung University of Science and Technology, Neipu, Taiwan
pnchou@g4e.npust.edu.tw

Abstract. This study aimed to investigate the effect of 3D digital design on students' spatial visualization skills. A 3D digital design program as one of afterschool clubs was created in a public elementary school. 10 students voluntarily participated in the program. A quasi-experimental pretest and posttest design was used to fulfill the research purpose. The educational experiment lasted for six weeks. Prior to the study, students were given a spatial visualization pretest. One week after the completion of the experiment, students received the same post-test. The results showed that the 3D digital design intervention significantly improved students' spatial visualization skills.

Keywords: 3D digital design · STEM education · Spatial visualization · Education reform

1 Introduction

Our previous study showed that elementary school students receiving 3D computer software instruction (Google SketchUp) significantly enhanced their basic engineering knowledge, particularly for spatial ability [1]. Based on this findings, in other words, the 3D digital design training had a potential for developing students' spatial visualization skill. In the current study, we adopted another 3D computer software (TinkerCad) with 3D printers to design an instructional intervention whose goal was to evaluate the effect of 3D digital design on students' spatial visualization skills.

In the literature, several studies also attempted to incorporate 3D digital design with 3D printers into the curriculum. However, few studies adopted a scientific view to evaluate the instructional effectiveness. For example, in McKay et al.'s study [2] high school students used emerging maker technologies such as 3D printers and Laser cutters to design their projects in one makerspace classroom. However, the study only described the learning process and did not report further information regarding students' learning performances. Similarly, Kalsioloudis and Jones [3] only proposed theoretical arguments regarding the learning benefits of 3D printers.

The purpose of the study was to examine the effect of one 3D digital design program (TinkerCAD) on elementary school students' spatial visualization skills. Specifically, the research question was:

- Did students receiving 3D digital design instruction improve their spatial visualization skills?

2 Research Method

2.1 Research Design

A quasi-experimental pretest and posttest without a control group design was used to investigate the effect of 3D digital design on students' spatial visualization skills. The educational experiment lasted for six weeks. Prior to the study, students were given a spatial visualization pretest. One week after the completion of the experiment, students received the same post-test with different item numbers.

2.2 Research Participant

Ten forth-grade students (male: 5; female: 5) from a public elementary school in Taiwan voluntarily participated in the study. Prior to the study, they had no experience designing 3D objects by using computer software. Figure 1 shows a student engaging in 3D digital design activities.

Fig. 1. A student engaging in 3D digital design activities.

2.3 Research Instrument

A test developed by Ou [4] was used to measure elementary school students' spatial visualization. The test contains 15 multi-choice questions. The score range of the test from 0 to 15. Ou [4] reported high validity and reliability of the test. Figure 2 shows one question example.

2.4 Teaching Schedule

The educational experiment was conducted in a computer lab. The 3D digital design program as one of after-school clubs lasted for six weeks (See Table 1). The weekly class was scheduled in a 3 h session. Student participants used 3D computer software called TinkerCAD to design their 3D objects. When students completed the 3D digital design in each week, the instructor collected the digital files and subsequently transferred them to one 3D printer. In the upcoming learning session, students obtained their tangible 3D objects.

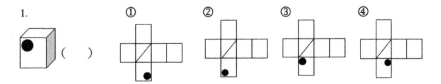

Fig. 2. One question example from the test (adapted from Ou's test).

2.5 Engineering Design Process

This study adopted Chou's [5] three-stage learning progression model (see Fig. 3) as engineering design process. In the first stage (copy), students only copy teacher-provided 3D design. When moving the second stage (tinker), students might modify the 3D design by incorporating their own ideas. In the last stage (create), students were asked to create their 3D objects.

Table 1. Teaching schedule.

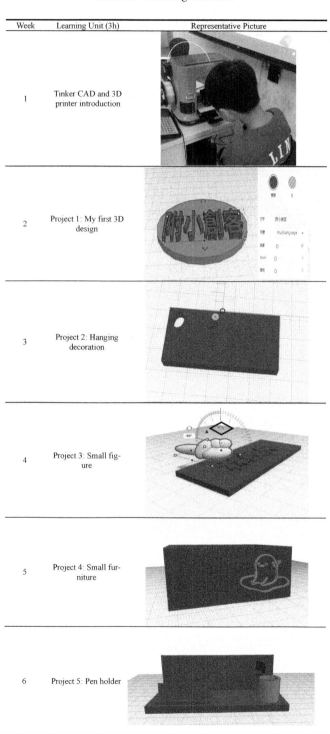

Week	Learning Unit (3h)	Representative Picture
1	Tinker CAD and 3D printer introduction	
2	Project 1: My first 3D design	
3	Project 2: Hanging decoration	
4	Project 3: Small figure	
5	Project 4: Small furniture	
6	Project 5: Pen holder	

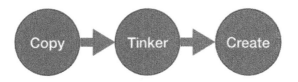

Fig. 3. Chou's three-stage learning progression model.

3 Preliminary Findings

Table 2 reports the results of t-test. The findings indicated that students' spatial visualization skills were significantly improved after a 6-week educational experiment ($t = 7.62$; $p < 0.01$). In other words, the 3D digital design intervention might show a learning benefit for elementary school students. The results supported Trumble's [6] study which reported that elementary school students significantly increased their spatial ability after the completion of a summer camp.

Table 2. Results of t-test.

Comparison	Mean difference	t	df	Sig.
Post-test & Pre-test	6.2	7.62	9	0.00**

$^{**}p < 0.01$ (Pre-Test: $M = 2.8$/$S.D. = 0.9$; Post-Test: $M = 9$/$S.D. = 2.3$)

4 Concluding Remark

Our preliminary research results indicated that the 3D digital design activity might support students learning spatial visualization. One possible explanation was that immerging in 3D digital design activities enabled students to greatly visualize spatial rotations, which directly influenced their spatial visualization skills. Our next research step was to interview students' learning responses. It will be expected that the qualitative results may support quantitative findings.

References

1. Chou, P.-N., Chen, W.-F., Wu, C.-Y., Robert, C.: Utilizing 3D open source software to facilitate student learning of fundamental engineering knowledge: a quasi-experimental study. Int. J. Eng. Educ. **33**(1b), 382–388 (2017)
2. McKay, C., Banks, T.D., Wallace, S.: Makerspace classrooms: where technology intersects with problem, project, and place-based design in classroom curriculum. Int. J. Des. Learn. **7**(2), 11–16 (2016)
3. Katsloloudis, P., Jones, M.: Using computer-aided design software and 3D printers to improve spatial visualization. Technol. Eng. Teach. **75**(4), 14–20 (2015)

4. Ou, R.L.: The study on the problem representation of spatial ability for sixth-grade students. Unpublished Master Thesis, National Taichung University of Education (2016)
5. Chou, P.-N.: Smart technology for sustainable curriculum: using drone to support young students' learning. Sustainability **10**(10), 3819, 1–17 (2018)
6. Trumble, J.: 3D digital design and elementary students' spatial visualization skills. In: Proceedings of Society for Information Technology & Teacher Education International Conference, pp. 114–117, Association for the Advancement of Computing in Education, Austin (2017)

Developing the Scale of Technology Product Imagination Disposition

Yi-Jin Wang[1], Hui-Min Lai[2], Tien-Chi Huang[1(✉)], and Pei-ling Chien[3]

[1] Department of Information Management, National Taichung University of Science and Technology, Taichung 404, Taiwan
tchuang@gm.nutc.edu.tw
[2] Department of Business Administration, National Taichung University of Science and Technology, Taichung 404, Taiwan
[3] Global Communication Faculty, Kobe Gakuin University, Kobe, Japan

Abstract. Due to the rapid development of information technology, not only did people begin to think about the rapid development of wireless networks, but also the development of products in other fields through various tools and applications, including the rise of audio-visual platforms and the popularization of mobile applications. They have made mobile games and mobile payments closer to our daily life. In this way, technology education has been widely used in the educational environment, showing the increasing demand for technology products in education. This study aims to develop and verify the characteristics of people's imagination of technology products. A total of 135 objects over the age of 18. Through exploratory factor analysis performed by principal component analysis of the varimax orthogonal rotation; item analysis uses comparisons of extreme groups so as to check item-total correlations and internal consistency; Confirmatory factor analysis compares the goodness of fit indices of the first-order model, the first-order four-factor model, and the second-order model. These analyses are conducted to determine and construct validity and reliability. A second-order model technology product imagination disposition scale is constructed, which contains 17 items in four facets, namely practical evaluation, positive preference, beyond reality and attitude, to measure people's imagination of technology products and help teachers understand the characteristics of students.

Keywords: Confirmatory factor analysis · Exploratory factor analysis · Technology imagination · Technology product · Scale development

1 Background

The rapid development of information technology has led to changes in various industries and fields. The future things seen on TV and movies are people's imagination of future inventions. Studies have pointed out that imagination is the foundation of creativity [1], indicating the source of creativity and invention. Because of its rich imagination, many inventions are mainly derived from people's use of imagination, through continuous thinking and experimentation, discovering many scientific theories and creating technologies that improve lives [2]. In the process of technology development, not only did people begin to think about the rapid development of wireless networks, but also the development of products in other fields through various tools and applications, including the rise of streaming platforms and the popularization of mobile applications. They have made mobile games and mobile payments closer to our daily life.

According to the literature, technology is an adaptation to environment tools for humans to use knowledge, tools, resources, and skills to solve life problems and expand capabilities [3]. In recent years, science and technology education has frequently appeared in the educational environment, showing the increasing acceptance of education for technology products. In the past, many studies have demonstrated the use of a single technology to help the learning environment [4–6], but there is very little research on people's imagination of technology. Therefore, this research aims to develop the technology product imagination disposition scale, defining technology products as covering software and hardware technologies, including APPs, websites, self-media, videos, and required equipment created by individuals. Discuss whether people have the qualities of imagining technology products so that teachers can understand the extent to which students imagine technology products.

2 Methods

2.1 Participants

In this study, Taiwanese people aged 18-year-old and over were the main respondents. To avoid the possibility of omission and mistakes caused by human error when inputting the data and the limitation of time and space, online questionnaires were selected for more distribution and questionnaire recovery. A total of 138 recovered questionnaires, with 135 valid and 3 invalid.

2.2 Research Tools

The research tool used in this institute is the "Technology Product Imagination Disposition Scale". This scale refers to the technology imagination disposition scale proposed by Lin [7] to discuss the correlation between grit and Internet addiction. It comes from three scale frameworks and is divided into six factors. Since this research is to explore the characteristics of imaginary technology products, it will be followed by an exploratory factor analysis. Based on the results of the item deletion, item analysis, and confirmatory factor analysis is conducted to unify the factors of technology product imagination.

The original scale is a Chinese version, without a translation process, a few inappropriate items that do not meet the purpose of this study are semantically revised or deleted and identified by four experts to delete the items that are not easy to understand the meaning of the question. A total of 4 items were deleted, and the remaining items were adjusted and revised, leaving 20 items. This research scale uses the 5-point Likert scale to quantify the measurement, and the scope ranged from 1 = Strongly Disagree to 5 = Strongly Agree.

2.3 Data Analysis

Statistical analyses were conducted using IBM SPSS Statistics Version 25.0 for exploratory factor analysis and item analysis as the basis for screening items, and then use Amos 26.0 for confirmatory factor analysis to confirm the construction validity of the technology products imagination scale.

3 Results

3.1 Exploratory Factor Analysis (EFA)

In this study, the exploratory factor analysis was the first to be carried out. The factor analysis was performed by principal component analysis of the varimax orthogonal rotation. The Kaiser-Meyer-Olkin (KMO) value was 0.89 (>0.5), and Bartlett's test of sphericity was 942.956 ($p < 0.05$), knowing that this scale is suitable for factor analysis [8]. Consider eigenvalue >1 [9], if the factor loading of the item is less than 0.5, or the item falls in more than one factor, delete it. The analysis results are shown in Table 1. A total of 3 items are deleted, resulting in 4 factors. By using the scale of Technology Imagination Disposition based on Lin [7] as a foundation to develop a new form of differentiation to distinguish the similar definition between the factors, which are practical evaluation, positive preference, beyond reality, and attitude; given that the fourth factor is a view refer to the way people feel toward a particular behavior [10], it is named "attitude". Practical evaluation refers to the possibility that individuals can imagine the practicability, mass production, acceptance and widespread of technology products; positive preference refers to the individual's positive emotions and preferences for imaginary technology products, which will produce happiness and interesting feelings, and the motivation to try to improve his imagination ability; beyond reality refers to improving the imagination for individuals to break through the limitation in the real world and construct unprecedented lifestyles or technology products as well as imagine plots or human things that transcend real characteristics from their ideas; attitude are used to assess the individual's attitude towards imaginative technology products. The variance explained is 62.19%.

Table 1. Exploratory factor analysis results.

Construct	Items	Factor loading			
		1	2	3	4
Practical evaluation	T3	0.792			
	T5	0.780			
	T7	0.639			
	T8	0.622			
	T10	0.592			
	T11	0.569			
Positive preference	T2		0.797		
	T4		0.714		
	T9		0.644		
	T17		0.588		
Beyond reality	T1			0.824	
	T6			0.738	
	T14			0.582	
	T15			0.567	
Attitude	T12				0.804
	T13				0.693
	T16				0.518

3.2 Item Analysis

The analysis of this research project uses comparisons of extreme groups so as to check Item-total correlations and internal consistency. The extreme group comparison method is to compare the difference between the total scores of the lowest 27% and the highest 27%. The difference in the results is called the Critical Ratio (CR). This was followed by conducting an independent sample t-test. All project levels reached a significant level ($p < 0.05$), ranging from 7.384 to 10.179 for practical evaluation, 6.935 to 8.903 for positive preference, 5.925 to 8.977 for beyond reality, and 3.788 to 6.968 for attitude factor. The correlation test checks the total correlation of each item and the total correlation of each item after correction. The correlation coefficient of all items is higher than 0.3 [11] and reaches a significant level ($p < 0.05$), ranging from 0.607 to 0.713 for practical evaluation, 0.623 to 0.691 for positive preference, 0.564 to 0.670 for beyond reality, and 0.443 to 0.653 for attitude factor. Furthermore, the corrected factor-scale total correlations were also above 0.3, ranging from 0.374 to 0.664. The Cronbach a coefficient after used to calculate the reliability of each scale. The Cronbach a coefficient after the deletion of all items did not exceed 0.903 of the original scale, indicating good internal consistency of the scale.

3.3 Confirmatory Factor Analysis (CFA)

This study conducted a confirmatory factor analysis on the four-factor model and observed the first-order model, the first-order four-factor model, and the second-order model. As shown in Table 2, when the first-order model ($\chi2 = 268.709$, $p = 0.000$, SRMR = 0.759, RMSEA = 0.097, TLI = 0.800, CFI = 0.825) is compared with the first-order four factors ($\chi2 = 230.292$, $p = 0.000$, SRMR = 0.2118, RMSEA = 0.087, TLI = 0.838, CFI = 0.864), most of them do not reach the ideal value in the goodness of fit indices. The second-order model ($\chi2 = 171.831$, $p = 0.000$, SRMR = 0.0611, RMSEA = 0.061, TLI = 0.921, CFI = 0.934), which is within the acceptable range according to the standard results [12]. Overall, the second-order model and sample data can be adapted, and the fit is good. The Akaike's Information Criterion (AIC) = 126.82, which is used to select among competing models [13]. It also indicates that the last measurement model is the most simplest as it displays the lowest value. Therefore, the second-order model (see Fig. 1) was used as the model for confirmatory factor analysis.

Table 2. Confirmatory factor analysis results.

	df	χ^2 (p)	SRMR	RMSEA	TLI	CFI	AIC
Criteria			<0.08	<0.08	>0.90	>0.90	
First-order model	119	268.709 (0.000)	0.759	0.097	0.800	0.825	336.709
First-order four-factor model	114	230.292 (0.000)	0.2118	0.087	0.838	0.864	308.292
Second-order model	115	171.831 (0.000)	0.0611	0.061	0.921	0.934	247.831

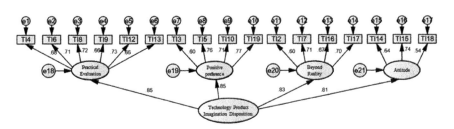

Fig. 1. The second-order model of technology product imagination disposition.

4 Discussion and Conclusion

This study develops the scale by constructing a second-order model of the technology product imagination disposition and distinguishes it into four factors, namely practical evaluation, positive preference, beyond reality, and attitude. In the future, this scale can be used to assess the tendency of students' technology product imagination. Students are evaluated before and after the implementation of relevant courses to evaluate the teaching effect. Teachers are able to design teaching courses and activities for students based on the four factors constructed in this study, using different teaching styles from the past, for example, use virtual reality to help students understand the spatial structure [14]. It not only increases the learning performance of students but also enables students to increases the tendency of using technology products. With diverse teaching methods, students are led to freely create personal works, from virtual to physical, to guide students to imagine and implement through life experience and learning content for enhancing the imagination ability of technology products.

Acknowlegments. This research is partially supported by the Ministry of Science and Technology (MOST), Taiwan (R.O.C.) under grant no MOST 108-2628-H-025-001-MY3, MOST 109-2511-H-025-005-MY3. We would like to thank them for its sponsorship and support.

Appendix

Items	
1	I could easily imagine the technology products that do not exist
2	I improve my imagination in many ways, such as reading fiction novels, attending creativity courses, and so on
3	I take practicality of my imaginative technology product into consideration
4	I found it pleasant to imagine technology product
5	I think of the presentation when imagining the technology product
6	I often think of the changes of the technology products nowadays
7	I take public acceptance of my technology product into account
8	I imagine the appearance and functions of technology product. Web screen, for instance
9	I consider that imagine technology product can spice up our life
10	I imagine technology product by combining different features, such as material, software, hardware, and so on
11	I evaluate popularity of the imaginative technology product
12	I consider that imagination can help to design a new technology product
13	I am able to connect things from imagination as well as virtual system and object to reality
14	I often imagine different kinds of tools that humans will use in the future
15	I expect customer demand from future technology product
16	I consider that imagination can help to create a technology product
17	I found it interesting to imagine technology product

References

1. Vygotsky, L.S.: Imagination and creativity in childhood. J. Russ. East Eur. Psychol. **42**, 7–97 (2004)
2. Wang, C.C., Ho, H.C., Wu, J.J., Cheng, Y.Y.: Development of scientific imagination model: a concept-mapping perspective. Think. Skills Creat. **13**, 106–119 (2014)
3. Mohr, J.J., Sengupta, S., Slater, S.F.: Marketing of High-Technology Products and Innovations, 3rd edn. Pearson, London (2010)
4. Aebersold, M.: Simulation-based learning: no longer a novelty in undergraduate education. OJIN Online J. Issues Nurs. **23**(2), 1–13 (2018)
5. Hainey, T., Connolly, T.M., Boyle, E.A., Wilson, A., Razak, A.: A systematic literature review of games-based learning empirical evidence in primary education. Comput. Educ. **102**, 202–223 (2016)
6. Sung, Y.T., Chang, K.E., Liu, T.C.: The effects of integrating mobile devices with teaching and learning on students' learning performance: a meta-analysis and research synthesis. Comput. Educ. **94**, 252–275 (2016)
7. Lin, M.H.: Developing the scale of technology imagination disposition and its correlation with grit and with internet addiction. Master's thesis (2019). http://rportal.lib.ntnu.edu.tw/handle/20.500.12235/90597
8. Williams, B., Onsman, A., Brown, T.: Exploratory factor analysis: a five-step guide for novices. Australas. J. Paramed. **8**(3), 1–13 (2010)
9. Horn, J.L.: A rationale and test for the number of factors in factor analysis. Psychometrika **30**(2), 179–185 (1965). https://doi.org/10.1007/BF02289447
10. Fishbein, M., Ajzen, I.: Belief, Attitude, Intention, and Behavior: An Introduction to Theory and Research. Addison-Wesley, Boston (1975)
11. Pallant, J.: SPSS Survival Manual. McGraw-Hill Education, London (2013)
12. Hu, L.T., Bentler, P.M.: Cutoff criteria for fit indexes in covariance structure analysis: conventional criteria versus new alternatives. Struct. Equ. Model. Multidiscip. J. **6**(1), 1–55 (1999)
13. Hu, L.T., Bentler, P.M.: Evaluating model fit. In: Hoyle, R.H. (ed.) Structural Equation Modeling: Concepts, Issues, and Applications, pp. 76–99. Sage, New York (1995)
14. Fogarty, J., McCormick, J., El-Tawil, S.: Improving student understanding of complex spatial arrangements with virtual reality. J. Prof. Issues Eng. Educ. Pract. **144**(2), 04017013 (2018)

Development of a VR STEAM Welding Project Course

Chih-Chao Chung[1], Chun-Chun Tung[2], Yuh-Ming Cheng[3], and Shi-Jer Lou[4(✉)]

[1] General Research Service Center, National Pingtung University of Science and Technology, Neipu, Taiwan
[2] College of Engineering, National Kaohsiung University of Science and Technology, Kaohsiung City, Taiwan
[3] Department of Computer Science and Information Engineering, Shu-Te University, Kaohsiung City, Taiwan
[4] Graduate Institute of Technological and Vocational Education, National Pingtung University of Science and Technology, Neipu, Taiwan
lou@mail.npust.edu.tw

Abstract. This research aimed to develop the teaching mode, ability indicators, and course content of a "VR STEAM Welding Course" for the Engineering Department of Universities of Science and Technology. The students of the Electric Welding Course in Universities of Science and Technology were taken as the subjects for the integration of the STEAM education concept, in order to integrate the VR technology into the teaching of the welding course. The Fuzzy Delphi Method was adopted as the research method, and an expert questionnaire analysis was conducted. The conclusions are summarized as follows: (1) a three-part, "student-centered" teaching mode was developed, which included welding knowledge and skills training, STEAM integrated learning, and the practical application of VR; (2) Eight ability indicators of the "VR STEAM welding course" were established; (3) the "welding construction" ability indicator for VR-assisted welding teaching was the most feasible; (4) the ability indicator of "welding construction" for STEAM education had the highest integrality into welding teaching; and (5) the mobile learning platform of the VR STEAM welding course had high real-time characteristics. The findings can serve as a reference for the subsequent content design, teaching activity planning and the implementation of the experimental teaching of this course.

Keywords: VR · STEAM · Welding · Education reform · Welding project course

1 Introduction

The rapid development of science and technology has brought about all kinds of conveniences that people can enjoy. The digitalization of science and technology knowledge makes it more convenient for people to accumulate, share, analyze, and apply it, and it also expands the horizons of mankind and enables people to grasp knowledge and information more accurately and predict the future [1]. A talent for innovation and invention, as well as a breakthrough and advancement in knowledge, will also be required for technological advancement, especially in the 21st century. Therefore, Virtual Reality (VR) is often used in operational learning activities; it allows learners to repeatedly operate the technology, there-by overcoming the limited operation times of such skills [2, 3]. VR can also present a real situation that is very similar to the actual situation, so it can effectively improve the motivation to learn and the effectiveness of learning [4, 5].

However, according to a statistical survey of the U.S. Federal Department of Education, most of the talent required for innovation and invention in the next 10 years will be related to the fields of Science, Technology, Engineering and Mathematics (STEM) [6]. In recent years, elements of Art (art and design thinking) have been integrated into STEM education, which aim to promote the students' problem-solving, critical thinking and innovative abilities. Engineering or design methods that are based on Mathematics and Science can be used to solve real-world problems, to restructure art education into an inquiry-based and discovery-oriented discipline, and to encourage creative problem-solving. This has become a new interdisciplinary STEAM course [7]. The integration of art encourages students to take risks, to tolerate different opinions, and it attracts more young people to invest in the fields of Science, Technology, Engineering and Mathematics. It can be seen that the educational orientation of STEAM contributes to the development and learning of an integrated curriculum in Engineering education [8].

Furthermore, the most basic course in Engineering education is the Factory Internship course. The main content of the course includes the training of students in correct and safe working habits, as well as in the knowledge and skills related to machine manufacturing, such as fitting, electric welding, lathing, mill machining, and so on. In the above-mentioned machine-operated skills, the training of electric welding skills is a primary and indispensable processing method in modern industry. Students can be also coached to pass the Technician's Certification examination that is organized by the Labor Development Agency for welders, cold work, general manual electric welding, electric welding, semi-automatic electric welding, argon gas tungsten electrodes, etc. [9, 10]. At present, the professional skills of the welding personnel in industry are considered for recruitment. Although there are currently robotic arms that can support electric welding, their accuracy is still not as good as that of professional masters. Welders need eye-hand coordination, and there are a wide range of employment opportunities for those with this skill [11, 12]. Coupled with the current government policies of promoting offshore wind power and national shipbuilding, the demand for welding manpower is still rising, which shows the necessity and importance of improving the effectiveness of welding courses in this plan.

In view of this, in order to verify the effectiveness of the learning model, this study planned to develop STEAM integrated welding courses and to teach design, and it also emphasize the application of emerging technology and virtual technology to courses and teaching [13], in order to construct the "VR STEAM welding course" curriculum and ability indicators for future Universities of Science and Technology to carry out practical applications and research. It is hoped that it will enable the students of Universities of Science and Technology to get early exposure to the application of VR technology and to opportunities for practical exercises and innovative ideas.

2 Research Design

This research was mainly divided into two parts, namely, the construction of ability indicators, and the development of courses. Firstly, through a literature analysis and research team meetings, the ability indicator framework of the "VR STEAM welding course" was developed to prepare the "VR STEAM" expert questionnaires related to welding courses. In addition, experts and members in related fields, such as VR applications, STEAM education, welding, and other related fields, were invited to participate, provide consultation, and implement the Fuzzy Delphi Method (FDM) expert questionnaire survey and analysis, as well as to complete the construction of ability indicators, which were used as the basis for curriculum development. For curriculum development, the expert focus group interview method was used to collect and gather opinions from all parties, and the literature analysis and research team meeting results were used as the reference basis for this.

This study used the FDM to construct curriculum ability indicators. By combining the Delphi method and the Fuzzy theory, the FDM makes use of triangular fuzzy numbers that can improve the shortcomings of the traditional Delphi method and also solve the limitations and ambiguity of human nature, and it is also an effective method for constructing indicators [14, 15]. Therefore, this study invited 15 experts to conduct an FDM expert questionnaire survey, in order to gather expert opinions. Then, ability indicators were constructed, and curriculum models, teaching strategies, teaching activities and a reference basis for the mobile learning platform were developed.

3 Results and Discussion

According to the purpose of this research and the literature review, the teaching mode, course content, ability indicators, teaching strategies, mobile learning platform, etc. of the "VR STEAM Welding Course" for the Engineering students of the Universities of Science and Technology are described as follows:

3.1 Developing the Teaching Mode of the "VR STEAM Welding Course" for the Engineering Students at Universities of Science and Technology

The teaching mode of the "VR STEAM Welding Course" in this study is mainly "student-centered", as shown in Fig. 1. Curriculum planning, which incorporates Problem-based Learning, includes three parts, namely, welding knowledge and skills training, STEAM integrated learning, and VR Practical application. In the student learning process, teachers can use virtual welding equipment, a digital learning platform and welding factory classrooms and other diversified environments and equipment to assist in their teaching, all of which emphasize the "learning-by-doing" mode. This allows students to carry out the inquiry-based learning of STEAM welding knowledge and skills in an appropriate way, to make a critical analysis of the data obtained by various media, and then to construct their own knowledge, to carry out meaningful learning, and to enhance their teamwork and problem-solving abilities. The main role the teacher is to assist, and a real and virtual hybrid method is used to become an innovative teaching mode of the VR STEAM welding course. In the follow-up, the research results will be evaluated to verify the effectiveness of the student's learning and the completeness and applicability of the curriculum design.

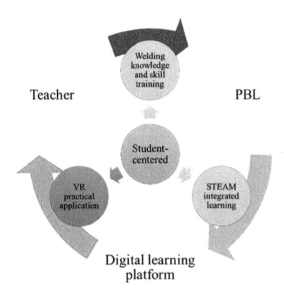

Fig. 1. Teaching mode.

3.2 Developing the Course Content of the "VR STEAM Welding Course" for the Engineering Students at Universities of Science and Technology

The course content of this "VR STEAM Welding Course" plans to apply VR technology mainly to the welding practice course, and it includes three major features, namely, Immersion, Interaction and Imagination. This course uses the VR Welding Simulator device to implement VR welding teaching. It enables students to enjoy pre-learning in a high-safety, low-cost environment, while interacting with VR welding scenes and interface devices, it provides a sense of presence, fun, immersive effect, exploration, maneuverability, dynamic interaction and real-time visual feedback, and it is a student-centered learning mode. While learning the skills of electric welding, students can also understand the development and application status of VR technology, so as to improve their scientific and technological literacy.

Fifteen experts and scholars were invited to give subjective scores on the "feasibility of the teaching of VR technology-assisted electric welding ability indicators", based on the current situation of electric welding knowledge and VR technology teaching applications, so as to obtain their evaluation of each question. The FDM expert questionnaire analysis results from 11 valid questionnaires (with the effective questionnaire recovery rate of 73%), are shown in Fig. 2. The teaching feasibility of

VR technology-assisted general manual welding scored between 0.635 points and 0.750 points. The item with the highest feasibility score was "welding construction", with a score of 0.750, followed by "drawing reading and drawing", with a score of 0.710, "test material processing and combination", with a score of 0.694, "welding inspection", with a score of 0.690, "operation preparation", with a score of 0.687, "industrial safety and hygiene", with a score of 0.677, "welding bead cleaning", with a score of 0.640, and "professional ethics of electric welders", with a score of 0.635.

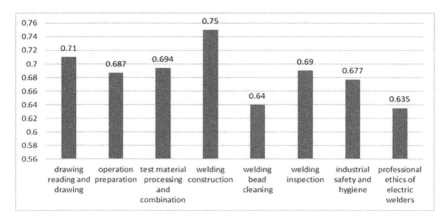

Fig. 2. Histogram of the feasibility of ability indicators of three major characteristics of VR auxiliary welding teaching.

3.3 Developing the Teaching Strategy of the "VR STEAM Welding Course" for the Engineering Students at Universities of Science and Technology

The teaching strategy of the "VR STEAM Welding Course" plans to integrate STEAM education mainly into the welding course, so that students can develop integrated thinking in Science, Technology, Engineering, Art, Mathematics, as well as other disciplines. Furthermore, the plan to replace the traditional welding course with VR welding courses and mobile learning platforms is to guide students to learn and provide them with diversified learning channels.

Fifteen experts and scholars were invited to give a subjective score of the "Integrality of STEAM Education and Welding Ability Indicators", based on the current status of the teaching application of welding knowledge and STEAM integrated thinking education, in order to obtain the evaluation value of experts and scholars for each question. The results of the FDM expert questionnaire survey on 11 valid questionnaires (with an effective questionnaire recovery rate of 73%) are shown in Fig. 3. The integrality scores of the STEAM education and welding ability indicators were between 0.633 and 0.736 points. The item with the highest integration score was "welding construction", with a score of 0.736, followed by "welding inspection", with a score of 0.715, "drawing reading and drawing", with a score of 0.708, "test material processing and combination", with a score of 0.692, "industrial safety and hygiene", with a score of 0.686, "operation preparation", with a score of 0.665, "welding bead removal", with a score of 0.664, and "the professional ethics of electric welders", with a score of 0.633.

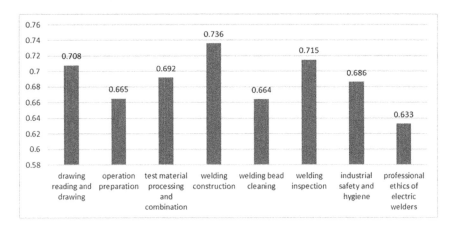

Fig. 3. Histogram of integrality of STEAM education and welding ability indicators.

3.4 Constructing a Mobile Learning Platform for the "VR STEAM Welding Course" for the Engineering Students at Universities of Science and Technology

In this study of the "VR STEAM Welding Course", the mobile learning platform, called the "Line Virtual Classroom", was built. Students were encouraged to join the "Line Virtual Classroom" course group, which provided them with a diverse learning environment, with a high real-time performance and no time-and-space constraints. At present, the most commonly-used communication software in Taiwan is the Line application [16]. The mobile learning platform of this course was built on the Line system because many teachers use Line social media to assist them in their teaching. The Line's group chat-room, notepad, photo album, reply, announcement, vote, and other functions, were used to build a "Line virtual classroom", as shown in Fig. 4. After students join this course, teachers can set learning assignments in the virtual classroom, according to the curriculum design, they can encourage students to explore, or have flipped teaching and other learning activities. It also allows students to hand in homework, they learn to give back and they can share their learned work.

1. **Notepad:** links to the textbooks of each unit, assignment announcement and submission, topic discussion.
2. Photo album: pictures of each unit course and submission of students' actual works.
3. File: sharing of each unit's extended learning files.
4. Other functions: voting, picking days, climbing ladders, etc. to be used by group students.
5. Chat room: teacher-student interaction, consulting service.

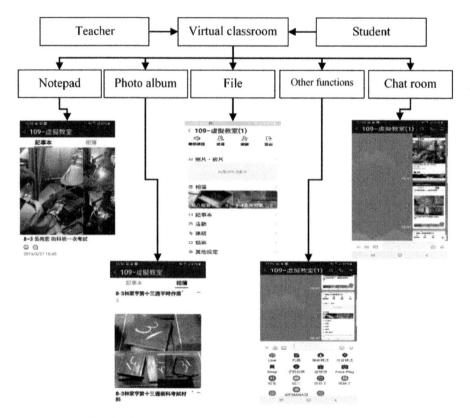

Fig. 4. VR STEAM welding course mobile learning platform.

4 Conclusion and Suggestions

This study aimed to integrate STEAM education into welding courses, and to apply VR technology and a mobile learning platform to assist in the teaching of welding. According to the analysis results of expert questionnaires, the conclusions are summarized as follows:

4.1 The "VR STEAM Welding Course" Develops a Student-Centered Teaching Mode

This "VR STEAM Electric Welding Course" is a student-centered teaching model. The key points of the course must include three parts: welding knowledge and skills training, STEAM integrated learning, and a practical VR application. The course planning was carried out from two directions, namely students' perspective and teachers' assistance. The problem-oriented learning and teaching strategies were used to guide students to learn electric welding knowledge and skills, to gain STEAM integrated knowledge, as well as related knowledge and skills that are related to the VR practical application.

4.2 The Item "Welding Construction" Had the Highest Feasibility in the Teaching of the VR Technology-Assisted Electric Welding Course Content

The course content of this "VR STEAM Welding Course" was determined by an FDM analysis. In terms of the feasibility of using VR technology to assist the teaching of the electric welding course content, the item with the highest score was "welding construction", followed by "drawing reading and drawing", "test material processing and combination", "welding inspection", "operation preparation", "industrial safety and hygiene", "welding bead removal", and "professional ethics of electric welders". In this way, the students were guided to learn welding-related knowledge and skills through the application of VR technology in the course planning and auxiliary course teaching.

4.3 The Item "Welding Construction" Had the Highest Integrality in the Teaching Strategy that Adopted and Integrated STEAM Education into the Welding Course

This research design integrated STEAM education thinking into the teaching activities of the welding courses. After an FDM expert questionnaire survey and analysis, in terms of the integration of this "VR STEAM Welding Course" and STEAM education, the item with the highest score was "welding construction", followed by "welding inspection", "drawing reading and drawing", "test material processing and combination", "industrial safety and hygiene", "operation preparation", "welding bead cleaning", and "the professional ethics of electric welders". These were used to develop a teaching strategy for students to learn welding courses with STEAM integrated thinking and to deepen the value of the students' STEAM learning and application.

4.4 The Mobile Learning Platform of the VR STEAM Welding Course Had High Real-Time Characteristics

The mobile learning platform of this course is based on the Line application, which is the most commonly-used communication software in Taiwan. It uses the Line group chat room, notepad, photo album, reply, announcement, vote, and other functions to build a "Line Virtual Classroom", it provides students with a diversified learning environment that is not limited by time and space, and it is highly real-time. It also provides a consultative and interactive communication platform between teachers and students, as well as between students and students.

References

1. Taiwan's Industrial Policy Prospective Research Project: 2030 my country's industrial vision and policy research. Taipei, Taiwan (2016)
2. Tang, Y.M., Au, K.M., Lau, H.C.W., Ho, G.T.S., Wu, C.H.: Evaluating the effectiveness of learning design with mixed reality (MR) in higher education. Virtual Reality **24**, 797–807 (2020). https://doi.org/10.1007/s10055-020-00427-9

3. Tao, S.-Y., Chuang, T.-Y.: Effects of motion sensing human computer interaction technology and game-based learning environment for elementary school students. Int. J. Digit. Learn. Technol. **9**(3), 115–136 (2017)
4. Radianti, J., Majchrzak, T.A., Fromm, J., Wohlgenannt, I.: A systematic review of immersive virtual reality applications for higher education: design elements, lessons learned, and research agenda. Comput. Educ. **147**, 103778 (2020)
5. Tseng, C.Y.: Immersive experience of seamless virtual space: virtual reality. Elem. Educ. J. **65**(3), 105–120 (2017)
6. Catterall, L.G.: A brief history of STEM and STEAM from an inadvertent insider. STEAM J. **3**(1), 5 (2017)
7. Allina, B.: The evolution of a game-changing acronym: why government recognition of STEAM is critical. Arcade **31**(2), 1–3 (2013)
8. Chung, C.-C., Lin, C.-L., Lou, S.-J.: Analysis of the learning effectiveness of the STEAM-6E special course—a case study about the creative design of IoT assistant devices for the elderly. Sustainability **10**(9), 3040 (2018)
9. Chen, Y.Z.: Welding. New Wun Ching Developmental Publishing, Taipei (2005)
10. Wu, L.D., Chuang, S.C.: Specification and qualification of welding procedures for metallic materials - welding procedure tests - Part 1: arc and gas welding of steels and arc welding of nickel and rickel alloys. Weld. Cut. **24**(3), 28–42 (2017)
11. David, D., Monroe, R., Thomas, E.: Exploring the Need to Include Cast Carbon Steels in Welding Procedure Specifications. Amer Welding Soc 550 NW Lejeuen Rd, FL, USA (2015)
12. Wu, L.D., Chuang, S.C.: Welding materials and technology CNS national standard revision-make persistent efforts. Weld. Cut. **22**(4), 29–33 (2012)
13. Zhang, Y., Zhang, J., Cheng, S.: Application of welding simulator trainer in aluminum welder training. Electric Weld. Mach. **46**(4), 127–130 (2016)
14. Chung, C.W.: Study on the construction of development indicators of recreational fisheries by the fuzzy Delphi method. Kaohsiung Normal Univ. J. Educ. Soc. Sci. **43**, 85–98 (2017)
15. Wu, C.T.: Educational policy analysis: concepts, methods, and applications. Higher Education, Taipei, Taiwan (2008)
16. Huang, Y.N., Chen, X.M.: Research on the Use Behavior of Instant Messaging Software-Taking LINE as an Example. Department of Graphic Communication Arts, 345–352 (2015)

Enhancing Students' Learning Outcomes of a STEAM Permutations Course Through a Game Based Visual Programming Environment with Qualifying Rank Strategy

Yu-Che Huang[1], Yueh-Ming Huang[1(✉)], and Andreja Istenic Starcic[2]

[1] National Cheng Kung University, Tainan 701, Taiwan ROC
yuche.kurt.huang@gmail.com, huang@mail.ncku.edu.tw
[2] University of Ljubljana, Ljubljana, Slovenia
andreja.starcic@gmail.com

Abstract. The main purpose of this research is to develop a visual programming game with a Qualifying Rank strategy (QRVPG), allowing learners to use this system to conduct a STEAM-oriented mathematics course, the content of which is permutation. In the QRVPG system, learners can perform learning tasks with lower cognitive levels in their personal game copies to understand and construct knowledge, as the level of the game role increases, levels with higher cognitive levels will also appear. Then, learners are necessary to analyze and apply the knowledge they learned to complete more difficult learning tasks. In addition, learners can compete in the QRVPG system. This research hopes to introduce the qualifying rank strategy to allow learners with similar abilities to compete with each other, through this way, enhance learners' learning motivation and engagement. In general, this research hopes to improve learners' core competence in all aspects of STEAM through the cooperation of game formation and the gradual development of cognitive level.

Keywords: STEAM education · Math learning · Game based learning · Visual programming language · Computational thinking · Qualifying rank strategy

1 Introduction

In recent years, STEAM education has received increasing attention from educator [1]. Many studies have introduced different teaching strategies or teaching models into STEAM education courses [2, 3]. In these studies, Project-Based Learning is often used for teaching. In this way, learners can cultivate the core competence of STEAM through the process of design and work practice [4, 5]. However, the content of STEAM courses conducted by Project-Based Learning is usually more complicated, and learners need to gradually combine trans-disciplinary knowledge during the learning process. Such a learning process can easily increase the cognitive load on learning. Therefore, in recent years, some studies have begun to introduce game strategies into STEAM courses [6, 7], through this approach can not only increase learners' learning motivation and effectiveness, but also effectively reduce learners' cognitive load [8]. According to the results of a systematic review research from [9], current STEAM-oriented game system uses cooperative learning as the bulk of the process usually. However, the element of competition is also an important part of game-based learning [10]. Similar to cooperative learning, the introduction of competitive elements into games can also improve learning motivation and effectiveness [11], but this kinds of research applications in STEAM teaching activities are still quite rare. Therefore, the primary purpose of this research is to explore how to add a competition mechanism to STEAM-oriented game-based teaching, and to explore the impact of this teaching approach on the learners' learning performance, learning motivation. In addition, according to the research findings from Leonard et al. [12] and Sengupta, Dickes and Farris [13], the ability of Computational Thinking (CT) skill is closely related to learners' STEAM core competencies. At the same time, there have also been studies on applying Visual Programming Language (VPL) such (i.e. Scratch) to the classroom for developing CT skills [12] and STEAM Competencies. Therefore, this research will develop a VPL game which combined a Qualifying rank strategy of a STEAM-oriented mathematic course. Then, it is hoped that learners can use VPL to solve learning problems of STEAM concepts, and enhance learners' STEAM core by using CT skills.

2 Literature Review

2.1 GBL of STEAM Education

Game-based learning refers to the application of game or game elements in teaching system. For students, it is an incentive to stimulate their learning motivation [13]. At the same time, while game-based learning allows students to learn in the process of learning through games, students need to have a clear learning goal on which they can build their cognitive ability [14, 15]. At the same time, some studies have pointed out that STEM courses conducted by Project-Based Learning can provide learners with a clear learning goal, and can improve their learning ability in all aspects through the practice of works.

The teaching concept of STEM means that subjects should not be taught in separate subjects, but should be introduced into the curriculum through a series of cross-domain knowledge learning activities, because these subject concepts are related to daily life and will not appear in us alone [16]. In 2018, Yakman proposed to incorporate the concept of "art" into STEM [17]. The "A" in STEAM not only refers to art in a narrow sense, but also refers to beauty in a broad sense and the humanistic atmosphere cultivated in STEM courses. Compared with STEAM, STEM courses without art indicate the lack of creativity and design thinking goals. However, the curriculum content of PjBL is usually more complex; learners need to combine cross-domain knowledge in the learning process, which often results in the cognitive load of learners. Because of this reason, in the recent years, some studies have begun to apply the game elements or strategy in the STEAM curriculum of PjBL [6, 7], which can effectively reduce the cognitive load of learners [8].

In related research results, researchers found that the ability of CT is closely related to the performance of learners' STEAM core competence. Therefore, in recent years, many studies have applied visual programming language (VPL) such as Scratch to the classroom for developing CT ability, as a teaching tool for STEAM-oriented related courses.

2.2 Qualifying Rank Strategy

According to the results of a systematic review research from [9], most of STEAM-oriented game systems were based on cooperative learning. However, the element of competition is also an important part of game-based learning [10]. Similar to cooperative learning, there have been many research point out that adding competitive elements in the game can also improve learning motivation and effectiveness [11]. But this kinds of research applications in STEAM teaching activities are still very few, so this topic is still worthy of further exploration. However, learning with a normal competitive strategy had some disadvantages. For example, learning through competition might let winners increase their sense of self-accomplishment with higher motivation, but it might make those who fail feel depressed about learning, and reduce their learning motivation or engagement [18]. The reason case this situation is that most games use a ranking points as a competitive element. When this kind of game strategy is used, when the score gap of the ranking is getting bigger and bigger, the students in lower achievements with backward scores will gradually lose the motivation to learn. Therefore, the elements of competition should be slightly modified when design a learning game.

Qualifying is a very interesting element of game competition too; there are many popular games in the game market in this way to allow players to engage in benign competition. The main implementation method is to divide the quality level of competition into several ranges. Players must compete with other players of the same level. The winner of the game can increase the qualifying score, and the loser will reduce the qualifying score. When the ranking score accumulates to a certain value, the quality level of the competition area will be increased, which means that the player's strength in the game is higher than other players in the original range. On the contrary, if the player's strength is insufficient, the ranking points will be continuously lost and the quality level of the competition area will be lowered. This phenomenon indicates that the player's ability is not enough to face other stronger players. Therefore, if this strategy can be introduced into learning games, learners with different cognitive levels and learning achievements can be separated, and learners of the same level can compete, and then gradually cultivate learning in the process of continuous competition ability. Through this way, the learner will not lack the motivation to learn because of the large gap with other peers, and has a clearer learning goal.

3 Research Method

3.1 Qualifying Rank Visual Programming Language Game (QVPLG)

In QVPLG, learners can perform game tasks in story mode. As more tasks are completed and the role experience accumulated in the game is worth increasing, the difficulty of the task will gradually increase. As shown in Fig. 1 below, learners can drag the program grammar puzzle on the left to the execution area in the middle, and observe the execution result of the program on the far right. If the learner can use the grammar puzzle correctly to make the game character defeat the monster, the role will be accumulated Experience points and gold coin rewards. After the character is upgraded, the attack power in the game can be improved. Through this method of developing strategies, learners can be more involved in the game. In addition, as the difficulty of the task increases, it will echo with the development of game character abilities and programming skills. The abilities developed in the story mode can also give learners more advantages in the competitive mode.

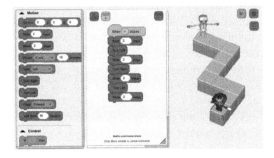

Fig. 1. Player playing a copy of a lower cognitive level.

As shown in Fig. 2 below, when learners use QVPLG to compete with their peers, two learners with similar programming abilities (qualifying score, QC) must each solve game tasks of the same difficulty level. At the same time, two learners will be able to watch the opponent's problem solving states when they were solving the problem, this design is to make the competition have a greater impact tension. In this mode, during a competition, two learners will have to solve the game tasks of three competitions respectively, and the content of the tasks of both parties are exactly the same. Therefore, the learner who completes the three tasks first will win and the QC value will increase. On the contrary, the other learner will lose the QC value due to the loss in the game. All learners can gradually develop the ability of programming and computational thinking in this process by constantly competing with others of comparable ability.

3.2 Research Framework and Hypothesis

The hypothetical diagram proposed by this study is shown in Fig. 3.

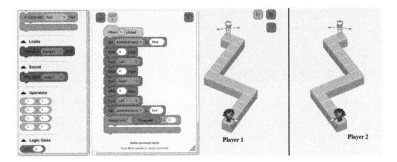

Fig. 2. The screenshots of learners using the QVPLG to carry on a qualifying competition with peer.

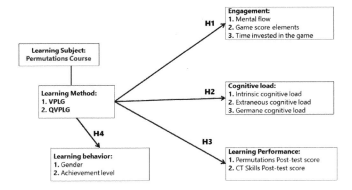

Fig. 3. The hypothetical diagram of this study.

This research intends to apply QVPLG to STEAM-oriented mathematics courses, and the main content of its learning is permutations. In the first research aspect H1, the main research question is to explore whether there is a difference in the degree of learning participation between the experimental group and the control group. The research items are the flow state of the learner, the score obtained by the learner in the game, and the length of time the learner spends in the game.

In the second research aspect H2, the main research question is to explore whether there is a difference in cognitive load between the experimental group and the control group, which includes intrinsic cognitive load, extraneous cognitive load, and germane cognitive load.

In the third research aspect H3, the main research question is to explore whether the experimental group and the control group have differences in learning achievement performance. This part will discuss the post-test scores of permutation ability and the post-test scores of CT skills.

Finally, in the fourth research aspect H4, this research expected to analyze the operational behavior records left by learners in the experimental teaching system through lag sequence analysis (LSA) method, and to explore the learning behavior of learners with different gender and different learning achievements in the experimental group and the control group.

4 Conclusions and Future Works

In this research, a visual programming language game (QVPLG) with a qualifying competition mechanism will be developed and applied to a STEAM-oriented math curriculum. Different from general game-based learning, learners can develop the ability of game characters by completing problem-solving tasks in the game copy of personal practice, and learn the knowledge of different cognitive levels in this way. In addition, learners can compete virtuously with peers of equal learning level by participating in qualifying competitions. Through this way, this research expects that as learners' ranking scores increase in the game, learners' core STEAM competencies will also grow.

In future experimental teaching, this research will use QVPLG to conduct STEAM-oriented mathematics courses, and explore the impact of this teaching method on learners' learning performance, cognitive load, learning engagement and behavior patterns. Then, according to the research findings, provide future researchers with more foundation in this kind of STEAM-oriented GBL environment.

Acknowledgements. This research is partially supported by the Ministry of Science and Technology, Taiwan, R.O.C. under Grant no. MOST 109-2511-H-006-011-MY3 and MOST 106-2511-S-006-001-MY3.

References

1. DeJarnette, N.K.: Implementing STEAM in the early childhood classroom. Eur. J. STEM Educ. **3**(3), 18 (2018)
2. Chen, Y., Chang, C.-C.: The impact of an integrated robotics STEM course with a sailboat topic on high school students' perceptions of integrative STEM, interest, and career orientation. EURASIA J. Math. Sci. Technol. Educ. **14**(12), em1614 (2018)
3. Lou, S.-J., et al.: Effects of implementing STEM-I project-based learning activities for female high school students. Int. J. Distance Educ. Technol. (IJDET) **12**(1), 52–73 (2014)
4. Fan, S.-C., Yu, K.-C.: How an integrative STEM curriculum can benefit students in engineering design practices. Int. J. Technol. Des. Educ. **27**(1), 107–129 (2015). https://doi.org/10.1007/s10798-015-9328-x
5. Nam, Y., Lee, S.-J., Paik, S.-H.: The impact of engineering integrated science (EIS) curricula on first-year technical high school Students' attitudes toward science and perceptions of engineering. EURASIA J. Math. Sci. Technol. Educ. **12**(7), 1881–1907 (2016)
6. Özdener, N., Demirci, F.: Determining students' views about an educational game-based mobile application supported with sensors. Tech. Know. Learn. **24**(1), 143–159 (2018). https://doi.org/10.1007/s10758-018-9368-x
7. Schneider, J., Schaal, S.: Location-based smartphone games in the context of environmental education and education for sustainable development: fostering connectedness to nature with Geogames. Environ. Educ. Res. **24**(11), 1597–1610 (2018)

8. Bressler, D.M., Bodzin, A.M., Eagan, B., Tabatabai, S.: Using epistemic network analysis to examine discourse and scientific practice during a collaborative game. J. Sci. Educ. Technol. **28**(5), 553–566 (2019). https://doi.org/10.1007/s10956-019-09786-8
9. Gao, F., Li, L., Sun, Y.: A systematic review of mobile game-based learning in STEM education. Education Tech. Research Dev. **68**(4), 1791–1827 (2020). https://doi.org/10.1007/s11423-020-09787-0
10. Rollings, A., Adams, E.: Andrew Rollings and Ernest Adams on Game Design. New Riders, Indianapolis (2003)
11. Chen, C.-H., Law, V., Chen, W.-Y.: The effects of peer competition-based science learning game on secondary students' performance, achievement goals, and perceived ability. Interact. Learn. Environ. **26**(2), 235–244 (2018)
12. Topalli, D., Cagiltay, N.E.: Improving programming skills in engineering education through problem-based game projects with Scratch. Comput. Educ. **120**, 64–74 (2018)
13. Prensky, M.: Digital game-based learning. Comput. Entertain. (CIE) **1**(1), 21 (2003)
14. Erhel, S., Jamet, E.: Digital game-based learning: impact of instructions and feedback on motivation and learning effectiveness. Comput. Educ. **67**, 156–167 (2013)
15. Plass, J.L., Homer, B.D., Kinzer, C.K.: Foundations of game-based learning. Educ. Psychol. **50**(4), 258–283 (2015)
16. DeCoito, I., Steele, A., Goodnough, K.: Introduction to the special issue on science, technology, engineering, and mathematics (STEM) education. Can. J. Sci. Math. Technol. Educ. **16**(2), 109–113 (2006). https://doi.org/10.1080/14926156.2016.1166298
17. Yakman, G.: STEAM education: an overview of creating a model of integrative education. In: Pupils' Attitudes Towards Technology (PATT-19) Conference: Research on Technology, Innovation, Design & Engineering Teaching, Salt Lake City, Utah, USA (2008)
18. Hwang, G.-H., et al.: Differences between students' learning behaviors and performances of adopting a competitive game-based item bank practice approach for learning procedural and declarative knowledge. Interact. Learn. Environ. **27**(5–6), 740–753 (2019)

A LUPDA Assessment Model for Activities in STEAM Education

Yu-Cheng Chien[1], Pei-Yu Chang[2], Hsin-Yu Lee[1], Tai-Yi Huang[3], and Yueh-Min Huang[1(✉)]

[1] Department of Engineering Science, National Cheng Kung University, Tainan, Taiwan
huang@mail.ncku.edu.tw
[2] Graduate School of Technological and Vocational Education, National Yunlin University of Science and Technology, Douliu, Taiwan
[3] Department of Learning Technologies, University of North Texas, Denton, USA

Abstract. The Science, Technology, Engineering, Arts, and Math (STEAM) has become the buzzword in the field of education. Many studies have revealed the importance of STEAM education and proposed different strategies to enhance it, nevertheless, these strategies are not in perfect alignment with five disciplines of STEAM. Therefore, this study proposed an assessment model which can match each discipline of STEAM activities respectively, including Learning, Using, Practicing, Designing, and Applying (LUPDA). We piloted and reviewed this model through the STEAM learning activities of the Micro: bit-Obstacle Avoidance Car. Finally, the LUPDA model provides effective measurement thorough STEAM hands-on activity.

Keywords: STEAM · LUPDA · Assessment

1 Introduction

The National Science Foundation (NSF) began to use the term "STEM" in the 1990s, which represents the abbreviations for Science, Technology, Engineering, and Math [1]. With the announcement of the "Education Innovation Plan" by former US President Obama in 2010, STEM has further drawn educators' attention (House, 2010). Many pieces of research and policy reports have indicated the demand of STEM education. Even, some countries believe STEM education is a crucial factor to maintain the competitiveness in the global economy [2–4]. Furthermore, Yakman [5] proposed that arts should be included in STEM to become STEAM (Science, Technology, Engineering, Arts, and Mathematics) which help students to build engineering background with artistic aesthetics, particularly for engineering design.

Moreover, according to the employment forecast report issued by the U.S. Department of Labor [6], it revealed that employment opportunities in future jobs will be inextricably related to STEM-related occupations which will massively increase from 2016 to 2026. However, to our best knowledge, few studies have focused on developing a sound evaluation model corresponding to five disciplines of STEAM activities [7]. Therefore, this study aims to develop a model that includes those actions of *learn, use, practice, design* and *apply* based on the intrinsic objective of STEAM education.

2 Method

2.1 The Design of a LUPDA Evaluation Model

STEM education has become a global education trend. As a result, both formal learning environments and informal learning environments have launched STEM education-related courses. No matter in which learning environment, instructors always need to plan a series of related learning activities to increase cross-field knowledge so as to cultivate students' interdisciplinary skills [8, 9].

This study identified the actions to be taken by students in STAEM activities as five types: learning, using, practicing, designing, and applying, which correspond to science, technology, engineering, art and mathematics respectively.

1. Science is the main subject for students to master scientific knowledge and scientific laws to form a scientific spirit.
2. Technology is the concretization of science, that is, learners' ability to master, apply, and invent technology.
3. Engineering refers to the practical application of technology, which means that learners can use technology to carry out a systematic development process and able to evaluate or reflect.
4. Art asks learners to be innovate and able to think about design with the ingredient of aesthetics.
5. Mathematics is that learners must master the knowledge of mathematics as a foundation to synthesize other abilities.

The detailed descriptions are shown in Table 1.

2.2 Model Design

To measure these STEAM objectives and students' skills, this study defines five actions taken by students through *learn, use, practice, design,* and *apply* in STEAM activities.

In this study, we invited several researchers and experts to review the assessment principles in scoring until consensus being reached. At the same time, they have piloted and reviewed the rubric, as shown in Table 2.

3 Experimental Design

3.1 Participants

This study participants were fifth and sixth-grade students from five primary schools in South Taiwan. A total of 30 volunteers were recruited to participate in training workshop on the Micro:bit-Obstacle Avoidance Car (see Fig. 1). The participants were

Table 1. LUPDA evaluation model.

STEAM element	Qualities for evaluation
Science (Learn)	1. establish experimental hypotheses and verify them 2. collect data and analyze experimental results 3. summary and reasonable inferences based on the analysis
Technology (Use)	1. choose correct and suitable materials and tools 2. use materials and tools by following specifications 3. modify or design models according to device measurement
Engineering (Practice)	1. understand the function of each component in the activity 2. combine components and build a system correctly 3. diagnose the correctness of the constructed system and make corrections
Arts (Design)	1. designed system is aesthetic 2. show unique design ability 3. have imagination or creativity
Math (Apply)	1. use appropriate tools for measurement 2. display data in graphs 3. analyze the trend of data measurement

Table 2. Rubric for LUPDA evaluation model.

	1-point (minimal)	2-point (solid evidence)	3-point (exceeds expectations)
Learn	Hypotheses and verify	Collect and analyze	Reasonable inferences
Use	Choose materials and tools	Use materials and tools	Modify or design tool measurement
Practice	Know each component	Combine components and build a system	Construct system and make corrections
Design	Designed with aesthetic	Show unique	WITH imagination or creativity
Apply	Use tools for measurement	Display data in graphs	Analyze data from measurement

asked to complete a series of learning activities that are the hands-on activities related the STEAM education. Because five students could not complete the experimental procedure, their experimental data were deemed invalid and eliminated. To ensure that all groups can able to complete the specific tasks, other 25 students (17 males and 11 females) were assigned to different groups according to their prior knowledge, and each group is three to four students.

Fig. 1. Micro:bit-Obstacle avoidance car.

3.2 STEAM Activity

In this study, the STEAM learning activity was designed as five-phased projects centered on the micro:bit-Obstacle Avoidance Car. The activity tasks are divided into five projects. The tasks classified according to the difficulty mentioned above, and the difficulty are organized from easy to difficult. As shown in Table 3, this activity conducted students a progressive way (from easy to difficult). Through this course, students can have basic knowledge and concepts of programming.

Table 3. The task of Micro:bit-Obstacle avoidance car in STEAM activity.

No.	Task	Task content	Level
1	Assembly	Let the Obstacle Avoidance Car perform 4 functions: forward, backward, left, and right	easy
2	Basic features	Use the gray value sensor to complete the track	easy
3	Follow the line	Use ultrasonic sensors to avoid obstacles on the track	medium
4	Avoid obstacles	Use Bluetooth to control Obstacle Avoidance Car's left and right to complete the track	medium
5	Remote control	Accelerate Obstacle Avoidance Car in a straight line and complete the track	Difficult

4 LUPDA for the Micro:Bit-Obstacle Avoidance Car Activity

4.1 Evaluation Implementation

This study develops a scoring rubrics for the Micro:bit-Obstacle Avoidance Car Activity based on the LUPDA model. To pilot and review the LUPDA model and rubrics, researchers and experts repeatedly revised the model based on Micro:bit-Obstacle Avoidance Car Activity. Table 4 shows the LUPDA model with a detailed assessment principle of this example.

Table 4. LUPDA for Micro:bit-Obstacle avoidance car activity.

Element	1-point (minimal)	2-point (solid evidence)	3-point (exceeds expectations)
Science (Learn)	Understand the task target and try their car that it can complete forward, backward, left, and right	Repeatedly try their car on the track, and making it can follow the route	In addition to following the route, it can remotely control their car through Bluetooth
Technology (Use)	Successfully operate gray value sensors and ultrasonic sensors	According to task requirements, use correct sensors which are gray value sensor or ultra-sonic sensor	Control the degree of the sensors: 1) different paths successfully detected; 2) read the distance value and successfully avoid obstacles
Engineering (Practice)	Assemble the car body and install the battery	Connect obstacle avoidance car and micro:bit	Connect gray value sensor and ultrasonic sensor with their car
Arts (Design)	Use LED of mircor:bit on obstacle avoidance car	Design a unique and distinctive LED	Design LED that fit the situation, such as marquee
Math (Apply)	Calculate the distance between the obstacle avoidance car and the obstacle	After judging the distance of the obstacle, calculate the turning angle	Make a successful turn before the their car approaches an obstacle

5 Discussion and Conclusion

With the development of STEAM education-related practices, educators need to evaluate student work that does not rely on traditional knowledge and is not limited to specific activities. This study's contribution provides a framework called LUPDA, which helps educators understand students' interdisciplinary integration and measure students' learning performance in STEAM. Nevertheless, in terms of the required resources and the applicability of education, to realize the LUPDA framework applies to multiple STEAM activities, the measure remains to be solved.

Acknowledgements. This research is partially supported by the Ministry of Science and Technology, Taiwan, R.O.C. under Grant no. MOST 109-2511-H-006 -011 -MY3, MOST 109-2811-H-006 -505 -, and MOST 107-2511-H-006 -014 -MY3.

References

1. Sanders, M.: STEM, STEM education, STEM mania. Technol. Teach. **68**(4), 20–26 (2009)

2. Anderson, E., Kim, D.: Increasing the success of minority students in science and technology. American Council on Education, Washington (2006)
3. Chen, X., Thomas, W.: Students who study science, technology, engineering and mathematics (STEM) in post-secondary education. U.S. Department of Education, National Center for Education Statistics, Washington (2009)
4. Dowd, A.C., Malcom, L.E., Bensimon, E.M.: Benchmarking the success of Latina and Latino students in STEM to achieve national graduation goals: Center for Urban Education (2009)
5. Yakman, G.: STEAM education: An overview of creating a model of integrative education. In: Pupils' Attitudes Towards Technology (PATT-19) Conference: Research on Technology, Innovation, Design & Engineering Teaching, Salt Lake City, Utah, USA (2008)
6. U.S. Department of Labor, B. o. L. S. Computer and Information Technology Occupations (2016). https://www.bls.gov/ooh/computer-and-information-technology/. Accessed 15 July 2020
7. Marshall, J.A., Harron, J.R.: Making learners: a framework for evaluating making in STEM education. Interdisc. J. Probl.-Based Learn. **12**(2), 1–13 (2018)
8. Bybee, R.W.: Advancing STEM education: a 2020 vision. Technol. Eng. Teach. **70**(1), 30–35 (2010)
9. Lin, K.-Y., Yu, K.-C., Hsiao, H.-S., Chu, Y.-H., Chang, Y.-S., Chien, Y.-H.: Design of an assessment system for collaborative problem solving in STEM education. J. Comput. Educ. **2**(3), 301–322 (2015). https://doi.org/10.1007/s40692-015-0038-x

Augmented and Virtual Reality in Education

A Testing Case of Simulation Learning in Nursing by Virtual Reality - Subcutaneous Injection Training

ChinLun Lai[1(✉)] and Yu-mei Chang[2]

[1] Communication Engineering Department, Oriental Institute of Technology,
New Taipei City, Taiwan
fo001@mail.oit.edu.tw
[2] Nursing Department, Oriental Institute of Technology, New Taipei City,
Taiwan
fk001@mail.oit.edu.tw

Abstract. In this paper, a virtual reality based nursing skill training is proposed to evaluate the learning efficiency improvement under the simulation learning theory. To perform this goal, a VR subcutaneous injection scenario is constructed and used as the skill training sample for the two-year college nursing students to understand their experience during the VR training process. The constructed training system includes completed step by step operations and the on line test function to fulfill the interactive self-training and skill evaluation functions. According to the designed goal, this learning methodology can achieve better learning performance and increasing the learning motivation while reducing the corresponding cost and effort significantly. It is observed from the students' feedback that the learning strategy, compared with the traditional teaching methods, can not only improves the student's interest in skill training but also enhances the learning performance. That is, the proposed teaching auxiliary system can improve both the student's interest and learning performance, and is practical to extend into other skill training fields in the future.

Keywords: Nursing skills training · Simulation learning · Subcutaneous injection · Teaching auxiliary system · Virtual reality technology

1 Introduction

The initiation of this research comes from two observation facts. First, it is observed that the nursing profession is facing a problem of shortage of nursing manpower due to the rapid development of high-tech medical care environment. Secondly, the simulated learning/training method is a powerful and fast growing strategy in modern education, which replicates the context of real case in a safe environment and provides interactive and feedback activities for students to achieve learning effect [1–6].

The cultivation of basic nursing skills is not only the core of nursing education, but also an important factor for clinical nursing staff to play their professional ability. The current nursing skills education method is that, with the help of simulated patients, nursing instructors first explain the principles of skills and then demonstrate the steps of skills. After that, students practice repeatedly according to the instructor's demonstration until they are familiar with whole process. At the same time, teachers can evaluate students' learning effect by observing students' operation or actual tests. However, due to the lack of standardization and repeatability of the instructor's operation demonstration, students lack of unified reference examples in practice, and students are not easy to detect errors in the operation process, which affects the learning effect.

In recent years, AR/VR/MR technology has been widely used in different fields of professional and technical fields, especially in the field of education [7, 8], thus educators must adapt teaching methods to develop the best teaching strategies. Since virtual reality provides an immersive learner experience, it is very suitable for professional skills training, and naturally also includes teaching in the field of medicine and nursing [9–17]. Virtual reality based applications are evolving rapidly in the field of health care due to the fact that VR applications can effectively save time and training costs, can practice operations quickly, as well as help coordinate the skills of medical professionals according to the relevant health care research. Kolb's [18] study describes how learners actively reflect on what they have learned in order to integrate new experiences into the current knowledge base. After acquiring a higher level of knowledge, learners actively try to integrate and reflect on knowledge in order to internalize it for personal development. In addition, in learning theory, learning outcomes are produced through continuous practice, rigorous evaluation and feedback mechanisms [19]. By exploring various methods including false attempts, learners can experience the immediate consequences and learn them. However, it is not acceptable in a real clinical environment by such 'tried by error' approach. Under this consideration, using VR operation does not cause patient safety risk and can provide learners with valuable learning experience, thus this experimental learning theory can be applied to the clinical education of VR simulation. In addition, numerous studies have shown that this principle of education not only effectively helps students learn clinical medicine, but also applies to expertise in aviation, sports, and musical performance.

The research shows that although nursing educators are incorporating immersive VR into the curriculum plan, few people in Taiwan have carried out relevant research on the application of immersive VR in nursing education. Compared with the traditional nursing teaching methods, simulation learning method will have more effective learning effect, and involves the use of innovative technology to convey knowledge. VR replaces reality with a computer-generated virtual environment, which inputs objects and information into the environment and describes the environment to users. Users can use sensors or controllers (for example, keyboard and mouse) to manipulate or interact with objects in the virtual environment. The results show that virtual reality education has greatly improved students' psychomotor ability [12]. Other studies have evaluated the learning results of VR education in students' emotional aspects, such as the improvement of communication ability and learning initiative, so the students can achieve good learning effect through repeated skill learning process more quickly.

Subcutaneous injection nursing skill is a basic nursing skill. Through subcutaneous injection, the drug can be absorbed slowly and produce continuous therapeutic effect. The route of subcutaneous injection is in subcutaneous fat layer. Since it is slower than intravenous injection, subcutaneous injection is often used as a way of administration of vaccines and drugs such as insulin for diabetic injection. It is an important part of subcutaneous injection skills to get into the appropriate depth. Medical staff suggest that the drug should be injected into the subcutaneous tissue, which is the fat layer under the skin. If the injection is too deep, the drug will be absorbed by the muscle layer, which makes the drug absorption faster and less lasting, thus will cause pain when the injection is to the muscle. On the contrary, if the injection is too shallow and does not reach the subcutaneous tissue, the drug will be directly absorbed by the epidermis, which will also affect the initial action and the action time of the drug. Therefore, injection technique is very important. In recent years, due to the increasing prevalence of chronic diseases and the aging of the population, the demand for subcutaneous injection has increased greatly. Through the correct nursing of subcutaneous injection, not only can achieve effective therapeutic effect, but also effectively prevent the occurrence of infection or side effects. Therefore, in addition to the clinical nursing staff in medical institutions, the nursing staff working in the field of family care must also be familiar with how to operate subcutaneous injection correctly, thus it is necessary to give them good skill training. However, due to the limited patients cases of volunteers in clinical practice, and the lack of a large number of nursing skills teaching manpower, most of the nursing staff in learning can only practice by simulating patients or mannequins themselves, resulting in poor training effect. On the other hand, in addition to the limited space, time, equipment and guidance manpower arrangement, a large amount of consumables consumption has also greatly increased the cost of practice, hence resulting in the reduction of training willingness of institutions and trainees.

In view of this, a simulated learning strategy for nursing skills training is implemented based on virtual reality technology and the subcutaneous injection skill is used as the training example to demonstrate the effect of this learning model. From this way, this learning strategy fulfills the concept of learning by practice while reducing the related cost and effort significantly. It is observed and expected, by some test samples feedback from the implemented system, that the learning strategy can not only improves the student's motivation in skill training but also enhances the learning performance than the traditional teaching methods. Furthermore, it is also easy to be applied into other skill learning and training fields thus is practical for the future education and training purpose.

2 The Research Methodology

Descriptions of the research methodology include two aspects: The system prototype implementation and the experimental design. For the system platform design, the helmet-mounted device with PC is adopted in hardware construction for good immersive fusion consideration, while the unity3D software package is used as the development platform for the reason of compatibility. On the other hand, simulation scenario contents and the feedback data collection method are also important. The whole research methodology concept is described as follows:

2.1 Building up the Simulation Platform

In the initial stage of the system construction, a PC-based head-mounted device, like HTC VIVE, is selected as the visual output equipment, while the complicated work of building 3D contents is done by a powerful desktop computer with specific graphic processing unit (GPU). At the same time, the UNITY3D software package is adopted as the development platform to build up the whole system including the 3D objects design, scenario flow, and interactive control strategies. The Maya software package is also used in building much detailed and complex 3D objects and scenes. On the other hand, to make the human–computer interaction easier and intuitive, the Leap Motion hardware unit is used in gesture recognition work thus users are able to control and interact with the system by simple hand gesture. Figure 1 shows the proposed VR learning platform architecture of this paper.

2.2 Nursing Experts Conduction

In order to confirm the clinical nursing skill in developing VR learning module, clinical expert consultation was built by six clinical practice experts. At the same time they are also served as a collaborative teaching faculty for the industry sector and help to listed important and basic clinical nursing skilled to be trained. These skills comprise subcutaneous injection, nasogastric tube care, urinary catheterization, intravenous administration, suction, and change position. In this paper, the VR subcutaneous injection is implemented and tested. Thus, the corresponding steps are defined and made according to the nursing textbooks and clinical nursing standards of major hospitals. After that, those operation process are programmed into the VR learning system as the training/learning contents.

2.3 Discussion on Learning Interest

Based on a small number of trainees, the change of learning interest and motivation caused by VR training system are explored in this paper. Qualitative analysis and interviews are used to understand the students' learning motivation and interest, as well as the experience feedback after using the self-learning system. The content of the interview includes the experience of VR learning experience, the subjective differences compared with traditional training methods, the subjective learning results caused by the training system, and the difficulties encountered in using the self-learning system. These results are used as the reference for future modification and improvement of the VR training system.

The focus group approach is used to collect user experience feedback in this paper. In the focus group interview, the researcher first introduced the basic process, defined the discussion topic, and explained the interview task to the group. In addition, participants were asked to approve the recording of interviews to ensure that they were fully covered. Finally, the researchers guaranteed the confidentiality of the information to the participants. In this paper, a teacher of the communication engineering department is served as the co-project leader of the research and the moderator of the focus group interview. The lecturer was trained to conduct quantitative research in focus groups. In addition, students' responses did not affect their assessment of course performance, thus protecting students' rights and ensuring the anonymity of transcripts. The relative experience materials discussed include: 1. The experience of VR skill learning, 2. What are the main differences between practicing in VR skill learning environment and using traditional skill learning methods, 3. How to help users to learn VR skills, and 4. What are their difficulties in learning.

3 Simulation Results and Discussions

The simulated learning/training system is implemented in a Laptop PC which runs Unity 2017 with i7 core, 16G RAM, and GeForce GTX 1070 display interface, while the HTC VIVE HMD with Leap Motion sensor is used as the display platform and intuitive gesture control unit. In order to achieve the reality effect, first of all, all the 3D models related to the subcutaneous injection training including space environment, equipment, and characters are constructed as Shown in Fig. 2, 3 and 4. Second, the standard operating procedure steps recommended by the consulting experts and the corresponding interactive action scripts are carried out by computer programming work. Moreover, the automatic assessment, operation step prompts, operation history video records, and the statistical analysis functions are also added into the designed learning system to improve the learning performance and provide as the teaching feedback usage. The implemented prototype and the snapshots during the training process are shown in Fig. 5, 6, 7 and 8.

To evaluate the performance of the proposed prototype system, at first a small number of sophomore nursing students in our school are examining the learning system to verify its operational fluency through informal testing methods and then collect their use experience feedback. After that, the system will be formally evaluated in the teaching class. The effect analysis includes learning interest and learning efficiency, and the results can be used as the basis for subsequent system modification and improvement.

Experimental results show that students have a higher motivation and interest in learning professional skills using this self-learning and training system than traditional methods. In fact, students generally report that they are less stressed, not afraid of operating errors, and willing to practice repeatedly. In addition, the feedback function of video playback can enable students to understand the operation errors at the first time thus they can correct the learning content immediately, so the learning efficiency will be effectively improved. Furthermore, the statistical result feedback of the student learning processes also helps the teachers to understand the students' learning status and can adjust their teaching strategies accordingly. These functional demonstrations can be observed in Fig. 9. Due to the paper page limitation, detailed description about interview questions and result tables are omitted.

Finally, the proposed learning system prototype was also presented in the 2019 ITEX International Innovation Invention Competition and won the gold medal awards in favor of expert review, which further highlights the use of this learning strategy while proves the advantages of adopting this self-learning/training system, and the practical value of such teaching aid system.

To sum up, the proposed teaching support system provides an eco-friendly and self-learning practical environment anytime and anywhere with gaining immediate learning feedback and practical experiences for the students. Thus, learning motivation, effectiveness, and efficiency can be improved dramatically by the proposed learning system than the traditional teaching auxiliary ones. Moreover, expensive resources such as nursing teaching aid, educational hardware, and realistic material can be reduced significantly by the virtual 3D models and scenario.

Fig. 1. The proposed VR learning platform architecture.

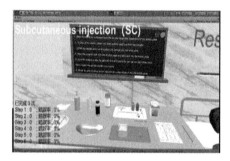

Fig. 2. The 3D models used in the VR system.

Fig. 3. The simulated patient 3D model.

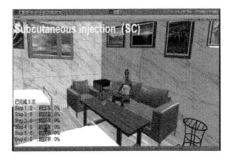

Fig. 4. The simulated environment of the ward.

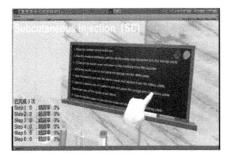

Fig. 5. The SOP directions of the SC operation process.

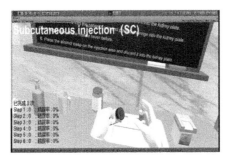

Fig. 6. A snapshot of the training process.

Fig. 7. A snapshot of the training process.

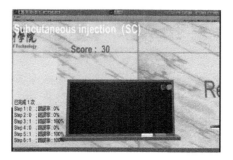

Fig. 8. Completing the training without limitation of tutor manpower, space, and time.

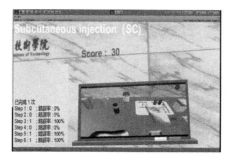

Fig. 9. Immediate feedback (video and statistics) both for students and teachers.

4 Conclusions

This paper proposes a powerful self-learning/skill-training assistant system based on virtual reality technique for learning performance evaluation. The subcutaneous injection operation skill is implemented in a VR system and applied to nursing department students for observation. According to the experienced feedback results, the advantages of the self-learning/skill-training, as well as the practical value of the proposed learning assistant system can be approved. Moreover, expensive resources such as teaching aid, educational hardware, and realistic material can be reduced significantly by the virtual 3D models and simulation scenario. That is, the proposed teaching support system provides an eco-friendly and self-learning practical environment in anytime and anywhere, in which the learning feedback and practical experiences for both the students and teachers can be obtained immediately. Moreover, it is also observed from the interview results that both the learning motivation and efficiency are quite satisfactory in the determined nursing skill test items and can be easily applied to other skill training fields, and can be a good simulation learning strategy in the nursing field.

References

1. Jeffries, P.R. (ed.): Simulation in Nursing Education: From Conceptualization to Evaluation. National league for Nursing, New York (2007)
2. Waxman, K.: The development of evidence-based clinical simulation scenarios: guidelines for nurse educators. J. Nurs. Educ. **49**(1), 29–35 (2010). https://doi.org/10.3928/01484834-20090916-07
3. Landeen, L., Nielson, A.: Focus on simulation-integrating simulation into teaching practice. J. Nurs. Educ. **47**(11), 487–488 (2008)
4. Khalaila, R.: Simulation in nursing education: an evaluation of students' outcomes at their first clinical practice combined with simulations. Nurse Educ. Today **34**, 252–258 (2014). https://doi.org/10.1016/j.nedt.2013.08.015
5. Ahn, H., Kim, H.: Implementation and outcome evaluation of high-fidelity simulation scenarios to integrate cognitive and psychomotor skills for Korean nursing students. Nurse Educ. Today **35**(5), 706–711 (2015)
6. Handwerker, S.M.: Transforming nursing education: a review of current curricular practices in relation to Benner's latest work. Int. J. Nurs. Educ. Scholarsh. **9**(1), Article 21 (2012). http://dx.doi.org/10.1515/1548-923X.2510
7. Freina, L., Ott, M.: A literature review on immersive virtual reality in education: state of the art and perspectives. In: Proceedings of eLearning and Software for Education (eLSE), Bucharest, 23–24 April (2015)
8. Hussein, M., Nätterdal, C.: The Benefits of Virtual Reality in Education-A Comparison Study, Bachelor Dissertation. Chalmers University of Technology, University of Gothenburg, Sweden (2015)
9. Lai, C., Chang, Y.-m.: Improving the Skills Training by Mixed Reality Simulation Learning. In: Wu, T.-T., Huang, Y.-M., Shadieva, R., Lin, L., Starčič, A.I. (eds.) ICITL 2018. LNCS, vol. 11003, pp. 18–27. Springer, Cham (2018). https://doi.org/10.1007/978-3-319-99737-7_2
10. Jenson, C.E., Forsyth, D.M.F.: Virtual reality simulation: using three-dimensional technology to teach nursing students. Comput. Inf. Nurs. **30**(6), 312–318 (2012). https://doi.org/10.1097/NXN.0b013e31824af6ae
11. Bayram, S., Biyik, C.N.: Effect of a game-based virtual reality phone application on tracheostomy care education for nursing students: a randomized controlled trial. Nurse Educ. Today **79**, 25–31 (2019). https://doi.org/10.1016/j.nedt.2019.05.010

12. Elliman, J., Loizou, M., Loizides, F.: Virtual reality simulation training for student nurse education. In: 2016 8th International Conference on Games and Virtual Worlds for Serious Applications (VS-GAMES), pp. S1–S2 (2016)
13. Farra, S.L., Smith, S.J., Ulrich, D.L.: The student experience with varying immersion levels of virtual reality simulation. Nursing Educ. Perspect. **39**(2), 99–101 (2018). https://doi.org/10.1097/01.NEP.0000000000000258
14. Foronda, C.L., Hudson, K.W., Budhathoki, C.: Use of virtual simulation to impact nursing students' cognitive and affective knowledge of evidence-based practice. Worldviews Evid.-Based Nurs. **14**(2), 168–170 (2017)
15. Zhu, E., Masiello, I., Hadadgar, A., Zary, N.: Augmented reality in healthcare education: an integrative review. PeerJ PrePrints **2**, 1–22 (2014)
16. Pugoy, R.A.D., et al.: Augmented reality in nursing education: addressing the limitations of developing a learning material for nurses in the Philippines and Thailand. IJODeL **2**(1), 11–24 (2016)
17. Carlson, K.J., Gagnon, D.J.: Augmented reality integrated simulation education in health care. Clin. Simul. Nurs. **12**(4), 123–127 (2016)
18. Kolb, D.: Experiential Learning: Experience as the Source of Learning and Development. Prentice Hall, Englewood Cliffs (1984)
19. Kilmon, C., Brown, L., Ghosh, S., Mikitiuk,: A.: Immersive virtual reality simulations in nursing education. Nurs. Educ. Perspect. (Natl. League Nurs.) **31**(5), 314–317 (2010)

Experiential Learning Through Controlling and Monitoring a Real-Time 3D House Using LabVIEW in a Virtual Laboratory

Bogdan M. Mîndruț[✉] and Claudiu A. Oprea

Technical University of Cluj-Napoca, 400114 Cluj-Napoca, Romania
Bogdan.Mindrut@mae.utcluj.ro

Abstract. This paper presents a new virtual laboratory based on a simulation environment for educational purposes. This virtual laboratory covers an important part of the smart home technology, acquiring and processing of different types of data and controls via the cloud technology. A smart house is a regular house that uses intelligent technology to efficiently gather information for the purpose of monitoring and controlling the home environment (e.g. temperature, lighting) and its electronic and mechanical devices. Its purpose is not only to make life easier for those who would benefit from these facilities on a daily basis, but also to create as much comfort as possible and a safer living environment. This paper presents a LabVIEW-based smart home simulator automation. In addition to this software created by National Instruments, a home simulator, HOME I/O developed by Real games, is used. The system can monitor and adjust the home temperature and is able to automatically adjust the brightness of every room's light fixtures or of the outside lights. At the same time, the alarm system can be controlled, with its motion sensors, doors and windows opening sensors for the occupants' enhanced safety and protection. The software was also designed with energy saving mindfulness making the home an eco-friendly place. To highlight the possibility of using the developed technology in a real environment, a hardware part of the system was implemented by using a MyRIO NI device.

Keywords: Smart home · Cloud control · Internet of Things · Virtual laboratory

1 Introduction

1.1 Purpose of Online Learning

Experiential learning has proven to be of great benefit to students. In universities, such teaching techniques are commonly accomplished through laboratory experiments. With the rapid rate of the development of new technologies, integration of industry practices, as well as simulation of industry environment have never been more necessary. However, the lack of facilities, equipment and laboratory space has been a major constraint for universities in the country.

Research in virtual environments, gamification and serious-games suggests that those tools can be very effective for education, and in certain contexts they provide unique advantages. Recent developments are making the technologies they are based on more widespread, with technologies such as 3D becoming widely available through web browsers and even on mobile devices [1].

1.2 Designing Smart Home Automations

Smart house is a system that uses information technology to monitor the environment, control the electric appliance and communicates with the outer world, an automation system that has been developed to automatically achieve some activities performed frequently in daily life to obtain more comfortable and easier life environment [2].

A control system of a smart home using LabVIEW is presented in [3] that consists of five parts, the most important devices being programed with the main objectives being alarm, lights, temperature that were also considered for this paper.

Smart house can also provide a remote interface to home appliances or the automation system itself, using wireless transmission protocols or the internet, to provide control and monitoring via a smart phone or web browser [4].

2 Research in Virtual Laboratory and Gamification Learning

The paper presents a very useful, innovative and compact laboratory, which is both simple and complex at the same time. HOME I/O is an interactive "smart house" simulation that also makes use of the surrounding environment. It is designed to cover a wide range of curriculum targets in science, technology and engineering. With the help of these simulations, it was possible to treat automation topics such as thermal behavior, light control, energy efficiency, even the protection provided by the alarm system, topics that are part of everyday life. The main purpose of the Home I/O simulator is to introduce the concepts of automation using an interactive smart home [5].

Equipped with the most common automation devices, HOME I/O requires the design of control solutions and the understanding of the energy impact of their commissioning. LabVIEW can be used to directly control Home I/O.

Alternatively, HOME I/O can also be used as an interface with external technologies, allowing the simulator to be easily connected with PLCs, Microcontrollers, Modbus or many other technologies.

In Fig. 1 it is shown a block diagram of a smart house automation that uses LabVIEW software as the main program and LabVIEW NXG for remote applications.

2.1 Communication Between Software

In order to communicate with the LabVIEW control program, in the Home I/O simulator all the inputs, respectively the outputs must be moved from the "wired" mode to the "connect" mode.

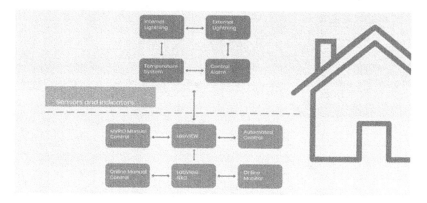

Fig. 1. Block diagram of the virtual laboratory.

This system uses LabVIEW for a logical design and LabVIEW NXG for developing the interface of the automated house to be used on almost every portable gadget that can access a page on a browser. For connectivity between programs, .NET VI's (LabVIEW's virtual instruments) are used from function palette, in the connectivity category. These are used with the selected class of Engine I/O that makes the nodes become memory maps for the simulator's inputs and outputs as shown in Fig. 2.

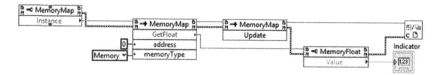

Fig. 2. Basic code for communication between the software.

2.2 Exemplification of a Simple Automation and Control

In the following chapter, the researchers have included a brief information on what this virtual laboratory has to offer and how profitably can it be used for experiential learning based on their experience of using the presented system.

Exterior Lighting. The Home I/O app benefits from several lighting fixtures outside the house. Each lighting source has a memory address that is retrieved via the access node by the LabVIEW program and is operated depending on the type of memory using the property block. All of these parts of the exterior lighting can be controlled both manually, from the LabVIEW program interface and automatically, depending on the external brightness. This varies depending on the time elapsed in the simulator, which can be accelerated with the use of the time bar. Students have the opportunity to understand and control the virtual environment and give free rein to their imagination to create different automated scenarios. For a brief example, in automatic mode, the

Fig. 3. House outside view and its exterior lightning command panel.

lights are turned on only in the evening according to the user's desired brightness level (Fig. 3).

Central Alarm. The alarm system of the house is provided with motion, windows and doors sensors. At the same time, the simulator contains two sirens, an external one for breaking open windows and doors, and one located inside, for the motion sensors. For instance, in armed alarm mode, if the motion sensor in one of the rooms, marked on the control panel as a LED, detects a movement, the internal alarm automatically starts and the color of the LED changes, warning the user in which room the movement occurred. Each value of the motion sensors is read via the memory map with the selected input type and the memory address (Fig. 4).

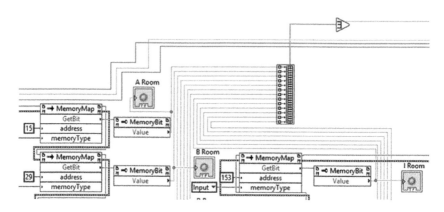

Fig. 4. Example of the LabVIEW code within the logic of the burglar alarm.

Heating. The automatic heating system aims to create a comfort that is as pleasant as possible from a thermal point of view for the people living in the house. By simply setting the temperature on the thermostat, this control takes the information and adjusts it according to the environment. The Home I/O simulator provides the LabVIEW control program with various parameters from the house sensors, such as the outside temperature, the chosen temperature in the room for control and the temperature set on the thermostat. The room temperature is influenced by both the radiator and the status of the doors or windows. The outside temperature varies in time and can be set between the minimum and maximum parameters on the Home I/O program interface.

Due to the existence of thermal inertia after turning off the radiator, a control loop that sends the set value to the property node, depending on the difference between the ambient temperature in the room and that set on the thermostat was used (Fig. 5).

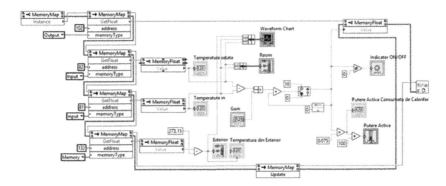

Fig. 5. Automation code of the heating system.

A night heating cycle can be seen on the graph, and with its help the heating phenomenon can be visualized. The set temperature is marked with green and it remains constant as long as the thermostat suffers no changes. The existing temperature in the room is marked with red and it is also greatly influenced by the outside temperature, marked with white on the graph (Fig. 6).

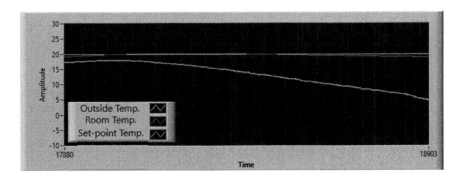

Fig. 6. Night heating cycle. (Color figure online)

Depending on the difference between the outside and the room temperatures, the program adjusts the value transmitted to the radiator so that at a larger difference, it operates at a maximum power. When the two temperatures start having closer values, in order to reduce the phenomenon of thermal inertia as much as possible, the value transmitted by the control loop will decrease until the two temperatures reach an approximately equal level.

Internal Lightning. The lightning scenarios can be a good way to learn how to create a complex user-defined automation. A brief algorithm for studying the internal lightning system would be that the user can define the value of the brightness he wants via the slider bar. During the day, if the cursor is set to the minimum brightness, the shades can close automatically, creating the visual comfort desired by the user. Otherwise, if the set brightness is higher than the room brightness, the shades will rise automatically, or stop at a level so that the value set and the value read by the brightness sensor are approximately equal. During the day, even if the desired brightness is set to maximum, as long as the room light does not fall below a certain minimum threshold, for a more efficient consumption, the LEDs do not light up. To create a pleasant comfort, in the automatic mode during the night, all drapes are closed. A real-time view of the opening and closing of the shades can be implemented in the front panel.

In Fig. 7, a loop is used in order to adjust the brightness in automatic mode, which makes a difference between the brightness selected by the user and the brightness outside.

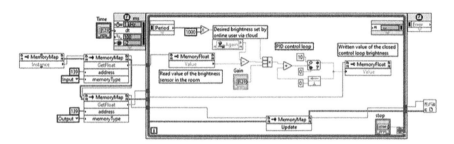

Fig. 7. Closed PID control loop for automation.

To control the blinds, the program compares the set brightness values with the interior of the room. If the set value is higher, the shades go up, as long as the two values do not reach equality. In the case where the set brightness is lower, the shades go down. When the two values become equal, the false value is sent to the curtain property node, stopping.

3 Experiential Learning and Cloud Control

3.1 MyRIO Implementation

Experiential learning is a process of acquiring knowledge through experience, and is more specifically defined as hands-on approach to learning that moves away from just the teacher at the front of the room verbally relaying their knowledge to students [6]. Experience-based learning is so effective because it helps establish lasting behavioral change. Rather than simply learning a new subject or gaining a skill, it develops new habits and behaviors, learning from trying new things, getting stuck and then resolving an issue, getting used to stepping out of one's comfort zone. In the field of engineering, having practical workshops is imperative for the development of the students. For this virtual laboratory, a MyRIO device from NI is used to demonstrates the basics of electronics and sensors and learning sample LabVIEW code. There are a multitude of usage options for this device that include a lot of sensors and measurements. This device can either be connected through USB cable to the PC or via wireless, the logic being made in LabVIEW (Fig. 8).

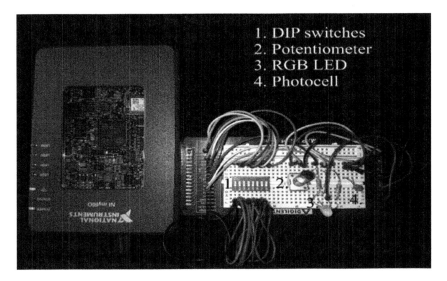

Fig. 8. MyRIO simple setup example for control of the brightness in a room.

For a simple demonstration, a MyRIO is used with a breadboard expansion, DIP switches, a potentiometer, RGB led and a photocell to emulate real existing equipment in a house. [7]. The switches can be assigned to do different tasks in the simulator, like controlling on-off lights, alarm, roll up or down shades, etc. The potentiometer can be used to manually control the brightness of the lights seen in the simulator. RGB Led can be used for numerous purposes like motion detection indicators, electrical heater indicator or even directly wired to show the brightness of the light controlled by the analog potentiometer. The photocell is placed to acquire real brightness data that can be then processed in LabVIEW to automate the lights in the simulator. There are a lot of experimental ideas that can be developed in this virtual laboratory with a little bit of imagination. Students given this opportunity, can start learning basic principles of home automation using a microcontroller and understanding sample electronic components (Fig. 9).

Fig. 9. Controlling the lights and shades from a smartphone.

3.2 System Link Cloud & NXG

As one of the core application domains in the Internet of Things, a smart home focuses on meeting the increasing demands of a modern living environment. LabVIEW NXG is used for the wireless control and monitorization of the simulator. After all, the logic of the program is designed in the diagram panel in LabVIEW, and all the information passes through one master VI that assembles the whole program via shared global variables of different types. In the same VI, the System Link library is used to share the desired data to the cloud, and then it is accessed by the webVI program developed in NXG [8]. This gives the user the ability to access the smart house from any place on any device that has an internet connection. The monitoring and the controlling of the simulator is being made through the browser in real-time. The data from the simulator is forwarded to the system link cloud via read or write tags, which can send or receive data with the specific path and type.

4 Conclusion

Since the creation of the first household appliances, electronics have evolved a lot. Today everyone can benefit from the slightest automation or control of electrical devices. Automated homes have become a common thing in our daily lives and more and more people can benefit from them. The increasing demand for specialists in the field of automation technology has led universities to treating smart home automation as a possible subject of learning. This research aims to bring an alternative solution to a laboratory that can have a lack of equipment and present safety concerns. The demand for virtually held laboratories and workshops is greatly increasing as the world tries to move as much as possible into an online environment.

The processes of the experiment can be executed multiple times, without any risk to the user or the equipment. Moreover, students can enhance their learning skills by using their creativity to discover and develop new scenarios of automation. This laboratory is based on the possibility of controlling the most common electrical components in a house. It can monitor and control home temperature, lights, alarm and even the access through garage doors or gates. The system-design platform used to control the simulator is LabVIEW which is a visual programming language used by technicians who work in the field of automation and not only.

Based on the authors experience after using the presented system, it can be concluded that the virtual laboratory is a great help for students and teachers. It is not only a more cost effective solution but it can be repeated in countless ways allowing students to use their imagination in creating something innovative and also fun.

Acknowledgement. This paper was supported by the project "Advanced technologies for intelligent urban electric vehicles – URBIVEL - Contract no. 11/01.09.2016", project co-funded from the European Regional Development Fund through the Competitiveness Operational Program 2014-2020.

References

1. Rodriguez-Gil, L., García-Zubia, J., Orduña, P: An architecture for new models of Online Laboratories: educative multi-user gamified hybrid laboratories based on Virtual Environments. In: 13th International Conference on Remote Engineering and Virtual Instrumentation (REV), p. 203 (2016)
2. Kumar, S.: Smart House Applications Control using LabVIEW, National Institute of Technology Kurukshetra, Haryana-136119 (2013)
3. Hamed, B.: Design & implementation of smart house control using LabVIEW. J. Soft Comput. Eng. (IJSCE) **1**(6), 98–106 (2012)
4. Travis, Jeffrey, Kring, Jim: LabVIEW for Everyone: Graphical Programming Made Easy and Fun, 3rd edn. Prentice Hall Professional, Upper Saddle River (2007). ISBN-10: 0131856723
5. Home I/O homepage: Simulation of a smart house and surrounding environment. https://realgames.co/home-io/. Accessed 10 Sept 2019
6. Growth Engineering site about Experiential Learning. https://www.growthengineering.co.uk/what-is-experiential-learning/. Accessed 10 Oct 2019
7. Doering, E. (ed.): NI myRIO Project Essentials Guide. National Technology and Science Press (2014)
8. LabVIEW NXG page manual. http://www.ni.com/documentation/en/labview-web-module. Accessed 11 July 2019

Students' Attitude Toward Learning and Practicing English in a VR Environment

Ying Ling Chen[✉]

Center for General Education, Oriental Institute of Technology, Taipei, Taiwan, Republic of China
Ci10226@mail.oit.edu.tw

Abstract. Virtual Reality (VR) technology has been engaged in educational content for students of all ages. A VR headset completes a new world with user-friendly interface, gesture controls, customized educational resources, and hands-on teacher controls. Learners are able to apply and practice their target language. Thus, the purpose of this study was to investigate learners' attitude and usefulness toward the implementation of VR technique in L2 learning. VR technique assists target language learning was designed according to the curricular objectives and the subject matter of a private electrical and technical university. Mixed method was applied and 117 freshmen participated in the study. A list of questionnaires of VR technique assists target language learning was applied for the first phase of data collection. Furthermore, a semi-structure interview and a field note techniques were carried out to be the main method for the detailed qualitative data. 15 participants were randomly involved in reflecting the experience of learning English in a VR environment. The results indicated that learning the target language in a VR environment was a practical intervention for developing independent motivator. L2 students have better attitudes toward their learning experiences. Meanwhile, the perceived satisfaction and usefulness positively affect learners' behavioral intention of VR usage and target language learning.

Keywords: Virtual reality · L2 · Attitude · Usefulness

1 Introduction

Virtual Reality technology has become a part of civilization in enhancing better education and quality life. Learning English has become a "must do" activity in Taiwan, many people attend a cram school; a language teacher lectures the lesson and corrects students' mistakes. It is the most traditional and effective way. However, some people do not have extra time to go to a private lesson, some people suggest they need more opportunities to practice what they learned in class; some people think when they have questions, they have trouble receiving assistance. There is another popular way of learning by reading L2 magazines and watching movies or YouTube. Students listen to the content and practice by themselves. Nevertheless, students may need help to distinguish if they perform their understanding correctly. In addition, Virtual Reality is able to act like a supportive intervention in improving performance and understanding in L2. VR technology has been applied in many uses, it is the support of high interactivity and the abilities for educational and training purposes for presenting a virtual environment that resembles the real world [1]. Consequently, this study was aimed to investigate whether the integration of Virtual Reality helped increasing L2 learners' learning attitude and usefulness. VR technology offers a platform about the autonomy of the students and makes them more motivated and passionate. It gives not only a groundbreaking way to mediate learning opportunities but also lead students to an immersive learning environment by stimulating onto the learner's physical reality.

2 Literature

2.1 Virtual Reality

Virtual Reality (VR) is highly considered as a capable technology for both computer-based training and simulation. An Immersive VR environment is usually performed on multiple, room-size screen or through a stereoscopic, head-mounted display unit [2]. Language learning opportunities and possibilities have been created and supported by the VR technology. VR has been employed extensively to a number of applications and highly interactive environment which allows users to become participants in a computer-generated world where they can interact with various stimuli [3]. VR is practiced as a media to offer target language learners an opportunity to apply and acquire the target curriculum in an ideal virtual space with reality essential. VR computer simulation has been defined as a highly interactive, 3-D computer generated program in a multimedia environment which provides the effect of immersion to the users [4]. Educators are willing to minimize the gap between the textbook and the real world. VR Scenario simulation practice makes leaning meaningful especially for students to review or retry specific parts of the environments to experience them more fully. Learning through specific customized contexts develop connections for learners to their target language.

2.2 VR Technology Assists English Learning

In a traditional teacher centered language classroom, learners' use of memory, cognitive, social and affective strategies to learn their target language [5]. However, learners these days are digital natives, they are keen on social networking via multiple media and involving in a range of activities for self-expression, individual and cooperative learning and negotiation of meaning [6]. In order to satisfy learners' needs and apply what they had learned in a language classroom, technology plays an essential role to offer more opportunities and make the proper use of practical activities on the language appropriation. Technology should role as tools in improving students' English communication skills and learning expertise [7].

VR technology creates opportunities for oral practice, VR technology also helps to link the world to meet learners' needs. Time and distance are not the obstacles because VR is able to provide an instant interactive training practically [8]. VR technology is full of potential for learners and educators to access flexibly. Additionally, users are always allowed to control, adjust, and modify the context, curriculum, target, and theme when using VR to assists teaching and learning.

2.3 Attitude of Learning

Students' learning and performance in the target language is affected by a number of factors, including students' attitude towards the subject, instructors, practices, and environment. Learning attitude is the key to effectiveness and achievement. Suitable assistance and support enable learners produce positive learning attitude for internalizing targeted information and knowledge. Researchers identified factors that influence learners' attitude include real life material and instructional material [9]. Previous studies were conducted that students' attitude and performance related to a significant correlation [10]. Additionally, teachers' background, teachers' personality, teachers' knowledge, teachers' emotional support, instructional practices, and classroom management [11]. Therefore, the creativity and innovation of educators require significant improvement in order to transform the learning attitude from a passive learner to an active producer. Positive learning attitude enables L2 learners to identify questions, participate classroom activities, and complete assignments.

3 Methodology

3.1 Design of VR L2 Learning System

In the VR English learning environment, the participants interact with the virtual machine and tools in a multimodal way combining haptic, audio and visual feedback, see Figs. 1, 2, 3 and 4. The VR L2 learning system provides an airport scenario in the real world, that help and guide the users during the practical process. Unity is a well-known game engine in dealing with 3D scene and objects, as well as a platform of integrating hardware and software [7]. The common approach with the VR training system emphasizes the physical interaction and literal skill to improve learners' L2 listening and oral ability. There are many development kits to choose to cooperative with unity such as Fuforia, MaYa, 3D Max, ARToolKit, Wikitude, and Unifeye. 3D Max and Maya are selected as the development tool because they are more economic and user-friendly. Thus, the support of unity, 3D Max and Maya enable L2 learners to interact with the designed VR scenes in the classroom, participants' positive learning attitude are greatly enhanced. The designed L2 learning VR system prototype are shown in Figs. 1, 2, 3 and 4.

3.2 Research Data Collection

This exploratory design mixed study investigated the essence of VR implementation based on the daily life scenario toward L2 students. Quantitative research approach was first used to discover the experience of participants after using the scenario-based VR L2 learning system. Next, the researcher designed a qualitative study to define the findings. Mixed methods research is valued for educational use and is discussed in the

Fig. 1. The prototype of the proposed VR language learning system.

Fig. 2. Demonstration of L2 practice by using the VR language learning system.

Fig. 3. Illustration of the airport scenario.

Fig. 4. Illustration of checking in at the counter by users.

research recently [12]. The use of quantitative and qualitative methods are components in a mixed methods study [13]. Therefore, students' experience in using VR to enhance language learning offered valuable data to improve the teaching and the system. 117 freshmen (101 males and 16 females) participated in the study. A list of questionnaires of students' attitude towards learning English via Virtual Reality learning system was rated on a five-point Likert scale. The Likert scale items explain different levels of formation toward changes in attitudes. L2 learners' emotions, liking, disliking (and the reason behind it) were designed and organized in the semi-structure interview questions to identify the factors that affected learners' learning attitude toward English learning. Participants were assigned to use VR language learning system with the given scenario after the lesson was taught. 7 female and 8 male students were randomly selected to provide the feedback on their VR learning practice. Observations on participants were conducted for an entire semester in the classroom and while students experienced the VR language learning system. A field journal was conducted for a researcher to maintain self-awareness [14]. Furthermore, three instructors with English, electronic engineering, and communication engineering backgrounds were the counselors for ensuring open-ended questions were in the research scope.

4 Results and Discussions

4.1 Quantitative Data

Participants' Positive Attitude of Learning English Through VR is Revealed. The first part of the survey investigate the areas in which attitude of learning English through VR system. Three characteristics of learning helpfulness, enjoyment, and effectiveness toward the VR were evaluated. Table 1 shows the mean value of the results. Students appreciate using VR to learn English was scored the highest ($M = 4.38$). Learning through VR helps participants in learning English scored as ($M = 4.22$). Learning from VR helps students remember and develop vocabulary effectively was scored as ($M = 4.02$). The use of VR makes learning English easier and faster was scored as ($M = 4.01$). Every part of participants' positive attitude of learning English through VR investigation was given ratings of above 4.0, students' attitude of learning English through VR is positive.

Table 1. Mean and standard deviation of student's attitude of learning English through VR. (from "strongly disagree" to "strongly agree").

Items	M	S.D
Attitude in Learning English through VR:		
Learning through VR helps me in acquiring English?	4.38	0.77
I like to use VR technology to learn and practice English?	4.22	0.54
Learning from VR helps me remember and develop vocabulary effectively?	4.01	0.95
The use of VR makes learning English easier and faster?	4.01	0.96

Areas Where Participants' Negative Attitude of Learning English Through VR is Revealed. The second part of the survey investigate the areas in which participants' negative attitude of learning English through VR. Three characteristics of uselessness, time waste, and dullness toward the VR English learning system were evaluated. Table 2 shows the scores of the students' feedbacks. Participants think the use of VR is useless in learning was scored the highest ($M = 1.48$), which means most of the students were rated between disagree and strongly disagree. Students feel bored while learning through VR was rated as ($M = 1.33$). When using the VR English learning system, students don't need an instructor was scored as ($M = 1.42$), which means most of the students still need the assistance from their instructor. Participants feel that they waste their time by using VR learning system was scored as ($M = 1.17$). Participants' negative attitude of learning English through VR were given scores of under 1.5, students' negative learning attitude toward VR system is very low (Table 2).

Table 2. The mean and standard deviation of students' negative attitude of learning English through VR: The Mean and Standard Deviation (from "strongly disagree" to "strongly agree").

Items	M	S.D
Participants' negative attitude of learning English through VR:		
Using VR language learning system wastes my time?	1.17	0.58
I feel bored while learning through VR?	1.33	0.66
VR language learning system is useless?	1.48	0.84
I do not need an instructor when using a VR language learning system?	1.42	0.78

Areas Where Participants' Perceived Usefulness in Learning English Through VR System is Revealed. The third part of the survey investigates three characteristics of usefulness, effectiveness, and enjoyment toward the VR English learning system. Item 1 presents the highest agreement of efficiency and effectiveness of VR and also indicates VR develops high quality of English learning ($M = 4.18$). Students enjoy learning English through VR language learning system ($M = 3.93$). Item 3 investigates by using VR language learning system, it has encouraged users to have more motivation in their learning ($M = 4.02$). Item 4 investigates that knowledge of capabilities is required to use VR was rated as ($M = 2.82$). Item 5 the VR language learning system is hands-on for learners was rated as ($M = 4.32$). Item 6 in participants' opinion using VR language learning system provides an effective way of solving problems in learning a target language was scored ($M = 3.18$) (Table 3).

4.2 Qualitative Data

Research Question 1: How VR language leaning system facilitates target language learning?
VR language learning system offers opportunities for students practice their target in an effective way after school. L2 learners were impressed by the interaction with the system during their use.

"I never thought I would use VR technology to learn and practice English. When I was in the scenario of airport, it was fun and real. I handed my passport to the ground crew and answered questions from her." (June, female student)"

"I would give a positive feedback for this VR system. My classmates and I enjoy having VR to facilitate our learning. I am more confidence in speaking English to a

Table 3. The usefulness of VR in English learning.

Items	M	S.D
The usefulness of VR in English learning		
VR language learning system provides an effective way of solving problems in learning a target language	4.18	0.87
Learning English through VR language learning system is enjoyable?	3.93	0.80
I have more motivation learning English by using VR language learning system	4.02	0.93
In order to use VR language learning system, knowledge of capabilities is required?	2.82	0.74
The VR language learning system is hands-on for users?	4.32	0.89
In my opinion using VR language learning system provides an effective way of solving problems in learning a target language	3.18	0.65

"VR" human instead of a real person. I practiced the conversation drills with less stress, and I don't worry about making mistakes. (June, female student)

"VR has given significant changes to my language learning; This is my first time using it. I felt like I am in the real environment. English learning becomes more entertained and interactive" (June, male student)

"VR provides opportunities for me to learn the target language which related to the daily life situation. I can practice the target language which related to real-life and the textbook material especially when I just learned from the class. I have ways to memorize new words and grammar rules." (May, male student)

Students addressed that feedback from the instructor is essential to facilitate improvement in the learning outcome. Students expressed their opinions on teachers' attitude and support; they anticipate their teachers to be well-prepared and motivated in teaching.

"Although VR enables me to practice my English before and after class. I personally like the instructor to provide specific feedback or suggestion to my practice right away." (June, female student)

"I think teacher with creative and innovative teaching method is important. Their open-minded and knowledgeable toward new learning activity motivate students learn and practice their English. (June, male student)

"I think interactive language learning is the best way to improve my English. If the instructor is passionate for his or her class, Students' learning outcome will be positive and motivated. I like to learn English through real-life material and like to connect the learning with VR" (May, female student)

Research Question 2: Students' attitude of usefulness of how VR facilitates their target language learning?

Opportunities of scenario-based learning were provided to L2 learners. Participants were welcomed to use VR language learning system to achieve better learning outcome.

"Using VR system to practice my English is very useful, I can image when I need to go abroad or transfer in an international airport, I will not be too shy in speaking English in the public. I will probably feel like I have understood the process of checking in and going through the custom. Although Covid-19 keeps everyone away from the airport, I believe when we have the cure. I will have the chance to go abroad and use what I learned from the class." (June, female student)

"I was shy in speaking English in the public, I used to worry that what should I do when I need to work at the hospital and use those medical terms at the work place. After practicing English with VR technology, I realize that speaking English is not that difficult. I was very shy and lack of confident but VR is very helpful. I think I improve a lot compares to the past." (May, male)

"I was not sure if VR can improve my English. I thought it was useless at the beginning. Then, I was forced to practice English with VR system after class. I think the motivation in learning English is very important, I used to feel bored in class because I don't like to join any conversation or activity. Honestly, after practicing English by VR technology, learning becomes real and assessable." (June, male student)

"VR is a very useful technology. It really helps me a lot by providing me easy access to the real-life English environment. Applying what I learned in the daily life is fun and stress free. I am satisfied with the technology this course provided. This course is valued and I become an active learner" (May, female student)

5 Conclusions

VR applications for language education will possibly become easier due to the development and popularity. This study specified that VR language learning system was a useful technology for developing autonomous language learners. According to [7] VR technology offers instant interactive exercise and provides real-life opportunity in language learning. Language learning with the technology support flourishes under innovative and inspired education. Effective practical opportunities develop students' positive attitude in L2 learning. VR English learning system plays a significant role in enabling students deal with their shortages. VR allows educators to take advantage on supporting students and reducing gap between lecture and practice. VR language learning system assists L2 teachers to develop understandable instruction and adapt curriculum-based activities and course work, moreover, assisting L2 learners improve their learning outcome [8]. Participants in this study shows positive attitude and motivation in using VR language learning system in acquiring their English ability. A high functioning VR L2 learning environment can be an effective assistance or a private tutor to meet the needs of the students before and after the class.

References

1. Lee, E.A.-L., Wong, K.W.: A review of using virtual reality for learning. In: Pan, Z., Cheok, A.D., Müller, W., El Rhalibi, A. (eds.) Transactions on Edutainment I. LNCS, vol. 5080, pp. 231–241. Springer, Heidelberg (2008). https://doi.org/10.1007/978-3-540-69744-2_18

2. Dalgarno, B., Hedberg, J., Harper, B.: The contribution of 3D environments to conceptual understanding. In: ASCILITE 2002, Auckland, New Zealand, pp. 149–158 (2002)
3. Limniou, M., Roberts, D., Papadopoulos, N.: Full immersive virtual environment CAVETM in chemistry education. Comput. Educ. **51**(2), 584–593 (2008)
4. Pan, Z., Cheok, A.D., Yang, H., Zhu, J., Shi, J.: Virtual reality and mixed reality for virtual learning environments. Comput. Graph. **30**, 20–28 (2006)
5. Dmitrenko, V.: Language learning strategies of multilingual adults learning additional languages. Int. J. Multilingualism **14**(1), 6–22 (2017)
6. Shen, H., Yuan, Y., Ewing, R.: English learning websites and digital resources from the perspectives of Chinese university EFL practitioners. ReCALL **27**(2), 156–176 (2015)
7. Chen, Y.: Augmented reality technique assists target language learning. In: Rønningsbakk, L., Wu, T.-T., Sandnes, F.E., Huang, Y.-M. (eds.) ICITL 2019. LNCS, vol. 11937, pp. 558–567. Springer, Cham (2019). https://doi.org/10.1007/978-3-030-35343-8_59
8. Chen, Y.: reducing language speaking anxiety among adult EFL learners with interactive holographic learning support system. In: Wu, T.-T., Huang, Y.-M., Shadieva, R., Lin, L., Starčič, A.I. (eds.) ICITL 2018. LNCS, vol. 11003, pp. 101–110. Springer, Cham (2018). https://doi.org/10.1007/978-3-319-99737-7_10
9. Yılmaz, Ç., Altun, S.A., Olkun, S.: Factors affecting students' attitude towards Math: ABC theory and its reflection on practice. Procedia-Soc. Behav. Sci. **2**(2), 4502–4506 (2010)
10. Mensah, J.K., Okyere, M., Kuranchie, A.: Student attitude towards Mathematics and performance: does the teacher attitude matter? J. Educ. Pract. **4**(3), 132–139 (2013)
11. Blazar, D., Kraft, M.A.: Teacher and teaching effects on students' attitudes and behaviors. Educ. Eval. Policy Anal. **39**(1), 146–170 (2017)
12. Ponce, O.: Investigación de Métodos Mixtos en Educación. Publicaciones Puertorriqueñas, San Juan (2014)
13. Caruth, G.D.: Demystifying mixed methods research design: a review of the literature. Melvana Int. J. Educ. **3**(2), 112–122 (2013)
14. Connell, P.J.: A Phenomenological Study of the Lived Experiences of Adult Caregiving Daughters and Their Elderly Mothers. University of Florida (2003)

The Impact of Applying Virtual Reality Technology to Spatial Ability Learning in Elementary School Students

Wen-Hung Chao[1] and Rong-Chi Chang[2(✉)]

[1] Department of Digital Media Design, Asia University,
Taichung City, Taiwan, R.O.C.
[2] Department of Technology Crime Investigation, Taiwan Police College,
Taipei, Taiwan, R.O.C.
roger@mail.tpa.edu.tw

Abstract. This study explored the effects of virtual reality (VR) technology applied to spatial ability learning in elementary school students. As supplement materials to the Geometry Unit in the curriculum, the learning materials were developed based on the mathematics competence indicators for fifth and sixth graders in Taiwan. Designed to enhance spatial concept and logical thinking, the materials tapped into VR technology to transform two-dimensional graphics into three-dimensional spaces, in view of effectively solving the problem of learning abstract 3D spaces. A quasi-experimental method was used to understand the influence of different learning methods on students' learning effectiveness and interest in learning. The experiment found that (1) the use of interactive VR learning materials significantly improved student's spatial ability; (2) using VR learning materials enhanced the learning effectiveness of students with low achievement in mathematics; and (3) the introduction of VR learning materials improved students' motivation for learning spatial concepts. The findings showed that the digital learning materials developed in this study were beneficial to the teaching effectiveness of teachers and the learning needs of students.

Keywords: Spatial ability · Mathematics · Virtual reality · Physical blocks · Digital learning materials

1 Introduction

Spatial ability is an important building block to mathematical ability. Its learning objectives include understanding the properties of geometric shapes, emphasizing the use of visualization, spatial inference, and geometric patterns to solve problems. The Geometry Unit in Taiwan's fifth-grade mathematics curriculum includes recognizing volumes and composite solids, where students are taught how to calculate the volume of stacked solids. When elementary school students learn about volume calculation in mathematics, they must be equipped with a basic understanding of spatial concepts.

Spatial ability is intimately tied to our everyday lives, as it helps us identify the position, size, shape of objects in the real world. Smith [1] proposed that spatial ability consists of three components: mental rotation, spatial visualization and spatial orientation. In the real world, there is a need for spatial ability training. For instance, space design, architectural modeling, graphic design and industrial design all require a good spatial competency foundation before one can understand and produce engineering and design drawings. Spatial orientation must be cultivated from a young age, and its related learning contents, e.g., length, area, surface area, volume, have a great impact on future ability development. Mathematics learning focuses on a logical framework in a stepwise manner. Conventional teaching of spatial ability usually uses three-dimensional perspective graphics as an aid to spatial concept formation. However, some students are unable to use perspective graphics to associate with three-dimensional solids, leading to frustration in the learning process and refusal to learn.

In recent years, the popularization of VR technology has given rise to various studies on VR in education [2]. The three characteristics of VR, i.e., immersion, interactivity and imagination, allow learners to learn as if they are in a real situation during the learning process, while the visual and auditory effects of VR create an immersive and imaginative learning experience. VR is able to attract learner attention, induce their feelings, and enhance the affective and cognitive learning effects [3, 4]. In addition, the tactile simulation and sensory feedback in VR devices allow users to interact with virtual objects [5] and promote active learner engagement [6, 7].

Learning mathematics should be an enjoyable experience, and its learning process should be embedded into a context that develops ways of understanding and thinking. In mathematics education, problem solving, a medium for learning math concepts and skills, is considered an important part of the curriculum and is a topic of ongoing interest by educational researcher [8]. In this study, an interactive VR-based three-dimensional space learning platform was developed in view of enhancing the development of spatial concepts on position, distance, and displacement in elementary school students. With this learning platform, such concepts in three-dimensional space can be enhanced through operating different actions, such as combination, stacking and movement of solids, in a constructed virtual space. An experiment was designed to understand the effectiveness of this platform on spatial ability learning and the impact of VR introduction on the learning motivation of students.

2 Application Implementation

The system was developed using Unity 3D game engine and designed with 3D objects, interactive scenes, learning situations and scoring functions. A complete VR interactive learning environment was created through the use of VR headsets, controllers, and base stations. The learning platform was designed with 2 units: unit 1 is the basic cognitive sense of space and three-dimensional concepts, involving the learning of volume, length, units and distance; and unit 2 focuses on the placement and creation of various three-dimensional objects, where learners are taught to use operations such as flipping, stacking, maneuvering, and assembling to construct three-dimensional structures. Virtual characters were put in place to guide learners through the learning process and score calculations (see Fig. 1).

(a) Virtual character guided learning (b) 3D space learning exercises

Fig. 1. Interactive VR learning scenario.

3 Research Methods

3.1 Research Design

This study was conducted using a quasi-experimental pre-post-test design. Two classes of fifth-grade students were the research subjects, where one class was the experimental group who were taught spatial orientation using the VR learning system, and the other class was the control group who were taught with the use of solid blocks. Before and after the experimental teaching, tests were conducted, and questionnaires were administered to the subjects to understand their spatial ability learning experience. Figures 2 and 3, respectively, show the use of learning aids in the control group and the experimental group.

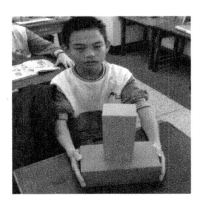 

Fig. 2. Control group students using physical blocks to assist in their learning.

3.2 Research Subjects

The subjects of this study were 50 fifth-grade students in an elementary school in Taiwan. The experimental group consisted 24 students, including 14 boys and 10 girls. The control group consisted 26 students, including 13 boys and 13 girls. At a total of 27 boys and 23 girls, the two classes were taught by the same teacher who had had 8

(a) 3D structure construction (b) Virtual object maneuvering

Fig. 3. Experimental group students using VR learning transform to assist in their learning.

years of mathematics teaching experience, and the learning content of the two classes was the same.

3.3 Research Tools

Spatial ability test (pre-post-test): Test questions on three-dimensional building block rotation, a common test for exploring spatial ability, were prepared to investigate students' spatial ability before and after the learning experiment.

Learning motivation scale: The learning motivation scale of this experiment was adapted from Hwang et al. [9]. The questionnaire consisted of two dimensions, intrinsic motivation and extrinsic motivation, with a total of 9 questions measured using the Likert 5-point scale to analyze the learning motivation difference between the two groups of students before and after the experiment.

The spatial ability pre-test and the learning motivation questionnaire were administered to both groups of students before the experiment started. At the beginning, students in the experimental group were given an introduction and demonstration on the operation of the VR system to ensure that they knew how to operate it. After that, the two groups of students were subjected to different learning methods. After the completion of the experimental course, the two groups were given post-tests and questionnaires. Figure 4 shows the experimental process. The experimental analysis and discussion are as follows.

4 Findings and Discussion

4.1 The Composition of the Experimental Group and the Control Group

The subjects of the experiment were 50 school students, including 24 students in the experimental group (14 boys and 10 girls) and 26 students in the control group (13 boys and 13 girls). The mathematics scores of both groups in the previous semester were analyzed. Independent sample t test showed that the mean score in the experimental group was 87.2, and that of the control group was 86.6 ($F(1, 48) = 0.051$, $t = 0.25$, $p > 0.05$), denoting no significant difference.

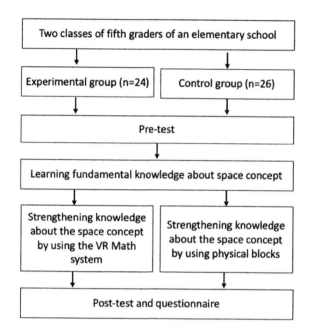

Fig. 4. Diagram of the experimental design.

4.2 Pre-post-Test Data Analysis of Experimental Group and Control Group

As shown in Table 1, the pre-test mean of the control group was 84.10 and post-test mean was 83.90, registering a slight 0.20 decrease. Meanwhile, the pre-test mean of the experimental group was 79.80 and the post-test mean was 86.80. After the introduction of VR learning materials, the mean score in the experimental group significantly increased 7 points. Table 1 shows that the pre-test and post-test in the control group using the conventional textbook did not reach a significant difference ($t = 0.05$, $p > 0.05$). On the other hand, the pre-test and post-test results of the experimental group using VR learning materials in the learning process were significantly different ($t = 5.22$, $p < 0.001$).

Table 1. t-test analysis of the learning motivation scale.

	N	Pre-test		Post-test		t
		M	S.D.	M	S.D.	
Control group	26	84.10	9.94	83.90	14.08	−0.05
Experimental group	24	79.80	12.12	86.80	11.77	5.22***

*** $p < 0.001$

4.3 The Learning Effectiveness of Students with Different Mathematical Abilities in the Experimental Group

Table 2 shows the data of the low-achieving subset, who were slower in math learning, and the high-achieving subset in the experimental group of students after using VR learning materials. According to data analysis, there were 14 students in the low-achieving subset (pre-test scores between 60–79). Their mean pre-test score was 69.14 (S.D. = 7.98) and the mean post-test score was 79.64 (S.D. = 13.07). The mean difference between the pre- and post-tests was 10.50 (= 79.64–69.14). Meanwhile, there were 10 students in high-achieving subset (pre-test scores between 80–100). Their mean pre-test score was 89.12 (S.D. = 5.51) and the mean post-test was 93.90 (S.D. = 5.41). The mean difference between their pre-test and post-test scores was 4.78 (= 93.90–89.12). Both the low- and high-achieving subsets reached a significant level in the score difference ($t = -4.89$; $t = -3.02$). In terms of the degree of difference, the enhancement of the learning effectiveness using VR materials in the low-achieving subset was higher than that of their high-achieving counterparts.

Table 2. Analysis on the learning effectiveness of students with different mathematical abilities in the experimental group.

	N	Pre-test		Post-test		t
		M	S.D.	M	S.D.	
Low achiever group	14	69.14	7.98	79.64	13.07	−4.89***
High achiever group	10	89.12	5.51	93.90	5.41	−3.02***

***$p < 0.001$

4.4 The Learning Effectiveness of Students with Different Mathematical Abilities in the Control Group

In the control group (Table 3), there were 10 students in the low-achieving subset (pre-test scores between 60–79). Their mean pre-test score was 72 (S.D. = 8.42) and the mean post-test score was 70.55 (S.D. = 13.80). The mean difference between their pre-test and post-test score was −1.45 (= 70.55–72). On the other hand, there were 17 students in the high-achieving subset (pre-test scores between 80–100). Their mean pre-test score was 89.23 (S.D. = 4.62) and the mean post-test score was 89.71 (S.D. = 9.78). The mean difference between their pre-test and post-test score was 0.48 (= 89.71–89.23). Neither the low- and high-achieving subsets reached a significant level in the score difference ($t = -0.31$; $t = 0.25$).

4.5 Comparison of Learning Motivation

A pre- and post-test analysis of learning motivation was conducted to understand the influence of different learning materials on students' spatial learning ability before and after the experiment. From the data analysis (Table 4), the mean pre-test and post-test scores in the experimental group's learning motivation were 3.89 and 4.41, respectively, which were statistically significant by the paired-sample t test ($t = 3.51$,

Table 3. Analysis on the learning effectiveness of students with different mathematical abilities in the control group.

	N	Pre-test		Post-test		t
		M	S.D.	M	S.D.	
Low achiever group	10	72.00	8.42	70.55	13.80	−0.31
High achiever group	16	89.23	4.64	89.71	9.78	0.25

$p < 0.01$). In the learning motivation of the control group, the mean pre-test and post-test scores were 3.97 and 3.77, respectively. The paired-sample t test ($t = -0.16$, $p < 0.876$) did not reach statistical significance (as shown in Table 4). Student learning motivation in the experimental group increased from 3.89 to 4.41 after using the VR learning platform, showing the integration of VR learning materials in learning can effectively enhance students' learning motivation. Meanwhile, the learning motivation of students in the control group dropped from 3.97 to 3.77, suggesting that the lack of variation and innovation in the conventional textbook-based learning model can lead to low learning motivation which in turn affects learning effectiveness.

Table 4. t-test analysis of the learning motivation scale.

	N	Pre-test		Post-test		t
		M	S.D.	M	S.D.	
Experimental group	24	3.89	0.79	4.41	0.58	3.51**
Control group	26	3.97	0.85	3.77	0.93	−0.16

**$p < 0.01$

5 Conclusion

The VR learning materials developed in this study aimed to create an interactive experience to enhance students' spatial ability. Students were given the chance to use rotation, stacking, maneuvering, and combination to explore the complete geometries of three-dimensional objects, thereby strengthening their ability to understand three-dimensional space. The experiment findings showed that the use of VR-assisted learning materials can arouse the interest and curiosity of learners with low mathematics ability, bringing into full play the advantages of integrating technology into learning. Kang, Hong, & Lee [10] suggested virtual simulation is an educational strategy that can effectively help students stay engaged in learning and achieve positive learning outcomes. The virtual environment created by VR allows students to have direct contact with the immersive, simulated world it presents, and the complete interactive experience motivates students to learn. Characterized by its elements of challenge and feedback, digital learning can reduce learning boredom or anxiety when the learning process is an immersive experience. Increased learning motivation enables learners to identify solutions through trial and error or imitation of examples [11].

Acknowledgement. This research is supported by the Ministry of Science and Technology, Taiwan, R.O.C. [grant number MOST 105-2511-S-261 -001 -MY2].

References

1. Smith, I.M.: Spatial Ability: Its Educational and Social Significance. University of London Press, London (1964)
2. Radianti, J., Majchrzak, T.A., Fromm, J., Wohlgenannt, I.: A systematic review of immersive virtual reality applications for higher education: Design elements, lessons learned, and research agenda. Comput. Educ. **147**, 103778 (2019)
3. Burdea, G.C., Coiffet, P.: Virtual Reality Technology, vol. 1, 2nd edn. John Wiley & Sons, New Jersey (2003)
4. Meyer, O.A., Omdahl, M.K., Makransky, G.: Investigating the effect of pre-training when learning through immersive virtual reality and video: a media and methods experiment. Comput. Educ. **140**, 103603 (2019)
5. Yao, H.P., Liu, Y.Z., Han, C.S.: Application expectation of virtual reality in basketball teaching. Procedia Eng. **29**, 4287–4291 (2012)
6. Zhou, Y., Ji, S., Xu, T., Wang, Z.: Promoting knowledge construction: a model for using virtual reality interaction to enhance learning. Procedia Comput. Sci. **130**, 239–246 (2018)
7. Padilha, J.M., Machado, P.P., Ribeiro, A., Ramos, J., Costa, P.: Clinical virtual simulation in nursing education: randomized controlled trial. J. Med. Internet Res. **21**(3), e11529 (2019)
8. Contreras, J.: BY way of introduction: posing and solving problems: the essence and legacy of mathematics. Teach. Child. Math. **12**(3), 115–116 (2005)
9. Hwang, G.J., Yang, L.H., Wang, S.Y.: A concept map-embedded educational computer game for improving students' learning performance in natural science courses. Comput. Educ. **69**(1), 121–130 (2013)
10. Kang, S.J., Hong, C., Lee, H.: The Impact of Virtual Simulation on Critical Thinking and Self-Directed Learning Ability of Nursing Students. Clinical Simulation in Nursing (2020)
11. Liu, C.-C., Cheng, Y.-B., Huang, C.W.: The effect of simulation games on the learning of computational problem solving. Comput. Educ. **57**(3), 1907–1918 (2011)

Educational Data Mining and Learning Analytics

Competence Mining to Improve Training Programs

Ildikó Szabó(✉), Katalin Ternai, and Szabina Fodor

Corvinus University of Budapest, Fővám tér 13-15, Budapest 1093, Hungary
{ildiko.szabo2,katalin.ternai,
szabina.fodor}@uni-corvinus.hu

Abstract. Analysing of competence and skill shortage or surpluses is essential for educational institutes to prepare their students for satisfying labour market needs in time and comprehensively. Currently, changes in labour market needs are influenced by not just economical but also technological factors. ICT and digitalization play key roles in transformations of business processes including employees' competences in executing these processes smoothly and effectively. Our research goal is to develop a competence mining method to identify and extract competences needed to fill job vacancies. Based on this new information the educational programs can be refined. This paper presents how to use business process models to extract competences from job vacancies and how this method evolved in time and what its contribution is to the training development based on learning outcome. Competence concept has a crucial role in this method, but it is defined on a broad scale that causes terminological diversity.

Keywords: Training program · Competence · Text mining · Business process model · Ontology transformation

1 Introduction

Educational institutes must meet different expectations. Globalization puts pressure on institutes to train students who can adapt to different culture and environments during their whole lifetime. Machines are unable to replicate judgement, empathy, persuasion, the ability to collaborate and communicate, and be flexible, adaptable, and resilient, though more AI change is coming [1]. These skills should be possessed by students. In 2018, JISC[1] in the UK surveyed 22,000 university students and while more than 80% of them felt that digital skills will be important for their chosen career, only half believed that their courses were preparing them well for the digital workplace [2]. The Universities need to start to develop an education 4.0 program in line with the 4th industrial revolution. The education 4.0 program should aim at providing graduates with capabilities and competencies required by the digital-driven industry [3]. The newest industrial revolution is boosted by technologies that creates new requirements. This transformation induced by Industry 4.0 requires continuous education processes

---

[1] Formerly the Joint Information Systems Committee (https://www.jisc.ac.uk).

performed by humans, educational programs fitting to information technologies, providing multidimensional mind development and deep understanding of subjects. These programs have to train such students who can learn and like analysing and discussing problems [4]. Higher educational institutions need to address needs of the labour market and this should be linked to research issues.

For the point of view to this study, monitoring competence needs of labour market is essential for educational institutes. Job vacancies published on a job portal aggregating posting from many sites (like indeed.com) are appropriate sources for ensuring this activity. These job ads are numerous and time varying, hence reflect dynamically changing needs well. The goal of our research is to develop a competence mining method to identify and extract competences needed to fill job vacancies. Based on this new information the educational programs can be refined. This paper presents how this method evolved in time and what its contribution is to the training development based on learning outcome. Competence concept has a crucial role in this method, but it is defined on a broad scale that causes terminological diversity. Section 2 presents some definitions and shows the role of this concept in training development. It clarifies this topic from the point of view of our method. Section 3 sheds light on some current research to emphasize our novelty in this field. Section 4 presents how competences can be mined from 192 warehouse manager jobs published the one of top job portals (indeed.com) in UK with using general text mining method and our process-based text mining method. Finally, it presents a competence dashboard for educators to improve their training programs. Conclusions and future works are drawn in Sect. 5.

2 Outcome-Based Training Development

Competence expresses "What is a human capable of?" [5]. Hecklau et al. [6] classified future competencies into four categories based on macroenvironmental analysis. Technical competencies are knowledge, skills and abilities related to work. Personal competencies are motivations and attitudes of people. Social competencies are abilities to cooperate, communicate with other people. Methodological competences are to support decision making and problem solving. Wikle & Fagin [7] distinguished hard/technical and soft skills as competences. Hard skills are learned or professional competencies, soft skills are generic ones. Lippman et al. [8 pp. 4] defined soft skills as "a broad set of skills, competencies, behaviours, attitudes, and personal qualities that enable people to effectively navigate their environment, work well with other and perform well". In the previous decades, there was a paradigm shift in education that put students in focus instead of teachers. European Qualification Framework represents this endeavour well. It advises to focus on what "students are expected to achieve and how they should demonstrate what they have learned" [9]. The emphasis was shifted from the learning output to learning outcome possessed by students. Conceptualizing learning outcomes helps in designing curriculum including teaching and learning activities, assessment methods and in creating transparent training programs. In Gagné's theory, the planning of education programs starts with the identification of learning outcomes followed by the construction of the task analyses – or in other words, the learning hierarchy – that are responsible for execution of measurable activities [10]. Technical/methodological competency and hard skill are very similar concepts. Social or personal competencies can be considered as soft skills. The original goal of Benjamin S. Bloom was to elaborate a better way to compare results of various training programs and test methodologies in 1956. His method provided guidelines for elaborating various training programs subordinated to learning outcomes. Terminology, structural changes, and changes in emphasis were made in its revised version. The Revised Taxonomy contains six categories: Remembering, Understanding, Applying, Analysing, Evaluating, Creating. Specific verbs are selected to describe these categories [11]. In summary, it was presented that outcome-based training development requires well-defined and measurable learning outcomes which are expressed by competences. Revised Bloom taxonomy presents six cognitive levels of complex thinking that are measurable by tasks achieved by students. Verbs describing these levels can be applied to extract competences or skills from job ads (see Sect. 4). Our research goal is to develop a competence mining method to identify, extract competences needed to fill job vacancies in order that training programs can be adjusted to this competence set. Business process model serves as a basis of this text mining process because it contains tasks which activity part can be connected to the revised Bloom taxonomy. It also provides additional information to understand the complexity of these tasks and other related factors. Hard skills or technical/methodological competencies are connected to tasks primarily that is why our purpose is to mine these competences instead of soft skills or social/personal competencies.

3 Related Work

OECD[2] Skills for Jobs database[3] is designed to measure skill shortage and surplus. Indicators to reveal these discrepancies were created based on five sub-indices: wage growth, employment growth, hours worked growth, unemployment rate, underqualification growth. These macro-economic indicators are to estimate changes in occupation groups and related skill sets [12]. CEDEFOP[4] Skill Forecast uses quantitative methods to forecast future trends in sector, occupations, and qualifications. Skill-OVATE is an online vacancy analysis tool for Europe. It provides insight into skills and jobs requested by employers. Data are fetched from job portals, employer's portals etc. but within a given time and not dynamically [13]. Bakhshi et al. [14] used occupations ranked by experts to create machine learning method for analysing future competence needs. Skill market gap analysis of SMART system is to identify gaps between competences can be acquired by a tourism-specific training program and labour market needs in tourism industry. This system also processes job ads but uses domain ontology and not process ontology to identify competences in them [15]. Skill gap analysis is a hot topic currently, hence the above-mentioned researches are just few examples among different projects and initiatives. However, they are different in

---

[2] Organisation for Economic Co-operation and Development.
[3] https://www.oecdskillsforjobsdatabase.org.
[4] Centre Européen pour le Développement de la Formation Professionnelle.

methods: quantitative and/or text mining, machine learning methods are applied. Our approach distinguishes from that based on the fact that it provides a tool to monitor labour market needs and it uses process ontologies as underlying knowledge.

4 Contribution: Process-Based Text Mining

Our main purpose is to analyse competences are required to fill a position. Several positions can be digitally transformed due to technological innovations (like self-driving forklift or mobile app). A reference business process model considering these innovations holds background information to process job vacancies in meaningful manner. The process-based text mining process is illustrated by Fig. 1. At the beginning, the structure of a process model is designed (task as process step, role as job role and required skill to execute this task by this role).

The business process model is implemented by using BOC ADONIS modelling platform[5]. ADONIS is a graph-structured BPM language. The ADONIS modeling platform is a business meta-modeling tool with components such as modeling, analysis, simulation, evaluation, process costing, documentation, staff management, and import-export. Its main feature is its method independence. Our approach is principally transferable to other semi-formal modelling languages. The models can be exported in the structure of ADONIS XML format. There are several parameters that can be set or defined when modelling a business process. The shell of a business process can be easily formed with activities, decision points, parallelism or merging objects, logical gateways and events. A prototypical java tool was developed to transform the business process into a process ontology in OWL format. For the mapping the conceptual models to ontology models meta-modeling approach have been used. The "conceptual model - ontology model" converter maps the Adonis model elements to the appropriate ontology elements in meta-level. The general rule used in our approach is to express each ADONIS model element as a class in the ontology and its corresponding attributes as attributes of the class.

Meanwhile a Python crawler fetches information about job vacancies from the selected job portal. Data cleaning and data prep process are executed before the text mining. The process-based text mining identifies patterns of part-of-speech tags (e.g. verb followed by noun) to get a list of expressions describing tasks (see Bloom taxonomy). The algorithm calculates the semantic distance of these expressions (e.g. create quality) from the business process elements of the process ontology (e.g. check quality). Similarity coefficients are used to do this calculation. The list of expressions is filtered by the value of the selected coefficient and by the descriptions of process elements. Remained expressions as descriptors identify process elements (like tasks) in job ads. Job ads contain information about when and where these process elements were required and by which position. An extended table is used to analyse task-related competences regionally, in time and based on positions. The theoretical background of

---

[5] BOC Group: Business Process Management with Adonis, http://www.boc-group.com/products/adonis/en/.

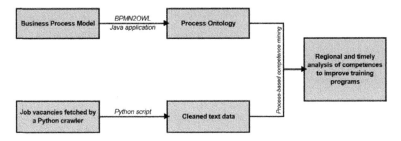

Fig. 1. Process-based text mining

this process has been presented in [16]. This paper presents how business process models can provide additional information in processing job vacancies versus basic text analytics method. The whole process is illustrated by the purchasing process including activities performed by warehouse managers.

4.1 Business Process Model and Its Transformation

A process from logistics was selected to present the applicability of the method. The warehouse manager has several responsibilities in this process, so this profession is well applicable to illustrate our method.

The warehouse manager's activities in the process are the following ones:

- Check Inventory: Stock-taking is the physical verification of the quantities and condition of items held in the inventory or warehouse.
- Check Quality: The quality assessment will be based on predetermined requirements and standards previously set by the company.
- Unload Goods: Safely prepare, lift, position and restrain goods on a vehicle platform and then unload goods at the destination.
- Manage Goods In: Provide the correct goods, at the correct amount, place, and time.
- Record Data: Record the purchasing information into the warehouse management information system.
- Treat Scrap: Sort the scrap into recyclables and unusable waste.
- Record Report: Record the waste information into the quality management system.

For the transformation process, a prototypical software tool was developed which transforms the BPMN model into OWL format[6]. The resulting file contains a partial ontology including classes and individuals of the input file [16].

---

[6] The BPMN model and the transformation program are available on the GitHub (https://github.com/szabinaf/BPM2OWL/).

4.2 Job Vacancies and Data Preparation

192 warehouse manager jobs were fetched from the UK labour market[7] by a Python crawler into CSV file. It was discovered that the important part of job descriptions starts with specific expressions such as responsibilities, accountability, looking for, candidate and so on. The 90% of job vacancies met these expectations, but the remained ones did not contain unnecessary texts (like company description). Hence the first part of these descriptions was cut off to get the relevant part of them.

Spacy, pandas, re and text distance Python library were used. List was created from the sentences of cleaned job descriptions. Sentences with at least 20 characters were processed, lemmatized, tokenized and their part-of-speech tags were determined.

4.3 First Approach: Text-Mining Based on Job Vacancies

Our first approach was to extract competence information based on only data downloaded from the career website. The cleaned and tokenized job description field was used for basic text analysis.

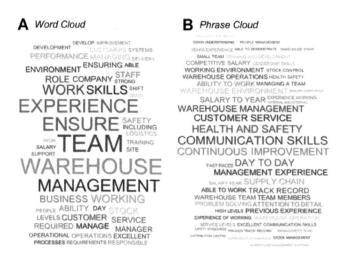

Fig. 2. Word and phrase cloud based on frequency

First, word, phrase frequency analysis was executed and word and phrase cloud was generated (see Fig. 2). From the point of gathering competence the most used words as *"TEAM"*, *"WAREHOUSE"* and *"ENSURE"* cannot add useful information.

---

[7] uk.indeed.com.

Looking into the most common terms like *"COMMUNICATION SKILLS"*, *"CONTINUOUS IMPROVEMENT"*, *"HEALTH AND SAFETY"* seem more relevant information. Analysis of the top 25% (1247 out of 4986) of used phrases provides valuable insight of needed competences such as *"PROBLEM SOLVING"*, *"EXCELLENT COMMUNICATION SKILLS"*, and *"MANAGING A TEAM"*.

A The 10 most important words

Word	FREQUENCY	% CASES	TF • IDF
TEAM	483	9.2%	501.4
WAREHOUSE	439	8.5%	470.5
EXPERIENCE	375	7.3%	426.3
ENSURE	378	7.5%	424.4
MANAGEMENT	343	6.6%	405.0
WORK	272	5.4%	345.4
SKILLS	241	4.7%	320.2
WORKING	222	4.4%	300.9
BUSINESS	189	3.7%	270.9
ROLE	182	3.6%	262.1

B The 10 most important phrases

Phrase	FREQUENCY	% CASES	TF • IDF
COMMUNICATION SKILLS	49	1.0%	98.4
CONTINUOUS IMPROVEMENT	44	0.9%	90.4
HEALTH AND SAFETY	43	0.9%	88.8
DAY TO DAY	40	0.8%	83.8
CUSTOMER SERVICE	38	0.8%	80.5
WAREHOUSE MANAGEMENT	36	0.7%	77.1
MANAGEMENT EXPERIENCE	35	0.7%	75.4
SUPPLY CHAIN	35	0.7%	75.4
SALARY TO YEAR	29	0.6%	64.8
TRACK RECORD	29	0.6%	65.3

Fig. 3. The 10 most important words and phrases based on TF·IDF

Figure 3 shows the most important words and phrases of job descriptions according to TF·IDF[8]. It provides good opportunity to find additional necessary competences like *"TEAM MEMBERS"*, *"ATTENTION TO DETAIL"*, *"PROBLEM SOLVING"*.

Then co-occurrence analysis was performed and different similarity coefficients (like Jaccard, Sorensen, Association strength, Adjusted Phi Coefficient) [17] were used to measure the distance between "ability/able"[9] keywords and words of job description field data (see Fig. 4). In groups made with different coefficients, many common words appeared like *"DEMONSTRATE"*, *"WORK"*, which confirms the importance of these words among the competencies of the warehouse manager position. It is also worth noting that among the words close to the keywords "ability" and "able" it can be found a number of verbs also used in Bloom taxonomy, such as *"DEMONSTRATE"* (in group Apply), *"MANAGE"* (in group Analyze), which confirms the effectiveness of our research. It worth mentioning that the similarity scores of text analytics are very low which indicates partial role in information.

---

[8] TF·IDF (term frequency-inverse document frequency): a statistical measure that evaluates how relevant a word is to a document in a collection of documents.

[9] The "ability" and "able" as keywords were used to describe the meaning of competence.

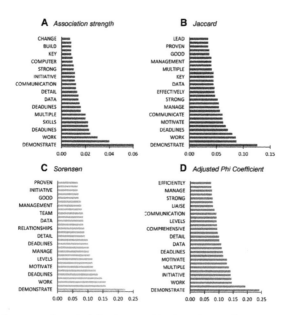

Fig. 4. 15 proximate words to "*ability*" and "*able*" based on different similarity coefficients

4.4 Second Approach: Process-Based Competence Mining

Please note that the even results of basic text analytics are too general, but it underlies the usability of Bloom taxonomy. Hence expressions in the form of verb and noun were extracted from these sentences. 1652 expressions were discovered in 4989 sentences. After removing duplicates 1324 expressions left as corpus.

The process steps were extracted from the process ontology. Jaccard normalized similarity coefficient was applied to determine which verb-noun expressions from the corpus are related to our role (warehouse manager) semantically. Expressions with greater than 0.5 Jaccard points were selected. Descriptions of process steps (see in Sect. 4.1) provided background information about the basic tasks that a warehouse manager has to do: check inventory (56% of 25), manage goods in (60% of 45), unload goods (50% of 6), check quality (80% of 5), record data (0% of 16), treat scrap (0% of 19), record report (39% of 23). Please note that if business process manager does not follow the professional terminology (e.g. treat scrap) or uses to general expressions (e.g. record data), the process model does not help in extracting competences from the descriptions. Otherwise it provides several descriptors to identify tasks in texts. All 57 descriptors were searched in each job descriptions. It was a good experience that not all job ads contained one or some of them. The reason behind this is that positions usually contain more than one role (e.g. executive, responsible roles etc.).

This study focused on only warehouse manager as a specific role. If the tasks executed by this role were not emphasized in the job ads but tasks related to other role (e.g. team leader activities) were, it diminished the hit rate aggressively. Our plan is to extend our business processes with more tasks related to other roles based on this analysis and filter our job ads by roles – not just positions - more precisely. Nevertheless, this method processed enough job ads to present how to use extracted tasks as technical/methodological competences or hard skills to improve curricula of training programs.

4.5 Potential Improvements in Training Programs

All job ads have information about where and when job vacancies were created in which position and at which company. The Python crawler stores this information beside job descriptions in a table. This table is extended with new columns named the above mentioned 57 descriptors and 7 process steps. Each row of these new columns has 1 or 0 value, depending on the fact that the job description in the row contain the given descriptor or not. Columns named process steps summarize these values. This extended table is appropriate to analyse competence needs from different viewpoints (regions, time, position, company, salary etc.). A new column was added to this table to examine digitalization needs in warehouse manager positions. This column represented that system knowledge was needed to fill the position or not. Advertising companies used mainly warehouse management systems in that time (mentioned in 18% of the job ads), but other 15 systems (such as stock control, operational management, ERP system etc.) appeared in the ads as well.

Figure 5 shows the *'manage goods in'* competence was required in the middle and south of United Kingdom, meanwhile system knowledge was also needed to fill warehouse manager positions there. It highlights the importance of this task and knowledge that can be taken into consideration by educational institute in this region. Additional information can be retrieved by other analyses. It can be presented timely distribution of competence needs to examine seasonal requirements. Training programs qualify students to fill given positions hence educators can be interested in seeing timely distribution of competences needs related to a specific position. Data can be drilled down in multidimensional analysis to reveal this kind of correlations. A system built on this method is capable of continually monitoring the labour market needs and providing information about competence trends and distributions. Future competence requirements can be predicated based on the trends. Programme leaders can get regional and temporal feedback to evolve their training programs with adjusting them to the actual or future needs of relevant jobs.

Fig. 5. The 'manage goods in' competence in a regional analysis

5 Conclusion

This paper presents how to use business process models to extract competences from job vacancies and how to use the results to improve training programs of educational institute. It illustrates through an example what competences are provided to stakeholders with using traditional text mining or process-based text mining Comparing these methods, it revealed that additional information are required to filter the corpus or glossary, to highlight system usage information, and to manage multiple roles in positions. The process model ensures these information, because systems, executors and tasks are connected in it. In this way, process-based text mining discovers more specific competences versus traditional text mining. A tool built on this method is capable of detecting what kind of systems and transactions should be operated by the warehouse manager. Information about mass competences needs distributing regionally and timely are used to reform training programs or optimize human resource training. Stakeholders can reorganize the educational portfolios, and also manage capacities. The key limitation of this study is that it largely depends on the phrases and terms used in the process model. In the future, alternative terms will be incorporated into our model and the scope of the business process model will be extended, and the pattern sets will be expanded.

References

1. JISC: Preparing for Education 4.0. https://www.timeshighereducation.com/hub/jisc/p/preparing-education-40. Accessed 2019
2. JISC: Digital skills crucial to the success of fourth industrial revolution. https://www.jisc.ac.uk/news/digital-skills-crucial-to-the-success-of-fourth-industrial-revolution. Accessed 2019
3. Rasika, L., Lim, F.C., Haslinda, A.: Strengths and weaknesses of education 4.0 in the higher education institution. Int. J. Innovative Technol. Exploring Eng. (IJITEE) **9**(2S3) (2019). ISSN: 2278-3075
4. Akgül, H.: Examining the impact of industry 4.0 on education. J. Awareness (JoA) **5**, 159–168 (2020)
5. Rowe, C.: Clarifying the use of competence and competency models in recruitment, assessment and staff development. Ind. Commercial Training **27**, 12–17 (1995)
6. Hecklau, F., Galeitzke, M., Flachs, S., Kohl, H.: Holistic approach for human resource management in industry 4.0. Procedia CIRP **54**, 1–6 (2016)
7. Wikle, T.A., Fagin, T.D.: Hard and soft skills in preparing GIS professionals: comparing perceptions of employers and educators. Trans. GIS **19**, 641–652 (2015)
8. Lippman, L.H., Ryberg, R., Carney, R., Moore, K.: Workforce connections: key "soft skills" that foster youth workforce success: toward a consensus across fields | VOCED plus, the international tertiary education and research database. Child Trends publication (2015)
9. Havnes, A., Prøitz, T.S.: Why use learning outcomes in higher education? Exploring the grounds for academic resistance and reclaiming the value of unexpected learning. Educ. Asse. Eval. Acc. **28**(3), 205–223 (2016). https://doi.org/10.1007/s11092-016-9243-z
10. Prøitz, T.S.: Learning outcomes: What are they? Who defines them? When and where are they defined? Educ. Asse. Eval. Acc. **22**, 119–137 (2010). https://doi.org/10.1007/s11092-010-9097-8

11. Forehand, M.: Bloom's taxonomy. Emerg. Perspect. Learn. Teach. Technol. **41**, 47–56 (2010)
12. OECD: Getting Skills Right: Skills for Jobs Indicators. OECD (2017)
13. Cedefop: Skill forecast. http://www.cedefop.europa.eu/en/publications-and-resources/data-visualisations/skills-forecast
14. Bakhshi, H., Downing, J.M., Osborne, M.A., Schneider, P.: The future of skills: employment in 2030. Pearson (2017)
15. Szabó, I., Neusch, G.: Dynamic skill gap analysis using ontology matching. In: Kő, A., Francesconi, E. (eds.) EGOVIS 2015. LNCS, vol. 9265, pp. 231–242. Springer, Cham (2015). https://doi.org/10.1007/978-3-319-22389-6_17
16. Ternai, K., Fodor, S., Szabó, I.: Business process matching analytics. In: Doucek, P., Basl, J., Tjoa, A.M., Raffai, M., Pavlicek, A., Detter, K. (eds.) CONFENIS 2019. LNBIP, vol. 375, pp. 85–94. Springer, Cham (2019). https://doi.org/10.1007/978-3-030-37632-1_8
17. Jackson, D.A., Somers, K.M., Harvey, H.H.: Similarity coefficients: measures of co-occurrence and association or simply measures of occurrence? Am. Nat. **133**, 436–453 (1989)

Personnel Learning Behavior in the Workplace: A Study of Workplace Habits

Waristha Saengrith[✉], Chantana Viriyavejakul, and Paitoon Pimdee

Department of Industrial Education, Faculty of Industrial Education and Technology, King Mongkut's Institute of Technology Ladkrabang, Bangkok, Thailand
61603009@kmitl.ac.th

Abstract. Workplace learning is becoming an essential part for an organization to enhance an employee's knowledge and skill to deliver an enterprise's business sustainability. To develop a suitable model for workplace learning, this paper aims to investigate learning behavior for personnel in a workplace and to understand the factors that influence learning behavior for technical staff of a plastic packaging company in Bangkok. The data was collected by using a questionnaire that included 3 parts; 1) personal factors 2) learning behavior of personnel in the workplace and 3) factors that influence learning behavior of personnel in the workplace. The target group was 75 technical staff members by a multi-stage sampling. The research findings were that from 3 ways of informal learning behavior in workplace are self-directed learning, networking, and coaching and mentoring, a target group behavior to agree with highest score of self-directed learning at the average score of 3.62, compared with network learning and coaching learning which neither agree nor disagree at average score 3.36 and 3.32, respectively. Moreover, challenges on their job is the most influential factor of their learning behavior in the workplace at average score 3.64 followed by a confidence level and support from the company with an average score 3.53 and 3.38, respectively. Results from the study show that mostly staffs were interested in learning by themselves with encouragement from challenges, confidence level, and support from the organization.

Keywords: Learning behavior · Workplace learning · Self-directed learning · Networking · Coaching and mentoring

1 Introduction

Nowadays, plastic packaging is the most contributing business to help grow economy in Thailand. Among the ASEAN countries, Thailand has the competitive advantage on production technology, services, and innovations over other countries in this region. However, Department of International Trade Promotion (DITP), Ministry of Commerce in Thailand, revealed that key challenges for growth in this business area in the future will be a lack of labor and low skills of labor problems. [1] From the survey, plastic manufacturers mentioned this root cause, the fundamental education system in

Thailand, i.e. the teacher treating students to be followers not for leaders. In addition, the education in the classroom does not facilitate learning activities to enhance self-paced learning [2]. Therefore, when they were employed by enterprises, new workers cannot utilize learning skills to find the answers for problem-solving situations and thus impacting the efficiency of the enterprise for competition in the market. To eliminate the labor skill problem, the enterprises would consider a method to develop knowledge and skill of their employees, especially with technical staff, who are responsible in the product quality control department and technical service support, as these are the most critical topics for plastic packaging manufacturers in Thailand. Therefore, workplace learning was focused on and defined as the Human Resource Development (HRD) program for developing a superior workforce for organization and individual employees who can achieve their work goals to best service the customers. That is the key importance for enterprises; to develop new knowledge delivery method that ensures skill competency. Moreover, lifelong learning and continuous learning were highlighted both for individuals operating in the learning system and for organizations competing in the international marketplace. In fact, workplace learning is recognized as moving from institutional education into normal life situations, taking place at work and other life areas and relating to improving the skills of employees and enhancing their knowledge, which may be either formal or informal. Presently, informal learning in the workplace has become an increasingly important tool for training employees. However, there is no specific way to prove how to effectively deliver knowledge and skill to employees in organizations since the differences of culture and the urgency of the enterprises to develop their employees varies greatly. In addition, when we talk about workplace learning, it is almost related to adult learning and can be defined as the acquisition of knowledge and skills by formal or informal means that occur in the workplace. To develop the suitable learning model for workplace learning, the understanding of current situations of learning behavior for personnel in the workplace is necessary. Therefore, the purpose of this study in context of workplace learning, or working with learning, is to explore the current state of learning behavior for personnel in workplaces around Thailand. Among the key research questions, two are very important, as follows:

1. How is the learning behavior way for technical people in workplace settings today?
2. How is the comparison between the 3 factors influencing to learning behavior of personnel in the workplace?

2 Literature Review

2.1 Workplace Learning

Since the early 1990s, workplace learning has expanded and recently the research in this field is both wide-ranging and interdisciplinary. This expansion reason is that learning, and working are both interconnected with the significantly rapid change in society and working life as well as being increasingly used in the development of future leaders and improve their impact on the effectiveness and competitiveness of an organization. Moreover, lifelong learning and continuous learning have become important both for individuals operating in the learning society and for organizations to compete in the international marketplace. Together with the business challenges in term of employee skill, workplace learning is now, therefore, the most important topic for discussion. There are various definitions of workplace learning, improving employee's skill and enhancing labor knowledge, which result from work-related interactions, a fact that contributes to the learning of both the individual employee and the organization as a whole [3–5]. In addition, workplace learning is concerned not only with immediate work competencies, but also better competencies to deal with problems and future challenges [6]. However, even broadly speaking, on definitions and composition of workplace learning, however, it was defined as the acquisition of knowledge and skill by formal and informal ways that occur in the workplace. Formal learning consists of qualifications and certified training, and no longer seen as the sole method of learning. Qualifications are more concerned in terms of a board structure that concerns workplaces and the employees, educational institutions, and various communities within organizations. While informal learning is unstructured and takes place away from traditional methods, or formal learning settings. It has no clear goals; often being unplanned and self-directed by the learner. In addition, informal learning is often conceived as learning that is tacit and integrated with normal work activities. From the research evidence, it is shown that informal learning is the most important type of learning for enhancing and developing skills and competencies in the workplace, while formal learning, such as classroom-based learning or training, is of minor importance [7–9]. Moreover, it was indicated that the employees learning only 20% learn from structured training programs, a feature of informal learning can be deliberately encouraged by an organization or it can take place despite an environment not highly conductive to learning [10]. The ratio of work-related learning was defined at 80% can occur informally through self- directed learning, networking, coaching, and mentoring [11]. As employees can benefit from this type of learning, beyond training, learners are self-directed, and the need to examine the context of and people involved with the learning including learner behavior. Therefore, workplace learning also can include a process of formal elements of learning, even if it is dominant due to being informal in nature and is often incorporated with workplace social interactions and everyday practices [12].

2.2 Learning Behavior in Workplace

Learning behavior in the workplace was defined by various approaches. The nature of learning, strategies, learning processes, and techniques have also been discussed. Examples of learning behavior are self-directed learning, networking, social learning, mentoring, coaching, and performance planning systems used in various contexts. The framework of self-directed learning practice [13] is considered to be the common practice of learning at work. Many research papers have been studied in adult education and andragogy, the need to examine and study as the multidimensional nature of self-directed learning in the context of workplace learning has been highlighted [14]. Recently, Organizations have begun to transfer power from the organization to the individuals in that organization learning for more flexible, effective, and faster operations [15]. Among the most recent learning behavior developments, is the forming of organizational networking, learning with that goal, which is to enhance knowledge sharing and creating new improved work practices. In Finland, the Ministry of Labor has launched a national program for learning networks which aims to develop cooperation between research institutes and working life organizations to advance organizational development. Network learning will establish with independent participants who can be either be individuals or organizations and can also be defined as a kind of loose organizations of learning in and outside of networks as a form of organizational learning [16, 17]. A general aim of network learning is usually to provide a forum for knowledge exchange, creation, and transformation. Therefore, typically for network learning, there is an exchange of knowledge, which takes place mutually but not necessarily symmetrically. From the training and development survey, it was found that over 80% of UK organizations were using coaching and mentoring to develop at least some of their employees in an organization [18]. This learning method concerned improving an employee's skills, performance, and behaviors within their present job role as a task-oriented form of personally, tailored training typically short-term with a task focus [19]. While mentoring is often oriented an exchange of support, learning or guidance for the purpose, it is not only for task focus, but also includes personal, career path and spiritual related areas. Together with 2 parts of coaching and mentoring, coaching also supports and helps people to know the way to do something more effectively in parallel to help deal with future changes and promotions.

2.3 Factors Influencing Learning in the Workplace

The factors influencing learning behavior in workplace broadly discuss both direct and indirect factors and other kinds of effects that may influence learning behavior in the workplace. The scope focuses on specific factors or on the overall culture of the unit, including communications and feedback, industrial relations, work design, continuity and training, as well as participation. The dominant finding from earlier research on mid-career learning was interesting due to factors of confidence, challenge, and support [20] that were mostly focused in this context. The relationship between all those factors was defined from the context of learning during working and occurs through doing something with the enthusiasm to seek for new learning opportunities that require a person's confidence. Therefore, being confident is the one key important factor to drive people to learn in the workplace. Moreover, the confidence level also rose from one person's success story to meet their challenges during work hours. In addition, when an organization provides sufficient support to learn, a person will be confident to deal with other challenges. In conclusion, if there is neither a challenge nor sufficient support to encourage learners to seek for or deal with challenges, then confidence level will decline and create a need for conditions for learning in the workplace.

To better understand learning behavior of our target audiences for plastic packaging manufacturers in Bangkok, this research has been conducted and defined as first step of the analysis stage. Further stages will design and develop a learning platform to apply for personal learning for final results with a learning model to enhance higher order thinking skill in the organization.

3 Research Objectives

1. To study and understand existing learning behavior.
2. To compare factors, influence to learning behavior for technical staff of flexible plastic packaging enterprises in Thailand.

4 Research Methodology

From the reviewed research methodology used in this field [20], it was found the most common ways have been survey study because it gave the proper approach to gain quick feedback from target respondents who are working in the manufacturing enterprises. The study employed a quantitative research design and research data was extracted from the fieldwork. A methodology based on inductivist approach was used to explore the participants' experiences, thoughts about learning behaviors.

4.1 Participants

The population on this research is technical staff who work for flexible plastic packaging companies in Bangkok 248 people. The sample was selected from multistage sampling from the location and size of the factory and become with 75 technical staff who were undergoing some type of workplace learning, through participant surveyed.

4.2 Research Instrument

For this study, the questionnaire was deliberately developed by the researcher using the previous study framework [11, 20]. It applied 5-points Likert's scale defined as 4.50–5.00 Strongly agree, 3.50–4.49 Agree, 2.50–3.49 Neither agree nor disagree, 1.50–2.49 Disagree and 1.00–1.49 Strongly Disagree. There are 3 parts questionnaires, first section related to the surveys respondent's background information about age, gender, level of education, job responsibilities and location of the company. Second section to survey the respondents' perception through 3 learning modes are self-directed learning, networking, coaching and mentoring and the last part is the comparison 3 factors; confidence, challenges, and support that influence personal learning of technical staff in the workplace. All those questionnaires were validated by three experts in the field of human resources in the workplace and education. The validation on both construction and content validity base on the Item Objective Congruent (IOC). A pilot survey was implemented before real data collection. It revealed that the reliability measurement using Cronbach's alpha of 0.7 was considered acceptable.

4.3 Data Collection and Analysis

Questionnaires were distributed by an electronic form to survey personnel who work at a technical department of flexible plastic packaging company in Bangkok with survey responded rate about 75%. All the participants rated the questionnaire for 3 parts according to their individual opinions. The last stage for data analysis, the statistic package, SPSS program, was used to analyze data gathered from questionnaires. With descriptive statistics, described information with percentage, means and standard deviation were computed and analyzed.

5 Results

According to the surveyed target audiences with 75 participants and data about general characteristic, learning behavior and factors influence learning of personal in the workplace were analyzed shown as follows.

5.1 General Characteristic of Respondents

From the above general characteristics, it was found most respondents is 59 females accounted for 78.7% of all participants with age dominate range of 20–30 year 42 persons as 56.0%. Almost all respondents 64 people, held a bachelor's degree at 85.3% and responsible mostly in Research and development department for 38 persons as 50.7% (Table 1).

Table 1. General characteristics of respondents.

Characteristics	Details	Number of People	Percentage
Sex	Male	16	21.3%
	Female	59	78.7%
Age	20–30	42	56.0%
	30–40	31	41.3%
	>40	2	2.7%
Education level	Under bachelor's degree	4	5.3%
	Bachelors' degree	64	85.3%
	Master's degree	7	9.4%
Job responsible	Research and Development	38	50.7%
	Technical customer service	29	38.7%
	Quality control	8	10.6%

5.2 The Perception on Learning Behavior of Technical Staff in Workplace

From the results of Table 2. It shows that the target audience agrees with learning through self-directed learning. With the average score of 3.62, on the other hands, network learning and coaching learning that neither agree nor disagree at average score of 3.36 and 3.32, respectively.

From the results of Table 3. It shown that the target audience agrees that challenge is the most influential factor to encourage labor learning with an average score of 3.64

and followed by a confidence factor of average level of 3.53 and the last with support from a company at an average score of 3.38.

Table 2. Learning perception of personal in workplace.

Learning mode	$\bar{X}$	SD	Level
Self-Directed Learning	3.62	0.52	Agree
Network Learning	3.36	0.57	Neither agree nor disagree
Coaching and Mentoring	3.32	0.44	Neither agree nor disagree

Table 3. Factors influence for personal learning in Workplace.

Learning mode	$\bar{X}$	SD	Level
Challenge	3.64	0.58	Agree
Support	3.38	0.64	Neither agree nor disagree
Confident	3.53	0.56	Agree

6 Discussion and Conclusion

Learning behaviors of personnel in the workplace were studied with technical employees of flexible plastic packaging manufacturers in Bangkok. The results of this study have helped us to find out the learning characteristics of target audiences. The comparison of 3 learning types following research study of informal learning in workplace through self-directed, networking, coaching and mentoring [11] was shown that target groups were interested in learning through self-directed ways, followed by coaching and mentoring and networking respectively. It is related to the previous research on continuing vocational education learners in Thailand dominated by self-directed learning [21]. Therefore, there are several ways that an organization enables labor to enhance self-directed learning, such as providing proper facilities or preparing a suitable environment for workplace learning. Moreover, the company could initiate and approach the education technology platform such as e-learning, mobile learning, chatbot learning and, etc. or their staffs as it is the basic knowledge of their employees to study by themselves. Moreover, from the studied factors that influence personal learning in the workplace, it was also found that challenges are the most influential factor for personal learning, followed by confidence and the last by support, respectively. That is related to the previous research from mentioned that high challenge task is directly influenced to motivation working and learning of employee [22]. Therefore, to motivate employees' learning, a company should consider approaching using an activity to enhance their challenge in order to build their confidence for working and learning in parallel. Similarly, the competition or reward for staff, who have initiative on new projects or may hold the conference for internal discussion between people in the organization can support confident level for working and to support learning behaviors of staff in the future.

This study indicated that self-directed learning is the most attractive learning behavior for a technical employee in Thailand to learn while they are in their workplace. Since this survey research is the first stage on the analysis to understand learning the characteristics of a person in the workplace. Therefore, the future, research is going to study and identification of a self-directed learning platform that is suitable for workplace learning and to come up with a final learning model to enhance personal skills of staff in the organization. Especially for technical staff, who are the key factors for plastic packaging manufacturers that the firm would like to use to increase business in a professional way. Moreover, to enhance learning activities for personnel in the workplace, the organization could consider creating activities to support challenge and build the confidence level of staff, such as competition in the organization or rewarding people [19] who have initiative for new projects to launch. A discussion session among people in the company could enhance the confident level for personnel in order to lead for learning behavior in future years to come.

References

1. Praveera, P.: Economic study report packaging industry, Bangkok (2018). http://oie.go.th/assets/portals/1/files/study_report/packaging_praveera.pdf. Accessed 5 Aug 2020
2. Supratana, C.: Importance of packaging to creating added value for export products, Department of Export Promotion Ministry of Industry Thailand, Bangkok (2003). https://www.ditp.go.th/contents_attach/78353/78353.pdf. Accessed 1 Aug 2020
3. Doornbos, A.J., Simons, R.J., Denessen, E.: Relations between characteristics of workplace practices and types of informal work-related learning: a survey study among Dutch police. Hum. Resour. Dev. Q. **19**(2), 129–151 (2008)
4. Felstead, A., Fuller, A., Unwin, L., Ashton, D., Butler, P., Lee, T.: Surveying the scene: learning metaphors, survey design and the workplace context. J. Educ. Work **18**(4), 359–383 (2005)
5. Fenwick, T.: Understanding relations of individual collective learning in work: a review of research. Manag. Learn. **39**(3), 227–243 (2008)
6. Boud, D., Garrick, J.: Understandings of Workplace Learning. Understanding Learning at Work. Routledge, New York (1999)
7. Ashton, D., Sung, J.: Supporting Workplace Learning for High Performance Working. International Labour Office, Geneva (2002)
8. Eraut, M.: Informal learning in workplace. Stud. Continuing Educ. **26**(20), 247–273 (2004)
9. Skule, S.: Learning conditions at work: a framework to understand and assess informal learning in the workplace. Int. J. Training Dev. **8**(1), 8–20 (2004)
10. Marsick, V., Watkins, K.: Informal and Incidental Learning in the Workplace Victoria J. Marsick & Karen Watkins. Routledge, London (1990)
11. Yeo, R.K.: How does learning (not) take place in problem-based learning activities in workplace contexts? Hum. Resource Dev. Int. **11**(3), 317–330 (2008)
12. Cacciattolo, K.: Defining workplace learning. Eur. Sci. J. **11**(10), 234–250 (2015)
13. Knowles, M.: Self-directed learning. Chicago (1975)
14. Rana, S., Ardichvili, A., Polesello, D.: Promoting self-directed learning in a learning organization. Eur. J. Training Dev. **40**(7), 470–489 (2016)
15. Rigby, C.S., Ryan, R.M.: Self-determination theory in human resource development: new directions and practical consideration. Adv. Dev. Hum. Resour. **20**(2), 133–147 (2018)

16. Alasoini, T., Halme, P.: Learning Organizations, Learning Society. National Workplace Development Programme Yearbook, Ministry of Labour, Helsinki, pp. 117–139 (1999)
17. Knight, L.: Network learning: exploring learning by interorganizational networks. Hum. Relat. **55**(4), 427–454 (2002)
18. Deeks E.: CIPD survey shows manual staff are poor relations in workplace training. People Management, 10 (2001)
19. Silverman, M.: Supporting Workplace learning: a background paper for IES research network members. The Institute for Employment Studies, pp. 1–22 (2003)
20. Eraut, M.: Non-formal learning and tacit knowledge in professional work. Br. J. Educ. Psychol. **79**, 113–136 (2000)
21. Suwat, W.: Self-directed learning of continuing vocational education learner. Thesis Doctor of Philosophy (Vocational Education) Kasetsart University, Bangkok (1997)
22. Anseel, F., Carette, B., Lievens, F.: Does career timing of challenging job assignments influence the relationship with in-role job performance? J. Vocat. Behav. **83**(1), 61–67 (2013)

Required English Communication Skill Levels of Mechanical Engineers at the Workplace in Taiwan

Judy F. Chen[1(✉)] and Clyde A. Warden[2]

[1] Business Administration Department, Overseas Chinese University, Taichung, Taiwan
jfc@ocu.edu.tw
[2] Marketing Department, National Chung Hsing University, Taichung, Taiwan
warden@dragon.nchu.edu.tw

Abstract. This study examines the required mechanical English communication skill levels in the workplace. We employed Google search tool to search job openings of mechanical engineers in Taiwan and then analyzed the English skill requirements listed on each individual mechanical engineer job opening. After keying in mechanical engineer, Google shows a total of 119 job openings. Among them, 12 job openings require high school degree, 49 job openings require associate degree, 52 job openings require bachelor degree, and 6 job openings require master degree. Associate and college required degrees account for the most of the job openings. Beginning with the associate degree required jobs, employers start to emphasize English communication skills. For the bachelor degree required job openings, intermediate English skills are most needed. Results of this study enable educators to prepare students to be equipped with the skills needed by workplaces and enable them to be more employable.

Keywords: Communication skill · English for mechanical engineering · Workplace · English for specific purposes

1 Introduction

Mechanical engineering is the base of industry. In fact, it is the foundation of industrial countries. All machinery and equipment must be designed by mechanical engineers. In the history of scientific and technological progress, mechanical engineering has always been the driving force behind the development of civilization. From the agricultural era to the industrial revolution, to various computer products in the current high-tech era, aerospace technology and micro-manufacturing, mechanical engineering has always been the mainstream of the industry [1]. Taiwan lacks natural resources and is an export-oriented country. It must rely on the creation, invention and innovation of machinery to manufacture products required by consumers worldwide and sell them all over the world. English is an international language. English communication skills are important aspect as companies attempt to grow internationally [2] found that "fluency in the English language is seen as an opportunity in engineering field to advance towards becoming a global engineer [3–6].

168   J. F. Chen and C. A. Warden

Not only academia but also industry have stressed the importance of engineering graduates' communication skills [7]. Communication skill is often one area to be examine when engineering programs are being evaluated for improvement [8]. Mechanical engineers not only have to possess mechanical skills (hard skills) but also need to acquire soft skills such as English verbal and non-verbal communication skills, presentation skills, selling skills, etc. [9]. Although English communication skills are being emphasized across the world, Accordingly, this study, by exploring the job openings of mechanical engineers, attempts to assess the required English communication skill levels of mechanical engineers at the workplace in Taiwan.

2   Method

For this study, we focus in the Taiwan's workplace. We used Google search tool to collect the data by keying in mechanical engineer (機械工程師), as shown in Fig. 1. Then, we retrieved the information listed on the job openings. Afterward, we sorted out the job openings based on the educational requirements. Next, we examined and analyzed the specific requirements of English skills for high school degree, associate degree, bachelor degree and master degree required jobs, respectively.

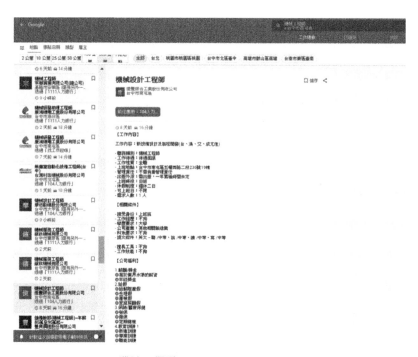

Fig. 1. Using Google (機械工程師) to search for mechanical engineer job openings.

3 Results

For the search of mechanical engineer job opening, Google shows a total of 119 job openings. Among them, Among them, 12 job openings require high school degree (Table 1), 49 job openings require associate degree (Table 2), 52 job openings require bachelor degree (Table 3), and 6 job openings require master degree (Table 4).

Most of the high school degree required job openings do not specified the needs for English listening, speaking, reading, and writing skill, as shown in Table 1.

Table 1. Proficiency requirements of English skills: high school degree required jobs.

Level	Skill							
	Listening	Ratio	Speaking	Ratio	Reading	Ratio	Writing	Ratio
Not specified	9	75.0%	9	75.0%	9	75.0%	9	75.0%
Elementary	3	25.0%	3	25.0%	3	25.0%	3	25.0%
Intermediate	0	0.0%	0	0.0%	0	0.0%	0	0.0%
Advanced	0	0.0%	0	0.0%	0	0.0%	0	0.0%

For associate degree required job openings, we can see more companies specifies the needs for English listening, speaking, reading, and writing skill, as shown in Table 2.

Table 2. Proficiency requirements of English skills: associate degree required jobs.

Level	Skill							
	Listening	Ratio	Speaking	Ratio	Reading	Ratio	Writing	Ratio
Not specified	22	44.9%	22	44.9%	23	46.9%	23	46.9%
Elementary	14	28.6%	14	28.6%	14	28.6%	14	28.6%
Intermediate	13	26.5%	13	26.5%	12	24.5%	12	24.5%
Advanced	0	0.0%	0	0.0%	0	0.0%	0	0.0%

For the bachelor degree required job openings, 26(49%) companies require intermediate English listening skill, 27(50.9%) companies require intermediate English speaking, reading and writing skill level. Intermediate English skills are most needed.

Table 3. Proficiency requirements of English skills: bachelor degree required jobs.

Level	Skill							
	Listening	Ratio	Speaking	Ratio	Reading	Ratio	Writing	Ratio
Not specified	14	26.4%	14	26.4%	14	26.4%	14	26.4%
Elementary	12	22.6%	11	20.8%	11	20.8%	11	20.8%
Intermediate	26	49.1%	27	50.9%	27	50.9%	27	50.9%
Advanced	1	1.9%	1	1.9%	1	1.9%	1	1.9%

Out of six job openings that require master degree, three require intermediate level of English listening, speaking, reading, and writing skill, as shown in Table 4.

Table 4. Proficiency requirements of English skills: master degree required jobs.

Level	Skill							
	Listening	Ratio	Speaking	Ratio	Reading	Ratio	Writing	Ratio
Not specified	2	33.3%	2	33.3%	2	33.3%	2	33.3%
Elementary	1	16.7%	1	16.7%	1	16.7%	1	16.7%
Intermediate	3	50.0%	3	50.0%	3	50.0%	3	50.0%
Advanced	0	0.0%	0	0.0%	0	0.0%	0	0.0%

4 Conclusion

As the educational requirement goes up, the required English skill levels also go up. Companies may expect employees who have college or master degree to be able to use English to communicate fluently at the workplaces. From the listings of the four English skills, we can see that when companies need employees to have the English skills, listening, speaking, reading and writing skills are equally important.

In Taiwan, because of the large English class size for non-English major students, most English classes for mechanical engineering college students focus on listening and reading skills training. This study's findings show that more resources need to be put in for training college students' speaking and writing skills in order to prepare them for the workplaces.

Acknowledgment. The authors are grateful to the Ministry of Science and Technology of the Republic of China, Taiwan, for financially supporting this research under Contract No. MOST 108-2511-H-240-001 –

References

1. Andrews, D.C.: An interdisciplinary course in technical communication. Tech. Commun. **50**, 446 (2003)
2. Kassim, H., Ali, F.: English communicative events and skills needed at the workplace: feedback from the industry. Engl. Specif. Purp. **29**, 168–182 (2010)
3. Darling, A.L., Dannels, D.P.: Practicing engineers talk about the importance of talk: a report on the role of oral communication in the workplace. Commun. Educ. **52**, 1–16 (2003)
4. Moslehifar, M.A., Ibrahim, N.A.: English language oral communication needs at the workplace: feedback from human resource development (HRD) trainees. Procedia Soc. Behav. Sci. **66**, 529–536 (2012)
5. Missingham, D.: The integration of professional communication skills into engineering education (2006)
6. Hashimoto, S.: Multidisciplinary learning extends communication skill, and helps cross cultural understandings: biomedical engineering. J. Syst. Cybern. Inform. **15**, 106–112 (2017)

7. Riemer, M.J.: English and communication skills for the global engineer. Global J. Eng. Educ. **6**, 91–100 (2002)
8. Gunn, C.J.: Engineering graduate students as evaluators of communication skill. Age **9**, 1 (2004)
9. Choudary, D.V.: The importance of training engineering students in soft-skills. Abhinav Int. Mon. Refereed J. Res. Manag. Technol. **3**, 1 (2014)

Research on the Implementation Status and Learning Satisfaction of Off-campus Internship Courses in the Department of Mechanical Engineering of the University of Technology

Dyi-Cheng Chen[1(✉)], Hsi-Chi Hsiao[2], Jen-Chia Chang[3], Su-Chang Chen[4], Kuo-Cheng Wen[1], Jia-Yue Guo[1], and Yu-Chen Gao[1]

[1] Department of Industrial Education and Technology, National Changhua University of Education, Changhua 500, Taiwan
dcchen@cc.ncue.edu.tw,
{m0831005,M0731009}@gm.ncue.edu.tw,
calerqazwsx@gmail.com
[2] Department of Business Administration, Cheng Shiu University, Kaohsiung, Taiwan
hsichihs@gmail.com
[3] Graduate Institute of Technological and Vocational Education, National Taipei University of Technology, Taipei, Taiwan
jc5839@ntut.edu.tw
[4] Department of Marketing and Logistics Management, National Penghu University of Science and Technology, Penghu, Taiwan
csc@npu.edu.tw

Abstract. This study explores 38 students of mechanical engineering at the University of Technology. The experiment group and the control group are used to compare the differences in the satisfaction of students with and without the intervention of topic-oriented teaching materials, and to understand the situation of learning satisfaction after the training with external students. This study uses a questionnaire distribution method for analysis and research. The content of the questionnaire is divided into two parts: student background attribute data and student learning satisfaction. The analysis is based on descriptive statistics and t test correlation.

The results show that there are significant differences between interventional teaching materials and student learning satisfaction. The value of "Course Teaching" is 4.965 $p < .001$; the value of "Internship Environment" is 2.183 $p < .05$, and the value of "Internship Tutoring" is 4.423 $p < .001$. The study found that the learning level of "Course Teaching", "Internship Environment" and "Internship Tutoring" has improved significantly. Before the internship, students conducted project-based off-campus internship teaching material teaching, so that students have a certain cognition for the enterprise during the internship. Preparing knowledge and standards can also improve self-study performance. Finally, on the basis of the research results, this study puts forward related suggestions, project-based and future research for improving undergraduate internships.

Keywords: Mechanical engineering · Off-campus internship · Learning satisfaction · Project-based off-campus teaching materials

1 Introduction

With the rapid changes of the world economy, higher education should train student to enhance their ability to face the future. Therefore, off-campus internships have played an indispensable role in higher education. The main core of off-campus internship is to strengthen and practice the employment. Off-campus internship is also to cultivate and strengthen students' sense of social responsibility, innovative spirit and practical ability [1]. Students can accumulate their work experience during the internship. They can gain an in-depth understanding of their strengths and weaknesses through internships, and recover their shortcomings in theoretical knowledge as soon as possible. In the future, they can enhance their competitiveness in the job market or develop their own careers ability [2]. According to this research, for students, the core focus of off-campus internship is to obtain employment experience. Students also highly value the experience of internship, and recognize that it is very beneficial to their future workplace development [3].

According to the above literature, we know that students gain experience through off-campus internships, and the lack of theoretical or business-related knowledge needs to be returned to school to make up. However, if we can use the Project-Based off-campus internship teaching materials as a guide, then we can understand the operation and standardization of internship institutions, effective communication and prior knowledge of teamwork before the internship, So that students can proceed smoothly during the internship. This study hopes that by analyzing whether teaching materials are involved in project-based off-campus teaching materials and after off-campus internships, students can evaluate the differences in learning satisfaction during their internships and understand the differences between off-campus internships and learning satisfaction after teaching materials intervention. Provide further suggestions for school teaching methods.

2 Literature Review

2.1 Analysis and Meaning of Learning Satisfaction

Education is an indispensable part of life, so effective learning is helpful to human beings, especially students are very important to improve the quality of education [4]. However, learning refers to changing a person's reaction or behavior due to experience. Satisfaction is one of personality traits, an attitude, a feeling, and an abstract and fuzzy term [5, 6]. Regarding satisfaction, many scholars have set many definitions. Learning satisfaction is a learner's pleasant feeling or attitude towards learning activities, that is, his desires and needs are met during the learning process. [7]. The study of learning satisfaction can understand the lack of courses and improve them, enhance the interests of learners, and guide the direction of course development [8].

2.2 Status of Off-campus Internships

What motivated the need for students to participate in internships during college? The main motivation is that most students say they want to understand the working environment and collect practical work experience. They hope that when they enter the labor market after graduation, they will help the workplace. Many people also hope that internships will help them find work in the future. The use of internships as a means of making money seems to be a secondary motivation [9]. Considering the impact of internships on students, students choose internships to understand jobs or industries that may be suitable for their profession [10].

According to the above research, in addition to the students' basic professional knowledge and skills, and the company's expectations of the students' ability to apply to the workplace. It is necessary to pay attention to the learning process of students in off-campus internships. Does the employer have the attitude and behavior to provide timely counselling and assistance to students when they encounter difficulties or obstacles? Analyze the learning satisfaction and make suggestions after researching and discussing the research characteristics.

3 Research Methods

3.1 Research Methodology and Framework

This research mainly explores the learning satisfaction of graduates of related majors in mechanical sciences from the University of Technology, allowing students to evaluate their own satisfaction with their learning and their internship institutions when participating in off-campus internships. Compare and discuss the differences between the two with and without teaching materials. This research adopts a quasi-experimental research method, which lasted 8 weeks of teaching activities; based on the teaching experiment and teaching experiment data of off-campus practice teaching materials as the analysis basis. The self-variable term is a teaching mode, which is divided into teaching material intervention teaching, which is used in the experimental group, and no teaching material intervention teaching, which is used in the control group; the dependent variable is learning satisfaction, and the questionnaire survey is used for students using the off-campus practice process as a test tool.

The research uses questionnaire survey methods and theoretical analysis methods to make a questionnaire for the satisfaction of off-campus internship learning. The content of the questionnaire is divided into two parts. In the first part, there are 10 options related to the satisfaction of outside school internship learning, The second part is to ask the interviewee's personal information, including: gender, grade of internship, and type of internship. Questionnaires were distributed to school students, and independent sample t-tests and reliability analysis were performed.

3.2 Research Object

The research object is 38 students in the third grade of a mechanical field in a university of technology, 19 students in class A (Control group) and 19 students in class B (Experimental group). In order to avoid unduly affecting the operation of the school and the normal teaching process, the second class of students taught by the researcher is used in groups without changing the school class and class time. Teaching experimental research, one class is experimental group. The experimental group has the intervention of project-based off-campus teaching materials, and the professor teaches the students in the classroom. One group is the control group, without the intervention of teaching materials. There were 19 people in each group.

3.3 Teaching Syllabus Before Off-campus Internship

In the experimental group, before participating in the off-campus internship, there is a project-based off-campus teaching material intervention teaching. The teaching materials before the off-campus internship is divided into five chapters, which are the operation and standardization of internship institutions, effective communication and teamwork, technical problem solving strategies, data collection, and internship report writing. Through the teaching materials before the internship, students can understand the prerequisite knowledge before the internship. It is hoped that the students can participate in the off-campus internship through the teaching materials and have a certain understanding of the enterprise specifications (Table 1).

Table 1. Teaching material units and outlines.

Course title	Off-campus internship
Chapter	Teaching unit
1. Operation and standardization of internship institutions	1-1 Understand the current status of the industry
	1-2 Company organization and department functions
	1-3 Work norms and professional ethics
	1-4 Standard operating procedures
	1-5 Internship content
2. Effective communication and teamwork	2-1 Effective communication
	2-2 Teamwork (understand the meaning of teamwork)
3. Technical problem solving strategies	3-1 Technical problem solving strategies
4. Data collection	4-1 Data collection (including patent search, application network, technical manual query, etc.)
5. Internship report writing	5-1 Internship report writing skills
	5-2 Internship report writing (including industry-academia cooperation technology training experience report, topics for practical topics)

*New add item.

3.4 Questionnaire Design

Through Ghaith M. Jaradat's perspective on training internship to explore the satisfaction of mechanical engineering students' out-of-school internship learning [11], and then add and modify the proportional items to produce a questionnaire. This questionnaire uses Likert's five-point scale. Subjects respond according to their actual feelings, ranging from "completely agree" to "completely disagree", with 5 to 1 points respectively. The higher the score, the better the student's learning satisfaction. The first part of the questionnaire is divided into three aspects, namely course teaching, internship environment, and internship guidance. Table 2 lists the Satisfaction Form of Mechanical Engineering Students' Off-campus Internship Study.

Table 2. Satisfaction form of mechanical engineering students' off-campus internship study.

Dimension	Indicator
1. Aspects of course teaching	1-1 The internship helped me find a job after graduation
	1-2 In the future, if the internship agency is willing to hire me, I will be willing to go to work
	1-3 Faculty's course arrangements and training help to use and complete internship tasks
	1-4 When there are difficulties or obstacles during the internship, the school instructor can provide me with guidance and assistance in a timely manner
2. Aspects of the internship environment	2-1 When encountering difficulties or obstacles during the internship, the internship institution can give me guidance and assistance in a timely manner
	2-2 The professional ability of the intern institution can meet my skills development
	2-3 Internship institutions provide my professional and safe internship environment
3. Aspects of internship counselling	3-1 I am satisfied with the administrative supporting measures of the internship system
	3-2 Pre-departure briefing sessions (including industrial safety and ethics workshops) helped me
	3-3 The teaching methods of internship institutions can be suitable for my learning

4 Results and Discussions

4.1 Attribute Analysis of Background Information of School Student Questionnaire

In this study, 38 questionnaires were distributed and 38 were recovered, all of which were valid questionnaires, and the recovery rate was 100%. The SPSS statistical software was used to analyze the questionnaires. Table 3 shows the background analysis results of the students. In the 38 samples, all students in the control group and the experimental group all participated in off-campus internships, and most of the students in the school participated in off-campus internships during the third year of college. In terms of gender, male students in both the control group and the experimental group accounted for 84.2% of the sample. For mechanical students, this ratio reflects gender differences in the field of mechanical learning. The categories of internship time for students are 100% for summer internships.

Table 3. Results of background analysis of questionnaires for school students.

Basic information	Control group			Experimental group		
		Times	Percentage		Times	Percentage
1. Have you taken an off-campus internship?	Yes	19	100%	Yes	19	100%
	No	0	0%	No	0	0%
2. Grades involved in off-campus internships	Sophomore	1	5.3%	Sophomore	2	10.5%
	Junior	11	57.9%	Junior	12	63.2%
	Senior	7	36.8%	Senior	5	26.3%
3. Field of study	Machinery field	19	100%	Machinery field	19	100%
4. Gender	male	16	84.2%	male	16	84.2%
	Female	3	15.8%	Female	3	15.8%
5. Internship category	Summer internship	19	100%	Summer internship	19	100%

4.2 Analysis of School Students' Learning Satisfaction Questionnaire

In the study, the t test was used for analysis, and the categories with different learning satisfaction were sorted out in Table 4 below. In the aspects of course teaching, internship environment and internship counselling, the learning satisfaction of the control group and the experimental group is very different.

In the aspects of course teaching, the question "The internship helped me find a job after graduation" has a t-value of 2.927 $p < .05$, and this learning satisfaction has improved significantly. "In the future, if the internship agency is willing to hire me, I will be willing to go to work" The question t value is 3.543 $p < .001$, and this learning satisfaction has improved significantly. "Faculty's course arrangements and training help to use and complete internship task". The t value of the question is 5.906 $p < .001$, and this learning satisfaction has improved significantly. "When there are difficulties or obstacles during the internship, the school instructor can provide me with guidance and assistance in a timely manner" The question t value is 4.170 $p < .001$, which has significantly improved the learning satisfaction. The t value of the "Course Teaching" facet is 4.965 $p < .001$, and the learning satisfaction of the "Course Teaching" has improved significantly. On the issue of "The internship helped me find a job after

Table 4. Analytical results of the satisfaction table of students' off-campus practice study.

	Control group $N = 19$		Experimental group $N = 19$		t test
	Mean	SD	Mean	SD	
1. Aspects of course teaching	3.11	.830	4.28	.606	**4.965*****
1-1 The internship helped me find a job after graduation	3.42	1.017	4.26	.733	**2.927***
1-2 In the future, if the internship agency is willing to hire me, I will be willing to go to work	3.00	1.247	4.16	.688	**3.543*****
1-3 Faculty's course arrangements and training help to use and complete internship tasks	2.74	1.046	4.37	.597	**5.906*****
1-4 When there are difficulties or obstacles during the internship, the school instructor can provide me with guidance and assistance in a timely manner	3.26	.933	4.32	.582	**4.170*****
2. Aspects of the internship environment	3.88	.705	4.33	.577	**2.183***
2-1 When encountering difficulties or obstacles during the internship, the internship institution can give me guidance and assistance in a timely manner	4.05	.705	4.37	.597	1.490
2-2 The professional ability of the intern institution can meet my skills development	3.42	1.071	4.37	.597	**3.368****
2-3 Internship institutions provide my professional and safe internship environment	4.16	7.65	4.26	.653	.456
3. Aspects of internship counselling	3.44	.609	4.32	.613	**4.423*****
3-1 I am satisfied with the administrative supporting measures of the internship system	3.58	.769	4.42	.692	**3.548*****
3-2 Pre-departure briefing sessions (including industrial safety and ethics workshops) helped me	3.47	.905	4.16	.688	**2.623***
3-3 The teaching methods of internship institutions can be suitable for my learning	3.26	.991	4.37	.597	**4.163*****

$*p < .05, **p < .01, ***p < .001$

graduation", although there are significant results, it is relatively low compared with other issues in the aspect of curriculum teaching. The reason can be seen in Table 4 "In the future, if the internship agency is willing to hire me, I will be willing to go to work". During the internship, I have a certain understanding of the current state of the industry. If the internship institution is willing to continue to hire students in the future, and willing to continue serving, so some people will continue to serve, and some will look for work after graduation. The reason for the above four points is that when the students first intern, they do not understand that the company will behave in a flustered manner and cannot concentrate on the internship. However, the off-campus internship course conveys work specifications, internship content, and standard operating procedures at work as well as the matters to be noted during the internship, these learning items allow students to know what kind of study and preparation they need to do during the internship, and can accurately focus on the internship project.

In the aspects of internship environment, the question "When encountering difficulties or obstacles during the internship, the internship institution can give me guidance and assistance in a timely manner" has a t-value of 1.490, which has not significantly improved the learning satisfaction. The t-value of the question "Pre-departure briefing sessions (including industrial safety and ethics workshops) helped me" is 3.368 $p < .01$, which has significantly improved the learning satisfaction. The question "Internship institutions provide my professional and safe internship environment" has a t-value of 0.456. There is no significant improvement in learning satisfaction. The t value of the "Internship Environment" facet is 2.183 $p < .05$, and the learning satisfaction of the "Internship Environment" has improved significantly. The "When encountering difficulties or obstacles during the internship, the internship institution can give me guidance and assistance in a timely manner" problem can be compared with the "When there are difficulties or obstacles during the internship, the school instructor can provide me with guidance and assistance in a timely manner" problem. It can be known that when encountering difficulties or obstacles during the internship, they will still first seek the guidance and assistance of the school guidance teacher.

In the aspects of internship counselling, the question "I am satisfied with the administrative supporting measures of the internship system" has a t-value of 3.548 $p < .001$, a significant improvement in learning satisfaction. "The pre-departure briefing session (including work safety and ethics lectures was helpful to me)" The question t value is 2.623 $p < .05$, and this learning satisfaction has improved significantly. The t value of the question "The teaching methods of internship institutions can be suitable for my learning" is 4.163 $p < .001$, which is a significant improvement in learning satisfaction. The face value of "Internship Counseling" is 4.423 $p < .001$, and the learning satisfaction of "Internship Counseling" has improved significantly.

5 Conclusions

In this study, through the above analysis, the differences between school students' satisfaction with off-campus Internship and teaching materials intervention were compared. It is hoped that by analyzing the differences between students' perceptions of off-campus internships and student satisfaction with learning after teaching materials intervention, further project-based for school teaching methods are proposed.

(1) Aspects of course teaching
    Significant standards have been achieved in the teaching aspects of the curriculum. Based on the results, it can be known that before the off-campus internship, it is useful to carry out the project-based off-campus teaching materials. The teaching materials mentions "Operation and standardization of internship institutions" and

"Technical problem solving strategies ", etc., to enable students to have a certain understanding of off-campus internships and to effectively solve problems when they encounter problems.

(2) Aspects of internship environment

In terms of the internship environment, only "The professional ability of the intern institution can meet my skills development" has reached a significant level. When the teaching materials were involved, "Technical problem solving strategies" were mentioned. The professional teachers can also solve technical problems when discussing professional technology, satisfy the students' skills development, and prove that teaching materials are useful.

(3) Aspects of internship counselling

In the aspect of internship counseling, they have reached a significant level, because before the internship, the supporting measures such as topic-oriented out-of-school internship teaching materials and pre-departure briefing sessions will be made to allow students to study smoothly during the internship and improve their self-improvement. Performance of learning satisfaction.

From the above three points, it can be seen that students conduct project-based off-campus teaching materials for off-campus internships before internships, so that students have certain prior knowledge and standards of the enterprise during the internship, and can also improve their self-study performance.

Acknowledgements. I am grateful to the Ministry of Science and Technology, Taiwan, for its support and funding for this research; Project Number (MOST 108-2511-H-018-014).

References

1. Wang, H.L.: Problems and countermeasures of college students' internships in China. J. Chifeng Univ. (Nat. Sci. Ed.) **32**(12), 239–240 (2016)
2. Chang, J.C., Hsiao, H.C., Chen, S.C., Chen, T.L.: The relationship between students' background and their off-campus internship conditions for departments of electrical engineering & computer science in technological universities. Int. J. Concept. Manag. Soc. Sci. **4**, 1–5 (2016)
3. Alpert, F., Heaney, J.G., Kuhn, K.A.L.: Internships in marketing: goals, structures and assessment–student, company and academic perspectives. Australas. Mark. J. **17**(1), 36–45 (2009)
4. Kamalluarifin, W.F.S.W., Aniza, F.N.F.M., Jayabalan, H., Saufi, M.L.H.M., Bakar, N.A.A., Karib, S.H.F.: Blended learning: satisfaction among accounting students in UNITEN KSHAS. Global Bus. Manag. Res. **10**(3), 547–557 (2018)
5. Yung, Chaur-Shin: Theory and Practice of Technical Vocational Education. Sanmin Bookstore, Taipei City (1985)
6. Wei, M.-T.: A Study of the Work Satisfaction on Activities of Vocational Exploration and Guidance of Junior High School Students for Vocational High School Teacher, Master's thesis, National Taipei University of Technology, Taipei, Taiwan (2002)
7. Knowles, M.S.: The Modern Practice of Adult Education: Andragogy Versus Pedagogy. Association Press, New York (1970)

8. Fujita-Stank, P.J., Thompson, J.A.: The effects of motivation and classroom environment on the satisfaction of noncredit continuing education student. (ERIC Document Reproduction Service No. ED: 3730646) (1994)
9. Margaryan, S., Saniter, N., Schumann, M., Siedler, T.: Do internships pay off? The effects of student internships on earnings, IZA Discussion Papers, No. 12478 (2019)
10. Rothman, M., Sisman, R.: Internship impact on career consideration among business students. Educ. + Train. **58**(9), 1003–1013 (2016)
11. Jaradat, G.M.: Internship training in computer science: exploring student satisfaction levels. Eval. Program Plan. **63**, 109–115 (2017)

Reviewing the Changes in Core Competencies for Undergraduates in Technological Universities

Jen-Chia Chang, Hsiao-Fang Shih(✉), and Kuang-Ling Chang

Graduate Institute of Technological and Vocational Education, National Taipei University of Technology, No. 1, Section 3, Zhongxiao East Road, Taipei, Taiwan
tch3214@goo.tyai.tyc.edu.tw

Abstract. The objectives of this study are to explore the core competency content of electrical engineering & computer science students, as well as the current situation of training. Literature review and focus group methods were adopted to design the questionnaire survey content. In addition, first-year students from the college of electrical engineering & computer science of a university of technology underwent questionnaire surveys before and after 2 years. There were 195 effective questionnaire copies, accounting for the effective recovery rate of 60.9%. Targeting the survey results, paired sample t-test analysis was carried out. The study found that the post-test scores of students after 2 years were lower than those of the first grade, especially in terms of general core abilities, and each ability had significant differences. It is recommended that the teaching objectives and course content be consistent with the core competencies. The curriculum content should also be designed for the core competencies, using situational education, problem-based learning, and integrated teaching methods and integrated teaching methods, so that students can understand the learning goals and the focus of teaching is to promote students to improve their core competencies.

Keywords: Core competency · Engineering technology education · Technology university

1 Introduction

Departments in the field of electrical engineering & computer science are closely related to high-tech industry development. Improving the core competency of students majoring in electrical engineering & computer science indeed ensures Taiwan's leading status in the global high-tech industry. Therefore, the core competency of students majoring in electrical engineering & computer science is especially important. It can be seen from the MOE's various programs and technical and vocational education policy outline contents that the MOE actively promotes collaboration between technical colleges and the industry, emphasizing the core competency of students studying in technical and vocational education in response to ever-changing future industrial changes. Hence, the purpose of this study is to understand the current situation of the core competency of students majoring in electrical engineering & computer science. We used a questionnaire related to core competency to investigate the students of the Institute of Electrical Engineering and Technology in a domestic university of science and technology. They surveyed that they had the core competency in the first year and before the end of the sophomore year. In our research, we'd like to explore the following questions:

1. What is the core competency content of electrical engineering & computer science students?
2. Will the core competencies of electrical engineering and computer science students vary by grade?

2 Literature Review

In 2014, UNESCO proposed the "2014–2021 Education Strategy". The strategy emphasizes that the future of the Technical and Vocational Education and Training system should aim to develop the world of work and emphasize evidence-based curriculum design [1]. Currently, countries around the world are emphasizing the importance of students' core competency. They believe that core competencies are related to future employability and combine core competencies with educational goals. They want to build students' ability to meet industry needs and the ability to work immediately.

2.1 Higher Educational Goals and Core Competency

The educational objective is to train students to achieve professional and achievements in three to five years after graduation in higher education [2]. Each school and department consider the cultivation of students' professional abilities related to future employment when setting educational goals. It is expected that students will be able to cope with various work problems when they are employed. Core competency refers to the main and important competitiveness that the future environment and society should possess [3]. The educational goal is to train graduates to achieve professional goals. After students study, students are expected to have professional knowledge and abilities, which is the core ability [4].

2.2 Core Competency in Engineering Education

The main mission of the *Accreditation Board for Engineering and Technology* (ABET) is to certify engineering and technology related departments and curriculums applied at US education institutions. The ABET led the global engineering education certification towards student learning result orientation in 2000, setting up new certification specifications known as EC2000. At present, the ABET deems the core competency of engineering technology education (TAC) as: demonstrate the ability to solve generalized engineering problems using mathematics, science, engineering, technology, skills, and modern tools, demonstrate the ability to design systems, components, or processes for broadly defined engineering technology problems, demonstrate the ability to carry out written, oral, and graphical communication in a technical and non-technical environment, demonstrate the ability to perform competency standard tests and measure, conduct, analyze, and explain experiments, demonstrate the ability to perform effective work as a technical team member [5]. The Youth Guidance Committee of the Executive Yuan of our country believes that the employment of college graduates should be based on their work attitude and cooperation ability, career planning and learning progress, and the ability to apply professional knowledge [6]. The Institute of Engineering Education Taiwan (IEET) pointed out at an engineering and technology education seminar in 2019 that the core competency items expected of engineering technology education (TAC) students are: demonstrate familiarity with knowledge, technology, skills, and tool competencies required for engineering practice, demonstrate the ability to properly execute standard operating programs and execute, analyze, explain, and apply experiments in practical skills, demonstrate the ability to apply creativity in engineering practical skills, demonstrate the ability to engage in plan management, effective communication, and teamwork, demonstrate the ability to confirm, analyze, and solve engineering practical and technical problems, recognize current issues, understand the impact of engineering practical technology on the environment, society, and the world, cultivate the habit and ability of continuous learning, understand professional ethics, recognize social responsibility, and respect pluralistic perspectives [7].

3 Research Method

In order to gain insight into the core competency of electrical engineering & computer science students and whether or not their core competency is enhanced after course learning, this study used document analysis, focus group, questionnaire survey, and other methods to carry out relevant research. The research methods and research design are described in detail below.

3.1 Document Analysis

Literature analysis is a form of qualitative research that uses systematic analysis of literature evidence and answers specific research questions [8]. Through data compilation and analysis of the current status of the core competency development of my country's Institute of Electricity and Information Technology, the teaching objectives of the Institute of Electricity and Technology of the four universities of science and technology are summarized, corresponding to the core competency that students of engineering technology education should have after graduation. Among them, the School of Electrical Engineering includes four departments: electrical engineering, electronic engineering, optoelectronic engineering, and information engineering.

3.2 Focus Group Interview

The focus group interview method refers to group interviews by selecting members who meet specific research conditions, with the purpose of collecting qualitative information [9]. Through the use of the "Focus Group," to collect and integrate the opinions of people with academic and practical experience in this field, analyze and discuss the content of the questionnaire in the form of a focus group. In order to ensure the appropriateness of the core competency questionnaire of the Institute of Electrical Engineering, the content of the questionnaire was organized through data analysis, and professors in the field of electrical engineering were invited to hold an expert meeting based on the core competency summary table of the Institute of Electrical Engineering, and confirm the questionnaire through discussion and exchange Content, developed the "Core Competency" scale. After pre-examination by 90 students from the University of Science and Technology in the field of electric capital, experts, and scholars from different fields of electric capital are invited to confirm the final content of the questionnaire.

3.3 Questionnaire Survey

This study took the first-year freshmen of the four technical day department of the 107th academic year of the School of Electrical Engineering (Department of Electrical Engineering, Department of Electronic Engineering, Department of Information Engineering, and Department of Optoelectronic Engineering) of T University as the research object, and used a seven-point scale to investigate. This time, 320 questionnaires were issued and 294 valid questionnaires were recovered in the pretest. The effective recovery rate was 91.9%, 241 valid questionnaires were recovered in the posttest, and the effective recovery rate was 75.3%. According to the before and after test data, there were a total of 195 before and after the test. Based on the survey results, a paired sample t test analysis was performed.

4 Research Results and Discussion

The Cronbach α values measured before and after this questionnaire were .946 and .969, indicating that the content had good internal consistency (Table 1).

Table 1. Reliability analysis of core competency questionnaire.

	Cronbach α	
	Pretest	Posttest
Core competency	.946	.969

According to the results of the questionnaire, after 2 years of study, students of the School of Electrical Engineering and Technology of T University of Science and Technology clearly dissatisfied with their performance in terms of Generic core competency, such as competitiveness regarding effective communication and teamwork, competency in discovering, analyzing, and handling problems, recognize current issues, understanding the impact of engineering practical technology on the environment, society, and the world, cultivate the habit and ability of continuous learning, competency in understanding professional ethics and social responsibility, work ethics, and attitude cultivation, competency in understanding new knowledge and new products, these core competency projects show that students feel that their performance is worse than that in the first grade. In Professional core competency, there are Competencies in mathematics, science, and engineering knowledge application, Competency in analysis and explanation, Competency in techniques, skills, and tools required for executing engineering practices, Competency in computer operations, and other items up to a significant difference (Table 2).

Table 2. Table of core competency paired sample t-test (N: 195).

Core competency	Paired sample t-test				
Item	Pretest		Posttest		t value
	M	SD	M	SD	
Generic core competencies					
5. Competency in effective communication and teamwork	5.49	1.03	5.09	1.35	3.53**
6. Competency in discovering, analyzing, and handling problems	5.51	0.98	5.13	1.32	3.51**
7. Recognize current issues, understand the impact of engineering practical technology on the environment, society, and the world, cultivate the habit and ability of continuous learning	5.35	1.13	5.01	1.27	3.11**
8. Competency in understanding professional ethics and social responsibility	5.42	1.13	5.03	1.31	3.63***
10. Work ethics and attitude cultivation	5.63	1.07	5.11	1.40	4.61***
14. Competency in understanding new knowledge and new products	5.48	1.2	5.08	1.37	3.90***
Professional core competencies					
1. Competency in mathematics, science, and engineering knowledge application	5.31	1.23	4.88	1.33	3.76***
2. Competency in experiment design and execution	5.06	1.26	4.89	1.27	1.42
3. Competency in analysis and explanation	5.17	1.16	4.93	1.25	2.11*
4. Competency in techniques, skills, and tools required for executing engineering practices	5.25	1.11	4.94	1.30	2.64**
9. Ability to design systems, components, or processes for broadly defined engineering technology problems	4.73	1.38	4.56	1.34	1.29
11. Competency in computer operations	5.39	1.22	5.15	1.33	2.15*
12. Document processing and reference reading	5.13	1.23	4.90	1.32	1.96
13. Competency in a foreign language in the professional domain	4.68	1.40	4.64	1.30	0.37
15. Competency in intermediate and advanced program language and data structure and algorithm and software equipment	4.49	1.08	4.53	1.33	-0.34

*$p < .05$, **$p < .01$, ***$p < .001$.

In 2010, Haishan, Xue conducted a questionnaire survey on 742 students from five universities in China and found that there were significant differences between students in schools and grades. With the increase of grades, students' self-study quality shows a downward trend [10]. Juan, Yu conducted a self-directed learning questionnaire on 362 college students in 2005. Senior students' self-directed learning was lower than that of first-year students [11]. They consider that freshmen who have just entered college have expectations of college life and are more willing to try than senior students. As they grow older and adapt to university life, students' interest and expectations for learning will decrease. From the results of this study and other related research, we can know that the students in the upper grades often feel that their learning performance is lower than that of the first grades. In terms of Professional core competency, although the students of the Institute of Electrical Engineering do not have too many significant differences in projects, they also have no increased performance. It can be seen that students still have insufficient self-confidence in the study of professional fields, and they do not think they can learn effectively the Core competencies in their professional field (Fig. 1).

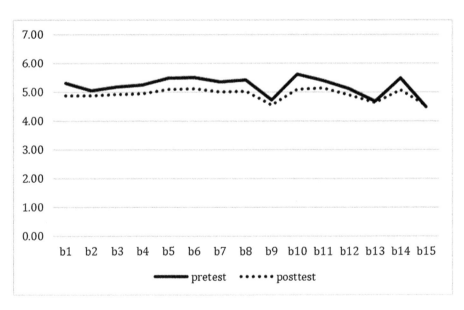

Fig. 1. Pretest and posttest results of core competency.

5 Conclusions and Recommendations

This study divides the Core competency of students from the School of Electrical Engineering into Generic core competency and Professional core competency. In the research results, the performance of the Generic core competency of sophomore students has a significantly lower self-evaluation than in the first grade. Professional core competency also had 4 items with lower scores than the first grade, and obtained significant differences. The results of this study are similar to those of scholars such as Xue and Yu. With age, students' learning and expectations will decrease. The research results are different from our expectations. We think that after nearly two years of study, students will think that their general core competency and professional core competency have improved. Students are clearly dissatisfied with their performance. This may be because the first-year freshmen believe that they can enter T Tech University because of their excellent grades, so they are very confident in their performance. After 2 years of study, students may become increasingly dissatisfied with their performance, so the post-test scores are lower than the pre-test scores. In addition, university courses will gradually become more difficult, especially in professional courses, the second year courses are obviously more difficult than the first year, so students will not be satisfied with their performance after 2 years.

The teaching objectives and core competencies of the School of Electrical Engineering should be as close as possible. The curriculum content should also be designed for the core competencies, using situational education, problem-based learning, and integrated teaching methods and integrated teaching methods, so that students can understand the learning goals and the focus of teaching is to promote students to improve their core competencies.

Acknowledgement. The researchers would like to express our thanks to the Ministry of Science and Technology's financial support by MOST 107-2511-H-027-001.

References

1. UNESCO Homepage. https://unesdoc.unesco.org/ark. Accessed 11 May 2019
2. Center for Education Innovation Homepage. http://celt.ust.hk/obe/download/. Accessed 11 May 2018
3. Kunchong, L.: The establishment of the university's core competence and competence indicators. Educ. Res. Mon. **2**, 107–122 (2010)
4. STUDYLIB Homepage. https://studylib.net/doc. Accessed 27 Sept 2019
5. Manchun, L.: US ABET Certification Norm Renewed. Eval. Bimonthly **47**, 55–56 (2018)
6. Youth Guidance Committee of the Executive Yuan Homepage. https://advisory.yda.gov.tw/. Accessed 11 Sept 2019
7. Institute of Engineering Education Taiwan Homepage. https://www.ieet.org.tw/. Accessed 30 Dec 2018
8. Frey, B.: The SAGE Encyclopedia of Educational Research, Measurement, and Evaluation. University of Kansas, USA (2018)
9. Yarong, Z.: Application of focus group method in investigation and research. Invest. Res. **3**, 51–73 (1997)
10. Haishan, X.: Research on the compilation of scale of undergraduates' learning quality and the investigation of the current situation. MS thesis, Fujian Normal University, Fujian (2010)
11. Juan, Y.: A survey of college students' learning autonomy. Int. Chin. J. Appl. Psychol. **2**(2), 112–116 (2005)

Theoretical and Designing Framework of Constructivist Learning Environment Model that Enhance Creative Thinking and Creative Expression of Science for Medical Illustration Students

Kan Komany[✉] and Sumalee Chaijaroen

Department of Educational Technology, Khon Kaen University, Khon Kaen 40002, Thailand
`kan.mdi.kku@gmail.com, sumalee@kku.ac.th`

Abstract. Creative thinking skills are one of the important skills of people in the 21st century, especially with science and medical personnel that, in addition to their scientific skills, they need creative expression of science together to enable to communicate or present complex information interesting and effective. Therefore, the purpose of this study is to synthesize the theoretical and designing framework of the learning environment according to constructivist theories approaches to enhance creativity and creative scientific expression. This research uses model research [3] that focuses on synthesis of the design process and development of learning models. It consists of 3 main steps which are 1) document analysis and learning context 2) analysis of learning theory principles and learning design theory 3) Synthesize and create theoretical framework and designing framework. The results show that the components of the theory that can support the research to achieve its objectives consist of 5 components: (1) learning theories, (2) Teaching model, (3) contextual base, (4) creative thinking and creative expression of science, (5) Media theories. The designing framework has 5 important goals which are (1) Stimulating the creation of intellectual structures, (2) Supporting intellectual balance, (3) Promoting creativity, (4) Promoting Creative expression of science, (5) Promoting and helping to balance intellectual. There are 7 components to designing this framework: (1) Problem situation, (2) Learning Resources, (3) Critical Thinking Center, (4) Collaboration Center, (5) Creative Thinking Center, (6) Creative expression of science Center, (7) Scaffolding Center.

Keywords: Constructivist theories · Creative thinking · Creative expression of science

1 Introduction

The progress of our world in the 21st century is a result of the advancement in Technology and Innovation that has been continuously created from the past to the present, an era in which Digital Technology plays a huge role in people. This makes people in the society need to have the skills to search for more complex information correctly and appropriately in order to combine new knowledge with their own knowledge and experience and create a new piece of work. Therefore, the quest for self-knowledge and creative thinking and creative expression skills are important skills for people of today and the future. These skills should be practiced at an early age, which allows students to have good skills before going into the real work context in society.

Scientific and medical personnel are a group of people with full potential in science that can help advance the global society. These groups can create new innovations, including the transmission of new and complex information for people in society to learn. Therefore, this group is highly necessary to have creative thinking skills in order to create new ideas. Scientific and creative expression skills to make the data transfer interesting and effective to the recipient. For this reason, the researcher sees the importance of how to create learning for students, especially in science students to develop intellectual skills, knowledge building skills, creative thinking skills and creative expression of science. Therefore, the purpose of this study is to synthesize the theoretical framework of the learning environment according to constructivist theories approaches to enhance creativity and creative scientific expression. This research uses model research (Richey & Klein, 2007) that focuses on synthesis of the design process and development of learning models.

2 Research Purpose

2.1. **To study the design and development of a learning environment model based on constructivist concepts to enhance creative thinking and creative expression of science for medical illustration students.**
2.2. **To synthesize the theoretical framework and designing framework of constructivist learning environment model to enhance creative thinking and creative expression of science for medical illustration students.**

3 Research Methodology

This research uses the Model research [3] by dividing the process into three phases which is currently in the process of Phase 1, that is the model development process by studying and analyzing documents and survey research. The goal of Phase 1 is to synthesize the theoretical framework and designing framework of constructivist learning environment model.

3.1 Target Group

Target group in this research consisted of 3 experts for the evaluation of the theoretical framework and the designing framework and 30 medical illustration students from faculty of Medicine, Khon Kaen University.

3.2 Research Instruments

Recording form for synthesize the designing framework of constructivist learning environment model to enhance creative thinking and creative expression of science. Evaluation form for the experts used in theoretical framework and designing framework of constructivist learning environment model to enhance creative thinking and creative expression of science.

3.3 Data Collection and Data Analysis

Gathering various information from research papers and documents related to theoretical principles and context of the sample group, for use in the study and synthesis of the framework as follows: (1) Documents and data are collected which are related to the theoretical framework such as Intellectual theory Constructivist theory, teaching theory, learning design theory, media theory and research that related to the Constructivist Learning Environment Model that enhance creative thinking and creative expression of science for medical illustration students. Then perform data analysis. (2) Student opinions related to the learning context are explored. After that, take the results from the survey for analysis by using summaries, interpretations and analytical explanations. (3) synthesize the theoretical framework and then create the designing framework through analysis by interpreting the data and using the descriptive analysis in the framework synthesis record (4) The composition of the model is presented to the consultant and experts to check the consistency between theory and designing framework using assessment forms through data interpretation and descriptive analysis. Its results and recommendations are used to improve the model.

4 Research Results

4.1 Theoretical Framework

The results of the synthesis of theories and research documents are found that the theoretical framework consists of 5 fundamental: 1) Learning theories consisting of Cognitivism and Constructivism, 2) Teaching model consisting of Open Learning Environment (OLE), Constructivist Learning Environment (CLE), Select Organize Integrate (SOI), 3) Contextual base of the target group is Medical Illustration (MDI), Faculty of Medicine, Khon kaen University, 4) Media theories consisting of Media symbol system and Color Theories that can stimulate creativity., and 5) Creative thinking and Creative expression of science that consists of Guilford's creative principles and the creative scientific expression principles of Sherry-Ann Brown, Department of Medicine, Mayo Clinic, Rochester, MN, USA. (see Fig. 1).

4.2 Designing a Framework

The designing framework of Constructivist Learning Environment Model that enhance creative thinking and creative expression of science for medical illustration students (see Fig. 2) showed the four stages as follows:

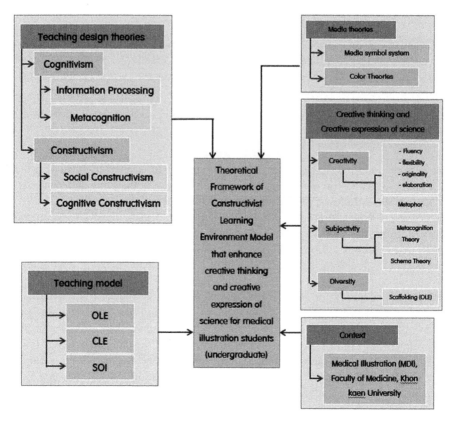

Fig. 1. Theoretical framework of constructivist learning environment model that enhance creative thinking and creative expression of science for medical illustration students

Stimulating the Creation of Intellectual Structures. It was designed on the basis of Cognitive Constructivism by Piaget. This foundation believes that students who are motivated by a problem situation lead to a state of intellectual conflict causing them to try to balance their cognitive balance. The process of enabling into the learning context or complex problems is another factor that helps students to create knowledge. Students also need to be stimulated by creative thinking. Guilford, 1967, while solving problems in various situations, with Functionalist theories of color is what helps stimulate creative thinking. All of this is the design of the **Problem situation**.

Supporting Intellectual Balance. This step is to help students adjust their cognitive balance or knowledge building after students encounter complex situations. What students are encouraged to do is chunking skills. Conceptualization of knowledge. Use of cognitive tools. Using the media symbol system. Communication, exchange of knowledge among students. All of this creates three important components: the **Learning Resources, Cognitive Center, Collaboration Center.**

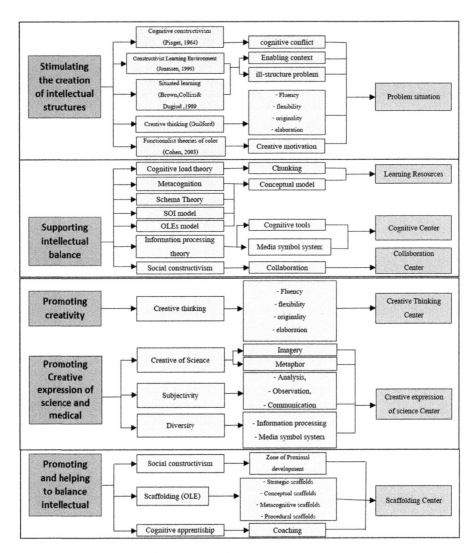

Fig. 2. Designing framework of constructivist learning environment model that enhance creative thinking and creative expression of science for medical illustration students.

Promoting Creativity. The component is designed according to Guilford's creative theory which consists of 4 areas: (1) Fluency, (2) flexibility, (3) originality, (4) elaboration. In which these skills are required for students to stimulate their creative thinking skills. All of this creates the **Creative Thinking Center.**

Promoting Creative Expression of Science and Medical. Students also need creative expression skills in addition to creative thinking skills that contains Imagery and Metaphor, including Subjectivity and Diversity. This was the design of Creative expression of science Center.

Promoting and Helping to Balance Intellectual. In the theory of Social constructivism, it is believed that learners with lower skills or knowledge need to be helped to upgrade and develop themselves. In Open Learning Environment (OLE) principles, students need to be assisted in four areas: Strategic, Conceptual, Metacognitive, and Procedural. Students need to receive advice or assistance from those who have expertise. All of this was designed as a Scaffolding Center.

5 Summary and Conclusion

The purpose of this study is to synthesize the theoretical and designing framework of the learning environment according to constructivist theories approaches to enhance creativity and creative scientific expression. This research uses model research (Richey & Klein, 2007) [3] that focuses on synthesis of the design process and development of learning models. The results show that the components of the theoretical framework consist of 5 components: (1) learning theories consisting of Cognitivism and Constructivism, 2) Teaching model consisting of Open Learning Environment (OLE) [5], Constructivist Learning Environment (CLE) [14], Select Organize Integrate (SOI) [8], 3) Contextual base of the target group, 4) Media theories consisting of Media symbol system [6] and Color Theories that can stimulate creativity., and 5) Creative thinking and Creative expression of science that consists of Guilford's creative principles [2] and the creative scientific expression principles of Sherry-Ann Brown [10]. The designing framework has 5 important goals which are (1) Stimulating the creation of intellectual structures. It was designed on the basis of Cognitive Constructivism by Piaget [4]. This foundation believes that students who are motivated by a problem situation lead to a state of intellectual conflict causing them to try to balance their cognitive balance that is consistent with the results of Sumalee [1], and Samat and Chaijaroen [11] research that designed problem situations to encourage students to create knowledge through problem solving. The process of enabling into the learning context or complex problems is another factor that helps students to create knowledge. Students also need to be stimulated by creative thinking (Guilford, 1967), while solving problems in various situations, with Functionalist theories of color is what helps stimulate creative thinking. (2) Supporting intellectual balance. This step is to help students adjust their cognitive balance or knowledge building after students encounter complex situations. What students are encouraged to do is chunking skills. Conceptualization of knowledge. Use of cognitive tools. Using the media symbol system. Communication, exchange of knowledge among students. (3) Promoting creativity. The component is designed according to Guilford's creative theory [2] which consists of 4 areas: fluency, flexibility, originality, elaboration. (4) Promoting Creative expression of science. Students also need creative expression skills in addition to creative thinking skills that contains Imagery and Metaphor [10, 16, 17], including Subjectivity and Diversity [10]. (5) Promoting and helping to balance intellectual. In the theory of Social constructivism [13], it is believed that learners with lower skills or knowledge need to be helped to upgrade and develop themselves. In Open Learning Environment (OLE) principles [5], students need to be assisted in four areas: Strategic, Conceptual, Metacognitive, and Procedural. Students need to receive advice or assistance from those who have expertise [12]. There are 8 components to designing this framework: (1) Problem situation, (2) Learning Resources, (3) Critical Thinking Center, (4) Collaboration Center, (5) Creative Thinking Center, (6) Creative expression of science Center, (7) Scaffolding Center.

Acknowledgements. This research was supported by Ph.D. Program in Educational Technology, Faculty of Education, Research Group for Innovation and Cognitive Technology, Khon Kaen, University, and Research and Technology Transfer Affairs Division, Khon Kaen University.

References

1. Sumalee, C.: The learner's creative thinking learning with learning innovation to encourage human thinking. Eur. J. Soc. Sci. **28**, 213–218 (2012)
2. Guilford, J.P.: The Nature of Human Intelligence. McGraw-Hill Book Company, New York (1967)
3. Richey, R.C., Klein, J.D.: Design and Development Research: Methods, Strategies, and Issues. Routledge, Abingdon (2007)
4. Piaget, J.: Part I: cognitive development in children: piaget development and learning. J. Res. Sci. Teach. **2**, 176–186 (1964)
5. Hannafin, M., Land, S., Oliver, K.: Open learning environments: foundations, methods, and models. In: Reigeluth, C.M. (ed.) Instructional Design Theories and Models Volume II: A New Paradigm of Instructional Theory. Lawrence Erlbaum Associates, New York (1999)
6. Klausmeier, H.J.: Educational Psychology, 5th edn. Harper & Row, New York (1985)
7. Sweller, J.: Cognitive load theory, learning difficulty, and instructional design. Learn. Instr. **4**, 295–312 (1994)
8. Mayer, R.E.: Designing instruction for constructivist learning. In: Reigeluth, C.M. (ed.) Instructional Design Theories and Models Volume II: A New Paradigm of Instructional Theory. Lawrence Erlbaum Associates, New York (1999)
9. Wilson, B.G., Cole, P.: Cognitive teaching models. In: Jonassen, D.H. (ed.) Handbook of Research for Educational Communications and Technology. MacMillan, New York (1996)
10. Brown, S.-A.: Creative expression of science through poetry and other media can enrich medical and science education. Front. Neurol. **6**, 3 (2015)
11. Chaijaroen, S., Samat, C.: Design and development of learning environment to enhance creative thinking and innovation skills for teacher training in the 21st century. In: 23rd International Conference on Computers in Education, pp. 667–672. Asia-Pacific Society for Computers in Education, Hangzhou (2015)
12. Brown, J., Collins, A., Duguid, P.: Situated cognition and the culture of learning. Educ. Res. **18**(1), 32–42 (1989)
13. Vygotsky, L.S.: Mind in Society: The Development of Higher Psychological Processes. Harvard University Press, Cambridge (1978)
14. Jonassen, D.: Designing constructivist learning environments. In: Instructional Design Theories and Models: A New Paradigm of Instructional Theory, vol. II, pp. 215–239. Erlbaum, New-Jersey (1999)
15. Augello, A., Infantino, I., Pilato, G., Rizzo, R., Vella, F.: Binding representational spaces of colors and emotions for creativity. Biol. Inspired Cogn. Archit. **5**, 64–71 (2013)
16. Musolff, A.: Creativity in Metaphor Interpretation (2019)
17. Barnden, J.A.: Unparalleled creativity in metaphor (2008)

Tracking At-Risk Student Groups from Teaching and Learning Activities in Engineering Education

Christopher Chung Lim Kwan

The Hong Kong Polytechnic University, Kowloon, Hong Kong SAR
ceclkwan@polyu.edu.hk

Abstract. Tracking student groups, in particular, at-risk student group is a challenging but meaningful work in a large class of an engineering mathematics course, enabling instructors to ascertain how well students are learning and when they need interventions of their studies during the delivery of teaching and learning activities. In the paper, two unsupervised learning algorithms, hierarchical clustering and k-means clustering, are used and compared with the use of LMS data such as the level of achievements in online class activities, assignments, a mini-project and a mid-term test for tracking at-risk student groups at the end of weeks 3, 5, 7, 9 and 11 in a 13-week semester of an academic year. Notwithstanding the higher accuracy of both clustering, the k-means clustering significantly outperforms the hierarchical clustering in terms of the precision, recall and f-measure at the end of week 11. It is found that the k-means clustering can be employed to track at-risk students with the recall of 0.640 and the f-measure of 0.533 for the initial intervention of their studies by the end of week 7.

Keywords: At-risk student · Hierarchical clustering · K-means clustering · Precision · Recall · F-measure

1 Introduction

Traditionally, educational data, generally generated from results of many assessment tasks like assignments, tests, laboratory reports and examinations, are used to grade student performance at the end of a subject or a course, informing students of how well they have learned for the progression of studies and graduation. These assessment results are further analyzed by course instructors to measure the achievement of the subject intended learning outcomes for quality assurance and accreditation purposes [2, 3, 11]. On the other hand, assessment can be regarded as formative feedback to students, providing them with frequent responses and precise information on how well they are on track during learning, and timely interventions of their studies if at-risk student group can be identified and tracked as early as possible during the delivery of teaching and learning activities [6, 7]. This is a particularly challenging work for lecturing in large classes [9].

With advances in artificial intelligence, it is possible to identify at-risk students in class and to predict students' success in a course [4, 5, 7, 10]. Marbouti et al. [8] built three logistic regression-based models to identify at-risk students in a large first-year engineering course at weeks 2, 4 and 9 in a semester. These models are highly predictive in identifying at-risk students. However, these models like other supervised learning models cannot be trained and tested in the absence of observed data or output variable such as students' final grade, addressing the value of creating unsupervised learning models like hierarchical clustering and k-means clustering for tracking and identifying at-risk student groups.

2 The Context of the Study

The dataset of an engineering mathematics course offered in a 13-week semester of an academic year is used for the present study and extracted from Blackboard LMS for hierarchical clustering and k-means clustering. In total, there are a total of 240 students participating in class activities and various assessment tasks, designed on the basis of the subject curriculum and the subject intended learning outcomes.

Identifying at-risk students with the aid of artificial intelligence is the focus of the study. The present study thus aims at addressing the following research questions:

What is the performance of hierarchical clustering and k-means clustering for tracking at-risk student groups in terms of the accuracy, precision, recall and f-measure?

Which clustering can be employed to track at-risk students for timely intervention of their studies by the end of week 7 with certain degrees of recall and f-measure?

For the dataset, there are 16 input variables such as 2 assignments, a mini project, a mid-term test, and 12 online class activities held in each week of the semester. The online class activities are done in face-to-face (F2F) sessions for recording the number of multiple-choice questions correctly attempted as well as students' attendance. The score of the online class activities is not counted in the calculation of the coursework assessment as these activities are designed for enhancing student engagement in class and checking their understanding of the topics, concepts, and theorems. The input variables used for hierarchical clustering and k-means clustering are summarized in Table 1.

The output variable is the final examination score which is always an unknown variable before the end of the 13-week course and is intended not to be used for clustering. As the final examination score is made available at the end of the semester, this variable is simply used for evaluating the performance of hierarchical clustering and k-means clustering respectively at the end of weeks 3, 5, 6, 7, 9 and 11 in terms of the accuracy, precision, recall and f-measure. A binary variable (i.e. 0 or 1) which indicates whether the student is at-risk or not is also defined. An integer "1" can be assigned to the binary variable which represents an at-risk student who either fails in the final examination or is absent from the final examination. Conversely, an integer "0" is assigned to a not-at-risk student passing the final examination.

Table 1. Input variables used for hierarchical clustering and k-means clustering.

Input variable	Completed by week	Type	Point
Assignment 1	5	Numeric	0–15
Mid-term test	7	Numeric	0–50
Mini-project	8	Numeric	0–20
Assignment 2	11	Numeric	0–15
1st Online class activity	1	Integer	0–3
2nd Online class activity	2	Integer	0–8
3rd Online class activity	3	Integer	0–4
4th Online class activity	4	Integer	0–6
5th Online class activity	5	Integer	0–2
6th Online class activity	6	Integer	0–3
7th Online class activity	7	Integer	0–6
8th Online class activity	8	Integer	0–2
9th Online class activity	9	Integer	0–3
10th Online class activity	10	Integer	0–3
11th Online class activity	11	Integer	0–1
12th Online class activity	12	Integer	0–1

3 Methodology

Initially, three input variables such as 1st, 2nd and 3rd online class activities are used for hierarchical clustering and k-means clustering respectively at the end of week 3. At the end of week 5, 1st–5th online class activities and assignment 1 are selected as input variables for clustering. Because of an in-class mid-term test held in week 7, clustering is also carried out for finding different groups of similar characteristics like at-risk student groups by the end of week 7. In this connection, nine input variables such as 1st–7th online class activities, assignment 1 and mid-term test are selected. Furthermore, twelve input variables such as 1st–9th online class activities, assignment 1, mid-term test and mini-project are chosen for clustering by the end of week 9. At the end of week 11, fifteen input variables except the 12th online class activity are used for clustering as shown in Table 1.

The goal of clustering is to categorize the data into similar groups. The distance between two data points are generally defined by "Euclidean distance", where k is the number of independent variables.

$$d_{ij} = \sqrt{(x_{i1} - x_{j1})^2 + (x_{i2} - x_{j2})^2 + \ldots + (x_{ik} - x_{jk})^2} \qquad (1)$$

As distance is highly influenced by scale of variables, it is customary to normalize the data first. Both hierarchical clustering and k-means clustering are then used and compared with the use of LMS data such as the level of achievements in online class activities, assignments, a mini-project and a mid-term test for tracking at-risk student groups at the end of weeks 3, 5, 7, 9 and 11 in a 13-week semester of an academic year.

3.1 Hierarchical Clustering

This hierarchical clustering is a bottom-up approach to construct a cluster dendrogram. The algorithm of hierarchical clustering is addressed as follows:

1. Assign a cluster to each data point initially such that 'n' clusters for 'n' data points;
2. Combine two nearest clusters by calculating the distance and the centroid;
3. Repeat to proceed the step 2 until all data points are in one cluster, then stop the iteration.

3.2 *K*-Means Clustering

This method is also one of the simplest unsupervised learning algorithms [1]. The algorithm of k-means clustering is used for categorizing groups of similar characteristics. Firstly, the number of 'k' cluster centers is specified and initialized randomly. Then, the distances between each data point and cluster centers are calculated by using Euclidean distance formula. Secondly, assignment of the data points to that cluster center whose distance from the cluster center is minimum as compared to all the cluster centers is made. In other words, the minimum-distance classifier can be used to separate the above data into k clusters, where a data x_t is in cluster i if $\|x_t - m_i\|$ is the minimum of all k distances. That is,

$$b_i^t = \begin{cases} 1 & if \|x_t - m_i\| = \min_k \|x_t - m_k\| \\ 0 & otherwise \end{cases} \quad (2)$$

The algorithm aims to minimize an objective function which is defined as

$$E\left(\{m_i\}_{i=1}^k | X\right) = \sum_t \sum_i b_i^t \|x_t - m_i\|^2 \quad (3)$$

Thus, taking its derivative with respect to m_i and setting it to zero yield

$$m_i = \frac{\sum_t b_i^t x_t}{\sum_t b_i^t} \quad (4)$$

The new cluster center can thus be updated by using the assigned data points and the Eq. (4). Thirdly, the distances between each data point and new cluster centers are recalculated by using the Eq. (2). Therefore, this is an iterative procedure. If there is no reassignment of the data points, then the iteration is stopped. Otherwise, the second step is repeated for assigning the data points.

4 Result

The mean scores of five student clusters were determined from hierarchical clustering and k-means clustering respectively at the end of weeks 3, 5, 7, 9 and 11 respectively. In particular, it is found that Cluster 3 of hierarchical clustering is tracked and identified to be the potential at-risk student group based on the mean scores of input variables up to the end of week 7 as shown in Table 2. The mean scores of 1st, 2nd, 4th, 5th, and 7th online class activities are not shown in Table 2 for simplicity. The number of students in this cluster is 26. Students were not actively engaged in the online class activities as a result of the second lowest mean score among five groups. Their performances on both Assignment 1 and the mid-term test were also unsatisfactory as their mean scores were the lowest among the clusters. In particular, the mean scores of Assignment 1 and the mid-term test were 9.94 out of 15 and 19.06 out of 50 respectively. They thus scored on average 29.00 out of 65 for the completed coursework comprising Assignment 1 and the mid-term test. It is also found that the final examination score which is the output variable not to be used for hierarchical clustering was also the lowest among five groups. As identified to be the at-risk student group, 46.2% of students (i.e. 12 students) in this group can be correctly identified as at-risk students (i.e. true positive), representing a precision of 0.462 of the present clustering. However, 53.8% of students (i.e. 14 students) who are not-at-risk students can be misclassified (i.e. false positive).

Table 2. Hierarchical clustering of student groups at the end of week 7 in a 13-week course.

Variable	Cluster 1	Cluster 2	Cluster 3	Cluster 4	Cluster 5
Group size	55	41	26	96	22
3th Online class activity	1.95	0.00	0.77	0.73	0.64
Assignment 1	13.21	13.45	9.94	12.63	13.16
6th Online class activity	2.38	0.00	0.04	0.97	1.09
Mid-term test	34.09	35.18	19.06	28.91	33.52
Coursework's score (wk.7)	47.30	48.63	29.00	41.53	46.68
Final examination	53.24	44.73	35.65	41.44	49.64
At-risk student %	3.6	17.1	46.2	27.1	13.6

Among these five clusters, students of Cluster 2 did not participate in any online class activity at all but they achieved the best performance on both Assignment 1 and the mid-term test. They obtained the highest mean score of the completed coursework up to week 7 but they only achieved the third highest mean score in the final examination. As Cluster 2 is identified to be the not-at-risk student group, 82.9% of students (i.e. 34 students) belonging to this cluster can be correctly classified as not-at-risk students (i.e. true negative). However, 17.1% of students (i.e. 7 students) who are really at-risk students can be misclassified (i.e. false negative).

Students belonging to Cluster 1 not only actively participated in online class activities, but also performed well on both Assignment 1 and the mid-term test. The final examination score was the highest among other groups. As Cluster1 is not to be identified as the at-risk student group, 3.6% of students (i.e. 2 students) assigned to this group cannot be correctly tracked and classified as at-risk students for early intervention (i.e. false negative) but 96.4% of students (i.e. 53 students) can be correctly identified as not-at-risk students in this group (i.e. true negative).

Clusters 4 and 5 of hierarchical clustering are not identified to be groups of at-risk students because students of Clusters 4 and 5 ranked the second lowest mean score and the third highest mean score of the completed coursework up to the end of week 7 respectively. They were engaged in the online class activities as well. Overall, 72.9% and 86.4% of students belonging to Clusters 4 and 5 respectively (i.e. 70 and 19 students) can be correctly classified as not-at-risk students (i.e. true negative). However, 27.1% and 13.6% of students assigned to clusters 4 and 5 (i.e. 26 and 3 students) can be misclassified respectively (i.e. false negative).

Clusters 1 and 3 of k-means clustering are tracked to be the potential at-risk student group based on the mean scores of input variables up to the end of week 7 as shown in Table 3. The mean scores of 1st, 2nd, 4th, 5th and 7th online class activities are not shown in Table 3 for simplicity. Students belonging to Clusters 1 and 3 were not much engaged in the online activities among other clusters. They obtained the second lowest and the lowest mean score of the completed coursework up to week 7 respectively. Even though the final examination score which is the output variable is not used for k-means clustering as well, they ranked the lowest and the second lowest mean score in the final examination respectively. As tracked to be at-risk student groups, 48.3% and 33.3% of students (i.e. 28 and 4 students) in these two groups can be correctly classified as at-risk students (i.e. true positive), representing an overall precision of 0.457 of the present clustering. However, 51.7% and 66.7% of students (i.e. 30 and 8 students) who are not-at-risk students can be misclassified respectively (i.e. false positive).

Table 3. K-means clustering of student groups at the end of week 7 in a 13-week course.

Variable	Cluster 1	Cluster 2	Cluster 3	Cluster 4	Cluster 5
Group size	58	57	12	44	69
3th Online class activity	0.47	1.12	0.33	1.84	0.25
Assignment 1	12.63	13.03	6.00	13.00	13.32
6th Online class activity	0.69	2.16	0.33	1.64	0.14
Mid-term test	22.03	31.18	20.29	35.17	35.94
Coursework's score (wk.7)	34.66	44.20	26.29	48.17	49.26
Final examination	33.22	49.02	37.83	50.45	48.75
At-risk student %	48.3	8.8	33.3	6.8	14.5

Clusters 2, 4 and 5 of k-means clustering are identified to be not-at-risk student groups because students of Clusters 2 and 4 actively participated in online class activities and did the coursework well. Clusters 2 and 4 ranked the third highest and the second highest mean score of the completed coursework by the end of week 7 respectively. Students of Cluster 5 showed the least participation in the online class activities but achieved the highest mean score of the completed coursework. As a result, 91.2%, 93.2% and 85.5% of students belonging to Clusters 2, 4 and 5 respectively (i.e. 52, 41 and 59 students) can be correctly identified as not-at-risk students (i.e. true negative). Conversely, 8.8%, 6.8% and 14.5% of students assigned to these three clusters (i.e. 5, 3 and 10 students) can be misclassified respectively (i.e. false negative).

Clusters 4 and 5 of hierarchical clustering are identified to be the potential at-risk student groups based on the mean scores of input variables by the end of week 11 as shown in Table 4. The mean scores of 1st, 2nd, 4th, 5th, 7th–11th online class activities are not shown in Table 4 for simplicity. Students assigned to Clusters 4 and 5 did not actively participate in the online class activities. They also obtained the second lowest and the lowest mean score of the completed coursework comprising two assignments, the mid-term test and the mini-project up to week 11 respectively. In fact, students of Cluster 4 did not submit Assignment 2 in week 11; some of them withdrew from their studies due to difficulties in handling tremendous workloads from studying 7 courses in a semester. Students of Clusters 4 and 5 ranked the lowest and the second lowest mean score in the final examination respectively. As detected to be at-risk student groups, 90.5% and 45.5% of students (i.e. 19 and 5 students) in these two groups can be correctly identified as at-risk students (i.e. true positive), representing an overall precision of 0.765 of the present clustering. However, 9.5% and 54.5% of students (i.e. 2 and 6 students) who are not-at-risk students can be misclassified respectively (i.e. false positive).

Table 4. Hierarchical clustering of student groups at the end of week 11 in a 13-week course.

Variable	Cluster 1	Cluster 2	Cluster 3	Cluster 4	Cluster 5
Group size	79	51	78	21	11
3th Online class activity	1.57	0.00	0.77	0.33	0.18
Assignment 1	12.96	13.26	12.63	13.48	6.36
6th Online class activity	2.06	0.02	0.87	0.81	0.00
Mid-term test	33.19	30.84	29.97	28.52	17.64
Mini-project	17.59	15.98	17.05	14.57	5.27
Assignment 2	12.96	12.63	13.04	0.00	8.41
Coursework's score (wk.11)	76.70	72.73	72.69	56.57	37.68
Final examination	53.28	47.45	46.09	7.86	33.64
At-risk student %	2.5	19.6	17.9	90.5	45.5

Clusters 1, 2 and 3 of hierarchical clustering are tracked to be not-at-risk student groups because students of Clusters 1 and 3 were actively engaged in online class activities and did the coursework well. Clusters 1 and 3 ranked the highest and the third highest mean score of the completed coursework by the end of week 11 respectively. Students of Cluster 2 had the least participation in the online class activities but achieved the second highest mean score of the completed coursework. As a result, 97.5%, 80.4% and 82.1% of students belonging to Clusters 1, 2 and 3 respectively (i.e. 77, 41 and 64 students) can be correctly classified as not-at-risk students (i.e. true negative). Nevertheless, 2.5%, 19.6% and 17.9% of students assigned to these three clusters (i.e. 2, 10 and 14 students) can still be misclassified respectively (i.e. false negative).

Clusters 2 and 3 of k-means clustering are tracked to be the potential at-risk student group based on the mean scores of input variables up to the end of week 11 as shown in Table 5. Students belonging to Clusters 2 and 3 were not much engaged in the online activities. They obtained the lowest and the second lowest mean score of the completed coursework up to week 11 respectively. They ranked the second lowest and the lowest mean score in the final examination respectively, despite the fact that the final examination was not included in the clustering. As tracked to be at-risk student groups, 50% and 91% of students (i.e. 6 and 20 students) in these two groups can be correctly classified as at-risk students (i.e. true positive), corresponding to an overall precision of 0.765 of the present clustering. Conversely, 50% and 9% of students (i.e. 6 and 2 students) who are not-at-risk students can be misclassified respectively (i.e. false positive).

Table 5. K-means clustering of student groups at the end of week 11 in a 13-week course.

Variable	Cluster 1	Cluster 2	Cluster 3	Cluster 4	Cluster 5
Group size	71	12	22	77	58
3th Online class activity	0.77	0.17	0.32	1.65	0.03
Assignment 1	12.57	6.83	13.45	13.01	13.21
6th Online class activity	0.97	0.00	0.77	2.10	0.02
Mid-term test	29.63	17.29	28.07	33.05	31.93
Mini-project	17.11	5.50	14.77	17.55	16.24
Assignment 2	13.00	8.33	0.27	12.95	12.97
Coursework's score (wk.11)	72.32	37.96	56.57	76.55	74.34
Final examination	46.28	33.33	8.86	52.69	48.64
At-risk student %	16.9	50.0	91.0	2.6	17.3

Clusters 1, 4 and 5 of k-means clustering are classified to be not-at-risk student groups because students of Clusters 1 and 4 were actively engaged in online class activities and did the coursework well. Clusters 1 and 4 ranked the third highest and the highest mean score of the completed coursework by the end of week 11 respectively. Students of Cluster 5 showed the least participation in the online class activities but achieved the second highest mean score of the completed coursework. Overall, 83.1%, 97.4% and 82.7% of students belonging to Clusters 1, 4 and 5 respectively (i.e. 59, 75 and 48 students) can be correctly classified as not-at-risk students (i.e. true negative). However, 16.9%, 2.6% and 17.3% of students belonging to these three clusters (i.e. 12, 2 and 10 students) can be misclassified respectively (i.e. false negative).

Accuracy, precision, recall and f-measure of a model are defined and calculated as follows:

$$Accuracy = \frac{TP+TN}{TP+TN+FP+FN} \quad (5)$$

$$Precision = \frac{TP}{TP+FP} \quad (6)$$

$$Recall = \frac{TP}{TP+FN} \quad (7)$$

$$F-measure = 2 \cdot \frac{Prescision \cdot Recall}{Precision + Recall} \quad (8)$$

where TP: true positive; TN: true negative; FP: false positive; FN: false negative

The performance of the present models is further evaluated in terms of accuracy, precision, recall (i.e. sensitivity), and f-measure as shown in Table 6. Despite the high accuracy of both models, it is found that the k-means clustering has achieved the higher recall of 0.640 and the f-measure of 0.533 by the end of week 7. Furthermore, it has achieved the higher precision of 0.765, the recall of 0.520, and the f-measure of 0.619 by the end of week 11.

Table 6. Accuracy, precision, recall and f-measure of hierarchical clustering and k-means clustering

	Week 7		Week 11	
	Hierarchical clustering	K-means clustering	Hierarchical clustering	K-means clustering
Accuracy	0.783	0.767	0.858	0.867
Precision	0.462	0.457	0.750	0.765
Recall	0.240	0.640	0.480	0.520
F-measure	0.316	0.533	0.585	0.619

5 Conclusion and Future Works

It is concluded that the k-means clustering significantly outperforms the hierarchical clustering in terms of the precision, recall and f-measure at the end of week 11. It is found that the k-means clustering can be employed to track at-risk students with the recall of 0.64 and the f-measure of 0.533 for the initial intervention of their studies once the results of the 1st–7th online class activities, assignment 1, and the mid-term test are made available at the end of week 7.

To further confirm that the differences between clusters of the five-cluster solution are distinctive and significant, F statistics from one-way ANOVAs will be calculated to examine whether there are statistically significant differences between the five clusters on each of the clustering variables such as assignments, mid-term test and online class activities, and each of two non-clustering variables such as coursework's score and final examination. The independent variable is cluster membership, and the dependent variables are the clustering variables and two non-clustering variables. The results will show that there are significant differences between clusters on most of these variables with the p-value being below 0.05. The significant F statistics provide an evidence that each of the five clusters is distinctive.

References

1. Alpaydin, E.: Introduction to Machine Learning, 2nd edn. MIT Press, Cambridge (2010)
2. Biggs, J.B.: Teaching for Quality Learning at University: What the Student Does, 2nd edn. Society for Research into Higher Education/Open University Press, Phildelphia/Buckingham (2003)
3. Hong Kong Institution of Engineers: Professional Accreditation Handbook (Engineering Degrees). Accreditation Board, pp. 1–35 (2013)
4. Kwan, C.L.C.: Identifying at-risk students from course-specific predictive analytics. In: 27th International Conference on Computers in Education, pp. 356–360 (2019)
5. Lackey, L.W., Lackey, W.J., Grady, H.M., Davis, M.T.: Efficacy of using a single, non-technical variable to predict the academic success of freshmen engineering students. J. Eng. Educ. **92**(1), 41–48 (2003)
6. Lu, O., Huang, A., Huang, J., Lin, A., Ogata, H., Yang, S.J.H.: Applying learning analytics for the early prediction of students' academic performance in blended learning. J. Educ. Technol. Soc. **21**(2), 220–232 (2018)
7. Macfadyen, L.P., Dawson, S.: Mining LMS data to develop an "early warning system" for educators: a proof of concept. Comput. Educ. **54**(2), 588–599 (2010)
8. Marbouti, F., Diefes-Dux, H.A., Strobel, J.: Building course-specific regression-based models to identify at-risk students. In: The American Society for Engineering Educators Annual Conference, Seattle, WA (2015)
9. Mulryan-Kyne, C.: Teaching large classes at college and university level: challenges and opportunities. Teach. High. Educ. **15**(2), 175–185 (2010)
10. Olani, A.: Predicting first year university students' academic success. Electron. J. Res. Educ. Psychol. **7**(3), 1053–1072 (2009)
11. Sazhin, S.: Teaching mathematics to engineering students. Int. J. Eng. Educ. **14**, 145–152 (1998)

Where Are the Students? A Study of Norwegian Technology Students' Perceptions of Emerging Trends in Higher Education

Frode Eika Sandnes[1,2(✉)]

[1] Oslo Metropolitan University, 0130 Oslo, Norway
frodes@oslomet.no
[2] Kristiania University College, 0153 Oslo, Norway

Abstract. Teachers in higher education in Norway have over the last decade reported reduced physical attendance in lectures, students not using the textbooks, and low academic performance. Also, there is an intensified institutional pressure to make use of digital tools and flipped classroom paradigms. To obtain better insight into students' perceptions of these issues a class of computer science students' perceptions were probed using a comprehensive questionnaire. The results confirm some of the claims that students want more digital learning such as videos, but perhaps not as black and white as it is often presented. Implications of the results is that one should not simply follow a single approach but employ an array of varied learning activities and materials.

Keywords: Student perceptions · Learning activities · Student preferences · Active learning · Textbook · Reading skill · Writing skill · Variation

1 Introduction

There are several key issues that emerged in higher education over the last decade and some claim that higher education is undergoing a major transformation. One of the widely discussed topics is that of distance education [1, 2] and digital education [3] where students can engage in learning activities across time and place. Issues such as MOOCs (Massive Open Online Courses) have received much attention [4]. More specifically, the use of streamed lectures and recorded lectures is a topic that is much discussed [5].

Another issue is to rely on the classical textbook versus emerging media [6]. Textbooks are often quality assured, and they are either purchased or borrowed. Traditionally, textbooks were only on printed paper but are increasingly being offered in electronic format [7]. However, the traditional textbook regime is being challenged by open and freely available online resources. Such resources take on many forms from freely available books, articles, blogs, discussion forums and videos.

Third, the student and teacher populations are becoming increasingly diverse [8, 9]. Student diversity evolves around multiple dimensions such as motivation and aspiration [10], background, and experience as well as socioeconomic and cultural backgrounds. The needs of such student populations are also diverse. The need for individual follow-up seems more important than ever.

Yet, as reported by many educators, auditoriums rapidly become sparse as the semester starts, students report not acquiring the textbooks, students do not contact the teachers – at least the students who should be contacting the teacher. The motivation of this study was therefore to obtain insight into students' perception of key questions related to current pedagogical issues. Our previous studies of student perceptions have been used to probe a range of issues including plagiarism [11], university life [12], internationalization and cultural differences [13], choice of university [14], learning tools [15], to mention a few. It was decided to focus this study on the use of the classic textbook, students' future plans, and students prior experience including prior higher education studies and work experience. Pedagogical issues addressed included the use of video or streaming versus traditional lectures, group versus individual learning, exams versus portfolio examinations, and so forth. Issues related to learning management systems [16] and digital organization of learning materials [17] were not addressed in this study.

2 Method

2.1 Experimental Design

A questionnaire-based study was chosen with mostly closed questions. Some questions were designed to allow for between group analyses, in particular for dividing students along the lines of those who have acquired the textbook, who had previous higher education experience (previous degree), previous work experience and future study plans.

2.2 Context

The questionnaire was employed in an undergraduate course of Human Computer Interaction where the students are taught a curriculum covered according to a traditional textbook [18]. This course is predominantly lecture-based but lectures are voluntary. The focus is on active learning through work on three projects, in which two are group works and one is individual work. One of these group projects involves design thinking which is intended to show train the students to get value from collaborating in teams [19]. The second group project involves a controlled empirical experiment [20–22]. The course is assessed based on a portfolio comprising three reports resulting from the three practical projects. Students get formative feedback on the projects and could submit a revised portfolio for assessment. The teacher was available for consultation and supervision throughout the semester.

2.3 Participants

Approximately 150 students were initially taking the course. The total number is approximate as some students sign up late and some students drop off and there is therefore no well-defined total number. A total of 42 students responded to the questionnaire yielding an approximate response rate of 28%. The questionnaire was anonymous and no information about demographic details were collected.

2.4 Materials

A comprehensive questionnaire with 58 questions were designed. Most of the questions were closed with 46 5-item Likert scale questions, 4 yes/no questions and 8 open free-text questions. The questionnaire addressed students' attitudes towards textbooks, streaming and video, details of the curriculum and usefulness and relevance. The questionnaire was implemented using Google forms.

2.5 Procedure

The questionnaire was distributed electronically during two weeks of October 2019 as part of the midterm course evaluation. This approach was chosen to prevent introducing an additional questionnaire but instead integrate the additional research-oriented questions as part of the regular obligatory course evaluation questionnaire to prevent evaluation fatigue. The questionnaire was totally anonymous and voluntary. The results were later presented and discussed in class and used as a case for statistical analysis and hence incorporated as part of the curriculum.

2.6 Analysis

The results of the questionnaire were analyzed using the statistical software JASP version 0.11.0.0 [23]. Non-parametric statistical tests (mostly Mann-Whitney U tests) were used as the Likert responses were ordinal. Only the questions related to the research questions are discussed herein. The questions related to the general course evaluation are not discussed herein.

3 Results

3.1 General Results

Figure 1 shows general responses to the questions. On the two extreme ends of the scale the results indicate that students were very much in favor of portfolio evaluation over traditional exams and video lectures – these items also have also few neutral responses. On the lower end of the scale, students were not in favor of student presentations in class. Students appears to have prioritized coursework over part-time jobs.

On the higher end of the scale students prefer a mixture of physical and video lectures, value developing writing abilities, students tend to prioritize other courses over the current course, value developing reading abilities, prefer fixed assignments over free assignments and value social interaction.

The responses to the remaining questions appear balanced on the scale and appear neutral, that is regarding students' opinions about the incorporation about research

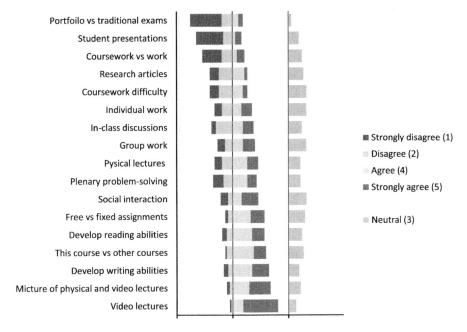

Fig. 1. Distribution of overall responses illustrated as a diverging stacked bar chart with issues sorted according to their responses falling on the left to the right side of the scale. Magenta responses (left) indicate the lower end of the Likert scales (1 and 2), and green responses (middle) indicate the higher end of the Likert scales (4 and 5). Grey (right) indicates neutral responses (3). (Color figure online)

articles, individual work, in-class discussions, group work, physical lectures and plenary problem solving.

3.2 Effect of Textbook

Of the responses 21 had acquired the course textbook and 16 had not. When separating the responses according the students who have acquired the textbook several interesting differences were observed among the two groups. First, there was a significant difference in how the two groups valued the importance of developing ones writing abilities ($W = 235.0$, $p = .034$). Those who had preferred the textbook had ranked the importance of developing writing abilities higher ($M = 4.1$, $SD = 0.8$) than those who had not acquired the textbook ($M = 3.1$, $SD = 1.5$). There was also a significant difference in the desire to have more scientific research articles in the curriculum ($W = 75.0$, $p = .013$). Those who had not acquired the textbook exhibited more positive responses towards more academic articles ($M = 3.4$, $SD = 1.2$) than the students who had acquired the textbook ($M = 2.3$, $SD = 1.0$).

There was also a significant difference between the two groups in terms of how easy they found the textbook ($W = 182.0$, $p = .022$), how interesting it as ($W = 209.0$, $p < 0.001$), and how relevant it was ($W = 201.5$, $p = .003$). Students who had acquired the textbook found it easier ($M = 4.6$, $SD = 3.7$) versus ($M = 3.7$, $SD = 1.2$) more interesting ($M = 4.1$, $SD = 1.1$) versus ($M = 2.8$, $SD = 1.0$) and more relevant ($M = 4.5$, $SD = 0.8$) versus ($M = 3.3$, $SD = 1.2$). There was no significant difference in the perceived cost of the textbook ($W = 180.5$, $p = .106$) as the mean indicate a neutral response ($M = 2.50$, $SD = 1.161$). Moreover, there was no significant difference in the perceived importance of training to read difficult texts ($W = 200.0$, $p = 0.317$) as the mean responses tended towards neutral ($M = 3.5$, $SD = 1.2$). Moreover, there were no differences across these student groups in any desire to have more video lectures ($W = 177.0$, $p = .764$) as both groups indicated that they would prefer more video-based lectures ($M = 4.4$, $SD = 1.0$). Moreover, both groups indicated a preference for a mix of traditional lectures and videos ($M = 3.9$, $SD = 1.2$). The perception of the importance of the traditional lectures was close to neutral ($M = 3.2$, $SD = 1.3$).

3.3 Effect of Plans for Further Study

Of the 42 participants 21 indicated that they had ambitions to pursue further education, while 16 did not express such plans. There was a significant difference between these two groups in terms of desire for more video lectures ($W = 234.0$, $p = .021$), as the students with plans for further education were more positive towards more video lectures ($M = 4.6$, $SD = 0.9$) than those without such plans ($M = 4.0$, $SD = 1.1$). There also a significant difference in attitude towards working alone ($W = 103.0$, $p = .042$). The students who wanted to continue their studies were significantly less enthusiastic about working alone ($M = 2.7$, $SD = 1.3$) compared to those who did not want to continue to study after obtaining their degree ($M = 3.6$, $SD = 1.2$). There was also a significant difference in the perceived price of the textbook ($W = 200$, $p = .045$) as those who had plans for further education perceived the textbook as less expensive ($M = 2.8$, $SD = 1.1$) than those who had no further study plans ($M = 2.1$, $SD = 1.5$). Interestingly, there were no observed significant differences in attitudes towards developing writing abilities ($W = 187.0$, $p = .555$), developing abilities for reading advanced texts ($W = 189$, $p = .505$), freedom to choose topics for assignments ($W = 191.5$, $p = .464$), and the inclusion of more scientific articles in the curriculum ($W = 173.0$, $p = .440$).

3.4 Effects of Prior Work Experience

Of the respondents who replied 18 indicated that they had several years of work experience prior to their current studies, while 19 participants did not have any work experience. When analyzing the data according to these two groups only one significant difference could be observed, namely that of the perceived useful knowledge acquired through the course ($W = 107.0$, $p = .048$). Those who had no previous work experience were more positive about what they have learned ($M = 3.7$, $SD = 0.9$) compared to those who had previous work experience ($M = 2.8$, $SD = 1.5$). Interestingly, there was no significant difference between the groups in their perceptions of how useful the course was to be in their future profession ($W = 109.5$, $p = .056$). Overall, students were moderately positive towards the usefulness of the course ($M = 3.5$, $SD = 1.4$). There was also no observed difference in attitudes over prioritizing part-time jobs over attending curricular activities ($W = 157.0$, $p = .671$). Respondents indicated a negative attitude towards prioritizing part-time work ($M = 2.5$, $SD = 1.4$).

3.5 Effects of Prior Higher-Education Experience

Of the valid responses 9 students indicated having studied at higher level prior to the current study while 28 had not studied at higher levels before. There were two noticeable differences between these two groups, namely in the opinion about the adequacy of groups problem solving activities ($W = 64.0$, $p = .026$) and the perception of the task difficulties ($W = 44.0$, $p = .003$). Those with no previous study experiences expressed a stronger indication that there were too little plenary based problem-solving activities ($M = 2.1$, $SD = 1.5$) compared to those who had studied before ($M = 3.4$, $SD = 1.2$). Moreover, those who had not studied before found the coursework more difficult ($M = 3.1$, $SD = 1.1$) than those with previous study experience ($M = 1.8$, $SD = 1.0$). No significant differences could be observed for the importance of physical lectures ($W = 122.0$, $p = .899$), more video lectures ($W = 108.0$, $p = .475$), usefulness of class discussions ($W = 95.0$, $p = .267$), social contact with other students ($W = 144.0$, $p = .521$), preferences for group work ($W = 94.5$, $p = .259$), compulsory student presentations ($W = 143.5$, $p = .518$), exams versus portfolio evaluation ($W = 143.5$, $p = .503$), importance of improving writing abilities ($W = 128$, $p = 0.956$), abilities to read advanced texts ($W = 94.0$, $p = .248$) and preference for freedom in choosing assignments ($W = 111.5$, $p = .606$).

4 Discussions

4.1 Effects of Textbooks

The results confirm the author's impression that only a fraction of the students acquires and actively uses the textbook, either through purchase, or via library loans. It is quite interesting that students who use the textbook were also more concerned with their writing abilities. One possible explanation is that some students were more text oriented and if they prefer to read, they may also prefer to write, or value the importance of good writing skills. On the other hands, students who were more hands-on who like to learn by trial and error rather than reading, may also be more interested in the actual artefacts created rather than describing these artefacts in words. One may also wonder whether the teachers who themselves usually are academically trained are text oriented and expect students to be so too, while some student may just want to get their degree and pursue a practical profession. On the other hand, although computer science is a practical field involving development and coding, it also involves reading of complex documentation and writing of the same documentation although the focus on documenting code has become less than what is used to be as code is to be self-documenting. Another speculation is that students may have an inflated belief in writing tools such as Grammarly [24].

It is somewhat surprising that the students who actively used the textbook were less in favor of using more research articles. On possible explanation could be that some students like predictability and system and a textbook with a complete presentation of the syllabus may be an attractive benefit, while a set of research articles may come across as less organized and more chaotic. Why those who do not actively use the textbook were more positive towards research articles could be explained that they are usually free of charge, or that articles can be more updated knowledge if used in such a manner, and present a topic in a more focused manner compared to an introductory textbook.

The students who used the textbook were all more positive regarding the textbook in terms of how easy it was to use, how interesting it was and how relevant it was. This raises the important question about how the students who do not use the textbook could form an opinion about the book without having used it? Could it be that they had browsed the textbook in a bookstore or library and decided that is was not suitable for them, or were these responses based on an impression of textbooks in general? The results did not support the commonly held impression that students do not purchase textbooks due to their high cost.

The results did not show any evidence that textbook users were less in favor of say videos than those who do not use textbooks. The results could be interpreted as if students would like more videos, but not just videos. It seems the variety, and balance of traditional lectures, reading and video when these respective parts are applied sensibly, will contribute to learning.

It is somewhat concerning that the students in general, irrespective of being text/textbook oriented or not, did not find it important to develop their abilities to read difficult texts. Could this be because the students had not been exposed to sufficiently difficult texts in their studies, or is it because they did not realize that they most likely would have to read advanced documentation in their future careers?

4.2 Effect of Plans for Further Study

Students who reported ambitions for further study were both more positive towards video lectures and group work than those who did not want to continue studying after their degree. One possible explanation for these results is that a student who has further study plans may by natural selection be more academically inclined and thereby more independent with respect to getting hands-on help from the teachers. Yet, one could argue that to appreciate the benefits of group work and slowing larger problems in collaboration with their peers.

Students who were interested in further study also did not perceive the textbook as expensive as those who did not want to continue studying. Again, could the perception of textbook cost be linked to the appreciation of the actual value of textbooks? Will a lower appreciation of the textbook result in the perception of higher cost?

It is a matter of concern that there was no difference between these two groups in how they valued the importance of academic articles as an academic research article is the stable ingredient of a researcher's life and we should expect that students who were purposing further study would have matured in their attitude towards research articles. The results indicate that students were quite impartial to the use of research articles in the curriculum. Perhaps students need to be better prepared for further education by motivating them for the importance and the general relevance of research articles? Also, it is concerning that there was no difference between the groups in terms of improving writing skills and abilities to read advanced texts as these are core academic skills needed in higher education. However, the scores were on the positive side for both groups suggesting that these skills were valued by most students.

4.3 Effects of Prior Work Experience

Although students were moderately positive towards the benefits of the course the students with prior work experience were less so compared to those without work experience. Possible explanations for this observation could be that the course perhaps is too theoretical and not sufficiently practical and therefore not matching their expectations. Or, perhaps these more experienced students simply were more critical than students recently finished secondary school? Another explanation could be that some of the students with prior work experience were already familiar with some of the contents of the curriculum such that they do not perceive that they have learned as much. However, it is also likely that their former work experience is not related to their future career plans and if so, the curriculum should cover new elements. The fact that there was no difference between the groups in terms of perceived usefulness for future career support this view that past working experience is different from the future career. The respondents therefore might have been unable to make an informed assessment of this question.

The results suggest that students do not prioritize jobs over studies. This is contrary to the impressions by the author and colleagues as students often report that they were unable to attend lectures and supervision meetings due to job obligations. Consequently, if students do not attend optional learning activities there may be other causes. Perhaps students do not find enough value to merit the investment of time and effort to attend?

4.4 Effects of Prior Higher-Education Experience

Students without previous higher education experience found there to be too little plenary problem-solving activities (typical of primary and secondary school), as well as finding the coursework more difficult is as we would expect. Students with more experience have learned to become more independent and tackle more difficult problems.

The results also revealed that there were no differences in perceptions of learning writing and learning skills. This is somewhat surprising as one would expect more experienced students to have realized the importance of written communication. But the scores were generally positive, and it may therefore be unrealistic to observe any difference.

4.5 Limitations

As the questionnaire was anonymous it is not possible to analyze the responses according to who attended lectures and not. In hindsight, a control question about lecture attending habits should have been included. One could expect that the perceptions of those who do regularly attend lectures and those who do not could be somewhat different.

5 Conclusions

A questionnaire-based study is reported where the goal was to probe students' perceptions towards emerging pedagogical issues in higher education. The results in general align with the new pedagogical ideas. In conclusion, the results support a mixed approach with a variety of learning activities and delivery methods are applied instead of just a single "silver-bullet" fix-it-all approach. One should also be careful not to necessarily follow requests from students uncritically, as students may prescribe the wrong medicine for "symptoms" that may be better addressed using other means.

References

1. Shih, T.K., Antoni, G.D., Arndt, T., Asirvatham, A., Chang, C.T., Chee, Y.S., et al.: A survey of distance education challenges and technologies. Int. J. Distance Educ. Technol. **1**(1), 1–20 (2003)
2. Gunawardena, C.N., McIsaac, M.S.: Distance education. In: Handbook of Research on Educational Communications and Technology, pp. 361–401. Routledge (2013)
3. Reeves, T.C.: Storms clouds on the digital education horizon. J. Comput. High. Educ. **15**(3) (2003). http://doi.org/10.1007/BF02940850
4. Ebben, M., Murphy, J.S.: Unpacking MOOC scholarly discourse: a review of nascent MOOC scholarship. Learn. Media Technol. **39**(3), 328–345 (2014)
5. Chen, C.M., Wu, C.H.: Effects of different video lecture types on sustained attention, emotion, cognitive load, and learning performance. Comput. Educ. **80**, 108–121 (2015)
6. Albrecht, U.V., Folta-Schoofs, K., Behrends, M., Von Jan, U.: Effects of mobile augmented reality learning compared to textbook learning on medical students: randomized controlled pilot study. J. Med. Internet Res. **15**(8), e182 (2013)
7. Irvine, V., Code, J., Richards, L.: Realigning higher education for the 21st-century learner through multi-access learning. MERLOT J. Online Learn. Teach. **9**(2), 172–186 (2013)
8. Lee, O., Luykx, A.: Science education and student diversity: race/ethnicity, language, culture, and socioeconomic status. In: Handbook of Research on Science Education, vol. 1, pp. 171–197 (2007)
9. El-Khawas, E.: The many dimensions of student diversity. In: Student Services: A Handbook for the Profession, vol. 4, pp. 45–52 (2003)
10. Law, K.M., Sandnes, F.E., Jian, H.L., Huang, Y.P.: A comparative study of learning motivation among engineering students in South East Asia and beyond. Int. J. Eng. Educ. **25**(1), 144–151 (2009)
11. Jian, H.-L., Sandnes, F.E., Huang, Y.-P., Cai, L., Law, K.: On students' strategy-preferences for managing difficult course work. IEEE Trans. Educ. **51**, 157–165 (2008)

12. Jian, H.L., Sandnes, F.E., Huang, Y.P., Huang, Y.M., Hagen, S.: Studies or leisure?: a cross-cultural comparison of Taiwanese and Norwegian engineering students' preferences for university life. Int. J. Eng. Educ. **26**, 227–235 (2010)
13. Jian, H.-L., Sandnes, F.E., Huang, Y.-P., Huang, Y.-M., Hagen, S.: Towards harmonious East-West educational partnerships: a study of cultural differences between Taiwanese and Norwegian engineering students. Asia Pac. Educ. Rev. **11**, 585–595 (2010)
14. Jian, H.L., Sandnes, F.E., Huang, Y.P., Huang, Y.M.: Cultural factors influencing Eastern and Western engineering students' choice of university. Eur. J. Eng. Educ. **35**, 147–160 (2010)
15. Jian, H.-L., Sandnes, F.E., Huang, Y.-P., Law, K., Huang, Y.-M.: The role of electronic pocket dictionaries as an English learning tool among Chinese students. J. Comput. Assist. Learn. **25**, 503–514 (2009)
16. McGill, T.J., Klobas, J.E.: A task–technology fit view of learning management system impact. Comput. Educ. **52**(2), 496–508 (2009)
17. Sandnes, F.E., Eika, E.: A simple MVC-framework for local management of online course material. In: Uskov, V.L., Howlett, R.J., Jain, L.C. (eds.) SEEL 2017. SIST, vol. 75, pp. 143–153. Springer, Cham (2018). https://doi.org/10.1007/978-3-319-59451-4_15
18. Sandnes, F.E.: Universell utforming av IKT-systemer, 2nd edn. Universitetsforlaget, Oslo (2018)
19. Sandnes, F.E., Eika, E., Medola, F.O.: Improving the usability of interactive systems by incorporating design thinking into the engineering process: raising computer science students' awareness of quality versus quantity in ideation. In: 2019 5th Experiment International Conference, pp. 172–176. IEEE (2019)
20. Sandnes, F.E., Eika, E., Medola, F.O.: Towards a framework for the design of quantitative experiments: human-computer interaction and accessibility research. In: Antona, M., Stephanidis, C. (eds.) UAHCI 2018. LNCS, vol. 10907, pp. 107–120. Springer, Cham (2018). https://doi.org/10.1007/978-3-319-92049-8_8
21. Sandnes, F.E., Eika, E.: Statistics-IDE: supporting the design of empirical experiments for non-experts during early stages of research projects. In: Karwowski, W., Ahram, T. (eds.) IHSI 2018. AISC, vol. 722, pp. 502–507. Springer, Cham (2018). https://doi.org/10.1007/978-3-319-73888-8_78
22. Sandnes, F.E., Eika, E.: Hostage of the software: experiences in teaching inferential statistics to undergraduate human-computer interaction students and a survey of the literature. In: Mikropoulos, T.A. (ed.) Research on e-Learning and ICT in Education. SIST, pp. 167–183. Springer, Cham (2018). https://doi.org/10.1007/978-3-319-95059-4_10
23. JASP Team: JASP (Version 0.11.1) [Computer software] (2019)
24. Kaushik, H.M., Eika, E., Sandnes, F.E.: Towards universal accessibility on the web: do grammar checking tools improve text readability? In: Antona, M., Stephanidis, C. (eds.) HCII 2020. LNCS, vol. 12188, pp. 272–288. Springer, Cham (2020). https://doi.org/10.1007/978-3-030-49282-3_19

Emerging Issues and Trends in Education

A Study of Learner's Computational Thinking Using Constructivist Universal Design Learning Package for Kindergarten Education

Chinnaphat Junruang and Issara Kanjug(✉)

Department of Educational Technology, Faculty of Education,
Khon Kaen University, Khon Kaen, Thailand
issaraka@kku.ac.th

Abstract. Computational Thinking has been defined as an important skill for students to have in learning, both from early childhood to college. To be able to deal with common problems in daily life as well as other problems Easily and systematically Combined with the advancement of science and technology Resulting in the development of artificial intelligence Resulting in human adaptation and learning the basic principles of artificial intelligence. The purpose of this research was study learners' computational thinking. The research participants were 40 kindergarten academic year 2019 students of Demonstration school of Khonkaen University. Experimental research was employed in this study. The instruments used in the experiment were Constructivist Universal Design Learning Package for Kindergarten Education. Data collection used the computational thinking test for kindergarteners. The results revealed that: the Learners' computational thinking average score was 9.33 or 77.50%. Computational thinking of learners is at a good level.

Keywords: Constructivist learning environment · Universal design for learning · Computational thinking · Learning innovation · Kindergarten Education

1 Introduction

Computational thinking is a skill that has been talked about a lot in modern times. Which is an important skill in problem solving using computer problem solving process [1]. Combined with the advancement of science and technology That humans have created technology or artificial intelligence That is as intelligent as humans It can think logically and reasonably. Make decisions and learn by themselves, called "Artificial Intelligence (AI)". Therefore, to be able to live in a dynamic world and constantly changing, that is, computational thinking. Computational Thinking is the prerequisite skill for understanding the technologies of the future. It is a thought process, rather than a specific body of knowledge about a device or language. Computational thinking is often associated with computers and coding, but it is important to note that it can be taught without a device. For that reason, computational thinking can be a part of any classroom, including the classrooms of our youngest learners in the primary grades. And, I would argue, it is quickly becoming a necessary foundational skill for students.

By explicitly teaching, and allowing space for the development of, computational thinking, teachers can ensure that their young students are learning to think in a way that will allow them to access and understand their digital world. Teaching computational thinking, in short, primes students for future success. Furthermore, it can be integrated into existing routines and curricula [2]. Ability in problem solving of preschool children and found that Problem solving in children aged 1 or 2 years can easily solve problems. And is a problem that is not complicated Until the child grows up, so he can solve simple problems and is a problem that is not complicated Until children grow up to be able to solve complex problems better. [3] Therefore, it is necessary to cultivate computational thinking from kindergarten to education in order to prepare according to the theory of development according to age. To the next level of complex thinking

Learning environment Is a new context in teaching design in which designers have to create situations or important events for learners with evaluation By allowing students to interact with various sources of knowledge In a variety of ways In which the learners are actively involved in the learning process And the new trend of learning theories that give more importance to learning than teaching is constructivist Therefore, the principles of environmental design in learning are based on constructivist concepts. As basic principles in design to promote computational thinking in conjunction with Universal design for learning (UDL) are well suited with each other because universal design for learning is "a systematic decision-making method for differentiation" [4]. While UDL is a principle for design curriculum that provides each learner equal opportunities to learn and support different learning need of divers student in inclusive classroom by using flexible instructional materials, teaching methods, and assessment. In this study Designing media for organizing learning experiences for a variety of formats and methods of accessing learning According to the characteristics of the learners with various learning styles Consists of 3 important principles which are 1) Representation 2) Action & Expression and 3) Engagement [5].

Therefore, the principles of constructivist learning environment in accordance with the Universal Design Principles are used as the basis for the Learning Package design to promote computational thinking for students in kindergarten.

2 Literature Review

2.1 Computational Thinking

Computational Thinking as solving problems designing systems, and understanding human behavior, by drawing on the concepts fundamental to computer science." [1]. Computational thinking skills in early childhood are included abstraction, algorithm, decomposition and Pattern Recognition Apart from exploring the effectiveness of such CT courses for K-12 students, the degree of preparedness of the teachers in teaching CT is another important issue. When CT becomes a necessary form of literacy all around the world, it will not only be a kind of expertise that, stereotypically, only computer engineers use. On the contrary, everyone should have positive attitudes toward CT in order to understand and make use of it.

2.2 Constructivist Learning Environment

The constructivist estimate of learning can be discover to Piaget [6] who believed that learning is not pass on passively but attained through well-defined stages by active participation of a learner. [7] Designing an environment for student centered. Blending between media and method base on Constructivist theory [8] with online learning by using technology and internet.

2.3 Universal Design for Learning

Universal design for learning (UDL) is a principle for instructional designing by using flexible instructional materials, teaching methods, and assessment in order to provide access to a wide range of students with and without disabilities in inclusive classroom [9]. Universally designed structures are more usable not only for individuals with disabilities but also has led to improved usability for everyone [10] In this Constructivist Learning Environment, the principles of designing a learning environment are combined with universal design principles. By providing a variety of learning materials such as images, videos, sounds, multimedia so that students can access learning equally and efficiently.

3 Method and Result

3.1 Research Participants

The target group of this research were students in kindergarten level 1, Demonstration School, Khon Kaen University. Kindergarten Department That are currently studying in the second semester, academic year 2019. A total of 40 people. The sample was chosen by Purposive Sampling. The average age of the students was 4.

3.2 Assessment Tool – Computational Thinking Ability Test

The learning performance of computational thinking includes four component of CT which are abstraction, algorithm, decomposition, and Pattern Recognition. In study, the research tools included the post-test of the computational thinking. The computational thinking test sheets were developed by teachers. There is a way to find quality by checking by experts. Evaluation Which has the following development steps 1) Study the theoretical concepts and research related to computational thinking the study uses the Wing 2006 framework. 2) Create a subjective test By defining the test of 4 items that cover all 4 elements of computational thinking which are the identification of the elements, finding the abstract thinking patterns and the algorithm 3) Create scoring rubrics for evaluating computational thinking from the above tests The researcher has assigned the scoring criteria in each question into 4 ranges from 0–3 points. 4) Set criteria for evaluating the students' computational thinking the researcher evaluated the computational thinking skills according to the 6 level criteria of Ling [15]. 5) Present the test and evaluation criteria which have been inspected by the advisor to the expert To determine the consistency between the exams and the learning objectives (Index of

Item Objective Congruence (IOC), including examining the characteristics of questions and the correctness of language usage According to the expert's consideration, all 4 tests have found that all tests have a consistency index of 0.67–1.00, which is considered to have passed the IOC of 0.5 or more, which the researcher has adjusted. Quiz to be more appropriate according to the recommendations of experts.

3.3 Experimental Process

Before the experiment, the students were given time to get used to the Constructivist Universal Design Learning Package for Kindergarten Education. Figure 1 shows the flow chart of the experiment. Each period in the computer class is 60 min in kindergarten school. At the beginning, the instructor spent 1 weeks teaching introduce learners about learning with a constructivist learning environment about component and how to use.

Thereafter, 8 weeks was spend on the enhancement of applying the four phases of CT and the integration of blockbased programming in a sixth-grade Mathematics course. After the effectiveness of involving the CT process with mathematics was confirmed in study one, this part (three periods) was later demonstrated in the teacher training course for the newly appointed principals to experience and observe the common sense of involving CT processes in learning. The students practiced this method six times, each time taking half a period. Therefore, there were totally six situated examples implemented during the three periods of the mathematics course.

Finally, they also spent one period on the post-test of the pen-and-paper-based mathematics test for measuring their learning achievements. There were totally 15 periods spent on the experiment, which lasted for a total of around three-fourth of a semester (i.e., 15 weeks). The experimental treatment after the pre-test was 5 weeks.

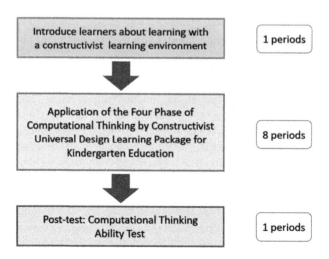

Fig. 1. Experimental process.

3.4 Learning Assistive

The participants used Constructivist Universal Design Learning Package for Kindergarten Education to learning. This series of the parts are shown in Fig. 2. This set of Learning Package is divided into two sections: the online learning material and the offline learning material in the classroom. First use Let's start with the problem situation. The teacher will guide students with problem situations before class. In which students will choose what kind of media they want to hear from. It has been prepared according to international design principles, divided into stills, audio and multimedia. The second step allows the learner to complete the learning mission. If stuck or need help can Get scans at the aid base or consult an expert to balance knowledge based on the cognitive constructivist theory. Through the learning of Constructivist Universal Design Learning Package for Kindergarten Education, participants could apply what they had learned into real-life and face the challenges in the future at a higher level.

Fig. 2. Constructivist Universal Design Learning Package for Kindergarten Education to learning.

4 Results and Discussion

4.1 Computational Thinking Ability

After applying the Constructivist Universal Design Learning Package for Kindergarten Education, the results of the learner's computational thinking ability test were analysis using Mean and S.D. The performances of the computational thinking ability overall average score was 9.33 or 77.50%, representing the computational thinking skill evaluation level at level 5, meaning good level, which was higher than the specified criteria 70% of the full score. Separated by computational thinking elements. The separation of elements the mean score was 2.05, or 68.3%. In the search for patterns, the score was 2.68 or 89.17%. The abstract thinking had a mean of 2.18, the mean score of 72.50 and the algorithm. Have an average score of 2.40, or 80.00% (Table 1 and Fig. 3).

Table 1. The learners' computational thinking ability.

No.	List assessment	Results of the expert (Percentage)	Results of the expert (Percentage)
1.	Decomposition	2.05	68.30
2.	Pattern recognition	2.68	89.17
3.	Abstraction	2.18	72.50
4.	Algorithm	2.40	80.00
		9.33	77.50
	Total	**9.33**	**77.50**

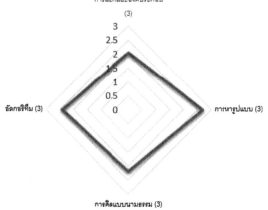

Fig. 3. The learners' computational thinking.

4.2 Discussion and Future Work

The learner has computational thinking ability in which the computational thinking elements are: 1) Decomposition 2) Pattern Recognition 3) Abstraction and 4) Algorithm. The results of this research are consistent with the research of Palts and Pedaste [14], which indicated that the nature of learning management that promotes computational thinking should begin by defining or defining a problem. Then find solutions to problems, plan designs and choose solutions. Therefore, the learning management characteristics according to STEM Education can develop students' computational thinking ability in line [17], stating that the practice of computational thinking ability can be used. Learning management through STEM education activities because it is based on using the problem as the base Problem situations are defined to challenge thinking and generate interest in students. In addition [14], stated that learning management according to STEM study allows students to think and design work pieces. Design solutions to problems that are based on real-life contexts. It can encourage students to have the ability to solve problems. This ability is related to computational thinking ability [1, 13, 16].

Future work includes in-depth discussion and analysis of the correlation of additional dimensions such as creative thinking, trial and errors and critical thinking.

References

1. Computational thinking Communications of the ACM. http://www.cs.cmu.edu/afs/cs/usr/wing/www/publications/Wing06.pdfMarkB. Accessed 10 June 2018
2. Early Learning Strategies for Developing Computational Thinking Skills. https://www.gettingsmart.com/2018/03/early-learning-strategies-for-developing-computational-thinking-skills/. Accessed 22 Oct 2019
3. Computational thinking in STEM classroom. https://robomatter.com/blog-ct-in-stem-classroom/. Accessed 22 Oct 2019
4. Udvari-Solner, A., Villa, R., Thousand, J.: Access to the general education curriculum for all: the universal design process. In: Villa, R., Thousand, J. (eds.) Creating an Inclusive School, pp. 134–154. Association for Supervision and Curriculum Development (ASCD), Alexandria (2005)
5. Hall, T., Stahl, S.: Using universal design of learning to expand access to higher education. In: Adams, M., Brown, S. (eds.) Towards Inclusive Learning in Higher Education: Developing Curricula for Disabled Students. Routledge, New York (2006)
6. Piaget, J.: The Construction of Reality in the Child. Ballantine Books (1975)
7. Vygotsky, L.S.: Mind in Society: The Development of Higher Psychological Processes. Harvard University Press, Cambridge (1980)
8. Jonassen, D.H.: Designing constructivist learning environments. In: Reigeluth, C.M. (ed.) Instructional-Design Theories and Models: A New Paradigm of Instructional Theory, vol. 2, pp. 215–239. Lawrence Erlbaum Associates, Mahwah (1999)
9. Haager, D., Klingner, J.: Differentiating Instruction in Inclusive Classrooms: The Special Educator's Guide. Pearson Education, Boston (2005)
10. Hall, T., Strangman, N., Meyer, A.: Differentiated instruction and implications for UDL implementation: Effective classroom practices report. National Center on Accessing the General Curriculum (2003)
11. Brackmann, C., Román-González, M., Robles, G., Moreno-León, J., Casali, A., Barone, D.: Development of computational thinking skills through unplugged activities in primary school (2017)
12. Palts, T., Pedaste, M.: Model of learning computational thinking. A new culture of learning: computing and next generations. In: The IFIP TC3 Working Conference Preliminary Proceedings, Vilnius University, Lithuania (2015)
13. Aho, A.V.: Computation and computational thinking. Comput. J. **55**, 832–835 (2012)

14. Chimkul, A.: Effects of biology learning management under the STEM education concept on abilities. In problem solving and biology class achievement of high school students (Master of Education), Department of Science Education Department of Curriculum and Instruction Chulalongkorn University (2016)
15. Ling, L.U., Saibin, C.T., Naharu, N., Labadin, J., Aziz, A.N.: An evaluation tool to measure computational thinking skills: pilot investigation. In: Bildiri, ICOTAL 2018, Melaka, Malaysia (2018)
16. Gonzalez, M.R., Gonzalez, J.P., Fernandez, C.J.: Which cognitive abilities underlie computational thinking? Criterion validity of the computational thinking test. Comput. Hum. Behav. **72**, 678–691 (2016)
17. Supkerd, S.: Learning activities. To strengthen computational thinking by Management of STEM education Academic program and application Secondary School Year 4 Anukulnari School (Master of Education), Computer Education Graduate school Rajabhat Maha Sarakham University (2016)

Constructing an Information Search Platform Using Data Mining to Improve Student Learning

Shu-Chen Cheng[1], Yu-Ping Cheng[2], Yueh-Min Huang[2(✉)], and I. Robert Chiang[3]

[1] Department of Computer Science and Information Engineering, Southern Taiwan University of Science and Technology, Tainan, Taiwan
kittyc@stust.edu.tw
[2] Department of Engineering Science, National Cheng Kung University, Tainan, Taiwan
n98061513@gs.ncku.edu.tw, huang@mail.ncku.edu.tw
[3] Gabelli School of Business, Fordham University, New York, USA
ichiang@fordham.edu

Abstract. There has been an ongoing proliferation of online articles and other materials on the World Wide Web for e-learning. Although a generic search engine can be used to find materials in a subject domain (for example, computer science,) the search results often have advertising, media, and news mixed in. To improve the search quality, in this study an information search platform based on data mining technology was constructed. Using term frequency-inverse document frequency (TF-IDF), this platform calculates all terms in each web article to automatically filter out non-computer science category keywords and articles. The search platform enables students quickly find and read information in articles for a given set of search keywords. The experimental results show improved learning performance with increased computer science knowledge and concepts and more computer science articles found using the information search platform by filtering out articles in non-computer science categories.

Keywords: Data mining · Term frequency-inverse document frequency · Information search platform · Learning performance

1 Introduction

E-learning can improve knowledge limitations and accessibility in traditional classrooms through combining big data and internet technology. Many studies have indicated that learning material combined with e-learning instruments can effectively improve learning performance and learning motivation in the classroom [1–3].

Although the Internet allows users and learners an easy search through web resources, the search result often contain contents unrelated to computer knowledge, such as advertising, media information, and news reports in the thousands mixing in. This is because generic search engines are not designed to filter out non-domain-specific articles and resources.

In this study, an information search platform based on data mining technology was design and built to retrieve keywords and computer science articles, as well as to filter out non- computer science category articles. Learners can quickly search for computer science materials and articles on the information search platform. The improvement in students' learning was measured using the information search platform and to compare the number of computer science articles retrieved by the students on the proposed platform vs. on the Google platform.

2 Literature Review

As the Internet has grown, big data has increased significantly. Users can search through thousands of web resources through the Internet. In order to calculate the importance of the terms in data or articles, the frequency of terms must be efficiently retrieved from the text [4].

Term frequency-inverse document frequency (TF-IDF) is a numerical statistical method used for the word weighting in data mining and information retrieval [5, 6]. It can calculate the importance of each word in articles or texts [7, 8]. Researchers Qaiser and Ali indicated that TF-IDF can be applied in a large amount of data, and they explained the calculation method and procedure for use of TF-IDF [9]. Researchers Christian, Agus, and Suhartono used TF-IDF to construct automatic text summarization in a single document. Their results showed that TF-IDF can calculate words effectively and can determine the importance of each word in a single document [10].

In addition, most studies have indicated that combining information platforms can help students effectively learn in the classroom [11–13]. Researchers Chin, Lee, and Chen developed a learning system where students can search for keywords to read additional information through a web page [14]. Researchers Barbagallo and Formica integrated semantic search and e-learning to show the feasibility and effectiveness of this approach [15].

According to the aforementioned literature review, TF-IDF and the application of information platforms have been proven to be effective. Meanwhile, they can improve the learning performance of students in the classroom. However, these platforms cannot automatically filter out articles in non-computer science categories, so students may end up searching for web articles that are not relevant to their learning materials. Therefore, this study is based on TF-IDF to construct an information search platform. This method can be used to calculate the weighting of all terms in each web article and automatically filter non-computer science articles, while it automatically provides computer science articles for users and students. They can effectively and quickly search keywords to read such articles on the information search platform.

3 Research Method

In this study, an information search platform using data mining was designed and built to improve student learning for computer related courses. Students in the experimental group searched three keywords using the information search platform; students in the control group instead used Google search platform for the same three keywords. Students from both groups then read the articles and recorded the number of links to such computer science articles. The learning performance of the students and the number of computer science articles in the two groups were then compared.

3.1 Participants

Students in their junior year in the Department of Computer Science and Information Engineering of a university participated in this study. There were 15 participants in the experimental group and 15 participants in the control group.

3.2 Construct an Information Search Platform Based on Term Frequency-Inverse Document Frequency

This study uses term frequency-inverse document frequency (TF-IDF) to calculate the keyword weight of each web article and order the weighting of the keywords in descending order. Figure 1 shows the system architecture diagram. First, the information search platform retrieves web articles through web crawler programs and filters the stop words in these articles through data pre-processing. Second, these articles are based on TF-IDF to calculate the term weighting so terms with high TF-IDF value can be used as the keywords for each article. Finally, the weighting of the keywords is ordered from high to low and stored in the database. In addition, each keyword must run through several rounds of calculations to select computer science keywords and filter out non-computer science articles.

Figure 2 shows the information search platform used in this study. This platform was based on TF-IDF to enhance the search for computer science articles, and reduce the search for non-computer science articles, such as advertising, news reports, etc. Learners could effectively search for and read articles that were informational and applicable to their learning process.

3.3 Experimental Process

Before the classroom experiment in this study, the teacher explained the experimental process, the pre-test, platform operations, and the post-test in the two classes. In this study, the pre-test and post-test included 3 quiz items, where the item content had all of the computer science category keywords. In addition, the answers to the questions included three options: correct, incorrect, and uncertain. Before the pre-test and post-test, the teacher told the students to avoid guessing the answer during the quiz. If the students did not understand a quiz item, they were instructed to choose the uncertain option.

Figure 3 shows the experimental process used in this study. The experimental group and the control group engaged in different learning activities in the two classes, where the experimental group used the information search platform, and the control group used the Google search platform. First, the teacher explained the experimental process and conducted the pre-test to determine the students' prior knowledge from the previous classes. Then, the researchers provided three keywords for the experimental

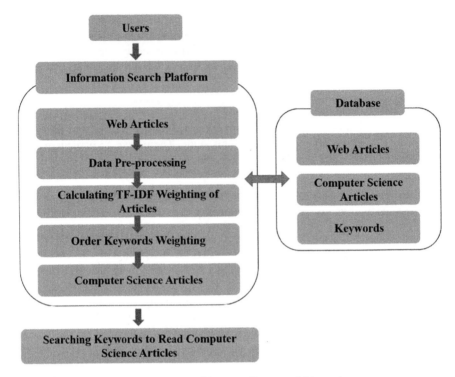

Fig. 1. System architecture diagram of this study.

Fig. 2. The information search platform used in this study.

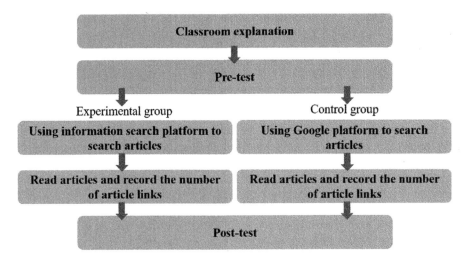

Fig. 3. The experimental process used in this study.

group and the control group and instructed them to use the information search platform and the Google search platform for keyword searches, respectively. In addition, students in the experimental group and the control group were instructed to read the content of the article they found and record the number of links to the computer science article. Finally, students took a post-test to complete the experimental process.

4 Experimental Results

This study was based on data mining to construct an information search platform and explore the learning performance of the students in the classroom. In addition, the number of links to computer science articles was compared between the two groups to explore which search platform was most effective in increasing learning computer science knowledge and encouraging reading of more of this type of article.

The independent sample t-test results for the pre-test showed that the mean of the experimental group was 1.47; the mean of the control group was 1.53, and the t value was -0.184 ($p > 0.05$). There were no significant between-group differences, which means that there was not much difference in the knowledge of the two groups prior to the learning activity.

Table 1 describes independent sample t-test results for the post-test. The mean of the experimental group was 2.07; the mean of the control group was 1.60, and the t value was 2.646 ($p < 0.05$). There were significant between-group differences, which means that the experimental group was able to use the information search platform effectively to understand computer science concepts and acquire knowledge, thus effectively improve learning performance.

Table 1. The independent sample t-test results for the post-test.

Group	N	Mean	SD	t
Experimental	15	2.07	0.26	2.646*
Control	15	1.60	0.63	

*$p < 0.05$.

Figure 4 shows the distribution of the answers to the pre-tests for the two groups. The horizontal axis represents the answer options, and the vertical axis represents the % of correct answers. As shown in Fig. 4, the blue line indicates the distribution of the experimental group's answers. In the experimental group, the % of correct answers was 48%; the % of incorrect answers was 29%, and the % of uncertain answers was 22%. The green line indicates the distribution of answers in the control group. The % of correct answers in the control group was 51%; the % of incorrect answers was 35%, and the % of uncertain answers was 13%.

Figure 5 shows the distribution of answers to the post-tests for the two groups. The horizontal axis represents the answer options, and the vertical axis represents the % of answers. As shown in Fig. 5, the blue line indicates the distribution of the experimental group's answers. In the experimental group, the % of correct answers was 68%; the % of incorrect answers was 29%, and the % of uncertain answers was 2%. The green line indicates the distribution of answers in the control group. The % of correct answers in the control group was 53%; the % of incorrect answers was 37%, and the % of uncertain answers was 9%.

According to the distribution of the answers to the pre-test and post-tests, the experimental group had a higher % of correct answers through the use of the information search platform than the control group using the Google search platform (the % of correct answers was 68% in the experimental group and 53% in the control group). In addition, the information search platform effectively provided appropriate computer science articles that improved their understanding of keywords that they had previously been uncertain about (the % of uncertain answers in the experimental group dropped from 22% to 2%).

Furthermore, the number of links to computer science articles in the experimental group and the control group was analyzed. As shown in Fig. 6, the blue line represents the number of links to computer science articles searched by the experimental group using the information search platform. The green line represents the number of links to computer science articles searched by the control group using the Google search platform. The experimental group searched for keyword 1, where a total of 16 articles were computer science in nature. The control group searched for keyword 1, where a total of 18 articles were computer science in nature. The experimental group searched for keyword 2, and a total of 15 articles were computer science in nature; the control group searched for keyword 2 and a total of 11 articles were computer science in nature. The experimental group searched for keyword 3, and a total of 30 articles were computer science in nature; the control group searches for keyword 3, and a total of 11 articles were computer science in nature.

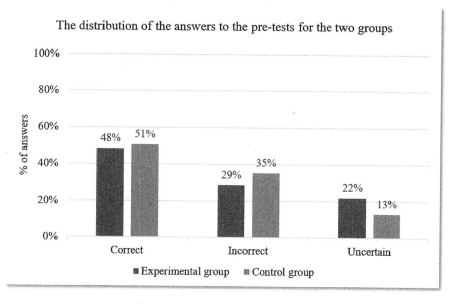

Fig. 4. The distribution of the answers to the pre-tests for the two groups.

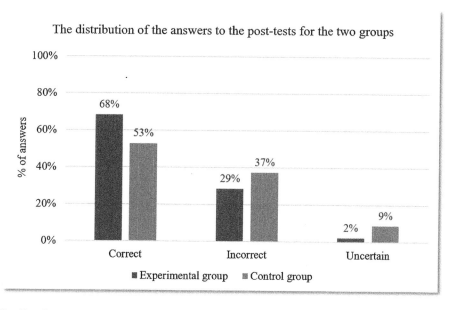

Fig. 5. The distribution of the answers to the post-tests for the two groups. (Color figure online)

Even though the Google search platform provides big data, there is no specific classification for computer science articles. When students are searching for keywords, they must filter out a lot of articles to find computer science articles. The information search platform thus effectively provides computer science articles, so the students were able to read and learn more quickly and efficiently.

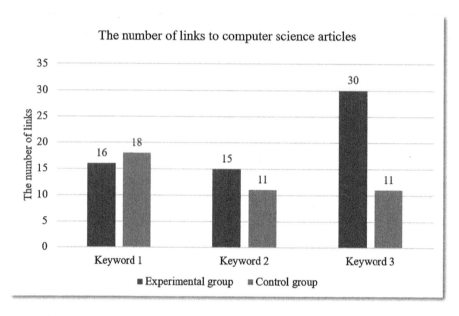

Fig. 6. The number of links to computer science articles. (Color figure online)

5 Conclusion

This study was based on data mining to construct an information search platform. Through TF-IDF, this platform calculates the weighting of all terms in each article, automatically filters non-computer science category keywords and articles, and automatically provides computer science articles. According to the experimental results, the experimental group was able to use the information search platform to search for keywords and read computer science articles, which in turn improved their base of knowledge and concepts and enhanced their learning performance. Furthermore, the information search platform can find such articles more easily than the Google platform. Therefore, the proposed information search platform can effectively provide computer science articles and also assist students to quickly read and learn related to computer science.

Acknowledgements. This study is supported in part by Ministry of Science and Technology, Taiwan under Contract No. MOST 106-2511-S-218-001-MY3 and MOST 108-2511-H-218-004.

References

1. Hung, C.Y., Sun, J.C.Y., Liu, J.Y.: Effects of flipped classrooms integrated with MOOCs and game-based learning on the learning motivation and outcomes of students from different backgrounds. Interact. Learn. Environ. **27**(8), 1028–1046 (2019)
2. Chin, K.Y., Wang, C.S., Chen, Y.L.: Effects of an augmented reality-based mobile system on students' learning achievements and motivation for a liberal arts course. Interact. Learn. Environ. **27**(7), 927–941 (2019)
3. Önal, N., Çevik, K.K., Şenol, V.: The effect of SOS table learning environment on mobile learning tools acceptance, motivation and mobile learning attitude in English language learning. Interact. Learn. Environ. 1–14 (2019). https://doi.org/10.1080/10494820.2019.1690529
4. Jones, K.S.: A statistical interpretation of term specificity and its application in retrieval. J. Doc. **28**, 11–21 (1972)
5. Schütze, H., Manning, C.D., Raghavan, P.: Introduction to Information Retrieval. Cambridge University Press, Cambridge (2008)
6. Rajaraman, A., Ullman, J.D.: Mining of Massive Datasets. Cambridge University Press, Cambridge (2011)
7. Havrlant, L., Kreinovich, V.: A simple probabilistic explanation of term frequency-inverse document frequency (TF-IDF) heuristic (and variations motivated by this explanation). Int. J. Gen Syst **46**(1), 27–36 (2017)
8. Zechner, K.: Fast generation of abstracts from general domain text corpora by extracting relevant sentences. In: COLING 1996 Volume 2: The 16th International Conference on Computational Linguistics (1996)
9. Qaiser, S., Ali, R.: Text mining: use of TF-IDF to examine the relevance of words to documents. Int. J. Comput. Appl. **181**(1), 25–29 (2018)
10. Christian, H., Agus, M.P., Suhartono, D.: Single document automatic text summarization using term frequency-inverse document frequency (TF-IDF). ComTech Comput. Math. Eng. Appl. **7**(4), 285–294 (2016)
11. Molinillo, S., Aguilar-Illescas, R., Anaya-Sánchez, R., Vallespín-Arán, M.: Exploring the impacts of interactions, social presence and emotional engagement on active collaborative learning in a social web-based environment. Comput. Educ. **123**, 41–52 (2018)
12. Firat, E.A., Köksal, M.S.: Effects of instruction supported by web 2.0 tools on prospective teachers' biotechnology literacy. Comput. Educ. **135**, 61–74 (2019)
13. Wijekumar, K.K., Meyer, B.J., Lei, P.: High-fidelity implementation of web-based intelligent tutoring system improves fourth and fifth graders content area reading comprehension. Comput. Educ. **68**, 366–379 (2013)
14. Chin, K.Y., Lee, K.F., Chen, Y.L.: Using an interactive ubiquitous learning system to enhance authentic learning experiences in a cultural heritage course. Interact. Learn. Environ. **26**(4), 444–459 (2018)
15. Barbagallo, A., Formica, A.: ELSE: an ontology-based system integrating semantic search and e-learning technologies. Interact. Learn. Environ. **25**(5), 650–666 (2017)

Digitalization of a Systematic Literature Review Process – Lean Startup and Data Analytics Solution for Scholars

Zornitsa Yordanova(✉)

University of National and World Economy, 8mi dekemvri, Sofia, Bulgaria
zornitsayordanova@unwe.bg
https://www.scopus.com/authid/detail.uri?authorId=57200724991

Abstract. The paper aims at analyzing how Lean Startup as a product and project management approach can be used in the context of Logic-Based Program Synthesis product development. The research is interdisciplinary and connects some technological and managerial aspects of data analytics, product development, and technology management. Both the concepts of Lean Startup and Logic-Based program synthesis have very similar approach for problem-solving and developing solutions. By combining them, the paper shows results, which lead to: 1.) Designing a Method for a common process for developing a Lean Startup Program Synthesis (LSPS) application development model and 2.) Probating a concrete application development through the identified stages. The developed application's purpose is the digitalization of systematic literature analysis via data analytics technics and the use of Qlik Sense software. Potential readers are scholars who are interested in digitalizing and automating the performance of systematic literature analysis replacing the usual reading of full papers with a cross wording filtering amongst words in titles, abstracts and author keywords of science papers.

Keywords: Lean startup · Data analytics · Technology management · Systematic literature review · Science digitalization · Science innovation

1 Introduction

In the last 20 years, interdisciplinary research has gained much focus and has resulted in many innovations between different sciences and industry fields. The present study aims to present the development of an application based on the popular Lean Startup product development approach, which was originally used only to start technologies, but now, 10 years later, it is a common management practice in large corporations, multinational companies, and yet in small product-oriented companies and startups. It is widespread in many industries such as banking, technology, services, manufacturing, etc. worldwide. At present, it covers not only product development and start-up functions [1], as it was in the beginning, but also the tasks of project management [2], innovation management [3], customer relationship management [4], etc. Lean Startup research in the context of technology development has grown tremendously in the last few years. One of the most common description of it is a hypothesis-driven entrepreneurship, in which entrepreneurs create a high level product, process and organization for an innovation and then through experimentations, continue to develop this product's vision and next actions according to the feedback of users, market, suppliers, etc. [5].

Program synthesis, on the other hand, refers to the development of a program in a systematic way, starting with a high-level specification, which is a declaration describing what the program should do [6]. So, comparing these two concepts from two different scientific fields and having a huge difference in their purpose and essence, several common elements emerge: their use refers to satisfying a high level of requirements, which can be further used as a validation of some hypotheses. This basically, very much converges to the most recent innovation-driven theories, which explain innovation as a problem-solution activity rather than an invention of a new product/process/organization or business model.

This research aims at analyzing both the concepts from the perspective of a fast verification approach for development of technologies, programs, applications, business models, products, etc., i.e. innovative technology. The methodology of the study presents the development of an application, based on Qlik software which usually is used for a Business Intelligence tool and Data Analytics software, which tool satisfies high-level requirements and might be used for validation of ideas. In the current case, the application development and an object of the research is a tool for digitalization of the process of systematic literature review as part of the research work of scholars and students.

2 Theoretical Background

2.1 Project and Product Management for Technology

Project management is that part of project knowledge that explores and studies the more successful management of these initiatives. Organizations are becoming more project-oriented [7], and projects are the preferred management instrument especially for implementation of new activities [8, 9]. However, because projects are constantly delayed, exceeding, and often technically unsuccessful, project management is often explored for opportunities for improvement. These threats increase with the complexity of the project. All these assumptions are extremely valid for science applied projects per se. As a structure, the methodology has been developed in nine main areas of knowledge and an additional one for integrity. The main areas of knowledge are: Integrity management; Project scope management; Project time management; Cost management; Quality management; Human resources management; Project communication management; Risk management; Procurement management [10]. An additional area added in recent years is the Management of the Code of Ethics in the project, which each project manager undertakes to comply with. Very often projects are implemented through processes. They are implemented by the project participants and fall into two categories: (1) Project management processes - for planning, organizing, coordinating and managing the project work. They are universal and standardized in the contractor's project management system. (2) Product Oriented Processes - to specify and create the project product.

2.2 Lean Startup Method

The Lean Startup model for development and subsequent innovation management is based on four main pillars for optimal innovation management: (1) systematic and continuous innovation management, (2) developed and two-way communication between the company and its potential customers, (3) the efficient use of resources and (4) the achievement of a cost-effective and optimal price.

The term Lean Startup was first mentioned by startup entrepreneur and consultant Eric Rees in his personal blog Startup Lessons Learned in September 2008. The name is borrowed from the philosophy of lean production developed at Toyota by Taiichi. Ono and Shigeo Shingo [11]. Some of the main principles of "lean" production are to give employees a tool to share their knowledge of production procedures and to develop the concept of production just in time, which increases innovation and reduces the consumption of unnecessary resources. Since its inception in 2008, the Lean Startup method has become widespread and recognizable among innovators and entrepreneurs around the world. Initially, its popularity was expressed as "Good Practice in Systematic Innovation Management" among companies in Silicon Valley, San Francisco, USA. Subsequently, with the accumulation of empirical data, research and results, it is built as a method. Officially, the method was published in 2011. by Eric Rees, who describes it in his book, Lean Start-Up: How Continuous Innovation is at the Heart of Successful Business [1]. Etymologically, the term is composed of two concepts - lean (tight) and startup. The category of startup, despite its wide distribution and usability, is not strictly defined and for the purposes of a comprehensive presentation of the Lean startup method, it should be clarified.

The Lean Startup method is based on five fundamental principles:

- Entrepreneurs are everywhere - by entrepreneurs, the author of the method means people or startups that create products or services in conditions of high uncertainty, regardless of the size or sector of the company. With this first principle, the Lean Startup method claims that it is applicable to any type of entrepreneurship.
- Entrepreneurship is management - and deserves a new type of management, focused on its specific challenges and opportunities.
- Validated learning - startups exist to learn how to build a sustainable business. Learning as a system, the author of the method accepts as a process of continuous testing and validation of ideas and vision of entrepreneurs to prove their rationality, the right direction and, if necessary, to be a signal for necessary correction.
- Action/build - Measure - Learn - the startup company must have predefined criteria and metrics that give an indication of the fulfillment of the set goals. Based on this reporting from the created metrics and set goals, entrepreneurs can assess whether the direction followed is correct or it is necessary to make a change.
- Innovation accountancy - although they are the result of creativity, experimentation or vision, in order to be successful, innovation must be measurable. This is necessary for them to be managed systematically: to take into account the progress, the priorities, to set the next goals and direction. The Lean Startup method introduces some terms that are the basis of its implementation as a management system for

startups and innovative projects in established companies. With their presentation, the main points in the concept of the method are clarified.
- Customer feedback - part of the systematic model of innovation management, which the method adopts is the continuous customer feedback. It is proactive, applied at the earliest stage and not only reflects the needs and desires of customers, but also takes into account side and side effects such as product perception, unwarranted validation (which is not based on analysis but on customer emotion and sensitivity).
- Minimum viable product (MVP) - The aim of the minimum applicable product is to test the business hypothesis through a quickly produced, clean product model that can be quickly and cheaply placed on the market and validate the concept of the idea.
- Continuous deployment - this is a development technique that involves continuous updating of products that are already on the market, based on feedback and even several times a day. This characterizes the products and services that have adopted the technique of "continuous implementation" as highly adaptable and flexible.
- Decomposition of the elements of the product and marketing of several different versions of the product or service simultaneously (split testing, versioning) - through the method different combinations of the product and the discovery of the optimal and preferred combination by customers are possible.
- "Significant" metrics and "Meaningless" metrics (Actionable metrics and vanity metrics) - Metrics are important, but their meaning is important and reporting of real and significant results. The metrics that startups need should be such that they carry specific information related to their business goals. Meaningless metrics are those on the basis of which no specific decision or action can be taken and are not appropriate.
- Change of direction (Pivot) - the concept of change of direction is the ability and need of the startup company to change elements of the product, marketing strategy or other elements of its existence as a result of customer feedback or metrics that it collects and analyzes. The change of direction is intended to minimize the loss of resources when there is reason to believe that the current direction is not correct and does not reveal potential.

3 Research Design

In the Scopus database, searching with different keywords, regarding Lean Startup from one hand and all possible project, product and innovation management practices, there are only six research papers referring to 'synthesis' and 'logic-based'. The results of the analysis are presented in the results' section, because the analysis was done with the developed application, following the development phases, defined in the next paragraphs, designing the research methodology.

The research design is based on the common elements of the analyzed Lean Startup management approach and the technical method Program Synthesis. The research design follows an application development for digitalization of literature review (at a limited extend). The process of developing will follow both concepts phase stages: 1.) Specification/Idea generation; 2.) Synthesizing/Building, development; 3.) Verification/Measure, data 4.) Feedback/Learn.

Both the concepts of Lean Startup and Program Synthesis are circular and follow these four common phases and are based on the cycle principle. By the presented below Figs. 1, 2 and 3, the main stages are presented for the purposes of resulting in a common process for developing a Lean Startup Program Synthesis (LSPS) application development model.

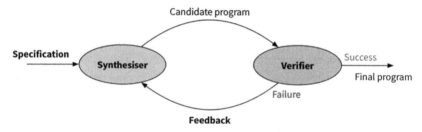

Fig. 1. General process in Program synthesis. Source: James Bornholt, Program Synthesis Explained, (2015), available at: https://www.cs.utexas.edu/~bornholt/post/synthesis-explained.html [12].

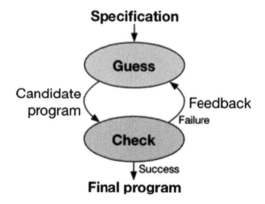

Fig. 2. Basic Program Synthesis process. Source: James Bornholt, Program Synthesis in 2019, (2020), available at: https://blog.sigplan.org/2019/07/31/program-synthesis-in-2019/ [13].

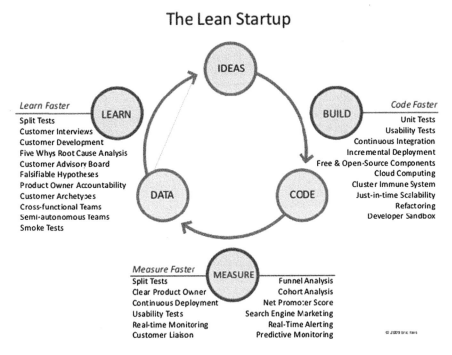

Fig. 3. Lean Startup process for development. Source: Eric Ries, Lean Startup Fundamental Feedback Loop and Workshop Info - from Web 2.0 Expo #leanstartup, (2009), available at: https://www.slideshare.net/startuplessonslearned/eric-ries-lean-startup-fundamental-feedback-loop-and-workshop-info-from-web-20-expo-leanstartup [14].

Concluding, the general phases for development of a Lean Startup Program Synthesis (LSPS) application development model are (improved by business modelling coming from Lean Startup requirement for not only technical verification and validation, but also customer and market validation):

1. Identification and description of high level business requirements (no matter if the development is coming from internal or external sources)
2. High-level design and development with features of Minimal Viable Product
3. Validation phase
4. Re-design and improvement

4 Results and Discussion

In this section of the paper, presentation of the application development process takes place with the respect of the above defined general process. In Table 1, the process and the performed actions as well as the results of each of them is presented.

Table 1. Developing application for digital systematic literature review

Phase	Actions	Results
High level business requirements	Digitalization of literature analysis – a common practice which usually takes long time and it is resource-consuming. Digitalizing it, the main assumption is its facilitation and assistance through digital techniques	Defining sub-requirements, incl. Scopus database search, identification of data analytics platform for performing the analysis
High-level design and development	Designing the work process in the developed solution (with different datasets, based on Scopus database searches, identifying different keywords across the different datasets, etc.)	Developing a Qlik Sense application which may contain several datasets from Scopus data searches and analyzing them accordingly
Validation phase	Defining a scope for Lean Startup application papers and analyzing them in the context of identification of knowledge gaps and fasten up the process of literature review of a large number of articles	Validation trough manual (traditional) systematic literature analysis and the results from the developed application
Re-design and improvement	After validation, some features are adding as not only analyzing science papers and articles based on words in titles and keywords, but also including words in abstracts (including context analysis based on the context of each sentence where the analyzed word is used originally)	The re-design was done by additionally sub-dividing (automatically) each word of an abstract and a search by these words is also possible

This is how the application works by filtering and high-level flexible requirements (Fig. 4).

There are several possibilities in the application: searching by words, which are either in titles, abstracts or keywords of different data sets, combining different words from the three filters, analyzing one or more datasets (coming from Scopus search), etc. The feature of combining sets of words from titles, abstracts or keywords of science papers might identify many hidden dependencies and linkages.

This is a wave analysis in the application, which is applied for searching the words 'logic-based' and 'synthesis' in abstracts of around 3000 science articles related to Lean Startup and product, project and innovation management (Fig. 5).

The wave analysis facilitates the systematic literature analysis by providing useful information on which are the topics discussed through titles. Keywords and abstracts with a proper selection of a word in one of the three analyzed components of a science paper.

Digitalization of a Systematic Literature Review Process 243

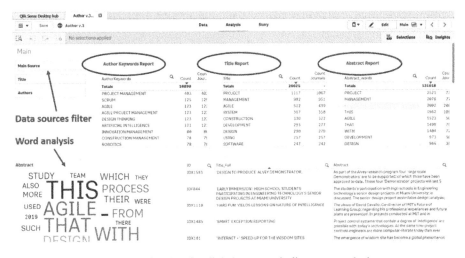

Fig. 4. Application for digital systematic literature analysis.

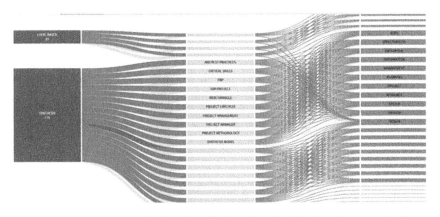

Fig. 5. Wave analysis in the developed application for digitalization of systematic literature review.

5 Conclusion

In conclusion of the presented model for developing applications, based on both the principle of continuing development Lean Startup and Logic-based programing, the readers may use the outcome for their own development approach. The presented model proposes not only technical valid process, but also its combination with a proven business model technique. In addition, here is presented this model validation through a concrete application, digitalizing (at some extend) the systematic literature analysis process which is common one for each researcher. Major benefits of the developed application are: 1.) Facilitating and digitalizing the systematic literature review process;

2.) Revealing some hidden dependencies and linkages between articles; 3.) Word and context analysis.

The future work of the author will be focused on collaborating with different scientists from diverse science fields for real implementation of the developed application and validating the possible results from its usage.

Acknowledgments. The paper is supported by the BG NSF Grant No KP-06 OPR01/3-2018.

References

1. Ries, E.: Lean Startup: How Today's Entrepreneurs Use Continuous Innovation to Create Radically Successful Businesses. Crown Publishing Group, New York (2011)
2. Hamerski, D.C., Torres Formoso, C., Luís Isatto, E., Cevallos, C.: Combining Lean and Agile Project Management in a Multi-Project Environment: Case Study in a Retail Company (2019)
3. Lichtenthaler, U.: Agile innovation: the complementarity of design thinking and lean startup. Int. J. Serv. Sci. Manag. Eng. Technol. (IJSSMET) **11**(1) (2020). https://doi.org/10.4018/ijssmet.2020010110
4. Eisenmann, T.R., Ries, E., Dillard, S.: Hypothesis-driven entrepreneurship: the lean startup. Harvard Business School Entrepreneurial Management Case No. 812-095 (2012)
5. Hossain, S.S., Jubayer, S.A.M., Rahman, S., Bhuiyan, T., Rawshan, L., Islam, S.: Customer feedback prioritization technique: a case study on lean startup. In: Misra, S., et al. (eds.) ICCSA 2019. LNCS, vol. 11623, pp. 70–81. Springer, Cham (2019). https://doi.org/10.1007/978-3-030-24308-1_6
6. Deville, Y., Lau, K.: Logic program synthesis. J. Log. Program. **19**(20), 321–350 (1994)
7. Morris, P., Pinto, K.J.: The Wiley Guide to Project, Program, and Portfolio Management. Wiley, Hoboken (2007)
8. Filippov, S., Mooi, H.: Innovation project management: a research agenda. J. Innov. Sustain. **1**(1) (2010). RISUS ISSN 2179-3565
9. Ghaben, R., Jaaron, A.: Assessing innovation practices in project management: the case of Palestinian construction projects. Int. J. Innov. Sci. Res. **17**(2), 451–465 (2015). ISSN 2351-8014
10. Project Management Institute: Project management body of knowledge, PMBOK (2017)
11. Ohno, T.: Toyota Production System: Beyond Large-Scale Production. Productivity Press, Portland (1988)
12. Bornholt, J.: Program Synthesis Explained (2015). https://www.cs.utexas.edu/~bornholt/post/synthesis-explained.html
13. Bornholt, J.: Program Synthesis in 2019 (2020). https://blog.sigplan.org/2019/07/31/program-synthesis-in-2019/
14. Ries, E.: Lean Startup Fundamental Feedback Loop and Workshop Info - from Web 2.0 Expo #leanstartup (2009). https://www.slideshare.net/startuplessonslearned/eric-ries-lean-startup-fundamental-feedback-loop-and-workshop-info-from-web-20-expo-leanstartup

Effect of Facebook Use on Social Comparison Perceptions

Fu-Rung Yang[1], Chih-Fen Wei[2], and Jih-Hsin Tang[3(✉)]

[1] Department of Education, University of Taipei, Taipei, Taiwan
yangfr928@gmail.com
[2] Department of Psychology and Counseling, University of Taipei,
Taipei, Taiwan
cfwei@utaipei.edu.tw
[3] Department of Information Management, National Taipei University
of Business, Taipei, Taiwan
jefftang@ntub.edu.tw

Abstract. People's perceptions after browsing Facebook can provide valuable insights. We investigated social comparison domains (agency vs. communion) and social comparison directions (upward vs. downward) in Facebook by manipulating the domains and directions using a simulated Facebook profile of a comparison target. In total, 126 college students participated in the study. We used a Latin square design for agency upward, agency downward, communion upward, and communion downward comparisons. Individuals rated perceptive social comparisons after browsing the profiles. In this study, t-tests were conducted to compare results for the four profiles. Individuals perceived social comparison domains and social comparison directions. Furthermore, individuals browsing the agency comparison profile perceived communion information, and those browsing the communion comparison profile perceived agency information. The halo effect was evident in individuals browsing Facebook. Theoretical implications and practical implications are discussed. Suggestions for teachers and counselors are also provided.

Keywords: Social networking sites · Facebook · Social comparison · Agency · Communion · Halo effect

1 Introduction

People obtain much information about their friends from social network sites (SNSs), which enable them to observe their friends' recent life events and acquire social comparison information. When people are unsure of their status in a particular area, they frequently compare themselves with others. Facebook was selected as the SNS platform for this study. Facebook is the most popular SNS and most theoretically relevant to social comparison [1]. On Facebook, people present idealized versions of themselves by posting flattering pictures and updates regarding their achievements [2]. People not only disclose their information but also remain informed on the lives of their relatives, friends, and colleagues on Facebook; thus, Facebook has become the ideal platform for social comparison [3].

Festinger (1954) [4] defined social comparison as the evaluation of an individual's own thoughts and behaviors in comparison with those of others (i.e., comparison targets) that are similar in terms of characteristics or background. According to social comparison theory, people compare themselves with others to assess their emotions, personality traits, opinions, and abilities [4–6]. People make judgments and decisions more effectively by performing comparisons with others [7].

Agency and communion are crucial social comparison domains as well as the most influential pairing of abstract psychological distinctions [8]. Values, motives, traits, and behaviors in the aforementioned domains provide an effective framework for distinguishing and organizing. Agency is a meta concept related to self-advancement in social hierarchies, and communion is a partner concept related to the retention of positive relationships [8, 9]. Individuals evaluate their agency characteristics, including authoritativeness, task performance, and intelligence, and communal characteristics, including agreeableness and empathy [10, 11]. Agency and communion are critical domains for individuals to compare themselves with others.

Social comparison can be divided into two types: upward and downward. An upward comparison involves individuals comparing themselves to those who they perceive to be better, whereas a downward comparison involves comparison with someone perceived to have less desirable characteristics. Although Facebook offers opportunities for both types of comparisons, people typically conduct more upward comparisons because SNSs enable people to present their most desirable traits [12].

The halo effect, first described by Thorndike in the 1920s, involves making unreasonable inferences concerning others' unknown characteristics on the basis of known but typically irrelevant information. For example, attractive women are perceived to have more desirable personality traits than less attractive women [13, 14]. Known traits tend to influence how other irrelevant traits are perceived because of the halo effect. Individuals prefer sharing content on Facebook that presents them in a positive light. Browsing Facebook enables individuals to infer unknown information from known information. Individuals who perceived agency comparison information may infer communion comparison information.

In the present study, we designed four Facebook profiles to evaluate which components of Facebook profiles have a greater effect on social comparison domains (agency vs. communion) and social comparison directions (upward vs. downward). We hypothesized that individuals perceive the agency and communion comparison domains as well as upward and downward comparison directions on Facebook.

2 Method

2.1 Participants

In total, 134 college students (48 male and 86 female students) from a university in Taipei were included. All of the participants were between 19 and 23 years old and used Facebook regularly.

2.2 Social Comparison Manipulation

This study designed Facebook profiles with real photos obtained from college students in their early 20s living in Taipei. The photos on the four profiles differed, but the responses on the profiles were the same. The agency upward comparison profile highlighted higher intelligence, authority, and superior task performance on Facebook wall posts (e.g., high Test of English for International Communication [TOEIC] scores, student council presidency, and excellent academic performance). By contrast, lower intelligence, lack of authority, and inferior task performance were emphasized on the agency downward comparison profile (e.g., lower TOEIC scores, absence of student council positions, and poor academic performance). The communion upward comparison profile exhibited increased empathy, agreeableness, and communion on Facebook wall photos (e.g., involvement in volunteer activities and pleasant interpersonal relationships). By contrast, a lack of empathy, agreeableness, and communion were highlighted in the communion downward comparison profile (e.g., decreased involvement in volunteer activities and poor interpersonal relationships). The appendix presents the agency upward comparison profile pages.

Except the aforementioned characteristics, the social media profiles were otherwise similar in terms of the name (the name for the male profile was for Guan Yu Xu, and the name for the female profile was for Zi Han Xu), interests (cycling), number of friends (113), and other content. Moreover, the profile pictures were the same for all experimental conditions and did not depict the face of either the male or the female target individual. Last, all conditions included four identical posts that enhanced the realism of the profiles. For example, one involved a status update concerning the environment with a picture of autumn trees and the caption "I love fall."

2.3 Procedure

All participants were asked to browse a Facebook profile and complete a questionnaire after providing informed consent. Participants visited the laboratory and completed an online questionnaire program individually. Participants were told that we were studying the retention of information found on Facebook. Subsequently, they were informed that they would browse four Facebook profiles. We manipulated the comparison domains (agency vs. communion) and comparison directions (upward vs. downward) using a simulated Facebook profile of a comparison target. We used a Latin square design for agency upward, agency downward, communion upward, and communion downward comparisons to explore individuals' social comparison perceptions on Facebook.

2.4 Manipulation Check

We asked four questions regarding the profiles to verify whether participants had browsed the Facebook profiles. Participants had to select the correct TOEIC score and identify the activity attended by the person in the agency upward comparison profile and the agency downward comparison profile. Furthermore, participants were required to identify the relevant person who participated in the volunteer activity in the communion upward comparison profile and the communion downward comparison profile. We excluded participants who answered two Facebook content questions incorrectly. Two questions were chosen as our cut-off because it suggested that participants had not considered the profiles sufficiently. In total, eight participants were excluded for this reason. Finally, 126 participants (46 male and 80 female participants) were included in the study.

2.5 Measurement

After viewing the profile, participants completed a 5-point Likert scale (1 = strongly disagree, 5 = strongly agree) that measured six items (the target person's intelligence, authority, task performance, empathy, agreeableness, and communion). The scores of the six items were combined to create agency (three items) and communion (three items) scores.

3 Result

In this study, *t*-tests were conducted to compare the four Facebook profiles. Descriptive statistics and t-values were calculated for all the variables (Table 1).

Table 1. Facebook social comparison domain and social comparison direction *t*-test results ($N = 126$)

Social comparison domain	Dependent variables	Social comparison direction		*t*-value
		Upward	Downward	
Agency	Agency	3.97 (0.69)	2.29 (0.72)	18.68**
	Communion	3.55 (0.76)	2.88 (0.76)	8.00**
Communion	Agency	3.48 (0.75)	3.13 (0.67)	4.84**
	Communion	4.02 (0.76)	3.59 (0.73)	7.05**

*$p < .05$, **$p < .01$

Higher scores were obtained for the agency upward comparison profile (mean [M] = 3.97, standard deviation [SD] = 0.69) than for the agency downward comparison profile ($M = 2.29$, $SD = 0.72$), and higher scores were obtained for the communion upward comparison profile ($M = 4.02$, $SD = 0.76$) than for the communion downward profile ($M = 3.59$, $SD = 0.73$; Table 1). Furthermore, individuals browsing the agency upward comparison profile perceived communion upward comparison information ($M = 3.55$, $SD = 0.76$), and those browsing the agency downward comparison profile perceived communion downward comparison information ($M = 2.88$, $SD = 0.76$). Individuals browsing the communion upward comparison profile perceived agency upward comparison information ($M = 3.48$, $SD = 0.75$), and those browsing the communion downward comparison profile perceived agency downward comparison information ($M = 3.13$, $SD = 0.67$). Individuals perceived agency and communion comparison domains as well as upward and downward comparison directions on Facebook. The results support our hypothesis.

4 Discussion

We assessed how individuals perceive social comparison on Facebook by simulating Facebook profiles that included elements of social comparison domains (agency vs. communion) and directions (upward vs. downward). Individuals perceived agency and communion comparison as well as upward and downward comparison. Individuals who browsed the agency upward profile perceived agency upward information, and those who browsed the agency downward profile perceived agency downward information. Individuals who browsed the communion upward profile perceived communion upward information, and those who browsed the communion downward profile perceived communion downward information.

Although we did not include communion information on the agency profile, individuals concluded that the owner of the profile had communion traits. Participants also attributed agency traits to the communion profile. In the agency upward profile, participants attributed communion upward traits ($M = 3.55$, $SD = 0.76$) to the profile. In the agency downward profile, participants concluded that the profile owner had communion downward traits ($M = 2.88$, $SD = 0.76$). In the communion upward profile, participants attributed agency upward traits ($M = 3.48$, $SD = 0.75$) to the profile. In the communion downward profile, participants believed that the owner had agency downward traits ($M = 3.13$, $SD = 0.67$). The halo effect was evident in individuals who browsed Facebook. Individuals tend to infer unknown characteristics of others on the basis of known information.

4.1 Theoretical Implications

When browsing simulated Facebook profiles, individuals perceived social comparison, including social comparison domains (agency vs. communion) and directions (upward vs. downward). The distinction between agency and communion is an influential pairing of abstract psychological distinctions. Social comparison domains and social comparison directions are essential in social comparison on Facebook.

Our results also support the halo effect in individuals browsing Facebook [15]. Individuals browsing the agency comparison profile perceived communion information, and those browsing the communion comparison profile perceived agency information. This could be a factor affecting individuals' well-being after browsing Facebook. Inferring unknown information from known information may affect people's evaluation of themselves and their well-being.

4.2 Practical Implications

Social networking sites such as Facebook and Instagram are very popular in student life. The amount of information on Facebook was so vast that offered students information and interests. Students can disclose themselves and know about the lives of their relatives, friends and colleagues on Facebook. Furthermore, Facebook has already become the ideal platform for social comparison. Individuals tend to focus their evaluations of themselves and others on the domains they most value. Paulhus (2002) [16] argued that agency and communion provide suitable summary labels for the content distinction of the two manners, in which people attempt to appear desirable during social comparison. Individuals might perceive social comparison domains (agency vs. communion) and directions (upward vs. downward) on Facebook. Students browse Facebook might trigger social comparison automatically and this might influence an individual's well-being.

Social comparison was a ubiquitous and far-reaching social process in human interaction. While browsing Facebook, individuals perceived agency and communion comparison information. In school, in addition to positive encouragement for agency domain, teachers should also give positive encouragement for communion domain. Encouraging students to demonstrate the traits of communion and replace competition with cooperation is also crucial in education. Teachers and counselors in school should be aware of how Facebook affects social comparison (domains and directions) in students and advise them to use Facebook wisely. Teachers can also teach students to compare by themselves, pay attention to their own learning and growth, and avoid negative effects caused by inappropriate comparisons with others.

Appendix

References

1. Morry, M.M., Sucharyna, T.A., Petty, S.K.: Relationship social comparisons: your Facebook page affects my relationship and personal well-being. Comput. Hum. Behav. **83**, 140–167 (2018). https://doi.org/10.1016/j.chb.2018.01.038
2. Chou, H.T.G., Edge, N.: They are happier and having better lives than I am: the impact of using Facebook on perceptions of others' lives. Cyberpsych. Behav. Soc. **15**(2), 117–121 (2012). https://doi.org/10.1089/cyber.2011.0324
3. Gonzales, A.L., Hancock, J.T.: Mirror, mirror on my Facebook wall: effects of exposure to Facebook on self-esteem. Cyberpsychol. Behav. Soc. Netw. **14**(1–2), 79–83 (2011). https://doi.org/10.1089/cyber.2009.0411
4. Festinger, L.: A theory of social comparison processes. Hum. Relat. **7**(2), 117–140 (1954). https://doi.org/10.1177/001872675400700202
5. Schachter, S.: The Psychology of Affiliation. Stanford University Press, Stanford (1959)

6. Thornton, D.A., Arrowood, A.J.: Self- evaluation, self- enhancement, and the locus of social comparison. J. Exp. Soc. Psychol. **1**(1), 40–48 (1966). https://doi.org/10.1016/0022-1031(66)90064-3
7. Mussweiler, T., Ruter, K., Epstude, K.: The why, who, and how of social comparison: a social-cognition perspective. In: Guimond, S. (ed.) Social Comparison and Social Psychology: Understanding Cognition, Intergroup Relations, and Culture. Cambridge University Press, New York (2006)
8. Trapnell, P.D., Paulhus, D.L.: Agentic and communal values: their scope and measurement. J. Pers. Assess. **94**(1), 39–52 (2012). https://doi.org/10.1080/00223891.2011.627968
9. Bakan, D.: The Duality of Human Existence: An Essay on Psychology and Religion. Rand Mcnally, Oxford, England (1966)
10. Campbell, W.K., Rudich, E.A., Sedikides, C.: Narcissism, self-esteem, and the positivity of self- views: two portraits of self-love. Pers. Soc. Psychol. Bull. **28**(3), 358–368 (2002). https://doi.org/10.1177/0146167202286007
11. Carlson, E.N., Vazire, S., Oltmanns, T.F.: You probably think this paper's about you: narcissists' perceptions of their personality and reputation. J. Pers. Soc. Psychol. **101**(1), 185–201 (2011). https://doi.org/10.1037/a0023781
12. Rosenberg, J., Egber, N.: Online impression management: personality traits and concerns for secondary goals as predictors of self-presentation tactics on Facebook. J Comput. Mediat. Commun. **17**, 1–18 (2011). https://doi.org/10.1111/j.1083-6101.2011.01560.x
13. Dion, K.K., Berscheid, E., Walster, E.: What is beautiful is good. J. Pers. Soc. Psychol. **24**, 285–290 (1972). https://doi.org/10.1037/h0033731
14. Landy, D., Sigall, H.: When beauty is talent: ask evaluation as a function of the performer's physical attractiveness. J. Pers. Soc. Psychol. **29**, 299–304 (1974). https://doi.org/10.1037/h0036018
15. Asch, S.E.: Forming impressions of personality. J. Abnorm. Psychol. **41**(3), 258–290 (1946). https://doi.org/10.1037/h0055756
16. Paulhus, D.L.: Socially desirable responding: the evolution of a construct. In: Braun, H., Jackson, D.N., Wiley, D.E. (eds.) The Role of Constructs in Psychological and Educational Measurement, pp. 67–88. Lawrence Erlbaum, Mahwah, New Jersey (2002)

Hands-on Statistical Methods: A Case Study with Hidden Markov Models Using Simulations and Experiments

Steinar Thorvaldsen[✉]

UiT The Arctic University of Norway,
PO Box 6050, Langnes, 9037 Tromsø, Norway
steinar.thorvaldsen@uit.no

Abstract. Biological processes are often very complicated compared with physics and chemistry. One of the newest and most challenging interactions between biology and computational science comes from modern molecular biology and bioinformatics, where Hidden Markov Models (HMM) are widely applied tools. This paper presents the background, theory and HMM algorithms based on examples from Gregor Mendel's classical plant experiments. This approach aims to achieve some intuitive advantages in a biological and bioinformatical setting, because the pedagogy goes from the known to the unknown. It only presumes basic knowledge of genetics, statistics and matrix algebra. The student may gain insight into the complex HMM methodology by running "experiments" with the application *MendelHMM* in a kind of "digital laboratory". The optimal model can only be sought in a certain probabilistic sense. This process is known as machine learning.

Keywords: Experimental mathematics · Bioinformatics · Markov chains · HMM · Machine learning

1 Introduction

Stochastic processes are among the most general objects of study in probability and statistics, but are normally not part of the introductory courses in statistics. Markov processes are special cases of such processes. Some genetic processes can be represented by Markov chains in the sense that the random variables are not independent, but rather the value of each variable depends on just the previous element in the sequence. Markov chains models such local interactions [1].

Hidden Markov Models (HMM) can be very useful tools for analyzing a wide range of linguistic and biological data, and are often included in a modern biological curriculum. However, the subject is considered to be rather difficult. The biological world is complex, and compared with physics and chemistry, it is only quite recently that a somewhat systematic offensive towards biological problems by using mathematical models has taken place. Modern students of biology have to learn more about mathematical modeling than in earlier days.

This paper presents HMM's background, theory and algorithms based on examples from Gregor Mendel's classical plant experiments. This approach is considered to have some intuitive advantages in a bioinformatical and biological setting, because the pedagogy goes from the known to the unknown. It presumes only basic knowledge of genetics, statistics and matrix algebra, and the student may gain insight into the complex HMM methodology by running "experiments" with the application *MendelHMM* [2] in a kind of "digital laboratory".

Mendel's famous experiments in plant hybridization were published in 1866 and are often considered an essential work of modern genetics. He had no prior knowledge of the diploid nature of genes, but through a series of experiments, he could anticipate the hidden concept and name it "Element". In his experiments, he examined seven simple traits in the common garden pea (named *Pisum*). A trait (called *phenotype*) occurs either in one variation or another, with no in-between. These plants are naturally self-pollinating and exhibited traits that occur in very distinct forms, as shown in Fig. 1.

Experiment number	Sample size N in F2-generation	Dominant expression	Recessive expression
1 Form of ripe seed	7324	smooth	wrinkled
2 Colour of seed albumen	8023	yellow	green
3 Colour of seed coat	929	grey	white
4 Form of ripe pods	1181	inflated 	constricted 
5 Colour of unripe pods	580	green 	yellow 
6 Position of flowers	858	 axial	 terminal
7 Length of stem	1064	 tall	 dwarf

Fig. 1. The 7 phenotypes that Mendel examined of the *Pisum* garden pea.

Today we know that such recessive expressions most often are mutations in the DNA molecule of the genes, and it is well known for Mendel's growth gene (trait 7) that a single DNA-nucleotide G is substituted with an A. The outcome is that the enzyme's 3D structure is altered, and no biochemical reaction can occur.

In his experiment, Mendel also examined in more detail the plant seeds with two and three simultaneous heredity factors. When he studied two traits, he used 1 and 2, and three traits 1, 2 and 3 in Fig. 1.

2 The Software

The interface of the program *MendelHMM* is shown in Fig. 2. There is a frame containing controls for loading and managing training data in the left part of the window. On the right side there is a frame holding controls for managing the Hidden Markov model. Button **Estimate (EM)** runs the estimation of a model from the selected training set. The button **Sample (new)** serves to produce new training sets according to the selected HMM model and sample size.

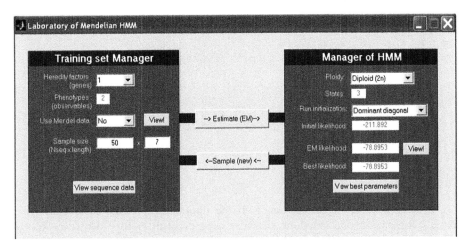

Fig. 2. The main window of the program *MendelHMM*, with buttons for loading models, training sets, viewing individual sequences and results.

3 To Estimate a Statistical Model According to a Training Set

The actual model and the actual sequence of hidden state values cannot be found stringently from the knowledge of the observations' sequence. The optimal model can only be looked for in a probabilistic sense, and to search for the most probable model is one of the common and often challenging tasks in Markov modeling. In an ideal case, the model is derived from knowledge about the objects we study and its configuration. However, in many practical situations, the available knowledge is insufficient. Still, knowledge can be improved with our training data. This iterative process is called *learning*.

There are two main kinds of learning. The first one, *supervised learning*, operates with a training set consisting of pairs (x_i, y_i), where y_i is a sequence of observations, and x_i is a sequence of corresponding states. The second possibility, the *unsupervised learning*, works with sequences of observations, y_i, only. In our situation, this case is adopted. A central question is the source of the training data and how it may influence the appropriate learning algorithm's choice. The *maximum likelihood (ML) estimate* is suitable when the training data are random samples from a probability distribution that can be searched for.

Supervised ML estimation is a pure counting of the relative frequency of occurrence of events. Additionally, ML estimation and the *Baum-Welch* re-estimation algorithm provide unsupervised learning, and it is a special case of the *EM algorithm* (Expectation Maximization). The algorithm is an iterative adaptation of the model to fit the training data. An HMM may often be slow to estimate because of its high number of parameters and many local maxima.

A presentation of model parameters estimated by the MendelHMM program is shown in Fig. 3.

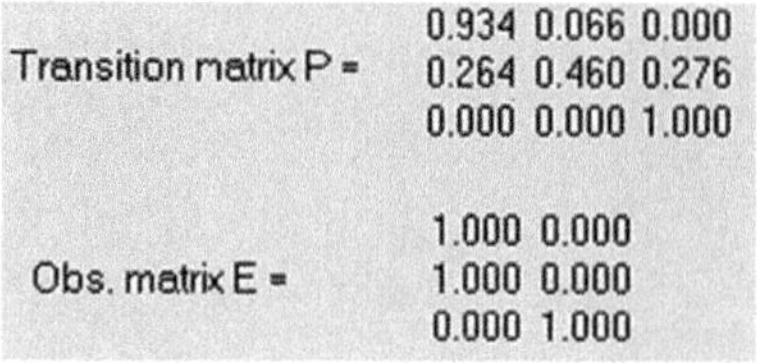

$$\text{Transition matrix } P = \begin{matrix} 0.934 & 0.066 & 0.000 \\ 0.264 & 0.460 & 0.276 \\ 0.000 & 0.000 & 1.000 \end{matrix}$$

$$\text{Obs. matrix } E = \begin{matrix} 1.000 & 0.000 \\ 1.000 & 0.000 \\ 0.000 & 1.000 \end{matrix}$$

Fig. 3. EM-estimation of model parameters based on two phenotypes and 50 sequences each of length 7. The results are sensitive to the initial values.

We may achieve higher efficiency in the optimization methods by employing special properties of the functions that arise as relevant in biology. However, global optimization is still in its early stage, and rapid progress is expected in this field by introducing techniques for data perturbation to escape local maxima (Simulated Annealing). Simulated Annealing [3] is an established methodology for introducing randomness into optimization by performing a random tour of the search space. Though, it has been proved that finding the globally-optimal ML parameters is NP-hard [4], so initial conditions matters a lot for success. Simulated Annealing is not implemented in the toolbox MendelHMM. However, initial values may be chosen by two methods, either by random or by a dominant diagonal method.

4   Sampling of New Training Data

The toolbox MendelHMM may also produce new data samples from our Markov model by running through it in a probabilistic way. A graphical outlook of the data sequences can also be provided, as displayed in Fig. 4.

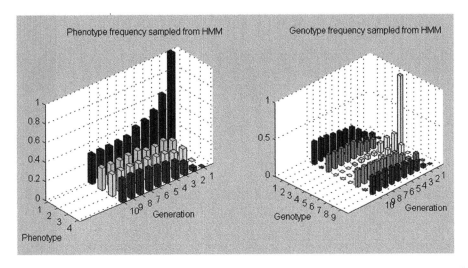

Fig. 4. A sequence sample distribution of observations and hidden states from the *MendelHMM* toolbox with two genes (4 phenotypes and 9 genotypes).

5 The Probability of a Given Sequence

Some fundamental problems have to be solved in the HMM process. The first is the problem of sequence evaluation. As a case study, the Mendel experiment gives us a simple example of such evaluation, often called the *forward/backward* procedure. If we, in the case of one gene, have a sequence of dominant (**A**) and recessive (**a**) observations:

$$y = (A, A, a, a, a) \qquad (1)$$

Note here that when writing a single letter **A** in **bold**, we mean the phenotype and not the genotype. How do we then calculate the probability that this sequence is derived from the model? In our particular Mendel model, we have initial state vector π, probability state transition matrix P_S, and emission probabilities P_E:

$$\pi = \begin{pmatrix} 0 & 1 & 0 \end{pmatrix}, \qquad P_S = \begin{pmatrix} 1 & 0 & 0 \\ 1/4 & 1/2 & 1/4 \\ 0 & 0 & 1 \end{pmatrix} \qquad \text{and} \qquad P_E = \begin{pmatrix} 1 & 0 \\ 1 & 0 \\ 0 & 1 \end{pmatrix} \qquad (2)$$

The first column in P_E tells that all genotypes of type number 1 (AA) and type 2 (Aa) will be observed as phenotype 1(**A**), and the second column tells that all genotypes of type 3 (aa) will be observed as phenotype 2 (**a**). In this rather simple case, only one possible state path can hide behind the given observations:

$$(0\,1\,0) \rightarrow (0\,1\,0) \rightarrow (0\,0\,1) \rightarrow (0\,0\,1) \rightarrow (0\,0\,1), \tag{3}$$

and calculating the probabilities in the defined model M gives:

$$\sum_{\text{all } x_{1:5}} \Pr(y, x_{1:5}|M) = \frac{1}{2} \cdot \frac{1}{4} \cdot 1 \cdot 1 = \frac{1}{8} \tag{4}$$

6 The Sequence of Most Probable Values of the States

As mentioned before, the actual sequence of hidden values cannot be found from the knowledge of the sequence of observations and the corresponding Markov model. The optimal sequence can only be looked for in a probabilistic sense. The search for the most probable sequence is another of the central questions in HMM. The *Viterbi algorithm* solves this task. This algorithm applies dynamic programming and can be interpreted as a search for the shortest path.

In our Mendel experiment, we may have a sequence of dominant observations:

$$y = (\mathbf{A, A, A, A, A}) \tag{5}$$

How should we find the most probable sequence of states (e.g. genotypes)? A predicted path through the HMM should estimate what the genotype sequence is in the emitted symbol sequence. We decode the observed symbol sequence to obtain the states and select the highest probability path (Fig. 5).

Obs:	A	A	A	A	A
	π_1				
AA:	0	1/4	→1/4	→1/4	→1/4
Aa:	1	→1/2	→1/4	→1/8	→1/16
aa:	0	0	0	0	0

Fig. 5. Analyzing an observation sequence by the *Viterbi algorithm*. The solution of the best state path is marked in **bold face**.

We are using the best preceding path (up to position t) to find the best possible score and path at position t+1. The sequence begins by default in state π_1, and we construct a table of the possible paths, each with a pointer from the previous position that generated it. After creating the table, the optimal state sequence will be found by backtracking, as in Fig. 5. In Fig. 6 shows a graphical illustration from the program MendelHMM with 10 generations.

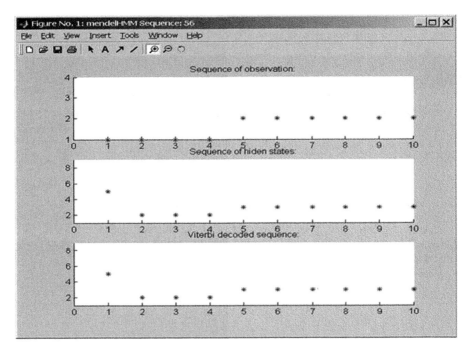

Fig. 6. A sample sequence of observations and hidden states from the *MendelHMM* model with 4 phenotypes and 9 hidden states. The Viterbi prediction based on the observed phenotypes alone is also presented and is very accurate in this example.

7 Concluding Remarks

Mendel created the first mathematical model for the transmission of heritable traits, based on the concepts of probability. He also studied in detail data from two and three independent pairs of genes. A resampled version of Mendel's data sets is available in our program *MendelHMM*. Even though Mendel's original "raw" data are lost, we have to regenerate them with the same sample size and ratios, as reported in his paper. In our program, the transition and emission probabilities may be estimated from the sequences of observations, and the number of hidden states may be varied.

The approach in MendelHMM is based on *experimental mathematics* in which computation is used to investigate mathematical objects and identify properties and patterns to achieve a better understanding [5, 6]. The method makes use of computational evidence instead of formal proofs. Experimental mathematics has long traditions in the history of science. It has re-emerged as a separate area of study in our time when computers vastly increase the range of achievable calculations. In this way, an innovative use of technology in learning a complex methodology may be realized.

Today HMMs are applied to a variety of problems in both language and DNA/protein sequence analysis, including gene finding and protein family classification and prediction. More background information and exercises may be found at the *MendelHMM* homepage [7]. The toolbox is implemented in *Matlab* and is freely available for nonprofit, academic use. Later on, the next version of the program will be available as an open-access web application.

References

1. Ross, S.M.: Introduction to Probability Models, 10th edn. Academic Press, Oxford (2009)
2. Thorvaldsen, S.: A tutorial on Markov models based on Mendel's classical experiments. J. Bioinform. Comput. Biol. **3**(6), 1441–1460 (2005)
3. Kirkpatrick, S., Gelatt, C., Vecchi, M.: Optimization by simulated annealing. Science **220**, 671–680 (1983)
4. Day, W.H.E.: Computationally difficult parsimony problems in phylogenetic systematics. J. Theoret. Biol. **103**, 429–438 (1983)
5. Borwein, J., Devlin, K.: The Computer as Crucible: An Introduction to Experimental Mathematics. CRC Press, Boca Raton (2008)
6. Santner, T.J., Williams, B.J., Notz, W.I.: The Design and Analysis of Computer Experiments. SSS. Springer, New York (2018). https://doi.org/10.1007/978-1-4939-8847-1
7. Mendel HMM Toolbox for Matlab. http://www.math.uit.no/bi/hmm/

Integrating Big Data in Introductory Statistics Education - Challenges for Instructors and Students

Jane Lu Hsu(✉) and You-Ren Chen

National Chung Hsing University, Taichung 402204, Taiwan
jlu@dragon.nchu.edu.tw

Abstract. Statistics education aims to equip students with theoretical concepts and analytical skills. In introductory statistics, training is focused on memorization of fundamental theorems and formulae with manual calculation. This study is in the first phase of a more comprehensive project to enhance undergraduate students' big data literacy in introductory statistics. Challenges for instructors and students are described based on qualitative findings. Four aspects are introduced: (1) software acquaintance; (2) big data applications; (3) understanding differences in statistical inferences between small data and big data; and (4) modification of teaching/learning module. Integrating big data applications into introductory statistics can be beneficial for students in practical training and in capacity building.

Keywords: Big data · Introductory statistics education · Challenges for instructors and students

1 Introduction

Big data has been integrated in curriculum for statistics education to equip students with advanced analytical skills to handle complicated data structures in reality. In introductory statistics education, big data is more of a concept than a subject in the course.

1.1 Characteristics of Big Data

Characteristics of big data have been described using 3Vs (Volume, Velocity, Variety) or 5Vs (Volume, Velocity, Variety, Veracity, and Value) [1]. Large volume data generated systematically in high speed is one major aspect of big data. Information stored in systems with structured or unstructured format for analytics are considered big data if certain characteristics can be possessed:

- Volume – size of data. Big data refers to huge amount of data points.
- Velocity – speed of data generation. Big data is generated, stored, and distributed in high speed.
- Variety – types of data. Big data has structured, semi-structured, or unstructured format.

- Veracity – quality of data. Big data needs to be accurate, consistent, secure, and reliable.
- Value – usability of data. Big data can be used for analytics, government policies, business strategies, and education.

1.2 Big Data in Statistics Education

Statistics education aims to equip students with theoretical concepts and analytical skills. In introductory statistics, training is focused on memorization of fundamental theorems and formulae with manual calculation. Software is supplementary in introductory statistics. Datasets in introductory statistics are simplified for manual calculation. For software training, subsets of data are provided to ease the burden of learning and practicing statistical formulae.

Statistics provides a foundation for advanced business analytics. In introductory statistics, big data is usually not introduced. Since introductory statistics can be the only statistical course students take in undergraduate education, lacking of the concept of big data can be a disadvantage for students to confront challenges of analytics in advanced study or in career development.

For students, the gap between handling 30 data points and tens thousands of data points is huge. Although statistical inferences apply to big data are extended from basic theorems, students in introductory statistics usually do not get opportunities to learn the skills needed for handling big data.

1.3 Research Objective

Introducing concept of big data in introductory statistics is in the beginning. Objective of this study is to provide some insights into challenges for instructor and students in integrating big data into introductory statistics education.

2 Literature Review

The development of statistics education incorporates big data applications, and further into business analytics in data science. For introductory statistics education, teaching objective is to train students with analytical skills using statistical concepts. Since statistical properties (unbiasedness, efficiency, consistency) are different between small data and big data, adding big data applications in introductory statistics means more materials for instructors and for students to cover within limited time frame of the course, which can be challenging.

Daniel [2] identifies critical issues with big data in education and explains the importance in conceptualization of implementation as big data in education becomes a mainstream. Klašnja-Milićević et al. [3] argue the rationales to associate big data and learning analytics together, and describe possibilities and techniques for extending the capabilities of educational systems.

François et al. [4] state the need to have big-data literacy integrated into statistical literacy. Bargagliotti et al. [5] emphasize the need to have big data analytic skills considered as one of the undergraduate students' learning outcomes.

3 Research Methodology

This study is in the first phase of a more comprehensive project to enhance undergraduate students' big data literacy in introductory statistics. Challenges for instructors and students are described based on qualitative findings.

Introductory statistics offered as a core course in college of management at a national university is selected for this study. Student enrollment is above 90. In addition to conventional statistics teaching, big data application is introduced in the course.

Students are offered an option to join this project with additional training in big data application. Signed consensuses are obtained before participation.

3.1 Project Design

Most students in introductory statistics class from the college of management are not familiar with programming. Hence, there is a step-by-step teaching method designed for students to help them learn how to use Python to process big data and visualize data. Teaching method is illustrated in Fig. 1.

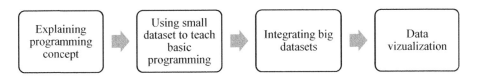

Fig. 1. Teaching method applied to introductory statistics.

After class, most students mentioned that they could understand the basic programming concept well, and enjoyed the learning process of the training.

4 Results

Sources of big data used in introductory statistics are from open source. Table 1 lists examples of open source data, descriptions, and organizations as data sources.

Based on preliminary findings in this study, challenges and opportunities for instructors and for students are summarized as follows. Challenges for instructors/ students are:

Table 1. Examples of open source data for introductory statistics.

Dataset	Short description	Data source
US station hourly climate	This dataset contains the weather change every hour from January 1, 2010 to January 31, 2010 in United States one station	NOAA
Gross domestic product	This dataset contains the GDP(US dollars) of different countries in different years. Data interval from 1960 to 2018	OECD
Crude oil production	This dataset contains the oil production of different countries in different years. Data interval from 1960 to 2018	OPEC
Industrial production index	This dataset contains the Industrial production index of different industries in different month in Taiwan. Data interval from January 1982 to June 2020	National statistics
Customer price index	This dataset contains the Customer Price Index of different categories in different month in Taiwan. Data interval from January 1981 to July 2020	National statistics
National income statistics	This dataset contains the national Income of different categories in different season in Taiwan. Indicators contains economics growth, GDP. GNI etc. Data interval from season1, 1961 to season1, 2020	National statistics
Total value of import and export trade	This dataset contains the total value of import and export trade in different month in Taiwan. Data interval from January, 2001 to July, 2020	National statistics
Business indicators	This dataset contains Taiwan's business indicators every month from January 1982 to June 2020. Business indicators contains leading factor, coincident factor etc.	National statistics
Taiwan's electricity supply and demand information	This dataset contains Taiwan's electricity supply and demand information every day from January 1, 2019 to June 30, 2020	Government information open platform
UV detection	This dataset contains the UV value every hour from August 10, 2020 to August 11, 2020 in Taiwan's different detection stations	Government information open platform
Dioxin information	This dataset contains the Dioxin value every day from March 6, 2017 to May 18, 2020 in Taiwan's different sites	Government information open platform

Software acquaintance – Python is a powerful software for data science. Instructors may have more knowledge than students in coding. For first-time statistics learners, training in software coding can be very challenging. Additional help sessions are needed for slow-learners to get acquainted with software.

Big data applications – Big data applications cover diversified topics. What instructors select for teaching materials may not be interested for students to learn. What students are interested, for example social media data, may not fit well in objectives of statistics teaching.

Understanding differences in statistical inferences between small data and big data – Big data holds certain statistical properties and is different from the content of introductory statistics. Instructors may need to spend extra time explaining the uniqueness of big data statistical properties, or may need to provide additional learning materials for students to understand big data statistical properties.

Modification of teaching/learning module – Conventional introductory statistics education has not been data-centered. Integrating big data in introductory statistics requires modification of teaching/learning modules.

5 Conclusion

This study provides some insights into challenges for instructors/students to integrate big data applications into introductory statistics education. Four aspects are introduced: (1) software acquaintance; (2) big data applications; (3) understanding differences in statistical inferences between small data and big data; and (4) modification of teaching/learning module.

In conclusion, introductory statistics education provides a solid foundation for students to learn advanced analytical skills in data science. Integrating big data applications into introductory statistics can be beneficial for students in practical training and in capacity building.

Research Funding. This research is supported by Ministry of Science and Technology (MOST-109-2511-H-005 -001) in Taiwan.

References

1. Younas, M.: Research challenges of big data. SOCA **13**(2), 105–107 (2019). https://doi.org/10.1007/s11761-019-00265-x
2. Daniel, B.K.: Big data and data science: a critical review of issues for educational research. Br. J. Edu. Technol. **50**(1), 101–113 (2019)
3. Klašnja-Milićević, A., Ivanović, M., Budimac, Z.: Data science in education: big data and learning analytics. Comput. Appl. Eng. Educ. **25**(6), 1066–1078 (2017)
4. François, K., Monteiro, C., Allo, P.: Big-data literacy as a new vocation for statistical literacy. Stat. Educ. Res. J. **19**(1), 194–205 (2020)
5. Bargagliotti, A., et al.: Undergraduate learning outcomes for achieving data acumen. J. Stat. Educ. **28**(2), 197–211 (2020)

Integration of LUPDA Theory and STEAM with Computational Thinking Concepts to Develop Assessment Principles for an AI Based STEAM Activity

Chih-Hung Wu[1] and Yueh-Min Huang[2(✉)]

[1] National Taichung University of Education, Taichung City, Taiwan, R.O.C.
chwu@mail.ntcu.edu.tw
[2] National Cheng-Kung University, Tainan City, Taiwan, R.O.C.
huang@mail.ncku.edu.tw

Abstract. This study uses learn, use, practice, design, apply/analyze (LUPDA) theory to combine science, technology, engineering, art, and math (STEAM) and computational thinking (CT) concepts to develop assessment principles. The STEAM teaching activity designs and implements an artificial intelligence (AI) webcam game with micro:bit technology, AI computer vision, and deep learning techniques to recognize the user's hand gestures via webcam. The game in our teaching experiment which can automatically interpret the user's gestures as scissors, stone, or cloth through the webcam, and then automatically react to the user through a motor. Finally, this study proposes a set of relevant assessment principles based on STEAM, LUPDA theory, and CT concepts.

Keywords: Artificial intelligence (AI) · STEAM · Computational thinking (CT) · LUPDA theory

1 Introduction

STEAM integrates science, technology, engineering, art, and mathematics across disciplines to cultivate problem solving skills by fostering cross-domain integration [1]. However, there has been very little research combining computational thinking (CT) concepts with STEAM education. Studies have shown that STEAM teachers who integrate CT concepts into lesson plans and curricula are more effective when they teach CT. In addition, CT training nurtures problem-solving attitudes and skills that are applicable not only to computer science, but to other disciplines as well [2]. However, few studies focus on developing assessment principles and questions for learning performance evaluation in science, technology, engineering, art, and math (STEAM) education.

Therefore, the purpose of this study is to develop a conceptual framework that includes a set of relevant assessment principles based on concepts of STEAM, LUPDA (learn, use, practice, design, apply/analyze) theory, and CT. The final assessment framework, and principles grounded in STEAM + LUPDA + CT were designed. Next, professors and experts were asked to revise the assessment principles and questions.

2   Literature Review

International research in the field of CT has increased dramatically in recent years; visual programming language is the most commonly used tool in CT studies. For example, the visual programming software Scratch has been used as a teaching tool in the past few years [3]. For educators, and especially for K-12 students, visual programming is a frequently used coding tool. For teachers, how to apply CT concepts to teaching is still an important issue that needs to be clarified [3]. A review of research on CT has used games in conjunction with learning theory to design contextual games to enhance students' CT skills [4].

3   Method

This study utilized the LUPDA theory to create and improve learning performance in STEAM education. LUPDA theory identifies the main purposes and guidelines for different STEAM learning components. The primary aims of LUPDA theory for STEAM are learning science content for science education, using technology (or coding) for technology education, practicing how to use tools for engineering education, designing works for art education, and applying/analyzing data for math education in STEAM learning activities. The detail descriptions are shown in Table 1.

This study combines LUPDA theory, STEAM, and CT to develop a framework of assessment principles and questions for STEAM education. This study invited several scholars and experts in STEAM and CT to help modify and revise the designed assessment principles/questions for each STEAM dimension to satisfy expert validity.

Designing a STEAM Activity. This study designed an AI-based webcam game with micro:bit technology and motors for a STEAM education activity based on the learning materials on the website [5]. Figure 1 presents the design of system. The science content includes the concepts of artificial intelligence (AI), Convolutional neural network (CNN), and mobile net. The technology content uses modified scratch visual language coding. The engineering content includes a webcam, micro:bit and motors. The art content encompasses the system design. The math content involves deep learning neural network accuracy calculation, and motor rotation angle calculation. The STEAM activity is used as an example of STEAM education activity in the proposed assessment framework and principles.

Fig. 1. AI webcam (scissors, stone, and cloth) game with micro:bit technology [5].

4 Data

This study develops a conceptual framework of relevant assessment principles and questions based on STEAM, LUPDA theory, and CT concepts. The framework and assessment principles were designed and asked the professors and experts to revised the assessment principles. The conceptual framework with detail assessment principles for STEAM with CT concepts are shown in Table 2, 3, 4, 5 and 6.

Table 1. LUPDA theory for STEAM education.

STEAM	Main purposes	Guidelines for educators
Science	Learn	The STEAM activities and courses in science part could focus on teaching students how to study and understand science content
Technology	Use	The STEAM activities and courses in technology part could focus on training students how to properly use technology, tools, and coding
Engineering	Practice	The STEAM activities and courses in engineering part could focus on training students how to properly use tools to assemble various materials in their work. Educators can design several activities to help students practice how to use these tools
Art	Design	The STEAM activities and courses in art part could focus on training students how to design beautiful unique works based on art theories. The teacher uses the designed activity to help students enhance their imagination and creativity
Math	Apply/Analyze	The STEAM activities and courses in math part could focus on training students how to use math to apply or analyze data and to discover trends in data

Table 2. Framework of assessment principles for the STEAM science dimension.

STEAM	LUPDA theory	Computational thinking	Score	Assessment principle
Science	Learn	Decomposition	+1 +2 +3	Being able to divide the science problem into several sub problems Being able to understand every useful science concepts or theories or algorithms for sub problems Being able to choose/use science correctly according to specifications in each sub problems

(continued)

Table 2. (*continued*)

STEAM	LUPDA theory	Computational thinking	Score	Assessment principle
		Pattern recognition	+1 +2 +3	The ability to figure out the pattern for each sub problems The ability to select the most appropriate science concept in each patterns Using science correctly in each patterns
		Abstraction	+1 +2 +3	The ability to design/plan several science sub programs to solve the problem Can choose the most appropriate science concepts/theories/algorithms and apply it in different sub problem and patterns Knowing how to build a good system or model (e.g. AI model)
		Algorithm	+1 +2 +3	Being able to design the flowchart that includes system/model/experimental hypotheses and then verify them The ability to collect data and analyze the experimental/simulation results Making generalizations and reasonable inferences based on the results of analysis

Teaching activity: building and training AI models

Table 3. Framework of assessment principles for the STEAM technology dimension.

STEAM	LUPDA theory	Computational thinking	Score	Assessment principle
Technology	Use	Decomposition	+1 +2 +3	Being able to divide the technology problem into several sub problems Being able to understand every useful techniques and tools for sub problems Being able to choose/use techniques and tools correctly according to specifications in each sub problems
		Pattern recognition	+1 +2 +3	The ability to figure out the pattern for each sub problems The ability to select the most appropriate materials and tools in each patterns Using materials and tools correctly according to specifications in each patterns

(*continued*)

Table 3. (*continued*)

STEAM	LUPDA theory	Computational thinking	Score	Assessment principle
		Abstraction	+1 +2 +3	The ability to design/plan several sub programs to solve the problem Using materials and tools/functions correctly according to specifications to finish the sub program The ability to modify or revise code based on the results
		Algorithm	+1 +2 +3	The ability to design/plan a flowchart to solve the whole problem Using and combine designed functions or subprograms based on the flowchart The ability to modify or revised the design of flowchart based on results

Teaching activity: being able to write program training data and improve training accuracy

Table 4. Framework of assessment principles for the STEAM engineering dimension.

STEAM	LUPDA theory	Computational thinking	Score	Assessment principle
Engineering	Practice	Decomposition	+1 +2 +3	Being able to divide the engineering problem into several sub problems Being able to understand every useful materials and tools for sub problems Being able to choose/use materials and tools correctly according to specifications in each sub problems
		Pattern recognition	+1 +2 +3	The ability to figure out the pattern for each sub problems The ability to select the most appropriate materials and tools in each patterns Using materials and tools correctly according to specifications in each patterns

(*continued*)

Table 4. (*continued*)

STEAM	LUPDA theory	Computational thinking	Score	Assessment principle
		Abstraction	+1 +2 +3	The ability to design/plan several components to solve the sub problems Using the components correctly to solve the sub program The ability to modify or revise components based on the results in each sub problems
		Algorithm	+1 +2 +3	The ability to design/plan a flowchart to solve the whole problem The ability to correctly combine components and build systems The ability to diagnose the correctness of the built system and modify it

Teaching activity: the ability to assemble motors from 1 to 2 motors

Table 5. Framework of assessment principles for the STEAM art dimension.

STEAM	LUPDA theory	Computational thinking	Score	Assessment principle
Art	Design	Decomposition	+1	The designed system is aesthetic Can show unique design ability Have imagination or creativity
		Pattern recognition	+2 +3	
		Abstraction		
		Algorithm		

Teaching activity: design the appearance of an AI rock-paper-scissors game

Table 6. Framework of assessment principles for the STEAM math dimension.

STEAM	LUPDA theory	Computational thinking	Score	Assessment principle
Math	Apply/Analyze	Decomposition	+1 +2 +3	Being able to divide the math problem into several sub problems Being able to understand every useful math functions for sub problems Being able to choose/use math formula or tools correctly according to specifications in each sub problems
		Pattern recognition	+1 +2 +3	The ability to figure out the pattern for each sub problems The ability to display trend of data in charts The ability to analysis the trend of data
		Abstraction	+1 +2 +3	Ability to use appropriate math for measurement Using the math correctly to solve the sub program The ability to modify or revise math formulas based on the results in each sub problems
		Algorithm	+1 +2 +3	The ability to design/plan a flowchart to solve the whole problem The ability to correctly combine math formula and tools The ability to diagnose the correctness of the built system and modify it

Teaching activity: the ability to calculate correct rate of AI rock-paper-scissors game

Based on our proposed assessment framework and principles, the steam capability diagnosis analysis can be conduct after the STEAM activity. The higher STEAM score in our framework, the higher capability students have. The score is calculated by the sum of each assessment principles in STEAM dimensions. An example of STEAM assessment result can be shown in Table 7. The capability diagnosis analysis for each student can be display in Fig. 2 based on the results of our proposed assessment framework. The high score in the dimension of STEAM denotes the student has high capability of this STEAM dimension.

Table 7. Example of STEAM assessment result.

Dimension	Sum of score
Science	4
Technology	5
Engineering	3
Art	6
Math	5

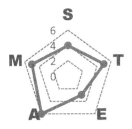

Fig. 2. STEAM capability diagnosis analysis.

5 Conclusions

This study used LUPDA theory to combine STEAM and CT concepts to develop assessment principles for STEAM and CT educators. The contribution of this study is the innovative integration of STEAM and CT for cross-disciplinary education, with a focus on building cross-disciplinary problem-solving skill in STEAM education. The concepts of CT, when applied to STEAM education, can help students cultivate problem-solving skills. If CT concepts are applied to STEAM education, they are useful for nurturing problem-solving skills and improving the learning performance of STEAM students. This study proposed LUPDA theory, which can help educators to design assessment principles and questions for measuring students' learning performance in their own STEAM with CT concepts activities.

Acknowledgement. Funding for the study was provided by the Ministry of Science and Technology (MOST), Taiwan, under Grant number: MOST 108-2511-H-142 -007 -MY2.

References

1. Pimthong, P., Williams, J.: Preservice teachers' understanding of STEM education. Kasetsart J. Soc. Sci. (2018)
2. Swaid, S.I.: Bringing computational thinking to STEM education. Procedia Manufact. **3**, 3657–3662 (2015)
3. Hsu, T.-C., Chang, S.-C., Hung, Y.-T.: How to learn and how to teach computational thinking: suggestions based on a review of the literature. Comput. Educ. **126**, 296–310 (2018)

4. Malizia, A., Fogli, D., Danesi, F., Turchi, T., Bell, D.: TAPASPlay: a game-based learning approach to foster computation thinking skills. In: 2017 IEEE Symposium on Visual Languages and Human-Centric Computing (VL/HCC), pp. 345–346. IEEE (2017)
5. GMII.TW. http://www.gmii.tw/gmiiblog/6031322. Accessed 2020

Project Management for Innovation Projects – State of Art

Zornitsa Yordanova

University of National and World Economy, 8mi dekemvri, Sofia, Bulgaria
`zornitsayordanova@unwe.bg`

Abstract. It has been largely researched what the factors which determine successful project management are. Most of the research show a huge dependency between project success and type of the projects in terms of size, industry, scope, market, etc. Much research analyze the type of project management and all specifics related to its application. This paper focuses on project management specifically for innovation projects as they are extremely different types of projects which require distinct project management approach. The purpose of the research is to determine the current state of art of the topic by revealing the research achievements in the science literature. The research applies a systematic literature analysis through a traditional approach as well as an advanced technique for digital systematic literature review so to reveal the current status of the state of art of the topic Project management for innovation projects. The systematic literature analysis went through 299 research papers from the Scopus database so to uncover the current accomplishment. The results are of interest to scientists and practitioners primarily from the management sciences, but are also extremely suitable for practitioners from any other industry related to innovation development.

Keywords: Project management · Innovation management · Technology management · Systematic literature review · Science management · Advanced analytics

1 Introduction

Over the last 40 years, project organization has been established as an effective tool for managing complex new activities within organizations. Project management handle many activities better than any other organizational structure [1]. Projects are the preferred management tool for the implementation of new activities, such as innovation development and innovation projects [2]. In recent decades, projects have become a parallel structure of the organization in almost every organization to engage in new activities [3]. Innovation developments are some of the optional new activities which take place in organizations. Developing innovations is exactly such activities which project organization is extremely appropriate for [4]. These kinds of projects are very often innovation projects per se [5]. For many companies, improving and increasing innovativeness and the ability to develop innovations is the most substantial factor for growth [6]. Unfortunately, while the value of these projects for companies is significant, their failure rate is also very high. This is why, the current research focuses on analyzing the management practices of innovation projects and to reveal by performing a systematic literature review, the state of art of this project management branch. The study design of the research steps on literature review of 299 science papers from Scopus database which are funneled for detecting the real research studies dealing with the topic. The findings show there is still gap no matter of the topicality on the matters. In addition, a specially developed Tool for Advanced Analytical Literature Review (AALR) is used so to detect some hidden for the manual literature review process dependencies.

2 Theoretical Background

The theoretical background in this section aims at briefly pointing out the main knowledge areas involved in the research. Deeper research analysis is performed in the 'results' section as part of the applied methodology.

2.1 Project Management

Project management is that part of project knowledge that explores and studies the more successful management of these initiatives. Organizations are becoming more project-oriented [7], and projects are the preferred management instrument especially for implementation of new activities [8]; [9]. However, because projects are constantly delayed, exceeding, and often technically unsuccessful, project management is often explored for opportunities for improvement. These threats increase with the complexity of the project. All these assumptions are extremely valid for science applied projects per se. As a structure, the methodology has been developed in nine main areas of knowledge and an additional one for integrity. The main areas of knowledge are: Integrity management; Project scope management; Project time management; Cost management; Quality management; Human resources management; Project communication management; Risk management; Procurement management [10]. An additional area added in recent years is the Management of the Code of Ethics in the project, which each project manager undertakes to comply with. Very often projects are implemented through processes. They are implemented by the project participants and fall into two categories: (1) Project management processes - for planning, organizing, coordinating and managing the project work. They are universal and standardized in the contractor's project management system. (2) Product Oriented Processes - to specify and create the project product.

There are plenty of science papers discussing innovation management, but still the connection between both sub-branches of management, dealing with project and innovation management remain unclarified.

2.2 Innovation Projects

According to During [11] innovation projects have to deal with three sub-processes concurrently: "These are problem solving, to bring about a new product or process;

internal innovation diffusion, to disseminate information and engender a positive attitude towards new developments; and change in the organization so that it may function successfully with new products or processes." His views still have no point on the matters of these innovations project management.

Innovation projects in this research are considered as projects which goal is developing an innovation. The definition adopted for innovation projects in this research is as follows: 'Innovation projects are systematically managed endeavors that use inputs in order to transform them into outputs with a certain scope and aims at achieving something new, in a new way or at improving something existing' [12]. It originates from both project management and innovation management theory.

3 Research Design for Revealing Project Management for Innovation Projects

The research design of the project is based on the principles of the systematic literature review. It was performed twofold by different approaches: in the traditional way by traditional manual means and secondly by using a digital tool for systematic literature review based on wording and context analysis in a specially developed data analytics software QlikSence.

The traditional systematic literate review steps on search in the Scopus database of science papers focusing on both project management and innovation projects. The used formula in Scopus advanced search was:

TITLE-ABS-KEY ("project management") AND TITLE-ABS-KEY ("innovation projects").

The advanced search feature of Scopus data source allows the search of all science papers, which have simultaneously the term 'project management' and 'innovation projects' in these papers' titles, abstracts and author keywords, no matter of the exact place. Doing this advanced search, the author assumes to scope all papers which purposefully target both project management and innovation projects or more focused "innovation projects management". No restrictions have been done to limit the science discipline of the papers because most of the research related to these methodologies are case studies and are very specific examples of their application. This data source gives the state of art of the topic in its full existence in the science literature.

The second research method used is applying the innovative digital Tool for Advanced Analytical Literature Review (AALR). A special tool has been designed and developed to serve the research. The tool is based on Qlik Sense application, which is amongst the best recognized business intelligence tools for data analytics. It is basically used for enterprise data analysis and its application in the current research through AALR is indeed an innovative method for deeper word and contextual analyzing the topic. It aims at revealing hidden connections between science papers with different focus from first impressions and hidden for analyses based on the traditional approaches. AALR is very useful and extremely appropriate for interdisciplinary research where the analyses include literature from diverse science fields.

The tool AALR integrates all the results from the Scopus research showed in the first step of the research design. AALR is configured with various filters by which the researcher can search and combine different words in order to compare and collate the use of different words within large amount of research papers in their titles, author keywords and abstracts. By doing this, the researcher is able to reveal hidden context, to discuss and analyze the use of words in their context, to make comparison and to identify links between different research. It might be also useful for defining knowledge gaps.

In the case of this research and the loaded data in the tool AALR, which data is Scopus sourced, the tool has this took, presented on Fig. 1.

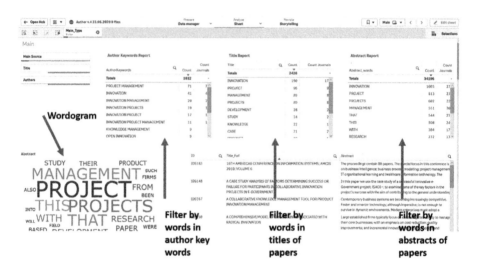

Fig. 1. AALR tool for digital literature analysis on words and word context.

In the tool AALR many analyses can be performed. They usually are iterative and consecutive based on the findings in the prior step. The results are demonstrated in the 'results' section of the paper.

4 Results and Discussion – Project Management for Innovation Projects

In this section of the paper, results from systematic literature review are presented based on the criteria put in the research design. The found science papers in the Scopus database are 299 papers. On Fig. 2 are shown all the papers according to the year of their publication.

It is obvious from the distribution of science research through the years that management of innovation projects has become of an interest of scientists after 2004 and especially in the last three years after 2017 (the data for 2020 is only for the first months and this is the reason for the big difference as well as the operational delay in indexing publications in the Scopus database). These are the journals which published more than 5 articles on the topic (inclusion criteria is shown in the research design):

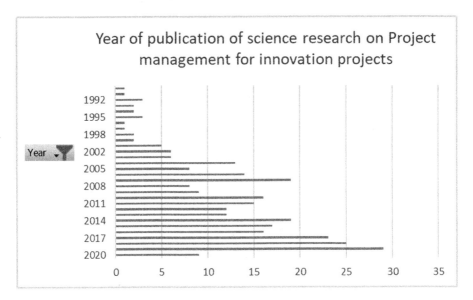

Fig. 2. Wave analysis in the developed application for digitalization of systematic literature review.

- Journal of Product Innovation Management - 15 articles
- Project Management Journal - 9 articles
- International Journal of Project Management - 9 articles
- International Journal of Technology Management - 7 articles
- IEEE International Engineering Management Conference - 6 papers
- Technovation - 5 articles

The relevance of the journals to both project and innovation management fields of the most publications on the matters confirms the suitable inclusion criteria set.

Reviewing the most cited articles showing the following results presented on Table 1.

The results show that top 10 of the golden source in the research topic are articles published in the period between 1994 and 2014. Going deeper into these research reveal that these studies do not really refer to project management for innovation projects but surely they are the knowledge base used for developing this particular management sub-branch. 60% of the cited paper more than 100 times are from the Journal of Product Innovation Management. This insight assumes with no science method but still relevantly for the research that project management for innovation projects in very closed also to product development.

Analyzing the scoped articles, by using filters in the titles and abstracts in excel with all 299 studies, with the inclusion criteria both containing "innovation" and "project" the results show 120 articles (the filters are first applied for abstracts as they contain much more information for the piece of research and then for the titles). By manually reviewing the titles and abstracts of these 120 articles, again they are not so focused in projects management for innovative projects. This is a reason to perform a

Table 1. Most cited science articles on project management for innovation projects.

Author	Title	Source	Cited by
Olson; Walker; Ruekert; Bonner [13]	Patterns of cooperation during new product development among marketing; operations and R&D: Implications for project performance	Journal of Product Innovation Management	287
O'Connor [14]	Market learning and radical innovation: A cross case comparison of eight radical innovation projects	Journal of Product Innovation Management	261
Keegan; Turner [15]	The management of innovation in project-based firms	Long Range Planning	191
Lettl [16]	User involvement competence for radical innovation	Journal of Engineering and Technology Management - JET-M	179
Moenaert; Souder; De Meyer; Deschoolmeester [17]	R&D-marketing integration mechanisms; communication flows; and innovation success	The Journal of Product Innovation Management	174
Moenaert; Meyer; Souder; Deschoolmeester [18]	R&D/Marketing Communication During the Fuzzy Front-End	IEEE Transactions on Engineering Management	162
Du J; Leten B; Vanhaverbeke [19]	Managing open innovation projects with science-based and market-based partners	Research Policy	135
Markham [20]	A Longitudinal Examination of How Champions Influence Others to Support Their Projects	Journal of Product Innovation Management	117
Brettel; Heinemann; Engelen; Neubauer [21]	Cross-functional integration of R&D; marketing; and manufacturing in radical and incremental product innovations and its effects on project effectiveness and efficiency	Journal of Product Innovation Management	109
Song; Thieme [22]	The role of suppliers in market intelligence gathering for radical and incremental innovation	Journal of Product Innovation Management	109

digital literature review for extracting real valued studies on the matters of the current research (with the availability to include more filters and funneling options).

The first analysis performed by the tool for digital literature review and analysis AALR, includes filtering the scoped 299 articles/papers by the author keywords "project management" and "innovative projects" which it should be the most précised search for the research topic. On Fig. 3 is presented a wordogram of the most frequently met words in the 87 articles that met these criteria. Words with less than 4 symbols and common words for abstracts are removed (ex. like, this, these, most, paper, have, been, such, from, case, more, used, which, etc.) from the wordogram.

Abstract

PRODUCT   RESULTS   BETWEEN
OTHER **KNOWLEDGE**
OPEN   2019   RISK   MODEL
                     TEAM
USING **RESEARCH**
PURPOSE   IMPACT   SOCIAL
DEVELOPMENT PROCESS
WORK   PERFORMANCE   APPROACH

Fig. 3. Most used words in abstracts of focused articles on project management for innovative projects.

The results show that usually research dealing with project management for innovative projects discuss also these topics: processes, development, research, open, impact, social, performance, product.

Analyzing deeper the focused 87 articles, some interesting ones paid attention. The topic for project management for innovative projects is research for example in the case of e-government in the article of Keefe, Bikfalvi, Beer and De La Rosa called "A case study analysis of factors determining success or failure for participants in collaborative innovation projects in e-Government" [23]. Some use and application of flexible project management methods is also detected as in the article 'Agility and the role of project-internal control systems for innovation project performance' of Lill, Wald and Gleich from 2019 [24]. Interesting insights are reveals from De Los Rios and Villa in 2019 about the management of science, technology and innovation projects under the PMI principles [25]. Again in 2019, a research of Midler is discussing the transformation of innovation project management, which additionally funnels the researched topic into a specific knowledge area of project management called 'innovation project management' [26].

The latest research on the topic is more and more focused and confirmatively prove the existence of the specific knowledge area of project management for innovation projects and development.

5 Conclusion

In conclusion of the presented analyses aiming at stating the art of project management for innovative projects the author clearly showed the interconnection between project management, innovation management and product management as closely relevant multidisciplinary approach for the newly more and more met term: 'innovative projects management'. The research provided to readers some insight about the currently done science work on the matters and reveal some contextual topics discussed meanwhile as: open innovation, process management, user involvement, the importance of performance.

The future work of the author will be focused on collaborating with different scientists from diverse science fields for using some of the collected knowledge on managing innovative projects.

Acknowledgments. The paper is supported by the BG NSF Grant No KP-06 OPR01/3-2018.

References

1. Gemünden, H.G., Lehner., P., Kock, A.: The project-oriented organization and its contribution to innovation. Int. J. Project Manag. **36**(1), 147–160 (2018)
2. Allahar, H.: A management innovation approach to project planning. Technol. Innov. Manag. Rev. **9**(6), 4–13 (2019). https://doi.org/10.22215/timreview/1245
3. Matinheikki, J., Artto, K., Peltokorpi, A., Rajala, R.: Managing inter-organizational networks for value creation in the front-end of projects. Int. J. Project Manag. **34**(7), 1226–1241 (2016). ISSN 0263-7863. https://doi.org/10.1016/j.ijproman.2016.06.003
4. Van Lancker, J., et al.: The organizational innovation system: a systemic framework for radical innovation at the organizational level. Technovation (2015). https://doi.org/10.1016/j.technovation.2015.11.008i
5. Maranhão, R., Marinho, M., de Moura, H.: Narrowing impact factors for innovative software project management. Procedia Comput. Sci. **64**, 957–963 (2015). https://doi.org/10.1016/j.procs.2015.08.613
6. Lopesa, A.: Innovation management: a systematic literature analysis of the innovation management evolution. Braz. J. Oper. Prod. Manag. **13**(1), 16–30 (2016). https://doi.org/10.14488/BJOPM.2016.v13.n1.a2
7. Morris, P., Pinto, K.J.: The Wiley Guide to Project, Program, and Portfolio Management. Wiley (2007)
8. Filippov, S., Mooi, H.: Innovation project management: a research agenda. J. Innov. Sustain. (2010). ISSN 2179-3565
9. Ghaben, R., Jaaron, A.: Assessing innovation practices in project management: the case of Palestinian construction projects. Int. J. Innov. Sci. Res. **17**(2), 451–465 (2015). ISSN 2351-8014
10. Project Management Institute, Project management body of knowledge, PMBOK (2017)
11. During, W.E.: Project management and management of innovation in small industrial firms. Technovation **4**(4), 269–278 (1986)
12. Yordanova, Z.: Innovation project tool for outlining innovation projects. Int. J. Bus. Innov. Res. **16**(1), 63–78 (2018)

13. Olson, E.M., Walker Jr., O.C., Ruekert, R.W., Bonner, J.M.: Patterns of cooperation during new product development among marketing; operations and R&D: implications for project performance. J. Prod. Innov. Manag. **18**(4), 258–271 (2001)
14. O'Connor, G.C.: Market learning and radical innovation: a cross case comparison of eight radical innovation projects. J. Prod. Innov. Manag. **15**(2), 151–166 (1998)
15. Keegan, A., Turner, J.R.: The management of innovation in project-based firms. Long Range Plan. **35**(4), 367–388 (2002)
16. Lettl, C.: User involvement competence for radical innovation. J. Eng. Technol. Manag. JET-M **24**, 53–75 (2007)
17. Moenaert, R.K., Souder, W.E., De Meyer, A., Deschoolmeester, D.: R&D-marketing integration mechanisms; communication flows; and innovation success. J. Prod. Innov. Manag. **11**(1), 31–45 (1994)
18. Moenaert, R.K., Meyer, A.D., Souder, W.E., Deschoolmeester, D.: R&D/Marketing communication during the fuzzy front-end. IEEE Trans. Eng. Manage. **42**(3), 243–258 (1995)
19. Du, J., Leten, B., Vanhaverbeke, W.: Managing open innovation projects with science-based and market-based partners. Res. Policy **43**(5), 828–840 (2014)
20. Markham, S.K.: A longitudinal examination of how champions influence others to support their projects. J. Prod. Innov. Manag. **15**(6), 490–504 (1998)
21. Brettel, M., Heinemann, F., Engelen, A., Neubauer, S.: Cross-functional integration of R&D; marketing; and manufacturing in radical and incremental product innovations and its effects on project effectiveness and efficiency. J. Prod. Innov. Manag. **28**(2), 251–269 (2011)
22. Song, M., Thieme, J.: The role of suppliers in market intelligence gathering for radical and incremental innovation. J. Prod. Innov. Manag. **26**(1), 43–57 (2009)
23. Keefe, T., Bikfalvi, A., Beer, M.; De La Rosa, J.L.: A case study analysis of factors determining success or failure for participants in collaborative innovation projects in e-Government. In: Proceedings of the European Conference on e-Government; ECEG, pp. 276–282 (2013)
24. Lill, P.A., Wald, A., Gleich, R.: Agility and the role of project-internal control systems for innovation project performance. Int. J. Innov. Manag. **24**, 1–29 (2019). 2050064
25. De Los Rios, V.C., Villa, J.L.: Analysis of the management of science; technology and innovation projects under the PMI principles [Análisis de la Gestión de proyectos de Ciencia; Tecnología e Innovación bajo los Principios del PMI]. In: Proceedings of the LACCEI International Multi-Conference for Engineering; Education and Technology (2019)
26. Midler, C.: Crossing the valley of death: managing the when; what; and how of innovative development projects. Project Manag. J. **50**(4), 447–459 (2019)

Innovative Learning in Education

A Comparative Study on Ethics Guidelines for Artificial Intelligence Across Nations

Tony Szu-Hsien Lee, Shiang-Yao Liu, Yin-Ling Wei, and Li-Yun Chang(✉)

National Taiwan Normal University, Taipei 10610, Taiwan (R.O.C.)
liyunchang@ntnu.edu.tw

Abstract. This study aimed to investigate the commonality and differences among AI research and development (R&D) guidelines across nations. Content analysis was conducted on AI R&D guidelines issued by more economically developed countries because they may guide the trend of AI-based applications in education. Specifically, this study consisted of three phases: 1) information retrieval, (2) key term extraction, and (3) data visualization. First, Fisher's exact test was employed to ensure that different AI R&D guidelines (e.g., the latest ones in the US, EU, Japan, Mainland, and Taiwan) were comparable. Second, the Key Word Extraction System was developed to retrieve essential information in the guidelines. Third, data visualization techniques were performed on key terms across multiple guidelines. A word cloud revealed the similarity among guidelines (e.g., key terms that these guidelines share in common) while a color-coding scheme showed the differences (e.g., occurrence of a key term across guidelines and its frequency within a guideline). Importantly, three key terms, namely, AI, human, and development, are identified as essential commonality across guidelines. As for key terms that only extracted from particular guidelines, interestingly, results with the color-coding scheme suggested that these key terms were weighted differently depends on the developmental emphasis of a nation. Collectively, we discussed how these findings concerning ethics guidelines may shed light on AI research and development to educational technology.

Keywords: Artificial intelligence · Data visualization technique · Education · Ethics guidelines · Text mining

1 Introduction and Related Work

The rapid advances in research and development (R&D) of artificial intelligence (AI) have yielded a number of ethics guidelines. These guidelines provide guidance for new AI technologies and applications and thus are important references for developing educational technology. Since Aiken and Epstein [1] initiated a conversation concerning what is desirable and what is not in using AI in education, over the past 20 years, the growing concerns in discussing ethical issues in AI (e.g., privacy, responsibility, autonomy, justice, transparency, and beneficence) highlighted the importance of AI ethics.

These ethics guidelines may vary across nations, which in turn, may influence the application of ethical principles in different fields such as industry, governments, and academia [2]. Although there are a few studies [3, 4] which compares different ethical guidelines across various stakeholders (e.g., policymakers, AI developers, key user groups or general users, educators and professionals), several critical issues exist. First, while Jobin et al.'s analysis is comprehensive, their contribution is merely descriptive [5], rather than normative. Second, while Zeng et al. attempted to use visualization techniques to explicitly establish the links among AI ethics guidelines, there approach of choosing keywords is manually-chosen, rather than data-driven. Third, the literary genre of various ethics guidelines is often neglected in previous comparative analyses. For instance, *Ethically Aligned Design* which released by IEEE [5] is 294-page long whereas *The Japanese Society for Artificial Intelligence Ethical Guidelines* [6] only has three pages. Without considering the length of content, in comparing ethics guidelines across different stakeholders, the results may be misleading.

To address the above issues, we focus on AI R&D guidelines issues by governments because these normative, official AI ethics guidelines play prominent roles in developing and implementing AI technologies. Moreover, we deliberately choose guidelines from more economically developed countries [4] given their leading statues in educational technology worldwide. Note that the length of these guidelines would be comparable. Furthermore, we utilize text mining and data visualization techniques to analyze the content. By adopting the more objective approach and by keeping in mind that we do not aim at a full analysis of all AI ethics documents, the goal of this study is to investigate the commonality and differences among these AI R&D guidelines.

Particularly, we raise the following research questions:

1. What is essential commonality across AI ethics guidelines in more economically developed countries chosen in this study?
2. What are the differences among these guidelines and how do they potentially relate to the developmental emphasis of different nations?

2 Research Method

We adopted content analysis and data visualization techniques to investigate commonality and difference of key terms among AI principles issued by governments. In particular, we focused on AI R&D principles considered by more economically development countries because they would guide the development of AI-based products.

2.1 Materials

AI R&D principles issued by the USA, EU, Japan, China, and Taiwan were selected as target content for analysis. The first three, representing more economically developed countries, together accounted for nearly half of all ethical AI principles, according to Jobin et al. [4]. The later two, China and Taiwan, were selected based on our research interest.

Below are brief sketches of these AI R&D principles, beginning from the latest one:

1. Guidance for Regulation of Artificial Intelligence Applications [7]: 10 principles from the USA.
2. Guidelines for Artificial Intelligence Technology Research and Development [8]: 8 principles and 3 core values from Taiwan.
3. Guidance for Research and Development of Artificial Intelligence [9]: 7 principles form Mainland China.
4. Ethical Principles and Democratic Prerequisites to form a responsible AI [10], 9 principles from EU.
5. The Japanese Society for Artificial Intelligence Ethical Guidelines [6]: 9 principles from Japan.

2.2 Instruments

The Key Term Extraction [11], a multilingual keyword extraction system for suggesting key terms from digital documents (PRC Patent No: ZL 00 1 22602.9.), was adopted for our content analysis. This research tool features in automatic keyword extraction, a fundamental technology in advance information retrieval system.

With a larger corpus, the precision rate of the Tseng's [12] keyword extraction algorithm is over 96% for news and over 90% for bibliographic materials, suggesting that its system quality is reliable. Moreover, this system affords both quantitative and graphical representations for the results. Resulting key terms would be ranked based on their frequency (by token) in the document, while the semantic relationship between these key terms would be shown by a key-term graph. This system is available via: http://rsp.itc.ntnu.edu.tw/SAMtool/SegWord_CGI.html.

2.3 Procedure

The procedure consisted of three phases: (1) information retrieval, (2) key term extraction, and (3) data visualization. In the phase one (information retrieval), for each guideline, number of principles and total length of principles were retrieved for examining whether they differ significantly across five guidelines. The Fisher's exact test was performed, respectively. Results showed that neither the length ($p \geq 0.05$) nor the number of principles ($p \geq 0.05$) differ across guidelines, suggesting the five guidelines were comparable. In the phase two (key term extraction), each guideline was processed by the Key Term Extraction [12]. All automatically-generated key-term graphs and the key terms were saved in a cloud drive (https://parg.co/bGGc). We examined each term carefully and kept content words, excluding function words, for further exploration. Finally, given that there were commonality and differences existed in the key terms from five guidelines, data visualization technique was adopted in the phase three.

3 Results and Discussion

We presented the commonality and differences of key terms across five guidelines by word cloud, an intuitive visualization technique to give our readers a glance into the most frequent words, and a color-coded table to show a more in-depth analysis on the coverage of different guidelines on various key terms.

3.1 Word Cloud as a Starting Point for Deeper Guideline Analyses

To derive an intuition of what information these guidelines may contain, we did the keyword summaries by HTML5 Word Cloud. Figure 1 showed the most frequent words of as a weighted list of key words. The top 5 frequent words (and times) were: AI (70), human (32), develop (24), society (18), and system (18). We also did the same analyses on separate guidelines (see cloud drive). Although font sizes of the words indicated their occurrence frequency in the guidelines, other properties did not encode specific information. Thus, in the following, we focused on the results of key term extraction.

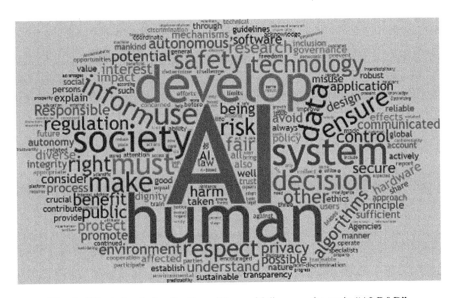

Fig. 1. Word cloud visualization of five guidelines on the topic "AI R&D".

3.2 Color-Coded Analysis Showing Commonality and Differences in Key Terms

The key term extraction was run on individual guideline. To reveal commonality and differences of the resulting five lists of key terms, we applied a color-coding scheme (see Fig. 2).

Key term \ Nation	Japan (2017)	EU (2018)	Beijing (2019)	Taiwan (2019)	USA (2020)	Cumulative frequency
AI	18	10	16	19	26	89
Human	2	9	7	8	4	30
Development	4	2	6	2	3	17
Data	0	6	3	5	2	16
Safety	3	5	2	0	3	13
Systems	0	7	7	0	3	17
Society	9	0	2	4	0	15
Information	3	2	0	0	8	13
Autonomous	0	8	0	2	2	12
Decisions	0	2	0	9	0	11
Ensure	0	3	5	0	3	11
Impact	2	0	3	0	3	8
Privacy	0	2	0	2	4	8
Fair	2	0	0	2	2	6
Risks	0	0	4	0	10	14
Benefit	0	0	2	0	9	11
Potential	0	0	4	0	7	11
Application	0	2	0	0	8	10
Nature	0	0	3	0	5	8
Respect	4	3	0	0	0	7
Security	0	2	0	0	5	7
Considered	0	0	3	0	3	6
Protection	0	4	0	0	2	6
Processes	0	2	0	0	4	6
Research	3	0	2	0	0	5
Responsibility	2	3	0	0	0	5
Rights	0	0	3	2	0	5
Integrity	2	0	0	0	3	5
Humanity	3	0	2	0	0	5
Human dignity	0	2	0	2	0	4
Environment	0	2	2	0	0	4
Implementation	0	0	2	0	2	4

Fig. 2. The distribution of key terms retrieving from AI R&D guidelines across nations. (Color figure online)

First, key terms were categorized into five colored sections to denote how common they were across five guidelines; for instance, green denotes a key term that was mentioned in five guidelines (green = 5, blue = 4, red = 3, and 2 = yellow; for a key term that only appeared in one guideline, see cloud drive). Also, darker color denotes more frequent that the key term was mentioned.

Second, within each colored section, key terms were sequenced based on their cumulative frequency. For example, for three key terms in the green section, while they were all mentioned across five guidelines, they were listed as follows based on weights: AI(89), Human(30), and Development(17).

4 Conclusions and Future Work

This study adopted content analysis and data visualization to investigate the commonality and differences among AI R&D guidelines across nations (i.e., the US, EU, Japan, Mainland, and Taiwan). Three key terms, AI, human, and development, are identified as essential commonality across guidelines. As for key terms that only extracted from particular guidelines (e.g., risk, benefit, responsibility, rights and more), they were weighted differently in the color-coding scheme. The findings echoed prior research which suggested that AI ethics guidelines may vary across nations and cultures [2, 4], with supportive evidence from a more objective, data-driven approach. This approach could be applied to guidelines that released by other stakeholders (e.g., AI developers, key user groups or general users, educators and professionals), letting the conversation [1] moves on.

Acknowledgements. This work was financially supported by the grant MOST- 109-2634-F-003-008 from Ministry of Science and Technology of Taiwan.

References

1. Aiken, R.M., Epstein, R.G.: Ethical guidelines for AI in education: starting a conversation. Int. J. Artif. Intell. Educ. **11**, 163–176 (2020)
2. Liu, S.Y., Chang, C.H., Chao, E., Chang, L.Y., Lee, S.H.: Challenges and reflections on ethics of artificial intelligence: a literature review. J. Inf. Soc. (in Press)
3. Zeng, Y., Lu, E., Huangfu, C.: Linking artificial intelligence principles. In: Espinoza, H., Héigeartaigh, S.Ó., Huang, X., Hernández-Orallo, J., Castillo-Effen, M. (eds.) Proceedings of the AAAI Workshop on Artificial Intelligence Safety, vol. 2301, pp. 103–106. Creative Commons CC0, Honolulu (2019)
4. Jobin, A., Ienca, M., Vayena, E.: The global landscape of AI ethics guidelines. Nat. Mach. Intell. **1**, 389–399 (2019)
5. The IEEE Global Initiative on Ethics of Autonomous and Intelligent Systems: Ethically Aligned Design (EAD1e) (2019). https://standards.ieee.org/content/dam/ieee-standards/standards/web/documents/other/ead1e.pdf?utm_medium=PR&utm_source=Web&utm_campaign=EAD1e&utm_content=geias&utm_term=undefined
6. Japanese Society for Artificial Intelligence: The Japanese Society for Artificial Intelligence Ethical Guidelines (2017). http://ai-elsi.org/wp-content/uploads/2017/05/JSAI-Ethical-Guidelines-1.pdf

7. Memorandum for the Heads of Executive Departments and Agencies: Guidance for Regulation of Artificial Intelligence Applications (2020). https://www.whitehouse.gov/wp-content/uploads/2020/01/Draft-OMB-Memo-on-Regulation-of-AI-1-7-19.pdf
8. Digitimes: MOST announces AI R&D guidelines (2019). https://www.digitimes.com/news/a20190923PD209.html
9. Beijing Academy of Artificial Intelligence: Beijing AI Principles (2019), https://www.baai.ac.cn/news/beijing-ai-principles-en.html
10. European Commission: Artificial intelligence: Commission takes forward its work on ethics guidelines (2019). https://ec.europa.eu/commission/presscorner/detail/en/IP_19_1893
11. Tseng, Y.H.: Multilingual keyword extraction for term suggestion. In: Proceedings of the 21st International ACM SIGIR Conference on Research and Development in Information Retrieval, pp. 377–378. Association for Computing Machinery, New York (1998)
12. Tseng, Y.H.: Automatic key feature extraction from digital documents, PRC Patent No: ZL 00 1 22602.9. Application date: August 4, 2000. Effective from April 26, 2006 to August 4 (2020)

Analysis on the Application of AI Technology in Online Education Under the Public Epidemic Crisis

Shuijing Li[1], Ming Yan[1], Xin Zhang[1], and Zhe Li[2(✉)]

[1] Communication University of China, Beijing 100024, China
[2] Fujian Normal University, Fuzhou 350007, China
lizheritetu@163.com

Abstract. In order to prevent the spread of COVID-19, online education has become a learning way for primary and secondary schools and universities. However, the rapid development of online education faces many challenges. In recent years, Artificial Intelligence (AI) technology has been developed rapidly and applied in different industries. Therefore, many problems in online education can also be improved through AI technology, so as to improve the quality of online education, and make education improve. This paper mainly analyzes the integration of AI technology and online education to solve the problems faced by students in online learning. At the same time of reducing the burden of education participants, let AI technology play a better role, and help education develop from traditional offline mode to online and offline complementary direction.

Keywords: COVID-19 · Artificial Intelligence · Online education · Integration

1 Introduction

With the outbreak of the epidemic, nearly 270 million students across the country need to learn online at home. Online education plays an unprecedented role and shoulder the responsibility of national students' learning. Schools in various regions respond to the call and organized online education. Multi-platform and multi type online education become a learning way for students of all grades during the epidemic period. The common platforms include Rain class, Tencent class, Massive Open Online Course (MOOC), China education channel, etc.

1.1 Education During the Epidemic

However, the sudden change of education mode will inevitably bring many problems, such as students' difficulty in focusing, platform easy to jam, teachers are not familiar with the online teaching mode, which can't be ignored. Therefore, this paper hopes to solve the difficulties of students and teachers in online education through the combination of Artificial Intelligence (AI) technology and online education, and help online education at the same time, innovate more functions and play a better role.

1.2 The Future of AI Education Integration

AI is a hot spot around people in recent years. Many achievements of AI have been applied in real life, such as license plate recognition, fingerprint recognition [1].

With the continuous development of AI, it has been able to replace some jobs. According to previous studies, AI competes with human lawyers for contract review, the accuracy of AI will be 10% higher than that of human, and the time used will be about 200 times shorter.

It can be seen that the integration of AI and education is the general trend. AI can provide the technology and tools needed for education development, make learning environment tend to build technology integration, improve teachers' teaching efficiency, provide a high-quality education solid foundation for students, so that students have more diversified learning environment. According to the analysis of Frost Sullivan prospective industry research institute, from 2019 to the next three years, China's AI education market will gradually expand and develop, reaching 719.8 billion yuan by 2023. Forecast of China's AI education market scale in 2019–2023 is as shown in Fig. 1.

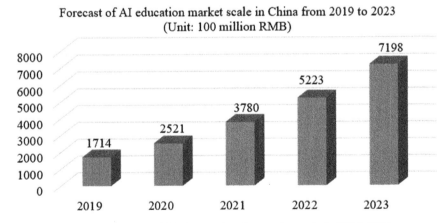

Fig. 1. Forecast of China's AI education market scale in 2019–2023.

2 Problems of Online Education During the Epidemic and AI Helps Education

2.1 The Necessity of Online Education During the Epidemic

We can use the mathematical model of infectious diseases to analyze and simulate the spread speed and scope of infectious diseases, so as to verify the necessity of home isolation and martial defense of epidemic situation. This paper uses Susceptible-Exposed-Infectious-Recovered (SEIR) model to analyze. SEIR model is a model to study the transmission speed, spatial range, transmission path, dynamic mechanism of infectious diseases by analyzing the relationship among susceptible, exposed, infectious and recovered people, so as to guide the effective prevention and control of infectious diseases.

S refers to the susceptible, E refers to the exposed, I refers to the infectious, R refers to the recovered, β refers to the infection rate, γ_1 refers to the recovery rate in the incubation period, γ_2 refers to the recovery rate in the patient, α refers to the development rate in the incubation period. The formula of SEIR model is:

$$\frac{dS}{dt} = -\beta IS + \alpha R \tag{1}$$

$$\frac{dE}{dt} = \beta IS - (\alpha + \gamma_1)E \tag{2}$$

$$\frac{dI}{dt} = \alpha E - \gamma_2 I \tag{3}$$

$$\frac{dR}{dt} = \gamma_1 E + \gamma_2 I \tag{4}$$

$$S(t) + E(t) + I(t) + R(t) = constant \tag{5}$$

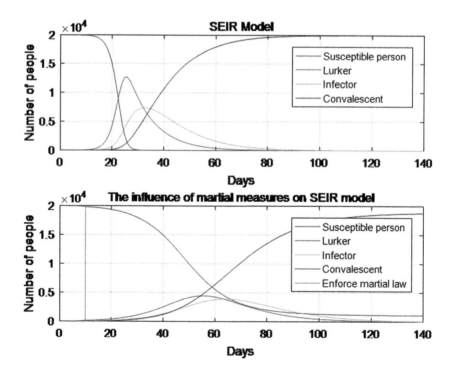

Fig. 2. Comparison of SEIR model for severe epidemic prevention.

The SEIR model with a total population of 20000 is established to compare the epidemic situation after no measures and martial law control. The simulation results are shown in Fig. 2. The right figure takes strict prevention measures on the 10th day. It can be seen that compared with the figure above, the high incidence date of infectious diseases in the figure below is delayed and the number of patients in the high incidence period is greatly reduced.

Therefore, it can be find out that it is wise to continue to study and work at home and isolate people. During the epidemic, the education of students can't be separated from the online education mode, but at the same time, the problem of online education has also been magnified.

2.2 Problems of Online Education During the Epidemic

While online education plays an important role, it also exposes a lot of problems and deficiencies. In the early stage of "non-stop learning", online education was entrusted with a heavy task in a hurry. The number of online classes exceeded 200 million, and various online class platforms have been stuck and overloaded. In the face of such a large-scale concurrent number of customers, the whole industry has no relevant data and experience, there is no time to conduct the drill in advance, which leads to the problem of network congestion and overall overload of interactive services for operators.

In addition to the problems of the platform operators, the sudden change of the teaching environment makes all the education participants face great difficulties. The change of teaching methods caught the teachers by surprise, suddenly changed the usual teaching methods and made different teaching plans, which is undoubtedly a big test for teachers. Most of the teachers did not have the experience of being "anchor". They had to prepare for the start of the class a long time in advance every day. After the start of the class, they either forgot to turn on the microphone or the camera, which caused a lot of embarrassment.

For a period of time, the vast majority of students said that it was difficult for them to have the immersion of traditional teaching mode, there was no learning atmosphere in class, excessively tested of consciousness, and it was difficult to focus on listening. And the interaction of online class is poor, students cannot communicate with teachers in time when they meet some problems, teachers can't ask questions as usual, and can't consolidate the effect of skilled knowledge points in the class. The courses on the Internet are also uneven. Some teachers can't give lectures live, so they choose the recorded and broadcast course resources on the Internet to study, but the high-quality courses also need to be carefully searched. At the same time, when students have classes at home, their parents also need to take care of them at all times. Part of teachers' tasks in the campus originally fell to their parents.

2.3 Problems Needing Attention at the Same Time of AI Helping Education

At the same time, there are many problems and hidden dangers that need to be paid attention to when AI helps education.

1. Network information security: The use of big data in online education makes the data of online education users displayed in the background. Without protection, it is easy to make users' privacy leaked. Therefore, relevant laws should be formulated to protect users' privacy and rights [2].
2. The relationship between technology and teachers: AI helps teaching, but it should also make teachers as the main teachers, learning knowledge and skills is very important, but learning to be human and improving moral cultivation is more important. AI can bring about the application of repetitive rules, but it can't give students creative aesthetic, emotional and ideological help. Compared with teaching knowledge, education is more important. We need to distinguish the ethical relationship in education.
3. Cannot implement technology from top to bottom: AI helps education should be promoted from the bottom up. The era of intelligence is coming. Students, teachers and educational institutions need to be prepared. Teachers and students need to adapt themselves to AI in order to play its effect. If top-down pressure is applied, students and teachers cannot adapt to sudden changes, they can't play their own role, lead to half the effort.
4. Focus on the education of students in remote and poor areas: The family conditions of students in most areas of our country can meet the network environment and hardware conditions needed for online education, but the remote areas and some poor families cannot meet the conditions for children's online learning [3]. In order to make these students receive equal treatment for teaching, we should speed up the construction of network environment in the remote areas, help students in poor areas to get a good learning environment, give them corresponding equipment support, and promote the equality of teaching level.

3 AI Helps Online Education

3.1 AI Helps Online Education Solve Problems

In order to give full play to the role of AI in education, we can associate the problems found in online education during the epidemic with AI. Using AI to help online education solve the existing problems can also add to the online education.

In the traditional teaching, the teacher not only plays the role of teaching in the classroom, but also shoulders the task of urging students to concentrate and avoiding students skulk away. In the live online class, it is difficult for teachers to observe whether students are distracted. The "eye of vision" of face recognition has entered the classroom in the early years. This technology can analyze the students' facial expression and body behavior posture, so as to judge the concentration of students. However, this project has been questioned before. It is believed that watching students' behavior in the classroom at all times will violate their privacy. Using this technology in online education can not only replace teachers' task of supervising students, solve the problem of low consciousness of students, but also avoid infringing their privacy.

In addition to solving the problem of students' consciousness, AI can also use its technologies to add more functions to online education [4]. It is possible to search the questions by taking photos through character recognition in computer vision technology, and search the questions intelligently to make up for the problems that students cannot answer [5]. At the same time, AI can also replace teachers' repetitive tasks, such as using image recognition, natural language processing for marking papers, correcting homework, sorting out mistakes, speech recognition for oral English test, AI intelligent scoring [6].

On March 19, 2020, High Technology Computer Corporation (HTC) held the first VIVE Virtual Ecology Conference (V^2EC 2020), which is a milestone international conference with full online significance. At the conference, thousands of participants from 55 countries participated in the conference using Virtual Reality technology (VR), with more than 500000 live video online views.

Big data can also play a significant role in online education [7]. For students, they can collect information through big data, for example, collect the wrong questions, summarize the types of frequently wrong questions, collect the question sets for practice, and give instructions for grammar and word replacement in writing. For teachers, they can master the teaching data, understand which part of the class students are absorbed and which part is unwilling to listen, understand the teaching methods that students like, and improve the teaching methods targeted. For enterprises, they can use big data to divide customers, collect online data in the background, analyze the subject content, difficulty and hobbies of students' search, divide the level of customers, supervise each index, help enterprises to make corresponding changes, and generate targeted solutions for different users [8]. The application of AI in education can be graded as shown in Fig. 3. The higher level of application, the more core it is in online education.

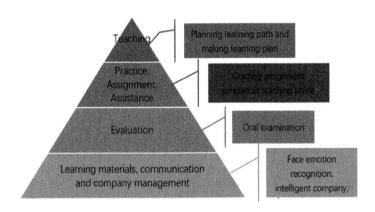

Fig. 3. Application of AI technology in Education.

With the advent of 5G (5th Generation mobile networks), online education has a stronger foundation, so that teachers can conduct online tutoring in a more timely manner. It can also gather high-quality teachers from all over the world, improve the quality of teaching, and solve the problems of uneven online teaching level and hard to find good courses.

With the rapid development of 5G technology, it has been widely used in business. Its advantages of high transmission rate and low latency can make online education under 5G network no longer suffer from problems such as high concurrent network access and poor network quality. 5G's ultra-high bandwidth will make 4K video, VR and Augmented Reality technology (AR) better supported by network environment, a better development environment provides favorable conditions for the future development of AI [9]. At present, China's educational resources are still very unbalanced, the online education and teaching mode in 5g environment may be able to slightly improve this situation [10]. 5G can make the live classroom highly similar to the offline classroom. The immersive learning environment can not only give students real experience in class, but also interact with teachers to improve teaching efficiency.

3.2 Teaching Mode of Man-Machine Dual Division

After the outbreak of the epidemic, the rise of online education makes online education become an important part of education, but it cannot completely replace the traditional teaching methods [11]. In 2015, the Organization for Economic Co-operation and Development (OECD) conducted a study on the relationship between the use of computers and students' academic performance. The results show that the use of computers is inversely proportional to students' academic performance. In other words, the higher the use of computers, the worse the performance. Therefore, in the change of teaching mode, the role of online education in the teaching process should be carefully considered. Online education will become a powerful supplement to offline teaching, AI technology will help upgrade the teaching environment and mode.

The man-machine dual teacher mode was a big discovery in online education industry in 2019. Teachers and machines work together to participate in the teaching process, giving full play to the different advantages of people and AI [12]. Teachers are responsible for the creative and emotional work that AI is difficult to learn, while machines are responsible for the repetitive and monotonous work. It can not only reduce the burden of teachers, but also make use of AI assistance to make learning personalized and diversified [13]. The flow chart of the teaching mode of human-machine dual division is shown in Fig. 4.

The man-machine dual teacher mode makes students' learning time fragmented, learning time and place more free and flexible, helps teachers have more time to interact with students, reduces teachers' and students' burden and improves efficiency [14]. Online and offline integrated education, using the construction of knowledge map and intelligent search to improve the efficiency of teachers' lesson preparation, according to AI assessment to understand students' learning situation, select the appropriate way of class, according to the Asian company iFLYTEK's analysis, structured lesson preparation can reduce teachers' lesson preparation time by an average of 53%. AI takes the place of teachers to evaluate the repetitive high questions such as composition, translation and oral English, so as to reduce the time for teachers to correct their homework. The system collects and summarizes the learning data of students, assists teachers to understand the weak links of students' learning, teachers can help students learn more accurately and specifically, and improves the interaction between teachers and students. Use AI to judge each student's knowledge weakness,

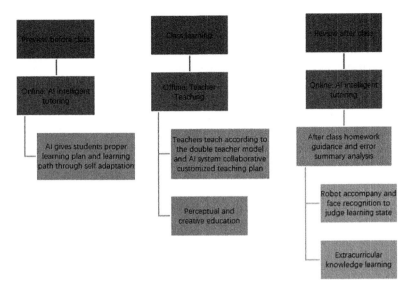

Fig. 4. Schematic diagram of man machine dual division mode.

develop each person's unique learning methods and contents, make learning personalized, and prevent learning blind and inefficient [15].

3.3 Research on AI + Education and Dual Teacher Model

In order to understand the problems that students and teachers encounter in online classes, and their views on AI + education and human-computer dual teacher mode, this paper uses online questionnaire to distribute nearly 200 students and teachers from multiple cities, the respondents are distributed in different ages. The questions in the questionnaire are:

1. Do you know the teaching mode of "man-machine dual division"?
2. Are you satisfied with the teaching mode of "man- machine dual teacher"?
3. What do you think the proportion of AI teachers in your study or teaching is about?
4. Do you think this kind of "man- machine dual teacher" teaching mode is helpful to your study?
5. What do you think are the advantages of the "man- machine dual division model"?

　①. The teaching form of double teachers is new, which is easier to attract students' attention.
　②. Increase interaction among teachers and teachers, students and students, and enhance classroom satisfaction.
　③. To reduce the burden of teachers and improve the efficiency of teachers' work.
　④. Improve the quality of classroom teaching and promote the development of students.

Analyze the survey results and get the results in Table 1.

According to the data analysis of the questionnaire, it can be seen that the teaching mode of man-machine dual teacher has not been widely used in teachers and students for the time being, and more than half of the experimenters have never heard this new teaching mode before, but most of the experimenters think that the teaching mode of man-machine dual teacher will play an auxiliary role in learning or teaching work, it will help learning to some extent, and this new learning method can arouse students' curiosity, help students to study and lighten the burden of teachers and parents. At the same time, the dual teacher model is also questioned by the experimenters, such as AI is difficult to teach students in accordance with their aptitude, human-computer dual teacher teaching reduces the communication between teachers and students, and the new model is difficult to be accepted by the public and difficult to promote. But on the whole, the experimenters have a positive attitude towards the teaching mode of human-computer dual division. Therefore, the man-machine dual teacher mode has a large and positive development space, and I believe that the combination of the two in education will bring benefits to all walks of life in the society

Table 1. Survey results.

Question number	Options	Results (%)
1.	Yes	42.86
	No	57.14
2.	Commonly	28.57
	Satisfied	57.14
	Very satisfied	14.29
3.	Less than 20%	39.81
	20%–50%	45.90
	50%–80%	14.29
4.	Yes	75.45
	No	24.55
5.	①	85.71
	②	42.86
	③	85.71
	④	57.14

4 Summary

The outbreak of the epidemic gives online education an opportunity to show its own role and the strengths of online education. In the era of AI big data and other technologies' high-speed development, in order to help the development of education, at the same time, promote the intelligent informatization of education, AI and education are integrated, make contributions to the collaborative development, and inject fresh blood into the education of the new era. All teaching participants should also actively respond to the call of the Education Bureau, face the upgrading and reform of education actively, build a flexible education system, and strengthen the integration of education and AI. The development of education mode needs the joint efforts of students, teachers, parents, schools, educational institutions and Education Bureau.

References

1. Yan, M., Li, Z., Yu, X., Jin, C.: An end-to-end deep learning network for 3D object detection from RGB-D data based on hough voting. IEEE Access **8**, 138810–138822 (2020)
2. Chen, Z.: Strong AI and super AI: technology rationality and its criticism. Sci. Manag. **5**(5), 25–33 (2016)
3. Heller, R.F., Strobl, J., Madhok, R.: Online education for public health capacity building in low- to middle-income countries: the peoples-uni experience. Int. Rev. Res. Open Distance Learn. **20**(1), 80–93 (2019)
4. Lin, L., Qv, S., Wang, D., Guo, X., Zheng, S., Yu, H.: Discussion on medical humanities education in artificial intelligence era. China Continuing Med. Educ. **12**(6), 55–59 (2020)
5. Zhang, S., Liu, Y., Shao, J.: Analysis on the competitive strategy of online education enterprises – taking new oriental online as an example. Manag. Adm. **5**, 71–75 (2020)
6. Jin, C., Tie, Y., Bai, Y.: A style-specific music composition neural network. Neural Process. Lett. (2020)
7. Liu, H., Ma, W., Yang, Y., Carbonell, J.: Learning concept graphs from online education data. J. Artif. Intell. Res. **55**, 1059–1090 (2016)
8. He, K.: The deep integration of information technology and subject teaching. Educ. Res. **10**, 39–47 (2018)
9. Jia, J.: Artificial intelligence empowers education and learning. J. Distance Educ. **1**, 39–47 (2018)
10. Wang, Z.: Internet plus air classroom helps education to tackle poverty: taking Xiji County of Ningxia as an example. Digit. Teach. Prim. Secondary Schools **5**, 80–82 (2020)
11. Wang, X.: Position reconstruction and organization implementation of online education and teaching—online teaching during the epidemic in Zhejiang Province. Digit. Teach. Primary Secondary Schools **5**, 67–68 (2020)
12. Guo, L.: No suspension in colleges and universities on the reform of teaching methods of finance major. Chin. Foreign Entrepreneurs **14**, 215–216 (2020)
13. Tsai, Y.: Exploring in-service preschool teachers' conceptions of and approaches to Online education. Australas. J. Educ. Technol. **33**(1), 134–147 (2017)
14. Bao, W.: COVID-19 and online teaching in higher education: a case study of Peking University. Hum. Behav. Emerg. Technol. **2**(2), 113–115 (2020)
15. Wang, Z.: How should education be transformed in the post-epidemic era. e-Education Res. **41**(4), 13–20 (2020)

Design Aspects of a Virtual Reality Learning Environment to Assess Knowledge Transfer in Science

Johanna Steynberg[✉], Judy van Biljon, and Colin Pilkington

School of Computing, University of South Africa,
Florida Park, Roodepoort, South Africa
hanlie@ssoftwaredesign.co.za

Abstract. Science educators need assessment tools to assess to what extent learners' knowledge and skills can be transferred to real-life situations. Virtual reality learning environments (VRLEs) can be used to create authentic virtual spaces where situated learning and assessment can take place. However, there are considerable design and implementation challenges when developing a VRLE. This research explored the design aspects of a virtual reality environment for the assessment of knowledge transfer in science education. A design science research approach was followed, implementing existing guidelines from literature in building a VRLE. Lessons learned from the implementation were formulated, and the theoretical contribution of this study is a set of literature-based, practice evaluated guidelines, synthesising lessons learned. From the study, it is apparent that there are many benefits from using a VRLE for assessment, and we hope that using these guidelines could mitigate some of the usability issues that remain.

Keywords: Virtual reality · Science education · Authentic assessment · Human-computer interaction · Usability

1 Introduction

Educators need a way to determine if, and to what degree, a learner can transfer his or her knowledge and skills learned in the science classroom to real-world situations. Computer-generated simulation platforms can provide the complex contexts that constitute realistic situations with authentic tasks. These simulations can be used to create authentic virtual spaces that provide safe and effective environments where situated learning, as well as assessment, can take place [29].

This paper focuses on the lessons learned during the development of a virtual reality learning environment (VRLE) for authentic assessment of the transfer of skills and knowledge in the secondary school science classroom. Existing guidelines for developing a virtual reality learning environment assisted in the design of the VRLE. The research question presented by this paper is as follows: What are the important design aspects of a virtual reality environment for the assessment of knowledge transfer in science education.

2 Background Literature

Learning in the 21st century is characterised by a large number of non-recurrent skills that have to be applied appropriately and with cognitive dexterity. In this paper an assessment model is proposed that moves away from the current linear model that focusses on content, isolated from real-life situations, toward an assessment model that accepts the complex, non-linear and possibly chaotic nature of real learning [2].

2.1 Learning, Educational Simulations and Virtual Reality Environments

An educational simulation is a learning platform designed with a real-life environment as its basis, presented as an abstracted reality, with structured tasks divided into levels and pedagogical tools to assist and guide the learner. Such a platform has many features that make it an ideal environment for performance-based assessment, such as the immersion of learners into a world that closely resembles reality and their interaction with it, the complexity of the possible responses and the analysis and synthesis of information [1, 28]. A VRLE supports complex, authentic environments and could emerge as a preferred technology for integrated instruction and formative assessment. VRLEs can increase engagement by immersing the learner fully in the learning environment in a sensory encompassing way, and may lead to better conceptual understanding and transfer of learning [26].

In this study, a fully immersive platform was created where the learner is immersed in a simulated world created by a collection of software and related hardware, rendering the illusion of being in a three-dimensional space and time [22] that facilitates motion tracking within a digitally created environment.

2.2 Current Limitations and Challenges of Virtual Reality Environments

Despite considerable progress in the field of virtual reality technology, technological and implementation challenges remain – high cost, uncomfortable headsets, eye strain from focusing close to the eyes for long periods, motion sickness, an empty room for room-scale virtual reality and educational material design challenges [2, 13].

However, the development of artificial intelligence has improved interaction between human and computer systems in VRLEs [21]. This, together with the decreasing cost of virtual reality hardware, free versions of virtual reality software development platforms such as Unity and Unreal Engine, as well as the steady improvement in hardware technology, minimises these limitations, and continues to do so [13].

3 Research Methodology

Guided by pragmatism, this study followed the design science research (DSR) iterative design-implement-evaluate process. The artefact development is divided into two iterations, each starting with the planning of the environment and actions, moving to development, and finally, an evaluation. The evaluations will include the usability of the artefact at the particular stage of development and the evaluation of the platform for validity and reliability as an assessment tool. As a theoretical contribution of this study, guidelines abstracted from literature will be updated and refined from the lessons learned through the two iterations.

4 Developing a VRLE for Assessment

VRLEs have unique usability and complexity challenges as the increased immersion can amplify the positive and negative aspects of the environment [8]. VRLE design should combine three different areas – pedagogy, technology and content – into an integrated environment [14], pointing to the need for VRLE development guidelines.

4.1 Guidelines for Pedagogy

The first step in developing the VRLE is to determine the scenario, the problem, the goal, the objectives and the audience [6, 22]. Storytelling in each scenario links the environment and the narrative to form a rich context that enhances learning [6, 18]. Designers choose content that supports spatial visualisation – especially content that cannot be seen in the physical world, but can be presented in a VRLE [22].

Learning is enhanced when material is presented in learner-directed segments rather than one continuous unit [20]. Knowledge engineering methodologies have been used to break down learning material to be used in virtual worlds [10]. They determine the entities in the environment, the constraints acting on these entities, the activities and their rules that can take place in the environment, and then create illustrations to describe these components.

To enhance learning, pedagogical support tools that will be provided should also be determined. The tools could be implemented through the environment or via the use of a character (or pedagogical agent, which is a virtual character that is designed to facilitate learning in multimedia-based environments), or through both [6, 7, 23].

The guideline for pedagogy thus includes defining a rich, authentic environment with units consisting of the learning material benefitting from visualisation. Additionally, proposed pedagogical agents should be employed.

In this artefact, we present magnets and visualise magnetic fields with rays of light in the shape of the magnetic fields as seen in Fig. 1, which were implemented using particle systems in Unreal Engine. When developing the second scene in the artefact, it became evident that, even though there is a vast collection of three-dimensional assets available online, there are only a few objects available to depict a science environment. There are almost no magnets, electrical current components used in a laboratory, test tubes or chemical apparatus available for purchase. Additionally, available assets are hard to modify and have to be practically redesigned to become usable. We experimented with three-dimensional modeling software (Adobe Photoshop, Maya and Blender) and found them all difficult to learn to use and time-consuming to execute. If VRLEs, and specifically in the science paradigm, are to be widely available in the future, there will be a huge demand for educational three-dimensional assets.

Fig. 1. Magnetic fields are visible when the magnets are picked up.

We use two virtual characters as pedagogical agents – a man and a woman. The learner never sees them, but their voices guide the learner through the tasks. The man is an announcer – to guide the learner into the environment and navigate from scene to scene, and the woman guides the learner to complete the activities and explain the results. We evaluated five different text-to-speech online tools: Natural Reader, Amazon Polly, fromtexttospeech.com, text2speech.org and ttsreader. Amazon Polly was found to sound the most natural, and we used it to implement the voices, adding sound effects with Audacity to add texture and interest to the speech. A storyboard for the design, implementation and evaluation of simulations has been used successfully in education [9, 11]. The guideline for using a storyboard is that the simulation design must include the learner, the environment, the interaction and triggers between a learner and the environment, as well as the changes that take place in the environment [13].

We propose that in a VRLE, the learner is not a separate entity but part of the simulation as he or she interacts with the environment. Two simulation environment design approaches [9, 13] have been synthesized (Fig. 2) where the environment now includes the details of a scene, the learner, the interactions and changes to the scenes.

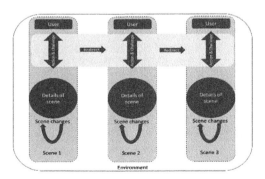

Fig. 2. The combination of the approaches of Fara and Liu to design the content of a VRLE

A detailed design of a virtual reality platform that assesses a student's scientific knowledge and skill transfer to a new situation about magnets was drafted as a storyboard. This included each scene in the environment, the objectives, details of the scene, action and challenges of the scene, cues and interactions, what learner response can be expected, change of scene, or redirection away from the scene after a learner's action.

4.2 Guidelines for Content

Level of Immersion and Realism. The levels of immersion and realism should be specified for every objective identified in the previous step to define the environment [6, 22, 27]. Passive participation is discouraged as merely watching a scene in VR does not mean learning is effective. Designers should use real-world metaphors, for example, a mailbox for leaving a message [15]. Visually realistic learning spaces help learners understand their environment as they know what to expect based on their existing mental models of the real world [18]. Learners expect real-world respect for personal space within a VRLE. Without careful consideration, discomfort can be created when another character stands too close to them or walks right through them, or an object passes through them. Additionally, side effects unique to virtual reality, such as eye strain, motion sickness, disorientation and headaches, have to be addressed and mitigated as far as possible at each step of the development process [8, 24, 25].

The guideline for immersion and realism is to design realistic learning spaces with real-world metaphors. The learner's personal space has to be respected and side-effects must be mitigated.

Our artefact is a VRLE of a deserted island in the year 2100. Earth has been destroyed, except for this island that holds the portal to a new world (Fig. 3). The scene starts with a short tutorial to familiarise the learner with the environment and the navigation methods. The learner is then guided through different tasks involving magnetism and on completion of the portal to the new world is opened, and the learner is transported there.

Fig. 3. Two of the scenes from the artefact: an ice landscape and the portal.

We found that working in Unreal Engine, collision and collision spaces are hard to control. In our prototype, a learner cannot walk into a table, but hands and arms can reach into the table. Additionally, when attaching an object such as a nail to a magnet, the nail seems to go through the magnet. We hope to clear up these issues in the second iteration of the DSR cycle.

Level of Interaction. Content should be realistic and interactive as high levels of reality and interactivity creates positive learning outcomes and better conceptual understanding in learning environments [22, 27]. The senses involved must be determined – will the environment be experienced via sight, sound, tactile or movement, or any combination thereof. This will also influence the level of control that the learner will have in the environment [27]. A problem manipulation space is critical – the learner must manipulate something and obtain feedback on how their manipulations affect the learning environment [6]. The guideline for interaction is to create an authentic environment where the learner must engage with the problem manipulation space.

Navigation: Locomotion, Entry Point and Way-Finding. Navigation in virtual worlds is one of the key usability problems [18]. A VR environment should have simple mechanics to minimise cognitive load so that the learner can concentrate on the task on hand, and not the navigation [8]. Walking-in-place, using a controller to direct the movement and teleportation are three of the locomotion systems commonly used in virtual reality environments [4].

Furthermore, the entry point of a VRLE should be carefully considered and designed as a key part of the environment [17, 18] The entry point should attract learners and allow a learner to survey his or her options of where to go next. Additionally, when entering a scene, care has to be given to the space around a learner, since it can be very jarring if a learner starts in an object such as in the middle of a table [8]. Additionally, spaces should provide an easy exit as interacting in confined spaces might trigger a phobic reaction. Learners should also understand that they can exit the VRLE at any point if they are uncomfortable or in any pain, physically or emotionally [8, 18].

Moving around in a virtual world can be described by the term 'wayfinding'. A learner should be able to move within a scene and between scenes, and can be guided to the next activity using maps, landmarks or paths in an environment.

The guideline for navigation in a VRLE is to use simple locomotion mechanics to move around in a comfortable environment. Guidance to move from one area to another should form part of the environment.

In our artefact, locomotion is controlled by thumbsticks on the hand controllers and it is based on the position of the learner's head. The thumbsticks control forward and backward movement in the direction the learner is looking. We experimented with adding a slight turn to the left/right movement of the thumbsticks; however, this resulted in vertigo and nausea in pilot tests. It was also evident from initial tests that learners should not be able to go where they are not supposed to; limits have been put into all scenes ensuring learners cannot walk off the world. We use areas changing colour, blinking shapes and a virtual character to guide the learner [17].

4.3 Guidelines for Technology

Hardware and Software Selection. Before development begins, the hardware and software to be used should be specified [6, 27], as various factors influence this selection. Firstly, the purpose and goal of the VRLE will determine which devices and software that will be acceptable. The choices of hardware and software will differ vastly from the final-year surgical student trying to perfect a life-threatening procedure to an elementary class experiencing a virtual field trip [16].

Secondly, hardware and software selection depends on properties that are unique to VRLEs, such as the levels of realism, immersion and interaction. The higher these levels, the more senses of the learner will be involved, and the devices and software to implement the environment will become more complex [10, 13, 27].

Thirdly, the audience of the VRLE also influences hardware and software choices, since different demographic groups will experience and use the devices differently. For example, the Oculus Rift is not recommended for children under the age of 13, since their eyesight is not fully developed yet; therefore, an alternative display should be chosen. Learners wearing glasses should be given extra support when fitting and adjusting headsets to allow them to see the environment clearly [19, 27].

Lastly, cost is often an overriding factor. The improvement of the teaching and learning process must be worth the cost, and the high cost of VR hardware and software has a negative influence on the adoption of VRLEs [12, 15, 27]. Costs may be financial costs, overhead setup time costs, and training costs for teachers and learners.

The guideline for technology specifies that appropriate hardware and software should be selected, considering the purpose, the level of immersion and realism, the audience and the cost.

For our artefact, we decided to opt for a middle of the road approach. We are using Unreal Engine 4.22 for the development – it is free for research use and has very good graphic rendering capabilities. Focusing on systems with handheld controllers, we are using Oculus Rift – a comfortable headset with integrated earphones and tracking to determine the position of the learner's head and two motion controllers with two desktop sensors to translate movement into the VRLE.

Implementation: Using a Finite-State Machine. The execution flow in games can be implemented through finite-state machines, which are abstract machines that can only exist in a finite number of states at any given time and can be easily represented using a graph. This allows for simplified design, implementing and testing as there is always only a finite number of states to consider [3, 5]. The guideline for implementation is to use a finite-state machine to implement interactive execution flow.

We added a short tutorial in the first scene of our environment to familiarise the learner with the controls and environment. When implementing the tutorial, the need for a better model for the algorithm was apparent – the usual if-then-else structure of a sequential model was not sufficient – the code was clumsy, repetitive and error-prone. Therefore, according to the suggestion of Seeman and Bourg [5], we used a finite-state machine to implement each scene in our artefact. The finite-state machine of the first action in our artefact is seen in Fig. 4.

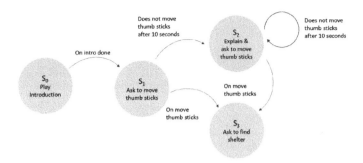

Fig. 4. Finite state machine of the first action in the tutorial, scene 1.

Table 1. Guidelines for developing a VRLE with the lessons learned from this study.

Guidelines			Lessons learned
Pedagogy	Create an authentic environment	[6, 18, 22]	There are very few three-dimensional science assets available to create an authentic environment
	Learning material should be divided into chunks	[20]	
	Implement visualised content	[22, 27]	Considerable time needed to design novel visualisations
	Pedagogical agents	[6, 7, 23]	Voices using text to speech can be added
	Storyboards	[9, 11, 13]	The learner is not a separate entity, but now becomes part of the simulation as he or she interacts with the environment
Content	Realistic learning spaces with real-world metaphors	[22, 27]	Collision and collision spaces are hard to control and needs extra attention
	Learner must engage with the problem manipulation space	[6]	
	Personal space has to be respected	[8, 24, 25]	Put restrictions into scenes to protect learner from harmful areas
	Side-effects must be mitigated	[8, 24, 25]	Movement that does not originate from the learner can cause vertigo and nausea
	Use simple locomotion mechanics to move around	[8, 18]	Do not use hand controllers to turn, only to move forward and backward
	Wayfinding via maps, paths or visual clues	[17]	Include visual clues such as blinking shapes

(*continued*)

Table 1. (*continued*)

Guidelines			Lessons learned
Technology	Consider purpose, level of immersion and realism, the audience and the cost when selecting hardware and software	[6, 10, 13, 16, 27]	There is a significant trade-off between monetary and time costs versus levels of immersion, realism and interaction
	Use a finite-state machine to implement interactive content	[3, 5]	The interactive nature of a learning environment moves away from sequential programming

5 Conclusion

This paper reports on the lessons learned during the first iteration of the study to define the key considerations and design aspects when building a VRLE for the assessment of knowledge transfer. Table 1 summarizes the contribution of this study: VRLE design guidelines, which were abstracted from literature, structured and implemented; and the lessons learned while implementing the design. Future work will involve the evaluation of iteration one and the development of iteration two. Considering the use of VRLEs to assess knowledge transfer, several challenges remain to develop usable assessment tools. However, in the light of the COVID-19 pandemic and the current world events, education needs to evolve into a new paradigm that meets the challenges of the complexity of learning in this new era. Online virtual reality classrooms, once considered an unaffordable luxury, may become a necessity as priorities adjust to the new reality. Future additions to this study could be the diversification of the learning process in the environment, based on specific learner's abilities. Another pathway could also be to explore science laboratories in a VRLE to bring knowledge and training to the parts in the world where experiencing a real-life laboratory is not possible.

References

1. Aldrich, C.: Learning Online with Games, Simulations, Strategies for Online Instruction. Jossey-Bass (2009)
2. Bailenson, J.: Experience on Demand: What Virtual Reality Is, How It Works, and What It Can Do. WW Norton, New York (2019)
3. Bevilacque, F.: Finite-State Machines: Theory and Implementation. https://gamedevelopment.tutsplus.com/tutorials/finite-state-machines-theory-and-implementation-gamedev-11867. Accessed 27 Apr 2020
4. Boletsis, C., Cedergren, J.E.: VR locomotion in the new era of virtual reality: an empirical comparison of prevalent techniques. Adv. Hum. Comput. Interact. **2019**, 1–15 (2019)
5. Bourg, D.M., Seemann, G.: AI for Game Developers. O'Reilly Media, California (2004)
6. Chen, C.J., et al.: The theoretical framework for designing desktop virtual reality-based learning environments. J. Interact. Learn. Res. **15**(2), 147–167 (2004)

7. Clarebout, G., Elen, J.: In Search of Pedagogical Agents' Modality and Dialogue Effects in Open Learning Environments. e-JIST **10**(1), 1–15 (2007)
8. Desurvire, H., Kreminski, M.: Are game design and user research guidelines specific to virtual reality effective in creating a more optimal player experience? yes, VR PLAY. In: Marcus, A., Wang, W. (eds.) DUXU 2018. LNCS, vol. 10918, pp. 40–59. Springer, Cham (2018). https://doi.org/10.1007/978-3-319-91797-9_4
9. Farra, S., et al.: Storyboard development for virtual reality simulation. Clin. Simul. Nurs. **12**(9), 392–399 (2016)
10. Górski, F., et al.: Effective design of educational virtual reality applications for medicine using knowledge-engineering techniques. Eurasia J. Math. Sci. Technol. Educ. **13**(2), 395–416 (2017)
11. Jeffries, P.R.: A framework for designing, implementing, and evaluating simulations used as teaching strategies in nursing. Nurs. Educ. Perspect. **26**(2), 96–103 (2005)
12. Kavanagh, S., et al.: A systematic review of Virtual Reality in education. Themes Sci. Technol. Educ. **10**(2), 85–119 (2017)
13. Liu, S., et al.: Exploring 3D immersive and interactive technology for designing educational learning experiences. In: Neto, F., et al. (eds.) Handbook of Research on 3-D Virtual Environments and Hypermedia for Ubiquitous Learning, pp. 243–261. IGI Global, Hershey (2016)
14. Mahdi, O., et al.: Towards design and operationalization of pedagogical situations in the VRLEs. In: EEE 18th International Conference on Advanced Learning Technologies (ICALT), pp. 400–402. IEEE (2018)
15. Merchant, Z., et al.: Effectiveness of virtual reality-based instruction on students' learning outcomes in K-12 and higher education: a meta-analysis. Comput. Educ. **70**, 29–40 (2014)
16. Mikropoulos, T.A., Natsis, A.: Educational virtual environments: a ten-year review of empirical research (1999–2009). Comput. Educ. **56**(3), 769–780 (2011)
17. Minocha, S., Hardy, C.: Navigation and wayfinding in learning spaces in 3D virtual worlds. In: Lee, M.J.W., et al. (eds.) Learning in Virtual Worlds : Research and Applications, pp. 5–41. AU Press, Edmonton (2016). https://doi.org/10.5860/choice.51-2973
18. Minocha, S., Reeves, A.J.: Interaction design and usability of learning spaces in 3D multi-user virtual worlds. In: Katre, D., Orngreen, R., Yammiyavar, P., Clemmensen, T. (eds.) HWID 2009. IAICT, vol. 316, pp. 157–167. Springer, Heidelberg (2010). https://doi.org/10.1007/978-3-642-11762-6_13
19. Nemec, M., et al.: Using virtual reality in education. In: Jakab, F. (ed.) 15th International Conference on Emerging eLearning Technologies and Applications (ICETA), pp. 1–6. Stary Smokovec (2017)
20. Parong, J., Mayer, R.: Learning science in immersive virtual reality. J. Educ. Psychol. **110**(6), 785–797 (2018)
21. Rique, T.P., et al.: Architectures for 3D virtual environments. In: Neto, F., et al. (eds.) Handbook of Research on 3-D Virtual Environments and Hypermedia for Ubiquitous Learning, pp. 115–147. IGI Global, Hershey (2016)
22. Ritz, L.T., Buss, A.R.: A framework for aligning instructional design strategies with affordances of CAVE immersive virtual reality systems. TechTrends **60**(6), 549–556 (2016). https://doi.org/10.1007/s11528-016-0085-9
23. Schroeder, N.L.: Pedagogical agents for learning. In: Choi, D., et al. (eds.) Emerging Tools and Applications of Virtual Reality in Education, pp. 216–238. Wright State University, Hershey (2016)
24. Serafin, S., et al.: Virtual reality musical instruments: state of the art, design principles, and future directions. Comput. Music J. **40**(3), 22–40 (2016)

25. Snowdon, C.M., Oikonomou, A.: Analysing the educational benefits of 3D virtual learning environments. In: Ntalianis, K., et al. (eds.) European Conference on e-Learning, pp. 513–522. Academic Conferences and Publishing International Ltd., Athens (2018)
26. Tsiatsos, T., et al.: Evaluation framework for collaborative educational virtual environments. J. Educ. Technol. Soc. **13**(2), 65–77 (2010)
27. Vergara, D., et al.: On the design of virtual reality learning environments in engineering. Multimodal Technol. Interact. **1**(11), 1–12 (2017)
28. Vos, L.: Simulation games in business and marketing education: how educators assess student learning from simulations. Int. J. Manag. Educ. **13**(1), 57–74 (2015)
29. Young, M.: Assessment of situated learning using computer environments. J. Sci. Educ. Technol. **4**(1), 89–96 (1995)

Research on Evaluation of Smart Learning Environment in Universities Based on AHP-FCE: A Case Study of Central China Normal University

Zhicheng Dai[✉], Mengting Wang, and Feng Liu

Central China Normal University, Wuhan 430000, Hubei, China
dzc@mail.ccnu.edu.cn

Abstract. With the rapid development of the Internet of Things (IoT), big data, Artificial Intelligence (AI) and other emerging technologies, the Smart Learning Environment (SLE) has emerged. This paper takes Central China Normal University as an example to evaluate SLE in universities. Taking the physical, resource and social of SLE as the first-level indexes of the evaluation index system, an index system with 3 first-level indexes and 26 second-level indexes was constructed by referring to relevant literature and the actual needs of teachers and students. According to this evaluation index system, a questionnaire was designed to collect data. Analytic Hierarchy Process (AHP) and Fuzzy Comprehensive Evaluation (FCE) were used to analyze the sample data and evaluate SLE, which can provide reference for the subsequent improvement of SLE.

Keywords: Smart Learning Environment (SLE) · Evaluation · Analytic Hierarchy Process (AHP) · Fuzzy Comprehensive Evaluation (FCE)

1 Introduction

With the development of emerging technologies such as Internet of Things (IoT), big data, Artificial Intelligence (AI) and other information technologies, the reform of information-based teaching has been advanced, and the informatization in Chinese universities has entered a new stage in the Smart Learning Environment (SLE). SLE is a new Learning Environment that supports students' effective learning in the information age. It can help to promote student participation and improve effective learning and change learning and teaching in a productive and desirable way [1]. Supported by Wi-Fi, 3G and 4G network environment, SLE enables learners to learn online anytime and anywhere [2].

Due to the limitation factors such as learners' age and their learning ability, the construction of SLE in primary and secondary schools is mainly based on the improvement of physical environment, and the teaching mode is still dominated by teachers. However, learners in universities have the ability of higher-order thinking, tend to study independently, and have an urgent need for resources and personalized learning. Besides, universities have the environment of independent innovation.

Therefore, SLE has more practical applications in universities. In recent years, Central China Normal University has been actively promoting the integration of information technology and education, reforming the learning environment, optimizing the infrastructure, and strengthening the development of high-quality teaching resources.

This paper took SLE as the research object, constructed the evaluation index system, and took Central China Normal University as the application case for evaluation and analysis. The structure of the paper is as follows: Sect. 2 briefly introduces the research object, the SLE of Central China Normal University; Sect. 3' contains evaluation index, which combined the literature and the actual needs of teachers and students; Sect. 4 describes the research methodology, the instruments, the participants, and data collection; Sect. 5 analyses the questionnaire data and obtain the evaluation results; and Sect. 6 concludes the research and suggests possible future the improving direction according to the evaluation results.

2 Research Object

SLE can be divided into three sub-spaces, physical space, social space and resource space [3]. Based on this learning space theory, Central China Normal University built its SLE. The system architecture of the SLE is shown in Fig. 1.

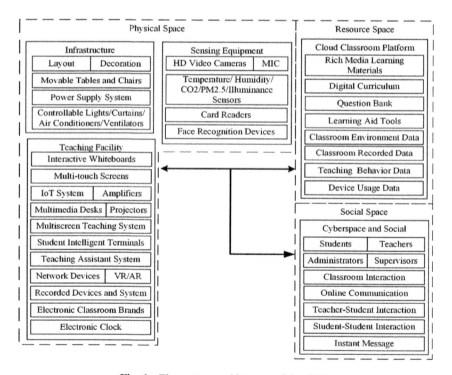

Fig. 1. The system architecture of the SLE.

Physical space includes infrastructure, sensing equipment and teaching facility, which is the basic support of the whole SLE, provides environmental protection services for various activities in the social space, and carries storage and presentation of various elements in the resource space. In terms of infrastructure, the smart classrooms are decorated in a simple and comfortable way, with reasonable layout. Desks and chairs can be dynamically combined. The lights, curtains, air conditioners and ventilators can be controlled by the central control host computer of IoT, to support teachers to carry out diversified teaching activities. Sensing equipment is the channel for data acquisition, including classroom environment data, audio and video data, identity identification information, etc. By analyzing the information available through SLE, it is possible to increase students' performance in learning and realizing goals [4]. Teaching facility is the core element of physical space, realizing the functions of teaching content presentation, teaching resources acquisition, classroom interaction and so on.

Resource space, the core element of SLE, is the bridge communicating between subjects in social space. "Cloud Classroom Platform" is the support service platform of SLE, provides teaching content component database, digital curriculum, quality question bank and learning aid tools, and gathers classroom environment data, device usage data and teaching behavior data of the whole teaching process.

The social space is the organism of SLE, including students, teachers, administrators and supervisors, who carry out learning activities in SLE and are interrelated under the support of "starC Multi-screen teaching system" and "Cloud Classroom Platform".

The teaching scene of SLE is shown in Fig. 2.

Fig. 2. The teaching scene of SLE.

3 Evaluation Index System

We took the physical, resource and social of SLE as the first-level index.

Physical space, as a formal learning place, is mainly composed of teaching infrastructure and educational equipment in the network environment. The second-level indexes of physical space were constructed by referring to relevant research results [5] of SLE application.

Resource space is an important guarantee to realize the integration of reality and virtual in SLE. Referring to the relevant evaluation literature on the website [6], the second-level indexes of the resource space were constructed.

Social space contains the interaction in student-student, teacher-student and human-computer. Social space is learner-centered. Fully considering learners' learning experience in SLE, the second-level indexes of the social space were constructed.

An evaluation index system with 3 first-level indexes and 26 second-level indexes was constructed, as Table 1 shows.

Table 1. Evaluation index system

Object	First-level indexes	Second-level indexes
SLE A	Physical B_1	Designability C_1; Structural C_2; Comprehensive C_3; Humanization C_4; Diversification C_5; Smart C_6; Perceptive C_7; Easy to access C_8
	Resource B_2	Compatibility C_9; Functional C_{10}; Security C_{11}; Operational C_{12}; Stability C_{13}; Connectedness C_{14}; Massive C_{15}; Scientific C_{16}; Open C_{17}; Well-formed C_{18}
	Social B_3	Applied consciousness C_{19}; Teaching method C_{20}; Information integration C_{21}; Technical mastery C_{22}; Interaction capacity C_{23}; Learning intention C_{24}; Class performance C_{25}; Cognitive load C_{26}

4 Method

4.1 Instruments

In this research, a questionnaire was conducted as an instrument. The questionnaire consisted of two parts: a demographic information questionnaire and an evaluation questionnaire.

Demographic information questionnaire was gathered from participants, including grade, major and gender.

A 5-point Likert scale (5 = strongly agree and 1 = strongly disagree) was used in this evaluation questionnaire. It measured participants' evaluation of SLE.

4.2 Participants

In this research, 336 students were selected as respondents. Eliminating the invalid questionnaires with missing answers and the same choices, we received 300 valid questionnaires. these samples involved 4 grades (freshman, 36.00%, sophomore, 33.67%, junior, 24.33%, senior, 6.00%), 2 majors (science and engineering, 54.67%, liberal arts, 45.33%) and 2 genders (male, 31.33%, female, 68.67%).

4.3 Procedure

Reliability. Reliability of this evaluation questionnaire was measured by Cronbach's α. The Cronbach's α of physical (B_1) was 0.829, resource's (B_2) was 0.871, social's (B_3) was 0.811, SLE's (A) was 0.910.

The Cronbach's α of the scale and subscales were all greater than 0.8. The results indicated good reliability and high internal consistency.

Validity. Validity of this evaluation questionnaire was measured by through Confirmatory Factor Analysis (CFA). Kaiser-Meyer-Olkin (KMO) was 0.898 (>0.700), the Bartlett test was significant ($P < 0.001$). The data was suitable for factor analysis.

Using principal component analysis (PCA) and Varimax, 3 first-level indexes were extracted from 26 second-level indexes. Their characteristic roots were greater than 1, and their cumulative variance contribution rate was 62.070%. For each second-level index in its first-level index, the value of factor loading was greater than 0.500, which meant that the model had significant convergent validity. For each second-level index in its different first-level index, the value of factor loading was close to 0, indicating adequate discriminant validity.

5 Data Analysis and Evaluation Results

AHP and FCE are commonly used traditional evaluation method [7, 8]. The evaluation method of SLE is based on the quantitative scoring of FCE, and the weight of evaluation index is determined by AHP.

5.1 Determination of Evaluation Index Weight

Hierarchical Model. The hierarchical model was built, as shown in Fig. 3.

Constructing Judgment Matrix. Compare the relative importance of the indicators of the same level by comparing the relative importance of relative weights to construct judgment matrix A. In this paper, 1–9 scale method was used to assign importance degree: 1, equally important; 3, the former is slightly more important than the latter; 5, the former is obviously more important than the latter; 7, the former is more important than the latter; 9, the former is extreme important than the latter; 2, 4, 6, 8, intermediate value between two adjacent judgments; reciprocal, if the ratio of the importance of element i to element j is a_{ij}, then the ratio of the importance of element j to element i is $a_{ji} = 1/a_{ij}$.

Calculating Weight. Asymptotic Normalization Coefficient (ANC) was selected to calculate the weight of the evaluation indexes. The steps were as follows:

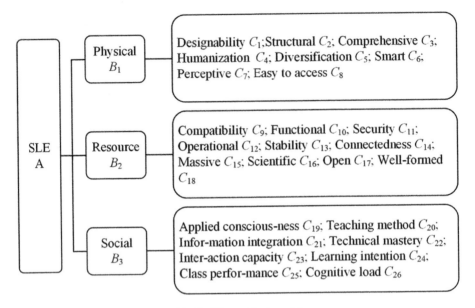

Fig. 3. Hierarchical model.

1. Normalized each column element of the judgment matrix A to get $\bar{A}$;

$$\bar{a}_{ij} = \frac{a_{ij}}{\sum_{i=1}^{n} a_{ij}} \quad i,j = 1, 2, \cdots, n \tag{1}$$

2. Summed each row element of $\bar{A}$ to get $\bar{W}$;

$$\bar{w}_i = \sum_{j=1}^{n} \bar{a}_{ij} \quad i = 1, 2, \cdots, n \tag{2}$$

3. Normalized $\bar{w}$ to get the weight W.

$$w_i = \frac{\bar{w}_i}{\sum_{i=1}^{n} \bar{w}_i}, \quad i = 1, 2, \cdots, n \tag{3}$$

Consistency Check. A consistency check is performed on the judgment matrix to test whether the weights of the indicators obtained by the judgment matrix are reasonable. There were three main steps:

4. Calculated the maximum eigenvalue λ_{max};

$$\lambda_{max} = \frac{1}{n}\sum_{i=1}^{n}\frac{(AW)_i}{w_i} \quad (4)$$

5. Calculated the consistency index CI;

$$CI = \frac{\lambda_{max} - n}{n - 1} \quad (5)$$

6. Calculated consistency ratio CR;

$$CR = \frac{CI}{RI} \quad (6)$$

When $CR < 0.1$, it is considered that the consistency of the judgment matrix is acceptable, that is, it indicates that the weight coefficient is assigned properly; otherwise, the judgment matrix needs to be adjusted until satisfactory consistency is achieved. RI is called the average random consistency index of judgement matrix; its value can be obtained in Table 2.

Table 2. Average random uniformity indicators RI

n	1	2	3	4	5	6	7	8	9
RI	0	0	0.58	0.9	1.12	1.24	1.32	1.41	1.45

Evaluation Index Weights. W After consistency check, All the 4 judgment matrixes have met the consistency requirement, $CR < 0.1$. The results were as follows:

Physical: $W_1 = [0.098 \quad 0.193 \quad 0.039 \quad 0.145 \quad 0.036 \quad 0.177 \quad 0.284 \quad 0.028]^T$
Resource: $W_2 = [0.065 \quad 0.131 \quad 0.215 \quad 0.032 \quad 0.048 \quad 0.123 \quad 0.230 \quad 0.111 \quad 0.029 \quad 0.016]^T$
Social: $W_3 = [0.047 \quad 0.195 \quad 0.062 \quad 0.109 \quad 0.269 \quad 0.097 \quad 0.187 \quad 0.034]^T$
SLE: $W = [0.413 \quad 0.260 \quad 0.327]^T$

5.2 FCE Process

Constructing Evaluation Factor Sets. U The factor set is the set of evaluation indexes of the evaluation object. Suppose that the evaluation object has m evaluation indexes, $U = \{u_1, u_2, \cdots, u_m\}$. For multi-level evaluation index system, multi-level factor set is established hierarchically. According to the established evaluation index system, the factor set U was established.

In this research, evaluation factor sets were as follows:

$$U = \{U_1, U_2, U_3\}$$

$$U_1 = \{C_1, C_2, C_3, C_4, C_5, C_6, C_7, C_8\}$$

$$U_2 = \{C_9, C_{10}, C_{11}, C_{12}, C_{13}, C_{14}, C_{15}, C_{16}, C_{17}, C_{18}\}$$

$$U_3 = \{C_{19}, C_{20}, C_{21}, C_{22}, C_{23}, C_{24}, C_{25}, C_{26}\}$$

Constructing Evaluation Set V. The evaluation set V is composed of all evaluation grades. In this paper, the evaluation set was selected as 5 grades, $V = \{v_1, v_2, v_3, v_4, v_5\}$ = {very good, good, average, poor, very poor}, corresponding to the percentile interval $\{[0.9 \sim 1), [0.75 \sim 0.9), [0.6 \sim 0.75), [0.5 \sim 0.6), [0 \sim 0.5)\}$.

Constructing Evaluation Matrixes R. If the evaluation set V has decision values of m evaluation levels and there are n indexes that need to be evaluated, the evaluation matrix R can be represented as:

$$R = \begin{bmatrix} r_{11} & r_{12} & \cdots & r_{1m} \\ r_{21} & r_{22} & \cdots & r_{2m} \\ \vdots & \vdots & \ddots & \vdots \\ r_{n1} & r_{n2} & \cdots & r_{nm} \end{bmatrix}$$

In this research, evaluation matrixes were as follows:

$$R_1 = \begin{bmatrix} 0.307 & 0.610 & 0.056 & 0.017 & 0.010 \\ 0.287 & 0.600 & 0.077 & 0.033 & 0.003 \\ 0.280 & 0.563 & 0.114 & 0.043 & 0.000 \\ 0.367 & 0.493 & 0.097 & 0.040 & 0.003 \\ 0.267 & 0.503 & 0.183 & 0.047 & 0.000 \\ 0.157 & 0.387 & 0.373 & 0.080 & 0.003 \\ 0.180 & 0.303 & 0.414 & 0.103 & 0.000 \\ 0.233 & 0.457 & 0.247 & 0.063 & 0.000 \end{bmatrix} \quad R_3 = \begin{bmatrix} 0.073 & 0.437 & 0.220 & 0.257 & 0.013 \\ 0.200 & 0.543 & 0.203 & 0.050 & 0.003 \\ 0.133 & 0.540 & 0.247 & 0.077 & 0.003 \\ 0.114 & 0.490 & 0.240 & 0.143 & 0.013 \\ 0.087 & 0.453 & 0.320 & 0.123 & 0.017 \\ 0.093 & 0.517 & 0.266 & 0.107 & 0.017 \\ 0.103 & 0.493 & 0.290 & 0.107 & 0.007 \\ 0.070 & 0.464 & 0.280 & 0.183 & 0.003 \end{bmatrix}$$

$$R_2 = \begin{bmatrix} 0.187 & 0.393 & 0.337 & 0.070 & 0.013 \\ 0.103 & 0.380 & 0.340 & 0.167 & 0.010 \\ 0.103 & 0.373 & 0.454 & 0.060 & 0.010 \\ 0.103 & 0.480 & 0.250 & 0.150 & 0.017 \\ 0.073 & 0.260 & 0.420 & 0.220 & 0.027 \\ 0.107 & 0.580 & 0.267 & 0.043 & 0.003 \\ 0.123 & 0.603 & 0.224 & 0.047 & 0.003 \\ 0.117 & 0.543 & 0.267 & 0.070 & 0.003 \\ 0.100 & 0.324 & 0.470 & 0.093 & 0.013 \\ 0.147 & 0.657 & 0.160 & 0.033 & 0.003 \end{bmatrix}$$

Calculating Result Vectors B.

$$B = W^T \times R \tag{7}$$

Index weight W has calculated in Sect. 5.1. In this research, result vectors were as follows:

$$B_1 = [0.245 \quad 0.454 \quad 0.24 \quad 0.062 \quad 0.003]$$

$$B_2 = [0.114 \quad 0.474 \quad 0.32 \quad 0.082 \quad 0.008]$$

$$B_3 = [0.117 \quad 0.493 \quad 0.27 \quad 0.112 \quad 0.010]$$

$$B = [0.169 \quad 0.472 \quad 0.268 \quad 0.084 \quad 0.007]$$

Calculating Score Values S. To calculate the exact score value of SLE, the evaluation score is determined according to a certain value rule. The quantized evaluation set V was defined as N.

$$N = [0.95 \quad 0.825 \quad 0.675 \quad 0.55 \quad 0.25]$$

The exact score value of SLE S can be calculated:

$$S = B \times N^T \tag{8}$$

In this research, score values were as follows:
Physical: $S_1 = 0.801$
Resource: $S_2 = 0.764$
Social: $S_3 = 0.762$
SLE: $S = 0.779$

6 Conclusion

The evaluation results showed that the overall performance of SLE in Central China Normal University was good (0.779). In the three sub-spaces of SLE, physical space got the highest score value (0.801).

Through the analysis of the sample questionnaire, in the physical space, the two indexes with the worst satisfaction were Smart C_6 and Perceptive C_7, and the two indexes with the best satisfaction were Designability C_1 and Structural C_2, indicating that students were satisfied with the infrastructure construction. Optimizing the IoT system in the smart classrooms can help to improve Smart C_6 and Perceptive C_7. The equipment in the smart classrooms is connected to the central control host of IoT, so that the teacher can control all kinds of teaching equipment through the teacher assistant or the teacher computer embedded in the desk, adjust temperature and humidity, etc., and improve the comfort level of the classroom.

In the resource space, the indexes with the worst satisfaction were Functional C_{10}, Stability C_{13} and Open C_{17}, and the indexes with the worst satisfaction were Massive C_{15} and Well-formed C_{18}, which showed that the content of the resource had meet the learning needs of students, but currently didn't have a high level of shared resources, information resources can only obtain some jurisdictions. The stability and functionality of the supporting platform can't meet the requirements of students, so developers should upgrade the supporting platform, improve its performance, optimize its response efficiency, and add new functions according to the actual demand.

In the social space, it was found that students didn't agree that the smart classrooms had a significant role in promoting learning and improving the interaction. The purpose of constructing smart classrooms is to improve the learning environment and enhance the teaching effect. However, teachers' nonproficiency in the use of equipment leads to the continuation of the teaching form of multimedia classrooms in smart classrooms, and the failure to develop diversified teaching modes has impeded improving classroom interaction. Teacher training which is focused on the correct use of smart classrooms and on the digital competence of teachers are critical to improve SLE [9]. Teachers should be guided to use the equipment in smart classrooms and develop innovative teaching mode.

Acknowledgements. This research is financially supported by the National Key Research and Development Program of China (Grant No. 2018YFB1004504) and Central China Normal University (Grant No. CCNU20ZN009).

References

1. Spector, J.M.: Conceptualizing the emerging field of smart learning environments. Smart Learn. Environ. **1**(1), 1–10 (2014). https://doi.org/10.1186/s40561-014-0002-7
2. Lee, J.S.R., Jung, Y.J., Park, S.R., et al.: A ubiquitous smart learning platform for the 21st smart learners in an advanced science and engineering education. In: The International Conference on Network-Based Information Systems, vol. 15, pp. 733–738 (2012). IEEE, Melbourne (2012)
3. Yang, Z.: Prospect on future education from perspective of ICT development. e-Education Res. **38**(6), 5–8 (2017)
4. Radosavljevic, V., Radosavljevic, S., Jelic, G.: Ambient intelligence-based smart classroom model. Interact. Learn. Environ., 1–15 (2019)
5. Oliver, B., Nikoletatos, P.: Building engaging physical and virtual learning spaces: a case study of a collaborative approach. In: The Australasian Society for Computers in Learning in Tertiary Education, Auckland, vol. 26, pp. 720–728 (2009)
6. Dickinger, A., Stangl, B.: Website performance and behavioral consequences: a formative measurement approach. J. Bus. Res. **66**(6), 771–777 (2013)
7. Wang, D.B., Lu, W.J.: The construction and application of functional indexes of colleges and universities in the development of sports industry-analysis based on fuzzy comprehensive evaluation method. Eurasia J. Math. Sci. Technol. Educ. **13**(8), 6027–6036 (2017)

8. Lin, H.H., Hsiao, S.W.: A study of the evaluation of products by industrial design students. Eurasia J. Math. Sci. Technol. Educ. **14**(1), 239–254 (2018)
9. Cebrian, G., Palau, R., Mogas, J.: The smart classroom as a means to the development of ESD methodologies. Sustainability **12**(7) (2020)

The Development of Simulation Web-Based Learning Environment to Enhance Ill-Structured Problem Solving for Engineering Students

Thawach Thammabut, Sumalee Chaijaroen, and Suchat Wattanachai[✉]

Department of Educational Technology,
Faculty of Education Khon Kaen University, Khon Kaen, Thailand
Suchat@kku.ac.th

Abstract. The ill-structured problem solving is the one important skill of the Engineer in 21st century. Thus, the purposes of this research was to develop of simulation learning environment to enhance ill-structured problem solving for engineering students and examine learners' ill-structured problem solving. The participants of this study consisted of 3 experts to evaluate the model and 30 students of electronics and telecommunication engineering department. The research instruments for data collection consisted of model evaluation form and learner's ill-structured problem solving interview form. The survey research was employed to this study. Then, the model evaluation data were analyzed by using summarization and interpretation description. Moreover, the learners' ill-structured problem solving were analyzed by using protocol analysis, summarization and interpretation description. The results of study revealed that the simulation learning environment model to enhance ill-structured problem solving for engineering students consisted of designing framework and there were 7 elements in this model as follows 1) simulation problem base, 2) resource center, 3) cognitive tools center, 4) scaffolding center, 5) enhancing problem solving center, 6) collaboration center, and 7) coaching center. The result of the model assessment revealed that the elements and function of the model were appropriate in 3 aspects follow as: con-tents, media, and designing. Thus, simulation learning environment may help engineering students to construct the knowledge and enhance ill-structured problem solving skill. Furthermore, the protocol analysis revealed that the learners solved problem by using 7 processes of ill-structured problems solving.

Keywords: Constructivist · Simulation · Learning environment · Electronics industrial

1 Introduction

Since 1st industrial evaluation in the 18th century until the present, the technology is rapidly change and impact our life in many aspect, especially, in engineering education. The engineering students cannot wait the knowledge from teacher because there are new knowledge every day. Therefore, they have to construct knowledge by themselves. Moreover, the one important skill of the engineer in 21st century is problem solving, especially, ill-structured problem [1]. Ill-structured problems are the kinds of problems that are encountered in everyday practice [2]. However, current instructional design focuses on transmitting and memorizing information. Furthermore, problems that engineering students found in the classroom are different from the workplace engineering problems. The workplace engineering problems possess conflicting goals, multiple solution methods, and non-engineering success standards [2]. In addition, learning to solve classroom problems does not necessarily prepare engineering students to future jobs. Thus, engineering students are lacking of construct the knowledge and ill-structured problems solving. Furthermore, engineering students need to prepare to practice engineer. Thus, they need to practice and experiment to promote students' understanding by using tools or equipment in laboratory. However, they are limited to practice in laboratory, few hours per week or equipment. Moreover, they need some laboratory assistance or teacher to help during practice [3].

For the above reasons, educator need to change strategies for the learning by apply theories to design the instructional. The constructivist theory is an approach to learning that people actively construct or make their own knowledge [4]. Moreover, simulation is an efficient and effective tool for engineering education [5]. Engineering students can learn anywhere and anytime. Furthermore, they can manipulate any parameters to test their hypothesis without risk.

Hence, this research aimed to develop simulation learning environment to enhance ill-structured problem solving for engineering students. The empirical findings are based on analyzing the learner's ill-structured problem solving process.

2 Purposes

To develop the simulation learning environment to enhance ill-structured problem solving for engineering students and examine learners' ill-structured problem solving.

3 Methodology

3.1 Participants

There were 3 experts for evaluation the quality of the simulation learning environment in 3 domains, contents, media, and instructional design. There were 30 students of 4th years in electronics and telecommunication engineering, who enrolled in the course of Electronics Industrial in 1st semester, 2019 academic year, Rajamangala University of technology Isan, Khon Kaen campus, Thailand, for examination ill-structured problem solving.

3.2 Research Instruments

For evaluation of simulation learning environment to enhance ill-structured problem solving for engineering students was used the model evaluation form to evaluate the quality in 3 domains as follows: contents, instructional design, and media. For evaluation learner's ill-structured problem solving were used the learner's ill-structured problem solving interview form.

3.3 Data Collection and Analysis

The evaluation of simulation learning environment were collected by 3 experts and were analyzed by using summarization, interpretation description. Then, the learner's ill-structured problem solving were collected by interviewing learners and data were analyzed by protocol analysis, summarization, and interpretation description.

4 Results

4.1 Synthesis the Designing Framework

The first process for development is synthesis the designing framework of simulation learning environment. The results revealed that the designing framework consist of 5 processes as follow:

Activating Cognitive Structure and Promoting Ill-structured Problems Solving.
The first process of designing framework was activating cognitive structure. The Cognitive constructivism [6] was used to disequilibrium or cognitive conflict of the learner. Then, the situated learning [7] were used to design the authentic problem in the real world. Moreover, the ill-structured problem solving [1] were integrated with decision making [8] and simulation [9] and above theories to design component called **"Simulation problem base"** shown in Fig. 1.

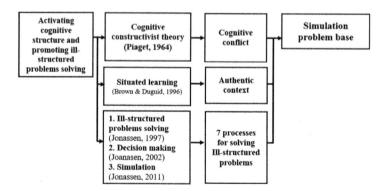

Fig. 1. The designing framework: Activating cognitive structure and promoting ill-structured problems solving.

Supporting for Adjusting of Cognitive Equilibrium. After learners' cognitive structure were disequilibrium, they need to adjust the cognitive structure from disequilibrium to equilibrium. Thus, the component called **"Learning resources"** will support learners to adjust cognitive structure. The information processing theory [10] and SOI model [11] was used to design this component. Furthermore, mental model theory [12], schema theory [12] and cognitive load theory [13] were used to design information into conceptual. In addition, the component called **"Cognitive tools center"** will support tools for supporting learner based on Open learning environments (OLEs) [14]. The cognitive tools comprise of seeking tools, processing tools, collecting tools, integrating tools, and generation tools were used to facilitate the learner' cognitive processing as shown in Fig. 2.

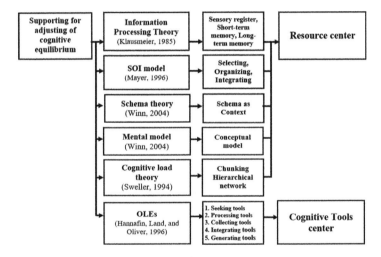

Fig. 2. The designing framework: Supporting for adjusting of cognitive equilibrium.

Supporting for Enlarging Cognitive Structure. For supporting for enlarge cognitive structure, social constructivism [15] used to design the component called **"Collaboration center"** for sharing knowledge and multiple perspectives as shown in Fig. 3.

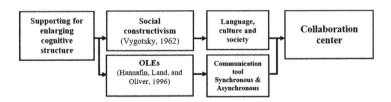

Fig. 3. The designing framework: Supporting for enlarging cognitive structure.

Enhancing Ill-Structured Problems Solving. In addition, enhancing ill-structured problem solving process were adapted from ill-structured problems solving [1] and design the component called **"Enhancing problem solving center"**. The processes of ill-structured problem solving skills were as follows: 1) learners identify problem space and contextual constraints, 2) identifying the stakeholder and their opinion, 3) generate possible problem solutions, 4) decision making of alternative solutions, 5) planning and monitor the performances, 6) implement and monitor the solution, and 7) adapt the solution as shown in Fig. 4.

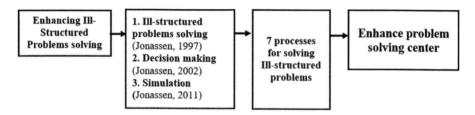

Fig. 4. The designing framework: Enhancing Ill-Structured Problems solving.

Promote and Assist Knowledge Construction. However, some learner may not construct the knowledge by themselves. Thus, for promote and assist knowledge construction, social constructivist, zone of proximal development [15] and OLEs, scaffolding [14] were used in design the component called **"Scaffoldings center"** to provide 4 Scaffolding as follow: conceptual scaffolding, strategic scaffolding, metacognition scaffolding, and procedural scaffolding. Furthermore, Cognitive apprenticeship [16] was used to design the component called **"Coaching center"** as shown in Fig. 5.

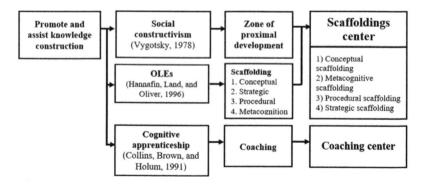

Fig. 5. The designing framework: Promote and assist knowledge construction.

4.2 Development of the Simulation Learning Environment

According to designing framework, there are 7 components of simulation learning environment as follow: 1) simulation problem base, 2) resource center, 3) cognitive tools center, 4) scaffolding center, 5) enhancing problem solving center, 6) collaboration center, and 7) coaching center, as shown in Figs. 6, 7, 8, 9 and 10.

The Development of Simulation Web-Based Learning Environment 333

Fig. 6. (A) Simulation learning environment (B) Simulation problem based.

Fig. 7. (A) Simulation problem based (B) Task of Simulation problem based.

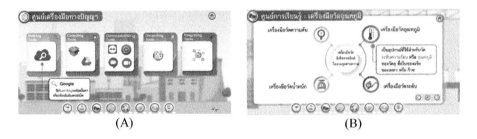

Fig. 8. (A) Cognitive tools center (B) Resource center.

Fig. 9. (A) Enhance problem solving center (B) Collaboration center.

Fig. 10. (A) Coaching center (B) Scaffolding center.

4.3 The Quality of the Simulation Learning Environment

The quality of the simulation learning environment were evaluated by 3 experts in 3 domain as follow: learning content, media, and instructional design. The results revealed that in Table 1.

Table 1. The quality of simulation learning environment.

No	List assessment	Expert no. 1	Expert no. 2	Expert no. 3
1	Learning content			
	1.1 Appropriate learning content	+1	+1	+1
2	Media			
	2.1 Appropriate navigator icon	+1	+1	+1
	2.2 Appropriate composition art	+1	+1	+1
	2.3 Appropriate images and animations	+1	+1	+1
	2.4 Stability	+1	+1	+1
3	Instructional design			
	3.1 Simulation problem base	+1	+1	+1
	3.2 Resource center	+1	+1	+1
	3.3 Cognitive tools center	+1	+1	+1
	3.4 Collaboration center	+1	+1	+1
	3.5 Enhance problem solving center	+1	+1	+1
	3.6 Scaffolding center	+1	+1	+1
	3.7 Coaching center	+1	+1	+1

According to Table 1, learning content aspect, experts agreed that the content is appropriate for learners. For media aspect, experts agreed that the navigator icon, composition art, images and animations are appropriate and stability. However, they suggest about fonts and color, it should be easier to read. The last aspect, instructional design, experts agreed that all components are appropriate and functional.

4.4 The Learner's Ill-Structured Problem Solving

The learners were asked to learn with simulation learning environment by start at **"Simulation problem base"**. After complete the tasks, they were interviewed for studying ill-structured problem solving process. The result of protocol analysis revealed that the learner solved the ill-structured problem by using 7 processes ill-structured problem solving process [1] as follow:

Learners Identify Problem Space and Contextual Constraints. The learner can identify initial state (current problem) and the goal state after solve the problem such the empirical evidence as *"They found spoiled milk and they can't deliver milk to customer. Thus, they want to deliver normal milk to customer"* or *"... spoiled milk and want normal milk for deliver"*.

Identifying the Stakeholder and Their Opinion. The learner can identify who are involve for this problem and what are their opinion such the empirical evidence as *"Stakeholders in this problem are Production manager, he need to produce milk for deliver to customer within 12 h and another stakeholder is chief executive officer (CEO), she provide budget for solving this problem only $1,000. The last stakeholder is process engineer, he need to measure the temperature in range 0–100 °C with accuracy ± 0.1 °C."* or *"Stakeholders are production manager who need to produce milk within 12 h, CEO who provide budget for $1,000, and process engineer who need to control temperature ± 0.1 °C."*

Generate Possible Problem Solutions. The learner generate solutions for solving the problem such the empirical evidence as *"We can generate 3 solutions as follow: 1) order the new temperature sensor, 2) repairing the damage sensor, and 3) order the whole new machine."* or *"There are 2 solutions for solving, 1) repairing the temperature sensor, and 2) order the new temperature sensor."*

Decision Making of Alternative Solutions. The learner can decision the suitable solution by using decision making model such the empirical evidence as *"We select the solution 1, order the new temperature sensor by using decision making model, rational choice, cost benefit, and risk assessment to evaluate 3 solutions. Then, solution 1 was found the highest score."* or *"We decision to order the new temperature sensor because this solution is highest score by using decision making model".*

Planning and Monitor the Performances. The learner can create the plan for the selected solution such the empirical evidence as *"step 1: order the new temperature sensor with appropriate specification. Step 2: Remove old temperature sensor and install new sensor instead. Step 3: check measure parameter for instance, range, accuracy, and precision."* or *"Step 1: order new temperature sensor, Step 2: replace new temperature sensor, and Step 3: checking accuracy and precision".*

Implement and Monitor the Solution. The learner can implement the plan and they can assess the performance such the empirical evidence as *"After we implement the plan. Then, we monitor the performance as follow: time for repairing, cost and measurement data."* or *"After replace the new temperature sensor, we have to check time for repairing, cost, and accuracy of temperature sensor."*

Adapt the Solution. The final process, the learner can tell the adapt solution if the performance are not meet the criteria such the empirical evidence as *"if the cost is higher than the budget we will find the cheaper new temperature with meet our requirements."* or *"We can improve both cost and accuracy of temperature sensor by finding the new temperature sensor which is better than current temperature sensor".*

5 Discussion

This study was descripted the development of simulation learning environment to enhance ill-structured problem solving for engineering students. The designing framework was synthesized and consisted of 5 processes and 7 components as above description. This results was consistent with Piyaporn W. [17] and Samat S. [18] which synthesized the designing framework of constructivist web-based learning environment. Their designing framework consist of 5 processes which may help learner to construct the knowledge and enhance high order thinking. Furthermore, the learner's ill-structured problem solving were found learners follow 7 processes from ill-structured problem solving [1]. This results was consistent with Samat S. [18] that study the learners' problem solving and transfer of learning. The implications of this finding revealed that the simulation learning environment to enhance ill-structured problem solving for engineering students may develop learners to construct knowledge and ill-structured problem solving skill for preparing them to be engineer for 21st century. In addition, leaners can learn with simulation learning environment in anywhere and anytime.

Acknowledgement. This research was supported by Ph.D. Program in Educational Technology, Faculty of Education, Khon Kaen University, and Research Group for Innovation and Cognitive Technology, Khon Kaen University which hereby giving the thankfulness all through this.

References

1. Jonassen, D.H.: Instructional design models for well-structured and ill-structured problem-solving learning outcomes. Educ. Tech. Res. Dev. **45**(1), 65–97 (1997)
2. Jonassen, D.H., Strobel, J., Lee, C.B.: Everyday problem solving in engineering: lessons for engineering educators. J. Eng. Educ. **95**(2), 139–151 (2006)
3. Campbell, J.O., Bourne, J.R., Mosterman, P.J., Brodersen, A.J.: The effectiveness of learning simulations for electronic laboratories. J. Eng. Educ. **91**(1), 81–87 (2002)
4. Stephen, N.E., Kratochwill, R.T., Coo, J.L.: Educational Psychology: Effective Teaching, Effective Learning, 3rd edn. McGraw-Hill College (2002)
5. Davidovitch, L., Parush, A., Shtub, A.: Simulation-based learning in engineering education: performance and transfer in learning project management. J. Eng. Educ. **95**(4), 289–299 (2006)
6. Piaget, J., Inhelder, B.: The Psychology of the Child. Basic Books, New York (1969)
7. Brown, J.S., Collins, A., Duguid, P.: Situated cognition and the culture of learning. Educ. Res. **18**(1), 32–42 (1989)

8. Jonassen, D.H.: Designing for decision making. Educ. Tech. Res. Dev. **60**(2), 341–359 (2012)
9. Jonassen, D.H.: Learning to Solve Problems a Handbook for Designing Problem-Solving Learning Environments. Routledge, New York (2011)
10. Klausmeier, H.J.: Educational Psychology, 5th edn. Harper & Row, New York (1985)
11. Mayer, R.H.: Designing instruction for constructivist learning. In: Reigeluth, C.M. (ed.) Instructional-Design Theories and Models: A New Paradigm of Instructional Theory, vol. II, pp. 141–160. Lawrence Erlbaum Associates, Mahwah (1999)
12. Winn, W.: Cognitive perspectives in psychology. In: Jonassen, D.H., (eds.) Handbook of Research for Educational Communications and Technology: A Project of the Association for Educational Communications and Technology, pp. 79–112 (2004)
13. Sweller, J.: Cognitive load theory. In: Mestre, J.P., Ross, B.H. (eds.) The psychology of learning and motivation: Vol. 55. The psychology of learning and motivation: Cognition in education, pp. 37–76. Elsevier Academic Press (2011)
14. Hannafin, M., Land, S.M., Oliver, K.: Open learning environments: foundations, methods, and models, instruction. In: Reigeluth, C.M. (ed.) Instructional-Design Theories and Models: A New Paradigm of Instructional Theory, vol. II. Lawrence Erlbaum Associates, NJ (1999)
15. Vygotsky, L.S.: Mind in Society: Development of Higher Psychological Processes. Harvard University Press (1978)
16. Collins, A., Brown, J.S., Holum, A.: Cognitive apprenticeship: making thinking visible. Am. Educ. **15**(3), 1–18 (1991)
17. Wonganu, P., Chaijaroen, S., Vongtathum, P.: Designing framework of constructivist digital learning environment model to enhance creative thinking for undergraduate students. Lect. Notes Comput. Sci. **1193**, 243–251 (2019)
18. Samat, C., Chaijaroen, S., Wattanachai, S.: The designing of constructivist web-based learning environment to enhance problem solving process and transfer of learning for computer education student. In: Rønningsbakk, L., Wu, T.T., Sandnes, F., Huang, Y.M. (eds.) ICITL 2019. LNCS, vol. 11937, pp. 117–126. Springer, Cham (2019). https://doi.org/10.1007/978-3-030-35343-8_13

The Study of Learner Context for the Development of Constructivist Learning Environment Model Combined with Mixed Reality Flipped Classroom to Enhance Creative Thinking in Product Design for the High School Students

Sathaporn Wongchiranuwat[1], Charuni Samat[2(✉)], Issara Kanjug[3], and Suchat Wattanachai[4]

[1] Doctor of Philosophy Student of Education Technology, Faculty of Education, Khon Kaen University, Khonkaen, Thailand
[2] Division of Computer Education, Faculty of Education, Khon Kaen University, Khonkaen, Thailand
thaibannok@hotmail.com
[3] Division of Educational Technology, Faculty of Education, Khon Kaen University, Khonkaen, Thailand
[4] Division of Surgery, Faculty of Veterinary Medicine, Khon Kaen University, Khonkaen, Thailand

Abstract. Creative thinking can promote creativity and innovation skills to a learner which important in this 21st century for unlimited innovation. This aimed to study the learner's context which basically used in the development of constructivist learning environment model. The 65 high school students were the target group. Survey research was employed by self-learner's survey form in Open-ended question and Likert ration scales in 5 scales; examined by 3 experts based on the consistency with theoretical framework. The results in 6 part revealed that (1) Demographics: 38 females or 58.46% and the revealed that learners 31 of them or 47.69% was in high level of GPA or 3.00–3.50 (2) Learning experience: 65 learners or 100% experienced in lecturing, demonstrating, practice and textbook learning (3) Technology experience: they were in neutral level or as $\bar{x} = 3.59$, S.D = 0.64 (4) Creative thinking experience: presented in low level as $\bar{x} = 2.98$, S.D = 0.73 as well as (5) Product design experience that $\bar{x} = 2.71$, S.D = 0.68 and (6) Expectations of the learner towards learning: most learners required flexible learning styles in variety and independent study based on interest or $\bar{x} = 4.89$, S.D = 0.74. The results hence were concluded that the current model of learning management should be a learning style that is flexible of environment, discovery, and knowledge construction. This includes supporting the use of technology as a cognitive tool to enhance the construction of knowledge and creative thinking.

Keywords: Learner context · Learning environment model · Constructivist · Creative thinking · Flipped classroom

1 Introduction

To strengthen the social development including job making in all industries, knowledge, innovative thinking, and creative thinking are important. They are the fundamental of such thinking and creativity in the 21st century [1, 2]. This is to focus on the development of economy based on creative knowledge along with integration of technology and innovation for the purpose of value-added business. Such creative economy that leads changing of epistemology seems to affect the learning paradigm shift. Since knowledge is dynamic and unlimited, learning in a classroom is not enough [3]. As that so, the recent studies have shown that the most learners have inadequate of creative thinking, discovery learning, and knowledge construction. The insufficiency of those skills resulted from rote learning style or traditional learning style while a teacher transmits knowledge and learner acts as passive one.

Learning style in these days should hence centered in creative thinking and construction of knowledge. Flipped learning classroom is one of learning styles that suggested to have well design in technology to enhance and give an opportunity to the leaners to search, find, and discovery based on various learning resources. They can have self- practice and construct their own knowledge from the knowledge in both inside and outside classroom with the help of a teacher who performs as a coach [4].

As that so, Constructivist theory that believes on knowledge discovery and construction as well as divergent thinking that is to invent and find a solution based on 1) fluency 2) flexibility 3) originality 4) elaboration [5] are fundamentally to enhance creative thinking based on the context of product design course that aims to have the learners with creative thinking by designing a new and useful product.

Consequently, the development of constructivist learning environment model combined with mixed reality flipped classroom to enhance creative thinking in product design for the high school students can be beneficial to learner efficiency in inventing and technology changing during the 21st century learning.

2 Literature Review

2.1 Creative Thinking

Creative thinking under the concept of Guilford [6]. The American psychologist believes that this is the development of structure of Intellect by consisting of 3 thinking dimensions as operation categories, content categories, and products categories. To clarify this, divergent thinking is the ability about creative thinking of each person to connect and adapt the relationship of thoughts in various directions and aspects. This can lead to the inventing or creating as well as finding concepts or solutions to solve the problem successfully. Creative thinking is defined as 1) fluency 2) flexibility 3) originality 4) elaboration [7].

2.2 Flipped Learning Model

Flipped learning model was designed and developed by Jonathan Bergmann and Aron Sams [8]. It is the learning style that emphasizes the changing of the traditional style that is the way a teacher transmits knowledge throughout lecturing in a classroom to a modern style. In other words, a learner has self-study and discovers knowledge outside classroom via provided technology or learning media by a teacher. The teacher then works on such the learner have learned by providing an inside classroom activity which the teacher guides and questions. The main purpose of the activity is to enhance learners to share knowledge and collaboratively solve a problem while having interaction between a teacher and learner through new kinds of technology and device such as a computer, mobile phone etc. This can help the learner to study by themselves in their own time not only classroom time while technology strengthen the connection between both [9].

3 Purposes

To study the context of the learners to be used as the basis of the development of constructivist learning environment model combined with mixed reality flipped classroom to enhance creative thinking in product design for the high school students.

4 Method and Result

4.1 Scope of Research

The model research was employed [10]. This is to intensively study the process of design and development a model which comprises 3 research as 1) Model development 2) Model validation and 3) Model use. In this study, research phase 1 Model development was implemented to present the results of the develop process by survey research in learner's context; such results were fundamentally used to design and develop the constructivist learning environment model combined with mixed reality flipped classroom to enhance creative thinking in product design for the high school students.

4.2 Target Group of the Study

The study target was the 65 high school students, science and technology learning substance group, who registered in product design course.

4.3 Research Design

Research phase 1 model development was employed by survey research.

4.4 Research Instruments

The survey form was used to study the context of learners. The form was developed by 3 procedures as 1) Define conceptual framework for developing a survey form 2) Synthesize a survey questions based on the theoretical framework and 3) Construct the survey form. It then was examined the consistency of both questions and concepts in theoretical framework by 3 assessment experts.

4.5 Data Collection and Analysis

The data of learner context was collected by the survey form which presented the following aspects as 1) Demographics 2) Learning experience 3) Technology experience 4) Creative thinking experience 5) Product design experience and 6) Expectations of the learner towards learning. The survey was in form of open-ended question and likert ration scales in 5 scales (5 = very high, 4 = high, 3 = neutral, 2 = low, 1 = very low) [11]. The data analysis was made by percentage, mean score, and standard deviation.

4.6 Research Results

The results of learner context in areas of characteristics of the learner, learning style, and factors influenced learners' patterns were hence used as a model developmental basis as the following.

- **Part 1 Demographics:** Demographics-basis information of the learners as by gender and GPA presented. The results were found that most of the learners were females or in amount of 38 learners or 58.46% and the data also revealed that the learners 31 of them or 47.69% was in high level of GPA or 3.00-3.50
- **Part 2 Learning experience:** The data of learning experience of the learners was found in 3 subtitles as 1) Learning theory 2) Learning media and 3) Learning model as shown in Table 1.

Table 1. Learning experience.

Learning experience	Number (n)	Percent (%)
▪ Learning theory		
A learner has had learning experiences by listening to lectures, demonstrating, and practicing.	65	100.00
A learner has had learning experiences by design thinking, making decision, and making-meaning based on multiple situations.	36	55.38
A learner has had learning experiences by discovery learning and self-knowledge construction	29	44.62

(*continued*)

Table 1. (*continued*)

Learning experience	Number (n)	Percent (%)
▪ Learning media		
A learner has had experience in web-based learning	43	66.15
A learner has had experience in the textbook learning	65	100.00
A learner has had experience in video based learning	27	41.54
▪ Learning model		
A learner has had experience in problem-based learning	32	49.23
A learner has had experience in collaborative learning	45	69.23
A learner has had experience in flipped classroom learning	14	21.54

According to Table 1, the results of learning experience were found that most learners had the experience in lecturing, demonstration, and practicing as 65 learners or 100.00%, 65 learner or 100.00% has had experience in the textbook learning, while 45 learners or 69.23% had collaborative learning experience.

- **Part 3 Technology experience:** The study of learners' technology experience based on the survey form was explained by the following aspects as 1) Use of technology device 2) Use of technology to support product design 3) Use of technology to explore knowledge 4) Use of knowledge as learning context to enhance action learning 5) Use of technology as social media for a conversation and knowledge sharing 6) Use of technology to reflex thinking. The technology experience data was shown in the below Table 2.

Table 2. Technology experience.

Technology experience	$\bar{x}$	SD	Performance level
■ Use of technology device			
Learner's ability to use a desktop computer	4.35	0.71	High
Learner's ability to use a laptop computer	3.98	0.62	Neutral
Learner's ability to use a smart phone	4.65	0.69	High
Learner's ability to use a tablet	2.45	0.74	Low
Total	3.84	0.65	Neutral
■ Use of technology to support product design			
Learner's ability to use Sketchup software for knowledge construction and product design	4.21	0.65	High
Learner's ability to use AutoCAD software for knowledge construction and product design	2.79	0.71	Low
Learner's ability to use 3D max software for knowledge construction and product design	2.15	0.69	Low
Total	3.05	0.68	Neutral

(*continued*)

Table 2. (*continued*)

Technology experience	$\bar{x}$	SD	Performance level
■ Use of technology to survey knowledge			
Learner's ability to use Google search engine for knowledge survey	4.85	0.56	High
Learner's ability to use Bing search engine for knowledge survey	3.78	0.70	Neutral
Learner's ability to use Yahoo search engine for knowledge survey	2.56	0.65	Low
Total	3.73	0.62	Neutral
■ Use of technology as learning context to enhance action learning			
Learner's ability to use Mixed Reality view software for practicing and modeling a product design	3.59	0.64	Neutral
Learner's ability to use HP Reveal software for practicing and modeling a product design	3.41	0.57	Neutral
Learner's ability to use 3D Warehouse software for practicing and modeling a product design	4.24	0.69	High
Total	3.74	0.63	Neutral
■ Use of technology to as social media for a conversation and knowledge sharing			
Learner's ability to use Facebook application for making a conversation and knowledge sharing	4.87	0.69	High
Learner's ability to use Line application for making a conversation and knowledge sharing	4.27	0.71	High
Learner's ability to use E-mail for making a conversation and knowledge sharing	3.70	0.74	Neutral
Total	4.28	0.72	High
■ Use of Technology to reflex thinking			
Learner's ability to use Mind Map software for building mind mapping and presenting ideas	3.67	0.65	Neutral
Learner's ability to use Web Blogger for building mind mapping and presenting ideas	2.49	0.59	Low
Total	3.08	0.62	Neutral
All Total	3.59	0.64	Neutral

According to Table 2, the results of technology experience were found that most learners in overall had the neutral level of technology using $\bar{x} = 3.59$, S.D = 0.64. Specifically, they had the high level of performance to use a social media platform for a conversation and knowledge sharing or $\bar{x} = 4.28$, S.D = 0.72, neutral level of technology device or $\bar{x} = 3.84$, S.D = 0.65 as well as the neutral level of technology use as learning context to enhance action learning or $\bar{x} = 3.74$, S.D = 0.63 respectively.

- **Part 4 Creative thinking experience:** Learners' creative thinking experience data collected from the survey form was presented in the following parts 1) fluency 2) flexibility 3) originality and 4) elaboration as shown in Table 3.

Table 3. Creative thinking experience.

Creative thinking experience	$\bar{x}$	SD	Performance level
■ Fluency			
Learner's ability to generate various ideas to search and discover needed answer/identify requirement/list possible alternatives for or a solution within limited time	3.97	0.79	Neutral
■ Flexibility			
Learner's ability to change/alternate for a variety of usefulness outcomes/transform a principle or limitation to achieve a goal	3.21	0.52	Neutral
■ Originality			
Learner's ability to create new ideas that leads to inventing based on the adjustment or prior knowledge	2.45	0.71	Low
■ Elaboration			
Learner's ability to perform details or solution guidelines with additional information for the purpose of elaborating/adjusting/improving for a new idea	2.30	0.64	Low
All total	2.98	0.73	Low

According to Table 3, the results of creative thinking experience were found that they had low performance in creative thinking experience or $\bar{x}$ = 2.98, S.D = 0.73. Among those 4 creative thinking components, the highest number was shown in fluency which in neutral level or $\bar{x}$ = 3.97, S.D = 0.79, flexibility presented $\bar{x}$ = 3.21, S.D = 0.52 in neutral level, while Originality shown $\bar{x}$ = 2.45, S.D = 0.71 and elaboration was at $\bar{x}$ = 2.30, S.D = 0.64 in low level respectively.

- **Part 5 Product design experience:** The results of product design experience of the learners based on the survey form was shown in Table 4 below.

Table 4. Product design experience.

Product design experience	$\bar{x}$	SD	Experience level
A learner has had the experience in product design such as furniture and life equipment	3.08	0.69	Neutral
A learner has had the experience in value-added product design	2.10	0.72	Low

(*continued*)

Table 4. (*continued*)

Product design experience	$\bar{x}$	SD	Experience level
A learner has had the experience in selecting of materials for product design	2.98	0.61	Low
A learner has had the experience in product presentation using an application software	2.65	0.74	Low
A learner has had the experience in design product 3D models	2.75	0.78	Low
All total	2.71	0.68	Low

According to Table 4, the results of product design experience were found that they had low level or $\bar{x} = 2.71$, S.D = 0.68 which they most had the experience in product design such as furniture and life equipment or $\bar{x} = 3.08$, S.D = 0.69 in neutral level. Meanwhile, the other kinds of product design experience as in selecting of materials for product design, product design 3D models, product presentation using an application software, and product design to value adding were in low level as $\bar{x} = 2.98$, S.D = 0.61, $\bar{x} = 2.75$, S.D = 0.78, $\bar{x} = 2.65$, S.D = 0.74, and $\bar{x} = 2.10$, S.D. 0.72 respectively.

Table 5. Expectations of the learner towards learning.

	Expectations of the learner towards learning	$\bar{x}$	SD	Expectation level
■ Content				
1	A learner requires an updated content which can be used in daily life	4.51	0.64	High
2	A learner requires an interesting presentation in various forms	4.54	0.72	High
3	A learner requires categorized content and consistent with learning topics	4.20	0.65	High
	Total	4.41	0.65	High

(*continued*)

Table 5. (*continued*)

	Expectations of the learner towards learning	$\bar{x}$	SD	Expectation level
■ Learning style				
4	A learner requires problem-based learning for knowledge discovery and construction	4.74	0.67	High
5	A learner requires group-based learning for knowledge sharing in both inside and outside classroom	4.79	0.77	High
6	A learner requires the flexibility of learning environment in form varieties based on each own interest	4.89	0.74	High
7	A learner requires learning style enhancing creative thinking	4.69	0.69	High
	Total	4.77	0.68	High
■ Teacher				
8	A teacher should design a lesson plan that compatible with each learner's ability in various styles	4.49	0.70	High
9	A teacher should support a learner to be an active learner for the achievement of self-learning	4.60	0.65	High
10	A teacher should provide multiple courses based on their interest for a selection of learners	4.78	0.72	High
	Total	4.62	0.67	High
	All total	4.60	0.74	High

- **Part 6 Expectations of the learner towards learning:** The study of the expectations of the learner towards learning comprised 3 parts as 1) Content 2) Learning style and 3) Teacher as shown in Table 5.

According to Table 5, the results of expectations of the learner towards learning were found that in high level or $\bar{x}$ = 4.60, S.D = 0.74. Accordingly, they presented the statistical data that $\bar{x}$ = 4.89, S.D = 0.74 $\bar{x}$ = 4.79, S.D = 0.77 $\bar{x}$ = 4.78, S.D = 0.72 for in topics that they required the flexibility of learning environment in various forms based on their own interests, they expected to have group-based learning for knowledge sharing in both inside and outside classroom, and they presented their expectation that a teacher should provide multiple courses based on their interest for a selection of learners respectively.

5 Conclusions

Consequently, the results of the study of learner context in terms of characteristics, learning style, and factors that affected their learning for the purpose of the development of constructivist learning environment model combined with mixed reality flipped classroom to enhance creative thinking in product design for the high school students were concluded that 1) Demographics: the majority was female and had GPA 3.00-3.50 or in high level 2) Learning experience: most of them had the experience in lecturing, demonstrating, practice and textbook learning 3) Technology experience: the learners were in neutral level 4) Creative thinking experience: they were in low performance level 5) Product design experience: they had low level of experience 6) Expectations of the learner towards learning: most learners expressed high expectation of learning. The results hence were that the learning styles of learners were not consistent with discovery learning and knowledge construction. Moreover, technology support was not adequate in knowledge construction and creative thinking enhancing [12]. In conclusion, the present learning styles should highlight knowledge construction and creative thinking by several and flexible learning methods. The learners should be enhanced to share and collaborate in both inside and outside classroom while the teachers act differently by transforming from a teller to coach (Coaching). Moreover, the learning style is suggested to focus on self-study with innovation improvement in order to foster a learner to be able to discover knowledge by themselves that beneficial to live [13].

Acknowledgement. This research was supported by Ph.D. Program in Educational Technology, Faculty of Education, Khon Kaen University, and Research Group for Innovation and Cognitive Technology, Khon Kaen University which here by giving the thankfulness all through this.

References

1. Dede, C.: Comparing frameworks for 21st century skills. 21st century skills: Rethinking how students learn, vol. 20, pp. 51–76 (2010)
2. Samat, C., Chaijaroen, S.: Design and development of learning environment to enhance creative thinking and innovation skills for teacher training in the 21st century. In: 23rd International Conference on Computers in Education, ICCE, pp. 667–672 (2015)
3. Chaijaroen, S., Samat, C.: The learner's creative thinking learning with learning innovation to encourage human thinking. Eur. J. Soc. Sci. **28**, 213–218 (2012)
4. Samat, C., Kampira, K.: Development of constructivist flipped classroom to enhance students' creative thinking for designing logo. In: 24th International Conference on Computers in Education: Think Global Act Local - Main Conference Proceedings, pp. 660–662 (2016)
5. Wongchiranuwat, S., Samat, C.: Synthesis of theoretical framework for augmented Reality learning environment to promote creative thinking on topic implementation of graphic design for grade 9 students. In: 24th International Conference on Computers in Education: Think Global Act Local - Main Conference Proceedings, pp. 639–641 (2016)
6. Guilford, J.P.: The Nature of Human Intelligence. McGraw-Hill Book Company, New York (1967)
7. Chaijaroen, S., Techapornpong, O., Samat, C.: Learner's creative thinking of learners learning with constructivist web-based learning environment model: Integration between pedagogy and neuroscience. In: 25th International Conference on Computers in Education: Technology and Innovation: Computer-Based Educational Systems for the 21st Century, Workshop Proceedings, pp. 565–571 (2017)
8. Bergmann, J., Sams, A.: Flip your classroom: Reach every student in every class every day. International Society for Technology in Education; ASCD, Alexandria, VA (2012)

9. Bergmann, J., Sams, A.: Before you flip, consider this. The Phi Delta Kappan **94**(2), 25 (2014)
10. Richey, R.C., Klein, J.: Design and Developmental Research. Lawrence, New Jersey (2007)
11. Likert, R.A.: Technique for the measurement of attitudes. Arch. Psychol. **25**(140), 1–55 (1932)
12. Chaijaroen, S., Kanjak, I., Samat, C.: The study of learners' critical thinking potential, learning with innovation enhancing thinking potential. Procedia Soc. Behav. Sci. **46**, 3415–3420 (2012)
13. Kanjug, I., Wattanachai, S., Kanjug, P., Nangam, C.: SOCIALClassnet as an LMS for online flipped learning environment. In: 6th IIAI International Congress on Advanced Applied Informatics, IIAI-AAI (2017)

Transparent Player Model: Adaptive Visualization of Learner Model in Educational Games

Danial Hooshyar[1(✉)], Emanuele Bardone[1], Nour El Mawas[2], and Yeongwook Yang[3]

[1] Centre for Educational Technology, University of Tartu, Tartu, Estonia
Danial.hooshyar@gmail.com, emabardo@gmail.com
[2] CIREL (EA 4354), University of Lille, Lille, France
nour.el-mawas@univ-lille.fr
[3] Department of Computer Science and Engineering, Korea University, Seoul, Republic of Korea
yeongwook.yang@gmail.com

Abstract. Despite the success of Learning Analytics (LA), there are two obstacles to its application in educational games, including transparency in assessing educational outcomes in real-time gameplay, and clarity in representing those results to players. Open learner model (OLM) is a valuable instrument with capability to improve learning that meets such challenges. However, OLMs usually suffer issues concerning interactivity and transparency, which mostly regard the assessment mechanism that is used to evaluate learners' knowledge. Tackling down transparency issues would offer context for interpreting and comparing learner model information, as well as promoting interactivity. As there is lack of studies investigating the potential of OLMs in educational games, we argue that this work can provide a valuable starting point for applying OLMs or adaptive visualizations of players' learner models within gameplay sessions, which, in turn, can help to address both issues of application of LA to game research and OLMs. As a case study, we introduce the proposed approach into our adaptive computational thinking game.

Keywords: Open learner model · Adaptive visualization · Learning analytics · Educational game

1 Introduction

Games that are designed for a specific educational purpose, or with secondary educational values can be defined as educational games. Educational games have gained the attention of researchers, governments, educators, as well as parents as they have been shown to be effective learning tools that both potentially engage and motivate students (e.g., [1, 2]). Findings from several studies suggest that educational games can also improve students' learning achievements (e.g., [2, 3]). For example, the study conducted by Partovi and Razavi [3] showed that students who learned through gameplay had significantly better academic achievement and motivation to learn science than those who learned with traditional approaches. Several researchers have addressed the key features of educational games stressing learner involvement through experimentation, cooperation, exploration, and competition (e.g., [4, 5]). One challenge for the successful deployment and adoption of educational games in formal education is how to measure the learning progress and outcomes achieved through educational games [1]. Since traditional educational measures are mostly highly invasive and compromise the flow, they are not suitable for educational games [6]. Conversely, LA has the capability to provide continuous non-invasive assessment for educational games by extracting and interpreting pertinent information from the real-time game data. Therefore, the application of LA to educational games can potentially improve the assessment of performance, game quality, progress, user appreciation, and learning outcomes [7, 8]. Despite the success of LA, there are two obstacles to its application in educational games. Firstly, transparency in assessing educational outcomes in real-time gameplay, and, secondly, clarity in representing those outcomes to the players.

According to Daniel [9], there exist three different models of LA: predictive, descriptive, and prescriptive. OLMs fall into the last category. Not only do OLMs provide educators with the chance to evaluate and monitor students' learning, but also provide opportunity for the students to monitor their learning by allowing them to visualize information concerning their learning process. Therefore, the application of OLMs to educational games can potentially help address the clarity issue that triggers reflection from the learners' side. Aside from the potential of OLMs in facilitating the representation of LA results to players, however, OLMs usually suffer from assessment transparency issues, as well as prompting users to actively engage with OLM [10, 11].

As the potentials of OLMs in educational games have been ignored, we argue that by adaptively displaying to players both the methods used in the game to measure their competencies and also the information on their acquired knowledge and skills (making the learner model open), issues associated to application of LA to game research, as well as assessment transparency and interactivity in OLMs, could potentially be solved. In other words, this work can provide a valuable starting point for the application of OLMs or adaptive visualization of players' learner models in educational games within gameplay sessions. As a case study, we introduce the proposed approach into our adaptive computational thinking game, AutoThinking, through an in-game character that adaptively prompts players to engage with real-time visualization of the game's Bayesian Belief Networks (the probabilistic method by which players' skills are assessed) and of metacognitive data on the player's educational progress (e.g., hints, warnings, suggestions, and feedback).

This paper is structured as follows. Section 2 reviews the related studies in the area of LA in educational games and OLMs. Section 3 presents the transparent player model (TPM) applied to our AutoThinking game. Section 4 concludes this paper and presents its perspectives.

2 Related Research

2.1 Learning Analytics in Educational Games

Most educational games record user (inter)actions, generating swathes of data useful for LA. Indeed, digital games already have in place the mechanics to respond to users' specific actions. What is missing from studies evaluating in-game performance, however, is how to apply this data educationally [8]. Some combination of visual, web, and LA promises an answer.

LA in educational games fits into two categories: in-game analytics which take place in real-time and post-game analytics which is offline [12]. The latter revolves around summative measurement of learning outcomes or diagnosing general learning patterns. Serrano-Laguna et al. [13, 14] put forward a two-step approach to any educational game with LA: first gathering game traces (start, end), phase changes or chapters, user input traces, and variables such as scores or attempts; then generating reports about student play. On the other hand, in-game LA is integrated within a game for two reasons: to offer analytic results as a ground for subsequent pedagogic decisions, or to adapt gameplay in real time. This embedded assessment is designed to be continuous and inconspicuous [1]. Basically, such non-invasive assessment links game activities that are observable to learning outcomes. Accordingly, it updates the learner model, which, in turn, facilitates monitoring and advancing learning in different ways, including reports on learners' progress, or adaptivity [15]. Such assessment was deployed in educational games brought about by the ELEKTRA and 80Days projects [16], which evaluated real-time learner responses to challenging situations by looking at skills, competence, and motivation. This input then triggered adaptations aimed at supporting the individual's needs and retaining motivation.

In short, LA shows great potential in enhancing educational games, but it still faces the two difficulties that this project seeks to address: 1) Transparency in assessment; and 2) the representation of the learning assessment to the user. The first difficulty involves exposing learners to the process of learner model aimed at helping them better understand and reflect on their own misconceptions, as they can compare and interpret their learner model information. The second difficulty requires an approach that presents pedagogic information to players in a visual way conducive to exploration and experimenting. These approaches must be empirically valid, user-friendly, and at the same time offer meaningful analysis of real-time evaluations. As pointed out by several researchers, e.g., [17, 18], using more visual LA tools enables instructors to provide personalized feedback, thereby promoting students' metacognitive skills development. Additionally, visual analytics offers the advantage of dealing with heterogeneous data sources, including demographic and historical data, which can help better understand the learning process, as prior learner experiences might affect future learning events. In combination, this approach promises to enhance LA's educational value within and beyond gaming.

2.2 Open Learner Models

In the artificial intelligent in education research field, the learner model is a key inner component of the conventional intelligent system design. It rests behind the user interface, collecting and assessing data on user-system interactions and then facilitating systemic adaptation to a specific user's needs [10, 11]. As Self [19] observes, an educational system must contain a learner model to discern and meet an individual student's needs. The educational system uses the learner model both as a frame of reference and source for all adaptive interactions. Yet the learner model is not always a black box behind the system: Self [19] argued that modular transparency could offer learners a valuable opportunity to self-reflect, which has led to a number of proposed OLMs in the recent years [10].

Opening the learner model to learners poses two difficulties. First and foremost is the problem of assessment transparency. Beyond opening the learner model directly (making available the representation of learning assessment to the learner himself/herself), there exist other instances that could potentially be open. Such instances include the means through which the model acquires information (e.g., [20]) and the assessment mechanism deployed to infer visualized or respective information in the domain model [10]. In fact, exposing learners to the process of learner model or domain content not only can be the key to interactive maintenance processes, but also would provide students with qualitatively better information to consider while reflecting on their own learning [21]. Furthermore, opening up such processes would help students to better understand and reflect on their own misconceptions, as they can compare and interpret their learner model information [22]. The second problem concerns the interactivity between the learner and the system, as processes of interpretation and reaction become partly dependent on the learner interaction. A number of interactive styles have been put forth to address such problems (e.g., [23, 24])—including inspectable, co-operative, editable and negotiated styles—but none have satisfactorily resolved the difficulties. As such, a new approach to human-computer interactions in OLMs is necessary to take advantage of their educational benefit. To this end, Minovic et al. [25] created a tool to visualize the learner model within gameplay sessions, allowing educators to track student progress. The fundamental difficulties remain, however, as its visualization reduces the learner model to a pie-chart in a corner of the screen. The visualization approach of OLM must be integrated with adaptive educational games in ways that motivate learner interaction with the visualized model. For example, that can be accomplished by adaptively visualizing metacognitive data (hints, warnings, suggestions, feedback) of the player's educational progress. Additionally, the proposed approach still ignores clarity and transparency in the assessment mechanism that is used to evaluate learners' knowledge. Adaptive engagement of learners with their OLMs and the method by which players' skills are assessed during gameplay could potentially solve issues associated with OLMs.

3 The Proposed Approach

3.1 Overview of the AutoThinking Game

AutoThinking is an adaptive educational game that aims to promote students' Computational Thinking (CT) [26]. The game is based on drag and drop icons instead of programming syntax. In a novel way, it promotes four CT skills, namely problem identification and decomposition, pattern recognition and generalization, debugging, and simulation. In addition to that, it fosters CT concepts of sequence, conditional, and loop (for more details, see [26]).

The game currently consists of three levels in which a player should, in the role of a mouse, develop different types of strategies and solutions (up to 20) to complete the levels, while collecting as many cheese pieces (there are 76 cheese pieces in the maze) and scoring as much as possible, and at the same time escaping from two cats in the maze (see Fig. 1). Adaptivity in both the gameplay and the learning process is integrated in the game. For example, according to the suitability of the solution for the current state of the maze (or player's skill), the game regulates the movement of one of the cats, and adaptively provides the player with various types of feedback (textual, graphical, or video) and hints, if necessary.

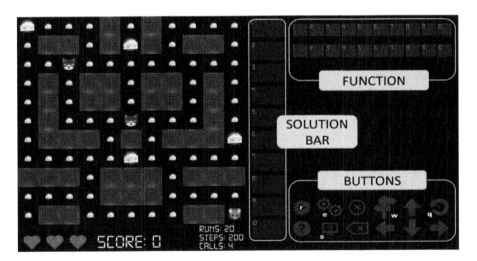

Fig. 1. Interface of AutoThinking.

3.2 The Transparent Player Model

Figure 2 illustrates the architecture of the TPM using real-time visual analytics on the AutoThinking game.

As Fig. 2 demonstrates, during the gameplay raw pixels and log data are stored in a repository. Log data are employed in learning analytics and real-time dynamic adaptation, while raw pixels are mainly stored to train and deploy virtual characters within

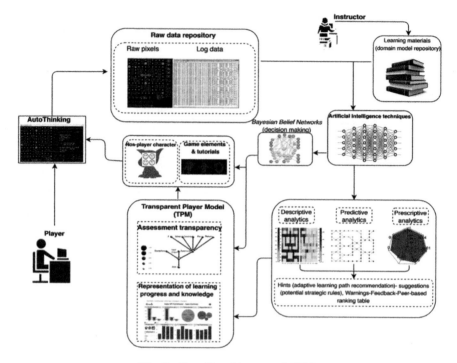

Fig. 2. Overall architecture of TPM.

the game from this data. These raw data are then employed in player-specific decision-making using various techniques such as Bayesian Belief Network (BBN), clustering, and classification algorithms.

In brief, the raw data are used to generate various types of analytics on players' learning process, namely descriptive, predictive, and prescriptive analytics. Various techniques can be used for this purpose, including clustering and classification methods. Results from these analytics are then visualized in various forms like hints (adaptive learning path recommendation and visualization), suggestions about potential strategic rules corresponding to the most recent move made by players, feedback, warnings, and peer-based ranking tables—included in the TPM. More explicitly, such visual analytics representing the players' cognition and competency will be used to communicate the information on skills acquired and learning progress to the players (representing players' learning model to them). Aside from this, visualization of the BBN in real-time will be used in the TPM to expose players to the assessment mechanism and reasoning used for evaluation of their competencies (when necessary).

The BBN from which player models are developed also mediates the TPM between game elements, tutorials, and a Non-Player Characters (NPC), thereby adaptively accessing the visualization features concerning player advancement and analytics in the TPM. When compared with previous approaches, TPM aids players by providing individually adapted visual analytics to explore, including metacognitive data on the player's educational progress (e.g., hints, warnings, suggestions, feedback), and the method by which their skills are assessed during gameplay. Finally, as shown in Fig. 2, the NPC prompts player adaptively to engage the TPM. Even expressions and emotions could be displayed by the NPC so players can reflect on and respond more productively to the situation [27].

4 Conclusions and Future Work

In this research, we studied two specific challenges associated with application of LA to educational games, namely, transparency in assessing educational outcomes in real-time gameplay and clarity in representing those results to players. To overcome those challenges, we proposed to apply the notion of OLMs to educational games. Such applications could visualize LA results from game data within educational games, including the current knowledge or skill levels of learners during active educational game sessions, relaxing the clarity issue. This could also help learners independently track, reflect on, and pace their learning processes. To address the assessment transparency issue, however, we propose to adaptively visualize the methods used in the game to measure players' skill. Such adaptive visualization of player's leaner model, called transparent player model or TPM, have the potential to not only relax the issues associated with application of LA to educational games, but also solve the interactivity issue of OLMs as a NPC prompts players adaptively to engage the TPM.

As a future work, we plan to implement the proposed TPM framework in the AutoThinking game. Additionally, we aim to investigate the possible effects of adaptively exposing learners to the process of learner model or domain content during the gameplay.

Acknowledgments. This research was supported by the University of Tartu ASTRA Project PER ASPERA, financed by the European Regional Development Fund.

References

1. Steiner, C.M., Kickmeier-Rus, M.D., Albert, D.: Making sense of game-based user data: learning analytics in applied games. In: International Association for Development of the Information Society, pp. 21–24 (2015)
2. El Mawas, N., Hooshyar, D., Yang, Y.: Investigating the learning impact of autothinking educational game on adults: a case study of France. In: CSEDU (2), pp. 188–196 (2020)
3. Partovi, T., Razavi, M.R.: The effect of game-based learning on academic achievement motivation of elementary school students. Learn. Motiv. **68**, 101592 (2019)
4. Zhonggen, Yu.: A meta-analysis of use of serious games in education over a decade. Int. J. Comput. Games Technol. **2019**, 1–8 (2019)
5. Hooshyar, D., Yousefi, M., Lim, H.: Data-driven approaches to game player modeling: a systematic literature review. ACM Comput. Surv. (CSUR) **50**(6), 1–19 (2018)
6. Van Eck, R.: Digital game-based learning: It's not just the digital natives who are restless. EDUCAUSE Rev. **41**(2), 16 (2006)

7. Westera, W., Nadolski, R.J., Hummel, H.G.K., Wopereis, I.G.J.H.: Serious games for higher education: a framework for reducing design complexity. J. Comput. Assist. Learn. **24**(5), 420–432 (2008)
8. Hauge, J.B., et al.: Implications of learning analytics for serious game design. In: 14th International Conference on Advanced Learning Technologies, pp. 230–232. IEEE (2014)
9. Daniel, B.K.: Big data and Learning Analytics in Higher Education. Springer, New York (2016)
10. Hooshyar, D., Pedaste, M., Saks, K., Leijen, Ä., Bardone, E., Wang, M.: Open learner models in supporting self-regulated learning in higher education: a systematic literature review. Comput. Educ. **154**, 103878 (2020)
11. Hooshyar, D., Kori, K., Pedaste, M., Bardone, E.: The potential of open learner models to promote active thinking by enhancing self-regulated learning in online higher education learning environments. Br. J. Edu. Technol. **50**(5), 2365–2386 (2019)
12. Westera, W., Nadolski, R., Hummel, H.: Serious gaming analytics: What students log files tell us about gaming and learning (2014)
13. Serrano-Laguna, Á., Torrente, J., Moreno-Ger, P., Fernández-Manjón, B.: Tracing a little for big improvements: application of learning analytics and videogames for student assessment. Procedia Comput. Sci. **15**, 203–209 (2012)
14. Serrano-Laguna, Á., Torrente, J., Moreno-Ger, P., Fernández-Manjón, B.: Application of learning analytics in educational videogames. Entertainment Comput. **5**(4), 313–322 (2014)
15. Shute, V.J., Ventura, M., Bauer, M., Zapata-Rivera, D.: Melding the power of serious games and embedded assessment to monitor and foster learning. Serious Games: Mech. Effects **2**, 295–321 (2009)
16. Kickmeier-Rust, M.D., Albert, D.: Micro-adaptivity: protecting immersion in didactically adaptive digital educational games. J. Comput. Assist. Learn. **26**(2), 95–105 (2010)
17. Vieira, C., Parsons, P., Byrd, V.: Visual learning analytics of educational data: a systematic literature review and research agenda. Comput. Educ. **122**, 119–135 (2018)
18. Kay, J., Bull, S.: New opportunities with open learner models and visual learning analytics. In: Conati, C., Heffernan, N., Mitrovic, A., Verdejo, M.F. (eds.) AIED 2015. LNCS (LNAI), vol. 9112, pp. 666–669. Springer, Cham (2015). https://doi.org/10.1007/978-3-319-19773-9_87
19. Self, J.A.: Bypassing the intractable problem of student modelling. Intelligent tutoring systems: at the crossroads of artificial intelligence and education, vol. 41, pp. 1–26 (1990)
20. Van Labeke, N., Brna, P., Morales, R.: Opening up the interpretation process in an open learner model. Int. J. Artif. Intell. Educ. **17**(3), 305–338 (2007)
21. Ginon, B., Boscolo, C., Johnson, M.D., Bull, S.: Persuading an Open learner model in the context of a university course: an exploratory study. In: Micarelli, A., Stamper, J., Panourgia, K. (eds.) ITS 2016. LNCS, vol. 9684, pp. 307–313. Springer, Cham (2016). https://doi.org/10.1007/978-3-319-39583-8_34
22. Johan, R., Bull, S.: Consultation of misconceptions representations by students in education-related courses. In: AIED, pp. 565–572 (2009)
23. Bull, S., McKay, M.: An open learner model for children and teachers: inspecting knowledge level of individuals and peers. In: Lester, J.C., Vicari, R.M., Paraguaçu, F. (eds.) ITS 2004. LNCS, vol. 3220, pp. 646–655. Springer, Heidelberg (2004). https://doi.org/10.1007/978-3-540-30139-4_61
24. Suleman, R.M., Mizoguchi, R., Ikeda, M.: A new perspective of negotiation-based dialog to enhance metacognitive skills in the context of open learner models. Int. J. Artif. Intell. Educ. **26**(4), 1069–1115 (2016)
25. Minović, M., Milovanović, M., Šošević, U., González, M.Á.C.: Visualisation of student learning model in serious games. Comput. Hum. Behav. **47**, 98–107 (2015)

26. Hooshyar, D., Lim, H., Pedaste, M., Yang, K., Fathi, M., Yang, Y.: AutoThinking: an adaptive computational thinking game. In: Rønningsbakk, L., Wu, T.-T., Sandnes, F.E., Huang, Y.-M. (eds.) ICITL 2019. LNCS, vol. 11937, pp. 381–391. Springer, Cham (2019). https://doi.org/10.1007/978-3-030-35343-8_41
27. Chen, Z.-H., Chou, C.-Y., Deng, Y.-C., Chan, T.-W.: Active open learner models as animal companions: motivating children to learn through interacting with My-Pet and Our-Pet. Int. J. Artif. Intell. Educ. **17**(2), 145–167 (2007)

Online Course and Web-Based Environment

A Study of Learner's Mental Model and Motivation Using Constructivism Online Learning Environment to Promote Programming in Rural School

Poramin Attane and Issara Kanjug(✉)

Khon Kaen University, Khon Kaen, Thailand
issaraka@kku.ac.th

Abstract. Programming is important for development of skills and thinking for the learners. but the problem of programming is abstract content. Learners can't imagine a result from their program during the programming. so, it makes programming is boring and difficult for learning. Mental model is understanding of learner to create mental representation in media and symbol. Development of student's mental model can help students to construct their knowledge in programming. Moreover, motivation is the one of important factor to success in learning. The purpose of this research was study leaners' mental model and motivation. The participants target 10 students at rural school. Experimental research was employed in this study. The instruments used in the experiment were Constructivist online learning environment. Data collection used the mental model interview recording form and motivation survey form. The results found that learner's mental model consists with 2 characteristics as follow: (1) Represent story or event by explaining in model (2) Change rule and procedure to solve problem. The learners' motivation was very motivated (mean = 3.93, $S.D.$ = 0.44). It was comprised of 2 components as follow: 1) Internal motivation was (mean = 4.1, $S.D.$ = 0.35) 2) External motivation was very motivate (mean = 3.75, $S.D.$ = 0.53). In conclusion, the Constructivism Online Learning Environment can improve programming and self-learning performance in rural school.

Keywords: Constructivism · Online learning environment · Mental model · Motivation · Programming

1 Introduction

Programming is important to develop important skills and thinking for students. Programming content are abstract, elaborate, and complex, so it is difficult for students to understand. Mental model is understanding of learner to create mental representation in media and symbol. Development of student's mental model make students understand and solve the complex problem. Moreover, programming content is bore because it has no graphic and colorful, so students need more motivation to help them to learn programming.

The reasons mentioned above, this study recognize the importance of computer classroom constructivist learning environment design. The researcher applied the mental model theory, motivation theory, constructivist theory, cognitive theory, the media attribution and symbols system used, textbook design and the specific context for the learning content synthesizing them as the framework for designing the constructivism online learning environment to enhance learner's mental model and motivation. Studies have reported increased student motivation, improved collaboration, knowledge construction and mental model.

2 Literature Review

2.1 Mental Model

Mental model is understanding of learner to create mental representation in media and symbol format. In this study use Kanjug [3] Mental models. There are consist with 2 characteristics as follow: 1) It was representation of understanding different topics or events explaining as model, 2) the understanding explained the changes from the things one understood to other things by being able to change rules and processes into problem solving.

2.2 Motivation

Student behavior that shows during learning with gamification for constructivism online Learning environment such as determination and effort to success. There are 2 types of motives: 1) Internal motivation 2) External motivation.

2.3 Constructivism Online Learning Environment

The constructivist estimate of learning can be discover to Piaget [8] who believed that learning is not pass on passively but attained through well-defined stages by active participation of a learner. Designing an environment for student centered. Blending between media and method base on Constructivist theory [9] with online learning by using technology and internet.

3 Methodology

3.1 Research Participant

The target group of this research were 7th grade students in Rural school. That are currently studying in the second semester, academic year 2019. A total of 10 people. The sample was chosen by Purposive Sampling.

3.2 Assessment Tool

Mental model interview recording form was developed by teachers. Finding quality by checking by experts which has the following development steps 1) Study the research and theory of mental model. This study uses the Kanjug [3] mental model framework. 2) Create a subjective test base on mental model elements 3) Create questions and evaluate by expert 4) edit and improve from expert suggestion.

Motivation survey form consist with motivation elements are internal motivation and external motivation. Finding quality by checking by experts which has the following development steps 1) Study research and theory of motivation. 2) Create scope and question of motivation survey form. 3) Evaluate by expert 4) edit and improve from expert suggestion.

3.3 Experimental Process

Before the experiment, the students were given time to get used to the Constructivist online learning environment to promote programming in rural school. Figure 1 shows the flow chart of the experiment. Each period in the computer class is 120 min in rural school. At the beginning, the instructor spent 1 weeks teaching introduce learners about learning with a constructivist online learning environment about component and how to use. Thereafter, 3 weeks was spent on the enhancement mental model and motivation by applying the mental model and motivation element and the integration of online learning. Learners face problems and do their task in Constructivism online learning environment. The role of teacher is coach to support and help learners. In the last period, Teacher interview student and let's student do motivation survey form. There were totally 5 periods spent on the experiment.

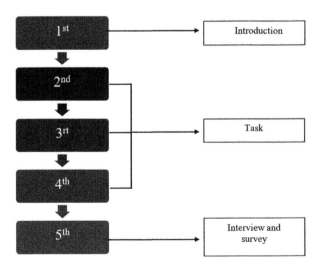

Fig. 1. Experimental process.

3.4 Learning Assistive

The participants used Constructivist online learning to learn. Constructivism online learning environment consist with 9 components as follows: 1) Problem base 2) Resource 3) Related case 4) Collaboration tools 5) Scaffolding 6) Coaching 7) Social support 8) Leaderboard and 9) Rules. This example element is shown in Fig. 2. First use let's start with the Problem base. Learners are challenged by a problem and task. Then, they can find answer from Resource and Related case. If they can't solve the problem. They can use Collaboration tools, Scaffolding, Coaching and Social support to support them to find the answer. Students can use Leaderboard when they want to see their score, badge and rank. If student want to know how to get badge, Rules will help them.

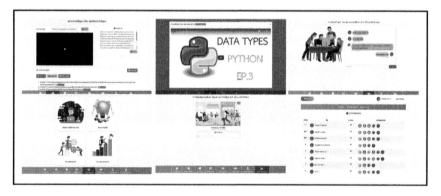

Fig. 2. Example of Constructivism online learning environment elements.

4 Results and Discussion

4.1 Learners' Mental Model

After applying the Constructivism online learning environment to promote programming in rural school. The result from mental model interview recording form was analysis by Protocol analysis. Learner's mental model consist with 2 characteristics 1) It was representation of understanding different topics or events explaining as model that can see in this sentence "When I make understanding, I draw concept map and I see the relation between programming content" and this sentence "Before we coding we have to know syntax and structure in programming. Then coding and execute". 2) the understanding explained the changes from the things one understood to other things by being able to change rules and processes into problem solving that can see in this sentence "In a moment, I can coding to solve the problem because I have been solved problem like this".

4.2 Learners' Motivation

The result from motivation survey form was analysis by mean and standard division. The learners' motivation result as follow: 1) Internal motivation was (mean = 4.1, S. D. = 0.35) 2) External motivation was very motivate (mean = 3.75, $S.D.$ = 0.53) (Table 1).

Table 1. The learners' Motivation.

No.	List assessment	Mean	S.D.	Motivation
1.	Internal motivation	4.10	0.35	Very motivated
2.	External motivation	3.75	0.53	Very motivated
	Total	**3.93**	**0.44**	Very motivated

4.3 Discussion

The learner's mental model consists with 2 characteristic are 1) It was representation of understanding different topics or events explaining as model 2) the understanding explained the changes from the things one understood to other things by being able to change rules and processes into problem solving. This result consistent with the research of Kanjug [3], which study Learners' Mental model learning with Learning Environments Model enhancing Expert Mental Model. The learners' motivation from Constructivism online learning environment to promote programming was very motivated. That was showing Constructivism online learning environment can promote learners' motivation by integrating between pedagogy, media symbol system and online learning. That motivation results consistent with the research of Teeramongkoljit (2015) and Tabpetch (2016) that describe the element of Constructivism online learning environment can attract learners to change their behavior, interaction, participation and promote motivation in learning.

References

1. Chaijaroen, S.: Theory to Practice, 2 edn. Pen printing (2016)
2. Kapp, K.M.: The gamification of learning and instruction: game-based methods and strategies for training and education (2012)
3. Kanjug, I.: Development of Learning Environments Model Enhancing Expertise Mental Model (2009)
4. Richey, R.C., Klein, J.: Design and Developmental Research. Lawrence, New Jersey (2007)
5. Hannafin, M.: Open Learning Environment: Foundation, Method, and Models. In Charles, New Jersey (1999)
6. Vygotsky, L.S.: Mind in Society: The Development of Higher Psychological Processes. Harvard University Press, Cambridge (1980)
7. McMillan, J.H., Forsyth, D.R.: What theories of motivation say about why learners learn. New Dir. Teach. Learn. **1991**(45), 39–52 (1991)

8. Piaget, J.: The Construction of Reality in the Child. Ballantine Books, New York (1975)
9. Jonassen, D.H.: Designing constructivist learning environments. In: Reigeluth, C.M. (ed.) Instructional-Design Theories and Models: A New Paradigm of Instructional Theory, vol. II, pp. 215–239. Lawrence Erlbaum Associates, New Jersey (1999)

Building an Online Learning Question Map Through Mining Discussion Content

Hei Chia Wang[(✉)] [iD] and Ya Lan Zhao

Institute of Information Management, National Cheng Kung University, Tainan, Taiwan
hcwang@mail.ncku.edu.tw

Abstract. Information and communication technology (ICT) has been widely accepted in education since the COVID-19 outbreak. Today, the convenience that ICT provides in education makes learning independent of time and place. However, compared to face-to-face learning, ICT online learning has the difficulty of finding student questions efficiently. One of the ways to solve this problem is through finding their questions from the online discussion content. With online learning, teachers and students usually send out questions and receive answers on a discussion board without the limitations of time or place. However, because liquid learning is quite convenient, people tend to solve problems in short online texts with a lack of detailed information to express ideas in an online environment. Therefore, the ICT online education environment may result in misunderstandings between teachers and students. For teachers and students to better understand each other's views, this study aims to classify discussions into a hierarchical structure, named a question map, with several types of learning questions to clarify the views of teachers and students. In addition, this study attempts to extend the description of possible omissions in short texts by using external resources prior to classification. In brief, by applying short text hierarchical classification, this study constructs a question map that can highlight each student's learning problems and inform the instructor where the main focus of the future course should be, thus improving the ICT education environment.

Keywords: ICT online education improvement · Question map · Short text analysis · Hierarchical classification

1 Introduction

With the rapid growth of information technology, our environment is always filled with information products such as smartphones, laptops, desktops, tablets, and game consoles. As information products become increasingly more ubiquitous around the world, various newly launched information products will break through the existing technologies and amaze the sensory experiences of human beings. In addition, the stunning interfaces of these devices have expanded the sensory desires of society. The advances in information technology have drastically shifted the channels people use to deliver ideas and communicate with one another. As a result, the significance of having the ability to grab people's attention and transmit and deliver targeted information to people in this digital age can never be overemphasized.

Thanks to the great assistance of information technology, currently, we no longer have to learn things face-to-face in a physical space. In contrast, we are able to enjoy the convenience of online learning spaces using networking, making it easier to learn at any time and any place. Furthermore, online learning environments are updated with the latest information in a much shorter time window, which definitely benefits us vastly in this modernized community. In short, technology-assisted learning environments break through the limitations of time and space between people.

Although the assistance of teachers indeed benefits students a lot, it is still inevitable that discussions between teachers and students may experience some communicative misunderstandings from time to time. However, it can be quite time-consuming and annoying to read carefully over every single word of the conversations in a group chat. On occasion, wordy and complex comments may make it even harder for students to solve their problems. Therefore, using text mining techniques to clarify teachers' main ideas from chat logs is a better method. By applying text mining techniques to form topic distributions, conversations between teachers and students become more efficient and effective [6].

Aiming to enhance the learning environment, the study offers an application environment for teachers and students to discuss. After collecting their discussions, the study will then analyze the chat logs between teachers and students using text mining techniques [1]. With the goal to enhance the learning process efficiency between teachers and students, the study conducts performance analysis of individual students' strengths and weaknesses in making presentations. Using this method, the study forms a better English presentation learning environment.

2 Research Methodology

By applying these four modules, this project hopes to improve the efficiency and performance of the ICT learning environment and current teacher training. Although some research [3, 10] has shown that the use of an online discussion board can improve teaching, it still has shortcomings in reading and repeated problems. We hope to establish a student problem classification, conduct subproblem grouping, and use the results of the grouping to detect the direction of students' problems and assist teaching by enriching the teaching material. We collect the chat records between the teachers and students of this course through a self-developed app, and then explain the NLP preprocessing of text mining in order to process the external resources. Deep learning algorithms have been found to be superb for classification [5, 8, 9]; therefore, we use a convolutional neural network (CNN) for our classification. The short text classification module uses a CNN based on theory-driven rubrics to classify the rich chat records into learning problem types. Then, it generates several question subclusters to clarify the details of each main category and let the teacher know the main question themes of the students in each subcategory. It also introduces the selection of the grouping methods and the final subject detection process. Finally, the resource-rich module is used to assist teachers in comparing the most similar parts of the students' subcategories with the textbook through their chat records after understanding the students' problems. For students, the method will provide information on some of the existing textbooks that may assist the students' understanding. The teacher's support part finds relevant resources on the Internet that can be used as a reference by the teacher. If the teacher finds that many students do not easily understand the material and keep asking questions, the teacher can incorporate external resources to improve the current teaching materials. The system architecture is shown in Fig. 1.

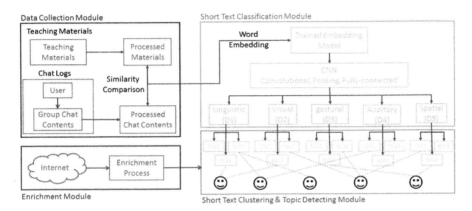

Fig. 1. Research architecture.

2.1 Data Collection Module

This app will collect the chat records between students and teachers. By uploading the chat history to the FireBase database, it will then further analyze the problem category of the internal conversation.

After collecting the chats of teachers and students, the research then preprocessed the text provided by teachers and students into several files based on the student ID. By marking the provider ID of the message when communicating in the app, this project can classify the related chat records of a single student. Figure 2 shows an example of the app.

2.2 Short Text Clustering and Topic Detection Module

This short text clustering module will continue to use a clustering method to find the types of questions for all the classified texts, use the grouping results in the chat records of each student to classify the question subtypes of each student, and use the TSF [7] method to identify the different themes and make correspondences between the students' subcategories and the topics in the textbook to assist students in learning.

In machine learning and natural language processing, a topic model is a statistical model used to discover abstract "topics" that appear in a document collection. The "topics" generated by topic modeling techniques are clusters of similar words. The topic model captures this intuition in a mathematical framework that allows examining

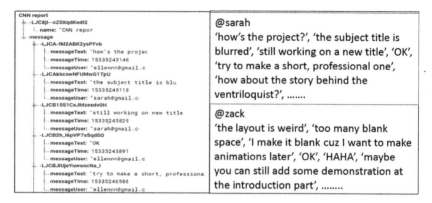

Fig. 2. Chat log example.

a set of documents and discovering what the topic might be based on the statistics of the words in each document.

Based on the above concepts, many researchers have proposed different topic models. Deerwester et al. [3] used Latent Semantic Analysis (LSA) to find the themes in documents. LSA converts TF-IDF with singular value decomposition into a document hidden topic and word hidden topic matrix. The document hidden topic matrix represents the hidden topics in each document, and the topic matrix of the hidden words represents the relationship between each word and the topic. Hofmann [4] later proposed Probabilistic Latent Semantic Analysis (PLSA), which proposed the concept of cooccurrence and the possibility that words and documents cooccur. Blei, Ng, and Jordan [2] later used the concept of the Dirichlet distribution and proposed Latent Dirichlet Allocation (LDA), which can obtain the distribution possibilities of each topic in each article and the setting of each topic in the input document as an LDA model.

Saura et al. [11] and Yun [12] showed that both LSA and LDA perform quite well in topic modeling, but LDA is more suitable for document clustering and word classification. The performance of LDA in document clustering and word classification is the most relevant to this project, especially since outperforms LSA. Therefore, this project chose LDA for topic modeling.

First, this project starts with data preprocessing, and methods applied to the resulting documents include tokenization, stop word deletion, lemmatization, and stemming. After that, the project built a Bag of Words model and TF-IDF using the obtained clustered documents to explore the words that appear in specific topics and their related weights. After obtaining the TF-IDF of each cluster document, the method then inputs the TF-IDF of each cluster document into the LDA model. Therefore, it can obtain the probability of the word distribution for each topic. In addition, it also obtains the probability that each cluster document is assigned to each topic. Once the topics are detected, an interface will be display to teacher. Two example interfaces are shown in Fig. 3(a) and Fig. 3(b). Therefore, we can determine the subject content of each student and understand the subjects of current students' problems, which can help teachers to improve the focus of their teaching materials.

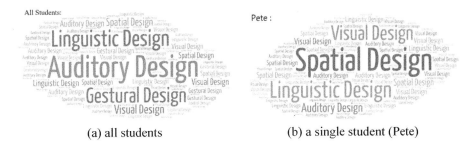

Fig. 3. Sample interface to show the problems of (a) all students and (b) a single student (Pete).

2.3 The Enrichment of Chat Logs

Since chat records are usually scattered and short, this project both understands students' problems and uses similar methods to determine the current teaching materials that are best suited for students' problems. Sometimes the content of the teaching materials may not be understood by students; therefore, this project attempts to use external resources to enrich the teaching and enhance the semantic meaning of chat records. By calculating the similarity between the preprocessed chat log document and the paragraph segment of the textbook, we can get a higher paragraph segment similarity score than the specific chat log document.

3 Summary of Proposed Methodologies

To allow teachers and students to better understand the viewpoints in an ICT education environment, this project aims to analyze short collections of students' discussion content and teachers' textbooks. First, this method defines the types of teaching topics. In this project, we expect to use the English presentation teaching of the Department of Foreign Languages as an example to demonstrate how the proposed app helps students and teachers to use online discussion. We first define the five presentation problem types {linguistic design, visual design, gestural design, auditory design, and spatial design} and the other categories are classified into the other.

In the information collection part, in order to obtain the log content, we expect that the data collection and preprocessing modules designed by us will collect and preprocess the chat records between teachers and students and the course materials. The short text classification module first embeds the chat content into the chat log matrix and classifies the chat corpus of each student as the main specific learning problem of the CNN. After establishing the short text clustering module, in addition to the original data, we also designed a method to enrich the chat records of each student and the most similar textbooks to improve the clustering performance. The short text clustering method is designed to cluster the chat record corpus to discover problem subtopics via topic detection. The subtopics can represent the current students' problems, and the topic modeling module can be used to detect the topics in the obtained cluster and provide a user interface for teachers to better understand each student's detailed questions. Finally, through the rich textbook model, the system assists teachers by suggesting supplementary textbooks for the questioner to enhance students' learning resources. Through the application of these modules, the project hopes to clarify the main learning problems of students and inform teachers where the focus of their teaching should be placed in the future.

References

1. Al-Samarraie, H., Teo, T., Abbas, M.: Can structured representation enhance students' thinking skills for better understanding of e-learning content? Comput. Educ. **69**, 463–473 (2013)
2. Blei, D., Ng, A., Jordan, M.: Latent Dirichlet allocation. J. Mach. Learn. Res. **3**, 993–1022 (2003)
3. Deerwester, S., Dumais, S., Furnas, G., Landauer, T., Harshman, R.: Indexing by latent semantic analysis. J. Am. Soc. Inf. Sci. **41**(6), 391–407 (1990)
4. Hofmann, T.. Probabilistic latent semantic analysis. Paper presented at the Proceedings of the Fifteenth conference on Uncertainty in artificial intelligence (1999)
5. Hou, W.F., Liu, Q., Cao, L.B.: Cognitive Aspects-Based Short Text Representation with Named Entity, Concept and Knowledge. Appl. Sci. Basel **10**(14) (2020)
6. Kale, U.: Technology valued? observation and review activities to enhance future teachers' utility value toward technology integration. Comput. Educ. **117**, 160–174 (2018)
7. Kern, R., Granitzer, M.: Efficient linear text segmentation based on information retrieval techniques. Paper presented at the Proceedings of the International Conference on Management of Emergent Digital EcoSystems (2009)
8. Njikam, A.N.S., Zhao, H.: CharTeC-Net: an efficient and lightweight character-based convolutional network for text classification. J. Electr. Comput. Eng. (2020)
9. Pota, M., Esposito, M., De Pietro, G., Fujita, H.: Best practices of convolutional neural networks for question classification. Appl. Sci. Basel **10**(14) (2020)
10. Raković, M., Marzouk, Z., Liaqat, A., Winne, P.H., Nesbit, J.C.: Fine grained analysis of students' online discussion posts. Comput. Educ. **157**, 103982 (2020)
11. Saura, J.R., Reyes-Menendez, A., Bennett, D.R.: How to extract meaningful insights from UGC: a knowledge-based method applied to education. Appl. Sci. Basel **9**(21) (2019)
12. Yun, E.: Review of trends in physics education research using topic modeling. J. Baltic Sci. Educ. **19**(3), 388–400 (2020)

Creating Interactive Non-formal Learning Opportunities in Resource-Deprived Distant Learning Institutions

Petra le Roux(✉) and Corné van Staden

School of Computing, University of South Africa,
Science Campus, 28 Pioneer Ave, Florida Park, Roodepoort 1709, South Africa
lrouxp@unisa.ac.za

Abstract. The rapid growth of technology has a profound effect on education, affecting both content and pedagogy and on the socio-cultural context in which it occurs. The term learning experience is used to reflect the pedagogical and technological shifts that have occurred in the design and delivery of education to learners. The importance of the socio-cultural context in which the learning takes place has a great impact on their learning. Creating such learning experiences is challenging, creating learning experiences in Open Distance e-Learning institutions (ODeL) is even more challenging. Furthermore, the evaluation of such an experience must address more than one discipline. The paper shows how data are drawn from an interactive learning experience that aligns academic goals and enrichment activities that support formal learning. To create the experience, the educational potential of social media was employed in a community of practice. Phenomenology as a philosophical worldview was used to study the experience of people in the context of open distance learning, using social media in a Computer Science environment. It is particularly useful and relevant for researchers interested in understanding the contextual realities of interactive learning communities. As a result, this contribution put forward specific attributes that affect mobile tutoring in resource-deprived distance learning environments. This study is yet unpublished, as it is part of a larger doctoral endeavor.

Keywords: User experience · Emotions · Qualitative research · Phenomenology · Open distance learning

1 Introduction

The South African government has recognised that distance learning has a vital role to play in the tertiary education sector and that it has huge potential to fill the skills gaps suffered by the country. In recognition of distance learning's importance, in 2012 the Department of Higher Education and Training (DHET) developed the Draft Policy Framework for the Provision of Distance Education in South African Universities. The framework states that distance learning has *"served the invaluable role of bringing higher education within the reach of students who would not otherwise have been able to study at this level"* [1].

The concept of distance learning focuses on open access to teaching and learning to free teachers and learners from distance, time, and space constraints to offer flexible learning opportunities to individuals and groups of learners. With Open Distance e-Learning (ODeL), it is assumed that every learner has access to and be able to make use of electronic technologies to accommodate the learning process [2]. Despite the promise of ODeL success, many students who have taken courses at a distance-based institution have been shown to face many challenges. However, there is a vast difference in the challenges experienced by developed countries and developing countries [3]. Many developing countries realise that many challenges resulting from discord between cultural, social, and geographical systems and the merging of ICT can be attributed to the digital divide [4–6].

Although it is widely recognised that the digital divide has multiple interpretations, technological inequity has been the dominant perspective in discourse relating to the inequalities experienced. At its most basic, the digital divide refers to the inequality of opportunities for a certain part of the population to benefit from the use of information and communication technologies (ICT). However, there is a move to a wider perspective of digital inequalities [7, 8]. Recent attempts to define the digital divide include, other than access and usage, the impact of ICTs on the individual and in societies.

Access to ICT technologies is manifested in both access to computing devices and the Internet. The main reason individuals and communities do not have access to a digital device or an up-to-date Internet service is twofold; an affordability gap due to low disposable income and a geographical gap, due to lack of infrastructure [9]. Although devices and the Internet provide a comparative model for the digital divide, neither captures the essence of how to use digital technologies. An individual can make use of this access to engage in meaningful social practices, specifically to communicate with people, to access information, and to utilise information [10, 11]. Equality in access and usage does not automatically lead to a more or less social equality. Some groups of society still benefit more from these technologies than others. This implies dominance and therefore an increasing social divide as the result of the social impact of ICT. Therefore, social inclusion will contribute to narrowing the social divide [7, 12].

Access and usage still pose many challenges in ODeL in the South African context, but there exists a body of knowledge on how to address it [13–15]. However, there is little evidence of the educational use of technology in developing countries addresses social equality. An investigation into and understanding of an individual's experience with educational technology is needed to understand how to address social inequalities. There is ample evidence that social media addresses social inclusion as well as its potential as an educational platform. Therefore, the possibility that social media can offer a space for social inclusion as well as addressing the ODeL challenges needs to be explored [13]. This paper presents a part of a larger, yet unpublished doctoral endeavor. One objective is to investigate non-formal interactive learning opportunities in a resource deprived distance-based education environment by looking into the experience of the participants of an interactive mobile tutoring application. Non-formal learning is one of three forms of learning defined by the Organization for Economic Co-operation and Development – OECD [16]. The other two are formal and informal learning. *Formal learning* is always organised and structured and has learning objectives and is intentional. *Informal learning* occurs in a variety of places, such as at home, work, and through daily interactions and shared relationships among members of society. *Non-formal* learning opportunities approach learning by creating learner-centered learning experiences. High-quality non-formal experiences are intentional and structured to engage the learner [17].

Our primary research question therefore is; What are the key attributes affecting mobile tutoring in a resource deprived distance learning environment? By answering this question, we put forward considerations that can be employed to address the challenges posed by the digital divide. We argue that this understanding can be accommodated through an online community of practice that contributes towards a better understanding of how learning takes place through everyday social practices rather than focusing on environments that are intentionally designed to support learning.

While the findings of the paper may be specific for the ODeL context, international readers may find this paper useful, as it provides possibilities to address the social impact of ICTs that can lead to social inequity in terms of age, gender, ethnicity, disability, social and economic status. We argue that understanding the experiences during tutoring and the subsequent dealing thereof, can contribute towards a conducive user experience that may alleviate the social pressures emanating from the digital divide. This paper further offers a unique contribution in that it combines user experience (UX) principles that primarily draws from HCI literature and phenomenology as a theoretical underpinning.

To position this research, the next two sections focus on the theoretical underpinnings of user experience including the measurement thereof and emotions as the basis for user experience measurement. This is followed by a discussion on the context of the research. Thereafter an outline of particularised methodological considerations is discussed, including conceptual considerations for enacting phenomenology in online environments, case study, data collection, and data analysis methods. The paper concludes with some research findings and a conclusion.

2 User Experience

User experience originated when there was a move in human-computer interaction (HCI) studies from usability concerns towards a wider set of problems to do with fun, enjoyment, aesthetics, and the experience of use [18–20]. Several models and theoretical approaches have been developed to help understand experience and examine experience from different perspectives. For example, Norman [21] describe an experience in terms of visceral, behavioral, and reflective levels. Hassenzahl [22] describes an experience in terms of goal fulfilling within a situated and dynamic context. Context is also an important component in frameworks described by [23–26]. Based on the review and analysis of the literature a conceptual framework of user experience was proposed and accompanied by the following definition of user experience as viewed by the authors: *A user's subjective appraisal about partaking in an interactive application in a certain context and time.* The framework models the four constituent elements and will now be introduced. An experience is created as the interaction between the user and the application which are both influenced by the context. Each of these is then further detailed through a set of sub-elements, e.g. the context is distinguished into physical, social, situational, cultural, and temporal. In real life, however, it is difficult to make a distinct separation of the constituent elements because user experience is interconnected in principle.

Measuring the user experience with interactive systems is a complex task as an experience is influenced not only by the characteristics of an interactive system (e.g. complexity, usability, functionality, etc., but also by a user's psychological state (such as predispositions, expectations, needs, motivation, mood, etc.), and the context (or environment) within which the interaction occurs (e.g. organisational or social setting, the meaningfulness of the activity, voluntariness of use, etc.) [27]. This study set out to draw a richer picture of the experiences of an e-tutor while using a tutoring application in resource-deprived distance learning environment. Thus, evaluating the emotions experienced during the tutoring and will allow for an in-depth understanding of the social-emotional and functional needs in using interactive tutoring applications.

3 Emotions

Emotions influence almost all interactions that an individual experienced daily, including human-human and human-technology interactions [28, 29]. The research aims to develop new knowledge on emotions experienced while using tutoring applications in resource-deprived distance learning environments to contribute towards an understanding of the social-emotional and functional needs of the online tutor in using interactive tutoring applications. This can be used to inform the development of tutoring applications where access to resources cannot be taken for granted.

Even though opinions and scientists vary widely regarding the nature and significance of this field, the theoretical and research contributions of the past years have established emotions as a legitimate field of scientific inquiry [30]. Due to the multi-dimensional nature of emotions, a straightforward definition it is still a matter of debate [31, 32]. However, most authors either explicitly or implicitly acknowledge that an emotion is not a simple phenomenon. Human emotions are, to a large extent, subjective and non-deterministic.

The identification of human emotional states is difficult and complex [29]. Therefore, to gain a better understanding of the subject, some models describing how we feel emotions can be found in the literature. These models help to convey a specific feature of human emotion and suggest perception as to how emotions are presented and interpreted by the human mind [33]. Some models describe the emotions using mainly a cognitive approach [34], whereas others consider multi-dimensional aspects such as pleasure and arousal [35, 36]. It is also possible to find models that describe emotions related to specific contexts; emotions elicited by products [22, 37], in a process-level approach [21] or an appraisal approach [38]. The Component Process Model (CPM) [39] is an emotion model based on appraisal theories. It allows the researcher to work with each component separately and can therefore choose appropriate methods to evaluate the different dimensions. Moreover, it has been successfully used in other HCI studies to support the investigation of emotional experiences in interactive contexts [40, 41].

Following appraisal theories, this work proposes a multi-component model to meet the requirements.

4 Context of Research - A Community of Practice

With the focus on non-formal teaching and learning in a social environment, a framework was selected that incorporates the concept of social learning. The theoretical construct of a community of practice [42] is grounded in an anthropological perspective that examines how learning takes place through everyday social practices rather than focusing on environments that are intentionally designed to support learning. This research utilises a community of practice as a theoretical lens through which the social context of the participants can be understood.

Wenger, McDermott, and Snyder's [43] definition states that a community of practice is a combination of *"a domain of knowledge, which defines a set of issues; a community of people who care about this domain; and the shared practice that they are developing to be effective in their domain"*. The discussion to follow addresses the three components of a community of practice: community, domain, and practice.

Community – Tutoring Participants. Cross-age tutoring refers to the experience of an older student (tutor) working with a younger student (tutee) in the context of an ODeL open and distance learning university. The interest in using students as instructional resources for each other is based on student's capabilities to play an active role in their education. There exist several benefits of cross-age (or peer) tutoring in the literature [44–46]. Furthermore, socially challenged participants may find communication easier online [47], especially as the use of social media platforms allows students to feel free to use abbreviations, slang, alternative spelling, and emojis [48]. The role of the e-tutor is summarised as being social, technical, pedagogical or intellectual and managerial or organisational and technical [49].

Domain - Social Media for Social Inclusion. Since their introduction, social media applications, such as Facebook and WhatsApp, have attracted millions of users, many of whom have integrated these applications into their daily practices. There is ample evidence in the literature that shows that students in higher education are on social media [35–37] and that social media can sustain learning [50, 51]. Finding ways to put social media to good pedagogical use is a task that remains to be fully explored, but it is one that holds significant potential in the context of mobile technology. The adoption of this technology in education introduces new learning strategies, based on the social learning theory [52].

Practice - Mobile Cross-age Tutoring. Adapting the definition of tutoring by Topping [53], the definition of tutoring that this paper assumes is a type of collaborative learning, in which students who are not professional teachers help others to learn, and learn themselves by teaching. Underlying theories applied to our model of interactive tutoring include the role model, behaviourist, and Gestalt theories and these theories are not mutually exclusive. *Role theory* uses the concept of *social role* to designate a set of expectations that are associated with positions in the social structure (e.g., teacher, learner). The *behaviourist theory*, associated with the work of the psychologist B. F. Skinner, asserts that effective learning occurs when every correct answer is rewarded. *Gestalt theory* asserts that learning occurs when the learner can *locate* an item in an intellectual structure or field or relate an idea to a larger context.

5 Research Methodology

This section discusses the research design and methodology used in the empirical phase of the research. It involved the researcher entering the field of the participant's involvement in online tutoring to answer the main research question: What are the key social-emotional and functional needs of the online tutor for effective tutoring in a resource deprived distance-learning environment? This qualitative, interpretive phenomenological inquiry, as part of uncovering meaning, will articulate the user experience of participants. Using the lens of the tutor's perspective, the focus will be on the participants' user experiences.

5.1 Phenomenology as a Philosophy and a Strategy

To answer the question of how we can understand the world as it is, one stream of philosophers investigated what is termed the "lived" experience. This experience included not only the visible and conscious aspects of the experience but also the subconscious aspects such as perception, thought, memory, and imagination. Phenomenology is a philosophical investigation of the phenomena of experience introduced by Edmund Husserl and proposes the adoption of a scientific attitude to experience by looking at experience with a scientific attitude laying aside all assumptions [54, 55].

Phenomenology as a strategy focusses on meaning-making from human experiences in situations as they spontaneously occur in the course of daily life. Phenomenology is the investigation and description of the common meanings participants share when experiencing the same phenomena to create an understanding of the participating individuals' lived experiences of a phenomenon. Descriptive Phenomenology focuses on subjective experiences and is personal whereas Interpretive Phenomenology attempts to describe accurately a phenomenon from an individual's perspective.

Martin Heidegger (1889–1976), a student of Husserl, challenged some of Husserl's assumptions and introduced the interpretive, or hermeneutic, research tradition [56]. Concerning the study of human experience, hermeneutic inquiry is on what humans experience rather than that what they consciously know.

5.2 Qualitative Data Collection

In qualitative research, the purpose of data collection is to provide evidence for a phenomenon under investigation and must be derived from an intensive exploration of the participants' experiences. The evidence was in the form of participants' accounts (experience journals) of their feelings and thoughts which were analysed to produce a core description of the experience. The methodology followed is discussed in this section and comprise of five phases [57]. The last phase, data analysis, is the topic of the next section.

- *Planning and Preparation.* To collect valid and reliable data e-tutors had to design and implement an online tutoring application using a social media platform and present at least five online tutoring sessions. Social media platforms used included Facebook, WhatsApp, Twitter, etc. The participants consisted of 17 fourth level Computing students who acted as tutors for first-level programming students and were engaged in tutoring for a minimum of five sessions. During these sessions they were required to keep an experience journal either online or offline.
- *Pre-study brief.* Emails were used to brief the participants. The concept of an experience was explained to the students. The participants were encouraged to describe each experience in terms of *situations, feelings,* and *thoughts* as depicted in Table 1. To describe an experience, students were provided with a list of adjectives to depict tone, feelings and emotions.
- *Logging period.* To support effective activity logging, participants were sent an email as notice that the tutoring and therefore journaling can commence. Regular emails were sent to remind participants of their journaling responsibilities.
- *Post-study follow-up.* After the data collection process, all the information provided by each participant was evaluated and an email of appreciation was sent out.

Table 1. Example template of an experience journal entry

Situation who, what, when, where?	Feelings	Thoughts
	A single word to describe feelings	What was going through your mind when you felt this way?
Day 1: 9 October 20.. First get-to-know session Lesson 1 - introduction	Depressed Encouraged	I feel depressed – thought it would be much easier. Struggle to start with the lesson I feel encouraged – tutee seems to be very excited

5.3 Data Analysis

Qualitative data analysis seeks to reduce and make sense of information in order that experiences that shed light on the research phenomena can emerge [58]. Thematic analysis is a method for identifying and analysing patterns (themes) within qualitative data and is a form of pattern recognition within data [59]. A theme captures something important about the data in relation to the research question and represents a level of patterned response or meaning within the data.

ATLAS.ti belongs to the genre of computer-aided qualitative data analysis software. The six steps of Braun and Clarke's [59] thematic content analysis can be translated for use with ATLAS.ti. According to Friese [60], when using ATLAS.ti, it is necessary to add an extra phase to the six phases. This phase entails the development of a structured coding system after the initial coding phase.

Some of the key findings obtained will now be presented. Four major themes emerged from assessing the events which correlate with the components needed to create an experience. The themes relate to the users (the tutor and tutee), the context, and the application. The first theme, *Tutor*, explored the experience of the tutor. The second theme comprises of the *Tutee*'s experiences in terms of participation, challenges as well as positive and negative experiences. The third theme addresses the impact of the application or *Tutoring Environment* and the final theme comprises the *Tutoring* process and explores the importance of procedures and processes during the tuition.

5.4 Findings and Discussion

Reading through the experience journals, the experience described when interacting with the tutee was the most intense and had the biggest impact on the tutoring activity and will be discussed below.

The social role of the tutor in online tutoring is one of the key critical success factors in online learning. In Atlas.ti, the *groundedness*, and *density* are code qualities that show the researcher how often they are used. The participation or the lack of participation of the tutee has a high groundedness (154). It can be concluded that the impact of tutee participation is high and therefore the influence on the tutor and tutoring process. Contact is made between the participants via an email sent to the tutee. Some experiences of e-tutors describing their feeling of negativity and despair if the tutee did not respond in an acceptable time. A positive experience to establish contact set the way forward. However, if contact has been established further tutoring was successful. Tutee cooperation led to feelings of excitement and encouragement.

- *I felt **good** when I realized that the tutee was interacting and asking questions.*
- *I felt **good** as the tutee showed his enjoyment and understanding*
- *I was **proud** to answering the questions that tutees had, they were really committed.*
- *I felt **encouraged** to see the ball rolling and the screenshots coming through*
- *I felt **delighted** to see that the tutee was able to write the program with minimal input*
- *I felt **anxious** – as time was elapsing and the tutoring sessions had not commenced*
- *I felt **nervous**: noting that hours later at 20h00 in the evening of the 1st day, tutee has not yet responded to the email nor acknowledged receipt of it.*

Tutee engagement with the content is essential for learning to take place. Almost all interaction where students engage with the tutoring content, led to positive experiences for the e-tutor as is evident by the use of emotion words.

- *I felt **good** as the tutee expresses their enjoyment and are cooperative during the sessions in such that the tutee feels comfortable to ask appropriate questions and also provide adequate feedback.*
- *I felt **happy** as the tutee enjoyed the one-to-one communication, as well as the experience of participating in the research project.*

The tutor had to create a tutoring environment based on a social media platform. The technical role of the tutor involves being familiar, comfortable and competent with the mobile device and social media platform of choice. Additionally, the tutor must be able to support tutees in becoming competent and comfortable themselves. The most used social media platforms were WhatsApp (44% representing 8 tutoring applications) followed by Facebook (33% representing 6 tutoring applications). Other platforms represent 23% and were platforms used once by tutoring applications. Both positive and negative experiences were described.

- *the tutee was eager and excited to learn using online application.*
- *it was great because enough tutorial information could be easily shared online*
- *it is not as easy as I thought it would be*
- *due to internet connectivity issue experienced by the tutee, downloading the day lesson content was difficult*

6 Conclusions

The thematic content that emerged from this study of participants' experiences provides potentially important information about to the development of online tutoring applications that address both the social aspects of the participants and system functionality needs. It can be concluded that the following attributes affect mobile tutoring in resource deprived distance learning environments: first, the impact of the tutee's experience on the emotional state of the tutor; and second the suitability of social media as an online tutoring platform for creating non-formal learning opportunities.

The evidence from this study suggests that tutor training must receive attention. There is a need for improved preparation and training for candidate tutors in their role as student and their transition to tutor. The finding also highlights the potentially pivotal role of the training institution in delivery of such training.

All the participants in this study indicated that the experience is directly linked to the experience of the tutee whilst engaging in the tutoring. Although operational issues did play a role in the effectiveness of the tutoring sessions, if addressed, it is the tutee's willingness to engage and participate that contributes towards the perception of success.

These findings agree with the theoretical underpinnings of Wenger's community of practice and Hassenzahl's user experience models.

References

1. Department: Higher Education & Training: Draft Policy Framework for the Provision of distance education., Pretoria (2012)
2. Ngubane-Mokiwa, S., Letseka, M.: Shift from Open Distance Learning to Open Distance e-Learning. In: Letseka, M. (ed.) Open Distance Learning (ODL) in South Africa. Nova Science Publishers, New York (2015)
3. Musingafi, M.C.C., Mapuranga, B., Chiwanza, K., Zebron, S.: Challenges for Open and Distance learning (ODL) students: experiences from students of the Zimbabwe Open University. J. Educ. Pract. **6**, 59–67 (2015)
4. Gulati, S.: Technology-enhanced learning in developing nations: a review. Int. Rev. Res. Open Distance Learn. **9**, 1–16 (2008)

5. Molawa, S.: The "first" and "third world" in Africa: knowledge access, challenges and current technological innovations in Africa. In: First International Conference on African Digital Libraries and Archives, pp. 1–14 (2009)
6. Oladokun, O.S.: ODL and the impact of digital divide on information access in botswana. Int. Rev. Res. Open Distance Learn. **12** (2011). https://doi.org/10.19173/irrodl.v12i6.1053
7. van Deursen, A., Helsper, E.: The third-level digital divide: who benefits most from being online? Commun. Inf. Technol. Annu. **9**, 29–52 (2015)
8. van Dijk, J.A.G.M.: Digital Divide: Impact of Access (2017)
9. Hilbert, M.: Technological information inequality as an incessantly moving target. J. Am. Soc. Inf. Sci. Technol. **26**, 1–26 (2013)
10. Warschauer, M.: A literacy approach to the digital divide. Cadernos de Letras **28**, 5–19 (2011)
11. Ghobadi, S., Ghobadi, Z.: How access gaps interact and shape digital divide: a cognitive investigation **34**, 330–340 (2015)
12. Lee, H., Park, N., Hwang, Y.: Telematics and Informatics a new dimension of the digital divide: exploring the relationship between broadband connection, smartphone use and communication competence. Telemat. Inform. **32**, 45–56 (2015). https://doi.org/10.1016/j.tele.2014.02.001
13. Stillman, L., Herselman, M., Marais, M., Boshomane, P.M., Plantinga, P., Walton, S.: Digital doorway: social-technical innovation for high-needs communities. Electron. J. Inf. Syst. Dev. Ctries. **50**, 1–18 (2012)
14. Siebrits, A., Stoltenkamp, J., Mokwele, T.: The impact of tutoring in the digital academic literacy programme on graduate attributes at the university of the western cape. Adv. Res. **5**, 1–31 (2015)
15. Unisa: myUnisa. https://www.unisa.ac.za/sites/myunisa/default. Accessed 03 May 2019
16. Werquin, P.: Recognising Non-Formal and Informal Learning. OECD Publishing, Paris (2010)
17. Blyth, D., LaCroix-Dalluhn, L.: Expanded learning time and opportunities: Key principles, driving perspectives, and major challenges. Youth Dev. Fall, New Dir, pp. 15–27 (2011)
18. Law, E., Vermeeren, A., Hassenzahl, M. (eds.) M.B.: Towards a UX Manifesto. Presented at the (2007)
19. Hassenzahl, M., Tractinsky, N.: User experience – a research agenda. **25**, 91–97 (2006). https://doi.org/10.1080/01449290500330331
20. Wright, P., Blythe, M.: User experience research as an inter-discipline: towards a UX Manifesto. In: Towards a UX Manifesto, pp. 65–70 (2007)
21. Norman, D.: Emotional Design. Basic Books, New York (2004)
22. Hassenzahl, M.: User Experience (UX): towards an experiential perspective on product quality, pp. 11–15 (2008)
23. McCarthy, J., Wright, P.: Technology as Experience. The MIT Press, Cambridge (2007)
24. Forlizzi, J., Battarbee, K.: Understanding Experience in Interactive Systems, pp. 261–268 (2004)
25. Desmet, P., Hekkert, P.: Framework of product experience. Int. J. Des. **1**, 13–23 (2007)
26. Mahlke, S., Thüring, M.: Studying antecedents of emotional experiences in interactive contexts, pp. 915–918 (2007)
27. Law, E.L.-C., Bevan, N., Christou, G., Springett, M., Lárusdóttir, M.: Meaningful measures. In: Proceedings of the International Workshop on Meaningful Measures: (VUUM), Reykjavik, Iceland (2008)
28. Mettrie, L., Picard, R.: Theoretical approaches to the study of emotion in humans and machines, pp. 1–20 (2010)

29. Picard, R.W.: Emotion research by the people, for the people. Emot. Rev. **2**, 250–254 (2010). https://doi.org/10.1177/1754073910364256
30. Turner, J.H., Stets, J.E.: Sociological theories of human emotions. Annu. Rev. Sociol. **32**, 25–52 (2006). https://doi.org/10.1146/annurev.soc.32.061604.123130
31. Barrett, L.F.: Solving the emotion paradox: categorization and the experience of Emotion **10**, 20–46 (2006)
32. Frijda, N., Frijda, N.H.: Emotion experience **9931**, 473–497 (2010). https://doi.org/10.1080/02699930441000346
33. Sreeja, P., Mahalakshumi, G.: Emotion models: a review. Int. J. Control Theory Appl. **10**, 651–657 (2017)
34. Ortony, A., Clore, G., Collins, A.: The Cognitive Structure of Emotions. Cambridge University Press, Cambridge (1988)
35. Plutchik, R.: Emotion: A Psychoevolutionary Synthesis (1980)
36. Russell, J.A.: A circumplex model of affect. J. Pers. Soc. Psychol. **39**, 1161–1178 (1980). https://doi.org/10.1037/h0077714
37. Singh, A.: Managing Emotion in Design Innovation. CRC Press, New York (2014)
38. Desmet, P.M.A.: a Multilayered Model of Product Emotions. Des. J. **6**, 1–13 (2003)
39. Scherer, K.: Appraisal Theories of Emotion: State of the Art and Future Development (2013). https://doi.org/10.1177/1754073912468165
40. Gao, Y., Zhu, W.: Detecting affective states from text based on a multi-component emotion model. Comput. Speech Lang. **36**, 42–57 (2016). https://doi.org/10.1016/j.csl.2015.08.002
41. Baveye, Y., Chamaret, C., Dellandrea, E., Che, L.: Affective video content analysis: a multidisciplinary insight. IEEE Trans. Affect. Comput. **9**, 396–409 (2018). https://doi.org/10.1109/TAFFC.2017.2661284
42. Wenger, E.C.: Communities of practice: learning, meaning, and identity (1998)
43. Wenger, E.C., McDermott, R.A., Snyder, W.: Cultivating Communities of Practice: A Guide to Managing Knowledge. Harvard Business School Press, Massachusestts (2002)
44. Bean, J., Bogdan Eaton, S.: The psychology underlying successful. J. College Student Retent. **3**, 73–89 (2002). https://doi.org/10.2190/6R55-4B30-28XG-L8U0
45. Boud, D., Cohen, R., Sampson, J.: Peer learning and assessment. Assess. Eval. **24**, 413–426 (1999)
46. Topping, K., Ehly, S.: Peer assisted learning: a framework of consultation. J. Educ. Psychol. Consult. **12**, 37–41 (2001)
47. Arasaratnam-Smith, L.A., Northcote, M.: Community in online higher education: challenges and opportunities. Electron. J. e-Learning **15**, 188–198 (2017)
48. Keogh, C.: Using WhatsApp to Create a Space of Language and Content for Students of Int'l Relations (2017). https://doi.org/10.5294/laclil.2017.10.1.4
49. Mcpherson, M., Nunes, M.B.: The role of tutors as an integral part of online learning support key words the role of the online tutor online learning skills, pp. 7–11 (2004)
50. Greenhow, C., Lewin, C.: Social media and education: reconceptualizing the boundaries of formal and informal learning. Learn. Media Technol. **41**, 6–30 (2016). https://doi.org/10.1080/17439884.2015.1064954
51. Manca, S., Ranieri, M.: Implication of social network sites for teaching and learning. Where we are and where we want to go. Educ. Inf. Technol. **22**, 605–622 (2017). https://doi.org/10.1007/s1063
52. Bandura, A.: Self-efficacy: toward a unifying theory of behavioral Change **84**, 191–215 (1977)
53. Topping, K.J.: The effectiveness of peer tutoring in further and higher education: a typology and review of the literature. High. Educ. **32**, 321–345 (1996). https://doi.org/10.1007/BF00138870

54. van Manen, M.: Researching Lived Experience: Human Science for an Action Sensitive Pedagogy. Routledge, London, New York (2015)
55. Katsirikou, A., Lin, C.: Revealing the "Essence" of things: using phenomenology in LIS research. Qual. Quant. methods Libr. **2**, 469–478 (2017)
56. Moran, D.: Introduction to Phenomenology. Routledge, London, New York (2002)
57. Flaherty, K.: Diary Studies: Understanding Long-Term User Behavior and Experiences. https://www.nngroup.com/articles/diary-studies/. Accessed 13 Mar 2020
58. Gray, D.: Doing Research in the Real World. SAGE Publications Ltd., London (2018)
59. Braun, V., Clarke, V.: Using thematic analysis in psychology. Qual. Res. Psychol. **3**, 77–101 (2006)
60. Friese, S.: Qualitative Data Analysis with ATLAS.ti. SAGE, London (2014)

Designing Framework of Constructivist Web-Based Learning Environment Model to Enhance Creative Thinking in Engineering Design Process for Grade 8th

Pasatorn Puratep[1(✉)] and Sumalee Chaijaroen[2]

[1] Nakhon Phanom University Demonstration School,
Nakhon Phanom University, Nakhon Phanom, Thailand
pasatorn@kkumail.com
[2] Department of Education Technology, Faculty of Education,
Khon Kaen University, Khon Kaen, Thailand

Abstract. Creative thinking is one of the most important characteristics of a person that drives innovation. It is a skill that helps countries succeed in the rapidly changing digital economy society in the 21st century [6]. Countries are therefore focused on developing creative populations. Most of today's innovations are created by the engineering design process. But the engineering design process itself still lacks effectiveness in promoting creativity in cognitive domain [5]. Therefore, the purpose of this study is to synthesize the framework of a web-based constructivist learning environment to enhance creative thinking [2] in engineering design process [3]. The document analysis and model research [1] were employed in this study The target groups used in this study were 1) 3 experts for assessment of the learning contents 2) 3 experts for assessment of the instructional design for theoretical framework 3) 3 experts for assessment of the instructional media design. 4) 3 experts for assessment of the gathering research instruments and 5) 30 eight-grade students of Khon Kean university Demonstration school who enrolled in a course of design and technology II. The instruments used were 1) survey form for collected instructional context 2) survey form for learning characteristic of students and 3) The recording form for synthesis of the theoretical framework. Summarization, interpretation and analytical description were employed to analyze the data. The result revealed that: The framework comprised of 6 stages as following: (1) Activating cognitive structure as problem-based component (2) Adjusting to cognitive equilibrium as learning resources component (3) Enlarging cognitive structure as cognitive tools and collaboration-based component (4) Enhancing creative thinking as creative thinking design-based component and (5) Fostering knowledge construction as scaffolding-based component. (6) Encouraging knowledge construction as coaching-based component.

Keywords: Constructivist · Creative thinking · Creative process · Engineering design process

1 Introduction

The rapid change of society in the 21st century. New innovations occur all the time, making it difficult to predict economic and social conditions. Innovation is therefore the key to adaptation to survive safely. With awareness of these issues, countries focus on the development of education to prepare and promote people's skills in facing and dealing with events in this field, using the 21st century skills development framework [12] for thinking skills such a creative. The Basic Education Core Curriculum BE 2008 (Revised BE 2017) in technology in Thailand has focused on allowing students to design innovations. By integrating knowledge in mathematics, science and others through the engineering design process. In which the engineering design process still lacks the effectiveness of creative promotion. Creative thinking is one of the most important characteristics of a person that makes humans successful and influence economic and social movements. For that reason, the researcher recognizes the importance of synthesis of design frameworks by using theory as the basis to help designers design their learning environment more efficiently, The purpose of this study is to synthesize the design of the constructivist web-based learning environment [15, 16, 18] to enhance creativity [17] in the engineering design process by integrating creative thinking.

2 Research Purpose

This study was aimed to synthesize the designing framework of the constructivist learning environment model to enhance creative thinking in engineering design process for grade 8th.

3 Research Methodology

This research employed by model research, phase 1 model development [1] via document analysis and survey research.

3.1 Target Group

Target group in this research consisted of 3 experts for the evaluation of the designing framework and 30 eight-grade students.

3.2 Research Instruments

Recording form for synthesize the designing framework of constructivist web-based learning environment model to enhance creative thinking in engineering design process for the students. Evaluation form for the experts used in designing framework of the model.

3.3 Data Collection and Data Analysis

The collecting data were used in framework synthesizing as the following: (1) The framework of the designing framework was synthesized by methods of data interpreting and descriptive analysis. (2) The designing framework was analyzed by data interpreting and using of descriptive analysis on the framework synthesis recording forms based on the theoretical framework. (3) Model components were proposed to advisor and experts to examine the consistency between theories and the designing framework by interpreting and descriptive analysis using data in the evaluation forms. The examined results were applied to improve the model.

4 Research Results

The results of the synthesizing of designing framework of constructivist web-based learning environment model to enhance creative thinking in engineering design process for eight-grade students were found that there were 6 stages of creative thinking enhancement as (1) Activating cognitive structure as problem-based component (2) Adjusting to cognitive equilibrium as learning resources component (3) Enlarging cognitive structure as cognitive tools and collaboration-based component (4) Enhancing creative thinking as creative thinking design-based component and (5) Fostering knowledge construction as scaffolding-based component. (6) Encouraging knowledge construction as scaffolding-based component.

The problem-based component (see Fig. 1) was designed to activate cognitive structures in accordance with constructivist theory when students are encouraged to create cognitive conflicts with specifies specific problems. Learners will try to balance the cognitive structure (equilibration) with the integration of external events (Assimilation) or adapting to that event in a particular environment (accommodation), Open-ended learning environments enabling context the perspectives taken in the environment to learner to engage in thinking and have a variety of perspectives. Externally induced specific problems with for novice learner, which helps promote divergent thinking component for creative thinking skills, fluency, flexibility, originality and elaboration. The design of Creative thinking design-based design to enhancing creative thinking, the component was designed based on the theory of creative thinking of Guilford [2] with 4 components as (1) Fluency means the ability of producing outcome in a limit time (2) Flexibility means the ability to construct something flexibly in various forms (3) Originality is defined to the ability to generate something originality (4) Elaboration is the ability to implement in details on original. By integrated creative components with the integrated creative design process model. Cognitive tools that was designed to the design stage 1 and 7 have the most opportunities to effective enlarge cognitive structure for originalities creative thinking (see Fig. 2) the design stage 2 and 6 are also the alternative to enhance creative thinking.

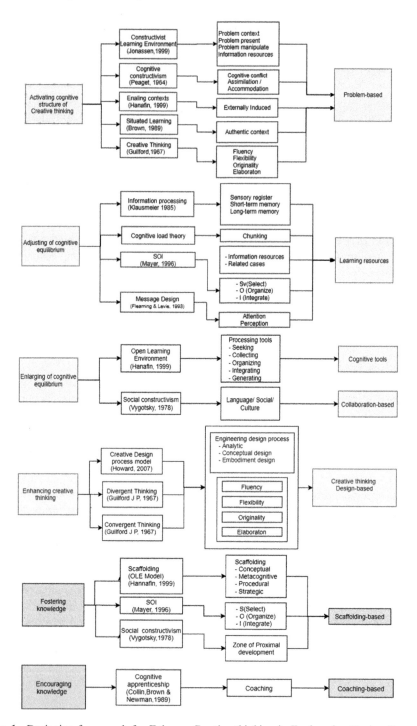

Fig. 1. Designing framework for Enhance Creative thinking in Engineering Design Process.

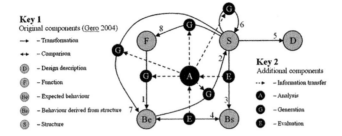

Fig. 2. Integrated creative design process model [3].

5 Conclusion

The results of synthesizing the designing framework of the constructivist web-based learning environments model to enhance creative thinking in engineering design process for eight-grade students comprised of 6 stages: (1) Activating cognitive structure as problem based component (2) Adjusting to cognitive equilibrium as learning resources component (3) Enlarging cognitive structure as cognitive tools and collaboration-based component (4) Enhancing creative thinking as creative thinking design-based component and (5) Fostering knowledge construction as scaffolding-based component. (6) Encouraging knowledge construction as coaching-based component. The design focus on the learner construct knowledge by themselves by constructivism paradigm. The creative thinking using Guildford's divergent thinking [2] during the use of engineering design processes in the operations Which is an integration of engineering and cognitive process together. These will enable educational designers to understand where and when creative thinking will occur to design the most effective cognitive tools for students.

Acknowledgements. This research was supported by Ph.D. Program in Educational Technology, Faculty of Education, Research Group for Innovation and Cognitive Technology, Khon Kaen, University, and Research and Technology Transfer Affairs Division, Khon Kaen University which hereby giving the thankfulness all through this.

References

1. Richey, R.C., Klein, J.D.: Design and Development Research: Methods Strategies and Issues. Lawrence Erlbaum Associates, Mahwah (2007)
2. Guilford, J.P.: The Nature of Human Intelligence. McGraw-Hill Book Company, New York (1967)
3. Howard, T., Culley, S., Dekoninck, E.: Describing the creative design process by the integration of engineering design and cognitive psychology literature. Des. Stud. **29**, 160–180 (2008)
4. Howard, T., Culley, S., Dekoninck, E.: Creativity in the engineering design process. In: International Conference on Engineering Design, ICED 2007 (2007)

5. Gero, J.S.: The situated function-behaviour-structure framework. Des. Stud. **25**(4), 373–391 (2004)
6. The Partnership for 21st Century Learning: Framework for 21st Century Learning (Final Report). The Partnership for 21st Century Learning, 2 (2015)
7. Piaget, J.: Cognitive development in children: piaget development and learning. J. Res. Sci. Teach. **2**(3), 176–186 (1964)
8. Vygotsky, L.S.: Mind in Society: The Development of Higher Psychological Processes. Harvard University Press, Cambridge (1978)
9. Jonassen, D.: Designing constructivist learning environments. In: Instructional Design Theories and Models: A New Paradigm of Instructional Theory, vol. 2, pp. 215–239. Erlbaum, New Jersey (1999)
10. Hanafin, M., Land, S., Oliver, K.: Open learning environment: foundation, methods, and models. In: Charles, M. (ed.) Instructional Design Theories and Model 2: A New Paradigm of Instructional Theory. Lawrence Erlbaum Associates, Mahwah (1999)
11. Mayer, R.E.: Designing instruction for constructivist learning. In: Instructional-Design Theories and Models: A New Paradigm of Instructional Theory. Lawrence Erlbaum Associates, New York (1999)
12. Klausmeier, H.J.: Educational Phychology, Sth edn. Harper & Row, New York (1985)
13. Kozma, R.B.: Learning with media. Rev. Educ. Res. **61**(2), 179–211 (1991)
14. Collins, A., Brown, J.S., Holum, A.: Cognitive apprenticeship: making thinking visible. Am. Educ. **15**(3), 6–11 (1991)
15. Chaijaroen, S.: Instructional design: principles and theories to practices. Department of Educational Technology, Khon Kaen University (2015)
16. Kanjug, I.: Development of learning environments model enhancing expertise mental model. Doctor of Philosophy thesis in Educational Technology, Graduate School, Khon Kaen University (2009)
17. Samat, C.: The development of constructivist web-based learning environment model to enhance creative thinking for higher education students. Doctor of Philosophy thesis in Education Technology, Graduate School, Khon Kaen University (2009)
18. Wattanachai, S.: Development of constructivist web-based learning environment model to foster problems solving and transfer of learning. Doctor of Philosophy thesis in Educational Technology, Graduate School, Khon Kaen University (2010)

Designing Framework of Constructivist Web-Based Learning Environments Model to Enhance Scientific Thinking for Secondary Students

Autsanee Seenonlee Maneeratana[✉] and Sumalee Chaijaroen

Department of Educational Technology, Faculty of Educational,
Khon Kaen University, Khon Kaen, Thailand
Autsanee.sl199@gmail.com

Abstract. Nowadays, Scientific thinking is important in the development of human learning. Therefore, the designing framework synthesis is the objective of this study. To promote the scientific thinking of students. The target audience was (1) experts for the assessment of the learning content (2) experts for the assessment of the instructional design for the framework (3) experts for the assessment of the instructional media design. (4) experts for the assessment of the collecting research instruments and 5) 35 Grade 7 students, 1st semester, the academic year 2020, Sri Kranuan Wittayakhom School, studying in a science course for the contextual survey. Model research type II [15] was employed by literature review to synthesize the framework. The process was as follows: study the principles and theories, to literature reviews research related to the design of the learning environment model. Assessment by experts consisting of content, design, media, and technology, measurement, and evaluation by the assessment from the expert assessment form. The research results consisted of 4 steps: (1) Activation of cognitive structure and enhance scientific thinking (2) Enhancement of cognitive equilibrium and expanding cognitive structure (3) Support and enhancement of scientific thinking and (4) Enhancement and support of knowledge construct. Also, the model has 6 components of were: (1) Problem based, (2) Resources, (3) Collaboration, (4) Scientific thinking, (5) Scaffolding, and (6) Coaching.

Keywords: Constructivist theories · Scientific thinking · Constructivist web-based learning

1 Introduction

The rapid development of information technology today makes every country around the world. There has been a change in the 21st-century world [19] such as digital technology. Technology to change the world (Disruptive technology) social, the economic, knowledge-based database has changed affecting education management. Conduct business and the world economy. Therefore, it is necessary to prepare resources for such changes, qualify in searching and knowledge creation to receive knowledge throughout life. By using technology together with including current information technology There are more information and knowledge. From the problem of teaching and learning by teachers being the only educator is not enough to build knowledge of learners. Educational management has changed from teaching or transfer by teachers or teaching media. Came to be an emphasis on student learning. Through action or real action that is related to the theory of Constructivist theory [14] focuses on self-knowledge by action or action.

Above all these important reasons, the learning strategy needs to be adjusted to reflect the characteristics of the 21st-century learner [19]. Thus, instructional design is necessary to support scientific thinking and construct the knowledge, instead of receiving knowledge from teachers. The instructional design theory [3] is applied in this design. The main theories that are based on the theory are constructivist theory. Cognitive theory: information processing and scientific thinking. These theories foster knowledge to construct and scientific thinking, particularly in science courses. Moreover, the media theories, media attributes, and symbols system include hypertext, hyperlink, and hypermedia [12] promote the knowledge construction and scientific thinking.

Nowadays, learning science emphasizes students' search for knowledge. The teacher acts as a coach to help learners build knowledge and achieve goals on their own. Which will result in the development of students' scientific thinking process This may help the student to expand their intellectual structure. Have scientific thinking and create meaningful knowledge.

From this importance, this research aims to design a learning environment for scientific thinking [5, 6] of secondary school students. Results in the development of learning skills and scientific thinking [5, 6] of students.

Researchers are focus on the importance of the designing framework. The framework can help designers to model. Also, it reaffirms its reliability and is a useful guide for designers to model.

2 Research Purpose

To synthesize the designing framework of a constructivist web-based learning environment model to support scientific thinking for secondary students.

3 Research Methodology

The Model research Type II [15], phase 1 Model development.

3.1 Target Group

The target groups were: (1) 3 experts for the assessment of the learning content (2) 3 experts for the assessment of the instructional design for designing framework (3) 3 experts for the assessment of the instructional media design. (4) 3 experts for the assessment of the collecting research instruments and 5) 35 Grade 7 students, 1st semester, the academic year 2020, Sri Kranuan Wittayakhom School.

3.2 Research Instruments

- Tools were used to synthesize the framework design concept model element design assessment form to confirm the quality of the model. The details are as follows: instructional management survey, theoretical conceptual framework synthesis record form, the memorandum of concept synthesis of the model. Opinion survey for learners about the context of learning management and survey for teachers on learning management context.
- Tool used for quality verification of learning environment models. For experts, such as the Learning Environment Model Evaluation Form, it is used for the quality examination of the model. By means of expert evaluation of the model, Question points consist of open-ended questions for the expert to assess on each issue. Along with giving reasons and opinions, as well as suggestions.

3.3 Data Collection and Analysis

Document study analyzes principles, theory, and literature review to the design of the model by studying the principles. Related theories are cognitive theory. Theories of constructivism in the pedagogy of scientific thinking. Media and technology theory the context of learning management; And neuroscience is to be used as a basis for research and to record information in a document audit record and document analysis. Conduct an assessment of the learning environment by introducing the learning environment to various experts consisting of content, 3 persons, design 3 persons, media 3 persons, and measurement and evaluation 3 persons by each specialist. Record the assessment results in the assessment form. With suggestions that have been improved.

4 Research Results

4.1 Theoretical Framework

The framework consisted of 6 elements: (1) Psychology based (2) Pedagogy based (3) Scientific thinking based (4) Media theory and Technology based (5) Contextual based and (6) Neuroscience based (see Fig. 1).

4.2 Designing Framework of Web-Based Learning Environment Model

The model includes 4 stages, as the following detail.

1. The activation of cognitive structure and enhance scientific thinking

The first fundamental of the framework is based on the cognitive constructivist theory [14]. It is believed that students who are motivated by the problems-based lead up to situations of intellectual conflict education must try to balance their cognitive strutures. The principle of authentic context based on Situated learning [1], believes that learning is an authentic activity, context, and culture. As well, the principle of scientific thinking [5, 6] along with 4 phases as inquiry phases, analysis phases, inference phases, and argument phases. It was designed as a Problem base (see Fig. 2).

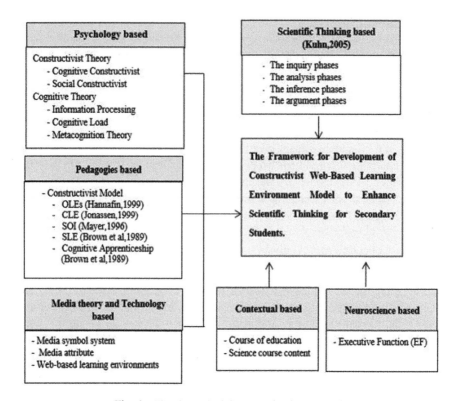

Fig. 1. The theoretical framework of the model.

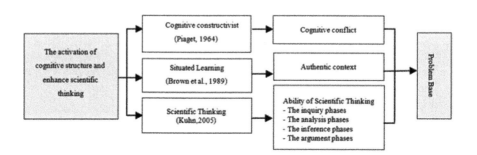

Fig. 2. The first of the designing framework of the model.

2. The enhancement of cognitive equilibrium and expanding cognitive structure

The second basis of this framework is based on Information processing theory [11], is believed that when the learners experience the environment by sensory register. Cognitive Load Theory [17] focuses on information content in many environments. Exceeds short-term memory capacity is only 7 ± 2 or 15–30 s, so chunking was used to categorizes information. SOI model [13] that help the learner to select, organize, and integrate information, and OLEs [8] consists of a learning resource that has a static resource and a dynamic resource that is information that can help to create new knowledge of learners (see Fig. 3).

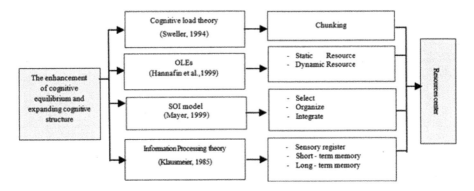

Fig. 3. The second of the designing framework of the model.

3. The support and enhancement of scientific thinking

The third of this framework is based on the relationship between the theories, scientific thinking and social constructivist [20] must be adopted as an important stream of cognitive development. Learners with the lower proximal development zone, there is a need for learning assistance, known as Scaffolding is the key to the development behind intelligence designed as the component of the Collaboration. Scientific thinking [8] consisted along with 4 phases as inquiry, analysis, inference, and argument (see Fig. 4).

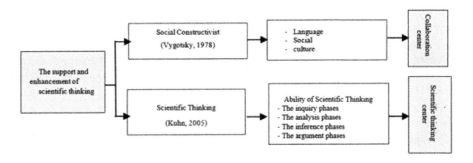

Fig. 4. The third of the designing framework of the model.

4. The enhancement and support of knowledge construct

The fourth of the model include Social constructivism [20] believes that the learners below the proximal development zone, there is a need for learning assistance, known as

Scaffolding [8] and Metacognition theory [7]. Cognitive apprenticeship [4] was designed as the Coaching Center (see Fig. 5).

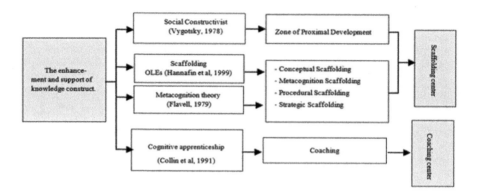

Fig. 5. The fourth of the designing framework of the model.

5 Conclusion

The theoretical framework of the model comprised of 6 elements: (1) Psychology based (2) Pedagogy based (3) Scientific thinking based (4) Media Theory and Technology based (5) Contextual based and (6) Neuroscience based, and designing framework comprised of 4 stages of (1) The activation of cognitive structure and enhance scientific thinking (2) The enhancement of cognitive equilibrium and expanding cognitive structure (3) The support and enhancement of scientific thinking (4) The enhancement and help of construct the knowledge including 6 elements as following: (1) Problem base (2) Resources (3) Collaboration (4) Scientific thinking (5) Scaffolding and (6) and Coaching. This research result consistent with the study of Chaijaroen [2, 3], Thitima, G. [18], Saowakon, S. [16], Kanjug and Chaijaroen [10]. From the research results, it was found that consisted of a learning environment that can support scientific thinking.

Fundamentals of theories of learning basis include: (1) psychology learning, including constructivist theory and cognitive theory (2) teaching and learning science designed together with constructivist theory, cognitive theory, and scientific thinking theory (3) principle of media theory and technology-based on learning includes: media symbol system and the media attribute (4) pedagogical of learning based on constructivist theories model consisted OELs [8], CLE [9], SOI [13], SLE [1], and Cognitive apprenticeship [4] (5) principle into contexts such as learners based on guidelines for teaching, course of education, and science course content, and (6) neuroscience-based of the executive function is a measure of the nerves in the brain region while performing scientific thinking tasks. Besides found that theoretical and designing frameworks that the researcher has designed and developed. It has been verified for quality by experts in content, media, and design to be correct and suitable for teaching and learning in current situations.

From the above importance the researcher, therefore, takes it as a basis for designing the model on the science courses. That enhances scientific thinking by integrating teaching science and neuroscience by the principle of constructivist theories, cognitive theories, and scientific thinking. Including features media symbol systems, media attributes and web-based learning environments that help in promoting student performance.

Acknowledgements. Thank you for support by Educational Technology, Faculty of Education and Research and Technology Transfer Affairs Division, Khon Kaen University.

References

1. Brown, J., Collins, A., Duguid, P.: Situated cognition and the culture of learning. Educ. Res. **18**(1), 32–42 (1989)
2. Chaijaroen, S.: Development of knowledge construction using information technology. Department of Educational Technology, Khon Kaen University (2004)
3. Chaijaroen, S.: Instructional design: principles and theories to practices. Department of Educational Technology, Khon Kaen University (2015)
4. Collins, A., Brown, J.S., Holum, A.: Cognitive apprenticeship: making thinking visible. Am. Educ. **15**(3), 6–11, 38–39 (1991)
5. Deanna, K.: Education for Thinking. Harvard University Press, Cambridge (2005). 218 p.
6. Deanna, K.: What is scientific thinking and how does it develop? In: Goswami, U. (ed.) Handbook of Childhood Cognitive Development (Blackwell), 2nd edn. (2010)
7. Flavell, J.: Metacognition and cognitive monitoring: a new area of cognitive-developmental inquiry. Am. Psychol. **34**, 906–911 (1979)
8. Hannafin, M.: Open learning environment: foundation, methods, and models. In: Charles, M. (ed.) Instructional Designing Theories and Model: A New Paradigm of Instructional Theory, vol. II. Lawrence Erlbaum Associates, Mahwah (1999)
9. Jonassen, D.: Designing constructivist learning environments. In: Instructional Design Theories and Models: A New Paradigm of Instructional Theory, vol. II, pp. 215–239. Erlbaum, Mahwah (1999)
10. Kanjug, I., Chaijaroen, S.: The design of web-based learning environments enhancing mental model construction. Procedia Soc. Sci. **46**, 3134–3140 (2012)
11. Klausmeier, H.J.: Educational Psychology, 5th edn. Harper & Row, New York (1985)
12. Kozma, R.B.: Learning with media. Rev. Educ. Res. **61**(2), 179–211 (1991)
13. Mayer, R.E.: Designing instruction for constructivist learning. In: Instructional-Design Theories and Models: A New Paradigm of Instructional Theory, vol. II (1999)
14. Piaget, J.: Cognitive development in children: piaget development and learning. J. Res. Sci. Teach. **2**(3), 176–186 (1964)
15. Richey, R.C., Klein, J.D.: Design and Development Research: Methods Strategies and Issues. Lawrence Erlbaum Associates, Mahwah (2007)
16. Saowakon, S.: The development of rish chemistry learning environments model to foster scientific thinking. Doctor of Philosophy thesis in Educational Technology, Graduate School, Khon Kaen University (2012)
17. Sweller, J.: Cognitive load theory, learning difficulty, and instructional design. Learn. Instr. **4**, 295–312 (1994)

18. Thitima, G.: The development of knowledge construction model to support scientific thinking for prathom suksa 6 learners. Doctor of Philosophy thesis in Educational Technology, Graduate School, Khon Kaen University (2010)
19. The Partnership for 21st Century Learning. Framework for 21st Century Learning (Final Report). The Partnership for 21st Century Learning, 2 (2015)
20. Vygotsky, L.S.: Mind in Society: The Development of Higher Psychological Processes. Harvard University Press, Cambridge (1978)

Development of Constructivist Web-Based Learning Environment Model to Enhance Problem-Solving and Transfer of Learning on Student in Industrial: Integration Between Pedagogy and Neuroscience

Chan Singkaew and Sumalee Chaijaroen(✉)

Education Technology Major, Faculty of Education, Khon Kaen University, Khon Kaen, Thailand
Sumalee@kku.ac.th

Abstract. This study aimed to design and develop the Constructivist Web-based Learning Environment Model to Enhance Problem-solving and Transfer of learning on students in industrial. The methodology in this study uses Developmental Research - Type I. That focusing on the principles of designing and developing a model, the model is designed and developed according to the following steps. (1) examine and analyze the principles theories, and research (2) study learner context (3) synthesize the theoretical framework (4) to synthesize the designing framework (5) developing the Constructivist Web-based Learning Environment Model and (6) assessing the efficiency. The results of the study found that: 1) The theoretical framework consists of 6 bases: (1) Learning theory base, (2) pedagogical base, (3) Media theory base, (4) neurological base, (5) Technological base, and (6) Context of instructional base 2) The designing framework consisted of 5 stages and 9 elements, were as follows: (1) Activate cognitive structure (2) Support for adjusting cognitive structure (3) Support for enlarging cognitive structures (4) Foster for problem-solving and transfer (5) promote and assist knowledge construction and 9 components were as follows: (1) Problem base (2) Resources (3) Cognitive tool (4) Collaboration for problem-solving (5) Center for enhancing problem-solving (6) Center for transfer of learning (7) Related cases (8) Scaffoldings, and (9) Coaching.

Keywords: Problem solving · Web-based learning environment · Constructivist learning · Transfer of learning

1 Introduction

The advancement of technology has influenced the increase of information in a knowledge-based and digital society. At the same time, the current problems are increasingly more serious and complicated. Therefore, a necessary skill for learners is problem-solving, especially for industrial students. However, in the present, instructional management emphasize transmitting information and content from teachers to learners. This results in a lack of seeking skills, knowledge construction, especially problem solving of the learners. Thus, it needs to adjust the instructional management to foster the learners to construct knowledge on their own, problem solving to solve problems in other situations. In response to solving such problems, the teaching and learning management should shift from teacher-centered content to learning management focused on students seeking knowledge. Build your own knowledge and problem-solving skills. A theoretical principle that is consistent with learning management that focuses on the students to seek and build knowledge on their own. Is the constructivist theory Which is a theory that focuses on seeking and construct knowledge by them self In addition, Problem Solving Principles [1] and principles of Learning Transfer [2] are aligned with the practice of industrial mechanics that need to solve the operational problems that face problems or new situation. So requires theoretical principles on media and network technology and media features Hyperlink symbol system, hyper-tech, hypermedia to connect knowledge nodes. that as a basis for understanding and expanding knowledge in each node and expanding knowledge by linking the features of the Internet to construct a learning environment. For this reason, the researcher recognizes the importance of designing and developing the Model based on constructivist approaches that promote problem-solving and Transfer.

2 Research Purpose

To design and develop a web-based constructivist learning environment model.

3 Research Methodology

3.1 The Sample Group

Divide into 2 groups: 1) The experts for validating and evaluating models' quality, 3 design professionals for examine the learning environment design, 3 media professionals for examine web-based media, and 3 professionals for examine the content of electronics. 2) The students for context instructional study, 30 high vocational certs industrial students, faculty of technical education Rajamangala University.

3.2 Research Methodology

The Model Research Phase I [3].

3.3 The Research Process

The research process is (1 Study principles, theories and related research. (2) studying the context of the learner, (3) synthesizing the theoretical framework, and (4) synthesis of the design framework (5) design and development of model and (6) Assessment quality

3.4 The Research Instruments

The research instruments included (1) learning environment model (2) ecological model evaluation form (3) theoretical framework form (3) design framework form.

4 Data Collection

4.1 The Theoretical Framework

After the researcher synthesis of the framework and then record that in recording form.

4.2 The Designing Framework

After the researcher synthesis of framework and then record that in recording form.

4.3 Development

After the designer design, the learning environment and then the developer developed according to designer.

4.4 Evaluation

Model efficiency is assessed by experts to validate and adapt to feedback on content, web media, learning environment, model design.

5 Data Analyses

5.1 The Theoretical Framework

The data analyses of the theoretical framework are summarizing, interpreting and analytical explanation.

5.2 The Designing Framework

The data analyses of the designing framework are summarizing, interpreting and analytical explanation.

5.3 The Efficiency

The Model Efficiency analyses by Interpreted and conclusion.

6 Result

6.1 Theoretical Framework

The theoretical Framework comprise 6 crucial bases include of 1) Learning theory base 2) Pedagogical base 3) Context of instructional, graduate features, learning management, main course 4) neurological base: Electroencephalography (EEG). 5) Technological base: 6) Media theory base. This study focuses on the identification of the sources of media and symbolic systems that help strengthen knowledge and memorization processes.

After reviewing the literature and all 6 bases researcher analyzed and synthesized the relationship between each base, illustrated in Fig. 1.

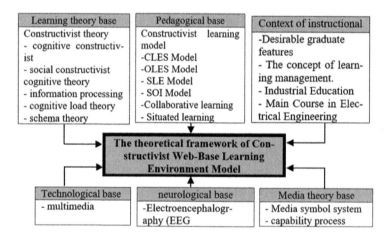

Fig. 1. Theoretical framework.

6.2 Designing Framework

From this study, it found that the synthesis of the design framework obtains by applying the theoretical framework as the basis for the design of model elements. The model consists of 5 crucial bases which are:

The Stimulate the Abandoned Structures, Problem-Solving, and Transfer. The first crucial base was activating cognitive structure, problem-solving, transfer, it shows the underlying theory used in designing components known as the "problem base" of the learning environments to promote problem-solving. The Theories that are important for stimulating cognitive structures are as follows: Cognitive constructivism [4]; cognitive conflict, situated learning [5]; Authentic context. These theories are transformed into problem situations to encourage learners to the learning process. The process of Ill-structure problem solving [1] as 1) Articulate Problem Space 2) Identify and clarify problem 3) Construct possible Problem Solutions 4) Select alternative Solutions 5) Planning and determination strategy solution 6) Implement the Solution and 7) Apply the Solution that theories use to design a learning environment to promote problem-solving. This theory may assist in stimulating cognitive structures and problem-solving as shown in Fig. 2.

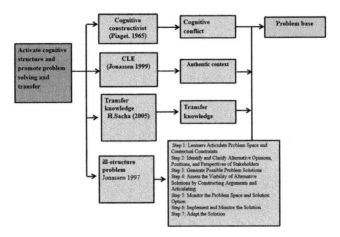

Fig. 2. The designing framework: activate cognitive structure and promote problem-solving and transfer of learning

Support Cognitive Restructuring. The second very important base of the designing framework was Support for adjusting cognitive structure, shows the underlying theory used in designing components known as the "Resources" of the learning environments to promote problem-solving and transfer. The underline theories used for Supporting for adjusting of the cognitive structure were as follows: information processing theory [7]: sensory register, working memory, long-term memory, Cognitive load theory [8]: Chunking, Hierarchical network, and media attribute symbol. These theories are transformed into designing framework as learning resources in order to provide information for the learners to construct knowledge. This may help learners processing information effectively and understand easily as shown in Fig. 3.

Foster for Problem-Solving and Transfer Practical Skills. The third base was support for enhance problem-solving and transfer of learning, it illustrated the theories used in designing the component called "Center for enhancing problem-solving" and "Center for transfer of learning" of the learning environments for promoting problem-solving and transfer. The theories used for Supporting for Foster for problem-solving and transfer learning were as follows: ill-structure Problem [1]. Analogical transfer (Transfer knowledge [9]: search a prior knowledge, mapping, and identical Structure, process, relational aspects, Inference, inference solution for solving the current situation. These theories use to design a learning environment to provide information for the learners to construct problem solving and transfer shown in Fig. 4.

Support for Enlarge Cognitive Equilibrium. The fourth important base was supported enlarge cognitive equilibrium, the theory used in the component design is called

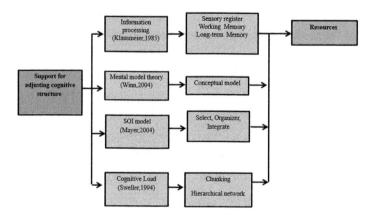

Fig. 3. The designing framework: Support for adjusting cognitive structure

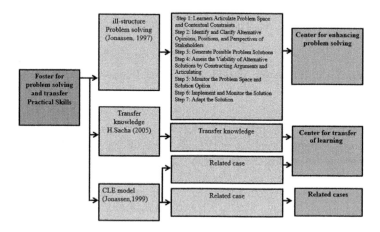

Fig. 4. The designing framework (Foster).

"Collaboration for problem-solving" and "Cognitive tool". The theories were as follows: Social constructivist theory [4]: Collaborative Activity Cognitive tool [5]: Seeking tool, collecting tool, generating tool, organizing tool, and Integrating tool. The theories transformed into learning resources in order to provide information for the learners to construct knowledge. This principle may be to help learners enlarge cognitive equilibrium as shown in Fig. 5.

Promote and Assist Knowledge Construction. The fifth base was support for promoting and assist knowledge construction, the theories used in design the element called "Scaffoldings" and "Coaching" for promoting and assist knowledge construction. The theories used for promotion and assist knowledge construction were as: Scaffolding [5] Conceptual Scaffolding, Strategic Scaffolding, Metacognition Scaffolding, Cognitive apprenticeship and Coaching. They transformed in order to provide information for the learners to construct knowledge. This may help promote and assist learners as shown in Fig. 6.

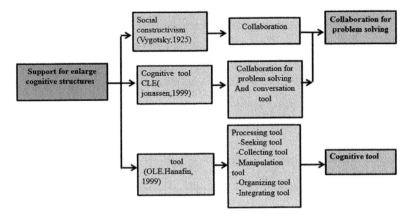

Fig. 5. The designing framework: support for enlarge cognitive equilibrium.

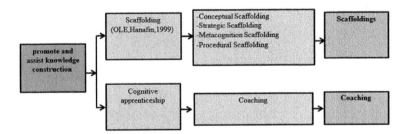

Fig. 6. Promote and assist knowledge construction.

6.3 Development

Result of design as present in the Figs. 7, 8, 9 and 10:

Fig. 7. Front page(main).

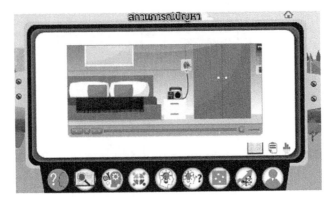

Fig. 8. Problem situation.

Fig. 9. Cognitive tool.

Fig. 10. Collaboration for problem solving.

7 Discussion

The development and design achieved using the Model Development Type I (Model Development). Model development process, study the context of the learners examine and analyze the principles, theories, and research, synthesize the theoretical framework, and synthesizing the designing framework, design and development of the model, and evaluation of the model efficiency and improvement with the expert. The research findings the theories and principles are 1) Learning theory base 2) Pedagogical base 3) Context of instructional 4) neurological base 5) Technological base 6) Media theory base. Model conceptual and components comprised (1) Problem base (2) Resources (3) Cognitive tool (4) Collaboration for problem-solving (5) Center for enhancing problem-solving (6) Center for transfer of learning (7) Related cases (8) Scaffoldings, and (9) Coaching. This finding was consistent with previous research [10] has found that students demonstrate problem-solving and transfer of learning and frameworks of theoretical designing for models based on theories. For the findings of this study that use theories especially the problem -solving theory [1] and transfer theory [9] as the foundation of the design. This has been demonstrated in the design framework of the constructivist web-based learning environment model to improve problem-solving and learning transfer. This may help learners to promote problem-solving and learning transfer. The theoretical validity of the design framework of the constructivist web-based learning environment model was also found based on expert assessment. The findings could support the design framework to improve problem-solving and Transfer of learning on Students in industrial.

8 Recommendations

The process of problem-solving and transferring learners' learning should be used as a basis for analyzing each learner's potential as part of the result analysis.

Acknowledgements. This research was supported by Ph.D. Program in Educational Technology, Faculty of Education, Khon Kaen University, and Research Group for Innovation and Cognitive Technology, Khon Kaen University which hereby giving the thankfulness all through this.

References

1. Jonassen, D.H.: Instructional design model for well-structured and ill-structured problem solving learning outcomes. Education Tech. Research Dev. **45**, 65–95 (1997)
2. Gentner, D., Holyoak, K.J., Kokinov, B.: The Analogical Mind: Perspectives from Cognitive Science. MIT Press, Cambridge (2001)
3. Richey, R.C., Klein, J.D.: Design and Development Research. Lawrence Erlbaum Associates, London (2007)
4. Piaget, J., Inhelder, B.: The Psychology of the Child. Basic Books, New York (1969)
5. Brown, J.S., Collins, A., Duguid, P.: Situated cognition and the culture of learning. Educ. Res. **18**(1), 32–42 (1989)

6. Klausmeier, H.J.: Educational Psychology, 5th edn. Harper & Row, New York (1985)
7. Sweller, J.: Cognitive load theory. In Mestre, J.P., Ross, B.H. (eds.) The Psychology of Learning and Motivation: Vol. 55: Cognition in Education, pp. 37–76, Elsevier Academic Press, San Diego (2011)
8. Sacha, H.: The Analogical Mind: Perspectives from Cognitive Science. MIT Press, Cambridge (2005)
9. Hannafin, M., Land, S.M., Oliver, K.: Open learning environments: foundations, methods, and models, instruction. In: Reigeluth, C.M. (ed.) Instructional-Design Theories and Models: A New Paradigm of Instructional Theory, vol. II. Lawrence Erlbaum Associates, Mahwah (1999)
10. Chaijaroen, S., Kanjug, I., Samat, C.: Learner's creative thinking learning with constructivist web-based learning environment model: integration between pedagogy and neuroscience. In: Rønningsbakk, L., Wu, T.-T., Sandnes, F.E., Huang, Y.-M. (eds.) ICITL 2019. LNCS, vol. 11937, pp. 663–671. Springer, Cham (2019). https://doi.org/10.1007/978-3-030-35343-8_70

Digital Accessibility of Online Educational Platforms: Identifying Barriers for Blind Student's Interaction

Isolda Lisboa[1], João Barroso[2], and Tânia Rocha[2(✉)]

[1] Open University, Milton Keynes, Portugal
ilisboa1@gmail.com
[2] INESC TEC and University of Trás-os-Montes e Alto Douro,
Vila Real, LISBON, Portugal
{jbarroso,trocha}@utad.pt

Abstract. e-Learning promotes asynchronous and synchronous access to education, free from geographical barriers, allowing a great number of people, that otherwise could not study, continue their academic life. Access, however, should be equally granted for All, not limited to the instrumental level, providing a dynamic model that meets the needs of the student user. e-Learning platforms have potential to both enhance learning quality and increase education access as long as is considered user's different needs. In this paper, we present the theoretical background about the current state of accessibility of e-Learning educational platforms and contents, by analyzing the Brazilian online educational context. This study intends to identify barriers and possible tools to enhance user experience for Blind students, and also present a UX methodology to reach that goal. For the latter, we propose a methodology based on obtaining qualitative and quantitative data to be obtained from online questionnaires. The ultimate goal is to make a global UX evaluation in order to present a complete perspective, on the actual Blind student's experience when interacting with the digital educational contents and platforms in specifics Brazilian universities digital platforms.

Keywords: Human-Computer Interaction (HCI) · Digital accessibility · e-Learning · Blind student · User experience (UX)

1 Introduction

Several factors make possible for teachers and students to find themselves in different geographical locations as well as in different time zones and still interact through e-Learning, opening up a new world of educational possibilities for students with disabilities and/or special needs.

With the advent of the Internet, new opportunities are presented for distance education and, according to [1], nowadays "this type of teaching-learning is an important means of acquiring knowledge, with universities and companies seeking to exploit the educational potential of the Internet to the maximum" [1]. Some examples are the popularization of Open Universities, where students and teachers have flexibility in terms of time and space [2].

The great diversity of cultural, socioeconomic, gender, ethnic and even people abilities of has been changing the context of universities and stimulating research. Furthermore, studying how these universities are dealing with this new reality, especially the treatment of people with disabilities is enhanced in several studies [3–7]. However, these studies showed a gap highlighting as essential more research to obtain specific knowledge of the needs of blind student in distance learning, thus promoting crucial changes and adaptations in the platforms.

In this paper, we aim at present a theoretical framework and validate a user experience methodology on the thematic Digital accessibility of online educational platforms: Brazilian blind student's case study.

This article is structured as follow: first, it is presented a brief theoretical framework based on: how technology can promote inclusion in education for students with diverse abilities; then, analyzed accessibility on digital educational contexts; also, presented assistive technologies to enhance digital access to Blind users, identifying Brazilian tools developed; and, the research methodology proposal is revealed with the objective of creating guidelines to maximize the blind student's experience; finally, conclusions and future work is highlighted.

2 Promoting Inclusion in Education for Students with Diverse Abilities Through Technology

The Brazilian Law of Directives and Bases of National Education (LDB), defines Distance Education, or e-Learning as being: "educational modality in which didactic-pedagogical mediation in teaching and learning processes occurs with the use of information and communication means and technologies, with students and teachers developing educational activities in different places or times" [8].

According to [9], e-Learning has the potential to improve the quality of learning, the access to education, reduces costs and improves its cost-effectiveness. The authors state that for the creation of quality experiences in e-Learning, one must consider: technology, pedagogy and organizational context. The way in which this educational environment is perceived by the student is still unclear, being necessary to focus on the students' experience in e-Learning and "listening to the students' voice in the search for the expansion of e-Learning knowledge, providing perspectives in the process of learning and the criteria used by him in his evaluation of e-Learning" [9].

Boroson states that "learning about the evolution of the educational system, in particular its treatment of students who are different in terms of ethnicity, gender and skills, can guide us as educators to lead the way forward". According to the author, the stigmatization of disability has always resulted in the social and economic marginalization of those with special needs, considering them incapable of contributing to society and excluding them from the public educational system [10].

Education is a fundamental right for All, enshrined in the Universal Declaration of Human Rights, and protected by several international conventions. This, in itself, was not enough to end the differences in educational policies offered to people with disabilities, and it has not yet resulted in enacted policies or, at significant levels, educational inclusion practices for people with disabilities. Peters points out that despite the large number of documents and standards, inclusive education has not yet "escalated" [11, 12].

Furthermore, [12] defines inclusive education as both a philosophy and a practice, based on specific theories of teaching and learning. The philosophy of inclusive education is based on the "right of all individuals to education with quality and with equal opportunities - that develops potential and respects human dignity - going beyond physical integration. Students with disabilities are entitled to adequate institutional support systems, which may include flexible curriculum, trained teachers, technologies, and acceptance" [12].

The author concludes that there is a political discourse between the different agencies that links economic development to inclusive education. This fact reveals that the growth in the number of people with disabilities and their exclusion from social opportunities has drawn the attention of these agencies. His analysis discloses that if the discourse in international policy documents continues to insist on an education that is "appropriate to the condition of the person with a disability, rather than preparing schools and educational institutions to reach these people and build an inclusive society, inclusive education may not become a reality for most people with disabilities, who are still excluded from education ", and quotes the [13] if people with disabilities are denied educational opportunities, then it will be the lack of educational inclusion, not disability, which limits their opportunities" [12, 13].

Despite the fact that some inclusive policies and practices are already present in higher education, there is still a long way to go. Gairín and Suárez even claim that inclusion is the hallmark for quality higher education [14].

Statistics confirm the growth in the number of students with disabilities seeking university, which according to Morina is due to the approval of laws and statutes to promote inclusion, namely the United Nations International Convention on the Rights of Persons with Disabilities in 2006, which determines the guarantee to people with disabilities, access, without discrimination and under the same conditions as other people, to higher education, professional training, adult education and continuing training. The United Nations created support plans and services to improve the access and educational inclusion of so-called non-traditional students, in the European strategic proposal - European Commission 2020. Similar actions have been taken by other countries in the direction of inclusive education, with the creation, in some universities, of departments that support the educational needs of students with disabilities and, through the incorporation of new technologies and/or inclusive education practices [15, 16]. However, the author does not mention which technologies.

Gibson and Thomas stress that ensuring access to higher education for people with disabilities is not sufficient without providing appropriate support to ensure their inclusion and permanence. It is necessary to incorporate the principles of inclusive education and a universal design for learning in university policies and practices, based on the social model of disability [17, 18].

Between 2004 and 2005, Morina conducted an analysis on the investigation of students' voices, with disabilities in higher education, regarding the barriers and supports of educational institutions. Regarding barriers, the biggest obstacle pointed out by the students was the negative attitude of the members of the institutions, namely, doubts about the veracity of the disability, non-adaptation of the teaching projects, questions about the ability to attend a university, architectural barriers, inaccessibility to information and technology, teaching methodologies that do not facilitate inclusion and the need for presence in the classroom - without flexibility for students with difficulties resulting from their deficiencies [15].

Yet, the technological resources that were supposed to function as facilitators were not used. Although, the students reported their performance was similar to the rest of the class, they felt that they had to try harder than the others, since they had to deal with their disability in addition to their studies. Morina concluded that students with disabilities should be encouraged, despite the barriers, to continue their academic life as a way to improve their quality of life, expand their work opportunities, contribute to society and achieve independence [15].

Similarly, Garrison-Wade points out that some universities have been implementing some interventions towards the inclusion of students with disabilities, such as, for example, through the use and providing assistive technologies [19].

These studies showed as technology can promote inclusion in an education context, especially for students with disabilities. Furthermore, e-Learning platforms can break physical barriers, giving universal access to education programs and contexts, allowing a truly accessible environment to promote apprenticeship for All students. However, as literature sustains, other barriers are lifted - the digital ones, as the main educational online platforms are developed with no accessibility or usability concerns.

3 Accessibility on Digital Educational Contexts

Accessibility, based on elaboration of the E_MAG (Electronic Government Accessibility Model), in its current version 3.0 (2014), takes on a broader dimension "it means allowing access by everyone, regardless of the type of user, situation or tool" [1].

Acosta-Vargas *et al.* claim there are now millions of higher education websites, developed with no accessibility concerns, with different styles and shapes, and that many of them are not in accordance with the guidelines proposed by the W3C and WCAG 2.0 - Web Content Accessibility Guidelines-"developed to guide web designers and developers to the elimination of errors in accessibility".

The authors emphasize that Web accessibility seeks to "guarantee satisfactory and barrier-free access to the Web for the greatest number of people, regardless of their physical limitations, environments or devices used by them." [22, 23].

There are several researches in the literature carried out to assess the accessibility of education websites, notably the e-Learning platforms' initial pages, and most point out errors in the (X) HMTL and CSS codes, indicating the need to improve them to allow a higher level of accessibility, since they are essential for the well-functioning of screen readers technologies [24–27, 28, 42].

Barros *et al.* carried out research on the situation regarding the "profile of students integrated in the Accessibility Project, developed in an e-Learning environment at Universidade Aberta, in Portugal - UAB". The authors' analysis revealed, as obstacles pointed out by the students: behavioral (looking); architectural (face-to-face exam locations), oral communication (deaf people) and materials visualization (blind people).

The aforementioned difficulty that stood out the most was for students with visual disabilities, despite using screen reader technologies. Such technology was not effective in accessing documents with different formats, namely, images and tables, pages made with a scanner without the possibility of reading the screen and powerpoint without accessibility to the screen readers.

Such information is crucial in adapting the materials [29].

Promoting accessibility on the websites of higher education institutions is an important need and must address all types of disabilities, including visual, hearing, physical, speech, cognitive and neurological.

4 Assistive Technologies to Enhance Digital Access to Blind Users

It is found in the literature several definitions of Assistive Technology (AT), altogether highlight the set of technological resources used to help people with disabilities with their functional skills, promoting their independence, quality of life, social inclusion, expanding their mobility, communication and learning skills [8, 34–36].

For the people with visual disabilities these resources are essential, not only for the maintenance of their daily activities, but, to have access to computers, smartphones and tablets, as well as any electronic and digital means of communication.

For example, operating systems most used in smartphones, computers and digital electronic devices in general, offer voice communication agents, who fulfill the role of personal assistants. Thus, the popular Android (Google), Windows (Microsoft) and iOS (Apple) have personal assistants Google Now, Siri and Cortana [37, 38] respectively.

Specifically, developed by the Electronic Computing Center of the Federal University of Rio de Janeiro (UFRJ), in 1993, and available free of charge on the Internet, the DOSVOX operating system allows blind people to use a common microcomputer (PC) to perform a series of tasks. Communication with the user takes place through voice synthesis, and "instead of simply reading what is written on the screen, DOSVOX establishes a friendly dialogue, through specific programs and adaptive interfaces". It is compatible with most existing speech synthesizers because it uses the standardized SAPI Windows interface, as well as with other programs, such as: Virtual Vision, Jaws, Window Bridge, Window-Eyes and screen magnifiers [39].

F123 is low-cost software that allows developers to make improvements to the system. One of the objectives of the program is to ensure that spreadsheets, documents and other programs are accessible to blind people. "It is not just speech synthesis, there is also a magnification of the screen, since many children need larger font sizes to use the computer effectively, …" explains Fernando Botelho, co-creator of F123 and CEO of the company. In 2019, his company launches VOISS and claims that is the cheapest talking computer on the planet. "The objective of this project was to democratize access to the digital world for blind people. Although the community received the project with great affection, sales have not been sufficient to maintain the necessary infrastructure for the assembly and sale of these machines", laments Botelho who was forced to close the sales [40, 41].

Other solutions are described in literature, for example, the combination of a multisensory and interactive approach with the support of technological resources allows users to access the same information thus ensuring the inclusion of those whom, in the majority, can only have access to education in this way [43]. Particularly, in 2014, a group of students from the Federal Institute of Education, Science and Technology of Mato Grosso do Sul, Brazil, won the award for best prototype at the Science and Technology Fair of Mato Grosso do Sul (Fecintec), with a stimulation plate tactile aid to the visually impaired to learn the signature and the Roman alphabet. According to the laureates, "…the project uses vibration to help the blind to feel the formation of the letter" [41].

For students with different visual abilities, the promotion of accessibility and usability must go beyond the use of the assistive technology used but also, in the technological development stage of the educational platforms. Furthermore, it should be encouraging the research and development of new ways, that could enhance the multisensory and multimodal users' interactions. To these users to be truly benefited, it will be necessary for the systems response to transcend the screens and reach devices that provoke tactile, auditory and even odors and flavors sensations.

5 Research Methodology Proposal Focusing on the Blind Student

In 2000, the Higher Education Census started collecting information on distance learning courses, in Brazil. Since then, this type of teaching has grown steadily, encompassing an important participation in Brazilian higher education. The number and percentage of students with disabilities, in Brazilian higher education, according to the Higher Education Census INEP/MEC/2008, is 11,412 students with disabilities (0.2%), out of a registered universe of 5,808,017 students [20].

The 2010 Census confirmed the growth trend of distance learning courses, which reach 14.6% of the total number of enrollments. The face-to-face courses reach a total of 3,958,544 bachelors' enrollments, 928,748 undergraduate degrees and 545,844 technological degree enrollments. On the other hand, Distance learning courses have 426,241 undergraduate enrollments, 268,173 undergraduate degrees and 235,765 enrollments in technological courses [20].

A recent analysis (January 2018), by the Higher Education magazine, on the 2016 Higher Education Census shows that "Only 0.45% of the total 8 million enrollments in higher education are from students with disabilities. In the private network, the percentage is even lower, 0.35%, while in the public network it reaches 0.73%" [21].

There are about 12,000 students entering courses, and only 4.800 are graduating students: "The dropout rate among students with disabilities is 27%, being higher in the private network: 31.5%. Physical disability is the most common among those enrolled and affects more than 12,700 people enrolled. After that come low vision (11,000 students), hearing impairment (5,000) and blindness (2,000)" [21].

Regarding the latter data, the importance of research on the profile of accessibility to online educational content of Brazilian distance-learning universities remains important and still justified.

For that, we intend to carry out research with two main objectives: (1) to assess the conditions of accessibility of educational content online, in Brazilian public institutions, from the perspective of the blind students' experience; and, (2) propose guidelines to maximize their user experience; truly enhance digital inclusion for these group of students. Furthermore, it is intended to identify distance learning as a form of inclusion in education for people with special needs, and the needs of the blind user in his/her interaction with the computer and online educational content, by assessing the educational resources and tools.

For this propose, the methodology followed will be the Design Science Research - DSR -which, according to Vaishnavi *et al.*, is a lens or set of techniques and perspectives in conducting research and which typically involves the creation of an artifact, knowledge, model or theory as a means to improve the current state. For this purpose, design, analysis, reflection and abstraction are used. Still, according to the authors, the areas of education, health, computer science and engineering make extensive use of DSR, sharing the same concerns to develop problem solutions and conduct evaluations [29].

The achievement of the proposed objectives implies conducting a research in two phases: (1) comprising an exploratory phase to obtain the theoretical foundation on the theme developed and to provide greater familiarity with the problem, followed by (2) a descriptive phase - with survey, analysis and interpretation of data - consistent with direct user interrogation through online qualitative and quantitative questionnaires.

According to Santoso *et al.*, the methodology suggested for the analysis of the user experience consists of a combination of qualitative and quantitative methods, such as the use of interviews, questionnaires, behavioral analysis and expert evaluation. Among the research frameworks currently on the market, the UEQ - user experience questionnaire stands out for its exceptional advantages in providing a "comprehensive impression of the user experience, ranging from classic aspects of usability to aspects of the user experience. The questionnaire also features a tool for accurate interpretation, easy to use and free of charge. Feedback collection can be done more efficiently with questionnaires, especially if they are used with an online tool, such as UEQ" [30].

In the first quantitative phase, we will apply the UEQ, with a additional field for users to add observations, difficulties or comments - as suggested by Nakamura *et al.*, to measure the user experience, considering pragmatic and hedonic quality aspects, as well as, through assessing the standard of the six quality measures, make assumptions about the areas where improvements will have the greatest impact on the user experience [31].

In the second, qualitative phase, we will apply a questionnaire with open questions to: diagnose the tasks and resources used by the user; evaluate the usability of the interaction; confirm or refute the assumptions obtained in the first phase to prepare a list of guidelines to be implemented in order to optimize the user experience.

The method of analysis for this phase will be the use of software for qualitative analysis of data such as texts, interviews and transcripts such as MAXQDA [32].

6 Conclusions and Future Work

The proposed study, involving field research and intending to suggest paths based on the results obtained, needs a physical spatial delimitation. In addition, the study of accessibility necessarily involves examining the legal norms about it, as this is where the requirements for equality to occur are fixed. And, even though it originated from international agreements and treaties, this standardization gains its own and unique state treatment for validity within the limits of each State, multiplying, in the Brazilian case, in rules edited not only by the Legislative authority, but also by the government agencies in charge of public policies, in the specific case of this investigation, the Ministry of Education [33].

In this way and with the proposed cut, the scientific importance and the social and political relevance of the present study on the profile of accessibility to online educational content of Brazilian distance-education universities by blind student is justified. We intend to identify and list difficulties experienced by the blind student in their interaction and propose ways to provide a positive and quality user experience.

As future work, we intend to present and implement the list of guidelines generated after the analysis of the data from the research two phases on at least one institution for its validation. The next phase is a repetition of the research first phase, but with the objective of assessing whether the implementation of the guidelines has had a positive effect on the user experience.

References

1. Morais, C., Mari, M.: Aprendizagem Para a Inclusão De Deficientes Visuais. Master dissertation. University Federal São Carlos, p. 96 (2011)
2. Tomás, C.: A Acessibilidade das Plataformas de Elearning em Instituições de Ensino Superior Público em Portugal: Contributos Iniciais. https://www.academia.edu/7308592/A_Acessibilidade_das_Plataformas_de_Elearning_em_Institui%C3%A7%C3%B5es_de_Ensino_Superior_P%C3%BAblico_em_Portugal_Contributos_Iniciais. Accessed 05 Feb 2020
3. Alahmadi, T., Drew, S.: Accessibility evaluation of top-ranking university websites in world, Oceania, and Arab categories for home, admission, and course description webpages. J. Open Flex. Distance Learn. **21**(1), 7–24 (2006)
4. Menzi-Çetin, N., Alemdağ, E., Tüzün, H., Yıldız, M.: Evaluation of a university website's usability for visually impaired students. Univ. Access Inf. Soc. **16**(1), 151–160 (2015). https://doi.org/10.1007/s10209-015-0430-3
5. Rodriguez-Ascaso, A., Boticario, J.G., Finat, C., Petrie, H.: Setting accessibility preferences about learning objects within adaptive elearning systems: user experience and organizational aspects. Expert Syst. **34**(4), e12187 (2017)
6. Abu Shawar, B.: Evaluating web accessibility of educational websites. Int. J. Emerg. Technol. Learn. (iJET) **10**(4), 4–10 (2015)
7. Acosta-Vargas, P., Lujan-Mora, S., Salvador-Ullauri, L.: Evaluation of the web accessibility of higher-education websites. In: 15th International Conference on Information Technology based Higher Education and Training (ITHET), Istanbul, Turkey, pp. 1–6. IEEE (2016)

8. Ministério da Educação: Direito à Educação Subsídios para a Gestão. Mec, pp. 1–344 (2006). http://portal.mec.gov.br/pec-g/192-secretarias-112877938/seesp-esducacao-especial-2091755988/12650-direito-a-educacao-subsidios-para-a-gestao-dos-sistemas-educacionais. Accessed 08 Mar 2020
9. Gilbert, J., Morton, S., Rowley, J.: e-Learning: the student experience. Br. J. Educ. Technol. **38**(4), 560–573 (2007)
10. Boroson, B.: Inclusive education: lessons from history. Educ. Leadersh. **74**(7), 18–23 (2017)
11. Declaração Universal dos Direitos Humanos. https://www.un.org/en/universal-declaration-human-rights/. Accessed 03 Feb 2020
12. Peters, S.J.: Education for all? A historical analysis of international inclusive education policy and individuals with disabilities. J. Disabil. Policy Stud. (JDPS) **18**(2), 98–108 (2007)
13. The World Bank. https://www.worldbank.org/. Accessed 10 Feb 2020
14. Castro, D., Gairín, J., Díaz-Vicario, A., Navarro, M., Muñoz, J.L., Suárez, C.: Estrategias de orientación y atención a colectivos vulnerables en la universidad Colectivos Vulnerables en la Univerdidad: refleciones y propuestas para la intervencion, 1a edición (2014). ISBN 978-84-9987-163-9. https://www.worldcat.org/title/colectivos-vulnerables-en-la-universidad-reflexion-y-propuestas-para-la-intervencion/oclc/900037087. Accessed 08 Mar 2020
15. Moriña, A.: Inclusive education in higher education: challenges and opportunities. Eur. J. Spec. Needs Educ. **32**(1), 3–17 (2017)
16. Convention on the Rights of Persons with Disabilities (CRPD). https://www.un.org/development/desa/disabilities/convention-on-the-rights-of-persons-with-disabilities.html. Accessed 04 Feb 2020
17. Gibson, S.: Narrative accounts of university education: socio-cultural perspectives of students with disabilities. Disabil. Soc. **27**(3), 353–369 (2012)
18. Thomas, L.: Developing inclusive learning to improve the engagement, belonging, retention, and success of students from diverse groups. In: Widening Higher Education Participation, pp. 135–159. Chandos Publishing (2016)
19. Garrison-Wade, D.F.: Listening to their voices: factors that inhibit or enhance postsecondary outcomes for students' with disabilities. Int. J. Spec. Educ. **27**, 113–125 (2012). https://eric.ed.gov/?id=EJ982866. Accessed 09 Mar 2020
20. Censo da Educação Superior. Instituto Nacional de Estudos e Pesquisas Educacionais Anísio Teixeira. http://portal.inep.gov.br/censo-da-educacao-superior. Accessed 10 Nov 2019
21. Revista Ensino Superior, Editora Segmento. https://revistaensinosuperior.com.br/. Accessed 04 Feb 2020
22. Acosta-Vargas, P., Acosta, T., Lujan-Mora, S.: Challenges to assess accessibility in higher education websites: a comparative study of Latin America universities. IEEE Access **6**, 36500–36508 (2018)
23. W3C. https://www.w3.org/WAI/fundamentals/accessibility-intro/#what. Accessed 08 Mar 2019
24. Pereira, A.S., Machado, A.M., Carneiro, T.C.J.: Avaliação da acessibilidade dos sítios eletrônicos das instituições de ensino superior Brasileiras. Informação Sociedade Estudos **23**(3), 123–142 (2013)
25. Mari, C.M.M.: Avaliação Da Acessibilidade E Da Usabilidade De Um Modelo De Ava Para Inclusão De Deficientes Visuais. Master dissertation - University Federal São Carlos, p. 96 (2011)
26. Ferati, M., Vogel, B., Kurti, A., Raufi, B., Astals, D.S.: Web accessibility for visually impaired people: requirements and design issues. In: Ebert, A., Humayoun, S.R., Seyff, N., Perini, A., Barbosa, S.D.J. (eds.) UsARE 2012/2014. LNCS, vol. 9312, pp. 79–96. Springer, Cham (2016). https://doi.org/10.1007/978-3-319-45916-5_6

27. Lobo, R.L., Souza, C.P.: Análise da acessibilidade para deficientes visuais no sistema moodle. SIED: EnPED-Simpósio Internacional de Educação a Distância e Encontro de Pesquisadores em Educação a Distância, pp. 1–7 (2016)
28. Dantas, E.M., Araújo, C.M.: Avaliação em ambientes virtuais de aprendizagem: desafios para uma abordagem colaborativa. In: III Colóquio Luso-Brasileiro de Educação a Distância e Elearning, pp. 1–15 (2013)
29. Vieira, D.M., Barros, I., Roboredo, I.: Projeto Acessibilidades: A Educação a Distância Inclusiva no Ensino Superior. Teoria e Prática da Educação **16**(1), 7–19 (2013)
30. Vaishnavi, S., Kuechler, V., Petter, W.: Design Science Research in Information Systems. http://desrist.org/desrist/article.aspx. Accessed 10 Mar 2019
31. Santoso, H.B., Schrepp, M., Yugo Kartono Isal, R., Utomo, A.Y., Priyogi, B.: Measuring user experience of the student-centered E-learning environment. J. Educ. Online **13**(1), 58–79 (2016)
32. Nakamura, W.T., Marques, L.C., Rivero, L., De Oliveira, E.H.T., Conte, T.: Are scale-based techniques enough for learners to convey their UX when using a Learning Management System? Braz. J. Comput. Educ. (RBIE) **27**(1), 104–131 (2019)
33. MAXQDA. https://www.maxqda.com/brasil/software-analise-qualitativa?gclid=Cj0KCQjw6575BRCQARIsAMp-ksPJ0Zb-6jnixDDZ1xcFPVAQbyc2xQ6M8UOeqXxxPUdUHiCGJs5AE48aAm8XEALw_wcB. Accessed 08 Mar 2020
34. MEC. http://portal.mec.gov.br/. Accessed 08 Mar 2020
35. MEC. http://portal.mec.gov.br/pec-g/192-secretarias-112877938/seesp-esducacao-especial-2091755988/12650-direito-a-educacao-subsidios-para-a-gestao-dos-sistemas-educacionais. Accessed 08 Mar 2020
36. Educa Mundo. https://www.educamundo.com.br/blog/curso-online-tecnologia-assistiva. Accessed 15 Jan 2020
37. Portal Educação. https://www.portaleducacao.com.br/conteudo/artigos/informatica/o-que-e-tecnologia/48269. Accessed 06 Jan 2020
38. Gomes, L., Salvino, M., Onofre, E.G.: Braile versus Byte: tecnologias tecendo caminhos de pessoas cegas. Revista Tecnologias na Educação (2015)
39. PROJETO DOSVOX. http://intervox.nce.ufrj.br/dosvox/. Accessed 10 Mar 2019
40. F123 – A tecnologia que possibilita. https://f123.org/?s=voiss. Accessed 20 Apr 2020
41. Premio Ceweb. http://premio.ceweb.br/2013/finalistas/F123_fernando_botelho.html. Accessed 15 Apr 2020
42. Schenini, F.: Projeto de instituto federal é voltado a deficientes visuais. Semana Nacional Ciência E Tecnologia - SNCT (2018). http://portaldoprofessor.mec.gov.br/conteudoJornal.html?idConteudo=3598. Accessed 08 Jan 2020
43. Reis, A., Martins, P., Borges, J., Sousa, A., Rocha, T., Barroso, J.: Supporting accessibility in higher education information systems: a 2016 update. In: Antona, M., Stephanidis, C. (eds.) UAHCI 2017. LNCS, vol. 10277, pp. 227–237. Springer, Cham (2017). https://doi.org/10.1007/978-3-319-58706-6_19
44. Rocha, T., Fernandes, H., Paredes, H., Barroso, J.: Combining NFC and 3D mapping to enhance the perception of spatial location for the blind. In: Antona, M., Stephanidis, C. (eds.) UAHCI 2016. LNCS, vol. 9739, pp. 607–615. Springer, Cham (2016). https://doi.org/10.1007/978-3-319-40238-3_58

Effect Analysis and Method Suggestions of Online Learning Under the Public Epidemic Crisis

Huimin Yuan[1], Ming Yan[1], and Zhe Li[2(✉)]

[1] Communication University of China, Beijing 100024, China
[2] Fujian Normal University, Fuzhou, China
lizheritetu@163.com

Abstract. In the context of a major national public epidemic caused by COVID-19, the education system has also been greatly affected, changing from traditional offline education to online education. In the case of changes in learning methods, the questions of how effective online learning is, whether it can achieve the learning effect of traditional offline education, and what measures should be taken if the online learning effect is not good are worthy of further analysis. To understand the general status of students' online learning effects, this paper analyzes the methods, effectiveness and problems of students' online learning at different stages, and puts forward appropriate suggestions on this basis. And through the questionnaire and predictive analysis method to verify the feasibility of the proposal, to provide a reference for the education objects and educators who try to improve the effect of online learning in the context of public outbreaks.

Keywords: Epidemic situation · Online education · Learning effect · Questionnaire

1 Introduction

The epidemic began to break out during the Chinese Spring Festival. The government took a series of strict travel restrictions to curb the spread of the epidemic, which not only restricted people's freedom of travel, but also had a huge impact on various industries and even the national economic development [1]. The traditional education mode requires students to have class together in the school and teachers to explain and guide on the spot. For some boarding schools and colleges, it also involves the dining hall, dormitory life, collective bathhouse and other inevitable collective life. In this complex environment, the contact distance between people is less than one meter, and the number of people in contact is too large. Once there are cases of epidemic infection, it will spread rapidly [2]. Considering many factors [3], all kinds of schools across the country choose to postpone the start of school to avoid the risk of epidemic infection caused by a large number of student flows. In order not to delay students' learning progress, the Ministry of Education advocates "no suspension of classes" and adopts online education mode to temporarily replace the traditional education [4], so as to ensure the smooth and orderly progress of students' academic plans.

Online education is a network-based education method. With the help of the Internet and information communication technology, teachers and students can break the limitations of time and space to learn and acquire knowledge in a more flexible and diverse way [5]. Online education can also realize the wide use of teaching resources, not only limited to the campus, library and other places, but also realize the system to automatically record the learning progress, attendance status, personal data of each student, so as to facilitate the management of teachers to the classroom.

The online education work does not go smoothly as expected [6], and encounters various obstacles. For example, the hardware equipment for online learning is insufficient, the platform is defective, the student's self-control is poor, the teachers' teaching burden is heavy, and the parents' supervision is exhausted. In a word, due to various factors, the effect of online education often can not reach the effect of traditional education.

The existing survey and analysis found that the longer the online class [7], the worse the learning effect of students, in other words, the lower the learning efficiency of students. However, due to the impact of the epidemic, students across the country have to stay at home for a long time online learning. It can be seen that the online learning effect of students in the public epidemic environment is generally not as good as that of traditional education [8]. This paper investigates and analyzes the effect of online learning through some specific cases. Based on the analysis results, some suggestions of learning methods are put forward to provide reference and help for all participants of online learning.

2 Case Analysis of Online Learning Effect of Students

The performance of students' online learning effect is different in different students. It is necessary to select several representative students' learning status, analyze and summarize their learning effect, and provide practical basis for proposing improvement measures.

2.1 The Case of Primary School Students

At present, the common way of online learning for primary school students is: on the one hand, relying on multiple channels of cable TV and IPTV to broadcast teaching content (one channel and one grade), and providing repeated viewing of computers, mobile phones and tablets. Supporting materials also provide students with paper and electronic versions for selection. On the other hand, teachers use a live platform like nails to conduct online live teaching and online attendance methods such as roll call, question, assignment and punch. At the same time, parents supervise students to finish their homework on time, and can communicate with teachers through WeChat and QQ [9]. Primary school students are still in the cultivation period of concept and habits, and are very vulnerable to the influence of people around them. Moreover, many primary school students have not strong learning awareness at present, and think that it is a holiday at home, and the phenomenon of online class perfunctory is more obvious. The main reasons that affect their online learning effect are: lack of self-awareness of learning, lack of serious attitude towards online classes, difficulty in resisting the temptation of online games and electronic products, and inadequate teacher discipline.

2.2 The Case of Senior Three Students

The common way for senior high school students to learn online is that teachers recommend some excellent courses in famous schools to let students learn independently in MOOC class. According to the teaching plan, teachers of each subject provide students with review guidance, knowledge point collusion and After class Q&A in the way of online live broadcast every day. The rest of the time is arranged by students themselves to learn and brush questions. When encountering problems, they can communicate with teachers at any time.

Senior three students are faced with the pressure of the coming college entrance examination. Under the traditional education mode, there are teachers' daily supervision and the atmosphere of students working together. Now, online learning at home is a test of students' self-learning ability and self-control. The main reasons that affect their effect are: the lack of hardware equipment, the inexperience of teachers and students in the operation of online class, the low classroom atmosphere, and the great pressure in all aspects.

2.3 The Case of Art Examinee

According to the original plan, art examinee should take part in the school examinations of major art schools in February and March, but the sudden epidemic disrupts everything. Some school examinations are canceled, some school examinations are moved to the college entrance examination, and cultural courses became the top priority at this time. Therefore, the art examinee all over the country have to study online at home, start to make up for cultural courses and strengthen professional courses. Most art examinee learn online with their classmates, and take time to strengthen professional courses after class.

Affected by the epidemic, this year's art examinee can't participate in the school test on time, some need to record art test videos at home, some change to only test cultural courses, which disrupts the original learning plan of art examinee, while the current online learning is not applicable to all art examinee. The main reasons that affect the online learning effect of art examinee are: the progress of cultural courses can not keep up, lack of one-on-one guidance from teachers, and great psychological pressure.

3 Suggestions on Improving the Effect of Online Learning

In view of the three special cases mentioned above, we put forward corresponding countermeasures and suggestions. Details as shown in the Fig. 1.

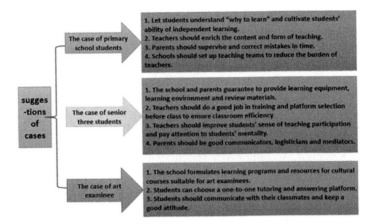

Fig. 1. Recommended block diagram for three case.

3.1 Student Level Suggestions

First of all, we need to make students understand "why we study" and cultivate students' independent learning ability. Because of the special situation of the epidemic situation, when students study at home, teachers cannot control too much. In a word, we should pay attention to guiding students to study independently. Therefore, it is suggested that three classes should be held in sequence: home epidemic prevention guidance class (focusing on how to live), home learning mobilization class (focusing on why to learn), home learning method guidance class (focusing on how to learn) [10]. Among them, the home-based learning mobilization class can inspire students' enthusiasm for learning with the help of the advanced deeds in the "anti epidemic war", and let students clearly realize that home-based learning is to prepare for the future as a patriot and defender. In the guidance course of home-based law, through sharing other students' efficient online learning methods and experience, we can provide guidance for other students' learning.

3.2 Teacher Level Suggestions

First, teachers should choose the right teaching platform in advance and make preparations before class. According to the operation of the teaching platform, teachers should be in a relatively stable state, and the unstable situation will affect the quality of the classroom to a certain extent. Before carrying out formal teaching, teachers should investigate the flow supported by the platform according to the number of students involved, so as to avoid the influence of such phenomena as incarceration on teaching effect. It is better to formulate the second plan to deal with emergencies. If it is a live classroom, teachers need to enter the classroom at least 10 min in advance, prepare various equipment, materials, etc., and pay attention to their appearance.

Second, the teaching resources should be simple and clear, and the content should be outstanding. When choosing teaching methods and preparing lessons, teachers should choose more concise and clear teaching resources, such as teaching courseware, audio and video resources, text resources, picture display, physical display (such as experimental operation steps, manual lessons, etc.), preview before class, classroom practice, after class work, and questionnaire feedback. And the teaching resources should be as simple, clear and prominent as possible, so as to avoid the influence of tedious teaching resources on students' class efficiency.

Third, students' participation in teaching needs to be strengthened. Teachers can arrange preview activities before class. For example, teachers can release syllabus in class in advance, and issue targeted preview tasks for each teaching content to attract students' attention. In the process of live broadcast, teachers need to avoid the students' learning weariness caused by the too fast pace of information transmission. For example, strategies such as retelling, content structuring, review and summary can be used to regulate the pace of information transmission. Teachers should assign homework to the students after class. If live class can be recorded and replayed, it's convenient for students who haven't heard to check and fill in the gaps and make a summary.

Fourth, the content of the class should be more abundant and the teaching form should be diversified. In the course of lectures, teachers should carry out various interactive activities. For example, online discussion, interactive survey, students' mutual evaluation, view sharing, online question answering and interactive whiteboard are carried out to enhance the attraction of online teaching. Teachers also need to pay attention to the principles and Strategies of game-based teaching design. If teachers are more able to apply the elements and mechanisms of games or games to online teaching, students may be able to improve the quality of online education.

3.3 Parent Level Suggestions

First, parents should do a good job in logistic support. To carry out online education, first of all, it is necessary to have relevant equipment, good network conditions and good learning environment. These all need the help of parents to reduce the influence and interference of other family members when students study online as much as possible. To ensure that students can study in a relatively comfortable, quiet and concentrated way, and try not to affect their learning mood because of these things.

Second, parents should be supervisors and administrators. As housekeepers are eager to cultivate their children's ability of independent learning, they still need to do a good job in supervision and management. On the one hand, parents should supervise their children to attend classes on time and finish their homework conscientiously. On the other hand, they should also supervise their children to use the Internet correctly and find and correct the bad behaviors in the use of Internet media in time. For example, addicting to online games, online novels, online shopping and other behaviors, which are unrelated to learning or excessive use of the Internet for entertainment.

Third, parents should be communicators and adjusters. Parents should pay more attention to students' learning situation and effect. After finding the problem, they can use QQ, WeChat, telephone and other contact information to communicate with the teacher in a timely manner. When parents find their children's learning pressure is too high, they should pay more attention to their children and guide them from the side to reduce their pressure.

3.4 School Level Suggestions

Not every teacher can quickly master the use of online teaching platform. The school should provide online teaching platform and tool training for teachers to ensure that teachers understand all teaching processes and operations before teaching and make full preparation. For example, providing teachers with an appropriate number of teaching assistants to help teachers do a good job in technology and other work. The purpose is to let professional people do professional things, so as to better improve efficiency and quality.

The school shall establish a teaching team according to the school section, grade and discipline, make class arrangement and prepare lessons in coordination. Each team can select online lesson preparation platform and software according to conditions and activity needs to support the development of online lesson preparation activities, such as video conference platform, cloud lesson preparation platform, social media (such as QQ group), etc. The establishment of teaching team can not only lighten the teaching burden of each teacher, but also concentrate the excellent resources of the school and give each student higher water quality education.

4 Model Prediction and Feedback

4.1 Initial Model of Online Learning

In this paper, a daily follow-up survey is carried out on the online learning of a junior high school class in Hubei Province. The teachers in this class assess and grade students' attendance, homework or examination, and teaching completion in online learning (full score is 10 points, once in two days). Record the initial learning situation of students just 20 days as the initial sample. Details as shown in the Fig. 2.

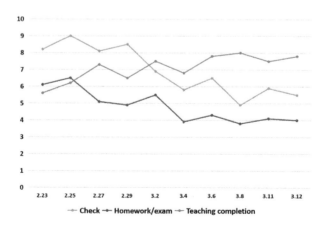

Fig. 2. Record of students' initial online learning.

From the line chart in Fig. 2, it can be intuitively found that students are enthusiastic about online learning at the beginning, attendance and homework are good, and teachers' teaching completion is only about half. With the increase of online learning time, the students' attendance and homework situation show a slow downward trend, and the teachers' teaching completion grows slowly.

4.2 Model Prediction After Online Learning Improvement

If readers refer to the above measures to improve students' online learning effect according to the actual situation, students' online learning effect will be improved. Continue to quantify the online learning effect of students from three directions of attendance, assignment or examination, and teaching completion. The following prediction will be made for the learning situation of 20 days with improvement measures, as shown in Fig. 3.

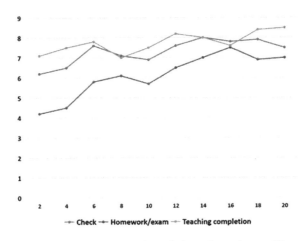

Fig. 3. Multi-angle demonstration of plane three-view to 3D model.

It can be seen from Fig. 3 that after the improvement of online learning, students' attendance, homework and teachers' teaching completion will be gradually improved, showing a slow growth trend.

4.3 Questionnaire Feedback

In order to verify whether the above-mentioned countermeasures and suggestions to improve the online learning effect of students are recognized and feasible, this paper adopts the method of questionnaire survey, and randomly selects 800 students, teachers and parents from 30 primary and middle schools in Hubei Province. The above suggestions are simplified and classified into 10 suggestions (10 points for each, 100 points in total), Students, teachers and parents are randomly selected and scored one by one. In addition to the invalid questionnaires, in the remaining 721 valid questionnaires, the proportion of people in different score segments were counted as shown in the Fig. 4.

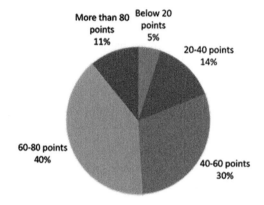

Fig. 4. Statistical chart of questionnaire scores.

Figure 4 shows that 51% of the students scored higher than 60 on the above suggestions for improving students' online learning, which shows that more than half of them think that these measures have certain effect and can be implemented.

5 Conclusion

Based on the impact of public epidemic on students' education in China, this paper analyzes the effect of online learning, and puts forward effective suggestions and solutions to improve the effect of online learning. This paper analyzes the problems existing in the online learning effect of the more common students and puts forward targeted improvement measures, including more general countermeasures and suggestions. This paper also uses the methods of questionnaire survey, prediction analysis and so on, through the investigation and Research on the students of primary and secondary schools and colleges in Hubei Province, it shows that the poor online learning effect of students is the prominent problem in the current online education. It also forecasts and compares the online learning efficiency of the students before and after taking the suggestions in the paper, and verifies the recognition and feasibility of the suggestions in the paper. This paper hopes to help improve the online learning effect of students.

References

1. Jon, M.W.: Sounding out synthesis: Investigating how educators in a teaching with technology course use sonic composition to remix reflection. E-Learn. Digit. Media **17**(3), 218–235 (2020)
2. Joseph, T., Edmund, T.: Assessment of the readability, availability, and quality of online patient education materials regarding uveitis medications. Ocul. Immunol. Inflamm. (2020)
3. Rice, M.F., Deschaine, M.E.: Orienting toward teacher education for online environments for all students. In: The Educational Forum, vol. 84, no. 2 (2020)

4. Jordan, R., Erik, M., Wolfswinkel, J.N.: COVID-19 video conferencing: preserving resident education with online meeting platforms (2020)
5. Fu, W., Zhou, H.: Challenges brought by 2019-nCoV epidemic to online education in China and coping strategies. J. Hebei Normal Univ. (Educ. Sci.) **22**(2), 14–18 (2020)
6. Li, M., Zhang, H.: A random talk on teaching during the epidemic. China Educ. Technol. **86**, 8–15 (2020)
7. Zheng, X., Wan, K.: Implementation logic, content and suggestions of home-school partnerships in large-scale K12 online. China Educ. Technol. **4**, 16–21 (2019)
8. Gao, J., Qian, H., Lai, D., Lun, Z., Wu, Z.: Human African trypanosomiasis: the current situation in endemic regions and the risks for non-endemic regions from imported cases. Parasitology (2020)
9. Yan, M., Li, Z., Yu, X., Jin, C.: An end-to-end deep learning network for 3D object detection from RGB-D data based on hough voting. IEEE Access **8**, 138810–138822 (2020)
10. Jin, C., Tie, Y., Bai, Y.: A style-specific music composition neural network. Neural Process. Lett. (2020)

Effective Blended Learning – A Taxonomy of Key Factors Impacting Design Decisions

Hanlie Smuts[1](✉) [iD] and Corlia Smuts[2]

[1] Department of Informatics, University of Pretoria, Pretoria, South Africa
hanlie.smuts@up.ac.za
[2] Department of Humanities Education, University of Pretoria, Pretoria, South Africa

Abstract. One of the keys to effective 21st century teaching is to integrate traditional pedagogical methods with the effective use of technology to foster student-centred learning. These increasingly sophisticated technologies are deployed in learning solutions, blending teaching techniques, learning styles, and delivery methods while creating a need for educators to gain new skills to meaningfully engage with these tools. The requirement is to scale blended learning and to design learning experiences that take full advantage of the digital platforms. This study presents a taxonomy with its dimensions and characteristics of the key factors impacting blended learning design. Such a taxonomy is useful not only for describing key factors impacting blended learning design, but also as a professional development tool for educators to increase efficacy of teaching and learning design. We constructed the taxonomy through a classification process following the taxonomy development approach of Nickerson et al.

Keywords: Educational technology · Blended learning · e-Learning · Taxonomy

1 Introduction

The world is experiencing revolutionary advances in technology labelled the 4th Industrial Revolution (4IR) [1, 2] and with the evolution of digital technologies, many opportunities realise through its application [3]. Both from a commercial perspective, as well as a knowledge and skill outlook perspective, digital technologies creates two possibilities: firstly, they provide multiple options for an organisation to embrace digital transformation [4] and secondly, they enable a world of visual and experiential learning in order to enhance skills and knowledge [5, 6].

For visual and experiential learning, many online platforms have bundled solutions to facilitate team-based learning, yet emerging learning spaces programmed in extended reality (XR) have the potential to create more engaging and personal experiences for students than any current developments in online course design [7, 8]. Blended learning designs to date are defined by the proportions of face-to-face versus online coursework, including media-rich elements [9]. The requirement is to scale blended learning and to design learning experiences that take full advantage of these digital platforms [8].

However, there is evidence in the literature that there is a lack of research investigating the effectiveness of computer-based instruction [10]. Some issues highlighted include lack of knowledge of the environment of computer-based instruction and virtual learning, and lack of knowledge and understanding regarding pedagogical issues and challenges in the context of computer-based instruction [11]. Furthermore, some educators are unable to use technology tools effectively to create a blended teaching- and learning environment without a clear understanding of the relationship between pedagogical knowledge and the role e-learning tools play as a medium for teaching and learning [12].

This study aims to consider the key factors impacting blended learning design. The primary research question that this study aims to address is: *"What are the key factors impacting effective blended learning design for education?"*. This was achieved through a review of the literature focusing on educational technology (Ed-Tech) and blended learning, and we used Nickerson et al.'s classification method for developing a taxonomy [15]. By applying the taxonomy of the key factors impacting blended learning design, educators will be able to increase efficacy of teaching- and learning design, as well as understand where they need to focus their own skills improvement.

Section 2 of this paper provides the background to the study and the approach to this study is discussed in Sect. 3. Section 4 provides an overview of the taxonomy development process, as well as the taxonomy of the key factors impacting blended learning design. Section 5 illustrates application of the taxonomy and Sect. 6 concludes the paper.

2 Background

Teaching practices are evolving, as student-centered approaches to instruction guides course design, accelerating the need for strategically planned teaching and instruction [8]. Consequently, the role of the educator has shifted – from a presenter of knowledge to a facilitator and curator [16]. This shift in role, further enabled by Ed-Tech, has completely reshaped the education landscape and required educators to implement more technology based teaching tools within and without the classroom [16].

In the following sections, we consider this shift in teaching practice and blended learning, as well as the impact of Ed-Tech.

2.1 Teaching Practice and Blended Learning

As technology has developed and now proliferates all areas of society, it is also impacting education and learning – specifically blended learning [13, 16]. Blended learning refers to innovative- and adaptable methods of education, teaching and learning through the usage of technological tools which allows learning to be student-centered and improve a students' interaction with the material [17]. These methods are informed by the type of technology, the system of delivery, and educational- and communication paradigms [16]. Research has shown that a blended-learning approach can greatly benefit students seeing as it combines online teaching and learning with in-class teaching and classroom time [18], allowing students to interact with the material comfortably at home, while more conventional content can be focused on in the classroom [16, 19].

One of the keys to effective 21st century teaching is to balance traditional pedagogical methods with the effective use of technology to foster learning [20]. Learning solutions are designed and deployed using increasingly sophisticated technology, creating a need for educators to gain new skills to meaningfully engage with those tools [20]. Therefore, professional development supporting the use of digital tools has evolved into collaborations with instructional design teams and other professionals in the learning science field, accelerating the application of new teaching practices [8]. The teaching practice impact on students entails increased collaboration, 24/7 access to learning, "flipping" the classroom (move direct instruction from the group learning space to the individual learning space), personalized educational experiences, attention-grabbing lessons, etc. [21]. For educators, impact lies in automated grading, classroom management tools, and paperless classrooms [22].

2.2 Impact of Ed-Tech

Seeing as technology is developing continuously, the concept of blended learning is also ever changing and dynamic [11]. It is therefore required that educators develop and acquire the skills necessary to navigate among the multiple options of interactive content technology, technologies that provide instant feedback [23], technologies with diagnostics capability for identifying student needs [24], technologies enabling learning assessment and storing of student work (student management systems), etc. [9]. However, successful blended learning, is more than a simple integration of information and communication technologies with face-to-face approaches [25]. With a student-centered construction of blended learning, the choices of what and when to blend are key [25]. Therefore, processes are required where educators are engages and supported to select fit-for-purpose Ed-Tech with the aim to facilitate and support teaching and learning [26].

Without sufficient access to sustained support and the tools and resources essential in the design of a student-centered environment, instructors are challenged to create these experiences on their own [14]. Furthermore, the myriad of Ed-Tech tools to consider such as software applications, web tools, data platforms and mobile applications, further amplifies the educator challenge and requires support to navigate and chose the best options [27].

2.3 Existing Technological Pedagogical Frameworks

Developing theory for educational technology is a complex endevour, because it requires a detailed understanding of complex relationships that are contextually bound. Moreover, it is difficult to study the cause and effect when educators, classrooms, politics, and curriculum goals vary from case to case [28]. Considering Ed-Tech, several theoretical frameworks are suitable for the evaluation of technology adoption such as the Technology Acceptance Model (TAM) [29], the extended Technology

Acceptance Model (TAM2) [30] and the Unified Theory of Acceptance and Use of Technology (UTAUT) [31]. Although these frameworks deal with a number of variables like perceived usefulness, perceived ease of use, performance expectancy, facilitating conditions, social influence, etc., they do not consider pedagogical attributes. The SAMR model uses 4 classifications: substitution (technology provides a substitute for other learning activities without functional change), augmentation (technology provides a substitute for other learning activities but with functional improvements), modification (technology allows the learning activity to be redesigned) and redefinition (allows for the creation of tasks that could not have been done without the use of the technology). Learning activities that fall within the substitution and augmentation classifications are said to enhance learning, while learning activities that fall within the modification and redefinition classifications are said to transform learning [32].

Mishra and Koehler [28] conducted a design experiment aimed at understanding educators' development toward enhanced uses of technology, while developing teaching with technology. The Technological Pedagogical Content Knowledge model (TPACK), is a concept created to assist in explaining sets of knowledge that educators need in order to teach to their students and effectively use technology in their teaching [28]. TPACK is a technology integration framework that identifies three types of knowledge which educators need to combine for successful Ed-Tech integration, namely; technological, pedagogical, and content knowledge [28].

Before the taxonomy of the key factors impacting blended learning design is presented, the research approach is discussed.

3 Research Approach

The objective of this paper was to design a taxonomy of the key factors impacting blended learning design. Firstly, we present an overview of the taxonomy development approach where after we share the taxonomy development process.

3.1 Taxonomy Development Approach

Nickerson et al. studied classification in IS [15] and as main contribution of their work, they defined a taxonomy, as well as proposed a classification method for a taxonomy [15]. The classification approach of Nickerson et al. [15] is an iterative method that commences with determining the meta-characteristics and determining the ending conditions. The meta-characteristics should be determined by the overall purpose of the taxonomy and Nickerson et al. defined the ending conditions as being objective or subjective. *Objective* ending conditions included confirmation that a representative sample of objects has been examined, and no object was merged or split in the last iteration of the taxonomy development approach; no new dimensions or characteristics were added in the last iteration of the taxonomy development approach, and no dimensions or characteristics were merged or split and at least one object is classified under every characteristic of every dimension (no 'null' characteristics). *Subjective* ending conditions relate to conciseness, robustness, comprehensiveness, extendibility and explanatory of the dimensions and characteristics classified [15].

In an *empirical-to-conceptual* iteration, the researcher identifies a subset of objects that have to be classified, and from an investigation of the objects, characteristics are identified. These characteristics are then refined into dimensions. In a *conceptual-to-empirical* iteration, the dimensions of the taxonomy are conceptualized in a deductive-, and often intuitive, way that is based on the researcher's knowledge. These dimensions are then refined by adding characteristics that allow for the classification of objects. It is necessary to note that for the development of a taxonomy, both types of iterations may be adopted, for instance, the first iteration might be conceptual-to-empirical, and a next iteration that refines the taxonomy could be empirical-to-conceptual. The iterations are performed until the ending conditions are met.

3.2 Taxonomy Development Process

In order to develop the taxonomy, we followed a number of steps. Firstly, we identified potentially relevant articles using a keyword search with the terms "characteristic" and "technology tool" and "higher education" and "student" and ("efficiency" or "effectiveness"). The keyword search was executed in common academic databases. We considered peer-reviewed journals and conference papers and identified 311 papers. Secondly, we screened the identified set of papers and extracted 105 papers as we excluded non-English papers, duplicates, and papers that did not contribute any considered key factors impacting educational technology decisions related to designing blended learning. We concluded a detailed screening of abstracts and analysis of the full text of the prospective papers and created a dataset (Appendix 1) that we utilized for the systematic development of the taxonomy dimensions and characteristics based on Nickerson et al.'s [15] taxonomy development method. This taxonomy development process [33, 34] was executed through a number of steps: firstly, we defined the meta-characteristics as the dimensions of blended learning design choices. We adopted Mishra and Koehler's [28] TPACK classification i.e. technology knowledge, content knowledge and pedagogical knowledge (Sect. 2.3), and framed our meta-characteristic therein. We proceeded through 4 iterations until all the extracted papers in our dataset were classified and the ending conditions were fulfilled as specified by Nickerson et al. [15].

In terms of the iterations, we initially adopted a conceptual-to-empirical iteration and integrated taxonomy dimensions identified in the literature review. The second, third and fourth iterations were empirical-to-conceptual and led to the classification of all the extracted papers in our dataset guided by the key factors impacting Ed-Tech decisions related to blended learning design. In these iterations, additional dimensions were identified namely how student learning takes place, student experience required, educator skills required, educator and students beliefs and attitudes and contextual determinants. We describe each dimension in the taxonomy in detail in the results section of the paper.

Lastly, we performed a thematic analysis for each dimension of the taxonomy to identify, analyse and report patterns or characteristics within the data [35]. The purpose of a thematic analysis is to interpret and organise the data in order to identify patterns or themes, emphasizing both organization and rich description of the data set and theoretically inform interpretation of meaning [36, 37]. We followed an iterative approach identifying patterns of themes until all characteristics in a particular taxonomy dimension were classified (Appendix 2).

In the next section, the design of the taxonomy of the key factors impacting educational technology decisions related to designing blended learning, is discussed.

4 Results: Taxonomy for Key Factors Impacting Ed-Tech Decisions Related to Blended Learning Design

The purpose of this study is to present a taxonomy of the key factors impacting blended learning design. In Fig. 1 the taxonomy of key factors impacting blended learning design is depicted consisting of eight dimensions, and each dimension with two to six distinct characteristics.

Dimensions	Characteristics					
Content knowledge	Cater to students needs		Availability		Variety	
Pedagogical knowledge	Assessment	Enrichment	Interaction	Learning approach	Learning objectives	
Technology knowledge	Access		Knowledge and skill		Usage	
How student learning takes place	Meaningfulness			Efficacy		
Learner experience required	Problem solving		Student interaction	Motivation	Performance	
Educator skills consideration	Communication	Creativity	Efficiency	Understanding	Management	Development
Beliefs and attitudes	Educator judgment regarding their own use of technology			Educator judgment regarding the use of technology by students		
Contextual determinants	Accessibility	Culture	Affordability	Environment	Policy	Skill determinants

Fig. 1. Taxonomy of key factors impacting blended learning design.

In blended learning design, content knowledge refers to the core requirement of an educator in terms of teaching a particular topic. The content knowledge dimension refers to a complete understanding of the subject knowledge and considers the question: *what content knowledge must the educator have to adequately meet the needs of students while making a variety of knowledge available to them?* The application of content knowledge in blended learning design should promote the *adaptation of teaching and learning content* to meet the needs and curiosities of a diverse population of students. *Variety* guides an approach to instruction that involves actively engaging students with the course material through multiple methods e.g. role plays, discussion boards, etc. Certain concepts may not readily be *available* for reflection, learning and critique and these concepts must be considered when content knowledge is applied for blended learning design.

For an educator to effectively convey their content knowledge, they also need to be in the possession of the appropriate pedagogical knowledge. Pedagogical knowledge points to the *how* of teaching, in other words what, the best methods of teaching content knowledge are that ensures that learning takes place and answers the question: *what are the best methods for enriching he learning experience and assessing whether the content knowledge had been effectively taught?* Learning objectives focus attention on, and awareness of the importance of what is to be learned. *Learning approach* entails the combination of different kinds of teaching materials (auditory, visual and kinesthetic materials) enabling the improvement and enhancement of the learning process. To be remembered, new information must be *enriched* and meaningfully connected to prior knowledge, and it must first be remembered in order to be learned. *Assessment* comprises of the ways in which students are assessed and evaluated, aligned to the learning outcomes. This is a powerful characteristic as it affects the ways students study and learn. *Interaction* promotes learning as it encourages communication and engagement among faculty, educators and students and is a means to provide feedback to students on their learning.

Seeing as blended-learning constitutes the effective incorporation of Ed-Tech tools into the teaching- and learning process, the educator needs to be familiar with- and be well acquainted with technical knowledge regarding the usage of Ed-Tech tools. Technology knowledge denotes the knowledge and ability to use Ed-Tech in combination with the relevant content- and pedagogical knowledge to create a blended-learning environment and answers the question: *how to access and use these Ed-Tech tools and which skills or knowledge are needed to do so?* The *knowledge and skill* characteristic refers to the skills and technology resources required to effectively integrate Ed-Tech into blended learning design. Mobile technologies enable mobility and has reduced the dependence on fixed locations for work and study, as well as accommodated synchronous and/or asynchronous communication. The proliferation of digital technologies enable multiple *usage* options such as immersive experiences, virtual reality, natural language processing, automatic speech recognition, etc. Irrespective of the usage options chosen, the ability to save and recycle materials previously created or annotated reinforces and extends the learning over a sequence of lessons. Having access to prior lessons may help students build on prior knowledge and educators locate and diagnose misconceptions. The *access* characteristic considers *accessibility* to material that students may require e.g. internet, web, internet sources etc. Additionally, the educator must also have sufficient knowledge on how certain tools operate and how to gain access thereto in order to guide students to be able to do the same. Furthermore, learning should not be impaired by malfunction of learning tools or information sources.

In order for learning objectives to be met, educators need to be familiar with how students learn. The how student learning takes place dimension focuses on creating meaningful learning experiences for students, and addresses the question: *how to teach for effective learning to take place?* The *meaningfulness* characteristic refers to the notion that learning is more effective and efficient when students have explicit, reasonable, positive goals, and when their goals fit well with the educator's goals. Apart from including collaborative, interactive, media-rich and personalised learning in blended learning design, an adequate pace – that may be managed with technology - in a lesson is important to the overall lesson success. *Efficacy* points to the meaningful organisation of information to ensure that it is more likely to be retained, learned, and used.

The importance of how students experience learning cannot be overlooked and a rapport between the educator and the students must be established so that the students' experiences can inform the teaching process. Student experience required refers to solving the problem surrounding how students experience learning and considers the question: *how can interaction between students be fostered while improving their performance and sustaining their motivation to learn?* The *problem solving* characteristic guides educators to design blended learning that is compatible with student determined objectives while identifying and addressing the challenges students are facing when attempting to learn with Ed-Tech tools. Furthermore, blended learning design needs to avoid over-reliance on technology and avoid the "lone student" syndrome where all possible interpersonal interactions are eliminated during the learning process. *Student interaction* highlights more opportunities for feedback, reflection and general support throughout the learning cycle between educators and students enabled through Ed-Tech. In addition, it enables interaction opportunities among students and learning communities, students and materials, and students and technology. *Motivation* focuses on the potential Ed-Tech offers students to own their own learning by embracing the opportunities available for transparent, collective-oriented learning processes. Blended learning design in the context of motivation must therefore aim to increase autonomy in learning, provide easy access to learning materials and act as a guide for both the educator and the student. Student *performance* may be impacted by Ed-Tech supporting the provision of information and resources to students. This characteristic focuses create better understanding by clarifying basic concepts in order to increase student success.

For educators to be able to achieve a sustainable and enriched blended-learning environment, they need to be in the possession of a certain skill set to be able to make the correct decision and execute the most effective teaching- and learning processes. Educator skills consideration denotes the ability that an educator has or needs to develop and considers the question: *what are the skills needed to make the best, informed choices regarding the institution of a blended-learning environment?* *Communication* from and educator perspective refers to the prompt and effective giving of feedback and the development of reciprocity and cooperation among students. *Creativity*, knowledge, and skills allow educators to utilize Ed-Tech's ability to address multiple acumens in order to differentiate instruction and to create a new learning environment that enables better personalization of the learning process. *Efficacy* refers to the more efficient use of the time by balancing levels of intellectual challenge and instructional support, while keeping track of deliverables. The *understanding* characteristic highlights that a student is not merely a consumer of content and materials, but an active participant in the learning process engaged and motivated through interactivity and collaboration. Learning tool specificity is fostered through an understanding that an information source provides results of direct relevance to a learning task accompanied by little irrelevant information. Educators need to *manage* their own capability to utilize Ed-Tech features to completely transform student achievement by implementing Ed-Tech purposefully. Furthermore, educator *development* need to take full advantage of the pedagogical affordances of technology, and develop a dynamic understanding of the features of Ed-tech, as well as learn how to interact fluidly with it during instruction.

Educators have certain preconceptions about how all educators and their students experience a blended-learning environment and these beliefs and judgements inform the choices that they make whether these attitudes reflect reality or not. Beliefs and attitudes points to an educators' judgement regarding the thoughts and beliefs of others when it comes to using Ed-Tech tools for teaching and learning, and answers the question: *what are the beliefs of educators when it comes to their own and their students' experiences when it comes to technology?* The fact that students utilise significant screen time does not imply that the use of a learning tool or information source is intrinsically pleasurable, that intellectual stimulation results from using a learning tool or information source or that the information about a learning domain captured by a learning tool or information source is complete.

The application of Ed-Tech tools are dependent on a wide range of variables originating from the environment surrounding an educational institution. Contextual determinants therefore refers to the physical factors that need to be taken into account when decisions are made regarding the institution of a blended-learning environment and considers the question: *what are the contextual determinants that will influence the Ed-Tech choices that need to be made?* It must be acknowledged that the characteristics related to the contextual determinants dimension are based on the papers that were extracted and classified. Characteristics identified through our classification process included *accessibility* (internet, web, internet sources, information source access anywhere, anytime), affordability (cost of Ed-tech ownership, total cost of education), environment (computing facilities, relationship between class size and efficacy of instruction, etc.) and policy (balance between promoting experimentation, working with student consent, and achieving transparency). *Culture* norms play an important role in how Ed-Tech is incorporated in education and is impacted by the homogeneity and diversity in computer usage, as well as students' background. *Skill determinants* focus on different capabilities of electronic learning and the adjustment to a digital environment, bringing in new curricula based on real world problems.

In the next section we share the application of the taxonomy with two exemplary studies.

5 Using the Proposed Taxonomy of Key Factors Impacting Blended Learning Design

The aim of this study was to present a taxonomy of the key factors impacting blended learning design. The taxonomy presented in the previous section could be applied as a professional development tool to guide new blended learning design, or to evaluate an existing design and close potential gaps. Figure 2 and 3 show how an exemplary module design was mapped as application of the proposed taxonomy. A practicing Further Education and Training (FET) teacher was supplied with the taxonomy and asked to map out her blended learning application. She utilised a typical red-amber-green (RAG) notation and assessed her module pre-COVID lockdown (Fig. 2) and the same module during COVID lockdown (Fig. 3) as adjustments were required as no face-to-face contact was possible. The characteristics that were able to be executed effectively and occurred often, were indicated alongside those who were less effective followed by identifying problem areas or characteristics which are lacking. Those aspects that were executed well and which the teacher managed were indicated as green whereas those that needed improvement and/or refinement were indicated amber. Aspects that were absent, or severely lacking were labelled red seeing as they were identified as being areas not supported in her blended learning design.

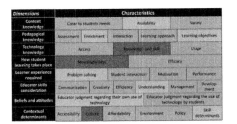

Fig. 2. Exemplary study mapped with the proposed taxonomy using heat map notation – before COVID-19 pandemic lockdown.

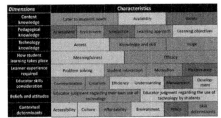

Fig. 3. Exemplary study mapped with the proposed taxonomy using heat map notation – during COVID-19 pandemic lockdown.

Seeing as the learners were unable to attend school, their most immediate need was to continue to receive schooling without physically attending classes. The impact on blended learning design is illustrated above where that which was effective versus areas that are problematic could be identified such as in the case of *variety* (changed from green to red). Due to the COVID lockdown circumstance, certain choices had to be made regarding the curriculum and what is teachable. Some topic areas needed to be removed to accommodate the new learning circumstances. This also impacted *assessment* seeing as all examinations were cancelled and assessment needed to be completed in a simpler manner by using a single summative tool.

When schooling returns to normal, this assessment against the taxonomy may be revisited and adapted to another change in circumstance.

6 Conclusion

In this study we presented a taxonomy of the key factors impacting blended learning design. The taxonomy was developed by applying Nickerson et. al's [15] taxonomy development process.

A taxonomy of key factors impacting blended learning design, consisting of 8 dimensions, were defined. Each taxonomy dimension consists of two to six characteristics. Such a taxonomy is useful not only for describing key factors impacting blended learning design, but also as a professional development tool for educators to increase efficacy of teaching and learning design. In order to illustrate the application of the taxonomy, an example assessment against the taxonomy using the heat map notation, was shared. The FET teacher reflected that it was a useful tool to identify what worked out well and what still needed further attention. She also mentioned that the fact that adjustments had to be made due to COVID-19 lockdown (red characteristics), the taxonomy highlighted potential risk areas that need to be attended to until such time as proper blended learning design may be applied again.

The characteristics of the first version taxonomy is quite coarse and further refinement of the classification may be implemented in future research. A study that specifically evaluates the applicability of the taxonomy across different teaching and learning initiatives may also be considered. Furthermore, the impact of the COVID-19 impact on blended learning design and how it impacts the 8 taxonomy dimensions, may be considered for further study.

Appendix 1 - Dataset Created from Papers Identified (Extract)

Paper title	Key factors	Reference
Podcasting: a new technological tool to facilitate good practice in higher education	• Encourages contact between students and faculty, • Develops reciprocity and cooperation among students, • Encourages active learning, • Gives prompt feedback, • Emphasizes time on task, • Communicates high expectations, • Respects diverse talents and ways of learning • Active learning, • Prompt feedback • More efficient use of the time	[38]

Note: where negatively formulated key factors were extracted, it was denoted with an "(N)"

Appendix 2 - Classification During Taxonomy Development Process (Extract)

Reference	Key factors	Dimension	Characteristic
[39]	Learner-centered	Learner experience required	Learner performance
[40]	(N) preventing the lone–learner syndrome interaction during the learning process	Learner experience required	Learner challenges/areas for improvement/problem solving
[11]	Access to material	Learner experience required	Learner motivation

References

1. Badri, A., Boudreau-Trudel, B., Souissi, A.S.: Occupational health and safety in the industry 4.0 era: a cause for major concern?. Safety Sci. **109**, 403–411 (2018)
2. Rajput, S., Singh, S.P.: Current trends in industry 4.0 and implications in container supply chain management: a key toward make in India. In: Kar, A.K., Sinha, S., Gupta, M.P. (eds.) Digital India. ATPEM, pp. 209–224. Springer, Cham (2018). https://doi.org/10.1007/978-3-319-78378-9_12
3. Ding, B.: Pharma Industry 4.0: literature review and research opportunities in sustainable pharmaceutical supply chains. Process Safety Environ. Prot. **119**, 115–130 (2018)
4. Bär, K., Herbert-Hansen, Z.N.L., Khalid, W.: Considering Industry 4.0 aspects in the supply chain for an SME. Prod. Eng. Res. Devel. **12**(6), 747–758 (2018). https://doi.org/10.1007/s11740-018-0851-y
5. Fadiran, O., Van Biljon, J., Schoeman, M.: How can visualisation principles be used to support knowledge transfer in teaching and learning?. In: Proceedings of the 2018 Conference on Information Communications Technology and Society (ICTAS 2018), Proceedings of the 2018 Conference on Information Communications Technology and Society (ICTAS 2018), Durban, South Africa. IEEE1 (2018)
6. Eppler, M., Burkhard, R.: Visual representations in knowledge management: framework and cases. J. Knowl. Manage. **11**(4), 112–122 (2007)
7. Saulnier, B.M.: Towards a 21st century information systems education: high impact practices and essential learning outcomes. Issues Inf. Syst. **17**(1), 168–177 (2016)
8. Horizon Report: Higher Education Edition, Educause (2019)
9. Roscoe, R.D., et al.: End-User Considerations in Educational Technology Design. IGI Global, New York (2018)
10. Zientek, L., et al.: Technology Priorities and Preferences of Developmental Mathematics Instructors. Community College Enterp. **21**(1), 27–46 (2015)
11. Sigaroudi, P.S., Mirroshandel, S.A.: A survey on electronic learning at smart schools. Int. J. Comput. Sci. Netw. Solutions **3**(6), 27–41 (2015)
12. Schneider, M., Stern, E.: The developmental relations between conceptual and procedural knowledge: a multimethod approach. Am. Psychol. Assoc. **46**(1), 178–192 (2010)

13. Gibson, R.T.: The experiences of high school English home language educators in preparing and delivering e- learning lessons to Further Education and Training (FET) learners: a qualitative study, University of KwaZulu Natal, Pietermaritzburg (2019)
14. Kinshuk, A.M., et al.: Teacher facilitation support in ubiquitous learning environments. Technol. Pedagogy Educ. **27**(5), 549–570 (2018)
15. Nickerson, R., Varshney, U., Muntermann, J.: A method for taxonomy development and its application in IS. Eur. J. Inf. Syst. **22**, 336–359 (2013)
16. Sangra, A., Vlachopoulos, D., Cabrera, N.: Building an inclusive definition of e- learning: an approach to the conceptual framework. Int. Rev. Res. Open Distrib. Learn. **13**(2), 146–160 (2012)
17. Protsiv, M., Atkins, S.: The experiences of lecturers in African, Asian and European universities in preparing and delivering blended health research methods courses: a qualitative study. Global Health Action **9**(1), 20–49 (2016)
18. Garrison, D.R., Kanuka, H.: Blended learning: uncovering its transformative potential in higher education. Internet Higher Educ. **7**(2), 95–105 (2004)
19. Basal, A.: The implementation of a flipped classroom in foreign language teaching. J. Distance Educ. **16**(4), 28–38 (2015)
20. Iqbal, M.D., Akter, B.: Technogagement: enhancing Student Engagement through edTech tools. In: Nordin, M.S., et al. (ed.) Humanising Technologies, pp. 29–32 (2018)
21. Reigeluth, C.M.: Instructional-Design Theories and Models: a New Paradigm of Instructional Theory. Routledge, Abingdon (2013)
22. Aljawarneh, S.A.: Reviewing and exploring innovative ubiquitous learning tools in higher education. J. Comput. Higher Educ. **32**(1), 57–73 (2019). https://doi.org/10.1007/s12528-019-09207-0
23. Watson, S.L., Watson, W.R.: The role of technology and computer-based instruction in a disadvantaged alternative school's culture of learning. Comput. Schools **28**, 39–55 (2011)
24. Adegbenro, J., Gumbo, T.M.: Exploring the conceptual relationship between teachers' procedural functional knowledge and pedagogical content knowledge. South Afr. J. Higher Educ. **29**(5), 29–47 (2015)
25. De George-Walkera, L., Keeffe, M.: Self-determined blended learning: a case study of blended learning design. Higher Educ. Res. Dev. **29**(1), 1–13 (2010)
26. Hollands, F.M., Escueta, M.: EdTech Decision-making in higher education. In: Working Group B for the EdTech Efficacy Research Academic Symposium, Center for Benefit-Cost Studies of Education (2017)
27. Bass, R.: The impact of technology on the future of human learning. Change Mag. Higher Learn. **50**(3–4), 34–39 (2018)
28. Mishra, P., Koehler, M.J.: Technological pedagogical content knowledge: a framework for teacher knowledge. Teachers Coll. Record **108**(6), 1017–1054 (2006)
29. Davis, F.D., Bagozzi, R.P., Warshaw, P.R.: User acceptance of computer technology: a comparison of two theoretical models. Manage. Sci. **35**(8), 982–1003 (1989)
30. Venkatesh, V., Davis, F.D.: A theoretical extension of the technology acceptance model: four longitudinal field studies. Manage. Sci. **46**(2), 186–204 (2000)
31. Venkatesh, V., et al.: User acceptance of information technology: toward a unified view. MIS Q. **27**(3), 425–478 (2003)
32. Romrell, D., Kidder, L.C., Wood, E.: The SAMR model as a framework for evaluating mLearning. Online Learn. J. **18**(2), 1–15 (2014)
33. Remane, G., et al.: The business model pattern database: a tool for systematic business model innovation. Int. J. Innov. Manage. **21**(1), 1–61 (2017)
34. Nakatsu, R.T., Grossman, E.B., Iacovou, C.L.: A taxonomy of crowdsourcing based on task complexity. J. Inf. Sci. **40**(6), 823–834 (2014)

35. Vaismoradi, M., Turunen, H., Bondas, T.: Content analysis and thematic analysis: implications for conducting a qualitative descriptive study. Nurs. Health Sci. **15**(3), 398–405 (2013)
36. Alhojailan, M.I.: Thematic analysis: a critical review of its process and evaluation. West East J. Soc. Sci. **1**(1), 39–47 (2012)
37. Leedy, P.D., Ormrod, J.E.: Practical Research: Planning and Design. 12th (edn.) Pearson, London (2018)
38. Fernandez, V., Simo, P., Sallan, J.M.: Podcasting: a new technological tool to facilitate good practice in higher education. Comput. Educ. **53**(2009), 385–392 (2009)
39. Chen, L.: A model for effective online instructional design. Literacy Inf. Comput. Educ. J. (LICEJ) **6**(2), 2303–2308 (2016)
40. Makuu, M., Ngaruko, D.: Innovation and development in blended learning mode in higher learning institutions: interactive experiences from OUT's postgraduate students and instructors. Huria J. **18**, 42–47 (2014)

Effective Utilization of the Constructivist Web-Based Learning Environment Model to Enhance Human Learning Efficiency Based on Brain-Based Learning

Wanwisa Wannapipat[1(✉)] and Sumalee Chaijaroen[2]

[1] Communication Arts Division, International College, Khon Kaen University, 123 Moo 16 Mittraphap Rd., Muang District, Khon Kaen 40002, Thailand
wanwwa@kku.ac.th

[2] Educational Technology Division, Faculty of Education, Khon Kaen University, 123 Moo 16 Mittraphap Rd., Muang District, Khon Kaen 40002, Thailand

Abstract. This presents the effective utilization and procedures for model use of the constructivist web-based learning environment model to enhance human learning efficiency based on brain-based learning. The Model Research Type II [1] phrase 3 Model Use was explored by Survey Research and Case Study in topics of 1) model use procedures 2) factors achieving model use and 3) model use achievements which illustrated as brain- based learning (BBL), learner's multiple intelligence (ML), relationship between ML and learning achievement, and learner opinion. The procedures, BBL, and opinion were examined by an in-depth interview while self-assessment was for ML and tests for achievements. The results showed procedures as 1) introducing learners to connect prior and new knowledge; 2) grouping them to share and elaborate thoughts; 3) learning with designed components as (1) Problem base (2) Resources (3) Meaningful experiences base (4) Collaboration base (5) Relaxing Room (6) Entertainment Corner (7) Brain Gym (8) Multiple Intelligences Room and (9) Scaffolding bases; and 4) reflexing knowledge to adjust conceptual thinking. The factors achieving model use resulted from context of designer, developer, learners, and teacher. The achievements illustrated by learner's 12 BBL principles; ML highest value was in language or $\bar{x} = 5.11$; while relationship between ML and achievement showed Positive Correlations at 0.88 level or 0.88 statistical significance. They satisfied with clear, direct, reachable, discoverable learning content, web-based learning, and model designed by pictures, animations, videos, graphs, navigators with icons and links.

Keywords: Constructivist web-based learning environment model · Multiple intelligences · Brain-based learning

1 Introduction

The knowledge society is becoming complex. As well, the technology has been developing in various ways which affects people's life that requires an ability to collaborate and compete. A language barrier is one of the important factors that most learners have faced with. English language should be used as a medium in academic communication [2]. Although English is needed, many learners cannot produce or use it well. The learning style could be a reason for that challenge that must be improved and updated. A learner must be able to be adaptive to the changing of the world. They cannot be just a passive one, but an active and skilled. Constructivism is the learning theory that mainly on knowledge construction made by the active learners through connecting the prior knowledge and new experiences. The knowledge construction made by the active learners is from the way of discovery, study, experiment, and inspection among their learner groups [3]. Likewise, Brain-Based Learning with 12 principles is learning design based on brain processes [4]. This compatible with media symbol system and attributions that emphasizing mental model construction [5].

Hence, the results of this study could be the evidence of effective utilization and procedures for model use of the constructivist web-based learning environment mod-el to enhance human learning efficiency based on brain-based learning that important to the complexity of the current world. The research was then aimed to study the effective utilization and procedures for model use of the constructivist web-based learning environment model to enhance human learning efficiency based on brain-based learning.

2 Literature Review

2.1 Constructivism

Constructivism is the learning theory that believes in the cognitive process that learners construct their own knowledge through experience meaningfully [6]. Also, Constructivism is defined as the method of learning that the learners actively construct their own learning experience or as their new knowledge [7]. This consistent with the belief that Constructivism encourages the learners to construct the knowledge and through cognitive processes where highlighting on the active learners by connecting the prior knowledge with the new knowledge and elaborate the schema [3]. So, Constructivism is the learning theory which mainly focuses on knowledge construction made by the active learners through connecting the prior knowledge and new experiences. The knowledge construction made by the active learners is from the way of discovery, study, experiment, and inspect among their learner groups. It encourages the learners to construct the knowledge and through cognitive processes where highlights on the active learners by connecting the prior knowledge with the new knowledge and elaborate the schema.

2.2 Brain-Based Learning

Brain-Based Learning is defined as the teaching method and learning design that are based on how the brain learns, including cognitive development and the way the students learn differently as they mature socially, emotionally, and cognitively. It is the learning process that based on 12 principles as 1) Brain is a parallel processor 2) Learning engages the entire physiology 3) The search for meaning is innate 4) The search for meaning occurs through patterning 5) Emotions are critical to patterning 6) Every brain simultaneously perceives and creates parts and wholes 7) Learning involves both focused attention and peripheral attention 8) Learning always involves conscious and unconscious processes 9) We have at least two types of memory systems: spatial and rote learning 10) The brain understands and remembers best when facts and skills are 11) embedded in natural spatial memory and 12) Every brain is unique [4].

2.3 Multiple Intelligences

Multiple Intelligences refer the intelligence nature that learners use them to solve problems and construct various outcomes. Each individual learner has a different level of dependent multiple intelligences. This theory relates human potentials or abilities in as 8 intelligences as 1) Verbal/Linguistic Intelligence 2) Logical/Mathematical Intelligence 3) Visual/Spatial Intelligence 4) Bodily/Kinesthetic Intelligence 5) Musical Intelligence 6) Interpersonal Intelligence 7) Intrapersonal Intelligence and 8) Naturalist Intelligence [8].

3 Purposes

The research was aimed to study the effective utilization and procedures for model use of the constructivist web-based learning environment model to enhance human learning efficiency based on brain-based learning.

4 Research Methodology

4.1 Research Scope

The Model Research Type II consisting 3 phrases as Phrase 1 Model Development Phrase 2 Model Validation and Phrase 3 Model Use. However, this study, Phrase 3 Model Use was explored by Survey Research and Case Study in topics of 1) model use procedures 2) factors achieving model use and 3) achievements of model use which defined as (1) brain- based learning (BBL), (2) learner's multiple intelligence (ML), (3) relationship between ML and learning achievement, and (4) learner opinion. In addition, in phrase 1 Model Development, the survey of learners' context, analysis and synthesis of theoretical and designing frameworks as well as developing of the model (web-based learning environment) were conducted; while in phrase 2 Model Validation in terms of internal and external validation was examined.

4.2 Target Group

The target group was the 35 students majored Information and Technology who registered in English for Science course.

4.3 Research Design

Regarding Model Research Type II [1], research phrase 1 Model Use by Survey research and Case study was employed.

4.4 Research Instruments

To find the effective utilization and procedures for model use, various instruments were used.

1. The constructivist web-based learning environment model to enhance human learning efficiency based on brain-based learning was used as learning model. It resulted from the expert examining in research phrase 1 and 2.
2. A recording form used to record procedures of model use.
3. An interviewing form in unstructured interview style for the purpose of collecting learner's protocol in about model use.
4. Self-assessment report for learner's multiple intelligences. Since the human learning efficiency in this study was theoretically designed as learning achievement and multiple intelligences.
5. The achievement tests to evaluate their achievement in the course topic Dealing with Problem due to the analysis that human learning efficiency in this study was theoretically designed as learning achievement and multiple intelligences.

4.5 Data Collection and Analysis

The model was examined by the experts during phrase 1 and 2. To manage the classroom for data collection, 35 learners were grouped into 10 groups by 2, 3,4 members each. Then, the introducing was made by guiding the learner how to use the model and connecting their prior and new knowledge based on the topic Dealing with Problem. While they were using or learning with the model, the teacher acted as a coach to guide, enhance, and coach them to discover knowledge by themselves. In the end of the session, both teacher and learners together concluded the ideas that had made. After finished, they were assigned to do ML self- assessment report, and achievement test whereas the target had an interviewing of model use and learning process.

To analyze the data, descriptive analysis and interpreting methods were used to study the results of model use, learning process, and opinions meanwhile their ML data was studied by percentage, mean value, and standard deviation. Furthermore, the relationship between ML and achievement was done by Correlation Analysis.

5 Results

The study of the Effective Utilization of the Constructivist Web-Based Learning Environment Model to Enhance Human Learning Efficiency Based on Brain-Based Learning was found the results as the following:

5.1 Procedures of Model Use

The procedures of model use for the Constructivist Web-Based Learning Environment Model to Enhance Human Learning Efficiency Based on Brain-Based Learning resulted from the study of data scope, designing resources, product characteristics and model use as the following:

1. Data scope: learners per each learning group as is the appropriate number for learning with a computer [1]/time allocation for each class: 1.30 h based on the findings in phrase 1 that all procedures as lesson introducing, prior and new knowledge elaborating, model using with all 10 components, knowledge reflexing and cognitive structure.
2. Designing resources: that comprised a) media as text, pictures, video, animation, sound, and hypermedia based on media attributes b) technology as a computer supported multimedia and internet connection signal and c) computer programs and applications as Macromedia Flash, Macromedia Dreamweaver, Adobe Photoshop Illustrator, LINE, Facebook.
3. Product characteristics: product's types and content as the developed web-based learning environment model which consisted of 9 components as a) Problem base b) Resources c) Meaningful experiences base d) Collaboration base e) Relaxing Room f) Entertainment Corner g) Brain Gym h) Multiple Intelligences Room and i) Scaffolding bases; while the content was in Dealing with Problems topic.
4. Model use: the data was collected from recording forms along with the interviewing. 4 model use processes were explored as the following: a) they were introduced to the lesson and model by elaborating prior and new knowledge as a question to their daily online shopping problems. This was related to their real life which induced them to have advance organizer in lesson benefits and categorized their own cognitive structure b) The grouping of learners was fundamentally from Social constructivism theory in emphasizing 'Social context learning'. They could suddenly adjust their cognitive structure while having discussion in groups. Having 3 members showed the best learning outcome that assisted each other and had good achievement while having 2 members consumed much time and some members paid low attention in 4-member group c) Learning with the constructivism model by designed and developed components as 1) Problem base (2) Resources (3) Meaningful experiences base (4) Collaboration base (5) Relaxing Room (6) Entertainment Corner (7) Brain Gym (8) Multiple Intelligences Room and (9) Scaffolding bases could enrich them to be an active learner since they could be fostered by a problem and task while provided rich learning environments based on brain- based learning [4]. They discussed, discovered, worked in group while being in disequilibrium which the teacher guide as a coach and d) In the last step, teacher and

learners together conclude and reflex knowledge in various methods as presenting in Facebook group and reporting in class presentation where the teacher discussed, explained, and guided them to have and construct their own knowledge.

5.2 Factors Achieving Model Use

The characteristics context of a designer, developer, teacher, and learners were studied. They were found as the following: 1) Characteristics of a designer: the designer had experienced in instructional design in online platforms as well as background in constructivism learning, media and cognition, and advanced multimedia interaction. 5 designers worked as a team to design the suitable content, storyboard, and screens. 2) Characteristics of a developer: the developer had background in computer education and experienced in learning innovation and environments, worked with other 3 developers to develop the model by Macromedia Flash, Macromedia Dreamweaver, Adobe Photoshop Illustrator. 3) Characteristics of the learners: their context was researched by the questionnaires in phrase 1 and 2 which found that they had experience in traditional learning style as lecturing in a classroom but familiar with technology as a computer, mobile phone, tablet as well as digital literacy as using Microsoft Office, Google, YouTube, LINE, Facebook, and Email. However, a number showed that they had slight experience in learning with the constructivist web-based learning environment model based on brain-based learning as shown in Table 1.

5.3 Factors Achieving Model Use

The characteristics context of a designer, developer, teacher, and learners were studied. They were found as the following: 1) Characteristics of a designer: the designer had experienced in instructional design in online platforms as well as background in constructivism learning, media and cognition, and advanced multimedia interaction. 5 designers worked as a team to design the suitable content, storyboard, and screens. 2) Characteristics of a developer: the developer had background in computer education and experienced in learning innovation and environments, worked with other 3 developers to develop the model by Macromedia Flash, Macromedia Dreamweaver, Adobe Photoshop Illustrator and 3) Characteristics of the learners: their context was researched by the questionnaires in phrase 1 and 2 which found that they had experience in traditional learning style as lecturing in a classroom but familiar with technology as a computer, mobile phone, tablet as well as digital literacy as using Microsoft Office, Google, YouTube, LINE, Facebook, and Email. However, a number showed that they had slight experience in learning with the constructivist web-based learning environment model based on brain-based learning.

Table 1. Learner's experience.

Learning experience	Number (n)	Percentage (%)	
Learning theory			
Experience in lecturing, demonstration, and practicing	35	100	
Experience in constructivism learning	5	16.67	
Learning media			
Experience in web- based learning	7	23.33	
Experience in learning environment	11	36.67	
Experience in learning environment based on brain-based learning	2	6.67	
Technology Experience	$\bar{x}$	SD	Performance level
Experience in a computer, mobile, tablet	4.50	0.57	Very high
Expectations of learning	$\bar{x}$	SD	Performance level
Learner's expectations of learning	4.39	0.58	Very high

The achievements of model use in terms of brain- based learning (BBL), learner's multiple intelligence (ML), relationship between ML and learning achievement, and learner opinion as that: 1) Brain- based learning (BBL). The learners were interviewed to have their protocol which found that they had learned through the model by 12 BBL principle. For example, they could function better after moving bodies, playing physical games, exercising to reduce stress via brain functions that adrenaline and cortisol hormone reducing affected the brain capability to input energy as oxygen and sugar; based on [4]. The situations also made meaning that enhance learning based on the principle that brain is social interaction and 2) Learner's multiple intelligence (ML). They took MI Self- assessment learned with the model. The results were presented in Fig. 1.

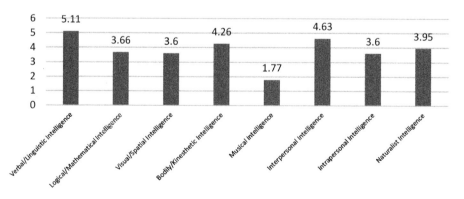

Fig. 1. Learner's multiple intelligence (ML).

The multiple intelligences of learners are illustrated in this table that their verbal/linguistic intelligence was the highest or $\bar{x} = 5.11$. 3) Relationship between learner's multiple intelligences and learning achievement. The data from the target was analyzed by Pearson product moment correlation coefficient as shown in Table 2.

Table 2. Relationship between learner's multiple intelligences and learning achievement.

Learner	X	Y	X^2	Y^2	XY
1	40	32	1600	1024	1280
2	40	32	1600	1024	1280
3	36	29	1296	841	1044
4	42	35	1764	1225	1470
5	32	24	1024	576	768
6	23	15	529	225	345
7	29	21	841	441	609
8	32	·23	1024	529	736
9	31	23	961	529	713
10	27	20	729	400	540
11	27	20	729	400	540
12	26	19	676	361	494
13	23	16	529	256	368
14	27	19	729	361	513
15	33	25	1089	625	825
16	31	23	961	529	713
17	31	23	961	529	713
18	33	24	1089	576	792
19	32	24	1024	576	768
20	26	19	676	361	494
21	30	22	900	484	660
22	33	25	1089	625	825
23	34	26	1156	676	884
24	26	18	676	324	468
25	25	17	625	289	425
26	31	22	961	484	682
27	25	18	625	324	450
28	26	19	676	361	494
29	30	22	900	484	660
30	27	19	729	361	513
31	32	24	1024	576	768
32	30	22	900	484	660
33	35	27	1225	729	945
34	27	20	729	400	540
35	38	30	1444	900	1140
Σ	1070	797	33490	18889	25119
r_{xy}			0.88		
$r2$			0.77		

The results found relationship between learner's multiple intelligences and learning achievement that Positive Correlations at 0.88 level or 0.88 statistical significance. The Correlation Coefficient was at 0.77 level ($r^2 = 0.77$) that means the ML value and achievement score had 77 percent of Covariance. 4) Learner opinion. The interview was implemented with the learners to have in-depth information based on 3 research opinion topics as content, web-based learning, and model design. *Aspect 1 Content*: they satisfied with the learning situations content which was related to real life. The content was categorized and inserted hyperlinks to multiple learning resources. It was also interesting by cartoons, animations, pictures, graphs, VDO. *Aspect 2 web-based learning*: the information was presented with architect design with categories. The icons, navigators, hypertext, hyperlinks, and hypermedia helped them to learn with ease while able to have discussion through Facebook and LINE. *Aspect 3 model design*: all components as Problem base, Resources, Meaningful experiences base, Collaboration base, Relaxing Room, Entertainment Corner, Brain Gym, Multiple Intelligences Room and Scaffolding bases could enhance them with ill-structure problem while able to discover and learn by learning resources. They could construct and related with the situation VDO in meaningful experience base. The relaxing room, brain gym, and entertainment corner provided physical activities that release stress and improve positive feelings. In addition, their MLs were enhanced through ML room where they could have collaboration with peers and a coach via chatroom and forum anytime.

6 Conclusions and Discussions

The effective utilization of the design and development of the constructivist web-based learning environment model to enhance human learning efficiency based on brain-based learning was examined by 1) model use procedures 2) factors achieving model use and 3) model use achievements which illustrated as brain- based learning (BBL), learner's multiple intelligence (ML), and learner opinions. The results showed procedures that are as 1) introducing learners to connect prior and new knowledge; 2) grouping them to share and elaborate thoughts; 3) learning with designed components and 4) reflexing knowledge. The model components as (1) Problem base (2) Resources (3) Meaningful experiences base (4) Collaboration base (5) Relaxing Room (6) Entertainment Corner (7) Brain Gym (8) Multiple Intelligences Room and (9) Scaffolding bases were designed which consistent with the study of [9]; and examined the internal and external validations [10, 11]. They were fundamental from psychological base, pedagogies base, learning base, media and technologies base, and contextual base [12] along with the context study in phrase 1 that found they experienced in lecturing and devices while requiring learning with technology enhance efficiency. The 12 BBL principles were enhanced to learners they could learn effectively based on brain processes. Linguistic intelligence showed the highest number among 8 ML, it seems they had improved language skills through the model. Furthermore, relationship between ML and achievement showed Positive Correlations which the ML affected achievement. Once the ML increased, the achievement consistently raised. For instance, the Cortex controls body movement while the model provides environments that they could exercise, the Occipital in Cerebral Cortex functions on visual processing and spatial circumstances. Finally, they satisfied with clear, direct, reachable, discoverable learning content, web-based learning, and model designed by pictures, animations, videos, graphs, navigators with icons and links. The designed and developed model could enhance their efficiency. It is recommended that other multiple intelligences should be fundamentally designed in the future study (Figs. 2 and 3).

Fig. 2. Multiple intelligences room. **Fig. 3.** Brain gym room.

References

1. Richey, R.C., Klein, J.: Design and Development Research: Methods, Strategies, and Issues. Lawrence Erlbaum Associates, Mahwah (2007)
2. Phanchan, T.: A comparative study of listening and speaking achievement of Matthayomsuksa four students of Rachineeburana school learning by using SON. Master's thesis, Silapakorn University, Nakhonpathom (2002)
3. Chaijaroen, S.: Educational Technology: Principles to Practice. Khon Kaen University, Khon Kaen (2008)
4. Caine, R.N., Caine, G.: Understanding a brain-based approach to learning and teaching. Educ. Leadersh. **48**, 66–70 (1990)
5. Mayer, R.E.: Learners as information processors: legacies and limitations of educational psychology's second metaphor. Educ. Psychol. **31**, 151–161 (1996)
6. Jonassen, D.H., Peck, K.L., Wilson, B.G.: Learning With Technology: A Constructive Perspective. Merrill, Upper Saddle River (1999)
7. Elliott, S.N., Kratochwill, T.R., Littlefield Cook, J., Travers, J.: Educational Psychology: Effective Teaching, Effective Learning. McGraw-Hill College, New York (2000)
8. Gardner, H.: Multiple Intelligences: The Theory in Practice. Basic Books, New York (1993)
9. Wannapipat., W., Chaijaroen, S.: Constructivist web-based learning environment model to enhance human learning efficiency based on brain-based learning: integrated with neuroscience. Dhammathas Acad. J. **17**, 155–176 (2017)
10. Khanjug, I., Chaijaroen, S.: The design of web-based learning environments enhancing mental model construction. Procedia Soc. Behav. Sci. **46**, 3134–3140 (2012)

11. Wattanachai, S., Chaijaroen, S., Poenimdang, C.: Design and development of constructivist web-based learning environment model to foster problem solving and transfer of learning. Acad. Serv. J. Prince Songkla Univ. **21**, 46–47 (2010)
12. Samat, C., Chaijaroen, S.: Design and development of learning environment to enhance creative thinking and innovation skills for teacher training in the 21st century. In: 23rd International Conference on Computers in Education, pp. 667–672. Asia-Pacific Society for Computers in Education, Ishikawa (2015)

Effects of AI Scaffolding on ZPD in MOOC Instructional RPGs

Clyde A. Warden[1] and Judy F. Chen[2(✉)]

[1] Marketing Department, National Chung Hsing University, Taichung, Taiwan
warden@dragon.nchu.edu.tw
[2] Business Administration Department, Overseas Chinese University, Taichung, Taiwan
jfc@ocu.edu.tw

Abstract. This study conducts development, application, and testing of artificial intelligence (AI) tools to both monitor learner ZPD and choose appropriate scaffolding for students in a large class, while students learn- by-doing through a Role Playing Game (RPG). Machine learning algorithms are developed and integrated into the cloud-based activity at both the individual and group level. Decision trees are developed that decide a range of scaffolding to supply individual learners and groups. Finally, data are tested across control and test groups. Research results show that learners in both the blended and fully online modalities accurately recall mere-exposure scaffolding (MES). Not only do learners recall seeing the MES, over the eight RPG rounds, they also accurately recall the main pedagogical message contained in the MES. Learners receiving MES in an online mode demonstrate more behaviors associating with the core pedagogical MES message content comparing to those in a blended mode. Fully online learners more frequently check their group's online RPG statistics and status information while also taking more time to prepare group attributes for a new RPG round.

Keywords: Communication skill · English for mechanical engineering · Workplace · English for specific purposes

1 Introduction

Use of groups and role-playing are common collaborative scaffolding approaches to facilitate self-regulated learning in blended and online modalities. We explore the efficacy of the well-known mere-exposure effect, where repeated minimal exposure increases positive affect, through the implementation of mere-exposure scaffolding (MES) in the form of low-cost, low-effort, digital messages focused on a core pedagogical goal. We test the effect of individual learner MES exposure on group collaborative behaviors across blended and fully online delivery modes—collecting group interactive behavioral trace data. Fully online groups receiving MES show behavior changes relating to the pedagogical message, while learners in the blended mode recall the MES message but do not change behaviors related to the MES message. Social network analysis shows the blended delivery mode constrains learners to follow established classroom norms—a concentrated social network with high connectivity. In contrast, the fully online mode, within a diffuse network, facilitates increased self-regulated learning that integrates the pedagogical goal targeted by the MES. Mere exposure is a well-established psychological effect that can change behavior through repeated exposure to a minimal stimulus [1, 2]. For this study, we combine mere exposure with scaffolding to implement *mere exposure scaffolding* (MES). This approach exposes learners to a core pedagogical goal attempting to positively influence group interactive behavior without curriculum revision. Through a rigorous experimental design collecting behavioral trace data, we test MES across blended and fully online modes. Social network analysis is employed to understand the implications of blended and fully online modalities, extending the work of Shu and Gu [3] who show differences in social patterns between face-to-face and blended instruction modes.

2 Literature Review

Administrators and instructors are confronted with the question of how much instructional scaffolding material to move online [4] as well as the differences in demands between blended and fully online modes [5, 6]. With decreasing face-to-face contact time and rising electronic mediation, instructors, and increasingly institutions, must consider the investments of time and money [7, 8]. Ever-increasing levels of support, both instructional and technical, need to be balanced against finite instructor and institutional time and resources [9, 10].

2.1 Scaffolding Through Mere Exposure Effect

The mere exposure effect (MEE) simply involves, "making a stimulus available to the individual's perception" even at a non-cognitive level [11]. This effect explains how repeated exposure increases a person's positive feeling for a stimulus. Children, for example, after systematic exposure to a particular food adjust their behavior to increase consumption of that specific food [12], while adults find familiar faces (repeated exposure) happier than novel ones [13]. The MEE is foundational and pervasive within the psychology domain, generally, and key to theories of attraction specifically [1, 2]. The effects of MEE are widely substantiated through numerous studies across diverse domains including diet [14, 15], ethics [16], and art criticism [17]. Currently, surprisingly little research or practice has focused on MEE in the education delivery context.

2.2 Collaborative Learning Partially and Fully Online

Support for individuals within groups to regulate the collaborative process is not well understood in the computer supported collaborative learning context [18]. Little data has been reported on the differences in social network dynamics between fully online and blended settings employing collaborative learning approaches. Classroom versus online interaction are shown to differ in their task emphasis through social network analysis [3]. This approach of social network analysis comes out of computer network research and is commonly combined with other research methods in studying networked and collaborative learning [19]. Although not yet widely used in educational research, this method is perfectly suited to analyzing group collaborative behaviors online, as in the current study.

2.3 Purpose of the Study

The goal of this study is to quantify the differential impact of MES on learner group social network tasks across fully online and blended instructional delivery methods. A rigorous research design tracks group-level behavior in the increasingly popular delivery modes of blended and fully online. This data collection approach avoids validity issues of survey approaches in favor of learner behavior trace data, an important trend in socially shared regulation of learning research [20]. Specifically, we explore the following research question:

Can individual exposure to MES, targeting a single pedagogical goal, affect group learning task social behaviors, related to the targeted goal, in blended and fully online class delivery modes?

3 Method

We design an experiment across two delivery formats, executing a university class focusing on skill acquisition. The current experimental class design results from a ten-year development cycle, iteratively adjusted for both blended and fully online delivery modes, integrating a role-playing game (RPG) where groups of learners seek to make virtual business agreements—a self-regulated learning context. Commercial negotiation is typical of business classes popular with non-business and business majors alike for the practical skill focus and cross-discipline applicability. The topic of commercial negotiation is a suitable research frame for the research question due the class emphasis on a clear pedagogical goal, task focus, and team-based behaviors, explained next.

The central pedagogical concept of negotiation is goal setting through planning, a skill that fits well within the average university undergraduate learner's zone of proximal development. While not a difficult skill to develop, it is not commonly associated with negotiation. This core concept is enacted through team planning. It is this core behavior of planning within a team that is adopted as the target behavior for the MES of this study to modify.

3.1 Self-regulated Learning Space

Numerous researchers have pointed out the common flow of role-playing games and self-regulated learning's stages of preparation, interaction, and reflection [21–25] as well as paralleling the spirit of Vygotsky's zone of proximal development scaffolding [26]. The negotiation RPG developed for this experiment draws heavily from pen-and-paper role-playing games, which is the genesis of modern video RPG games firmly embedded in the zeitgeists of Generation Z. For example, the most anticipated video game of 2020 is Cyberpunk 2077, directly adapted from and closely follows the pencil and paper RPG by Mike Pondsmith and starring Keanu Reeves—RPG video game production regularly cost as much as major Hollywood films to produce and generate similar profits for their game studios.

Role-playing games traditionally include the stages of genesis, i.e., character creation, (parallel to self-regulated learning's preparation), game world interaction and elaboration (matching self-regulated learning's interaction), and character realization, i.e., actualization, (analogous to self-regulated learning's reflection) [27]. The RPG gamemaster (GM), resembles an instructor, preparing fictional circumstances where players (learners) are free to interact and construct their own space [28, 29] and the gamemaster is the ultimate arbitrator of any disputes. Both blended and fully online learners, in groups simulating negotiation teams of virtual companies, interact with counterpart teams through the RPG, described next.

3.2 Instructional RPG Design

Like table-top RPGs, and the videogame genres they spawned, our simulated negotiation is mathematically based, involving learners in increasing levels of self-efficacy behaviors as they try to understand the implications of in-game decisions. We have observed behaviors similar to table-top RPG players who are highly involved in shaping their in-world characters attempting to achieve the maximum statistical advantage—a behavior called min-maxing.

Our experiment's RPG represents character class as either buyer or seller whose attributes are mirrored in product price and quality, production, inventory capacities, and delivery times. Lastly, buyers and sellers spend or accrue points in a system resembling RPG hero point game mechanics. These game intricacies increase task interdependency, improving player performance over extended iterations of play time [30]. The online context allows each negotiation RPG round to play out over a week, followed by instructor feedback and instruction, leading into the next negotiation round.

This study focuses on the impact of MES messages on behaviors and performance in blended and fully online modalities where learners are engaged in the negotiation RPG. The design differences between blended and fully online are limited to direct teacher contact, while the MES is distributed to a random selection of learners across both class designs. These experiment design details are covered next.

3.3 Common Class Design

The core instructional focus is on basic business concepts, fundamental negotiation strategies, and tactics. All instruction in the fully online class mode takes place through on-demand video lectures. Blended mode learners access the same materials, with review sessions held in the blended classroom. Identical online quizzes, through the semester, test lecture comprehension in both modalities over the 18-week semester.

Motivational and volitional e-mail (MVEM) [31, 32] is sent weekly email, following recommended design practice [32], updating and motivating students, keeping everyone on schedule, and supplying easy to use hyperlinks to class materials. A team of teaching assistants responds to any support request over email and the instant messaging platform Line.

3.4 MES Manipulation

We implement the MES (beginning with the third RPG) embedded within the weekly update email, sent to each individual learner. The MES manipulation includes an anamorphic animal graphic (400 × 200 pixels) with a speech balloon containing the phrase, "Winners Plan!" This message aligns with the core pedagogical target of planning before entering a negotiation and is quantified with the two variables of the RPG behavior tracking data (preparation stage). Learners in control groups receive the same email, but with a different animal graphic and no pedagogical MES in the speech balloon.

4 Measures

The current study relies on digital trace data from the online RPG [33, 34], an approach that is more accurate than self-reported behaviors [35, 36], generating learning analytics of actual behaviors and more actionable results [37, 38]. We collect six main variables of trace data across the three main phases of self-regulated learning (see Table 1).

Table 1. Study constructs and group RPG trace variables.

Construct	Trace variable	Explanation
Preparation		Intragroup behaviors of building RPG character (min-maxing)
	Assemble	Hours used to distribute points from dice roll to building the character skills
	Refresh	Times online group data is accessed by group members to review or modify
Interaction		Intergroup relationships
	Transact	Number of agreements (between buyers and sellers) over the six-day period
	Engage	Number of hours a group uses until their final deal over the six-day period
Reflection		Post-deal corrections and preparation for future rounds
	Adjust	Number of agreements canceled or nullified
	Parlay	Number of point donation to other groups

5 Results

Data from the six trace data variables are collected over eight iterations with 26 groups in the fully online mode ($n = 128$) and 12 groups in the blended mode ($n = 57$). In total, the groups completed 1,115 simulated business trades (587 fully online and 528 blended negotiation deals). Female learners account for 82% in the fully online mode and 59% in the blended mode all drawn from across a range of majors and grade levels. Crucial to the experiment is that the MES manipulation is received by test subjects, but not control, and test subjects do not communicate the MES content to control subjects, which we report next.

5.1 Manipulation Check

We check the manipulation through a question included in every weekly online quiz asking each respondent which animal he/she has seen inside class communications from the instructor, i.e., the MVEM.

5.2 Social Network Analysis

We next explore the influence of instructional delivery mode on group task social interaction. Our approach of social network analysis follows [3] analysis of communication patterns across instructional modalities. The first stage of social network analysis examines data from each game round followed by a global analysis, allowing comparison between the two modalities as groups experience a range of game roles (buyers versus sellers, weak versus strong starting positions, competitive advantage versus disadvantage). All network analysis uses the software R v3.5.3 [39] and the package igraph v1.2.4.1 [40].

5.3 RPG Round-Measures

Visual examination of 16 RPG network maps, through force-directed graphs, eight maps for each of the two delivery modes, shows a consistent difference between delivery modes and across the eight RPG rounds. The seventh RPG is typical of this difference (see Figs. 1 and 2), where the blended mode groups exhibit more interconnectivity and the fully online groups evidence more isolated arms (Edges connecting vertices are directed and the graphs are force-directed using Fruchterman-Reingold drawing algorithm layout). This tendency exists from the second RPG to the last. Figures 1 and 2 show, social network maps of RPG rounds including edges (trades) between vertices (groups). Vertices include direction (arrows) representing a group (e.g., Seller A) submitting a deal to a specified counterpart group (e.g., Buyer B). The counterpart (Buyer B) should also submit a deal in return (reciprocity) to the deal initiator (Seller A) in order to complete the deal. As Table 2 shows, during any single RPG round, reciprocity for both modalities approach unity (0 = no reciprocity and 1 = perfect reciprocity). This measure supports validity of the data collection as nearly every group who receives a connection reciprocates with one, i.e., a seller sells to a buyer and that buyer buys from that seller.

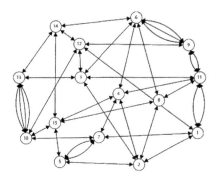

Fig. 1. Blended mode representative social network map (RPG round 7).

We next quantify levels of connectivity with the social network measures of edge density and mean distance. Edge density measures the percentage of total possible links made among vertices (groups), while mean distance is the average of the shortest number of vertices needed to pass through to reach any two vertices. The blended delivery mode groups end RPG 1 by making roughly the same proportion of connections (16%) as the fully online mode (14%). Afterwards, however, the blended mode groups make connections at two to three times higher a proportion than the fully online mode groups. Fully online groups appear to restrict interactions to a few counterparts, occasionally just one. This can be seen in Fig. 4's online mode with groups 19, 21, and 6. Although the fully online mode groups are making deals with fewer counterparts during any single RPG round, the question remains as to whether these groups are often the same, i.e., forming small subgroups or cliques. If so, the online mode is detrimental to the self-regulated learning goal of the RPG. Thus, we next test if the online mode groups are restricting interaction to small subgroups.

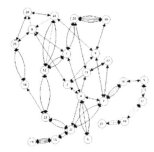

Fig. 2. Fully online mode representative social network map (RPG round 7).

5.4 Global Measures by RPG Mode

Edge density and transitivity measures are conducted with all the RPG rounds' data simultaneously, split by instructional delivery mode. Edge density for the fully online groups is 42% of all possible connections and 84% for the blended mode (see Table 2:

bottom line). This global result shows while the fully online groups make less connections during each round, ranging from 10–18%, they do not restrict their interactions to the same counterparts across every RPG round. Rather, fully online groups consider a range of participating groups as candidates for a transaction, although a narrower range compared to the blended mode groups.

Blended learners use the classroom to ease discovery when looking for counterparts. In contrast, fully online learners face one of the main challenges of online education—overcoming the distance between learners. Results show fully online mode group members use a range of online communication channels: Line (87%), email (51%), face-to-face (30%), Facebook messaging (20%), and the class supplied posting board (14%).

Table 2. Social network connectivity measures

	Edge density		Mean distance		Reciprocity		Transitivity	
	Fully online	Blended	Fully online	Blended	Fully online	Blended	Fully online	Blended
RPG1	.12	.27	3.31	2.75	.98	10	0	0
RPG2	.11	.31	4.50	2.28	.96	.91	0	0
RPG3	.15	.34	3.61	2.11	.97	.97	0	.03
RPG4	.16	.40	3.38	2.50	.99	10	0	0
RPG5	.11	.32	2.13	1.92	10	.99	.05	0
RPG6	.18	.38	3.58	2.37	.96	1	0	0
RPG7	.10	.43	3.48	1.94	.91	1	.07	0
RPG8	.42	.84	4.13	1.85	10	1	0	0
All RGPs	.12	.27	1.6	1.16	.97	.99	.52	.86

5.5 MES Uptake

For each class mode, digital trace data of the eight behavioral based variables in the RPG (assemble, refresh, transact, engage, adjust, parlay) are converted to the ordinal category values of low, medium, and high (a binning procedure based on standard deviation). All statistical tests employ chi-squared comparing the three discrete values between test and control groups independently for the two class modes—blended and fully online. Confirming test and control groups begin the experiment with equivalent behaviors, data from RPG rounds one and two are combined and tested. Before MES begins, both instruction delivery modalities exhibit no statistically significant difference between their respective test and control groups in any of the six measures. Digital trace data is combined from the third to the eighth RPG round to test for MES efficacy.

For the blended mode, no statistically significant result is exhibited between the test and control groups for any of the eight measures: assemble ($F = 1.52; p = .47$), refresh ($F = 3.1; p = .22$), transact ($F = 0.22; p = .9$), engage ($F = 1.4; p = .5$), adjust ($F = 0.58; p = .75$), and parlay ($F = .94; p = .63$).

For the fully online mode, two of the six variables are statistically significantly different, assemble ($F = 10.86$; $p = .004$) and refresh ($F = 8.2$; $p = .02$), as detailed in Table 3, while the remaining measures exhibit no impact from MES: transact ($F = 3.92$; $p = .14$), engage ($F = 1.32$; $p = .52$), adjust ($F = 1.97$; $p = .37$), and parlay ($F = 3.53$; $p = .17$).

Table 3. Statistically significant chi-squared results.

		Fully online mode					
		Refresh (times)			Assemble (hours)		
Mean (SD)		17.48 (13.26)			0.46 (0.61)		
p-value		< 0.05			< 0.01		
$x2$		8.2			10.86		
Cramer's V		0.23			0.27		
Level		No MES scaffold	MES scaffold	Marginals	No MES scaffold	MES scaffold	Marginals
Low	Observed	32	21	53	32	21	53
	Expected	24.28	28.72		24.28	28.72	
	Column %	45.07	25		45.07	25	
	Residual	7.72	-7.72		7.72	-7.72	
	Std. Residual	1.57	-1.44		1.57	-1.44	
	Adj. Residual	4.03	-3.4		4.03	-3.4	
Med.	Observed	17	35	52	17	35	52
	Expected	23.82	28.18		23.82	28.18	
	Column %	23.94	41.67		23.94	41.67	
	Residual	-6.82	6.82		-6.82	6.82	
	Std. Residual	-1.4	1.29		-1.4	1.29	
	Adj. Residual	-3.63	3.06		-3.63	3.06	
High	Observed	22	28	50	22	28	50
	Expected	22.90	27.1		22.90	27.1	
	Column %	30.99	33.33		30.99	33.33	
	Residual	-0.90	0.90		-0.90	0.90	
	Std. Residual	-0.19	0.17		-0.19	0.17	
	Adj. Residual	-0.5	0.42		-0.5	0.42	
Marginals		71	84	155	71	84	155

Learners in both the blended and fully online modalities accurately recall MES. Not only do learners recall seeing the MES, over the eight RPG rounds, they also accurately recall the main pedagogical message contained in the MES. Learners receiving MES in an online mode demonstrate more behaviors associating with the core pedagogical MES message content comparing to those in a blended mode. Fully online learners more frequently check their group's online RPG statistics and status information while also taking more time to prepare group attributes for a new RPG round. Both behaviors relate to the planning stage for the RPG. This result aligns with reports on mere exposure. While blended-mode learners did accurately recall the MES content, their group behaviors did not reflect any modification, which we examine next.

6 Conclusion

Teachers, administrators, and learners all face challenges from the unique aspects of the blended and fully online modalities—requiring careful scaffolding for self-regulated learning. Moving fully online presents a challenge to social capital [41] such that constructing learning spaces through peer support is problematic. We examine how the well-established mere exposure effect can be applied as educational scaffolding. While the MES affects learner behavior within the online mode, it does not show the same effect within the blended class. Within the online mode, exposure, to a fundamental pedagogical message results in learners exhibiting congruent behavior patterns.

The current study has numerous limitations. The current sample frame focuses on group work within an RPG. While role-playing is a common teaching practice, as is group work, it is not suitable for all instructional topics and MES may differ in its impact on other instructional approaches. Next, behavioral variables, in this study, are limited to the six collected through the group RPG interface Webpages. Other behaviors may be influenced by MES but are not currently measured.

Acknowledgment. The authors are grateful to the Ministry of Science and Technology of the Republic of China, Taiwan, for financially supporting this research under Contract No. MOST 108-2511-H-240-001 -.

References

1. Bornstein, R.F.: Exposure and affect: overview and meta-analysis of research, 1968–1987. Psychol. Bull. **106**, 265 (1989)
2. Montoya, R.M., Horton, R.S., Vevea, J.L., Citkowicz, M., Lauber, E.A.: A re-examination of the mere exposure effect: the influence of repeated exposure on recognition, familiarity, and liking. Psychol. Bull. **143**, 459 (2017)
3. Shu, H., Gu, X.: Determining the differences between online and face-to-face student–group interactions in a blended learning course. Internet High. Educ. **39**, 13–21 (2018)
4. Owston, R., York, D.N.: The nagging question when designing blended courses: does the proportion of time devoted to online activities matter? Internet High. Educ. **36**, 22–32 (2018)
5. Adekola, J., Dale, V.H., Gardiner, K.: Development of an institutional framework to guide transitions into enhanced blended learning in higher education. Res. Learn. Technol. **25**, 1973–1997 (2017)
6. Park, Y., Yu, J.H., Jo, I.H.: Clustering blended learning courses by online behavior data: a case study in a Korean higher education institute. Internet High. Educ. **29**, 1–11 (2016)
7. Roby, T., Ashe, S., Singh, N., Clark, C.: Shaping the online experience: How administrators can influence student and instructor perceptions through policy and practice. Internet High. Educ. **17**, 29–37 (2013)
8. Wingo, N.P., Peters, G.B., Ivankova, N.V., Gurley, D.K.: Benefits and challenges of teaching nursing online: exploring perspectives of different stakeholders. J. Nurs. Educ. **55**, 433–440 (2016)
9. Boling, E.C., Hough, M., Krinsky, H., Saleem, H., Stevens, M.: Cutting the distance in distance education: perspectives on what promotes positive, online learning experiences. Internet High. Educ. **15**, 118–126 (2012). https://doi.org/10.1016/j.iheduc.2011.11.006

10. Spector, J.M.: What makes good online instruction good?: new opportunities and old barriers. In: Visser, J., Visser-Valfrey, M. (eds.) Learners in a Changing Learning Landscape, pp. 251–266. Springer, Dordrecht (2008)
11. Zajonc, R.B.: Attitudinal effects of mere exposure. J. Pers. Soc. Psychol. **9**, 1 (1968)
12. Hausner, H., Olsen, A., Møller, P.: Mere exposure and flavour–flavour learning increase 2–3 year-old children's acceptance of a novel vegetable. Appetite **58**, 1152–1159 (2012)
13. Carr, E.W., Brady, T.F., Winkielman, P.: Are you smiling, or have I seen you before? Familiarity makes faces look happier. Psychol. Sci. **28**, 1087–1102 (2017)
14. Cooke, L.: The importance of exposure for healthy eating in childhood: a review. J. Hum. Nutr. Diet. **20**, 294–301 (2007)
15. Schaffhauser, D.: 06/11/15: Research: 6 in 10 Millennials Have "Low" Technology Skills. https://campustechnology.com/articles/2015/06/11/report-6-of-10-millennials-have-low-technology-skills.aspx. Accessed 15 Jul 2019
16. Kouchaki, M., Smith-Crowe, K., Brief, A.P., Sousa, C.: Seeing green: mere exposure to money triggers a business decision frame and unethical outcomes. Organ. Behav. Hum. Decis. Process. **121**, 53–61 (2013)
17. Hollingsworth, P.L.: The combined effect of mere exposure, counter attitudinal advocacy, and art criticism methodology on upper elementary and junior high students' affect toward art works. Stud. Art Educ. **24**, 101–110 (1983)
18. Järvelä, S., et al.: Socially shared regulation of learning in CSCL: understanding and prompting individual-and group-level shared regulatory activities. Int. J. Comput. Support. Collab. Learn. **11**, 263–280 (2016). https://doi.org/10.1007/s11412-016-9238-2
19. De Laat, M., Lally, V., Lipponen, L., Simons, R.-J.: Investigating patterns of interaction in networked learning and computer-supported collaborative learning: a role for social network analysis. Int. J. Comput. Support. Collab. Learn. **2**, 87–103 (2007). https://doi.org/10.1007/s11412-007-9006-4
20. Järvelä, S., Järvenoja, H., Malmberg, J.: Capturing the dynamic and cyclical nature of regulation: methodological progress in understanding socially shared regulation in learning. Int. J. Comput. Support. Collab. Learn. **14**(4), 425–441 (2019). https://doi.org/10.1007/s11412-019-09313-2
21. Cleary, T.J., Zimmerman, B.J.: Self-regulation differences during athletic practice by experts, non-experts, and novices. J. Appl. Sport Psychol. **13**, 185–206 (2001)
22. Kitsantas, A., Zimmerman, B.J.: Comparing self-regulatory processes among novice, non-expert, and expert volleyball players: a microanalytic study. J. Appl. Sport Psychol. **14**, 91–105 (2002)
23. Leggett, H., Sandars, J., Roberts, T.: Twelve tips on how to provide self-regulated learning (SRL) enhanced feedback on clinical performance. Med. Teacher **41**, 147–151 (2019)
24. Panadero, E.: A review of self-regulated learning: six models and four directions for research. Front. Psychol. **8**, 422 (2017)
25. Zimmerman, B.J.: Attaining self-regulation: a social cognitive perspective. In: Boekaerts, M., Pintrich, P.R., Zeidner, M. (eds.) Handbook of Self-Regulation, pp. 13–40. Academic Press, San Diego (2000)
26. Chaiklin, S.: The zone of proximal development in Vygotsky's analysis of learning and instruction. In: Kozulin, A., Gindis, B., Ageyev, V.S., Miller, S.M. (eds.) Vygotsky's Educational Theory in Cultural Context, pp. 39–64. Cambridge University Press, Cambridge (2003)
27. Bowman, S.L., Schrier, K.: Players and their characters in role-playing games. In: Zagal, J. P., Deterding, S. (eds.) Role-Playing Game Studies: A Transmedia Approach, pp. 395–410. Routledge (2018)

28. Bowman, S.L.: The Functions of Role-Playing Games: How Participants Create Community, Solve Problems and Explore Identity. McFarland & Company Inc. Publishers, Jefferson (2010)
29. Lankoski, P., Björk, S.: Game research methods: an overview. Lulu.com (2015)
30. Choi, B., Lee, I., Choi, D., Kim, J.: Collaborate and share: an experimental study of the effects of task and reward interdependencies in online games. CyberPsychol. Behav. **10**, 591–595 (2007)
31. Keller, J., Suzuki, K.: Learner motivation and e-learning design: a multinationally validated process. J. Educ. Media **29**, 229–239 (2004)
32. Kim, C., Keller, J.M.: Effects of motivational and volitional email messages (MVEM) with personal messages on undergraduate students' motivation, study habits and achievement. Br. J. Educ. Technol. **39**, 36–51 (2008)
33. Hernández-García, Á., Acquila-Natale, E., Chaparro-Peláez, J., Conde, M.Á.: Predicting teamwork group assessment using log data-based learning analytics. Comput. Hum. Behav. **89**, 373–384 (2018)
34. Lerche, T., Kiel, E.: Predicting student achievement in learning management systems by log data analysis. Comput. Hum. Behav. **89**, 367–372 (2018)
35. Emmerich, K., Bogacheva, N., Bockholt, M., Wendel, V.: Operationalization and measurement of evaluation constructs. In: Dörner, R., Göbel, S., Kickmeier-Rust, M., Masuch, M., Zweig, K. (eds.) Entertainment Computing and Serious Games. LNCS, vol. 9970, pp. 306–331. Springer, Cham (2016). https://doi.org/10.1007/978-3-319-46152-6_13
36. Zhou, M., Winne, P.H.: Modeling academic achievement by self-reported versus traced goal orientation. Learn. Instruct. **22**, 413–419 (2012)
37. Broadbent, J., Poon, W.: Self-regulated learning strategies & academic achievement in online higher education learning environments: a systematic review. Internet and High. Educ. **27**, 1–13 (2015)
38. Nistor, N., Hernández-Garcíac, Á.: What types of data are used in learning analytics? An overview of six cases. Comput. Hum. Behav. **89**, 335–338 (2018)
39. R Core Team: A language and environment for statistical computing. R Foundation for Statistical Computing, Vienna, Austria (2013)
40. Csardi, G., Nepusz, T.: The igraph software package for complex network research. InterJ. Complex Syst. **1695**, 1–9 (2006)
41. Coleman, J.S.: Social capital in the creation of human capital. Am. J. Sociol. **94**, S95–S120 (1988)

Survey Results of Learner Context in the Development of Constructivist Learning Environment Model to Enhance Creative Thinking with Massive Open Online Course (MOOCS) for Higher Education

Benjaporn Sathanarugsawait[1], Charuni Samat[2(✉)], and Suchat Wattanachai[3]

[1] Faculty of Education, Khon Kaen University, Khon Kaen, Thailand
[2] Division of Computer Education, Faculty of Education, Khon Kaen University, Khon Kaen, Thailand
thaibannok@hotmail.com
[3] Division of Surgery, Faculty of Veterinary Medicine, Khon Kaen University, Khon Kaen, Thailand

Abstract. One of the essential skills for learners in the 21st century learning era is creative thinking that can help them to be productive in innovations. This study aimed to study the context of learners in terms of learner characteristics, learning design, and factors influence their learning. The data can be fundamentally used in the model design and development process. Survey research was employed by using a survey form in Open-ended question with 5 Likert rating scales. The consistency in between theoretical framework and survey results was examined by the experts. The results were found in 6 aspects as 1) Demographics: 18 females and 12 males or 60 and 40% respectively 2) Learning experience: every learners or 100% had the experience in lecturing, demonstrating, and practice 3) Technology experience: the learners were in moderate level or as $\bar{x} = 3.01$, $S.D = 0.64$ 4) Creative thinking experience: the learners was in low level shown as $\bar{x} = 2.41$, $S.D = 0.56$ 5) Website design experience: presented value as $\bar{x} = 2.18$, $S.D = 0.55$ and 6) Learning expectation of learners: it was in very high level or $\bar{x} = 4.29$, $S.D = 0.58$. It thus revealed that they only had experience in traditional style while requiring to learn with media and technology as an active learner for knowledge construction and creative thinking developing.

Keywords: Learner context · Learning environment model · Constructivist · Creative thinking · MOOCs

1 Introduction

The 21st century learning skills are fundamental for the learners in this technology-based era which the skills of creativity and innovation are particularly emphasized. Since the ability to think creatively is one of the underlying patterns of invention which is important to living among multiple real-world situations [1]. The enhancing of creative thinking as divergent thinking is beneficial to people to think with fluency, flexibility, originality, and elaboration [2]. This can be the preparation of a learner for the complex and competitive working environments.

The world nowadays has been changing in many ways including learning paradigm. Conversely, in the past, a classroom could be a passive classroom where they acted as an inactive learner while the teacher transmitted the knowledge in front of the class. On the contrary, a learning theory as Constructivist believes that knowledge is dynamic which learner's cognitive structure is provoked to be disequilibrium; and it requires assimilation and accommodation processes for their prior and new knowledge as the learner has to be an active learner [3]. The role of teacher is as a coach who helps them to be able to learn by their own. Significantly, Massive Open Online Courses or MOOCs are one of the outstanding trends in higher education in current years [4]. It is open learning system which unlimited learners can access to learn via online platforms with flexible time and place [5]. MOOCs can enhance life-long education that related technologies due to their content creation and delivery in forms of flexible learning styles with preferable classes with own place and time to study [6].

As mentioned earlier, the study of learner context was implemented for the purpose of developing the Constructivist Learning Environment Model to Enhance Creative Thinking with Massive Open Online Course (MOOCS) for Higher Education to advantage learners to construct their own knowledge to think and invent creatively.

2 Literature Review

2.1 Constructivist Learning Theory

Learning is the way the learners construct knowledge, think, and learn through experience [7]. In addition, Constructivist learning is to construct knowledge for each individual appropriateness more than to perceive it. Learning environment is essential to make the knowledge meaningful as well as being an active learner [8].

2.2 MOOCs

Massive Open Online Courses or MOOCs is defined as the open learning system which widely provided and accessed to unlimited learner amount to enroll in a class and learn through online platform with time and place flexibility [5]. The learners can learn by video lectures or video-based instructional content, classroom note, discussion forum and finally be graded by a computer-based.

2.3 Creative Thinking

Creative thinking is the ability to think which defined as the cognitive process that as Divergent Thinking. It is the thinking in various ways that each person connects, adjusts, integrates prior knowledge into new ideas. Creative thinking comprises

Fluency, Flexibility, Originality, and Elaboration [2, 9]. Creative thinking can promote a learner innovation and creativity in the 21st century [10].

3 Purposes

This study aimed to study the context of learners defined to characteristics and learning design of the learners as well as factors influenced their learning. Their results could be used in the design and development of constructivist learning environment model to enhance creative thinking with massive open online course (MOOCs) for higher education.

4 Method and Result

4.1 Scope of Research

The Model Research [13] with 3 phases which Phases 1 Model Development was employed. The results were the fundamental data in other 2 phases as Phases 2 Model Validation and Phases 3 Model Use. Regarding the scope of these phases, Survey method was conducted to collect data of learner context as the basis in the design and development process of the model development.

4.2 Target Group of the Study

The target group was the 30 higher education students who registered in Web Design and Development for Digital Business course, Sripatum University Khon Kaen Campus, Thailand.

4.3 Research Design

Research Phases 1 Model development was employed by Survey research. The Survey Research was implemented for both qualitative and quantitative data. The questionnaire was used to examine 1) learning context 2) learner characteristics and 3) factors influenced learning in aspects of 1) Demographics 2) Learning experience 3) Technology experience 4) Creative experience 5) Website design experience and 6) Learner's expectation towards learning.

4.4 Research Instruments

The instruments used in the study was the survey used to study context of the learners who studied in Web Design and Development for Digital Business course. Which purposive to examine 1) learning context and 2) learner characteristics. There were 3 developing processes as 1) synthesize and set up basis conceptual framework 2) align the summarized data of the framework with the questions to be used in the survey and 3) construct the context survey. The 7 following question groups were developed as 1) Demographics 2) Learning experience 3) Technology experience 4) Creative experience 5) Website design experience and 6) Learner's expectation towards learning. The survey was in Likert ration scales in 5 scales (5 = very high, 4 = high, 3 = neutral, 2 = low, 1 = very low).

4.5 Data Collection and Analysis

The constructed survey was used to collect data in areas of learner characteristics, learning style, and factors affected learning. The forms were allocated to students by the link via google form. After two weeks, the data was collected and analyzed by statistics as percentage, mean score, and standard deviation.

5 Research Results

The results revealed the learning context, learner characteristics and factors influenced learning in aspects of 1) Demographics 2) Learning experience 3) Technology experience 4) Creative experience 5) Website design experience and 6) Learner's expectation towards learning as the following.

- Aspect 1 Demographics

    They were 18 males and 12 females or 60 and 40%, respectively.

- Aspect 2 Learning experience (Table 1)

Table 1. Learning experience.

Learning experience	Number (n)	Percent (%)
Learning theory		
Experience in lecturing, demonstration, and practicing	30	100
Experience in design thinking, decision making, and meaning making based on multiple situations	25	83.33
Experience in discovery learning and self-knowledge construction	20	66.67
Experience in constructivism learning	7	23.33
Learning media		
Experience in web-based learning	7	23.33
Experience in learning environment	11	36.67
Experience in learning environment enhancing creative thinking	10	33.33
Experience in MOOCs enhancing creative thinking	5	16.67
Learning model		
Experience in problem-based learning	5	16.67
Experience in learning style enhancing creative thinking	7	23.33
Experience in collaborative learning	13	43.33
Experience in Massive Open Online Course (MOOCS)	6	20.00
Experience in Massive Open Online Course (MOOCS) enhancing creative thinking	2	6.67

The data in Table 2 presented that all 30 learners or 100% had experience in lecturing demonstration, and practicing while 25 learners or 83.33% experienced in design thinking, decision making, and meaning making based on multiple situations and 66.67% or 20 learners used to have discovery learning and self-knowledge construction.

- Aspect 3 Technology experience

Table 2. Technology experience

Technology experience	$\bar{x}$	S.D	Performance level
Use of technology device			
Ability to use a desktop computer	4.57	0.50	Very good
Ability to use a laptop computer	3.97	0.67	Good
Ability to use a smart phone	4.43	0.77	Very good
Ability to use a tablet	2.83	0.53	Moderate
Total	3.95	0.62	High
Use of technology for knowledge construction enhancing			
Ability to use Wordpress program to construct knowledge and design a website	2.07	0.69	Poor
Ability to use Wix program to construct knowledge and design a website	1.93	0.83	Poor
Total	2.00	0.76	Poor
Use of technology to explore knowledge			
Ability to use Google search engine for knowledge survey	4.40	0.56	Very good
Ability to use Bing web browser for knowledge survey	3.03	0.85	Moderate
Ability to use Yahoo search engine for knowledge survey	2.90	0.66	Moderate
Total	3.44	0.69	Good
Use of technology as learning context to enhance action learning			
Ability to use Adobe Dreamweaver software for practicing and build a website design	2.63	0.56	Moderate
Ability to use Weebly software for practicing and build a website design	2.73	0.74	Moderate
Total	2.68	0.65	Moderate
Use of technology to as social media fora conversation and knowledge sharing			
Ability to use Facebook application for making a conversation and knowledge sharing	3.73	0.45	Good
Ability to use Line application for making a conversation and knowledge sharing	3.77	0.57	Good
Ability to use E-mail for making a conversation and knowledge sharing	4.07	0.52	Good
Total	3.86	0.51	Good

(*continued*)

Table 2. (*continued*)

Technology experience	$\bar{x}$	S.D	Performance level
Use of technology to reflex thinking			
Ability to create Vlog to present ideas	2.33	0.66	Poor
Ability to create Web Blogger to create a mind map and present ideas	2.03	0.56	Poor
Total	2.18	0.61	Poor
All total	3.01	0.64	Moderate

The results of learner context in technology experience were found that in moderate level or $\bar{x} = 3.01$, $S.D = 0.64$ which the highest value of performance level in use of technology device is $\bar{x} = 3.95$, $S.D = 0.62$, use of technology to as social media for a conversation and knowledge sharing is $\bar{x} = 3.86$, $S.D = 0.51$, and use of technology to explore knowledge is $\bar{x} = 3.44$, $S.D = 0.69$ respectively.

- Aspect 4 Creative thinking experience

Table 3. Creative thinking experience

Creative thinking experience	$\bar{x}$	S.D	Performance level
Fluency			
Ability to create numerous conceptual thinking and solution in limited time	2.73	0.58	Moderate
Flexibility			
Ability to differentiate or select other thinking solution for the purpose of usefulness in various ways	2.40	0.62	Poor
Originality			
Ability to produce ideas that different to the original thinking by adjusting and applying and that for an inventing	2.23	0.5	Poor
Elaboration			
Ability to generate details or solution with information to completely improve or elaborate main ideas	2.27	0.52	Poor
Total	2.41	0.56	Poor

This Table 3 illustrates the overall performance level of a learner in creative thinking skills for all those four thinking characteristics that in poor level which is $\bar{x} = 2.41$, $S.D = 0.56$. Their ability to think as Originality is at $\bar{x} = 2.23$, $S.D = 0.50$, Elaboration is $\bar{x} = 2.27$, $S.D = 0.52$, Flexibility is $\bar{x} = 2.40$, $S.D = 0.62$, and Fluency is $\bar{x} = 2.73$, $S.D = 0.58$ respectively.

- Aspect 5 Website Design Experience (Table 4)

Table 4. Website design experience

Website design experience	$\bar{x}$	S.D	Experience level
Experience in website design learning	2.07	0.52	Low
Experience in website design	2.27	0.52	Low
Experience in website design for added value in business	2.17	0.59	Low
Experience in website design by using an application	2.23	0.57	Low
Total	2.18	0.55	Low

The overall experience level of a learner in website design experience is in low level which the experience in website design learning showed the lowest value as $\bar{x} = 2.07$, $S.D = 0.52$.

- Aspect 6 Learner Expectation of Learning (Table 5)

Table 5. Learner expectation of learning

Learners expectations of learning	$\bar{x}$	S.D	Expectation level
Content			
Expectation to have learning content that can be used in daily life	4.43	0.57	Very high
Expectation to have various interesting content forms	4.27	0.52	Very high
Expectation to have content in categories under learning topics	4.37	0.67	Very high
Expectation to have the clear content and consistent with learning topics	4.50	0.57	Very high
Total	4.39	0.58	Very high
Learning styles			
Expectations to have problem-based learning for knowledge discovery and construction	4.00	0.64	High
Expectations to have group-based learning to interchange knowledge in a classroom and outside classroom	4.43	0.63	Very high
Expectations to have the flexible and various learning environment depends on interest	4.47	0.51	Very high
Expectations to have a coach who can give a guideline closely	3.93	0.64	High
Expectations to have learning style enhancing creative thinking	4.23	0.63	Very high
Total	4.21	0.61	Very high
Media and technology			
Expectations to have web-based learning	4.27	0.45	Very high
Expectations to learn with e-books	4.33	0.66	Very high
Expectations to learn with an application	4.10	0.61	High
Total	4.23	0.57	Very high

(*continued*)

Table 5. (*continued*)

Learners expectations of learning	$\bar{x}$	S.D	Expectation level
Evaluation			
Expectations to have an evaluation based on learning activities and learner's development	4.23	0.57	Very high
Expectations to have a guideline for learning outcomes	4.17	0.59	High
Expectations to have the clear and precise evaluation	4.13	0.63	High
Expectations to have feedback for self-improvement	4.30	0.60	Very high
Expectations to have different evaluation methods	4.37	0.49	Very high
Total	4.24	0.58	Very high
Teacher			
A teacher is expected to design learning based on curriculum in a variety that consistent with each learner's difference	4.33	0.61	Very high
A teacher is expected to promote learning by doing for knowledge construction	4.43	0.57	Very high
A teacher is expected to provide numerous and closeable courses based on their interest	4.40	0.56	Very high
Total	4.39	0.58	Very high
All	4.29	0.58	Very high

The overall of learner expectation of learning is in very high level which is as $\bar{x} = 4.29$, $S.D = 0.58$. In addition, the expectations in teacher and content was found in same very high level or as $\bar{x} = 4.39$, $S.D = 0.58$.

6 Conclusions and Discussion

Regarding the results, they were found that in Aspect 1 Demographics that most of the learners was male or 60% out of all 30 learners. To deeply consider in each aspect, Aspect 2 Learning experience which examine 1) Learning theories 2) Learning media and 3) Learning model, it was found that every learner had the experience in lecturing based learning which possibly that they were familiar with the traditional learning style. This can be the passive class that does not enrich them to be an active learning in discovery learning and hence construct their knowledge. In contrast, not a vast number of them experienced in Constructivist learning, web-based learning, learning environment enhancing creative thinking, MOOCs enhancing creative thinking, and MOOCs. This obvious difference could be used in the design and development of this study since the attributions of MOOCS that provides video lectures and class note could be an familiarity for them while experience in such collaborative-based learning could be fundamental to enhance them to learn collaboratively. As well, the principles of active learning would be emphasized to foster them to learn among Constructivist learning environments. Aspect 3) Technology experience, their experience level was in the moderate level which they could use a personal computer and notebook, tablet, and smart phone to learn through Facebook, LINE, and email as well as to discover learning by search engine as Google; however; Wordpress, Wix, Dreamweaver were not the programs for website design that they were familiar with. Hence, to design the learning environment model should base on media attributions of such Facebook, LINE, email that allow them to share and assimilate prior and new knowledge through collaboration as discussion. Technology can foster learner's creative thinking for meaning making [11]. Aspect 4 Creative experience, the outstanding data showed that they had low performance level of all 4 creative thinking characteristics as 1) Fluency 2) Flexibility 3) Originality and 4) Elaboration based on Guilford [10]. Similarly, the number of the results presented the low level of their experience Website design experience or Aspect 5. This supported the importance of the learning environment model development to enhance learner's creative thinking. In the final part, Aspect 6 Learner's Expectation towards Learning, they desired to have learning environment in terms of Content, Learning Style, Media and Technology, Assessment, and Teachers that the content needs to be various, adaptive and updated, categorized and consistent. Furthermore, it should provide problem based and group activity that allows them to discover and construct knowledge among cognitive friends. As well, the flexible and ubiquitous learning was required since they could learn by their comfortable time and place along with coaching. They strongly expected to be enhanced by creative thinking learning. Moreover, web-based learning, e-book, and learning applications were the suggested platforms to develop and assess learning performance. Hence, Massive open online course (MOOCs) can be used to promote the creative thinking of learners by interacting with the learning environment [12].

Acknowledgement. This research was supported by Ph.D. Program in Educational Technology, Faculty of Education, Khon Kaen University, and Research Group for Innovation and Cognitive Technology, Khon Kaen University which here by giving the thankfulness all through this.

References

1. P21-The Partnership for 21st Century Learning. P21 Framework Definitions (2015). http://www.p21.org/storage/documents/docs/P21_Framework_Definitions_New_Logo_2015.pdf
2. Guilford, J.P.: The Nature of Human Intelligence. McGraw-Hill Book Company, New York (1967)
3. Piaget, J., Cook, M.T.: The Origins of Intelligence in Children. International University Press, New York (1952)
4. Baturay, M.H.: An overview of the world of MOOCs. Procedia - Soc. Behav. Sci. **174** (2015), 427–433 (2015)
5. Kaplan, A.M., Haenlein, M.: Higher education and the digital revolution: About MOOCs, SPOCs, social media, and the Cookie Monster. Bus. Horiz. **59**(4), 441–450 (2016). https://doi.org/10.1016/j.bushor.2016.03.008
6. Dasarathy, B., Fisher, D.H.: The past, present, and future of MOOCs. In: Proceedings FOSE 2014: Future of Software Engineering Proceedings, May 2014, pp. 212–224 (2013). https://doi.org/10.1145/2593882.2593897
7. Jonassen, D.H., Peck, K.L., Wilson, B.G.: Learning with Technology: A Constructive Perspective. Prentice Hall, Upper Saddle River (1999)

8. Chaijaroen, S., et al.: Educational technology theories and approach into practice. Klaungnana-wittaya, Khon Kaen (2008)
9. Wadsworth, B.J.: Piaget's Theory of Cognitive and Affective Development: Foundations of Constructivism. Longman, New York (2004)
10. Samat, C., Chaijaroen, S.: Design and development of learning environment to enhance creative thinking and innovation skills for teacher training in the 21st century. In: The 23rd International Conference on Computers in Education, ICCE, pp. 667–672 (2015)
11. Kwanman, T., Samat, C.: Design framework of constructivist mobile application learning environment to foster creative thinking on basic photography skill for high school students. In: Journal of Physics: Conference Series, International Annual Meeting on STEM Education (I AM STEM), Avani Khon Kaen Hotel, Thailand, 13–15 August 2018, vol. 1340 (2018)
12. Sathanarugsawait, B., Samat, C.: Synthesis of theoretical framework of constructivist creative thinking massive open online courses (MOOCs) for higher education. In: Wu, T.-T., Huang, Y.-M., Shadieva, R., Lin, L., Starčič, A.I. (eds.) ICITL 2018. LNCS, vol. 11003, pp. 146–150. Springer, Cham (2018). https://doi.org/10.1007/978-3-319-99737-7_14
13. Richey, R.C., Klein, J.: Design and Developmental Research. Lawrence, New Jersey (2007)

The Development of Constructivist Web-Based Learning Environments to Enhance Learner's Information Processing and Reduce Cognitive Load

Nat Chaijaroen, Sarawut Jackpeng, and Sumalee Chaijaroen[✉]

Department of Educational Technology, Khon Kaen University, Khon Kaen, Thailand
Nat_ch@kkumail.com, Sumalee@kku.ac.th

Abstract. Nowadays information processing is human internal process which essential in information transferring. This procedure first begins in sensory memory, then short-term memory and encoded into long-term memory. The study aimed to synthesize the theoretical and designing frameworks of the constructivist web-based learning environment model to enhance learner's information process and reduce cognitive load. Model Research Type I Model Development [1] was employed by Document Analysis. Data collection processes were conducted by 1) reviewing and analyzing related theories as well as research 2) examining instructional context and 3) synthesizing theoretical and designing frameworks. The results showed that frameworks comprised 5 basis and 4 components. Those 5 bases were as 1) Psychological 2) Pedagogical 3) Information processing and cognitive load 1 4) Media theory and technological and 5) Instructional context bases while 4 model components were to 1) activate structure of cognition 2) boost the equilibrium of cognition 3) strengthen the construction of knowledge and 4) supporting and fostering knowledge construction which all by promoting information processing and decreasing level of cognitive load. In addition, 7 model elements were explored as (1) Problem Base (2) Vocabulary Plaza (3) Brainstorming Center (4) Center of Information Processing Enhancing and Cognitive Load Reducing (5) Friendly Cognitive Tool (6) Center of Scaffolding and (7) Coaching Desk. Hence, the designed constructivist learning environment model can help learners to enhance learner's information process and reduce cognitive load.

Keywords: Web-based learning environments model · Constructivist theories · Information processing theory · Cognitive load reducing

1 Introduction

The changed the society world and the advanced technology entering the Information and Knowledge Society affect the globalization society. Access to information is an important factor that differentiates the status and quality of education. Which changed the humans need to learn for life-long learning, especially 21st century. The role and importance of technology will increase. The new generation will grow with technology.

Thailand today, enters the Thailand 4.0 era, Thailand has driven by intensive digital technology and innovation to enhance the country's economic development, so therefore education is necessary. Developing human potential to enter the learning society is therefore a tool used to capture the enormous amount of information and knowledge that comes with today's technology.

According to the current problem situation, the quality of education and learning of Thai humans is still quite low. Although, now these people have higher educational opportunities, which the average number of academic years in the labor age population aged 15–59 years continuously increasing 9.3% in 2015. Learning problem in Thailand shows average English score of Grade 6 student of the O-Net test in 2016 at 34.59 scores [2]. The 2017 survey of English language proficiency index of Thai humans by Education First (EF) in the world was ranked the 56th [3]. Also, the placement test of English was revealed very low proficiency level [4]. From the above described, it showed that Thai humans must improve English skill. An important way to help solve this problem is student-centered learning. The development of learners with this rapid social change include the method related pedagogical theories and principles such as Constructivism theory which encourage students to create self-knowledge and the information processing which help the student to record and retrieve in long term memory, especially English vocabulary. The English vocabulary is not native language for Thai human, and it is the important foundations in the create sentence. So, if Thai humans cannot record recall vocabulary, they cannot be able to learn English efficiency.

Cognitive load theory [5] is mainly about decreased internal while information processing in working memory (exceed limit or 7 ± 2). Including media featured and symbol systems, which showed in hypertext, hyperlink, and hypermedia help to enhance information processing that focus on cognitive process and reduce cognitive load.

All the above reasons, the researcher is interested to study for synthesizing the theoretical framework, especially in learning that required memory such as English vocabulary, which results in the learners developing language as well.

2 Research Methodology

The Model research phase I: Model development was employed in this study.

2.1 Research Objective

The objective of research was to synthesize the theoretical and designing framework of the constructivist web-based learning environment model.

2.2 Target Group

This groups consisted as following;

1. 9 experts for evaluation of model quality consists 3 experts for evaluation of the model content, 3 experts for evaluation of the media quality, and 3 experts for model designing by used ID theory.
2. 3 experts for evaluation of instrument
3. 30 students from grade 11 of Demonstration school, Khon Kaen University
4. 1 model designer for evaluation of model designer characters
5. 1 model developer for evaluation of model developer characters
6. 1 English teacher for evaluation of his characters

2.3 Research Instruments

The instruments consisted as follows;

- Instrument for synthesize and analyzed the theoretical and designing framework
- And survey form for the experts to used evaluation of 3 domains of the theoretical framework qualities, such as media, contents, and instructional design.

2.4 Data Collecting and Analysis

The data of synthesized and developed this theoretical framework was collected as follows;

1. To analyze and review the matter
2. To literature review related research
3. To explore instructional context
4. To synthesize and developed theoretical and designing framework

Then, they were analyzed the principles & theories and research. Finally, the quality of the theoretical framework was assessed analyzed by experts used method of data summarization and interpretation.

3 Research Result

The theoretical framework consists of 5 bases, as follows;

1. Basic of learning psychology
2. Basic teaching sciences
3. Basic information processing
4. Fundamental of media theory
5. Basic contextual (see Fig. 1)

The first phase for development is the synthesizing and developing of the designing framework. The results revealed that 4 stages as following;

Activating Cognitive Structure and Enhancing Information Processing with Reducing Cognitive Load. In this process was activating cognitive structure. The Cognitive Constructivism theory by Piaget [7] said that the learner who is stimulated with situation problems and leaded to make them disequilibrium, then they need try

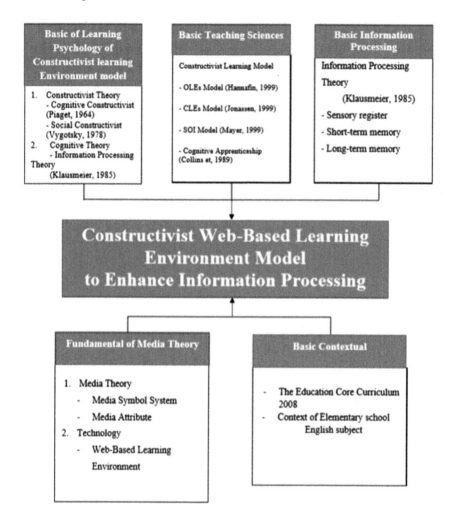

Fig. 1. Theoretical framework of constructivist web-based learning environment model to enhance learner's information processing and reduce cognitive load.

into equilibrium. The information processing theory [6] consisted of 3 processes: sensory register, short-term memory, and long-term memory with retrieved. The SOI model [6], which consists 3 processes in order to select, organize and integrate information. Furthermore, cognitive load theory by Sweller, chunking method, hierarchical network and Schema theory were used for designing the components called Problem base (see Fig. 2).

Supporting Cognitive Equilibrium and Enhancing Information Processing Along with Reducing Cognitive Load. After disequilibrium learner's cognitive structure, they need to adjust to equilibrium. The information processing Klausmeier [6] helps learners. Cognitive load theory [5] was used to design to reduce external cognitive load, such as chucking principle, which reduced the over limited English. Moreover,

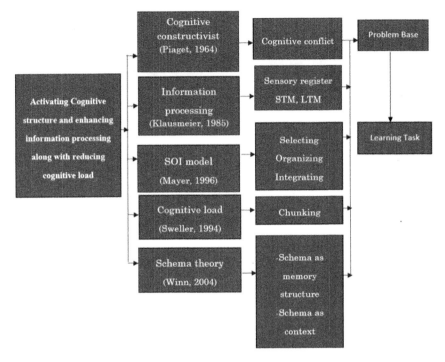

Fig. 2. The problem base.

SOI model and Schema were used to design information into component Vocabulary bank (see Fig. 3).

Enhancing Knowledge Construction and Enhancing Information Processing with Reducing Cognitive Load. Theory of social constructivism works collaboratively via sharing their multi-experiences and change their misconception including improve cognition. All mentioned, Brainstorming center was designed. Cognitive Theory [5] and SOI model enhance learners to store memory. OLEs [8] is a form of learning management together with technology that focus on student-center who promote knowledge building. The component was Cognitive tool center (see Fig. 4).

Supporting and Fostering Knowledge Construction. However, some learners may not construct knowledge by themselves or under the zone proximal development. The social constructivism theory [10] and principle of Open Learning Environments (OLE) [9] including 4 scaffolding were used to design the "Scaffolding center". Cognitive Apprenticeship [11] is a theory process that an expert of teaching skills to an apprentice. It was to use to design the "Coaching center" (see Fig. 5).

The theoretical framework of web-based learning environment model as following bases: 1) Psychological base 2) Pedagogical base 3) Information processing and cognitive load 4) Media theory and technology 5) Instructional Context The bases were used to design the model 7 components which comprised (1) Problem bases (2) Vocabulary bank (3) Collaboration center (4) Cognitive tools center (5) Center

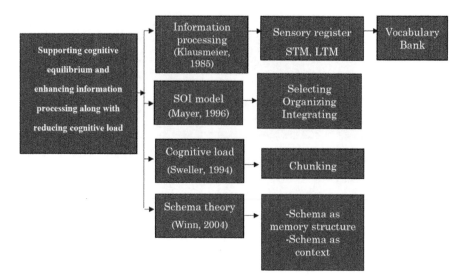

Fig. 3. The Learning Resources (Vocabulary bank).

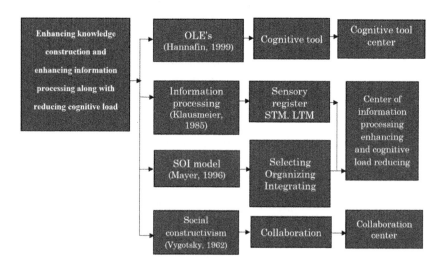

Fig. 4. The cognitive tools, enhance information processing, and collaboration center.

information processing enhancing and cognitive load reducing (6) Scaffolding center and (7) Coaching center.

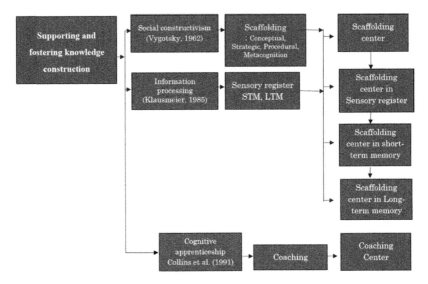

Fig. 5. The scaffolding and coaching center.

4 Discussion and Conclusion

The result of synthesis and development the theoretical framework to enhance learner's information processing and reduce cognitive load such as English vocabulary comprised 4 processes and 7 components as above described.

This research results congruent with [12], [13], and [14], was shown that theoretical and Designing framework to enhance learner's information processing reduce cognitive load which may help learners to remember English vocabulary and to be able to use.

Acknowledgements. This research was supported by Ph.D. Program in Educational Technology, Faculty of Education, Research Group for Innovation and Cognitive Technology, Khon Kaen, University, and Research and Technology Transfer Affairs Division, Khon Kaen University.

References

1. Richey, R.C., Klein, J.D.: Design and Development Research Methods, Strategies and Issues. Lawrence Erlbaum Associates, New Jersey (2007)
2. Ministry of Education: National Institute of Educational Testing Service 2014. Ministry of Education, Bangko2k, Thailand (2014)
3. The Nation: Thailand ranks near bottom in English proficiency: survey (2013)
4. Sritiwong, U.: Using school newspaper project to promote english writing ability and self-efficacy of mathayom suksa 6 Students. Thai thesis database, Bangkok, Thailand (2542)

5. Sweller, J.: Cognitive load theory. In: Mestre, J.P., Ross, B.H. (eds.) The Psychology of Learning and Motivation, vol. 55. The Psychology of Learning and Motivation: Cognition in Education, pp. 37–76 (2011)
6. Klausmeier, H.J.: Educational Psychology, 5th edn. Harper & Row, New York (1985)
7. Piaget, J.: Part I: cognitive development in children: Piaget development and learning. J. Res. Sci. Teach. **2**, 176–186 (1964)
8. Mayer, R.E.: Designing instruction for constructivist learning. In: Reigeluth, C.M. (ed.) Instructional Design Theories and Models Volume II: A New Paradigm of Instructional Theory. Lawrence Erlbaum Associates, New York (1999)
9. Hannafin, M., Land, S., Oliver, K.: Open learning environments: foundations, methods, and models. In: Reigeluth, C.M. (ed.) Instructional Design Theories and Models Volume II: A New Paradigm of Instructional Theory. Lawrence Erlbaum Associates, New York (1999)
10. Vygotskie, L.S.: Mind in Society: The Development of Higher Psychological Processes. Persons and Their Minds. Harvard University Press, Cambridge (1978)
11. Brown, J.S., Collins, A., Duguid, P.: Situated cognition and the culture of learning. Educ. Res. **18**, 32–42 (1989)
12. Kwanguang, P., Chaijaroen, S.: Designing framework of the learning environment model to enhance learners' information processing integration between pedagogy and neuroscience. Panyapiwat J. **8**(3), 188–201 (2016)
13. Chaijaroen, S., Techapornpong, O., Samat, C.: Learner's creative thinking of learners learning with constructivist web-based learning environment model: integration between pedagogy and neuroscience. In: 25th International Conference on Computers in Education: Technology and Innovation: Computer-Based Educational Systems for the 21st Century 32, pp. 565–571. Asia-Pacific Society for Computers in Education, Christchurch (2017)
14. Chaijaroen, S., Kwanguang, P., Samat, C., Kanjug, I., Somabut, A.: The design and development of the cognitive innovation to enhance problem solving. In: The 24th International Conference on Computers in Education, India (2016)

Theoretical and Designing Framework of Constructivist Web-Based Learning Environment Model to Problem Solving

Pitchaya Pimsook[✉] and Sumalee Chaijaroen

Department of Educational Technology, Khon Kaen University,
Khon Kaen, Thailand
pitchayapimsook@gmail.com

Abstract. The purpose of this research was to synthesize theoretical framework of constructivist web-based learning environment for problem solving. The target groups used in study were 1) 3 contents experts for evaluation of the contents 2) 3 experts for evaluation of the instructional designers 3) experts for evaluation of the instructional media expert. 4) 3 experts for evaluation of the collecting tools and 5) 20 students of regional special education center 9, Khon Kaen in a course of intellectual disability unit in the 2st semester, 2019. The instruments used were 1) survey form for learning contextual 2) survey form for students characteristic and 3) The recording form for synthesis of the theoretical framework of constructivist web-based learning environment model to problem solving. Summarization, interpretation and analytical description were used to analyze the data. The result revealed that: Theoretical framework of constructivist web-based learning environment comprise of 5 components as following 1) Psychological base 2) Pedagogy base 3) Problems Solving base 4) Media theory and Technology base 5) Contextual base.

Keywords: Web-based learning environments · Constructivist theories · Problem solving

1 Introduction

The changing of world society and advancement of technology is influenced society in globalization. This change affects human being need to learn all their life or life- long learning, especially 21 century learning focuses on learning creative and problem solving skills. However, at present instructional management focuses on transmitting and memorizing information. This results in lacking of problem solving and information seeking skills of the learners. Teaching in special education centers in the present day, emphasis on teaching and learning that allows learners to learn develop knowledge and skills from classroom instruction from teachers students must wait to receive knowledge from teachers. Teachers are educators. Focus on memorizing and following the process the steps that teachers have placed.

Most teachers are based on the study style. By using the lecture method and making it look as an example and allow students to follow the process steps placed making students have a variety of ways to think and did not dare to think or using methods that are different from what teachers assign and can not solve problems that occur beyond the classroom. But because of the current information and the learning environment has happened a lot and has changed over time students must therefore develop knowledge to make changes. The important thing that students lack is problem solving and experience for solving problems in various situations that occurred beyond the teacher to memorize and follow the process.

Special education centers therefore must develop teaching and learning to be modern and appropriate for the learners to learn and develop aiming to engage students in the learning process by using various techniques and activities to stimulate learning and develop ideas to solve problems in students. Changes in classroom teaching and learning into learning information and communication technology therefore being used to increase the learning efficiency of the learners in accordance with such concepts the design of teaching and learning by using information technology with the characteristics of the media to support the creation of knowledge of learners according to constructivist theory.

For the above reasons, researchers realize the importance of synthesizing the theoretical and designing framework of constructivist web-based learning environment model to problem solving.

This framework may help designer to effectively design the constructivist web based learning environment model. In addition, it will help to confirm the credibility and provide beneficial guideline for the designer to design the constructivist web based learning environment model.

2 Research Methodology

2.1 The Purpose

The purpose of this research was to synthesize theoretical framework of constructivist web-based learning environment for problem solving.

2.2 Research Design

Document analysis and survey research were employed in this study.

2.3 Target Group

1. 3 contents experts for evaluation of the contents.
2. 3 experts for evaluation of the instructional designers.
3. Experts for evaluation of the instructional media expert.
4. 3 experts for evaluation of the collecting tools and
5. 20 students of regional special education center 9, Khon Kaen in a course of intellectual disability unit in the 2st semester, 2019.

2.4 Research Instruments

The instruments in this study consisted of 2 instruments as following:

1. The expert review record form for checking the quality of the designing framework.
2. The synthesis of the designing framework record form for record the data for synthesis of the theoretical framework of constructivist web-based learning environment for problem solving.

2.5 Data Collecting and Analysis

The procedure of gathering and analysis data were as follows:

1. Synthesis of theoretical framework of constructivist web-based learning environment for problem solving. The data were collected by using the recording from for synthesis of the theoretical framework. Summarization, interpretation and analytical description were used to analyze the data.
2. Synthesis of theoretical framework of constructivist web-based learning environment for problem solving. The data were collected by using the recording from for synthesis of the designing framework.

Summarization, interpretation and analytical description were used to analyze the data.

3 Research Results

The theoretical framework for the development of a learning environment on the network found that the theoretical framework consists of 5 basic areas: (1) the basis of learning psychology (2) basic science (3) basic of solve complex structural problems (4) Fundamentals of media theory and technology (5) Contextual basis.

1. The basis of teaching science has introduced the teaching design (ID Theory) that focuses on applying various learning theory principles to become the basis for teaching design to promote knowledge creation and cognitive process development, namely intellectual constructivist theory, with the principle that learning processes begin with problems that cause causing suspicion or intellectual conflict. Therefore, it must be invented or searched for additional information to eliminate the internal intellectual conflict. Which is brought into practice by applying it as a design basis problem situation and social constructivist theory, with principles of knowledge creation based on social interaction, namely language, society, culture. Help create knowledge expand various perspectives and concepts that are brought into practice by applying as a design basis. Help base including the theory of learning, cognitive groups including information processing theory that with human information processing begins with information coming into the record of the sensory register. Then will go to collect long-term memory by integrating with previous knowledge is an intellectual structure schema theory and menthol model theory.

2. The basis of learning psychology of constructivist learning is knowledge about learning and teaching so that students can learn from changes that focus on technology to be applied in the teaching and learning of learners the researcher therefore introduced constructivist principles and theories as a basis for teaching and learning design. Including 1) Hannafin's Land & Oliver (1999) open learning environments (OLEs) model that focuses on solving open learning problems. Including learning resources, intellectual tools and help base 2) Jonassen's Constructivist Learning Environments (CLEs) model (1999) that focuses on developing knowledge in solving complex problems. Which students must link to their previous knowledge and experience 3) The SOI Model of Mayer (1999) that focuses on creating knowledge by using text and images that consist of selecting (S), organizing information (O) and information integration (I) 4) The Mclellan (1996) course learning that focuses on the real-life context in which the situation is connected in relation to the problem in real condition.
3. The basic structure for solving complex problems will use a complex problem-solving framework based on the Jonassen (1997) framework with 7 steps: (1) Learners Articulate Problem Space and Contextual Constraints (2) Identify and Clarify Alternative Opinions, Positions, and Perspectives of Stakeholders (3) Generate Possible Problem Solutions (4) Assess the Viability of Alternative Solutions by Constructing Arguments and Articulating Personal Beliefs (5) Monitor the Problem Space and Solution Options (6) Implement and Monitor the Solution and (7) Adapt the Solution.
4. Fundamentals of media theory and technology the researcher introduced the media symbol system, which is a multi-dimensional media (Hypermedia) that offers both animation, graphics, letters, sounds and the ability to process media that is a multiple link. Hyperlink that is a link in linking knowledge nodes. And using network technology to manage learning with the features of the internet network that offers both text, still images, sound animations and relies on the media symbol system that has the processing capability that can be stopped or reverted to information. Which allows learners to create concepts and promote intellectual structure expansion by the symbol system of the media on the network with the characteristics of hyperlinks, both images, sounds as well as other symbols.

Allowing learners to create various concepts or have new or use video that helps to expand the concept further from the existing experience thereby helping to solve problems with complex structures in learning from that information allowing learners to create their own knowledge anywhere, anytime, according to the principles of developing learners in the age of society, news and technology prosperity that responds to lifelong learning (Sumalee Chaicharoen, 2004).

5. Contextual basis consists of the curriculum of early intervention (EI) students in intellectual disability.

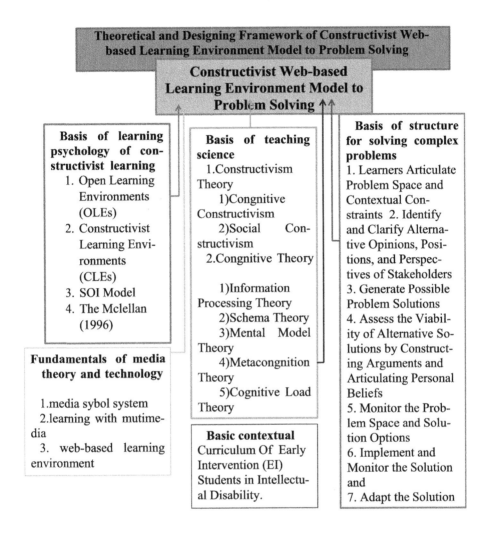

4 Conclusion

The results of this theoretical framework synthesis found that there is a clear theory of the principles outlined above. May be due to there are research documents that are reviewed documents. Study the relevant context and receive quality checks by experts which the results of the examination there is a consistency between principles clear theories which consists of 5 basic aspects. 1. The basis of learning psychology consists of a group of constructivist theory and cognitive theory groups which results in the synthesis of theoretical concepts in line with the research of Pina Sukcharoen and Sumalee Chaicharoen (2016), which uses the foundation of constructivist learning theory that focuses on creating knowledge of learners 2. The basis of teaching science consists of the OLE model, CLE model, SOI and similar learning model, which results in the synthesis of theoretical frameworks in line with Seksan Yampinin (2011) research that uses the teaching model as the basis for the design of learning environment elements that promote fix the problem. 3. The basic problem solving structure with complex structure consists of solving complex problems with Jonassen (1997), which is consistent with Suchart Wattanachai (2010) that has adopted this solution basis to encourage learners to develop solve problems with complex structures. 4. The basis of the theory of media and technology consists of the symbol system of the media. Multimedia learning and network technology which corresponds to Pina Sukcharoen and Sumalee Chaicharoen (2016) who have used technology on networks that can offer multimedia together with the use of the media symbol system to emphasize the creation of knowledge of learners. 5. Contextual basis consists of context related to regional special education center 9, Khon Kaen in a course of intellectual disability unit. Focused on problem solving skills.

Based on the results of this theoretical framework synthesis found that the inspection results there is a consistency between principles clear theories resulting in the synthesis of theoretical frameworks, network learning models based on constructivist concepts that promote problem solving effective can lead to further design and development of learning environment. Which is consistent with the research of Watcharaphon Tham Klang and Sumalee Chaicharoen (2017), which studied the theoretical conceptual framework of the constructivist learning environment that promotes problem solving processes which results in this may encourage learners to solve complex problems that which is necessary for intellectual disability students who need to continue to work in which the researcher will develop into a learning environment and continue to use.

References

1. Mai, N., Tse-Kian, N.: Engaging students in multimedia-mediated constructivist learning students' perception. Educ. Technol. Soc. **12**(2), 254–266 (2009)
2. Fosnot, C.T.: Constructivism: a psychological theory of learning. In: Fosnot, C.T. (ed.) Constructivism: Theory, Perspectives, and Practice, pp. 8–33. Teachers College Press, New York (1996)
3. Fer, S., Akyol, S.: Effects of social constructivist learning environment design on 5th grade learners' learning. Procedia - Soc. Behav. Sci. **9**, 948–953 (2010)
4. Cobb, P.: Where is the mind. constructivist and social cultural perspectives on mathematical development. Educ. Res. **23**(7), 13–20 (1994)
5. Wang, Y., et al.: Perspectives on cognitive computing and applications. Int. J. Softw. Sci. Comput. Intell. **2**(4), 32–44 (2010)
6. Yuan, S.: The teacher's role in problem-solving: a study of elementary mathematics programs from teachers' perspectives. A Research Paper Submitted in Conformity with the Requirements For the degree of Master of Teaching Department of Curriculum, Teaching and Learning Ontario Institute for Studies in Education of the University of Toronto (2016)
7. Richey, R.C., Klein, J.D.: Design and Development Research Methods. Strategies and Issues. Lawrence Erlbaum Associates, New Jersey (2007)

8. Huy, P.P., Bing, H.N., Alexander, S.Y.: School of education institute for positive psychology and education. Achiev. Optim. Best Instr. Effic. Use Cogn. Load Theor. Math. Probl. Solving **29**(3), 667–692 (2016)
9. Krulik, S., Rudnick, J.A.: Problem Solving. Allyn and Bacon, Boston (1987)
10. Piaget, J.: Judgment and Reasoning in the Child. Translated by Marjorie Warden. Roultedge & Kegan Paul, London (1989)
11. Vygotsky, L.: Interaction between learning and development. In: Gauvain, M., Cole, M. (eds.) Readings on the Development of Children. Scientific American Books, New York (1978)
12. Klausmeier, H.J.: Educational Phycology, S thed edn. Harper & Row, New York (1985)
13. Wilson, B.G., Cole, P.: Cognitive dissonance as an instructional variable. Ohio Media Spectr. **43**(4), 11–21 (1991)
14. Guilford, J.P.: The Nature of Human Intelligence. McGraw-Hill BookCompany, New York (1967)
15. Hannafin, M.J.: Video assessment of classroom teaching practices: lessons learned, problems & issues. Educ. Technol. **50**(1), 32–37 (1999)
16. Mayer, R.E.: The origin and decline of two rural resistance ideologies. In: Mayer, P. (ed.) Black Villagers in an Industrial Society: Anthropological Perspective on Labor Migration in South Africa. Oxford University Press, Cape Town (1999)
17. Mayer, R.E.: Designing Instruction for Constructivist Learning. Instructional Design Theories and Models: A New Paradigm of Instructional Theory. Lawrence Erlbaum Associates, Newjersy (1996)
18. Brown, C., Duguid, P.: Situated cognition and the culture of learning. Educ. Res. **18**(1), 32–42 (1989)
19. Donald, D.M.: Augmented reality on mobile devices to improve the academic achievement and independence of students with disabilities. Doctoral Dissertations, University of Tennessee, Knoxville (2014)
20. Solvie, P., Kloek, M.: Using technology tools to engage students with multiple learning styles in a constructivist learning environment. Contemp. Issues Technol. Teach. Educ. **7**(2), 7–27 (2014)
21. Dikaya, L.A., Ermakov, P.N., Dikiy, I.S.: EEG correlates of professional creative problem solving with insight. Int. J. Psychophysiol. **3**(85), 361–430 (2012)
22. Samat, C., Chaijaroen, S.: Design and development of learning environment to enhance creative thinking and innovation skills for teacher training in the 21st century. In: Proceedings of the 23rd International Conference on Computers in Education, ICCE 2015, pp. 667–672 (2015)

Technology-Enhanced Learning

A Study of Students' Context-Aware to Be Used as a Basis for Designing and Developing a Model of Mobile-Based Learning Environment to Enhance Computational Problem Solving in Programming for the High School Students

Kanyarat Sirimathep[1], Issara Kanjug[2], Charuni Samat[3(✉)], and Suchat Wattanachai[4]

[1] Doctor of Philosophy Student of Education Technology, Faculty of Education,
Khon Kaen University, KhonKaen, Thailand
kanyarat.siri@kkumail.com
[2] Division O of Computer Education, Faculty of Education,
Khon Kaen University, KhonKaen, Thailand
issaraka@kku.ac.th
[3] Division O of Educational Technology, Faculty of Education,
Khon Kaen University, KhonKaen, Thailand
thaibannok@hotmail.com
[4] Division of Surgery, Faculty of Veterinary Medicine, Khon Kaen University,
KhonKaen, Thailand
suchat@kku.ac.th

Abstract. Mobile-based learning as a rich environment to manage learning in a variety of learning contexts. It opens up opportunities to expand the learning experience of students, students can access to information anytime and anywhere to perform authentic activities, learning programming through mobile devices helping students to improve programming skills at all times and they can enhance computational problem solving which important competence to support the design and development of the program correctly. In developing any mobile learning environment, learner's context-aware are necessary for consideration. The research target was the 45 high school students. The Questionnaires are an open-ended question and Likert ration scales with 5 levels and the data were analyzed through descriptive analysis. which were examined by 3 experts based on the consistency with theoretical framework. The results showed that 1) the participants were 25 males were 55%, 20 females were 45% in high school. Most of the students had the learning experience of lecturing. 2) In the basic ability in using technology, it was found that the students are very familiar with mobile devices and its applications in high level ($\bar{x}$ 3.89 $s.d$ = 0.56) 3) Experience in computational problem solving found that some students have experience. 4) Programming experience Some students have experience in c programming and they can create program flowcharts. The findings show strong evidence that students are positive towards mobile-based learning and see it as an opportunity for a more flexible programming learning experience.

Keywords: Context-Aware · Learner's Context-Aware · Learning environments · Constructivist theories · Computational thinking · Programming · Mobile-based learning

1 Introduction

Computational Thinking (CT) is a type of skill that is necessary to students of the 21st century, to develop human resources by the Thailand 4.0 policy on the driving of the Thai economy through innovation. One of the innovations that appear in digital content or digital media. With both basic learning materials such as teaching and learning applications, e-book. Cheng [1] said that Computational Thinking (CT) skills should be added to every child's analytical ability to be an important component of learning. The teaching and learning process must encourage students to develop to their full potential. Teacher must provide a variety of content and teaching activities following the interests, aptitudes, and differences of students Practice thinking processes, management, coping situations, and applying knowledge to solve problems, organize activities for students to learn from real experiences. Emphasize the idea of making and solving problems as Including promoting the environment, atmosphere, equipment or learning materials to be able to facilitate learning at all places and all times.

Satyanarayanan proposed mobile devices [2] can (a) engage students in experiential and situated learning without limitation (place, time and device) (b) enable students to continue learning activities, inside the classroom, outside the classroom through their constant and contextual interaction and communication with their classmates and their teachers (c) support on-demand access to educational resources (d) allow for new skills or knowledge to be immediately applied. And (e) encourage learners to participate more actively in the learning process by engaging them to authentic and situated learning embedded in real-life context.

Mobile-based learning is the concept of using wireless technology devices such as mobile phones, smartphones, tablets, iPads, the teaching and learning model can be managed both in support of students to learn on their own. And learning to promote collaboration among students. Mobile-based learning makes teaching and learning happen anywhere, anytime, without limits, only in the classroom Students can access various information including slide data, audio, video, easy to find information. There is an interaction between students and instructors or students themselves immediately [3].

Programming is more than just coding. During programming, students are exposed to computational thinking, it exposes students to computational thinking which involves problem-solving [4] using computer science concepts like abstraction and decomposition. Even for non-computing majors, computational thinking is applicable and useful in their daily lives. The three dimensions of computational thinking are computational concepts, computational practices, and computational perspectives [5]. Programming through mobile that we carry around with us at all times means instant gratification for students, as they can show their games and applications to their friends, and it means that students can do their homework or additional practicing at all times.

Students use of computational thinking concepts such as abstraction, debugging, remixing and iteration to solve problems [6]. This form of thinking can be considered to be fundamental for students because it requires "thinking at multiple abstractions" [7], and computational thinking is the important aspects of 21st century competencies such as creativity, critical thinking, and problem-solving [8].

From the importance and problems mentioned above the researcher, studied the learner context-aware based on the basis of development from the Theoretical framework derived from relevant theoretical principles and from various research studies Which related to students' characteristics Learning management model and factors affecting students to be used as a basis for designing and developing a model of mobile-based learning environment to enhance computational problem solving in programming for the high school students.

2 Literature Review

2.1 Computational Thinking in Programming

Computational Thinking (CT) in relation to programming is an emerging field in K-12 education,Brennan and Resnick conceptualized CT in a programming context as comprising three key components: (1) CT concepts, such as sequences, loops, and conditionals; (2) CT practices, such as testing, debugging, abstraction, and modularization in programming; and (3) CT perspectives, such as students' views on connecting with the digital world. These components, taught while introducing the fundamentals of programming in K-12 education, enable students to develop CT-based problem-solving skills as they produce artifacts and become digital producers.

2.2 Mobile-Based Learning

Mobile-based learning is learning based on mobility often through mobile devices like laptops and smartphones, iPads, and wearable technology, Mobile-based learning model can manage learning both in support of self-learning, students can search from various sources of knowledge anywhere, anytime, according to the readiness of each student and mobile-based learning can support collaboration among students. Mobile-based learning is the suitable environment for 21st century learning [9] with have these powerful solutions provided by Education Apps to students.

Provides Systematic and Smart Learning. The Educational apps are arranged in both systematic and smart learning that it becomes possible for students to go with the flow.

Enhanced Interaction. The educational apps can make student active and create better interactive engagement between students. The interaction tendency is also increased in students by mobile-based Learning apps.

Bridges the Gap Between Parent and Teacher. The educational apps support teachers to the queries of the parents anytime and anywhere via an education app. Education apps foster transparency in student's learning at their schools.

Tracks Learning Progress. The educational apps are helping students improve their skills such as reading, learning new languages, math, and much more. Teacher can Tracks student's learning Progress.

E-books and Online Study Materials. The educational apps come with many benefits for students, as it saves a lot of money for buying study material from shops and libraries. Learning apps allow students to read the study material from the education app with a few simple clicks. Students can also discover miscellaneous study material by using education apps.

Anytime/Anywhere. The educational apps are available for students and they can learn at a convenient time.

Promotes Self-learning. The educational apps come with numerous material resources so that students can enjoyably interact with them.

Mobile-based Learning provide smooth peer-to-peer interactions along with a better learning experience. The mix of education and technology creates a positive step toward better learning experience and student engagement.

3 Purposes

To study of learner context-aware related to students' characteristics, Learning management model and factors affecting students to be used as a basis for designing and developing a model of mobile-based learning environment to enhance computational problem solving in programming for the high school students.

4 Method and Result

4.1 Scope of Research

The Model research (Richey & Klein) was employed [10]. This is to intensively study the process of design and development a model which comprises 3 research phrases as 1) Model development 2) Model validation and 3) Model use. In this study, research phrase 1 Model Development was implemented to present the results of the develop process by Survey Research in learner context-aware; The results were fundamentally used to design and develop a model of mobile-based learning environment to enhance computational problem solving in programming for the high school students.

4.2 Target Group of the Study

The study target was the 45 high school students, who enrolled computer science subject attending Surathampitak School, Muang District, Nakonratchasima Province, Thailand in the first semester of the academic year 2020.

4.3 Research Design

Research Phrase 1 Model development was employed by Survey research.

4.4 Research Instruments

The survey form was used to study the context of learners. There are 2 sections, the first section was Student profile Data which had 5 parts as follow 1) Demographics 2) Learning experience 3) Technology experience 4) Computational thinking experience 5) Programming experience, and the second section was students learning management expectations. The Survey were an open-ended question and 5 scales Likert [11]. Likert scale between 1 and 5, where 1 indicates extreme strongly disagree and 5 indicates strongly agree. The internal consistency and trustworthiness of the questionnaire results were estimated using Cronbach's alpha.

4.5 Data Collection and Analysis

This study was survey research using qualitative data collection. The data analysis was made by percentage, Mean and Standard Deviation by descriptive analysis using charts and simple percentages.

4.6 Research Results

The results of the study of learner context-aware regarding the characteristics of the students Learning management and factors affecting students as a basis for designing and developing a learning environment model, divided into 2 sections, with the following details:

Student's Profile Data

Demographics. Demographics-basis information of the learners as by Gender and GPA presented. The Data were analyzed by using the descriptive analysis function. The outputs are tabulated as seen in Table 1.

Table 1. Demographics-basis information of the learners.

Gender	(n)	(%)
Male	25	55
Female	20	45
TOTAL	45	100

The results were found that most of the Respondents were males or in amount of 25 learners or 55%; the data also revealed that 31 of them or 68.88% was in very good level of GPA or 3.00–3.50.

Learning Experience. The data of learning experience of the learners was found in 3 subtitles as 1) Learning theory 2) Learning media and 3) Learning model. The outputs are tabulated as seen in Table 2.

Table 2. Learning experience.

Learning Experience		Number (n)	Percent (%)
Learning Theory			
1	A learner has had the experience in lecturing, demonstration, and practicing	43	95.55
2	A learner has had the experience in design thinking, decision making, and meaning making based on multiple situations	30	66.66
3	A learner has had the experience in discovery learning and self- knowledge construction	25	55.55
Learning Media			
4	Students have experience in learning with mobile	41	91.11
5	Students have experience in learning with a mobile-based learning environment	20	44.44
6	Students have experience in learning with a mobile-based learning environment to enhance computational problem solving in programming	22	48
Learning model			
7	Students have experience in learning by using problem-based learning	32	71.11
8	Students have experience in learning to enhance Computational problem solving in programming	29	64.44
9	Students have experience in learning by using collaborative learning	39	86.66
10	Students have experience in learning by using mobile-based learning to enhance computational problem solving in programming	17	37.77

The results of the study of learning experience were found that most learners have the experience in lecturing, demonstration, and practicing as 43 students or 95.55%, 41 students or 91.11% have experience in learning with mobile, and 39 students or 86.66% have collaborative learning experience.

Technology Experience. The study of learners' Technology experience based on the survey form was explained by the following aspects as 1) use of technology device 2) use of technology to support knowledge construction 3) use of technology to explore knowledge 4) use of knowledge as learning context to enhance action learning 5) use of technology as social media for a conversation and knowledge sharing 6) use of technology to reflex thinking. The outputs are tabulated as seen in Table 3.

Table 3. Technology experience.

	Technology Experience	$\bar{x}$	S.D.	Level
	Use of Technology Device			
1	Desktop computer	4.50	0.20	Very High
2	Laptop computer	3.98	0.62	High
3	Smart phone	4.65	0.69	Very High
4	Tablet	2.45	0.74	Average
	Total	3.89	0.56	High
	Use of Technology to Support Knowledge Construction			
5	Use of Scratch as a tool for programming	3.98	0.65	High
6	Use of Code.org as a tool for programming learning	3.89	0.71	High
7	Use of Microbit as a tool for programming learning	2.45	0.69	Low
	Total	3.44	0.68	Average
	Use of Technology to Survey Knowledge			
8	Use Google search engine for knowledge survey	4.85	0.56	Very High
9	Use Bing search engine for knowledge survey	3.44	0.70	Average
10	Use Yahoo search engine for knowledge survey	2.56	0.65	Low
	Total	3.61	0.62	High
	Use of Technology as Learning Context to Enhance Action Learning			
11	Use of Flowgorithm for flowchart creating	3.59	0.64	High
12	Use of Flowdia Diagrams Lite android application for flowchart creating through mobile	2.45	0.57	Low
13	Use of Pydroid 3 android application for Python programming	2.45	0.65	Low
	Total	2.83	0.62	Average
	Use of Technology to as Social Media for a Conversation and Knowledge Sharing			
14	Facebook application	4.87	0.69	Very High
15	Line application	4.27	0.71	High
16	E-mail	3.70	0.74	High
	Total	4.28	0.71	High
	Technology Experience	$\bar{x}$	S.D.	Level
	Use of Technology to Reflex Thinking			
17	Use of Mind Map software for building mind mapping and presenting ideas	3.67	0.65	High
18	Use of Padlet application for building mind mapping and presenting ideas	2.49	0.59	Low
	Total	3.08	0.62	Average
	All Total	3.52	0.76	High

The results of the study of Technology experience were found that most student in overall had the high level of technology using Specifically, they had the good level of performance to use a social media platform for a conversation and knowledge sharing or $\bar{x} = 4.28$, S.D. = 0.71, High level of technology device or $\bar{x} = 3.89$, S.D. = 0.56 as well as the high level of Use of Technology to Survey Knowledge $\bar{x} = 3.61$, S.D. = 0.62.

Computational Problem Solving Experience. The study of learners' Computational Problem Solving Experience based on the survey form was presented in the following parts 1) decomposition problem 2) pattern recognition 3) abstraction 4) Algorithm and 5) Evaluating solutions. The outputs are tabulated as seen in Table 4.

Table 4. Computational problem solving experience

	Computational Problem Solving Experience	$\bar{x}$	S.D.	Level
	Decomposition problem			
1	Break down a complex problem or system into smaller parts that are more manageable and easier to understand	3.59	0.79	High
	Pattern recognition			
2	Find the similarities or patterns among small problem, decomposed problems that can help to solve more complex problems more efficiently	3.21	0.52	Average
	Abstraction			
3	Filter out–essentially, ignore - the characteristics that students don't need in order to concentrate on those that we do	2.45	0.71	Low
	Algorithm			
4	Plan, a set of step-by-step instructions to solve a problem	2.30	0.64	Low
	Evaluating solutions			
5	Make sure the solution does the job it has been designed to do and to think about how it could be improved	2.30	0.64	Low
	All total	2.77	0.73	Low

The results disclosed that they had low level in Computational Problem Solving Experience or $\bar{x} = 2.77$, S.D. = 0.73. Among those 5 Computational Problem Solving Experience, the highest number was shown in Decomposition problem which in High level or $\bar{x} = 3.59$, S.D. = 0.79, Pattern recognition presented $\bar{x} = 3.21$, S.D. = 0.52 in low level, Abstraction shown $\bar{x} = 2.45$, S.D. = 0.71, while Algorithm shown $\bar{x} = 2.30$, S.D. = 0.73 in low level, and Evaluating solutions shown in low level $\bar{x} = 2.30$, S.D. = 0.73.

Programming Experience. The study of learners' Programming Experience based on the survey form. The outputs are tabulated as seen in Table 5.

Table 5. Programming experience.

	Programming Experience	$\bar{x}$	S.D.	Experience Level
1	The experience in Programming learning such as web programming, mobile apps programming or software programming	4.21	0.69	High
2	The experience in project programming such as web programming, mobile apps programming or software programming	2.10	0.72	Low
3	The experience in programming such as text-based programming, block-based programming	3.21	0.61	Average
4	The experience in C Programming language	3.21	0.61	Average
5	The experience in Programming using a mobile application software	2.45	0.74	Low
	All total	3.03	0.68	Average

Their overall product Programming Experience was in Average level or $\bar{x} = 3.03$, S.D. $= 0.68$ which they most had the experience in Programming learning or $\bar{x} = 4.21$, S.D. $= 0.69$ in High level. Meanwhile, they had low level in the other kinds of Programming Experience as in project programming and Programming using a mobile application software as $\bar{x} = 2.10$, S.D. $= 0.72$, $\bar{x} = 2.45$, S.D. $= 0.74$.

Student's Expectation. The study of the student's expectation towards learning comprised 3 parts as 1) Content 2) Learning style and 3) Teacher. The outputs are tabulated as seen in Table 6.

Table 6. Student's expectation towards learning.

	Student's Expectation towards learning	$\bar{x}$	S.D.	Level
Content				
1	Modern content that can be applied in daily life	4.57	0.64	Very High
2	Interesting content, and diverse content	4.54	0.72	Very High
3	The content is organized into clear categories. And consistent with the study topics	4.20	0.69	High
	Total	4.43	0.65	High
Learning Style				
4	Problem-based Learning	4.77	0.69	Very High
5	Collaborative Learning	4.79	0.77	Very High
6	Flexible learning environment with a diverse learning and personalization based on students' interests	4.89	0.74	Very High
7	Learning that enhance computational problem solving	4.69	0.69	Very High
	Total	4.77	0.68	Very High

(*continued*)

Table 6. (*continued*)

	Student's Expectation towards learning	$\bar{x}$	S.D.	Level
Teacher				
8	A teacher should design a lesson plan that are consistent with the curriculum and able to organize a variety of learning experiences with individual differences	4.49	0.74	High
9	A teacher should support a learner to be an active learner for the achievement of self-learning	4.60	0.65	Very High
10	A teacher should arrange a variety of courses for students to choose according to student needs, interests and ability	4.78	0.72	Very High
	Total	4.62	0.67	Very High
	All total	4.60	0.74	Very High

The results revealed the student's expectation in learning that in very high level or $\bar{x} = 4.60$, S.D. = 0.74. Accordingly, they presented the statistical data for in topics that they required the Flexible learning environment with a diverse learning and personalization based on students' interests $\bar{x} = 4.89$, S.D. = 0.74, they expected to have group-based learning for knowledge sharing in both inside and outside classroom $\bar{x} = 4.79$, S.D. = 0.77, and they presented their expectation that a teacher should arrange a variety of courses for students to choose according to student needs, interests and ability $\bar{x} = 4.78$, S.D. = 0.72.

5 Conclusions

The present learning styles should highlight knowledge computational problem solving by several and flexible learning methods. The learners should be enhanced to share and collaborate in both inside and outside classroom while the teachers act differently by transforming from a teller to coach (Coaching). Moreover, the learning style is suggested to focus on self- study with innovation improvement in order to enhance a learner to be able to discover knowledge by themselves.

Acknowledgements. This research was supported by Ph.D. Program in Educational Technology, Faculty of Education, Khon Kaen University, and Research Group for Innovation and Cognitive Technology, Khon Kaen University which hereby giving the thankfulness all through this.

References

1. Cheng, Y.B., Huang, C.W.: The effect of simulation games on the learning of computational problem solving. Comput. Educ. **57**(3), 1907–1918 (2008)

2. Satyanarayana, M.: Mobile computing: the next decade. In: 1st Proceedings of the ACM Workshop on Mobile Cloud Computing & Services: Social Networks and Beyond (MCS'10), pp. 5:1–5:6. Association for Computing Machinery, New York, United States (2010)
3. Elgamel, L., et al.: Mobile learning (M-learning) and educational environments. Int. J. Distrib. Paralled Syst. (IJDPS) **3**(4), 31–48 (2012)
4. Wing, J.M.: Computational thinking and thinking about computing. Philos. Trans. R. Soc. **366**, 3717–3725 (2008)
5. Brennan, K., Resnick, M.: New frameworks for studying and assessing the development of computational thinking. In: Proceedings of the 2012 Annual Meeting of the American Educational Research Association, pp. 1–25. Vancouver, Canada (2012)
6. Barr, V., Stephenson, C.: Bringing computational thinking to K-12: what is involved and what is the role of the computer science education community. ACM **2**(1), 48–54 (2011)
7. Wing, J.M.: Computational thinking. Commun. ACM **49**(3), 33–35 (2006)
8. Ananiadou, K., Claro, M.: 21st century skills and competences for new millennium learners in OECD countries (Education Working Paper No. 41). http://www.oecd.org/officialdocuments/publicdisplaydocmentpdf/?cote=EDU/WKP%282009%2920&doclanguage=en. Accessed 15 July 2020
9. Charoula, A.: A K-6 computational thinking curriculum framework: implications for teacher knowledge. J. Educ. Technol. Soc. **19**(3), 47–57 (2016)
10. Richey, R.C., Klein, J.: Design and Developmental Research. Lawrence, New Jersey (2007)
11. Likert, R.A.: Technique for the measurement of attitudes. Arch. Psychol. **25**(140), 1–55 (1932)

Assistive Technologies for Students with Dyslexia: A Systematic Literature Review

C. Smith and M. J. Hattingh[✉]

University of Pretoria, Private Bag X20, Hatfield 0028, South Africa
marie.hattingh@up.ac.za

Abstract. The goal of this research review is to identify assistive technologies available to support students with dyslexia. The study reports on how accessible these technologies are, as well as the impact these technologies can have on the students if they are adopted. The main focus of the review lies on identifying assistive technologies that can help students with dyslexia but investigation is also done into the surrounding and closely related topics of accessibility, acceptance and impact of the technology as well as trying to understand some aspects of the dyslexia disability to better understand how the technologies can aid these students and help to rehabilitate them. Based on information gathered from previous research, the study tries to find a weak spot in the field of assistive technologies and tries to determine how it can be bettered.

Keywords: Systematic literature review · Learning disabilities · Learning aids · Dyslexia

1 Introduction

Dyslexia is a neurobehavioral disorder that very commonly affects children with rates up to 17.5% [1]. More research and observations made from The National Institute of Child Health and Human Development (NICHD), indicates that 17% to 20% of the United States population has some form of a reading disability, which means that one out of five children in the United States struggles with this problem and will most likely keep struggling with it through their teenage and young adult lives [2]. Dyslexia is a disorder where the person affected struggles with seemingly normal actions like word recognition, spelling and formulating sentences [3]. Since dyslexia is a problem that individuals have with language and phonological processing [1, 4] students really struggled in the past without technology to help them to overcome their disabilities and learn to move past it. With the world becoming more technological each day, people with learning disabilities have gotten the chance to utilize these new emerging technologies to help and assist them with their studying and progression in the academic system [5]. Diagnosis of the condition is happening more frequently, since new technology becomes available that helps to identify students with dyslexia traits and tendencies, like the use of EEG signal patterns [6]. The technological aids that these students require can get complex and can include different special hardware and software assistance [7]. Students with learning disabilities have always struggled to obtain access to the needed aids and technology, and even with institutions providing more resources in recent times, there are still students in many demographics that cannot obtain access to these needed aids [8]. In this literature review the focus will be on dyslexia and the technology that can be used to assist students with the disorder rather than learning disabilities in general, which will allow narrowing the research field down and producing better quality results on one specific topic in the overwhelmingly large field.

2 Research Method

The research question to be answered by this study is: What technologies are available to assist students with dyslexia? The following search terms were used: ("dyslexia" and "technology") OR ("dyslexia" and "learning" and "technology") OR ("assistive" and "technology") OR ("dyslexia" and "assistive" and "technology").

The selection criteria include a set of inclusion criteria and exclusion criteria that was pre-defined by the author based on information needed to answer the research question. The following inclusion criteria were used to select the sources, any article not conforming to this were excluded: (1) Studies in English (2) Articles that focus on the characteristics and description of dyslexia as a learning disability are included (3) Articles that define and describe different technological assistance initiatives are included (4) Studies from 2009 to 2019 (6) Peer reviewed academic journals.

Articles were obtained from ScienceDirect and Emerald Insight databases. Initially 1286 articles were identified, which were reduced to 168 after screening the title and key words. 164 articles were read and based on their eligibility to the research question, 80 articles were included in final review.

3 Analysis of Findings

The use of EEG signals and MRI (Magnetic Resonance Imaging) have been mentioned and briefly looked at in relation to identifying dyslexia or dyslexic traits within individuals [6], but there are many technologies being used to actually assist learners that are suffering from dyslexia with studying and performing their academic duties. Some of these technologies include speech recognition software, text-to-speech software, mind mapping software, scanning software, hand reading pens, spell checkers, smart pens, software on multimedia devices like cell phones and tablets, and computer-based learning programs. These technological options are very popular options when it comes to assistive technology according to the Dyslexia Association and will be investigated further. In this review it was discovered that dyslexia is a learning disability that is largely misunderstood to the world and every aspects from identifying individuals with dyslexia to the point of obtaining technological aid to assist them is a very difficult task and all these steps are investigated in more detail to follow. To be able to assist and obtain proper technological help for individuals who suffer from dyslexia, it is very important to correctly diagnose and identify the conditions beforehand. Although many researches would argue on the different types of dyslexia and how it can be identified, a common identifying method that is used consistently is the double deficit hypothesis, which proposes that individuals who have problems with phonological processing as well as naming speed represent independent dyslexic traits [9]. Many other reports attribute the identification of dyslexia in individuals because of the identification of a dissociation between phonological and visual attention span [10]. There are many traits that can be associated with the dyslexia learning disability and can be used to hypothesize that an individual may suffer from the disability, but there are also quite a few technologies available to help identify and diagnose individuals who have dyslexia. Some of these technologies to help identify the condition include DTI (Diffusion Tensor Imaging), EEG (Electroencephalography), ERP (Evoked Response Potential), and MRI (Magnetic Resonance Imaging). DTI (Diffusion Tensor Imaging) is technology branching from MRI (Magnetic Resonance Imaging) and is used generally to detect and investigate the white matter and fibre in the brain, and can be used for multiple learning disorders beyond just dyslexia as well as other brain-oriented diseases like Alzheimer's disease and Parkinson's Disease [11]. The DTI technology provides the ability to do extremely detailed investigation into white matter damage in the brain and is used in practice to investigate both the macro structural and microstructural integrity of white matter. MRI (Magnetic Resonance Imaging) is used for bigger and more overall investigations of the human body and is done by forming images of the human body through magnetic fields in combination with chemical contrast agents [12]. MRI technology is frequently used in practice to aid the identification and investigation of different cancers as well as neurological illnesses and conditions like dyslexia, Alzheimer's disease, and schizophrenia. As with all technologies, MRI technology does not come without any form of drawbacks and many researchers have investigated the effect of the chemical composition, that is needed for the MRI technology to produce imaging, on the human body and many are actively trying to determine if those chemicals are actually damaging the organs of people who go for these scans [13]. EEG (Electroencephalography) is technology that makes use of elctrophysiological monitoring to investigate and record the electric activities in the human brain and is generally used mostly for the identification and possible treatment of more physical problems like brain trauma and other injuries to the head, but can also be used to investigate some diseases that are of a neurological origin like dementia [14]. Despite the fact that EEG technology is more commonly used with more physical problems with the human brain does not mean it has no place to be leveraged when it comes to dyslexia and other diseases that are neurological in nature. Many studies have been conducted using EEG technology to help identify dyslexia and dyslexic traits or tendencies in individuals as well as the EEG technology being leveraged to help create a treatment and rehabilitation program with great success in helping children who participated to better their reading skills and speeds by quite a big margin [15]. Evoked potential is a method that also employs the use of visual, auditory, and sensory stimulation and subsequently using electric signal monitoring. There are different types of evoked potential studies to investigate neurological deficiencies, which include VER (Visual Evoked Responses), BAER (Brain stem Auditory Evoked Responses), and SSEP (Somatosensory Evoked Potentials), and these different studies all focus on different cognitive brain functions [16].

3.1 Identification of Dyslexia

There are quite a few technologies that can be leveraged to identify dyslexia and dyslexic traits in individuals but one important aspect that has been reiterated by so many researchers is the fact that early identification of the disorder is very important to be able to help the individual to overcome their difficulties and problems caused by dyslexia. Once dyslexia or dyslexic traits has been identified and diagnosed in an individual, the individual can start looking at sources that can aid in overcoming the disorder, like assistive technologies to aid studying and therapy to learn how to deal with the disorder in everyday life. A study looking at the use of assistive technologies and how it is impacted by the social structure of everyday life found that individuals who use assistive technologies are more likely to abandon the use thereof if these technologies excludes them or makes them feel different in any way to their peers [17]. It is also recommended that individuals who are diagnosed with dyslexia should undergo therapy since a lot of people never come to acceptance with the fact that they have the disorder, which in turn makes it much more difficult to rehabilitate and overcome the disorder. It is important to distinguish between assistive technology and learning technology before any further findings and statements can be made. In a broad overview, learning technology can be explained as technology that is used to help an individual to learn [18]. Assistive technology, on the other hand, can be described as technology that is assistive, adaptive, and rehabilitative in nature and is designed to aid individuals with learning disabilities, who struggle to learn with the normal medium and resources provided [17]. Although these technologies are very similar in the sense of helping and aiding individuals to learn, they are used by different demographics and under different circumstances. Even though there are amazing assistive technologies available to aid students, there is still a socio economic factor that causes most individuals that are suffering from dyslexia to not be able to obtain access to these technologies because of financial or other similar reasons. The implementation of assistive technologies is no simple task either, and comes with both positive and negative aspects [19]. Some advantages coming with assistive technology implementation include access to new innovative technology and that the school will have expertise knowledge on the assistive technology. Some of the drawbacks of implementing assistive technologies include expensive training, long implementation time and a lot of funding required to make the implementation successful [20]. It is very important, despite the cost implication of implementing assistive technologies that schools attempt to create a safe and inclusive learning environment for students who are affected by dyslexia and other neurological disorders, through the means of different assistive technologies as well as an interactive classroom environment [21]. The way a teacher runs or presents his/her class can make a big difference when they have knowledge and understanding on different cognitive disabilities and can help a student with a learning disability to fit in much easier [22].

3.2 Assistive Technologies for Dyslexia

One of the most popular assistive technologies to aid students with dyslexia is the use of speech recognition software which helps students that struggle with cognitive problems like reading and writing by allowing these students to speak the sentence they wish to convey. The software takes a recording of the spoken sentence and breaks it down into individual sounds, and by making use of different algorithms, will analyse the individual sound and will then write down a word that it finds most similar to the spoken word [23]. More research efforts have gone into using speech recognition software as a base and branching into more specific assistive technology like fully automated closed captioning. Fully automated closed captioning is technology that leverages speech recognition software to produce very accurate captions on video material for students that may struggle with their hearing cognition [24]. Speech recognition software has not only helped students to improve their learning ability, but also to boost their confidence since many students have no problem speaking, but because of the effects of the disorder, struggle with their reading ability [23]. Another frequently used assistive technology is text-to-speech software and would basically work in the complete opposite way as speech recognition software, catering for the students who have trouble puzzling together the words they hear in a way that makes sense or even more commonly used for students who have visual issues. Text-to-speech technology is a form of speech synthesis that takes text as input and converts this input into a voice generated output which enables the student to listen to what is written down instead of having to see and read the text [25]. One study in particular shows that readers who were using a text or speech assistive software were able to read at about 165 words per minute, while the average reader is at about 200 words per minute, showing that even though these software technologies are able to help people, they are still producing results that are 17% less effective than the average reader [26]. Another highly technological innovation which has been uncovered to aid students with dyslexia and other learning disabilities, is the smart pen. The smart pen is a pen that can be used by students in a very similar way to that of writing with a normal pen, but the smart pen has technology built in that records words that are spoken and synchronizes them with words that a user has written down on a special paper [27]. The biggest concern about the smart pen that was raised by users has to do with privacy issues, where the users are not comfortable with their conversations being recorded, seeing as the smart pen records spoken word in order to perform synchronization with the written words on the paper [27]. Another widely used assistive technology for students with dyslexia, is spell checking software. Spell checking software checks the spelling and sentence structure of the words the user is typing and has the ability to correct words that are misspelled and indicate where a phrase or word has not been used correctly [28]. One more medium exists that also plays a very important role in the field of assistive technologies, and that is the use of multimedia devices like smartphones, tablets, and even desktop computers. In recent years there has been an immense increase in the amount of applications being created for assisting students with their learning journey, because almost everyone in today's society has a smart phone or tablet and can leverage these devices to gain access to software applications aimed at assisting them in a way tailored especially for the learning disorder they might associate with [29]. The ability to leverage multimedia devices as a host or platform where assistive technologies can be used enables developers to really customize and develop user interfaces and features specifically tailored to the exact needs and preferences of students with learning disabilities [30]. Another example of software that can be used to help students with dyslexia is the use of courseware. Courseware is software that assists students through the means of any multimedia device that can be used in schools or even for self-improvement and studying at home, and is presented in the structure of an academic course, with different work pieces, assignments, tests, and self-evaluation exercises [31].

3.3 Accessibility and Inclusiveness of Assistive Technologies

Even though there are amazing technologies available nowadays in the field of assistive technologies, the reality remains that there is a big financial gap between the people who are able to obtain access to these technologies and those who cannot. It was found that through primary, secondary, and tertiary school structures in Nigeria, assistive technologies for students with visual impairments only have an availability rate of 3% to 6%, assistive technologies for the hearing impaired only have an availability rate of 2% to 4%, assistive technologies for students who are affected by learning disabilities only have an availability rate of 2% to 8% [32]. The biggest obstacle in today's world is the accessibility to these technologies and how the education system can become more inclusive towards students with learning disabilities. Because students with dyslexia, or any other cognitive illness for that matter, perceive situations in life differently than other students, it can be a difficult task for teachers to include them into their studying methodology without any flaws [33]. Different studies have already confirmed accessibility to assistive technologies as a problem in not only the educational system, but also in society. As such, even regular activities, like working on the internet becomes a problem for these students [34]. An innovative attempt to solve the problem of navigating and accessing the web for students with dyslexia is the use of a customized toolbar to improve web accessibility. The aim of this technology is to provide a web browser extension that allows students with dyslexia to customize the web pages to their liking and to have it in a way that they understand and feel comfortable working with [35]. More research into web accessibility, specifically with dyslexic users, shows that these users experience problems very similar to most users, which shows that developers do not necessarily have to go to extremes with their development and design in order to include these users who have different disabilities [36]. Some of these problems that are experienced when using the web include confusing design layout, no clear navigation method, making poor use of colors in design, small and unreadable text, and overcomplicated use of language. Inclusive design can be seen as developers understanding diversity in a population of potential users and addressing the diversity to deliver a design or product that is suitable for all the different users [37]. Design that is more focused on specifically dyslexic users usually incorporate the above mentioned qualities, as well as being minimalistic and incorporating the use of plain, easy to read and understand language and sentence structure [36]. Taking into account that accessibility is a big issue with assistive technologies, there are quite a few communities that are trying to fix the issue by establishing an online environment where individuals have open source access to assistive technology software, with the goal that individuals in society can benefit from this and that the adoption of assistive technologies in schools can increase to help learners overcome their learning difficulties and improve their livelihood [38]. The idea behind this online "directory" of open source software is to create an environment where developers can come together and contribute their ideas and software solutions that can be used freely by anyone who may not necessarily have the financial means to obtain help in another way. Another problem that was briefly touched on in this study is not only the accessibility of the technologies but the abandonment thereof even when students have access to it. The biggest contributing factor to abandonment of assistive technology can be attributed to students and individuals not accepting that they have a condition or an illness, as well as other conditions that may be caused because of the knowledge of their illness, like depression and anxiety [39]. More factors contributing to the abandonment of assistive technologies include financial reason, where users may not be able to sustain the use of the technologies financially and the fact that the use of these technologies make the users feel different than their peers. These statements are further backed up by research findings that the use and idea of assistive technologies are still very foreign and alienated in the minds of society and have not yet been accepted into their norms of living, and thus causing the users of these technologies to feel self-conscious and out of place [40]. Cultural diversity is also a factor that comes into play when investigating the accessibility that students have to assistive technologies. Some researchers have made statements that the first thing to do when trying to remediate the inaccessibility to assistive technologies is to try and close the gap between the different cultures and their ability to obtain these technologies [41]. Steps that can be taken to achieve this include aiding schools in more rural areas to incorporate assistive technologies into their classrooms and to provide training and courses for teachers to be able to teach and run the classroom in a more inclusive manner. By incorporating these changes students from all cultures have a better chance at obtaining aid as well as different cultural societies may learn more about dyslexia and other cognitive disabilities which can lead to a more accepting and inclusive society outside of an academic view [42]. Establishing a culture of inclusive design and development will greatly benefit these individuals in the academic world and in society as a whole.

4 Conclusion

It is found in this study that a very large number of research articles are based on a young population who are affected by the dyslexia learning disability, which stems from researchers having found that it is very important to identify and start treating the condition at a young age to be able to see more effective results. It was found that there are numerous assistive technology innovations and products available in the industry and that these technologies come with both positive as well as negative impacts for the students that are able to obtain and use them. The acceptance for assistive technologies and even people who are seen as "different" because of their cognitive disabilities are still very low in society, making it extremely difficult for these students to be able to adapt and fit into the educational systems that are in place. This leads to a high rejection rate of assistive technologies. More problems leading to students not being able to fit into the educational system are results of teachers not understanding and having enough knowledge of cognitive disabilities or schools not being able to incorporate a more inclusive learning experience because of the expenses involved in obtaining and incorporating the needed technological solutions. The main problem that arose after investigating numerous research, was that assistive technologies are extremely inaccessible to individuals since it is generally very expensive or it simply is not available in a lot of areas where the residents are in a low socio-economic class, such as some third-world and developing countries. The main problem of the accessibility to assistive technology should be addressed around the world and how these technologies can be made available in a financially sustainable way.

Acknowledgement. Publication funded by NRF UID/127494.

References

1. Shaywitz, S.E., Shaywitz, B.A.: Dyslexia (specific reading disability). Biol. Psychiatry **57**, 1301–1309 (2005). https://doi.org/10.1016/j.biopsych.2005.01.043
2. Wadlington, E.M., Wadlington, P.L.: What educators really believe about dyslexia. Read. Improv. **42**, 16 (2005)
3. Tunmer, W., Greaney, K.: Defining dyslexia. J. Learn. Disabil. (2009). https://doi.org/10.1177/0022219409345009
4. Bond, R.R., et al.: Automation bias in medicine: the influence of automated diagnoses on interpreter accuracy and uncertainty when reading electrocardiograms. J. Electrocardiol. **51**, S6–S11 (2018). https://doi.org/10.1016/j.jelectrocard.2018.08.007
5. Braddock, D., Rizzolo, M.C., Thompson, M., Bell, R.: Emerging technologies and cognitive disability. J. Spec. Educ. Technol. **19**, 49–56 (2004)
6. Perera, H., Shiratuddin, M.F., Wong, K.W., Fullarton, K.: EEG signal analysis of writing and typing between adults with dyslexia and normal controls. Int. J. Interact. Multimed. Artif. Intell. **5**, 62 (2018). https://doi.org/10.9781/ijimai.2018.04.005
7. Draffan, E.A., Evans, D.G., Blenkhorn, P.: Use of assistive technology by students with dyslexia in post-secondary education. Disabil. Rehabil. Assist. Technol. **2**, 105–116 (2007). https://doi.org/10.1080/17483100601178492
8. Kouroupetroglou, G., Pino, A., Kacorri, H.: A model of accessibility services provision for students with disabilities in higher education. In: International Conference Universal Learning Design, p. 11. Athens (2012)
9. Araújo, S., Pacheco, A., Faísca, L., Petersson, K.M., Reis, A.: Visual rapid naming and phonological abilities: different subtypes in dyslexic children. Int. J. Psychol. **45**, 443–452 (2010). https://doi.org/10.1080/00207594.2010.499949
10. Peyrin, C., et al.: Neural dissociation of phonological and visual attention span disorders in developmental dyslexia: FMRI evidence from two case reports. Brain Lang. **120**, 381–394 (2012). https://doi.org/10.1016/j.bandl.2011.12.015
11. Stebbins, G.T., Murphy, C.M.: Diffusion tensor imaging in alzheimer's disease and mild cognitive impairment. Behav. Neurol. **21**, 39–49 (2009). https://doi.org/10.3233/BEN-2009-0234
12. Bennett, C.M., Miller, M.B.: How reliable are the results from functional magnetic resonance imaging. Ann. N. Y. Acad. Sci. **1191**, 133–155 (2010). https://doi.org/10.1111/j.1749-6632.2010.05446.x
13. Geraldes, C.F.G.C., Laurent, S.: Classification and basic properties of contrast agents for magnetic resonance imaging. Contrast Media Mol. Imaging **4**, 1–23 (2009). https://doi.org/10.1002/cmmi.265

14. Müller-Putz, G.R., Riedl, R., Wriessnegger, S.C.: Electroencephalography (EEG) as a research tool in the information systems discipline: foundations, measurement, and applications. Commun. Assoc. Inf. Syst. **37**(1), 46 (2015). https://doi.org/10.17705/1CAIS.03746
15. Penolazzi, B., Spironelli, C., Vio, C., Angrilli, A.: Brain plasticity in developmental dyslexia after phonological treatment: a beta EEG band study. Behav. Brain Res. **209**, 179–182 (2010)
16. Stefanics, G., Fosker, T., Huss, M., Mead, N., Szucs, D., Goswami, U.: Auditory sensory deficits in developmental dyslexia: a longitudinal ERP study. NeuroImage **57**, 723–732 (2011). https://doi.org/10.1016/j.neuroimage.2011.04.005
17. Shinohara, K., Wobbrock, J.O.: In the shadow of misperception: assistive technology use and social interactions. In: Proceedings of the 2011 Annual Conference on Human Factors in Computing Systems - CHI'11, p. 705. ACM Press, Vancouver, BC, Canada (2011). https://doi.org/10.1145/1978942.1979044
18. Oliver, M.: Learning technology: theorising the tools we study. Br. J. Educ. Technol. **44**, 31–43 (2013). https://doi.org/10.1111/j.1467-8535.2011.01283.x
19. Ault, M.J., Bausch, M.E., Mclaren, E.M.: Assistive technology service delivery in rural school districts. Rural Spec. Educ. Q. **32**, 15–22 (2013). https://doi.org/10.1177/875687051303200204
20. Alnahdi, G.: Assistive technology in special education and the universal design for learning. Turk. Online J. Educ. Technol. - TOJET **13**, 18–23 (2014)
21. Hayhoe, S.: Learning in a Digitalized Age: Plugged in, Turned on, Totally Engaged, pp. 257–274. John Catt Educational Ltd, Suffolk (2014)
22. Thomas, L., Heath, J.: Institutional wide implementation of key advice for socially inclusive teaching in higher education. A practice report. Int. J. First Year High. Educ. **5**, 125–133 (2014)
23. Athanaselis, T., Bakamidis, S., Dologlou, I., Argyriou, E.N., Symvonis, A.: Making assistive reading tools user friendly: a new platform for Greek dyslexic students empowered by automatic speech recognition. Multimedia Tools Appl. **68**(3), 681–699 (2012). https://doi.org/10.1007/s11042-012-1073-5
24. Federico, M., Furini, M.: Enhancing learning accessibility through fully automatic captioning. In: Proceedings of the International Cross-Disciplinary Conference on Web Accessibility, pp. 1–4. Association for Computing Machinery, New York, NY, USA (2012). https://doi.org/10.1145/2207016.2207053
25. Taylor, P.: Text-to-Speech Synthesis. Cambridge University Press, Cambridge (2009). https://doi.org/10.1017/CBO9780511816338
26. Robson, L.: Additional help, additional problem – issues for supported dyslexic students. In: HEA STEM Annual Conference, p. 7. University of Edinburgh, Scotland (2014)
27. Olabisi, S.B., David, A.A.: Digital smart pen: a portable media with endless benefits. Int. J. Comput. Appl. **74**, 28–30 (2013). https://doi.org/10.5120/12954-0041
28. Gotesman, E., Goldfus, C.: The impact of assistive technologies on the reading outcomes of college students with disabilities. In: Chais Conference on Instructional Technologies Research 2009. Israel (2009)
29. Doughty, K.: SPAs (smart phone applications) – a new form of assistive technology. J. Assist. Technol. **5**, 88–94 (2011). https://doi.org/10.1108/17549451111149296
30. Borblik, J., Shabalina, O., Kultsova, M., Pidoprigora, A., Romanenko, R.: Assistive technology software for people with intellectual or development disabilities: design of user interfaces for mobile applications. In: 2015 6th International Conference on Information, Intelligence, Systems and Applications (IISA), pp. 1–6 (2015). https://doi.org/10.1109/IISA.2015.7387976

31. Abdullah, M.H.L., Hisham, S., Parumo, S.: MyLexics: an assistive courseware for dyslexic children to learn basic malay language. ASAC **95**, 3–9 (2009). https://doi.org/10.1145/1651259.1651260
32. Yusuf, M.O., Fakomogbon, M.A., Issa, A.I.: Availability of assistive technologies in nigerian educational institutions. Int. J. Soc. Sci. Educ. **2**, 12 (2012)
33. Pino, M., Mortari, L.: The inclusion of students with dyslexia in higher education: a systematic review using narrative synthesis. Dyslexia Chichester Engl. **20**, 346–369 (2014). https://doi.org/10.1002/dys.1484
34. de Santana, V.F., de Oliveira, R., Almeida, L.D.A., Baranauskas, M.C.C.: Web accessibility and people with dyslexia: a survey on techniques and guidelines. In: Proceedings of the International Cross-Disciplinary Conference on Web Accessibility, pp. 1–9. Association for Computing Machinery, New York, NY, USA (2012). https://doi.org/10.1145/2207016.2207047
35. de Santana, V.F., de Oliveira, R., Almeida, L.D.A., Ito, M.: Firefixia: an accessibility web browser customization toolbar for people with dyslexia. In: Proceedings of the 10th International Cross-Disciplinary Conference on Web Accessibility, pp. 1–4. Association for Computing Machinery, New York, NY, USA (2013). https://doi.org/10.1145/2461121.2461137
36. McCarthy, J.E., Swierenga, S.J.: What we know about dyslexia and web accessibility: a research review. Univers. Access Inf. Soc. **9**, 147–152 (2010). https://doi.org/10.1007/s10209-009-0160-5
37. Waller, S., Bradley, M., Hosking, I., Clarkson, P.J.: Making the case for inclusive design. Appl. Ergon. **46**, 297–303 (2015). https://doi.org/10.1016/j.apergo.2013.03.012
38. Buehler, E., et al.: Sharing is caring: assistive technology designs on thingiverse. In: Proceedings of the 33rd Annual ACM Conference Human Factors Computimg Systems - CHI 15, pp. 525–534 (2015). https://doi.org/10.1145/2702123.2702525
39. Cruz, D.M., Emmel, M.L.G., Manzini, M.G., Braga Mendes, P.V.: Assistive technology accessibility and abandonment: challenges for occupational therapists. Open J. Occup. Ther. **4**(1), 10 (2016)
40. Shinohara, K., Wobbrock, J.: Self-conscious or self-confident? a diary study conceptualizing the social accessibility of assistive technology. TACC **8**(2), 1–31 (2016). https://doi.org/10.1145/2827857
41. Wood, D.: Problematizing the inclusion agenda in higher education: towards a more inclusive technology enhanced learning model. First Monday (2015). https://doi.org/10.5210/fm.v20i9.6168
42. Alasuutari, H., Jokikokko, K.: Intercultural learning as a precondition for more inclu-sive society and schools. Finn. J. Ethn. Migr. **5**, 27–37 (2010)

Assistive Technology for ADHD: A Systematic Literature Review

Emily Black and Marie Hattingh[✉]

Department of Informatics, University of Pretoria, Pretoria 0001, South Africa
{emily.black,marie.hattingh}@up.ac.za

Abstract. This paper reports on a study that aimed to identify different assistive technologies that are currently available to support children living with ADHD. This review is conducted by using a systematic approach by collecting and analyzing academically acknowledged qualitative as well as quantitative studies between 2011 and 2019. For the purpose of this study, assistive technologies were divided into three categories namely: 1) Wearables, 2) Mobile technology and applications and 3) Computer-based technology. It was also found that some believe that the use of technology cannot be the aid to support children living with ADHD in a school environment. These results indicate that even though there are several assistive technology solutions that are currently present, there were mixed conclusions on the effectiveness of utilizing assistive technology as an aid of ADHD.

Keywords: Assistive technology · ADHD · Children · School performance

1 Introduction

The treatment for Attention Deficit Hyperactivity Disorder (ADHD) is not one of medication alone, thus multimodal treatments are currently recommended when one is treating ADHD [1, 2]. ADHD includes characteristics and symptoms of absent-mindedness, impulsivity, and hyperactivity [3]. Further, an ADHD child will also display signs of other characteristics such as not listening with understanding of the context, being forgetful, struggling to stay still or may be fidgety, being restless and talkative [4]. These behaviors can make it difficult for any educator or parent who needs to teach ADHD children, especially in a mainstream school environment.

An average of 8.4% of children worldwide is estimated to be diagnosed with ADHD, making it one of the most prevalent mental disorders that are currently affecting children [3]. Poor academic performance shows a positive correlation with ADHD.

ADHD may cause a cognitive impairment for people who suffer from the disability and results in a deficit in executive functioning of cognitive processes, problem-solving abilities and working memory [5]. These difficulties have a high impact on academic – and occupational performance [6]. Treatment for ADHD requires one to look at various components, such as individual - and family knowledge, collaboration and support from educators and other school personnel, management of a child's behavior, as well as medication to treat the psychological aspect [1].

Previously, educators had to rely on individually created visual and audio means of teaching. They used tools such as 16 mm projectors and tape recorders as support to better reach and teach children who learn differently [7]. Today, the means of teaching has become more technically orientated and computerized, with different media and audio functions that can support educational environments. An immense number of technological advances have increased humans' dependence on technology and computers to assist them with day-to-day activities.

Assistive Technology (AT) should not only adapt to support each learner's individual needs, but should also comply with the rules and regulations of assessments and examinations [4]. AT is a set of mechanical, electronic or computerized equipment designed for - and used by people with disabilities to help them function in their everyday lives [7]. Each child is different, which means that there is not only one AT solution that can help all children living with ADHD to learn better and that existing AT must be able to adapt to a student's individual need [4]. Hence, AT should not only be designed for students with visible or physical disabilities, but rather for all those who need help in order to succeed in a mainstream school environment.

This paper aims to critically evaluate struggles that children, living with ADHD, have concerning their school performance and how assistive technology can support these learners with their learning and developmental difficulties to excel in a mainstream school environment.

2 Research Method

The research question to be answered by this study is: *What aspects needs to be considered when utilising assistive technology as an aid to support ADHD in a school environment?* The following search terms were used: ("Assisting Technology" OR "Assistive Technology" OR "educational technology" OR "app*") AND ("Learning disability*" OR "learning difficult*") AND ("ADHD" OR "Hyperactivity Deficit Attention Disorder" OR "cognitive disability" OR "behavioural disorder" OR "conduct disorders" OR "disruptive disorders") AND ("School Performance" OR "grade average" OR "education") AND ("child*").

The selection criteria include a set of inclusion criteria and exclusion criteria that was pre-defined by the author based on information needed to answer the research question. The following inclusion criteria were used to select the sources, any article not conforming to this were excluded: (1) Studies in English, (2) Studies where participants were younger than 18, diagnosed with ADHD and/or learning disabilities, (3) Studies where participants display problems signs in regards to school performance, (4) Studies from 2011 to 2019, (6) Studies from peer reviewed journal articles and books using qualitative measures for analysis, seeking to understand the impact ADHD and learning disabilities has on school performance.

3 Analysis of Findings

This section describes the analysis of data found as well as a discussion on each topic. All the findings are divided in sections that relates to the different parts of the research question that served as a guide for this literature review. Of the 32 articles, eight discussed assistive technology intervention for ADHD, eight discussed educator's knowledge of ADHD and possible interventions, six articles discussed ADHD in correlation with learning disabilities, poor executive functioning and poor school performance, six discussed the prevalence of ADHD and five discussed guidelines when developing assistive technology for ADHD. Each of these aspects will be discussed in more detail in the following sections.

3.1 The Impact of the Environment on a Child with ADHD

Figure 1 shows that the school environment for a child with ADHD is influenced by the type of AT technology, the knowledge of the Educator and the performance of the child. Each of these aspects will be discussed in the following sections.

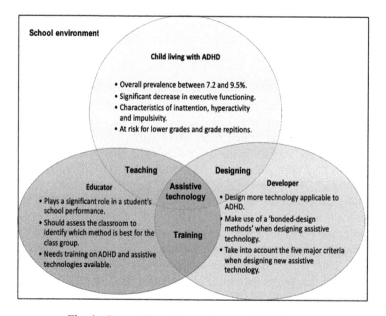

Fig. 1. Summation of the environment that impacts.

The Impact of ADHD on a Child. Analyzing the collected research materials, it was found by [9] and [14] that ADHD is one of the most common disorder affecting children.

Children living with ADHD shows a significant decrease in executive functioning [8]. Executive functioning is classified as the cognitive processes that allow us to respond accordingly in certain circumstances. It enables us to make decisions, develop new habits, evaluate risks, plan, prioritize and sequence activities [15]. Research done by [8] states that ADHD children exhibits a decrease in executive functioning skills. This compliments statements made by [9] and [10], that an average of 75% of ADHD children will have another psychiatric disorder, such as learning disabilities, anxiety, depression and aggression, which is impacting the quality of life and academic success for these children. Children need to use their executive functioning abilities to achieve daily goals in classrooms.

Educator Knowledge and Training on ADHD and Assistive Technology. Educators may be aware that cognitive abilities plays a significant role in a child's learning process and how this influences their academic success, yet they are less aware of the impact and symptoms of ADHD in the classroom [8]. The majority of textbooks to educate teachers on how to interact and teach children with special needs appropriately, only conveyed brief statements with explanations about learning disabilities in the classroom [11, 12].

In simple terms a classroom is that where children gets taught by an educator, yet the simplicity of this statement is influenced by many factors that vary internally as well as externally [13]. These factors can have a significant influence on the amount of effort that is spent of efficiently teaching children in that environment [13]. Optimal learning for students cannot occur without capturing their attention [14] and teachers should continually refocus a student's attention to the implied target once they notice that they lost their attention [13]. In order for teachers to make the best choice they need to have a prior understanding of the child and what he/she understands of the content as well as good knowledge about what the capabilities are of each specific technology that can be utilized in the classroom [14]. It is common for ADHD children to receive psychological help and medicine to help improve their cognitive processes, yet without the support the educator's understanding of the problem at hand and continuous motivation, these children is at risk of falling behind in school environments [11].

Developing Assistive Technology for ADHD. Assistive technologies refers to a wide variety of technology that can be utilized to support learning, teaching and the assessment of school activities [15]. Computer-assisted technology has been used as a form of special education for children who expressed a need with learning difficulties [15]. Smartphones, iPads and tablets has become more accessible to everyday lives. The capabilities of these devices has also been adopted in many classrooms worldwide as a form of learning and teaching [20].

There is evidence of many different assistive technologies used to improve a child's knowledge and skills when they live with difficulties such as ADHD. Several ongoing studies on many different assistive technologies and many assistive technologies were presented over the past years, yet most of them focus on Autism disorder and not ADHD [11]. People may mistake these two disorders to have many similar characteristics, however they are indeed very different. Thus the technologies developed for Autism disorder cannot automatically be adopted as an assistive technology solution for ADHD [16]. The challenge with developing these technologies to support children living with ADHD is to keep younger children entertained as well as older children or adolescents [2].

Benton and Johnson [17] argue that researchers and developers should have a 'bonded design' method when designing new assistive technology for children with ADHD. This is when the children who will possibly be users of the program is involved throughout the process [17]. This will help to increasing the value of the technology and make the design better [17]. After empirical research was done in the ADHD domain, [16] identified five major criteria's that assistive technology for ADHD should adhere to: 1) All technologies should be unobtrusive to wear, 2) Systems should be robust enough to handle ADHD behavior in the classroom and outside, 3) Avoid technology that may expose children to bullying and stigmatization in school, 4) The system should always deliver real time and continuous feedback, 5) It should be relatively easy to set up in order to avoid frustration for the child. These devices should recognize certain activities and movements made by a child in the classroom, it should then analyses the data, detect the changes that trigger inattentiveness in class and assist the child to regain attention in a non-intrusive way [16]. Abbott et al. [18] state that technology is increasingly used by humans to become more efficient and this contributed to rapid and multiple changes in the development domains, enabling technology to become cheaper, easily accessible, more efficient, reliable and flexible.

3.2 Discussion of Different Types of Assistive Technology for ADHD

This section aims to provide insight into the different methods that can be used as alternative ways to teach and support children living with ADHD in a mainstream school environment. Four main topics are covered namely: 1) Wearable technology to assist ADHD, 2) Mobile technology and applications to assist ADHD, 3) Computer-based technology to assist ADHD and 4) Arguments against technology intervention.

Wearable Technology that Can Assist with ADHD. Wearable technology is known as an accessory that can be worn, whether it is part of one's clothing, implanted in your body or tattooed on one's skin [24]. It is a hands-free gadget, used to make one's life more efficient that can be used in many practical ways by using microprocessors to send and receive information to-and-from the internet [24].

Rijo et al. [21] researched Child Activity and Sensitivity Training Tool (CASTT) as a wearable device for children living with ADHD. This prototype was built around three important components that needs to be taken into account when one is developing assistive technology for special needs, especially ADHD, namely: sensing, recognising and assisting. In 2012, the CASTT device could be combined with Dolce Ultra-lite (DUL) sensors, a smartphone, and HR monitor and an Electroencephalography (EEG) headset to sense the child's physical and psychological state when taking part in different activities [16]. They have found that the DUL sensors, smartphone and HR monitor were all comfortable to use by the children. This was magnified when a child went out for play time and only took off the EEG headset [16].

Finding solutions to help a child living it ADHD is extremely important, as their focus that is kept during the day in the classroom play a big role in their overall end year performance. During the rest of the study [16] made the notification on the smartphone vibrate every 15 min. They noticed that the vibrating notifications from the smartphone did not disturb the rest of the children in class, while at the same time reminding the student applicable to stay focused [16]. The average child did return to his current assignment after the smartphone vibrated and afterwards stayed focused for an average of 10–12 min of the intervention.

There is currently another smart watch called WatchMinder which can be used to help ADHD children set such reminders, with each reminder the watch vibrates [25].

Mobile Applications that Can Assist with ADHD. Today, mobile applications are part of the everyday lives of the average human being and the increase in users has come from more people being constantly on the move that can make use of the different applications anywhere at any time to aid several everyday tasks.

The different applications tend to satisfy different needs for different users living with ADHD as everyone living with ADHD does not exhibit the same characteristics and does not struggle with the same difficulties.

The iPad, as a useful mobile technology, has gained a substantial following over the past decade. It is found to be a feasible solution to enhance participation and inclusivity in the classrooms and many schools have adopted the technology as a means of learning and teaching, as it supports a wide range of educational needs [20]. The iPad is a tool to that encourages Universal Design for Learning (UDL) in a school environment and allows educators to teach children with different needs in different ways that can help them be successful and improve their overall school performance. Many parents, teachers and children across the world already own smartphones and tablets. Due to this, learning how to use the device will take the minimum amount of time for the applicable party. Educators can use this method to create a more inclusive classroom and incorporate learning methods based on all children's multiple complex needs. In order to implement the use of an iPad successfully the organization or school needs to provide the teachers as well as the learners with the needed support to gain the necessary skills and knowledge to efficiently use the device and the apps applicable [20].

ProceduralPal is a mobile application that aims to aid children living with ADHD and who has access to a smartphone to rehearse common daily tasks [25]. The application allows you to break these tasks up into separate smaller steps that can each be represented by a picture if needed [25]. Users can then view the images and read the instructions to know how to accurately and efficiently complete the task at hand step-by-step [25].

TaskTracker, like ProceduralPal is a mobile application that is designed to aid children living with ADHD to complete daily tasks efficiently. On the app, each user can log certain tasks that they may find difficult [25, 26]. For each tasks the app has a progress bar, alarm reminders and motivational messages that has been designed to encourage successful task completion with time managed, rather than focusing on remembering to complete the task alone [25], [19, 20].

While there are many other assistive technologies that can assist children living with ADHD during execution of everyday tasks and memory, the developers of the mobile applications mentioned above has included some basic needed features that others have not. Both ProcedurePal and TaskTracker are apps that not only focuses on task management, but they also place focus on time management.

The Training Attention and Learning Initiative (TALI) program, is a computerized software that is specifically designed to improve attention skills [21]. When working with this program you have 4 activities to complete on a touch screen tablet or smartphone. Each activity lasts 4 min and the exercises for the day takes approximately up to 20 min. By using an inbuilt criterion, the software is able to determine the level of difficulty for each individual user and will automatically adjust it regarding their performance in each activity. The developers created a visual and verbal guide in order to sufficiently help the child work on the system and through every activity. When a child's attention is trained, attention can be better maintained during strenuous school activities. [21] found that when the children used this app for a 3 month period, had selective improvements in both short- and long term attention.

Computer-Based Training and Gamification that Can Assist with ADHD. Computer-based training is seen as a form of training done on a computer. A computer has the capabilities to teach a student in more forms than one by making use of audio, video, graphical information and text. The system can be tailored to each individual's needs. This form of training can be beneficial when different students in the class each has different means of processing and gaining new knowledge. When the right training is offered as an intervention to the right children, who experience a deficit in certain cognitive functions, it is evident that this type of training will keep the children engaged and have many noticeable and favorable outcome [21].

Cogmed Working Memory Training is a computer-based application that is aimed to improve attention difficulties, caused by working memory inefficiencies, that children living with ADHD experience [21]. This program is designed to challenge the capacity of its user's working memory and target cognitive functioning that is needed to enhance its user's everyday lives. This goal is reached through cognitive exercises, developed by neuroscientists, that can be done by each user. It is developed in such a way that the difficulty level is set in real-time based on the user's performance when completing the different exercises for the day [21].

Plan it commander is a specific program or software aimed to help ADHD, to play at home, developed by the Ranj Serious Game Project. This program helps the children to plan for certain events by requiring the player to solve many different problems in a certain situation [21, 22]. The game consists ten main mission, all with submissions. These missions consist of activities that improve cognitive functioning by training complex and critical thinking skills, time management, planning and organizing skills [22]. Once the one mission is completed, the next will become available. There is an enclosed space provided where players can ask each other questions and in turn other players provide assistance [22].

Arguments Against Computer-Assisted Technology as an Aid for ADHD. Weisberg [25] argues that even though several new assistive technologies have been developed to assist ADHD and other executive functioning factors over the past years, some solutions may be intrusive. Many assistive devices display reminders and vibrate, this may cause a child living with ADHD to constantly be distracted by the device instead of it aiding the child to be more efficient when completing tasks.

Children who are allowed to substantially increase screen time to assist them with different tasks, may become dependent on media [23]. As the child gets older and child-parent conflict arises, children may seek support from other sources such as media, smartphones tablets and computers [23]. These children are at risk of becoming addicted to these devices and can increase their risk for other comorbid disorders that is common in children living with ADHD, such as anxiety and depression [23]. Side effects may occur when technology is used continuously, such as changes in behaviours, cognitive functioning and emotions [23]. This can be due to the amount of information one needs to process when working on technology and the constant change between platforms used.

4 Conclusion

Computer-assisted technology has become more popular as an aid to use in schools worldwide and is especially used to teach children with special needs. This is attributed to the fact that learning technology has a gained a reputation of when used appropriately it can substantially improve a child's experience and performance in a mainstream school environment. Even though there are verified arguments why technology is not the best solution to support children living with ADHD in a mainstream school environment, the positive feedback is far greater. Today, there is an increasing need to create an environment where access to education is equal for all students, while also creating a learning process that empowers the child to excel irrespective of their individual abilities or lack of. Attention should be placed on finding new ways to make an impact through different teaching practices to accommodate children living with ADHD learning disabilities or learning difficulties.

Acknowledgement. Publication funded by NRF UID/127494.

References

1. Silver, L.B.: Advice to parents on ADHD. Harmony (1999)
2. Sonuga-Barke, E., Brandeis, D., Holtmann, M., Cortese, S.: Computer-based cognitive training for ADHD. Child Adolesc. Psychiatr. Clin. N. Am. **23**, 807–824 (2014). https://doi.org/10.1016/j.chc.2014.05.009
3. Parekh, R.: What Is ADHD? https://www.psychiatry.org/patients-families/adhd/what-is-adhd. Accessed 30 Oct 2019
4. Bester, H.: New Hope For ADHD. Tafelberg, Cape Town (2014)
5. Ek, U., Westerlund, J., Holmberg, K., Fernell, E.: Academic performance of adolescents with ADHD and other behavioural and learning problems—a population-based longitudinal study: academic performance of adolescents with ADHD. Acta Paediatr. **100**, 402–406 (2011). https://doi.org/10.1111/j.1651-2227.2010.02048.x
6. Young, A.R., Beitchman, J.H.: Specific learning disorder. In: Gabbard's Treatments of Psychiatric Disorders. American Psychiatric Publishing (2014). https://doi.org/10.1176/appi.books.9781585625048.gg05
7. Blackhurst, A.E.: Perspectives on applications of technology in the field of learning disabilities. Learn. Disabil. Q. **28**, 175 (2005). https://doi.org/10.2307/1593622
8. Langer, N., Benjamin, C., Becker, B.L.C., Gaab, N.: Comorbidity of reading disabilities and ADHD: structural and functional brain characteristics. Hum. Brain Mapp. **40**, 2677–2698 (2019). https://doi.org/10.1002/hbm.24552

9. Skogli, E.W., Teicher, M.H., Andersen, P.N., Hovik, K.T., Øie, M.: ADHD in girls and boys – gender differences in co-existing symptoms and executive function measures. BMC Psychiatry **13**, 298 (2013). https://doi.org/10.1186/1471-244X-13-298
10. Birchwood, J., Daley, D.: Brief report: the impact of attention deficit hyperactivity disorder (ADHD) symptoms on academic performance in an adolescent community sample. J. Adolesc. **35**, 225–231 (2012). https://doi.org/10.1016/j.adolescence.2010.08.011
11. Liontou, T.: Foreign language learning for children with ADHD: evidence from a technology-enhanced learning environment. Eur. J. Spec. Needs Educ. **34**, 220–235 (2019). https://doi.org/10.1080/08856257.2019.1581403
12. Lucas, A.G., Passe, J.: Are social studies methods textbooks preparing teachers to support students with disabilities in social studies classrooms? J. Soc. Stud. Res. **41**, 141–153 (2017). https://doi.org/10.1016/j.jssr.2016.06.003
13. Bester, G., Brand, L.: The effect of technology on learner attention and achievement in the classroom. South Afr. J. Educ. **33**, 1–15 (2013). https://doi.org/10.15700/saje.v33n2a405
14. Dennis, M.S., et al.: A meta-analysis of empirical research on teaching students with mathematics learning difficulties. Learn. Disabil. Res. Pract. **31**, 156–168 (2016). https://doi.org/10.1111/ldrp.12107
15. Liu, G.-Z., Wu, N.-W., Chen, Y.-W.: Identifying emerging trends for implementing learning technology in special education: a state-of-the-art review of selected articles published in 2008–2012. Res. Dev. Disabil. **34**, 3618–3628 (2013). https://doi.org/10.1016/j.ridd.2013.07.007
16. Sonne, T., Obel, C., Grønbæk, K.: Designing real time assistive technologies: a study of children with ADHD. In: Proceedings of the Annual Meeting of the Australian Special Interest Group for Computer Human Interaction – OzCHI 2015, Parkville, VIC, Australia, pp. 34–38. ACM Press (2015). https://doi.org/10.1145/2838739.2838815
17. Benton, L., Johnson, H.: Widening participation in technology design: a review of the involvement of children with special educational needs and disabilities. Int. J. Child-Comput. Interact. **3–4**, 23–40 (2015). https://doi.org/10.1016/j.ijcci.2015.07.001
18. Abbott, C., Brown, D., Evett, L., Standen, P., Wright, J.: Learning difference and digital technologies: a literature review of research involving children and young people using assistive technologies 2007–2010 (2011)
19. Hribar, V.E.: The TaskTracker: assistive technology for task completion. In: The proceedings of the 13th International ACM SIGACCESS Conference on Computers and Accessibility (ASSETS 2011), pp. 327–328. Association for Computing Machinery, New York (2011). https://doi.org/10.1145/2049536.2049631
20. Weisberg, O., et al.: TangiPlan: designing an assistive technology to enhance executive functioning among children with adhd. In: Proceedings of the 2014 Conference on Interaction Design and Children – IDC 2014, Aarhus, Denmark, pp. 293–296. ACM Press (2014). https://doi.org/10.1145/2593968.2610475
21. Rijo, R., et al.: Mysterious bones unearthed: development of an online therapeuticserious game for children with attention deficit-hyperactivity disorder. In: Conference on ENTERprise Information Systems/International Conference on Project MANagement/Conference on Health and Social Care Information Systems and Technologies, CENTERIS/ProjMAN/HCist 2015, 7–9 October 2015, vol. 64, pp. 1208–1216 (2015). https://doi.org/10.1016/j.procs.2015.08.512
22. Bul, K.C.M., et al.: Development and user satisfaction of "plan-it commander", a serious game for children with ADHD. Games Health J. **4**, 502–512 (2015). https://doi.org/10.1089/g4h.2015.0021

23. Steve, A., Grubb, H.J.: The prevalence of ADHD in American society: the influence of parent-child and child-technology interactions. Eur. Sci. J. ESJ. **14**, 41 (2018). https://doi.org/10.19044/esj.2018.v14n8p41
24. Kenton, W.: The Ins and Outs of Wearable Technology. Investopedia 25 July 2019. https://www.investopedia.com/terms/w/wearable-technology.asp. Accessed: 15 Oct 2019
25. Weisberg, O., et al.: TangiPlan: designing an assistive technology to enhance executive functioning among children with ADHD. In: Proceedings of the 2014 Conference on Interaction Design and Children - IDC 2014, Aarhus, Denmark, pp. 293–296 (2014)
26. Becker, L.: WatchMinder History (2019). https://www.watchminder.com/about-us/history. Accessed 20 Oct 2019

Chinese Students' Motivations to Adopt E-Learning

James O. Stanworth[✉]

Department of Business Administration, National Changhua University
of Education, Changhua, Taiwan R.O.C.
stanworth.j@gmail.com

Abstract. Culture influences how students give meanings to, and engage with, e-learning. Since the predominance of research draws on models construed with values from the Western world they risk lacking congruence with other contexts. This study aims to identify the motives of students in Chinese culture towards e-learning and explain how these predict behavior. I use a form of laddering to identify students' motives and associating organizing schema. Results show 37 motives draw students towards while 31 push them away from e-learning. The analysis reveals that students are drawn towards the temporal spatial benefits of e-learning. They, however they feel debilitated and lack a sense of mo-qi with both their classmates and the teacher. These results point towards a different conceptualization of e-learning motivations than seen so far in the literature.

Keywords: Technology adoption · Chinese learner · Culture · E-learning

1 Introduction

1.1 Research Background

Notions about education and its delivery vary greatly across cultures and these translate into the way e-learning is also understood. Studies find that students may have different reactions and understanding to educational approaches that are based on the practices of a different cultural context [1]. The literature on the structure and approaches to e-learning is currently dominated by assumptions of educational values and norms that anchor in the Western world. This translates into a narrative that anticipates that e-learning facilitates interaction [2] and the development of critical thinking [3, 4] in environments that encourage the co-construction of knowledge [5]. Culture is already recognized, for example, as affecting online presence and learner perceptions [6].

Of particular relevance to Chinese learners who have markedly different understanding about education norms and values than their Western counterparts. Self-directed learning, for example is an anomaly in an environment where learning is still heavily directed by teachers and lectures are regarded as central to passing on knowledge of any substance [1, 7, 8]. Consequently, e-learning is understood differently by Chinese learners [9, 10]. The success of e-learning as a form of instruction is contingent on learners' willingness to engage with this form of learning.

Questions about what explains people's willingness to engage and use technology are of enduring interest [11, 12] and this is particularly so in terms of e-learning technologies [8, 13, 15]. This literature, however, largely overlooks how culture shapes e-learning technology adoption. This is surprising given the significance of culture in influencing, "the successful implementation and use of information technology." [16, p. 357] It is important to consider the cultural backgrounds of learners if we are to understand how they react to and consider adoption of e-learning educational technologies. This then frames significant questions about how and why Chinese e-learners want to adopt and use e-learning.

I draw on the perspective that adoption is effectively understood and explained from a motivation perspective. This breaks from the traditional technology acceptance or technology adoption perspectives. A motivation perspective frames adoption as motivational goals expressed through schema that reveal individuals' intentions towards technology adoption [17, 19]. This perspective aligns effectively with the aspiration in this project to construct a grounded model (i.e., in Chinese culture norms and roles) that explains goals (i.e., Chinese e-learners' motives) towards e-learning adoption (i.e., explaining their intention to use such technologies).

I frame two main objectives in order to incrementally advance our understanding of student adoption of e-learning:

- RO1: To identify Chinese students' motives towards e-learning adoption.
- RO2: To model Chinese students' motives as predictors of e-learning adoption.

2 Research Method

The goals of this project lead to a qualitative and phased approach. The first phase of study establishes the basis for the second. Under the first phase the e-learning materials and platform and developed and customized to the current teaching context. This provides a base for data collection in the second (i.e., surfacing motives towards e-learning).

2.1 First Phase

A significant dilemma for educators is how to resolve the dilemma between using commercially available classes and designing material in house [20]. The intuitional support that educators often have in-house often comes a significant pedagogical price [21]. This is a significant issue for those trying to retain control of both their materials and delivery approach. Establishing control over pedagogy through material design and delivery was considered particularly important for this research project.

I understood an opportunity to implement my own technologies (e.g., servers and video recording studio) to maintain greater control of my educational resources and their delivery). This do-it-yourself approach is increasingly possible as technologies become more accessible to the untrained [22]. To support this first stage I implemented a virtual server (ESXI 6.0) (See Fig. 1) that acted as platforms for my two main virtual servers. The first server, an Ubuntu based interactive website (for delivery of online course materials). The second, also Ubuntu based, was the BigBluebutton online classroom (Fig. 2). I also developed a studio (Fig. 3) for recording teaching material which integrated a series of camera angles on a virtual set. Over 20 h of course video were shot and edited spread across 52 discrete videos (i.e., each segment varied in length) (Fig. 4). On line quizzes were developed to supplement the material.

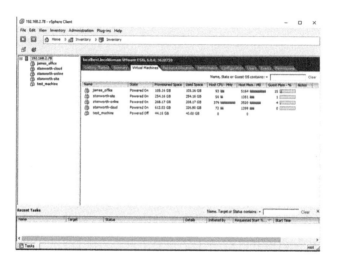

Fig. 1. Virtual servers for online instruction.

Fig. 2. Implementation of blended class (BigBluebutton). (Color figure online)

Fig. 3. Studio for e-learning.

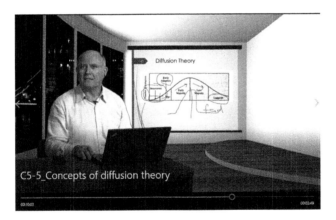

Fig. 4. Screenshot of online learning material (from lab).

Post design the courses was delivered, and refined to resolve inconsistencies or errors between all the multiple constituent parts (e.g., course schedules, online videos, scheduled times for online class, and links to quizzes). With these delivery issues resolved the course was delivered for a second time.

2.2 Second Phase

A primary objective of this study is to explore how students, socialized to Chinese culture, are motivated to engage with and take online courses. This necessitates an approach elaborate cognitive schema that relates experiences (i.e., of e-learning) to more abstract reasons for engaging in this behavior. There is long standing discourse on goal setting and striving within the domain of organizational behavior [23]. Laddering [24] provides a methodology for examining how explicating the relationship between goals and values. Bagozzi and colleagues [18, 19, 25] operationalizes this perspective as a means of explaining individual behaviours; such as, technology adoption. This approach, primarily qualitative, has two main strengths that align well with the purposes of this study. First, it captures actual expressions (i.e., students' own words) about their reasons for engaging with the online class. This helps to avoid the risk of prescribing concepts that might be relevant in one culture (i.e., Western students' concepts about e-learning adoption) but not in another (i.e., here, students under Chinese culture) (an imposed etic [26]. Students' motives once categorized and analyzed, can be said to express a cultural norm about engaging with an online class. Second, by drawing on the broad notion of goal setting as it relates to behavior it gives researchers latitude to develop theoretical explanation that are culturally congruent [27]. This represents the researcher exercising their "disciplined imagination" in the selection and development of the most qualified theoretical explanation [28].

The student participants took either a completely online or a blended class. The fully online class, in business, was structured so students learned the core theoretical material through online videos. These were put online and students could elect when to view them and take the associating quizzes. Class groups had to coordinate amongst themselves to work through a business simulation that ran interactively through the semester. As with the rest of the course this was completely online but supported by teaching assistants. The blended course, also in the business area, drew on the platforms and materials developed above. Students reviewed core-course material as online video with associating quizzes. They met with the instructor approximately every fourth class for face-to-face instruction.

Students were invited to participate the data collection via e-mail. To show appreciation for their time, I sponsored their lunch and offered a coupon (100NT$). To surface students' self-explicated motives for their behaviours, I ask open-ended questions following Bagozzi et al. [18]. Students began completing the open questionnaire by giving up to three reasons that drew them towards engagement with the online class. Next, students were asked to think of the first reason that they had provided and explain why it was important to them in the adjacent column. Students were then asked a final time to consider the explanation they had just given and make a further justification for it in the next column. I repeated this procedure for the second reason. Finally, students were asked to provide up to three reasons that explained what pushed them away from engagement with the online class. I applied the above procedure to both consequences. Ideally, this resulted in students creating two matrices of 9 motives.

To start the data analysis, I focused on data from the completely online class. My 81 informants, from this class, provided 1,448 discrete motives that explained their thinking towards engagement with online courses. The first stage of analysis leads to 37 categories explaining what draws students towards e-learning and 31 categories elaborating what pushes them away. The second stage of analysis yields for draws me towards e-learning 416 linkages and for pushes me away 364 linkages between categories.

3 Results and Discussion

3.1 Preliminary Results

For the fully online class Table 1 show the categories that explain what drew students towards learning in the online class. While Table 2 show the categories explicating students motivates for being pushed away from online course.

Table 1. Student defined motives pushing them towards adopting e-learning.

Attribute		Consequence		Value	
Code	Motive	Code	Motive	Code	Motive
A1	Learning flexibility	B1	Manage my study time	C1	Not limited by space or time
A2	Less time constraints	B2	No need to go to the classroom	C2	Learn to manage my schedule
A3	Manage study time by myself	B3	Flexible time management	C3	Effective use of my time
A4	Convenience	B4	Resource saving	C4	Save resources
A5	High efficacy	B5	Avoiding course time conflict	C5	Less time constraints
A6	Following the trends	B6	Time to do other things	C6	Develop friendship
A7	Making new friends	B7	Learning flexibility	C7	New experiences
A8	Resource saving	B8	Advantageous when lacking vitality	C8	Take more credits
A9	Class is interesting	B9	Own pace to study	C9	Self-development
A10	Schedule more classes	B10	Curious to try	C10	Increasing my understanding
A11	At ease	B11	Feeling relaxed		
A12	Review hard sections	B12	Expand the social network		
A13	Learn new things	B13	Skills for future		
A14	Extensive learning resources				

Table 2. Student defined motives pushing them away from e-learning.

Attribute		Consequence		Value	
Code	Motive	Code	Motive	Code	Motive
A1	No cooperating or coordinating	B1	Bad coordination in group work	C1	Hard to create friendship
A2	Cannot get the feeling of closeness	B2	Hard to fully communicate	C2	Lifeless communication
A3	Missing face-to-face interaction	B3	Cannot immediately solve problems	C3	lack of mò qì (默契)
A4	Hard to ask questions	B4	Lack of pressure to study	C4	Debilitating
A5	Cannot interact directly	B5	Cold interaction	C5	Hard to take care of the grade
A6	Health issues	B76	Unfamiliar with technology	C6	Lack learning efficacy
A7	Unfamiliar way of having class	B7	Bad for eyes	C7	Extra time consuming
A8	Easy to lack self-discipline	B8	Monotonous class	C8	Inconvenience
A9	Need access to computer	B9	Lack dedication		
A10	Overwhelmed by e-mail information	B10	Unfair grading		
A11	Rigid schedule	B11	Low efficiency in learning		
		B12	Knowledge feels scanty		

The next stage of the data analysis involves building implication matrices which show how one motive leads to another. At this stage, the analysis, is still partial and show only reveals the direct relationships (i.e., how often motive "A" leads to motive "B"). Indirect relationships (i.e., how often motive "A" leads to "C" but not directly through "B") are also significant. Further analysis will also consider centrality (how often a motive is a target of other motives) and prestige (how often a motive acts as a source to others) [18]. Figure 5 shows an example of the developing implication matrix.

	B1	B2	B3	B4	B5	B6	B8	B9	B10	B11	B12	B13	B14	B17	C1	C2	C3	C4	C5	C6	C7	C8	C9	C10	C12	C13	C16	C17
A1	5	4	10	2	3	2	0	0	0	0	0	0	0	0														
A2	3	1	8	0	3	0	4	2	0	0	0	0	0	0														
A3	1	2	1	0	1	0	2	1	2	0	1	0	0	0														
A4	0	28	5	3	3	2	0	2	3	0	3	0	0	0														
A5	2	1	0	0	0	0	1	0	2	0	1	0	0	0														
A6	0	0	0	0	0	0	0	0	1	16	0	0	2	1														
A9	0	0	0	0	0	0	0	1	0	0	0	9	2	0														
A11	0	4	1	1	0	3	0	0	0	0	0	0	0	0														
A12	0	0	0	0	0	0	0	0	1	0	0	2	0															
A13	0	0	0	0	7	0	0	0	0	0	0	0	0	0														
A14	0	1	0	0	0	0	2	0	0	2	1	0	0															
A15	0	0	1	0	0	0	0	0	9	1	0	0	0	0														
A16	0	1	0	0	0	0	0	0	0	1	0	1	17	0														
A17	0	4	1	0	1	0	0	1	1	0	0	0	1	0														
B1															1	3	2	0	0	0	1	0	0	0	2	3	1	0
B2															12	5	3	3	4	0	1	1	4	0	1	4	3	2
B3															1	6	6	0	4	0	0	0	4	0	1	2	1	0
B4															1	0	1	2	0	0	0	1	0	0	0	0	0	0
B5															2	0	2	1	1	0	0	0	10	0	0	0	1	0
B6															0	1	5	0	0	0	0	0	0	1	0	0	0	0
B8															2	2	1	0	0	0	0	0	1	0	1	1	0	0
B9															0	2	1	0	0	0	0	0	0	0	2	4	0	0
B10															1	1	0	0	0	0	2	0	0	0	4	1	0	6
B11															1	0	0	0	0	0	1	7	1	2	0	0	2	2
B12															2	0	1	0	0	0	2	0	0	0	0	3	0	0
B13															0	0	0	0	0	7	0	1	0	3	0	0	0	0
B14															0	0	0	0	0	0	0	1	0	22	1	0	0	0
B17															0	0	0	0	0	0	0	0	1	0	3	0	0	0

Fig. 5. Implication matrix of student defined relationships between motivates and e-learning.

The implication matrix provides the basis for developing a cognitive map of schema which shapes students under Chinese culture engagement with e-learning. The map needs sufficient complexity to capture respondents' thoughts while avoiding being overly cluttered. At this stage I have set a cut-off of four or more motives to arrive at Fig. 6 and Fig. 7.

Discussion: Reaction to Preliminary Analysis. The results show that students understand and are drawn towards e-learning by the temporal (e.g., *less time constraints, schedule more classes*) and spatial benefits (e.g., *convenient (place & process)*). As such these show some alignment with the existing literature on e-learning adoption [13, 29].

A significant exception is the notion of following the *trends* that leads students to be *curious to try* so as to have *new experiences*. Understanding something as fresh or novel under Chinese culture is signal of an emerging trend that might be significant. Literature in marketing shows queueing (i.e., the visible presence of and engagement by others in a new/significant phenomena) act to stimulate consumption [30]. I suspect this motive may be significant in explaining what draws students towards this form of learning.

The motives explicating what pushes students away contain much that is novel and significant to this cultural context. Students feel it is *easy to lack self-discipline* as they *lack pressure to study* while blaming themselves for *a lack of dedication* and this results in the overall sense that e-learning is *debilitating*.

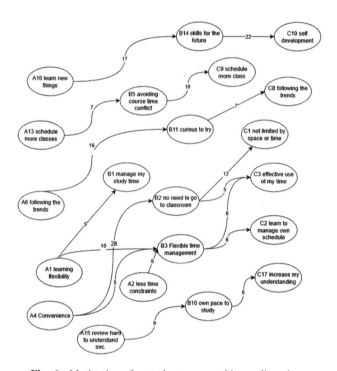

Fig. 6. Motivations for students approaching online class.

Students *cannot get the feeling of closeness* through *cold interactions* that means they *lack mò qì* (默契) with either the instructor or classmates.

These reactions points towards students being demotivated by interactions that might characterize as inauthentic (fake?) or lacking the genuineness of interpersonal contact [31]. These findings some broad alignment with work from business management research [32]. Understanding the implications of these findings, however, requires more reflection about the meanings around core categories through selective coding [33].

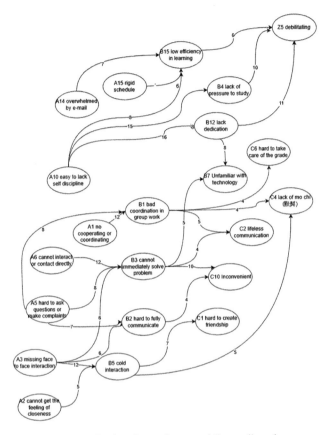

Fig. 7. Motivation for students avoiding online class.

4 Conclusions

The aim of this project is to explore the motives of Chinese students towards engaging with e-learning. I identify a discrete set of motives that explain what draws Chinese students towards and what pushes them away from e-learning. I also find a series of significant connections between these motives that lays the foundation for elaborating a contextualized explanation for Chinese students' motives towards e-learning. What draws Chinese students towards e-learning shows some alignment with existing literature (e.g., time and spatial benefits of e-learning) [13, 29, 34]. Whilst what pushes them away, however, grounds in more fundamental elements about how students understand the nature of learning and education. The Chinese understand learning process as lead by the relationships between the learner and teacher and between learners. [35] Consequently, they appear to feel pushed away from e-learning as they struggle to replicate this model in the online setting.

References

1. Chang, C.-Y., Tsai, C.-C.: The interplay between different forms of CAI and students' preferences of learning environment in the secondary science class. Sci. Educ. **89**(5), 707–724 (2005)
2. Puntambekar, S.: Analyzing collaborative interactions: divergence, shared understanding and construction of knowledge. Comput. Educ. **47**(3), 332–351 (2006)
3. Herold, D.K.: Mediating media studies - stimulating critical awareness in a virtual environment. Comput. Educ. **54**(3), 791–798 (2010)
4. Jamaludin, A., Chee, Y.S., Ho, C.M.L.: Fostering argumentative knowledge construction through enactive role play in second Life. Comput. Educ. **53**(2), 317–329 (2009)
5. Warden, C.A., Stanworth, J.O., Chang, C.-C.: Leveling up: are non-gamers and women disadvantaged in a virtual world classroom?". Comput. Hum. Behav. **65**, 210–219 (2016)
6. Zhu, C.: Student satisfaction, performance, and knowledge construction in online collaborative learning. Educ. Technol. Soc. **15**(1), 127–136 (2012)
7. Zhao, G., Jiang, Z.: From e-campus to e-learning: an overview of ICT applications in Chinese higher education. Br. J. Educ. Technol. **41**(4), 574–581 (2010)
8. Zhao, J., McConnell, D., Jiang, Y.: Teachers' conceptions of e-learning in Chinese higher education: a phenomenographic analysis. Campus-Wide Inf. Syst. **26**(2), 90–97 (2009)
9. Kember, D.: Misconceptions about the learning approaches, motivation and study practices of Asian students. High. Educ. **40**(1), 99–121 (2000)
10. Kember, D.: Reconsidering Open and Distance Learning in the Developing World: Meeting Students' Learning Needs. Routledge (2007)
11. Ivanović, D., Ho, Y.-S.: Highly cited articles in the information science and library science category in social science citation index: a bibliometric analysis. J. Librariansh. Inf. Sci. (2014). https://doi.org/10.1177/0961000614537514
12. Straub, E.T.: Understanding technology adoption: theory and future directions for informal learning. Rev. Educ. Res. **79**(2), 625–649 (2009)
13. Cheung, R., Vogel, D.: Predicting user acceptance of collaborative technologies: an extension of the technology acceptance model for e-learning. Comput. Educ. **63**, 160–175 (2013). https://doi.org/10.1016/j.compedu.2012.12.003
14. Hung, M.-L., Chou, C., Chen, C.-H., Own, Z.-Y.: Learner readiness for online learning: scale development and student perceptions. Comput. Educ. **55**(3), 1080–1090 (2010). https://doi.org/10.1016/j.compedu.2010.05.004
15. Persico, D., Manca, S., Pozzi, F.: Adapting the technology acceptance model to evaluate the innovative potential of e-learning systems. Comput. Hum. Behav. **30**, 614–622 (2014). https://doi.org/10.1016/j.chb.2013.07.045
16. Leidner, D.E., Kayworth, T.: Review: a review of culture in information systems research: toward a theory of information technology culture conflict. MIS Q. **30**(2), 357–399 (2006)
17. Bagozzi, R.P., Wong, N., Abe, S., Bergami, M.: Cultural and situational contingencies and the theory of reasoned action: application to fast food restaurant consumption. J. Consum. Psychol. **9**(2), 97–106 (2000)
18. Bagozzi, R.P., Leone, L., Bergami, M.: Hierachical representation of motives in goal setting. J. Appl. Psychol. **88**(5), 915–943 (2003)
19. Bagozzi, R.P.: The legacy of the technology acceptance model and a proposal for a paradigm shift. J. Assoc. Inf. Syst. **8**(4), 244–254 (2007)
20. Loftus, J., Stavraky, T., Urquhart, B.L.: Design it yourself (DIY): in-house instructional design for online pharmacology. Adv. Health Sci. Educ. **19**(5), 645–659 (2014). https://doi.org/10.1007/s10459-013-9492-2

21. Giuntini, P., Venturini, J.-M.: Highjacking the MOOC: reflections on creating/teaching an art history MOOC. Curr. Iss. Emerg. ELearn. **2**(1), 9 (2015)
22. Petrie, C.: The age of DIY. IEEE Internet Comput. **17**(6), 93–94 (2013). https://doi.org/10.1109/MIC.2013.120
23. Oettingen, G., Gollwitzer, P.M.: Goal setting and goal striving. In: Tesser, A. (ed.) EdIntraindividual Processes. Blackwell, Malden, pp. 329–347 (2001)
24. Reynolds, T.J., Gutman, J.: Laddering theory, method, analysis, and interpretation. J. Advert. Res. **28**(1), 11–31 (1988)
25. Bagozzi, R.P., Dabholkar, P.A.: Consumer recycling goals and their effect on decisions to recycle: a means-end chain analysis. Psychol. Mark. **11**(4), 313–340 (1994)
26. Berry, J.W.: Imposed etics-emics-derived etics: the operationalization of a compelling idea. Int. J. Psychol. **24**(6), 721–736 (1989)
27. Hsu, R.S., Stanworth, J.O.: Work as good-minded undertakings and effortless assignments: Chinese meaning of working for hospitality workers and its motivational implications. J. Organ. Behav. **39**(1), 52–66 (2017)
28. Weick, K.E.: Theory construction as disciplined imagination. Acad. Manage. Rev. **14**(4), 516–531 (1989). https://doi.org/10.2307/258556
29. Roca, J.C., Chiu, C.-M., Martínez, F.J.: Understanding e-learning continuance intention: an extension of the technology acceptance model. Int. J. Hum Comput Stud. **64**(8), 683–696 (2006)
30. Ackerman, D., Walker, K.: Consumption of renao at a Taiwan night market. Int. J. Cult. Tour. Hosp. Res. 6(3), 209–222 (2012). http://dbs.ncue.edu.tw:2235/10.1108/17506181211246366
31. Gao, G.: Don't take my word for it– understanding Chinese speaking practices. Int. J. Intercult. Relat. **22**(2), 163–186 (1998)
32. Stanworth, J.O., Hsu, R.S., Wang, J.T.: Chinese metaphors and narratives in self-service technology adoption. In: Presented at the 15th International Research Conference in Service Management, La Londe, France, June 2018
33. Strauss, A.L., Corbin, J.M.: Basics of Qualitative Research: Grounded Theory Procedures and Techniques. Sage Publications, Newbury Park (1990)
34. Henrie, C.R., Halverson, L.R., Graham, C.R.: Measuring student engagement in technology-mediated learning: a review. Comput. Educ. **90**, 36–53 (2015)
35. Li, J.: US and Chinese cultural beliefs about learning. J. Educ. Psychol. **95**(2), 258 (2003)

Designing Freirean-Inspired Community Relevant STEAM Curriculum for Underserved Students in Pakistan Using Action Research Process

Midhat Noor Kiyani(✉) [ID], Imran Haider, and Fahad Javed

National University of Sciences and Technology (NUST), Islamabad, Pakistan
mkiyani.msitel8seecs@seecs.edu.pk

Abstract. This study constituted community-based, action research that sought to identify community needs and design indigenous community relevant STEAM projects in a local community of underserved students in Pakistan. This Community-Based Action Research is conducted in "The Tent School System"; a slum school in H-11 Islamabad, Pakistan. The five-phase cyclic action research process is implemented that involved: diagnosing and identifying community problems using Freirean process of generative themes, creating STEAM lesson plans for identified problems, designing useful products using lesson plans to solve problems, evaluation of this STEAM workshop and then specifying learning for next interaction of this STEAM action project. Drawing on needs assessment survey, post feedback survey and field notes, this mixed methods study explored the experiences of low-socioeconomic students participating in contextually authentic STEAM Projects. Based on the students' feedback, it was revealed that the main sources of student engagement in this action research project were: the overall impact of these STEAM projects on their community and the skills they inculcated in them that made them capable of solving local community challenges on their own. The major strength of this study was its successful practical application of Freire's theory of critical pedagogy for designing community relevant learning environment for the students. Key learnings of this study imply a useful example of how students can contribute their knowledge and skills to promote general community well-being. Furthermore, the fusion of critical pedagogy of place in STEAM model offers a unique pedagogical innovation to education practitioners all around the world.

Keywords: Critical pedagogy · STEAM education · Action research · Community relevant · Authentic learning · Contextual

1 Introduction

This section below highlights the need and motivation to conduct this study.

1.1 Problem Statement

According to the 2018 report of UNESCO Institute for Statistics (UIS), one out of every five (nearly 262 million) children, adolescents and youth (between the ages of 6 and 17) are out of school [1]. In case of low and lower-middle-income countries, the situation is even worse as it increases to one out of every three children for these socially disadvantaged areas. In Pakistan, nearly 22.6 million boys and girls (44% children) are out of school. According to the same study, the gross enrollment rate is 70% but almost 50% of the children drop out of school before reaching fifth grade. Findings of the report 'The Silent Epidemic: Perspectives of High School Dropouts' commissioned by Bill & Melinda Gates Foundation connect increasing dropout rate with the lack of content relevance with the students' lives [2]. According to this report, 50% of the total 470 surveyed dropouts said that they left the school due to classroom content that was irrelevant to their lives or career choices. The research article by The Washington Post [3] further relates the increasing drop out ratio with the decreasing motivation and interest. Multiple research studies suggest that the student engagement plays an important part in understanding increasing drop-out rate [4]. These research findings imply that contextually irrelevant and unauthentic education system is producing disengaged students who drop out of school and deem education purposeless.

1.2 Literature Survey for Problem Analysis and Solution

The subsequent section highlights why this study is important to solve the aforementioned problem.

Science Technology Engineering Mathematics (STEM) education is the key driver of future innovation and economic growth [5]. However, it is often argued that the focus on scientific and technical STEM skills alone fails to meet the needs of innovation required in 21st century global society [6]. The integration of 'Arts' in STEM education gives rise to a transdisciplinary approach that increases creativity, motivation and problem solving skills [7]. Hence, producing young learners that have the capability to solve global challenges in today's world.

STEAM Model with Authentic Learning Approach. To ensure meaningful learning experiences required for global problem-solving, authentic learning is incorporated in Science Technology Engineering Arts Mathematics (STEAM) education. Research studies [8] show that arts-infused STEM education allow students to connect their meaningful experiences with the real world. Researchers from Indonesia [9] developed a contextual project-based learning model to integrate STEAM model in the chemistry classroom to explore the solution of their daily life problems. Same conclusions were made in collaborative autoethnography that STEAM allows students to develop personally relevant connections with their education [10].

Authentic STEAM Education to Engage Underserved Students. Researchers are now employing authentic and culturally responsive STEAM education models to engage the minority and underserved students. An exploratory case study was conducted in South Dakota, United States in which native American high school girls were engaged using culturally relevant STEAM experiential learning activities [11]. In the public schools of low-income community of Brazil [12], underserved groups of students were engaged using community-relevant pedagogical approach. In this research, a project titled "The City That We Want" was conducted in which students were given daily-life projects to critically in active case-based learning to solve their local contextually authentic issues. Through these projects, students get an opportunity to develop a learning environment of their interest; shift focus from curriculum in community to curriculum for community.

Freire's Theory of Critical Pedagogy and Authentic STEAM Content. For contextually relevant and authentic learning in communities, it is recommended to use the critical pedagogy approach introduced by the Brazilian author Paulo Freire. This critical pedagogy approach demands the use of problem-posing materials so as the students may think critically about their lives [13]. The major implication of Frere's theory of critical pedagogy is to analyze the revolutionary possibilities offered by unique educational practices that have the capability to fulfill the hopes of oppressed and marginalized community [14]. However, there are two shortcomings with the current research carried out in the development of authentic STEAM content for engagement of underserved students in the domain of critical pedagogy.

1. The practitioners of critical pedagogy believe that authentic education is one that allows the students to transform their life conditions [15]. The current research work explores possibilities of using problem-based learning environment, but not real community problems are considered i.e. students do not get a chance to work on their community problems and transform their personal and community lives. This implies that content which doesn't provide societal transformation opportunities to students is contextually unauthentic.
2. According to one research study [16], Freirean perspective suggests that people and their needs and issues must be the basis of the curriculum planning and content designing. However, the current STEAM content, often tagged as authentic, is not based on the community generative themes i.e. community members and stakeholders are not involved in problem identification process of the research.

In this study, we aim to address these shortcomings by designing contextual STEAM projects based on community generative themes which also allow students to promote community welfare.

2 Methodology

To design and conduct contextual STEAM projects based on community themes that engage underserved students for social community action, the recommended approach is Community-Based Action Research.

2.1 Action Research (AR) as Research Design

The research design that aligns with the goals and objectives of this study is the community-based Action Research (AR). Action research is known as "systematic and orientated around analysis of data whose answers require the gathering and analysis of data and the generation of interpretations directly tested in the field of action" [17].The selection of action research as research design of this study is remarkably significant and outcome-oriented. It was chosen because:

- It supports the agenda of social change where data is collected not only for problem identification but also problem resolution with a definite action plan [17].
- Roots of action research can be scientifically traced back to Freire's theory of critical pedagogy which implies that critical consciousness development is crucial for personal and social change [18]. As this consciousness development requires individuals to be known of the social, political and economic issues to take an action against them [13], action research is the most suitable research methodology.
- For technology-implication studies like STEAM education that involves economically and digitally marginalized populations, action research has been reported to be an effective research methodology [19].

2.2 Research Context: Underserved Community

In this study, the STEAM education model explored is applied in a relatively isolated social setting considerably different from contexts for which conventional solutions are usually developed. Hence, in this study, an important concern was to identify and specify an idiosyncratic setting where problems exist and can be solved.

Site and Sample. Located in the slum area of the capital territory of Pakistan, The Tent School System was selected as a research site (context) which serves almost 100 children from kindergarten through grade 10. It is a low-tech trust school with three rooms; two classrooms and one office. The community surrounding the school lacks the basic facilities of electricity, water and gas.

Through critical case sampling, fifteen students from years 8 to 14 (mean age = 12.3 years, SD = .99; 47% female) took part in this action research (the 'AR group'). To identify the needs prevalent in the community through needs assessment surveys, random sampling was used to select eleven community members from years 20 to 80 (mean age = 35, mean community stay = 15 years, 73% female).

2.3 Data Collection Tools and Analysis

Various mixed methods data collection tools were used within and after the STEAM based action research. The primary data collection tools included needs assessment survey and post feedback survey while classroom observations, field notes, pictorial evidence and STEAM project evaluation rubric served as supplementary performance evaluation tools.

Needs Assessment Survey. To identify the needs and problems prevailing the selected community, needs assessment survey questionnaire is used for data collection from the community members. This survey comprised of quantitative close ended questions triangulated by qualitative open-ended questions to collect comprehensive data on the community problems based on responses of community residents.

The questionnaires are analyzed using descriptive statistics and content analysis linked to the themes that emerged from the responses of community members. This content analysis was based on concept of 'Thematic Analysis' suggested by the Brazilian educator Paulo Freire [13] i.e. community generative themes. It helped us to develop a socially and culturally relevant curriculum that addresses the actual needs of the community.

Post Feedback Survey. The purpose of this survey is to explore the learning experience of students in this STEAM projects: the feedback of students on community relevant STEAM projects and if it has any positive impact on their motivation and engagement level. This survey contains close-ended questions which are triangulated by open-ended questions to validate the quantitative data.

The collected data was analyzed using content analysis on qualitative data (open-ended questions) and descriptive statistics for the quantitative data (close-ended questions).

3 Action Research in Community School: Stepwise Procedure with Observations and Findings

The section below details the comprehensive process of action research conducted in the Tent Schools System while discussing the observations and findings obtained from the data collection tools employed within this action research.

3.1 Phases of Action Research

According to Blum [20], there are two primary stages of the action research: diagnostic and therapeutic stage which involve collaborative analysis of the social situation and formulating change experiments as action plan, respectively. However, in this study we used a five-phase cyclical process by Susman and Evered [21] for rigorous and comprehensive action research project. Before implementation of five-phase process, this approach first requires developing a research environment (also called client-system infrastructure), which has been discussed briefly in Sect. 2. The five identifiable phases in this technique of conducting an action research are: Diagnosing, Action Planning, Action Taking, Evaluating and Specifying Learning.

3.2 The Tent School Action Research Project

To design community-relevant STEAM content, a five-phase cyclical action research by Susman and Evered [21] was conducted in the Tent school system. Each phase of this STEAM workshop is discussed in detail in the section below. Although, this STEAM workshop was observed by a school teacher and facilitated by the study's first author, it is important to note that students were considered expert learners in this project. The classroom teacher and facilitator were only responsible for coordination, moderation and overall administration of the Action Research project.

1. Diagnosing Community Problems. In this phase, researcher worked with the community school 'The Tent School System' administrative staff and community members to identify the primary problems that are being faced by the community residents. This was done by using needs assessment survey that contained a mixed set of questions (needs assessment survey responses available online [22]. For this purpose, researcher visited the community homes and collected responses from 11 community members of years 20 to 80 (mean age = 35, mean community stay = 15 years, 73% female), each from a different family and home who have been living in the same community for at least more than 5 years. The sample size of surveyed community members was limited to 11 due to the data saturation. By performing thematic analysis (Freirean process of generative themes) on the needs assessment survey responses, seven themes were collected as community problems as shared by the residents, see Table 1.

Table 1. Problems identified by community members with repetition frequency

Sr. no	Problem identified by community members	Repetition frequency
1	Poverty	1
2	Electricity shortage issues; solar system is used that won't work for long, especially in summers and rainy season	8
3	Hard commute; muddy streets to walk in, especially rain	1
4	Have to bring woods from jungle to burn as no gas connection	4
5	Water shortage issues; pump gets broken/damaged after every few days	5
6	Poor standard of education in our community	1
7	Political workers visit us only when they need votes	1

Then, based on the commonality of issues in the community i.e. repetition frequency of the theme, three major generative themes were identified.

1. No Gas Connection (use woods instead)
2. Electricity Shortage Issues (due to solar system)
3. Water Availability Issues (water pump breakdown)

One hinged theme (term coined by Freire) was also collected that wasn't highlighted by the community members but was evident when authentic observations of the community were taken.

4. Waste Disposal Issues (mainly due to livestock and improper waste management)

Some of the resources and key strengths of the community as identified by the community members in this survey included livestock, nearby fresh and vegetables market, easy transportation and cost-effective place of living.

2. Designing STEAM Projects to Solve Identified Problems. In this phase, community-relevant and project-based STEAM lesson plans were developed (available online [22]) for three of the selected generative themes i.e. Ineffective waste disposal, electricity shortage and non-availability of the gas in the community. These lesson plans used in the STEAM workshop were designed to relieve or at least lessen the primary problems identified in the above phase. To make STEAM projects cost-effective and reproducible for the students, daily life household items were used in the project. Students were appreciated and encouraged to use the recycled items like newspapers and plastic bottles in their projects. These lesson plans were designed according to the Freirean process of critical pedagogy which states that people and their needs must be the basis of curriculum and content planning [16].

Use of STEAM education model provided an opportunity to create interdisciplinary and meaningful projects that appeal to students with multiple intelligences for enhanced engagement in the workshop. Moreover, it provided students a good opportunity to display their creativity and innovation skills.

3. Students Designing Useful Products in Workshop. After designing community-relevant STEAM lesson plans to solve the identified problems, students started working on their chosen projects/programs under guidance of in-class facilitator and a local teacher from the school. In this study, the directive classroom-based intervention was selected to take action for solving the identified problems. In this intervention, the underlying research i.e. problems identified in phase 1 directed the change i.e. design of useful products by the students to solve the problems identified by community members. While students were working on the project, inquiry, dialogue and critical thinking were promoted aligning with the STEAM model of education.

STEAM Biogas Generator: As indicated in needs assessment survey, community lacked the facility of gas connection and had plenty of livestock (also, compost which would otherwise spread diseases). Hence, the project-based lesson plan 'STEAM Biogas Generator' was designed to solve this problem. In this project, students discussed about the project's impact in community, watched animated Urdu videos on biogas generator's design and learnt key project-related terms, processes and working of biogas generator. Then, students assembled the materials and started working on the project.

STEAM Waste Management Program: In the next project, two groups of students participated in the activities of STEAM Waste Management Program. The project activities included the motivational discussion on why this project was chosen, animated short Urdu videos on waste management, vocabulary and brief lesson on waste management techniques and processes, creating waste bins from recycled biscuits' boxes, a waste sorting game between 2 groups, recording evidence from community and practicing waste sorting, waste sorting game competition and the recycled products' activity where they designed plastic bottle baskets with unique creativity.

STEAM Recycled Electronic Products: To solve the electricity shortage issues, students used their waste management knowledge and designed electronic products from recycled plastic bottles. Students learnt the importance of plastic waste management by watching animated videos and discussions. Then, plastic bottles were re-used to design two very useful electronic products: battery powered portable flashlight and table fan.

The detailed pictorial evidence of this STEAM workshop is available online [22].

4. Evaluation of Workshop Outcomes. After the action had been taken against the defined community problems by designing useful products to solve them, next step was to evaluate the workshop outcomes. For evaluation, field notes taken during the workshop and performance-based assessments (project evaluation rubric) were used (project rubric and rubric scores are available online [22]). In this phase, it was determined whether the opted solution for each community problem was successful in relieving that problem. In case of biogas generator designed by students to solve the non-availability of gas in the community, the project remained unsuccessful. Even after multiple days, the designed biogas generator was unable to produce biogas for their use due to some design flaws that caused gas leakage. However, the students reported that they were able to learn and understand all about the biogas generator design and were determined to design it on their own again (prototype 2). Except biogas generator, students successfully relieved the identified problems of ineffective waste disposal and electricity shortage. Students used recycled items like cardboard and plastic bottle to create useful daily-use items like baskets and birdfeeders. The battery powered fan and flashlight designed by students were in working condition that we tested ourselves.

5. Specifying Learning. In this workshop, one of the observations noted was that the products designed by students in phase 3 were able to relieve problems at small scale only. Hence, in the next action research cycle, it was determined that the objective would be to design products for problem solution at mega scale.

4 Student Feedback and Comments

To collect student feedback and their perception on outcomes of action research project, post feedback survey was conducted after concluding STEAM workshop (the detailed responses are available online [22]). Almost 93% students reported that they found this action research project of community-relevant STEAM workshop engaging and interesting to perform. It was very interesting to note that all of the students showed their interest in performing more of such action research projects and 87% even stated to recommend this approach to their other teachers in the school, see Fig. 1.

Based on field notes and students' comments in open-ended questions of post survey, it was revealed that there were multiple reasons behind high student engagement, motivation and interest to participate again. After qualitative analysis of the data obtained through open ended questions, three themes were identified. These themes included:

1. Impact. Realization that each of the STEAM project they did in the action research had significant impact on their cognitive abilities, formal/informal learning, community and the environment around them.

2. Problem Generalization. While participating collaboratively in the projects, they learnt how can they use this new information and skills to solve other local community problems in their areas.

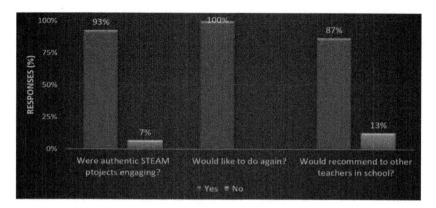

Fig. 1. Graphical Description of students' responses when asked about engagement.

3. Alternative Solutions. Due to community-relevant projects, students were able to suggest alternative ideas on how to solve the identified community problems using several other techniques and methods. Table 2 summarizes some of the students' responses according to the themes defined above.

Table 2. Students' responses to post survey feedback

Theme	Student response
Impact	We learnt to never throw plastic in the oceans rather make items from it like plastic bottles' products
	We can learn it now and then teach it to other kids; we can use these recycled bottles to make items and then teach it to others as well
	We can re-use a lot of items here in the community now. We learnt about various new items like compost that we can re-cycle or re-use
	If this biogas generator works, then gas availability is biggest impact. Otherwise, I learnt that there is an alternative solution of biogas for gas availability
	The flashlight we made can be used at night and fan in summers
Problem Generalization	Pick up bricks lying in the mid of path and dispose them off properly: waste disposal and also, we will be helping other people
	If your house has no floor and becomes muddy (especially after rain): Cut each plastic bottle in half, then use them to cover the muddy ground.
	Reduce cow manure by using it in biogas generator and prevent diseases in community
	Waste reduced in the community (cow manure); Save trees in the forest as we no longer have to go and cut trees to burn for cooking
	Waste management along with useful electronic products

(continued)

Table 2. (*continued*)

Theme	Student response
Alternative Solutions	Should try to make a proper place for waste disposal
	Use waste disposal vehicles/trucks and use them to pick waste from our community and dispose it off at some waste management cite
	Put compost in a landfill, cover it, then waste vehicles will come and pick it up. We can practice this activity
	I think biogas generator was the best solution to solve gas issues
	Make any battery powered heavy-duty light
	We can make mobile charger to solve charging issues in homes

5 Conclusion

In this paper, we discuss the lessons learnt from implementing Freire's theory of critical pedagogy by designing community relevant STEAM curriculum for underserved students in Pakistan. The research design employed for the paper was 5-phase cyclic action research that allowed us to systematically design authentic and contextual curriculum. However, the whole process was pragmatically small scale due to the rigid timetable, constrained school calendar and limited school resources. Moreover, due to the inadequate human resources and narrow timeframe, there were limitations on the scope of this study, which is exactly what Flicker [23] highlights about action research projects. Even with these real-world limitations, the study produced some key results and outcomes. The student engagement and empowerment as observed from the student feedback responses validate the notion that authentic and community relevant pedagogy can engage underserved students, as implied by the Freire's theory of critical pedagogy. An interesting breakthrough while conducting action research was when students mentioned how their useful knowledge will create a greater impact on their community and help them solve other local community challenges as well. Results obtained from this study will be used to inform the teachers, schools, parents, policy makers and NGO's to engage with the communities and teach students how to solve their local problems for community welfare.

Funding. This study was funded by the National University of Sciences and Technology (NUST), Islamabad, Pakistan.

References

1. New Education Data for SDG 4 and More. UNESCO Institute of Statistics (2018)
2. Bridgeland, J.M., DiIulio, J.J., Morison, K.B.: The Silent Epidemic: Perspectives of High School Dropouts, p. 44 (2006)
3. Douglas, D.: An alarming number of teenagers are quitting school to work (2015). https://www.washingtonpost.com/news/wonk/wp/2015/04/16/an-alarming-number-of-teenagers-are-quitting-school-to-work-heres-how-to-help-them/

4. Shernoff, D.J.: Optimal learning environments to promote student engagement. Springer New York : Imprint : Springer, New York, NY (2013)
5. Adesoji, F.A.: National and global trend on stem education and economic development. Adv. Soc. Sci. Res. J. (2018). https://doi.org/10.14738/assrj.56.4534
6. Hobbs, L.: STEAM: powering the digital revolution. In: de la Garza, A., Travis, C. (eds.) The STEAM Revolution, pp. 237–246. Springer, Cham (2019). https://doi.org/10.1007/978-3-319-89818-6_16
7. Perignat, E., Katz, J.: STEAM in practice and research: an integrative literature review. Think. Skills Creat. **31**, 31–43 (2019). https://doi.org/10.1016/j.tsc.2018.10.002
8. Chen, C.W.J., Lo, K.M.J.: From teacher-designer to student-researcher: a study of attitude change regarding creativity in STEAM education by using *Makey Makey* as a platform for human-centred design instrument. J. STEM Educ. Res. **2**(1), 75–91 (2019). https://doi.org/10.1007/s41979-018-0010-6
9. Rahmawati, Y., Ridwan, A., Hadinugrahaningsih, T., Soeprijanto: Developing critical and creative thinking skills through STEAM integration in chemistry learning. J. Phys. Conf. Ser. **1156**, 012033 (2019). https://doi.org/10.1088/1742-6596/1156/1/012033
10. Sochacka, N.W., Guyotte, K.W., Walther, J.: Learning together: a collaborative autoethnographic exploration of STEAM (STEM + the Arts) education. J. Eng. Educ. **105**, 15–42 (2016). https://doi.org/10.1002/jee.20112
11. Kant, J., Burckhard, S., Meyers, R.: Engaging high school girls in native american culturally responsive STEAM activities. J. STEM Educ. **18**, 15–25 (2018)
12. Cavallo, D., Blikstein, P., Sipitakiat, A., Basu, A., Camargo, A., de Deus Lopes, R., Cavallo, A.: The city that we want: generative themes, constructionist technologies and school/social change. In: IEEE International Conference on Advanced Learning Technologies, 2004, Joensuu, Finland. Proceedings. pp. 1034–1038. IEEE (2004). https://doi.org/10.1109/ICALT.2004.1357744
13. Freire, P., Macedo, D.: Pedagogy of the Oppressed, 30th Anniversary Edition. Continuum (2000)
14. Ferguson, J.: Book review: the student guide to freire's pedagogy of the oppressed. J. Transform. Educ. **17**, 195–197 (2019). https://doi.org/10.1177/1541344618824933
15. Aliakbari, M., Faraji, E.: Basic principles of critical pedagogy, p. 9 (2011)
16. Mahmoudi, A., Khoshnood, D.A., Babaei, D.A.: Paulo Freire critical pedagogy and its implications in curriculum planning. J. Educ. Pract. 5, 8 (2014)
17. Greenwood, D., Levin, M.: Introduction to Action Research. SAGE Publications, Thousand Oaks (2007). https://doi.org/10.4135/9781412984614
18. Maguire, P.: Doing participatory research: a feminist approach (1987)
19. Chetty, M., Tucker, W., Blake, E.: Using voice over IP to bridge the digital divide-A critical action research approach (2009)
20. Blum, F.H.: Action research–a scientific approach? Philos. Sci. **22**, 1–7 (1955). https://doi.org/10.1086/287381
21. Susman, G.I., Evered, R.D.: An assessment of the scientific merits of action research. Admin. Sci. Q. **23**, 582–603 (1978)
22. Kiyani, M., Javed, F., Haider, I.: Designing a freirean-inspired community relevant STEAM curriculum for underserved students in Pakistan using action research process. 3152900 Bytes (2020). https://doi.org/10.6084/m9.figshare.12673622
23. Flicker, S.: Who benefits from community-based participatory research? A case study of the positive youth project. Health Educ. Behav. (2006). https://doi.org/10.1177/1090198105285927

Digital Natives and Educational Traditions. What Changes When Exchanging Textbook Content with Internet Search?

Lisbet Rønningsbakk(✉)

UiT the Arctic University of Norway, Box 6050 Langnes N-9037, Tromsø, Norway
`Lisbet.ronningsbakk@uit.no`

Abstract. Use of technology challenge traditional concepts of learning in school. But what is actually changing? The paper shows result from a study that finds that the shift from textbook to internet content implicates significant changes. Textbooks present qualified content that is well adapted to the cognitive development of students of certain ages. Using internet content gives no such guarantees. The content validation has to be taken care of by the students. The internet search demands more complex skills than accessing content through the textbook. The students have to find relevant search terms, review and validate the results they find, select relevant content, use relevant strategies for storing and retrieving content and having the ability to present abstracts of their findings that are adapted to their learning purpose.

Collaboration works well for searching for content online because the students can benefit from each other's prior knowledge when discussing and reflecting during the learning work. Communicative and collaborative skills are important. So are good relations, to able students to work through obstacles and keep focus on the task even when internet searching takes them everywhere. Internet content has a flexibility that makes it easy adaptable to all students' learning prerequisites. Student collaboration between heterogeneous peers can work well because the complexity of the task involves a lot of different tasks to manage and are easy to distribute. It also makes possible for high performing students to find engaging content that will motivate and nourish the learning motivation.

Keywords: Digital content in school · Learning content · Technology supported teaching · Learning with technology · Profession oriented digital competence for teachers · Didactics · Content

1 Introduction

To be able to understand how new technologies can benefit learning in classrooms, we need to understand the changes that come with teaching with technologies. This paper sum up how using technologies can impact the didactical categories content and methods in teaching when exchanging textbook content with internet search. The paper is based on a recent phd-study with a broader focus on students' learning with technology.

Research show that the use of technology in Norway so far tends to being adapted to a traditional teaching practice. After using technology in schools for decades, the expected pedagogical innovations have not occurred [1, 2]. This was the background for a phd-study which aimed to understand how the use of technology impact the ways students work, emphasizing content, methods and students' role behavior [2]. The aim of the study was to question the needs of revising the didactics when new technologies were introduced to a field of old professional practice in school teaching.

The study documented that using technologies in many ways challenged teachers' practices. It also put forward some perspectives on how didactical theory needs to change to meet new perspectives on teaching and learning when using technologies in classrooms. This paper will present the study's results on the changes that occurred when exchanging the textbook content with internet search.

2 Method

The study was conducted as a multi-case study at two schools in the North of Norway, including 25 students at 4th (9–10 years old) and 10th grade (15–16 years old), selected on the background of their teachers' special interest and engagement for using technology, categorized as excellent cases. The empirical basis of the study mainly build on reflection notes from participating observations, students' products, notes from meetings and other documents, as documented in the thesis [2].

The case study strategy meets the need to investigate a phenomenon thoroughly through different sources of information [3, 4], even if it has some challenges generalizing results based on few units. However, literature supports the idea that knowledge generated from a case study can have general value for similar phenomenon [5, 6].

The data collection took place during five weeks during one academic year through participating observations. I conducted open observations to situations where students worked with technology, to try to capture what they really were doing and describe it. All observations were written down immediately after classes. Then the texts were elaborated into reflection notes which were distributed to the teachers within a week after observations. The teachers could respond to these narratives, and add and change if they wanted, but that never happened. The general response was that I had captured well what they tried to do and that my observations were more nuanced and detailed than expected. As a previous teacher I rapidly got the role as an extra teacher in both classes. This gave me solid experiences of the students and the teachers. But it also gave some challenges concerning the contradictive roles as teacher and researcher. These have been handled with a hermeneutic approach considering the researcher's preoccupations caused by professional experience within the field [7, 8].

To be sure I had understood the situation well, I discussed my observations and preliminary findings with the school leaders at each school and also presented the data describing each child in a specific report to their parents. This should assure that all participants would be well taken care of in the matter of informed consent.

Later, all texts were analyzed using qualitative methods and the digital platform NVivo. Through repeatedly reading, coding and reflections, the theoretical categories emerged. Finally, the empirical data where elaborated into two narratives, one for each class/school. They contented a selection of specific narratives which could enlighten the research questions of the study. The narratives were analyzed, using a selection of theory of learning, knowledge and didactics, to be able to understand the matter in a general way and draw the final conclusions.

The thesis also contents a thorough review of theories of learning and teaching to establish a conceptual framework that makes it possible to value the results in a future perspective where knowledge and learning conditions are rapidly changing due to technological development [2]. It is not room for a full presentation of the framework here, but the next subchapter will present some of the perspectives that is important for the research question presented here.

3 Digital Technologies and New Perspectives on Content in School's Education

An important prerequisite for the study was to be sure that concepts of knowledge and learning in school meets future standards for education. The need to measuring learning outcome has increased in Norwegian Education as result of Norway's participation and focus on international programs like PISA [9]. This tendency is worrying policy makers and Education scientist in Norway who point at the importance to develop sustainable competence instead of remembering bits of information. New technologies bring new concepts of what knowledge is or should be and challenge the traditional school's content [10, 11]. Hence, revisions of concepts of knowledge and learning is important to able teachers to develop profession oriented digital skills.

School knowledge in a European tradition is closely connected with content. Norwegian education is strongly influenced by the German Bildung tradition which emphasizes the transformation that certain content brings to the learner. An important issue for teachers were then to find the right content that could serve this purpose [12]. School knowledge is often connected with what is viewed as appropriate content. But this concept needs a revision for a future use. A sustainable concept of knowledge must meet the constant changes that occurs when information is nonstop available through digital sources. Technologies extend the abilities to store and retrieve knowledge and dismiss our need to remember in a traditional way [13, 14]. Hence the need of storing content as part of the individual learning process is no longer the main issue for education, but rather to develop good strategies to search and validate knowledge for certain purposes in certain contexts [15].

3.1 Learning as an Infinite Movement Between Previous Learning Experiences and Future Expectations

Danish professor Mads Hermansen describes learning as positioned in the actual point of *now* and stretched out between the two positions; *feed-forward* and *feedback*. Feed-forward is the expectation of new learning outcome while feedback relates to prior understanding. The learning process is an infinite movement between these positions and changes both dynamically from the perspective of the actual now [16, 17]. This means that prior and future knowledge is continuously changing when the learning process develops. This is also the situation when students learn in school.

Before starting learning something new, the previous knowledge has to be put forward. This is important to establish a zone of proximal development (ZPD). This process involves creating expectations to new learning (feed-forward) based upon the review of what you already know (feedback). In class the teacher will start the new learning task with asking the students what they know about the new learning task, what they can recall from previous, involve students in concept mapping, mediate discussions and so on, to establish the feed-forward. When feed-forward is established, it will work dynamically with the actual learning outcome. As the learning task is going on, students will revise their prior knowledge which will impact their feed-forward. All learning leads to new perspectives on both what they know and what they expect of future learning.

Hermansen adds two more dimensions to his model; a dynamic movement between *habitus* and *reflection,* and between *toil* and *exuberance* [16]. The two pairs point at important movements that are crucial for learning. Through the learning process, students' cognition moves between the outer positions of habitus and reflection, meaning that they move between acting on automatized scripts and on conscious actions. The habituated skills and knowledge makes it possible to build new knowledge upon the existing because it releases cognitive capacity for conscious processes. Learning as an interaction between toil and exuberance, points at the fact that learning drives forward through both flow and resistance. The will to struggle when meeting resistance, is important to achieve results.

Hermansen's dynamic model embody learning as an infinite process moving forward through shifts between feed-forward-feedback, habitus-reflection, and toil-exuberance. The model and the concepts can be used directly to show how technology impacts learning as shown later in the paper.

3.2 Tiller's Learning Sun as Motivational Power

Norwegian scholars Rita and Tom Tiller are occupied with motivation for learning. Their model of the Learning Sun [18] is useful to understand how the learning process are nourished. Learning in school should carefully consider what the students will find meaningful. Like Freire who view education as the means to meaningful existence [19, 20], Tiller and Tiller state that schooling should enrich students' lives. Hence, school has to adapt to its students instead of students' adapting to school [18, 21].

Tiller and Tiller's metaphor, the *Learning Sun,* embodies four important prerequisites for motivation and learning in school. The four dimensions are presented as four learning suns with mutual effect on each other. The first sun, learn to know, is about the intellectual dimension of learning and point at the individual's need of knowledge [18]. The need to know is a natural force for humans and a motivation in itself. The second learning sun, learn to do, is connected with practical knowledge or skills [18]. Some knowledge is embodied in the individual without being possible to describe in words. In my work I understand this dimension as the tacit knowledge [22, 23], which is necessary for performing within a social and cultural context. The third sun, learn to be, is about belonging and appreciation within a social group [18]. Taking turns, communication skills, and well behaving towards others etc. are social skills that promote a good adaption to the group and the class, are important for the third sun. The fourth learning sun, to learn to live, has to do with general well-being [18]. The importance of peers and companions who want will promote your well-being, to understand the needs of those around you and being willing to scarify something for others when it is needed. Empathy is important for this. It has to do with generally having a good time together with humor and a good spirit to make learning thriving. Tiller and Tiller add important prerequisites to Hermansen's concepts, and show that motivation is the basic force in learning. issues are important to understand the impact of technology in school.

4 When Content Moves from Textbooks to Internet

The study showed that technology changes the way students work with content in different ways, with more or less significant impact. The study findings present these changes: the changes that occur when the content moves from textbooks to internet; the technology's possibility to support content creation in new ways; and the fact that online resources can provide content that are updated and adapted to the local context. This paper will focus specifically on the changes occurring when textbook content is exchanged with internet search.

The internet is a never ending source of information of more or less relevance and trust value. When using the textbook, the teacher can control and trust the quality of the content. When students search for information online, the teachers no longer control this and the responsibility of the content validation is distributed to the students.

Also the search for content in itself demands more complex skills on internet. Students have to decide what kind of information they need and find relevant search terms for the purpose. They need to review and value the results to be able to pick relevant information before storing what they find useful. And they need strategies to store and retrieve the essence of the content for various purposes. All these activities demand different strategies than working with textbooks. Textbooks have undergone quality control and present the information in a way that is adapted to the students' level of cognition and previous knowledge. With internet content, quality control, valuing relevance and adapting to students' level of cognition, needs to be implemented in the search strategies [2]. Narratives from the study will exemplify this.

4.1 Internet Search and Heterogeneous Collaborations. Vivian and Thor

Vivian and Thor are collaborating to find information about the planet Jupiter for a joint presentation. Sitting together by the computer, the two 10 year olds have to perform different tasks: first discuss and agree about relevant search terms and then review and validate their findings before they choose the content best suited for their task. The two enter the collaboration with different prerequisites. Vivian is an eager student with high level of achievement in all theoretical subjects. Thor is not so fond of theory and tend to miss focus when the matter is not interesting. But they have a very good relationship and often play together in the breaks. The good relation makes it easy to work through the obstacles they meet about the task and the collaboration itself. When they search together for information about planet Jupiter, they have to calibrate their different conceptions, views and strategies. This is a complex process that depends on collaborative skills from both since their prerequisites are so different. Making this a real learning situation for both, require that both get the possibility to recall their former knowledge about the matter and communicate this to their mate to establish a common assumption of what they are looking for at the internet.

It is easy to picture a situation where Vivian, with her solid competence and advanced strategies, would take over the task and direct what Thor should do. But here they manage to create a collaborative situation where they both participate on an even level. Thor has some prior knowledge and interest for planets, and is also ahead of Vivian in digital skills. Their good relationship makes it easy to communicate well about the task and to established a common zone of proximal development where they both engage in the task and make their feed-forward-feedback-dynamic work. The work flow is good and motivating, nourishing the learning suns. This is obvious when listening to their learning dialogues during the search. They focus on the task and seem to communicate with intentions of scaffolding each other's thoughts and understanding. The result becomes very good.

4.2 Internet Search and High Performing Students. Margaret and Sean

In the same assignment, Sean and Margaret is presenting the planet Mercury. They show a different pattern of collaboration than Vivian and Thor. They are both high performing and ambitious students who rapidly settle for a common understanding of the task and start searching for proper information. In their communication about the content during the search, they don't spend time to negotiate about other things than the pure content. They look through a lot of sources and discuss how it will fit their purpose, quite a lot more sources than the average for the class. Margaret and Sean are used to working together and often prefer each other in collaborative tasks. But Sean's ability to focus is not as good as Margaret's. Sean's attention is often drawn to the other students because the tendency to compare his performance to them. But when the students work directly on screen, it is easier for Sean to focus on the content. This makes the collaboration with Margaret also easier. She doesn't have to repeatedly call on his attention to focus on their work, like she sometimes needs to.

4.3 Internet Search Demands New Learning Strategies. William. Theresa, Margaret and Vivian

For another multimedia presentation, the 4th graders were searching for pictures to illustrate folk tales. They worked in pairs and started with defining some search terms. William was disappointed with his search terms because they gave too many different results. He was annoyed to find that when he searched for pictures of a wood he also got portraits of people named Wood. It is not possible to avoid situations where students stumble upon content which is irrelevant or even abusive, when working with open google search.

During this activity we experienced the latter when one of the students retrieved a picture of a man holding his hands on a woman's breasts. Even quite so innocent, a picture like this can offend a child at this age. But the teachers in this class welcomed the situation because they got the chance to talk about abusive content on internet. They told me that they preferred to have these incidents in class instead of when students were sitting alone somewhere else, to be able to discuss digital awareness.

Another situation also showed that using internet for content search depends on having sufficient competences. Vivian and Margaret was involved in this situation together with Theresa. The three girls were usually good friends but this day some relational issues disturbed their collaboration. They had worked out a set of search terms to find pictures for their task. But they did not manage to agree about using any of the results. This was a stressful experience and they expressed doubt about how to fulfill the task. Theresa went back to the computer and ran the same search terms again. Vivian and Margaret got very angry at her because they meant that running them again showed lack of trust in what they previous had done. This led to an intermezzo which ended with agreement that Theresa agreed to change learning partner, which solved the problem. It came up that the girls had had a conflict the day before at home and that this had fostered some insecurity that had strong impact on their communication. They did not manage the task because of the underlying conflict. It can be argued that this situation is not about internet content in itself but the class as a learning environment is full of relational issues that also impact learning tasks. When the work with content gets more complex because it has to undergo discussions, it is also important that the students have the communicative skills and guts to say what they mean and to confront each other's different opinions.

5 Discussion and Conclusion

The narratives above document various challenges that occurs when changing from textbooks to content retrieved from internet search.

They all demonstrate the necessity of good collaborative skills to work together with searching for information on the internet. Internet search is a more complex task than looking it up in the textbook. When students collaborate they have to start with defining a joint understanding of the task. This involves a calibration of what they think the task is about and how they can work to fulfill the task. Communication is important to establish a feed-forward, an expectation of what the task is about based on the feedback to prior knowledge and understanding. They establish a feedforward together based on their previous knowledge and skills and the resources they both bring in to the collaboration, and they support each other's dynamic movement between habitus and reflection through discussing the task [16, 17].

The collaborative peers will have different prerequisites to take part in the common task. Prior knowledge will vary and make the dynamic between feed-forward and feedback different. They will also experience differences between habitus and reflection. While some have an intuitive understanding of what to do, others need to reflect to be able to decide what is the right action. Therefore, good communication is important. If the relations between the peers are good they will be able to communicate well and be motivated to do a good work together. The learning sun will get energy and learning will thrive.

The situation with Thor and Vivian shows that students can form well-functioning collaborative partnerships with different levels of basic knowledge and attitudes towards learning in school. The use of technology, as in internet searching, seems to frame their collaborative learning well. Using technology increases the field of task specific knowledge and opens for using skills and knowledge gained from other activities than school work. When Vivians' learning strategies are more developed than Thors', he adds his interest for planets and his digital skills to their collaboration. A more complex task demands more complex strategies and opens for distributed learning. In practice more different tasks will need attention and makes it possible to draw on both students' resources. Vivian's advanced learning strategies and basic school knowledge will benefit Thor's learning and his knowledge of planets and digital skills will be of use to her. Even if what is learnt are different for Thor and Vivian they will experience the collaboration as meaningful. Their good relation will support their dynamics between habitus and reflection [16], and feed the learning energy and all four learning suns [18] are nourished and they will be motivated for further learning and further collaboration. The collaboration will form a strong force to overcome exuberance when occurring [16].

Margaret and Sean experiences something similar in their work. But here the actual content is the driving force. Since they both have high ambitions and are high performing, they extend the use of internet content to a high level. For them the source of information is the main issue, and they use it to deepen and widen their understanding of planet Mercury. Their discussions show that they are reviewing their search results thoroughly in a way the textbook never would promote with its' quality secured content. Margaret and Sean have together the ability to elaborate the information with a critical view, looking for real information to use in their presentation. They discuss and discard, discuss and accept, source after source, before they agree about something they can decide to use. The feedforward-feedback-dynamics are fed with a lot of information which they never would have found in the textbook alone. Finding advanced content online motivates them for further investigation. Students with high academic performance can get the extra stimulation that they need to find to extend their feedforward – feedback and habitus – reflection-movements [16]. For these two the textbook content will limit their learning instead of nourish it they are highly motivated for the work and the collaboration and the learning sun shines.

When working with different content the possibility of comparison with other peers is not the same as when you can cast a look towards your peer's textbook to find out how much he has read compared to yourself. For Sean, whose attitude was quite competitive, this is an advantage.

William's frustration about search terms might on the other side, be an example that shows how literally children at the age of 10 understand their results. Open internet search doesn't discriminate between adults and children and it is impossible for teachers to determine searches to assure that they don't get unwanted results, either of irrelevant or abusive kind. Using internet as a source of content therefore involves work with critical review of all results and general digital awareness. Students need to know about the dangers of meeting unwanted and abusive content to develop strategies to handle these situations.

Finally, the narratives show that good relations are important prerequisites for a successful internet search collaboration. Retrieving content from internet demands the ability to question and be critical towards the peers' arguments. Without confronting and questioning the content, the validation process can be too shallow and the content will be accepted without the necessary discussions. Therese, Vivian and Margaret couldn't work themselves through the obstacles that a present conflict gave them, and all their feed-forward – feedback-processes was about their relationship and not the content. It is always a danger of losing focus at the actual content when collaboration problems occur. Teaching therefore also must have focus on learning communication and social skills to be able to establish a good situation that makes the learning suns shine [18].

References

1. Hatlevik, O.E., Egeberg, G., Gudmundsdóttir, G.B., Loftsgarden, M., Loi, M.: Monitor skole 2013. Om digital kompetanse og erfaringer med bruk av IKT i skolen. Senter for IKT i utdanningen, Oslo (2013)
2. Rønningsbakk, L.: Når didaktikken møter de digitalt innfødte: teknologistøttet læringsarbeid i skolen i lys av tradisjonell og nyskapende undervisning. UiT Norges arktiske universitet, Tromsø (2019)
3. Blaikie, N.: Designing Social Research. Cambridge Polity Press (2000)
4. Yin, R.K.: Case Study Research: Design and Methods, 3rd edn. Sage, Thousand Oaks (2003)
5. Flyvebjerg, B.: Five misunderstandings about case study research. In: Seale, C., Gobo, G., Gubrium, J.F., Silverman, D. (eds.) Qualitative Research Practice. Sage Publications, London (2007)
6. Gilje, N., Grimen, H.: Samfunnsvitenskapenes forutsetninger Oslo. Universitetsforlaget (1993)
7. Hammersley, M.: Case study. In: Lewis-Beck, M.S., Bryman, A., Liao, T.F. (eds.) The Sage Encyclopedia of Social Science Research Methods. Sage Publications, Thousand Oaks (2004)
8. Hodgson, J., Rønning, W., Tomlinson, P.: Sammenhengen mellom undervisning og læring. En studie av læreres praksis og deres tenkning under Kunnskapsløftet. NF-rapport, Sluttrapport (2012). http://www.udir.no/Upload/Rapporter/2012/SMUL.pdf?epslanguage=no
9. Ludvigsen, S.: Fremtidens skole: fornyelse av fag og kompetanser: utredning fra et utvalg oppnevnt ved kongelig resolusjon 21. juni 2013: avgitt til Kunnskapsdepartementet 15. juni 2015, vol. NOU 2015:8). Departementenes sikkerhets- og serviceorganisasjon, Informasjonsforvaltning, Oslo (2015)
10. Ludvigsen, S., Kunnskapsdepartementet: Elevenes læring i fremtidens skole: et kunnskapsgrunnlag: utredning fra et utvalg oppnevnt ved kongelig resolusjon 21 juni 2013: avgitt til Kunnskapsdepartementet 3 September 2014. In Norges offentlige utredninger (tidsskrift: online), Vol. NOU 2014:7 (2014)
11. Gundem, B.B.: Europeisk didaktikk: tenkning og viten. Universitetsforlaget, Oslo (2011)

12. Salomon, G. (Producer) Lecture at NYU Steinhardt, 25 September 2009 (2009). http://vimeo.com/7163245
13. Salomon, G., Perkins, D.: Learning in Wonderland. What do computers really offer education?. In: Kerr, S.T. (ed.) Technology and the Future of Schooling. Ninety-fifth Yearbook of the National Society for the Study of Education. Part II. University of Chicago Press, Chicago (1996)
14. Siemens, G.: Connectivism: a learning theory for the digital age. Int. J. Instruct. Technol. Dist. Learn. **2**, 3–10 (2005)
15. Hermansen, M.: Omlæring. Århus Klim forlag (2003)
16. Hermansen, M.: Motivasjon og den gode læring. In: Postholm, M.B., Tiller, T. (eds.) Profesjonsrettet pedagogikk, pp. 8–13. Cappelen Damm akademisk, Oslo (2014)
17. Tiller, T., Tiller, R.: Den andre dagen: det nye læringsrommet (2002)
18. Livet som lærer- og de unges rett til å gjøre ingenting. In: Tiller, R. (ed.), pp. 129–159. Høyskoleforl, Kristiansand
19. Freire, P., & Berkaak, O. A. (2003). De undertryktes pedagogikkinnledende essay. In S. Lie & O. A. Berkaak (Eds.). [Oslo]: De norske bokklubbene
20. Freire, P., Freire, P.. Teachers as Cultural Workers. Letters to Those Who Dare Teach. The Edge: Critical Studies in Educational TheoryFirst letter: Reading the word, reading the world, pp. 17–26. Westview Press, Boulder (1998)
21. Tiller, T.. Hvor går Nord-Norge? B. 2 Et institusjonelt perspektiv på folk og landsdel. Når skolen skulker sin omverden. In: Jentoft, S., Nergård, J.I., Røvik, K.A. (eds.), pp. 127–136. Orkana akademisk, Stamsund (2012)
22. Lave, J., Lave, J., Wenger, E.: Situeret læring - og andre tekster. Reitzel, København (2003)
23. Polanyi, M., Ra, E.: Den tause dimensjonen: en innføring i taus kunnskap, vol. nr 5. Spartacus, Oslo (2000)

Experiences Using Three App Prototyping Tools with Different Levels of Fidelity from a Product Design Student's Perspective

Amanda Coelho Figliolia[1,2], Frode Eika Sandnes[1(✉)], and Fausto Orsi Medola[2]

[1] Oslo Metropolitan University, 0130 Oslo, Norway
frodes@oslomet.no
[2] Sao Paulo State University (UNESP), Bauru, Brazil
{amanda.figliolia, fausto.medola}@unesp.br

Abstract. Prototyping has become a widely embraced technique in different design fields to facilitate early user involvement to ensure that the end-product meets the users' needs. Each design field has its tools and traditions for working with prototypes. This paper documents experiences with smartphone app prototyping from a product design student's perspective. Three prototyping tools with different fidelity levels were explored. Based on these experiences we reflect upon the prototyping tool characteristics and their suitability for non-computer scientist. We envisage that our experiences may be useful for other product designers who want to develop smartphone apps.

Keywords: Smartphone app prototyping · Product design · Interaction design

1 Introduction

Revolutionary prototyping is a well-established part of product development were ideas are tested early before committing to time-consuming and expensive productions. Prototyping is used within several fields such as architecture, product design, interior design, and computer science. Each field have specific techniques and methods for working with concept development and prototyping. This study focuses on prototyping smartphone apps. The prototyping of smartphone apps involves certain constraints [1], i.e., the interface communicates via the smartphone display with limited real estate, audio, and vibrator for tactile sensations, while input is provided via on-screen gestures such as taps and swipes. Other input modalities are possible such as tilting, in air-gestures, speech, etc., but these will not be discussed herein.

Concept sketches are sometimes mistaken for prototypes. Buxton gives an informed explanation of the differences [2], namely that prototypes are intended to be used for testing, and are therefore concrete and solution oriented, while sketches are used to represent ideas, facilitate communication among designers and generate discussion and evolvement of ideas. Prototypes can be realized with simple hand drawings [3]. Some argue that the organic nature of hand-drawings is beneficial, while others criticize these for not being aesthetically pleasing and argue for drawing aids such as

GUI-control stencils [4]. Our experiences also show that many computing students prefer to design visual layouts using software (Photoshop) to achieve more realistic-looking results.

Still, computer assisted prototyping tools are popular. Clearly, a prototype generated with a computer tool appears more realistic and holds potential for smoother user testing sessions. Yet, the danger of computer-assisted prototyping is a shift in focus from the concept to technical details resulting in more time being wasted on prototype creation. Moreover, a realistic-looking prototype is more likely to raise customers' expectations giving them a false sense of product completion.

This study explored three prototyping tools with different levels of fidelity [5], namely Adobe XD, Figma and React Native. The experiences with the tool is documented with a product design student who is well trained in design-thinking and prototyping of physical objects using rapid prototyping and 3D printing [6–9], and basic experience with software development and interface prototyping.

2 Related Work

Prototypes are often used to test technologies that are not easily available such as augmented reality displays [10–12], public kiosks [13, 14], or technologies that do not yet exist such as novel application-specific smart devices [15]. Such prototypes can be simple mockups that leave much to the imagination, or it can be more complete implementations such as using Arduino to prototype mobile technology [16]. The calder toolkit [17] is another example of making complex hardware more easily available for simple and rapid prototyping. Prototyping of objects in three-dimensional space is also a much-studied area [18–25] since the three dimensions somewhat need to be represented using the two-dimensional computer screen. Holograms allows three-dimensional objects to be visualized on two-dimensional planes, and prototyping of holograms using abrasions has also been explored [26]. A general review of prototyping tools and techniques can be found in [27, 28]. For a review of the history of graphical user interface prototyping tools see [29, 30].

Much have been written about prototyping of mobile technology. Raento et al. [31] discussed a prototyping platform for context-aware mobile applications that gets better access to the hardware than other prototyping platforms. Mora, Gianni and Divitini [32] presented an approach for prototyping internet-of-things applications that usually require detailed domain specific knowledge about the underlying technologies. Sabbir et al. [16] discussed the use of the Arduino toolkit to make mobile prototypes.

Bochmann and Ritz [5] classified mobile prototyping along several dimensions such as requirements for hardware functionality, target device, audience, prototype creator, range, focus, stage of project, speed, fidelity and longevity. Bochmann and Ritz [5] reviewed several mobile prototyping tools including Balsamiq Mockups, Axure RP and Adobe Fireworks. Bähr [33] proposed 16 requirements for mobile prototyping tools. Leiva and Beaudouin-Lafon [34] described a system where paper prototypes can be inserted into existing videos using markup points and green-screen areas to avoid re-shooting video montages.

3 Method

Smartphone apps holds great promise for health and rehabilitation. Advanced technology can bridge the gap between health professionals and users at a lower cost than was previously possible. Examples include oral health promotion [35], diabetes self-management [36], and blood donation [37]. This project involved the design of a smartphone app concept to facilitate the communication between rehabilitation professionals and users of prosthetic assistive technologies. The concept was identified during practical work with the development of a customized prosthesis. First, the vision of the app was determined followed by early concept sketches (see Fig. 1).

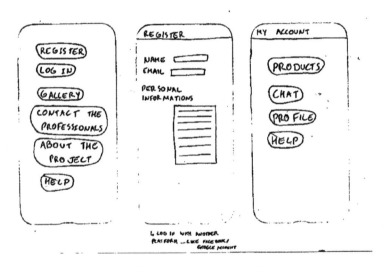

Fig. 1. Initial paper sketches of the app.

Next, app prototypes were created. The first prototypes were created using Adobe XD and used for preliminary user tests. These tests showed the need of a more detailed prototype with more responsive features and more interactivity. For this, React Native was used. Development with React Native proceeded at a low pace and towards the end of the project the React Native was replaced with Figma. In this study we focus on the experiences with the prototyping tools, and not the artefact per se.

The product design student found the process of developing the application very interesting and educational specially as the approach was quite different to typical product design practices. Product designers tend to focus on the details in the beginning of the project development, while with app development it is not equally relevant to focus on details in the beginning. Also, with app development it is very common to conduct many user tests early in the development as the feedback provides clues to relevant adjustments. This is especially helpful when the application is being developed for a specific user group.

It is worth noting that the product designer had no previous experience with the three prototyping tools. Although Figma and Adobe XD are quite different, their interface and workflow have several similarities. It was therefore easier to switch between Figma and Adobe XD than between these and React Native.

3.1 Product Design Versus Interface Design

This project explored design from the perspectives of product design and computer science. Product designers typically design and develop products by analyzing all the aspects of a product and its interaction with the user. A product can be defined as having three functions, namely practical, symbolic, and aesthetic. When designing a product, it is also common to focus on the usability and the user experience. Many products are developed with a user-centered design approach, where the user is involved in the process of development, increasing the chances of a successful product that is adaptable especially customizable assistive technology products. The computer science perspective on user interface design often focus on usability and user experience, as well as accessibility and appeal. What both disciplines have in common is the focus on the needs and requirements of the user, the creation of prototypes to evaluate ideas by the participation of the user during the process. The final prototype serves as the requirements specification to be used to code the final product and put it into production.

3.2 Prototyping Tools

Three prototyping tools were explored, namely Adobe XD, React Native and Figma. Adobe XD [38] is a simple prototyping tool allowing the designers to define the layout of the views and connect these with navigation structure. Adobe XD had the lowest fidelity of the three tools but for user testing it was found to be more suitable than Figma overall. The student was unable finish any React Native prototypes and this tool was therefore not used for user testing.

React Native [39] can both serve as a prototyping tool and an implementation tool as the final products can be deployed and put into production. React Native require programming in JavaScript and design of views that are then connected. React Native is the most high-fidelity tool of the three tools. Yet, the general nature of the tool means that it can be used for cross platform development with the same codebase, that is, develop apps for both the IOS and Android platforms simultaneously. See Dalmasso et al. [40] for a survey of cross-platform mobile application development tools.

Figma [37, 41, 42] is a mid-fidelity prototyping tool that allows the designer to use several interface controls and connect these together. The designs can be immediately tested and users get a realistic impression of the application.

4 Results and Discussion

4.1 Adobe XD

At the time of writing Adobe XD is freely available. Adobe XD has the lowest fidelity of the tools explored, and the easiest tool to get started as no programming is needed. It is relatively efficient to operate with some templates provided. The interface (see Fig. 2) was perceived as intuitive and easy to use. The interface is consistent with other Adobe software such as Photoshop and Illustrator allowing designers with experience from such tools to reuse existing experience and skills. It was relatively easy to make changes to designs, once exception being changes that involved multiple modifications in connections between pages which may require many time-consuming edits. Adobe XD designs can be stored in the cloud and updates deployed to the smartphones. This allows for easy and rapid user testing. It also simplifies the sharing of the project with other designers and testers. To access the prototype, one only need to install the app on the smartphone via a shareable link. Adobe XD support more complex interactions, however these were not perceived as straightforward to use. It was easy to view changes to the design using the desktop preview. The prototype quality was perceived as good but did not fully meet the expectations in terms of features and experiences during testing. One problem was the mismatch between available fonts in the desktop tool and the Android test app.

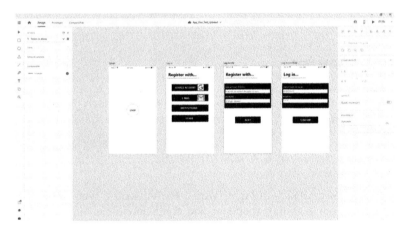

Fig. 2. App prototype in Adobe XD.

When testing the prototype on a smartphone we found that the swipe action could be enabled, but there was not a straightforward way to realize the swipe flow according to the artboards linking order. When swiping to go back to the previous page, the system was only going back to the previous linked artboard, even when it was connected to a different artboard. It was possible to share the project with other designers. Our tests showed that the Adobe XD Android app gave the most realistic experience despite the problems with swipe.

We found that the tool could be learned quickly. The first prototype did not require advanced functions as the attention was on the interaction, intuitiveness of the steps, and aesthetics. Some features were not responding realistically, such as swipe, popups, and textual field input. Consequently, the workflow could not be fully analyzed during the preliminary user testing.

4.2 Figma

Figma is a commercial product, but it has a free edition with fewer features. Figma can be classified as a medium fidelity prototyping tool. It was therefore more intricate and time-consuming to operate than Adobe XD. However, more advanced features such as popups and long screen with scrolling were perceived as more intuitive than the Adobe XD static views. Many tutorials facilitate exploring more advanced features. It is seemingly easier to make changes to existing designs as changes involves fewer operations than with Adobe XD. Figma is browser-based platform (see Fig. 3) with similarities to Adobe XD but with some differences, notably the prototype mode.

Fig. 3. App prototype in Figma.

The prototypes created with Figma were more interactive than Adobe XD hence giving users a more realistic experience and continuous flow. Figma also supports different templates giving more realistic prototypes. Most of the difficulties that occurred with Figma were relatively easy to solve due to the available tutorials and examples. More challenging issues included pages extending beyond the height of the screen.

It was straightforward to test the prototypes on the desktop. It took several attempts to make the prototypes run on a smartphone because the Figma Mirror app needed to work together with the Figma tool in the web browser and the frame to be tested need to be selected. This procedure complicates user testing.

4.3 React Native

React Native is both a high-fidelity prototyping tool and a development tool for cross platform development. React Native can thus also be used for incremental prototyping where the final prototype is the actual product. React native require programming. Development is thus slower than with Adobe XD and Figma and programming knowledge is needed. Changes are easily made if the code is well structured. Hence, it is hard to maintain and make changes to code that is made in a rush. Clearly, React Native gives easier access to the hardware functionality than the other two platforms. React Native is not visually oriented to the same degree as the two other tools. The lack of visual orientation was perceived as negative as product designers usually work visually.

The product designer had some coding knowledge. However, difficulties arose already during the installation of React Native CLI Quickstart (Development OS Windows and Target OS Android) as the process was perceived as confusing with much trial and error. Note that Node, Android Studio and Visual Studio Code (see Fig. 4) were also installed. After many difficulties compiling example code snippets and smartphone deployment following the tutorial steps, the debugging tools on Sandbox Code website was used instead. Eventually, React Native was abandoned as the time invested did not yield any concrete results. The curve was too steep. It seems that one needs extensive coding experience, and investment in time to use React Native. This tool seems not suitable for non-designers.

Fig. 4. React Native interface.

5 Conclusion

Experiences with smartphone app prototyping tools with varying levels of fidelity were reported. Our experiences show development took much longer than expected. Using React Native proved quite challenging, and we would conclude that implementation-oriented tools such as React Native requires too much programming experience and knowledge to be practical for individuals without a computer science background. Adobe XD and Figma are both pragmatic alternatives, with Figma being perceived as the most practical tool. Our experiences show that much time went into the operation of the tools diverting attention away from the concept. We would therefore argue for using even simpler means such as hand drawn prototypes, or software package the designer masters, if this cuts prototyping time and help maintain the attention on exploring the design space rather than aesthetics [43]. Especially, as product designers are trained in sketching. Also, choosing tools that facilitate simple prototype development may benefit the design process and the product quality. Our experiences support separating design from implementation as designers should focus on the concept development and user testing, leaving the implementation to programmers.

References

1. Sandnes, F.E.: Universell utforming av IKT-systemer. Universitetsforlaget, Oslo (2018)
2. Buxton, B.: Sketching user experiences: getting the design right and the right design. Morgan Kaufmann (2010). https://doi.org/10.1075/idj.18.1.13pur
3. Sandnes, F.E., Jian, H.L.: Sketching with Chinese calligraphy. Interactions **19**(6), 62–66 (2012). https://doi.org/10.1145/2377783.2377796
4. Chowdhury, A.: Design and development of a stencil for mobile user interface (UI) design. In: Chakrabarti, A. (ed.) Research into Design for a Connected World. SIST, vol. 135, pp. 629–639. Springer, Singapore (2019). https://doi.org/10.1007/978-981-13-5977-4_53
5. Bochmann, S., Ritz, T.: Prototyping Tools for Mobile Applications. Steinbeis-Ed. (2013)
6. da Silva, L.A., Medola, F.O., Rodrigues, O.V., Rodrigues, A.C.T., Sandnes, F.E.: Interdisciplinary-based development of user-friendly customized 3D printed upper limb prosthesis. In: Ahram, T.Z., Falcão, C. (eds.) AHFE 2018. AISC, vol. 794, pp. 899–908. Springer, Cham (2019). https://doi.org/10.1007/978-3-319-94947-5_88
7. Ferrari, A.L.M., dos Santos, A.D.P., da Silva Bertolaccini, G., Medola, F.O., Sandnes, F.E.: Evaluation of orthosis rapid prototyping during the design process: analysis of verification models. In: Di Nicolantonio, M., Rossi, E., Alexander, T. (eds.) AHFE 2019. AISC, vol. 975, pp. 298–307. Springer, Cham (2020). https://doi.org/10.1007/978-3-030-20216-3_28
8. Figliolia, A., Medola, F., Sandnes, F., Rodrigues, A.C.T., Paschoarelli, L.C.: Avoiding product abandonment through user centered design: a case study involving the development of a 3D printed customized upper limb prosthesis. In: Di Nicolantonio, M., Rossi, E., Alexander, T. (eds.) AHFE 2019. AISC, vol. 975, pp. 289–297. Springer, Cham (2020). https://doi.org/10.1007/978-3-030-20216-3_27
9. Usó, V.G., Sandnes, F.E., Medola, F.O.: Using virtual reality and rapid prototyping to co-create together with hospitalized children. In: Di Nicolantonio, M., Rossi, E., Alexander, T. (eds.) AHFE 2019. AISC, vol. 975, pp. 279–288. Springer, Cham (2020). https://doi.org/10.1007/978-3-030-20216-3_26
10. Huang, I.W.: Exploring low-fidelity prototyping methods for augmented reality usability tests. Master's thesis, University of Twente (2018)
11. Sandnes, F.E., Eika, E.: Visual augmentation of printed materials with intelligent see-through glass displays: a prototype based on smartphone and Pepper's Ghost. In: 2018 IEEE International Conference on Artificial Intelligence and Virtual Reality, pp. 267–273. IEEE (2018). https://doi.org/10.1109/aivr.2018.00063

12. Sandnes, F.E., Eika, E.: Enhanced learning of jazz chords with a projector based piano keyboard augmentation. In: Rønningsbakk, L., Wu, T.-T., Sandnes, F.E., Huang, Y.-M. (eds.) ICITL 2019. LNCS, vol. 11937, pp. 194–203. Springer, Cham (2019). https://doi.org/10.1007/978-3-030-35343-8_21
13. Hagen, S., Sandnes, F.E.: Toward accessible self-service kiosks through intelligent user interfaces. Pers. Ubiquit. Comput. **14**(8), 715–721 (2010). https://doi.org/10.1007/s00779-010-0286-8
14. Sandnes, F.E., Tan, T.B., Johansen, A., Sulic, E., Vesterhus, E., Iversen, E.R.: Making touch-based kiosks accessible to blind users through simple gestures. Univ. Access Inf. Soc. **11**(4), 421–431 (2012). https://doi.org/10.1007/s10209-011-0258-4
15. Sandnes, F.E., Herstad, J., Stangeland, A.M., Medola, F.O.: UbiWheel: a simple context-aware universal control concept for smart home appliances that encourages active living. In: 2017 IEEE SmartWorld. IEEE (2017). https://doi.org/10.1109/uic-atc.2017.8397460
16. Sabbir, A.S., Bodroddoza, K.M., Hye, A., Ahmed, M.F., Saha, S., Ahmed, K.I.: Prototyping arduino and android based m-health solution for diabetes mellitus patient. In: 2016 International Conference on Medical Engineering, Health Informatics and Technology. IEEE. (2016). https://doi.org/10.1109/meditec.2016.7835360
17. Lee, J.C., Avrahami, D., Hudson, S.E., Forlizzi, J., Dietz, P.H., Leigh, D.: The calder toolkit: wired and wireless components for rapidly prototyping interactive devices. In: Proceedings of the 5th Conference on Designing Interactive Systems: Processes, Practices, Methods, and Techniques, pp. 167–175 (2004). https://doi.org/10.1145/1013115.1013139
18. Sandnes, F.E.: PanoramaGrid: a graph paper tracing framework for sketching 360-degree immersed experiences. In: Proceedings of the International Working Conference on Advanced Visual Interfaces, pp. 342–343. ACM (2016). https://doi.org/10.1145/2909132.2926058
19. Sandnes, F.E.: Communicating panoramic 360 degree immersed experiences: a simple technique for sketching in 3D. In: Antona, M., Stephanidis, C. (eds.) UAHCI 2016. LNCS, vol. 9738, pp. 338–346. Springer, Cham (2016). https://doi.org/10.1007/978-3-319-40244-4_33
20. Sandnes, F.E., Eika, E.: Head-mounted augmented reality displays on the cheap: a DIY approach to sketching and prototyping low-vision assistive technologies. In: Antona, M., Stephanidis, C. (eds.) UAHCI 2017. LNCS, vol. 10278, pp. 167–186. Springer, Cham (2017). https://doi.org/10.1007/978-3-319-58703-5_13
21. Sandnes, F.E.: Sketching 3D immersed experiences rapidly by hand through 2D cross sections. In: Auer, M.E., Zutin, D.G. (eds.) Online Engineering & Internet of Things. LNNS, vol. 22, pp. 1001–1013. Springer, Cham (2018). https://doi.org/10.1007/978-3-319-64352-6_93
22. Sandnes, F.E., Lianguzov, Y.: Quick and easy 3D modelling for all: a browser-based 3D-sketching framework. iJOE **13**(11), 121 (2017). https://doi.org/10.3991/ijoe.v13i11.7734
23. Sandnes, F.E., Lianguzov, Y., Rodrigues, O.V., Lieng, H., Medola, F.O., Pavel, N.: Supporting collaborative ideation through freehand sketching of 3D-shapes in 2D using colour. In: Luo, Y. (ed.) CDVE 2017. LNCS, vol. 10451, pp. 123–134. Springer, Cham (2017). https://doi.org/10.1007/978-3-319-66805-5_16
24. Sandnes, F.E., Lianguzov, Y.: A simple browser-based 3D-sketching framework for novice and infrequent users. In: 2017 4th Experiment@ International Conference, pp. 155–156. IEEE (2017). https://doi.org/10.1109/EXPAT.2017.7984422
25. Sandnes, F.E., Eika, E.: Modelling 3D objects using 2D sketches through radial renderings of curvature maps. In: Karwowski, W., Trzcielinski, S., Mrugalska, B., Di Nicolantonio, M., Rossi, E. (eds.) AHFE 2018. AISC, vol. 793, pp. 203–213. Springer, Cham (2019). https://doi.org/10.1007/978-3-319-94196-7_19

26. Sandnes, F.E., Eika, E.: Drawing abrasive hologram animations with auto-generated scratch patterns. In: 2017 IEEE International Symposium on Multimedia, pp. 318–321. IEEE (2017). https://doi.org/10.1109/ism.2017.57
27. Beaudouin-Lafon, M., Mackay, W.E.: Prototyping tools and techniques. In: Human-Computer Interaction, pp. 137–160. CRC Press (2009). https://doi.org/10.1201/b11963-ch-47
28. Hartmann, B.: Gaining design insight through interaction prototyping tools, pp. 19–22. Stanford University, Stanford (2009)
29. Silva, T.R., Hak, J.L., Winckler, M.: A review of milestones in the history of GUI prototyping tools. In: 15th IFIP TC 13th International Conference on Human-Computer Interaction (2015). hal-01343040
30. Silva, T.R., Hak, J.L., Winckler, M., Nicolas, O.: A comparative study of milestones for featuring GUI prototyping tools. J. Softw. Eng. Appl. **10**(06), 564 (2017). hal-02146010
31. Raento, M., Oulasvirta, A., Petit, R., Toivonen, H.: ContextPhone: a prototyping platform for context-aware mobile applications. IEEE Pervasive Comput. **4**(2), 51–59 (2005). https://doi.org/10.1109/MPRV.2005.29
32. Mora, S., Gianni, F., Divitini, M.: RapIoT toolkit: rapid prototyping of collaborative Internet of Things applications. In: 2016 International Conference on Collaboration Technologies and Systems, pp. 438–445. IEEE (2016). https://doi.org/10.1109/cts.2016.81
33. Bähr, B.: Towards a requirements catalogue for prototyping tools of mobile user interfaces. In: Marcus, A. (ed.) DUXU 2015. LNCS, vol. 9187, pp. 495–507. Springer, Cham (2015). https://doi.org/10.1007/978-3-319-20898-5_48
34. Leiva, G., Beaudouin-Lafon, M.: Montage: a video prototyping system to reduce re-shooting and increase re-usability. In: Proceedings of the 31st Annual ACM Symposium on User Interface Software and Technology, pp. 675–682 (2018). https://doi.org/10.1145/3242587.3242613
35. Nolen, S.L., Giblin-Scanlon, L.J., Boyd, L.D., Rainchuso, L.: Development and testing of a smartphone application prototype for oral health promotion. Am. Dent. Hygienists Assoc. **92**(2), 6–14 (2018)
36. Petersen, M., Hempler, N.F.: Development and testing of a mobile application to support diabetes self-management for people with newly diagnosed type 2 diabetes: a design thinking case study. BMC Med. Inform. Decis. Mak. **17**(1), 91 (2017). https://doi.org/10.1186/s12911-017-0493-6
37. Nasta, L.G.S., Faria, L.P.P., Mares, T.F.: A very short story for a new future. In: Smart Healthcare for Disease Diagnosis and Prevention. Academic Press (2020). https://doi.org/10.1016/b978-0-12-817913-0.00001-8
38. Schwarz, D.: Jump Start Adobe XD. SitePoint (2017)
39. Eisenman, B.: Learning react native: Building native mobile apps with JavaScript. O'Reilly Media, Inc (2015)
40. Dalmasso, I., Datta, S.K., Bonnet, C., Nikaein, N.: Survey, comparison and evaluation of cross platform mobile application development tools. In: 2013 9th International Wireless Communications and Mobile Computing Conference, pp. 323–328. IEEE (2013). https://doi.org/10.1109/iwcmc.2013.6583580
41. Design, F.: Figma: the collaborative interface design tool (2017). https://www.figma.com/. Retrieved 17 September 2017. Downloaded 20 May 2020
42. Teplov, D.: Development of a mobile online banking UX/UI prototype, Thesis (2019)
43. Sandnes, F.E., Eika, E., Medola, F.O.: Improving the usability of interactive systems by incorporating design thinking into the engineering process: raising computer science students' awareness of quality versus quantity in ideation. In: 2019 5th Experiment International Conference, pp. 172–176. IEEE (2019). https://doi.org/10.1109/expat.2019.8876490

How Engineering Design Ability Improve via Project-Based Truss Tower STEM Course?

Wan-Hsuan Yen[✉] and Chi-Cheng Chang

Department of Technology Application and Human Resource Development, National Taiwan Normal University, No. 162, Sec. 1, HePing E. Rd. 106, Taipei, Taiwan
gordonwyen@gmail.com

Abstract. Engineering design ability is critical in today's society due to the vast development of technology. However, the development of it is not easy. The introduction of STEM (Science-Technology-Engineering-Math) and the utilization of PBL (Project-based Learning) seem to promise a bright future in the development of such ability. We adopted Atman's Engineering Design Process to evaluate the progress that students made after learning from a project-based Truss Tower STEM course. Students were grouped in six to design and construct a light-weight water tower type truss structure that can withstand severe earthquake. 137 students participated in this course and took pre-test as well as post-test. Students demonstrated significant progress in Developing Alternative Solutions and Project Realization. However, students did not show significant progress in Problem Scoping. Our research result echoes earlier research that some of engineering abilities might be trainable in classroom while other abilities might need other development methods.

Keywords: STEM · Science-Technology-Engineering-Math · PBL · Project-based learning · Truss tower · Engineering design process

1 Introduction

Engineering design ability is critical in today's world because more jobs rely on technology or artificial items. Besides, engineering education is more than making students to become engineers. Engineering education should also train students to become problem solvers, systematic thinkers, and hands-on makers. However, in most of the world, engineering education is not systematically provided until college level. This approach might hinder high school students from familiarizing themselves with this subject before making their decisions in future career. More importantly, this might also exclude those who do not choose engineering as their majors from basic engineering know-hows that are critical in today's society. As a result, the overall engineering readiness is not as sufficient as it could and should possibly be.

In the United States, according to National Science Board, NSB, and President's Council of Advisor on Science and Technology, PCAST, the demand for scientific and technical qualified employee is increasing but the supply of suitable talents is continuously decreasing for years [1, 2]. This challenge is even more severe as American's

PISA score remained at mediocre level or lower level comparing to other OECD countries for decades. The difficulty in training engineering capability and the lack of science and math ability both worsen the rate in developing such talents.

To respond to this challenge, STEM (Science-Technology-Engineering-Math) education was proposed for K-12 students. The idea of STEM focuses on the integration of Science, Technology, Engineering, and Mathematics. In short, one of the goals of STEM Education is to let students be able to perform and also learn the relating knowledge. However, many researchers cautioned unclearness of the goal of STEM education may let STEM education less effective. Furthermore, multiple facets of STEM education remained quite challenging in reality [3].

Although Taiwanese students performed better in PISA than their peers in the United States, the problem of Taiwanese education system is the mere emphasis of knowledge while insufficient efforts on attitude and applications. Some educators hoped the adoption of STEM can help students gain interests in such aspects. As we can see here, the seamless integration between learning subjects and the physical realization from abstract knowledge is quite important. Project-based learning (PBL) allows students to learn through completing a task that is challenging but well-designed [4]. With appropriate support and guidance, students are able to learn prior, during, or after the process. PBL is considered to be beneficial to STEM education since the challenging task will trigger students to actively search for know-hows that fit into the challenge. These knowledges may come from various subjects, such as Science, Technology, Engineering, Mathematics, and even the combination of them. It is supported that project–based learning did increase the integration attitude and behavior as well as the attitude toward Science, Engineering and Technology. Project-based learning also shew to have benefits to specific engineering techniques [5]. However, whether such method can greatly increase the whole and overall engineering design ability remains questionable.

We hereby developed a course around the challenging project that aims to build a water tower that can withstand earthquakes. Students are required to design and build a water tank with truss structure. The challenge of this task is to build the truss tower with minimum material while withstanding the maximum earthquake possible. Students will learn the knowledge pieces of STEM in the introductory classes and also combine them together when implementing the model construction. In the following text, we will describe the specialty of PBL, its usage in STEM education, and the engineering learning outcome expected.

2 Literature Review

2.1 Project-Based Learning (PBL) and Its Benefit for STEM Education

Project-based learning (PBL) is a model that organizes learning around projects [6]. Projects are complex tasks, based on challenging questions or problems, which involve students in design, problem solving, decision making or investigative activities. They give students the opportunity to work with relative autonomy over extended periods of time; and culminate in realistic products or presentations [6]. Erdogan and Bozeman [4] considered Project-based Learning (PBL) is a pedagogical method containing several features, including: (a) authentic assessment and content, (b) challenging projects with complex tasks, (c) decision making and problem solving, (d) explicit objectives with individual and collective learning, (e) realistic products to real-world problems, (f) student directed and teacher facilitated and (g) time limited.

Although many PBL models exist, a lot of them use different words to describe similar concepts. For instance, Buck Institute [7] define PBL as "Standards focused PBL is a systematic teaching method that engages students in learning knowledge and skills through an extended inquiry process structured around complex, authentic questions and carefully designed products and tasks." On comparison, "knowledge and skills" was mentioned as "various learning outcomes" in the Aggie STEM Center definition referring to what students gain through PBL [8]. In addition, both definitions indicate that students participating in PBL go through a series of investigative processes. Finally, both definitions describe an "engaging" process for those students learning STEM content through PBL [4].

Why is PBL such an ideal method for STEM education? This is probably because it is natural for scientists and engineers to solve problem or optimize solution. On the contrary, traditional scientific or engineering teaching method is through one way lecturing and lacks the experience in real-world problems, or the scenarios where decisions are not clear-cut and requirements conflicts. In addition, with the back-up of constructivist theory, PBL approach to STEM education can improve students' achievement in higher-level cognitive tasks that are not easily fulfilled by other teaching methods.

2.2 Engineering Design Process

Engineering design is a critical element of engineering education. It is also considered as a critical competency that engineering students need to acquire. In K-12 Technology and Engineering Education (TEE), the traditional models used to illustrate engineering content and design practice are shown as Fig. 1. It is represented as a circular cycle by a representation of a series of steps. Teacher are expected to teach all the steps when engaging students in designing engineering solutions.

However, although TEE model fit the engineering requirement well, it is not adequate in conveying the ideas used in STEM education. Wells [9] suggested that the primary goal of Integrated-STEM education is to teach students the content and practice of Technology and Engineering as well as Science and Mathematics. Wells [9] believes the current monodisciplinary STEM model cannot serve as the framework for conveying the integration of concurrent pedagogies.

The PRIPOSAL model, although also convey the engineering design process as a circle, it tries to categories each step as phase of engagement encountered when attempting to resolve an engineering challenge [9]. It is suggested the engineering students should learn from such approach to gain higher level of learning achievement when designing a solution (Fig. 2).

Another way to evaluate the learning outcome of an engineering student is to compare the student's performance level to the expert's performance level. Atman et al. [10] suggested five themes should be adopted when evaluating the engineering design

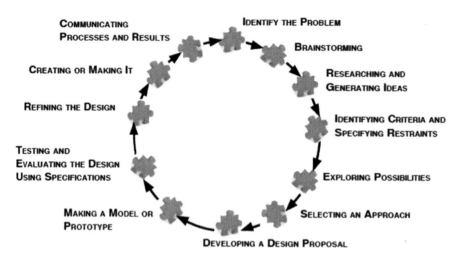

Fig. 1. Typical engineering design loop [9]

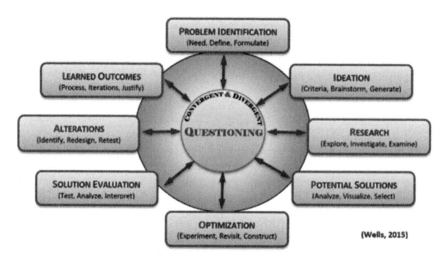

Fig. 2. PIRPOSAL model of integrative STEM education [9]

ability: problem scoping, project realization, alternative solutions generation, distribution of activity over time, and solution quality. With a further trimming based on the engineering textbook, Atman et al. [10] proposed the below design process with three design stages and ten design activities. The three stages are: Problem Scoping (including three activities: Identification of a Need, Problem Definition, and Gathering Information), Developing Alternative Solutions (including four activities: Generating Ideas, Modeling, Feasibility Analysis, and Evaluation), Project Realization (including three activities: Decision, Communication, and Implementation). Not only did Atman et al. [10] find engineering experts spend more in problem scoping, they also found experts gather more information covering more categories. They also considered these two stages (problem scoping and information gathering) are important competencies for engineering students to develop.

In our research, we'd like to explore the following questions:

1. What is the learning outcome of truss tower STEM course?
2. Is there difference in improvement among different engineering design process stages?

3 Method

3.1 Participants and Procedures

One hundred and thirty-seven high school students from twenty different schools registered the truss tower STEM class voluntarily. Seventy-five students are male (54.7%) and sixty-two students are female (45.3%). Due to the massive requests for the class, only parts of the intending students were recruited due to the limit of capacity.

The aim of this course is to help students build a truss tower with minimum weight that withstands the maximum earthquake possible (Fig. 3). The course lasts 10 weeks and its activities include: The introduction of earthquake and building safety, the analysis of truss tower structure, using of CAD system (2D), using of CAD system (3D), using of 3D printer, truss tower structure manufacturing and assemble, strength test and analysis, re-design and re-test. Before the course begin, each student needs to fill out the pre-test of Atman et al.'s (2007) Engineering Design Process. After finishing the course, the students would fill out the post-test of the same questionnaire to evaluate their progress.

Since earthquake is a common phenomenon in Taiwan, students are quite familiar with the possible consequences of it. The building process also requires students to calculate and structure design, which consists of the elements of M and E. The course also taught the cause of earthquake and the use of 2D/3D drawing, which added the S and T components to the whole setting.

Before and after the course, we surveyed the students' engineering design ability. We then analyzed the progress in each category to see if there is improvement in the engineering design process.

3.2 Engineering Design Process Inventory

To assess students' progress in engineering design ability, we adopted Engineering Design Process Inventory developed by Atman et al. [10]. Atman's model categorized engineering design process into three stages and ten activities. The three stages are: Problem Scoping (including three activities: Identification of a Need, Problem Definition, and Gathering Information), Developing Alternative Solutions (including four activities: Generating Ideas, Modeling, Feasibility Analysis, and Evaluation), Project

Fig. 3. Water tower truss structure

Realization (including three activities: Decision, Communication, and Implementation). According to Atman et al., the first and the last activity is not included in survey. We also delete the "other" questionnaire as it is not relevant to our research purpose. The final questionnaire consists of 28 items such as: "I know how to evaluate whether the designed product fit the constraint and requirement." and "I will consider the variety of engineering design as many as possible in the beginning." Students rated their perception on Likert 5-point scale.

3.3 Data Analysis

We used SPSS 23 for the descriptive statistics and paired t-test to examine whether the course make a difference in students' engineering design ability. If the paired t-test between pre- and post-test of certain design activity/stage is significant, the students' aspect for that shows the course make an impact on that dimension.

4 Results

4.1 Descriptive Analysis

The mean and standard of pre-test and post-test of each design activity is listed in Table 1. As shown in Table 1, the lowest ability in pre-test is Modeling (3.94) and the highest ability is Problem Definition (4.58). In post-test, Problem Definition is still the highest (4.56) but the lowest changed to Feasibility Analysis (4.32).

Table 1. Mean and standard deviation of pretest and posttest of each engineering design activity

Design activity	Mean of pretest	SD of pretest	Mean of posttest	SD of posttest
Problem definition	4.58	.41	4.56	.41
Gathering information	4.51	.50	4.53	.43
Generating ideas	4.04	.65	4.38	.51
Modeling	3.94	.66	4.34	.53
Feasibility analysis	3.96	.52	4.32	.48
Evaluation	4.03	.62	4.35	.50
Decision	4.15	.59	4.39	.55
Communication	4.30	.46	4.46	.40

4.2 Progress Between Pre-test and Post-test

The paired t-test result is shown in Table 2. Six out of eight items show significant differences between tests: Generate Ideas, Modeling, Feasibility Analysis, Evaluation, Decision, and Communication all show significant advancement. On the other hand, Problem Definition and Gather Information did not show significant differences.

Table 2. Paired t-test for pre- and post-test

Item	Pre-Post Mean Diff.	S.D.	t	p
Problem definition	.02	.38	.62	.54
Gathering information	−.03	.53	−.57	.57
Generating ideas	−.34	.61	−6.50***	<.00
Modeling	−.40	.61	−7.68***	<.00
Feasibility analysis	−.36	.49	−8.40***	<.00
Evaluation	−.32	.51	−7.17***	<.00
Decision	−.24	.64	−4.42***	<.00
Communication	−.16	.43	−4.25***	<.00

*$p < .05$, **$p < .01$, ***$p < .001$

5 Discussion and Conclusion

Our research shows that, prior to the truss tower course, the variance of students' ability in each engineering process is larger. Students were less confident and knowledgeable in Modeling and Feasibility Analysis. They were also not competent in Evaluation, Generating Ideas, and Decision. On the contrary, students were quite confident in Problem Definition and Gathering Information. They also considered Communication is one of their top three abilities.

After learning from the truss tower course, all of the ability perception level were higher than 4.3. Students shew biggest gain in Modeling, Feasibility Analysis, Generating Ideas, and Evaluation.

Our research found students gain significant progress after truss tower class in: Generate Ideas, Modeling, Feasibility Analysis, Evaluation, Decision, and Communication. Among all the above items, the score in post-test are all higher than the score in pre-test. This shows the ability of "Developing Alternative Solutions" and "Project Realization" may possible to be developed by training. Atman et al. (2007) also found the time spent on "Project Realization" by senior engineering students is also significantly higher than freshman engineering students. This might imply these abilities are trainable in classroom.

On the other hand, students did not show significant improvement in Problem Definition and Gather Information after truss tower class. When comparing the level of each items, Problem Definition and Gather Information are two of the highest items at Pre-test. The average of these two items were both close to the maximum value, 5.0. Accordingly, there is a possibility of no significant growth due to the fact that these pre-test scores are already at high level and the room of improvement is quite small.

However, comparing to Atman et al.'s [10] result, they also found the differences of time spent for Problem Scoping Stage, aka. Problem Definition and Gathering Information, was also not significantly different between freshman and senior engineering students. On the contrary, Atman et al. [10] found experts did spend significant more time than senior and freshman students. This could imply that although these abilities are not teachable in classroom, but only learnable in a workplace or by experience.

6 Limitations and Future Direction

There are several limitations of this research. First of all, the sample of high school students might be biased since only the self-registered and selected students enrolled the course and completed the study. Since students who voluntarily participated in STEM related courses may be more interested or confident in their STEM ability. Furthermore, their parents might emphasize more in similar direction and make them more knowledgeable or less scared about relating issues. This may decrease the external validity of our research. In the future, it is suggested to include all kinds of students or the combination of different type in our study. Second, since the questionnaire is self-evaluated, it is not avoidable that the common method bias may influence the reliability. For the future research, it might be better if other's evaluation such as teacher's evaluation or peer's evaluation can be included to avoid such bias. Last but not least, the progress of the engineering process perception might not come from the teaching only. Since truss tower is a group activity, the group level knowledge and group level atmosphere might have influence on students' gain. In the future, it would be better if the influencing factors from group dynamic can be included for analysis to achieve better understanding about the mechanism of the advancement of high school students' engineering design ability.

References

1. Casey, B.: STEM Education: Preparing Jobs of the Future (2012). https://www.jec.senate.gov/public/index.cfm/democrats/2012/4/stem-education-preparing-jobs-of-the-future. Accessed 18 May 2020
2. Raju, P.K., Clayson, A.: The future of STEM education: an analysis of two national reports. J. STEM Educ. Innov. Res. **11**(5), 25–28 (2010)
3. Margot, K.C., Kettler, T.: Teachers' perception of STEM integration and education: a systematic literature review. Int. J. STEM Educ. **6**, 2 (2019)
4. Erdogan, N., Bozeman, T.D.: Models of project-based learning for the 21st century. In: Sahin, A. (ed.) A Practice-based Model of STEM Teaching: STEM Students on the Stage (SOS)TM, pp. 31–42. Sense Publishers, Rotterdam (2015)
5. Moore, T., Miller, R., Lesh, R., Stohlmann, M., Kim, Y.R.: Modeling in engineering: the role of representational fluency in students' conceptual understanding. Res. J. Eng. Educ. **102**(1), 141–178 (2013)
6. Ozer, O., Ayyildiz, I., Esch, N.: Project-based learning in a world focused on standards. In: Sahin, A. (ed.) A Practice-Based Model of STEM Teaching: STEM Students on the Stage (SOS) TM, 63–73. Sense Publishers, Rotterdam (2015)
7. Markham, T.H., Larmer, J., Ravitz, J.: Project Based Learning Handbook a Guide to Standards-Focused Project Based Learning for Middle and High School Teachers. Buck Institute for Education, Novato (2003)
8. Capraro, R.M., Slough, S.W.: Why PBL? Why STEM? Why now? an Introduction to STEM Project-Based Learning. In: Capraro, R.M., Capraro, M.M., Morgan, J.R. (eds.) STEM Project-Based Learning: An Integrated Science, Technology, Engineering, and Mathematics (STEM) Approach, pp. 1–5. Sense Publishers, Rotterdam (2013)
9. Wells, J.G.: PIRPOSAL model of integrative STEM education: conceptual and pedagogical framework for classroom implementation. Technol. Eng. Teacher **75**(6), 12–19 (2016)
10. Atman, C.J., Adams, R.S., Cardella, M.E., Turns, J., Mosborg, S., Saleem, J.: Engineering design processes: a comparison of students and expert practitioners. J. Eng. Educ. **96**(4), 359–379 (2007)

Improving Student Learning Satisfaction in Lectures in English as a Medium of Instruction with Speech-Enabled Language Translation Application

Rustam Shadiev[1(✉)], Narzikul Shadiev[2], Mirzaali Fayziev[2], and Yuliya Halubitskaya[1]

[1] Nanjing Normal University, No. 122, Ninghai Road, Nanjing 210097, China
rustamsh@gmail.com
[2] Samarkand State University, No. 15, University Blv, Samarkand 140104, Uzbekistan

Abstract. Speech-enabled language translation (SELT) was applied to support learning of students during lectures in English as a medium of instruction (EMI). We aimed to investigate whether SELT support can facilitate students' learning satisfaction in EMI lectures. A qualitative research method was used in this study to address the research question. Thirty-three university students were hired for the study. All of them were non-native speakers of English and attended lectures in EMI. Their learning satisfaction was measured via a questionnaire and compared across two groups (i.e. low and high English as a foreign language ability). The results showed that all students had high level of learning satisfaction. In addition, we found that level of perceived learning satisfaction of low language ability students was significantly higher compared to that of high language ability students. Based on the results of this study, we suggest that educators and researchers may consider applying SELT technology during lectures in EMI because it is beneficial for the students with low linguistic competency as to have high level of learning satisfaction.

Keywords: Speech-enabled language translation · Learning satisfaction · English as a medium of instruction

1 Introduction

Many countries have been using English in education in general and expanding teaching in English as a medium of instruction (EMI) in particular in the last few decades (Tsui 2018). In EMI teaching, the instructors use English to teach academic subjects for students whose first language is not English (Chang 2010). Although, the number of EMI courses remarkably increases, scholars argued that some issues (with student linguistic incompetency as the most important among them) are not taken into considerations so that EMI courses result in lower student achievement. For example, scholars suggested that because of linguistic incompetency not every student attending foreign language-medium lectures fully understands the lecture content (Barnes and

Lock 2010). This notion was clearly reflected in the study of Chang (2010), who surveyed perceptions of 370 undergraduate students in Taiwan regarding the implementation of EMI for content courses, and found that about 13% of students could understand less than 24% of lecture and about 23% of students could understand less than 50% of lecture. Huang (2009) suggested that students who "suffer" from such learning via English are mostly students with low language ability.

In order to understand the reason behind student inability to understand content of lectures in EMI we need to refer to the notion of information processing. Information processing in EMI lecture is very complex. It involves taking in information, organizing and storing it to be retrieved at a later time (Siegler 1998). That is, first, a learner pays attention to information and brings it in; after that, information is actively manipulated in working memory and passively held in long-term memory (Slate and Charlesworth 1988; Smith and Kosslyn 2013). As working memory has limited capacity it is possible that it may become overloaded because information from EMI lecture is difficult to understand (Chow and Conway 2015). If students are not able to fully comprehend lecture content, this may negatively influence their learning satisfaction.

Scholars use various approaches to support learning and comprehension of students attending lectures in EMI. For example, the instructor provided real-time transcription of the lecture content during lectures (Kushalnagar et al. Kushalnagar et al. 2014) or lecture notes (Goodman 2014), audio-recorded (Soruç et al. 2018) or video-recorded (Shimoyamada et al. 2019) files after lectures to help enhance student comprehension. In this study, we employed SELT technology in EMI lectures. SELT receives speech input in one language and then simultaneously translates it into different language. Such approach was used in cross-cultural learning project in Shadiev and Huang (2016), Shadiev et al. (2018) and Shadiev et al. (2019). Participants representing different nationalities communicated with each other in their mother tongue and SELT was employed to translate their communication content for student to be able to understand it.

It is important to measure learning satisfaction. According to Keller (2010), learning satisfaction is a positive or negative affective response to the technology-supported learning environment. Jung (2014) defined learning satisfaction as the degree to which a student senses a positive association with the overall learning experiences. Keller (2010) argued that satisfaction can result from extrinsic (e.g. grades) and intrinsic (e.g. feelings of self-esteem) factors. Hui et al. (2008) highlighted that three essential satisfaction determinants are learning effectiveness, perceived course learnability, and perceived learning community support. That is, students' learning satisfaction can be enhanced if they believe that they have acquired specific skills, the course materials are easy to learn, and a learning environment created an active, strongly bonded community. Baturay et al. (2010) suggested that learning satisfaction is an important consideration for future participation in learning. One reason is because it is a critical variable that contributes to consistent participation and activation in learning and it affects continuing learning (Hui et al. 2008).

Informed by related literature, in this study, we administered lectures in EMI for non-native speakers of English and applied SELT technology to facilitate student comprehension of lecture content. Students perceived learning satisfaction during lectures in EMI supported by SELT was investigated. In this present study, we assumed that translating lecture content into student native language could be useful for learning so that students will be able to comprehend lecture content. As a result, we expect that student learning satisfaction will be positive. Our investigation was carried out with respect to students' language ability, i.e. we were interested in what satisfaction of all students, of students of low language ability and students of high language ability are. The following research question was addressed in this study:

- What is perceived learning satisfaction of students during lectures in EMI supported by SELT?

2 Method

A qualitative research method was used in this study to address the research questions. Thirty-three students from one university in Taiwan were recruited. They were between 18 and 23 years old. The participants were native speakers of Mandarin Chinese. English was their foreign language (EFL).

The participants attended two lectures on general topics given in English as the medium of instruction. We applied SELT during lectures to facilitate participant comprehension of lecture content. SELT received speech input from the instructor and simultaneously translated it from English into Mandarin Chinese. Translated texts were displayed for the participants during two lectures. After lectures, a questionnaire survey was administered to the participants to measure their perceived learning satisfaction with SELT support. In addition, one-on-one semi-structured interviews with the participants were conducted.

Demographic information was collected using a questionnaire and we measured the participants EFL ability using scores from their officially-recognized Test of English for International Communication (TOEIC) certificates.

The participants were divided into low and high EFL ability groups with 16 students in the former and 17 students in the latter.

One-on-one semi-structured interviews were conducted with the participants to explore their experiences during lectures in EMI. Each participant was interviewed for approximately 30 min. An open-coding approach was used for the interview data analysis. That is, all interviews were audio-recorded first, and then the recorded content was fully transcribed for the purpose of the analysis. The text segments that met the criteria for providing the best research information were highlighted and coded. Codes with similar meanings were sorted into categories, and the established categories produced a framework within which to illustrate findings of the study.

3 Results

The questionnaire results demonstrated that the students had high level of learning satisfaction ($M = 3.38$, $SD = 1.10$). High standard deviation value suggests high variability in student perceptions. When we compared perceptions of low EFL ability students ($M = 4$; $SD = 0.82$) and high EFL ability students ($M = 2.73$; $SD = 0.98$), we found a significant difference, $t = 6.944$, $p = 0.000$. That is, low EFL ability students had higher level of perceived learning satisfaction compared to high EFL ability students (Table 1).

Table 1. Learning satisfaction with SELT.

Variable	All		LA*		HA		t	p
	M	SD	M	SD	M	SD		
Learning satisfaction	3.38	1.10	4.00	0.82	2.73	0.98	6.944	0.000

*LA – low EFL ability; HA – high EFL ability.

4 Discussion and Conclusion

When we considered all students in general, our results showed that their level of learning satisfaction with SELT was high. We also noted that standard deviation value was high which suggests high variability in students' perceptions. When we considered different EFL ability, we found that low EFL ability students had significantly higher perceived learning satisfaction than high EFL ability students. The reason is because SELT were beneficial for low EFL ability students but not so useful for high EFL ability students. Some possible reasons were revealed during interviews with the students. For example, low EFL ability students mentioned that they were always anxious before lectures in English because of their low EFL ability. However, they were relieved after SELT technology was applied during lectures as they could read translated texts and understand content of the lecture. On the other hand, high EFL ability students mentioned that their language ability is high enough so they do not need any additional support. When SELT texts were shown to them they were distracted and confused because the instructor spoke in English but SELT texts were in Chinese. These findings are in line with those obtained in previous related research (Shadiev and Huang 2016; Shadiev et al. 2018; Shadiev et al. 2019).

Based on our results, we suggest that educators may consider applying SELT technology during lectures in EMI. Such approach, as we found from our study, can be useful for the students with low linguistic competency to comprehend lecture content and may satisfy learning needs of the students. Furthermore, as we found that SELT texts can be distracting for some students, an adaptive approach to use SELT texts can be used. That is, all students should have an option to choose whether to be exposed to SELT texts or not. In this situation, students who do not need SELT support may decide not to turn SELT option on whereas students who need SELT support may decide to turn it on. Future studies may also consider extending applications of SELT technology to other media. That is, SELT texts were presented as pure texts to the students in this study and future studies may consider embed them with other media such as figures, charts and tables. So that the students will receive not only pure texts but also figures, charts and tables accompanied with relevant textual captures in their native language to enhance their comprehension of content. Another promising future research direction is to design collaborative learning activities around SELT texts.

Perhaps, in the future, the students may collaborate and discuss with each other lecture content with translated texts by SELT technology.

References

Baturay, M.H., Daloglu, A., Yildirim, S.: Language practice with multimedia supported web-based grammar revision material. ReCALL 22(3), 313–331 (2010)

Barnes, B.D., Lock, G.: The attributes of effective lecturers of English as a foreign language as perceived by students in a Korean University. Aust. J. Teach. Educ. 35(1), 139–152 (2010)

Chang, Y.Y.: English-medium instruction for subject courses in tertiary education: reactions from Taiwanese undergraduate students. Taiwan Int. ESP J. 2(1), 53–82 (2010)

Chow, M., Conway, A.R.A.: The scope and control of attention: Sources of variance in working memory capacity. Mem. Cogn. 43(3), 325–339 (2015). https://doi.org/10.3758/s13421-014-0496-9

Goodman, B.A.: Implementing English as a medium of instruction in a Ukrainian university: challenges, adjustments, and opportunities. Int. J. Pedagogies Learn. 9(2), 130–141 (2014)

Huang, Y.P.: English-only instruction in post-secondary education in Taiwan: voices from students. Hwa Kang J. English Lang. Lit. 15, 145–157 (2009)

Hui, W., Hu, P.H., Clark, T.H., Tam, K.Y., Milton, J.: Technology-assisted learning: a longitudinal field study of knowledge category, learning effectiveness and satisfaction in language learning. J. Comput. Assist. Learn. 24(3), 245–259 (2008)

Jung, H.J.: Ubiquitous learning: determinants impacting learners' satisfaction and performance with smartphones. Lang. Learn. Technol. 18(3), 97–119 (2014)

Keller, J.M.: The ARCS model of motivational design. In: Motivational Design for Learning and Performance, pp. 43–74. Springer, New York (2010). https://doi.org/10.1007/978-1-4419-1250-3_3

Kushalnagar, R.S., Lasecki, W.S., Bigham, J.P.: Accessibility evaluation of classroom captions. ACM Trans. Accessible Comput. 5(3), 1–24 (2014)

Shimoyamada, S., Nakazawa, A., Fujimoto, T.: Blending online and offline learning: a study on the development of an English as a medium of instruction workshop. In: Proceedings of the 2019 8th International Conference on Educational and Information Technology, pp. 141–146. Association for Computing Machinery, New York (2019)

Siegler, R.S.: Information processing theories of development. In: Siegler, R.S. (ed.) Children's Thinking. Prentice-Hall, Upper Saddle River (1998)

Shadiev, R., Huang, Y.M.: Facilitating cross-cultural understanding with learning activities supported by speech-to-text recognition and computer-aided translation. Comput. Educ. 98, 130–141 (2016)

Shadiev, R., Sun, A., Huang, Y.M.: A study of the facilitation of cross-cultural understanding and intercultural sensitivity using speech-enabled language translation technology. Br. J. Edu. Technol. 50(3), 1415–1433 (2019)

Shadiev, R., Wu, T.T., Sun, A., Huang, Y.M.: Applications of speech-to-text recognition and computer-aided translation for enhancing cross-cultural learning: issues and their solutions. Educ. Tech. Res. Dev. 66(1), 191–214 (2018)

Slate, J.R., Charlesworth Jr., J.R.: Information processing theory: classroom applications. Retrieved from ERIC database, ED293792 (1988)

Smith, E.E., Kosslyn, S.M.: Cognitive Psychology: Mind and Brain. Pearson Higher Education, New York (2013)

Soruç, A., Dinler, A., Griffiths, C.: Listening comprehension strategies of EMI students in Turkey. In: Kırkgöz, Y., Dikilitaş, K. (eds.) Key Issues in English for Specific Purposes in Higher Education. ELE, vol. 11, pp. 265–287. Springer, Cham (2018). https://doi.org/10.1007/978-3-319-70214-8_15

Tsui, C.: Teacher efficacy: a case study of faculty beliefs in an English-medium instruction teacher training program. Taiwan J. TESOL **15**(1), 101–128 (2018)

Model of Technology Enhanced Affective Learning

Satu-Maarit Frangou(✉) and Minna Körkkö

University of Lapland, Rovaniemi, Finland
{satu-maarit.frangou,minna.korkko}@ulapland.fi

Abstract. In this paper, the concept of affective learning is discussed in today's context, in which technology plays a significant role, with the objective of developing a model of affective learning. The study is guided by Frangou's [6] embodied knowledge construction model of affects in writing and Körkkö's [18] holistic model of learning and guiding reflection. The models are examined and then merged to form a model of affective learning that can serve as a pedagogical framework to facilitate teaching and learning in a holistic learning environment that takes into account the learner's motivations, interests, and experiences. In this context, the learner's sensory and motor perceptions, together with embodied cognition, are intertwined into a technology-enhanced holistic pedagogy that considers the learner's individual embodied learning environment. This paper concludes with discussing the model and providing ideas for future research.

Keywords: Affective learning · Embodied cognition · Emotions in learning · Holistic learning · Technology enhanced learning

1 Introduction

The use of technology has become pervasive in classrooms around the world; therefore, affective learning is bound to be technology enhanced, as with other forms of learning. Learning is also inherently an emotional and embodied experience in which one is continuously exposed to feelings of failure and success, as well as challenges that can be both psychological and physical [4, 8]. Personal emotions are the key driving force that influence an individual's behaviors, attitudes, engagement in learning, and faith in one's abilities; in other words, learning is a process in which body, mind, and brain are interdependent [10, 11, 23]. New neuroscientific findings have confirmed that emotions, rational thinking, perceiving, and performing an action have the potential to support memory retrieval and decision making, highlighting the connection between emotional functions and cognitive processes [8, 11]. Technology, given its far reaching uses and potential, can then be used as a tool to enhance learning through applications that engage embodied cognition.

Each learner has an individual set of experiences and a unique way of perceiving. Also, they process their learning experiences through their own emotions, which suggests the need for an individualized and flexible approach to learning [13]. However, the emotions' influence on learning is often neglected due to their instinctive nature [8, 9, 12, 21] and difficulties in measuring learners' emotional and affective states, particularly during interactions [2]. Most theoretical models of learning seem to highlight the learners' experiences, actions, and reflection on the two, which can be summed up as the rational side of learning (e.g. [14, 22]). Some models address personal, emotional, and motivational sides of learning as well [3, 15]; however, those models do not consider the use of technology in the learning process, so there is a call for models that aim to combine these different aspects of learning while also integrating the role of technology.

To respond to this research gap, the principal aim of this study was to synthesize the concept of affective learning by zooming in on technology enhanced affective learning in which the emotions, technologies, and, embodied cognition all play a role. The authors wish to contribute to the scientific debate on affective learning by identifying its idiosyncrasies and peculiarities and thereby developing a model of technology enhanced affective learning. In what follows, we first present and discuss key insights from Frangou's [6] embodied knowledge construction model of affects in writing and Körkkö's [18] holistic model of learning and guiding reflection. Based on the review and interrelation of the two models, we argue for their suitability for merging and further development to provide a didactical approach that supports learner knowledge construction holistically. Then, we introduce a reflection of the created model and an elaboration of its adaptability to different settings. The paper ends by recapitulating our perspective and by discussing how it can lay the ground for a new way of approaching affective learning.

2 An Embodied Knowledge Construction Model of Affects in Writing

Although there is general agreement regarding the centrality of processing external and internal stimuli in embodied cognition, theoretical conceptualizations in the past have overlooked the emotions and affect, not to mention subjectivity and motivation [6, 19, 24]. Indeed, today's scientific literature on embodied cognition draws on multidisciplinary perspectives, highlighting the entirety of cognition in which motor functions and emotions are interrelated and function in conjunction with one another [6, 24]. Recent neuroscientific research underscores the harmonious synergy of the two separate but parallel processes of perceiving and registering the emotions and subsequently utilizing them in one's decision making processes [2]. Furthermore, according to the theory of embodied cognition, perceiving an action and performing the same action activate the same sensory-motor circuitry within the brain [11]. This means that the mind is not only in charge of the body, but that the body affects the mind, demonstrating their interrelation and the intersubjectivity of embodied cognition.

The embodied knowledge construction model of affects in writing [6] takes into consideration particularly the mind's learning environment and the intertwined spatial and temporal factors influencing the learning moment (Fig. 1). The model connects the six aspects of embodied cognition listed by [25] together with Hayes's [7] framework for the cognitive process of writing.

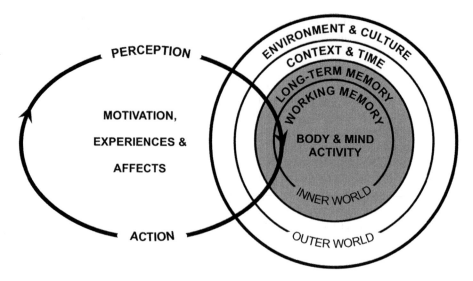

Fig. 1. The embodied knowledge construction model of affects in writing [6].

To consider the possibilities involved in developing a model of technologically enhanced affective learning, the significant factors we examine are taken from the embodied knowledge construction model of affects in writing [6] (Fig. 1). Knowledge construction is influenced by several factors in and around the learner. The Perception and Action sequence is fundamental and pervasive, having a connection to both the learner's inner and outer worlds. The learner's earlier experiences can influence their self-perception of their abilities and skills, as well as motivation by increasing or inhibiting it. Motivation affects learner predisposition to the task at hand; additionally, goals and benefit estimates also play a role. The Outer World of the learner incorporates first, the learner's sociocultural history and background along his/her learning environment and the classroom culture. Second, the outer world includes the physical task environment, which in this case contains the technology being used. It also includes the context and any time pressure, or lack of it. These can affect the learner's approach to the learning task. The Inner World's core is the body and mind activity of the learner, and beside it runs the working memory and long-term memory, which incorporate also the influence of actions on cognition. Additionally, the long-term memory holds significant knowledge about one's earlier experiences and learning, sociocultural background, and context. The long-term memory guides the learner to behave in an appropriate manner in a given context and time. The component of working memory also contains within itself the cognitive processes that motor activation has initiated by the consequent brain activation. In sum, the learner's body, mind, and brain form an active learning environment in which the learner's body and mind perceive the sensations inside oneself as well as outside in the surroundings, use imagination, and propagate emotions that affect the learning moment.

3 Holistic Model of Learning and Guiding Reflection

Today, it is increasingly highlighted that in addition to theoretical knowledge, factors that may remain subconsciously experienced, such as the emotions, motivation, and self-efficacy, determine learning and behavior [17]. Some researchers have pursued approaches that consider the multidimensionality of learning. For instance, Korthagen [15, 16] argues that learning occurs in the theory-practice-person connection and that learning from experience requires meaning-oriented reflection, which means an awareness of the essence of the problem under consideration. To find a deeper meaning in their experiences, learners must reflect carefully on emotional and motivational dimensions and their self-identity. According to Korthagen's [17] holistic approach, learning is a multidimensional process, which means that it can be rational and non-rational and can include motivation and emotions. Moreover, from a holistic perspective, learning is also seen as multilevel, which means that reflection starts from individual experience and is pondered in relation to the environment, competencies, beliefs, identity, mission and core qualities, such as individual strengths and developmental needs. These aspects form the layers of the onion model of reflection [16], which highlights the fact that learners must reflect on the inner layers in order to understand the meaning of their experiences. Blömeke et al. [3] share similar ideas when discussing the affective and motivational aspects of teacher behavior.

In the holistic model of learning and guiding reflection [18] (Fig. 2), the ideas of Korthagen's holistic approach were combined with the writings of theorists of reflective practice [1, 5, 14, 24]. Following the principal ideas of Korthagen, the model is comprised of the cognitive, emotional, and motivational dimensions of learning. persona forms the core of learning. Learning is based on experience, occurs in a certain context, and develops during interaction with others. Learning and behavior are determined by the learner's self-efficacy beliefs, which are affected by, e.g., the learner's prior experiences, motivation, self-concept, and environmental factors. At the same time, the teaching profession is influenced by wider social, cultural, and ethical aspects of schooling. The model (Fig. 2), originally designed for student teachers, can serve as a practical and theoretical guide for learners and learning facilitators at all levels of education. Learners can use it as, for example, a guide for their individual or peer reflection during learning and learning projects. The model helps learners to consider various dimensions of learning and ponder their actions from different viewpoints, e.g., theoretical and environmental factors or their personal strengths. Teachers and learning facilitators can benefit from the model in seeking to elaborate on discussions and encourage productive reflection.

As Fig. 2 shows, the model consists of eight parts, with a persona in the middle. The parts are connected to personal development and, through that, to student teachers' professional development. All parts of the model interact with one another. Following the ideas of the holistic approach, the persona forms the heart of the model. Inside the persona are one's personal characteristics and qualities, which can be regarded as strengths and developmental needs. Moreover, the persona includes one's mission—i.e., what student teachers aim for in the teaching profession. The environment in the model refers to those factors that are essential in a student teacher's lessons and that affect

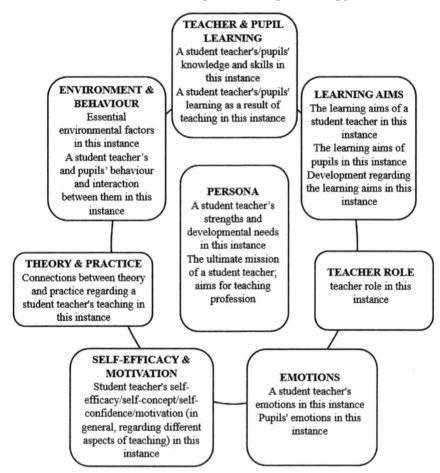

Fig. 2. Holistic model of learning and guiding reflection [18].

teaching and learning. Behavior refers to the behavior of student teachers and learners and the interactions between them. The model includes both teacher and learner learning and learning aims. Because part of teacher learning is unconscious and relates to the emotions and motivation, the model encourages student teachers to recall their emotions in specific moments. Regarding the emotional aspect, the model draws attention to student teachers' self-efficacy, motivation, self-concept, and self-confidence, as well as the relationship between these and student teachers' self-efficacy beliefs. The aim of the model is for student teachers to find connections between their practical experiences and educational theories. The model refers to specific teaching instances under focus. This is because reflection and learning always occur in certain contexts [5, 22]. Outside the circle, there are social, cultural, and ethical issues of schooling that are beyond the context and affect everything that happens in learning situations.

In what follows, the two theoretical models of Frangou [6] and Körkkö [18] are used as a platform to develop a model of technology enhanced affective learning and as a lens that affords a theoretically robust background for the exploration of affect related issues emerging from the synthesized theories.

4 Model of Technology Enhanced Affective Learning

Learning design involves the consideration of several factors simultaneously. Today, learners' individual differences are taken into account all the more when developing new pedagogies. Patience [20] stated that, "Affective pedagogy is as much about feelings and emotions as it is about learning outcomes". To contribute to this development direction, we have unified two theories to form a pedagogical framework for the facilitation of teaching and learning in a technology enhanced holistic learning environment that takes into account the learner's inner learning environment. Technology is in a central position in this model due to its potential to significantly improve and support learning. However, we refrain from pointing to any particular technological device, because the used technology and its meaningfulness in the specific learning moment is defined by the teacher and learners (Fig. 3).

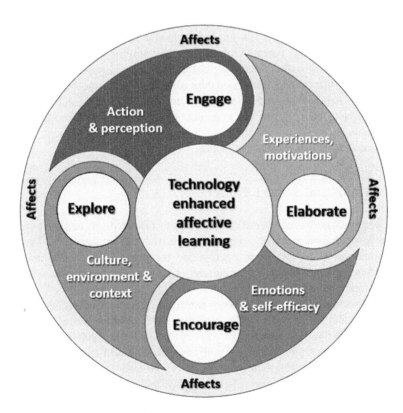

Fig. 3. Model of technology enhanced affective learning.

The synergy of the underlying theories [6, 18] is particularly influential and fitting for the design of a flexible and adaptive pedagogy that can support teachers in changing contexts to improve learning outcomes. Experiences of action and perception are at the very core of embodied cognition [25], highlighting the significance of the embodied self-experience of action or perception. This means that initiating a high level of engagement in learning improves learning achievement and develops agency, and through engagement, technology can play a significant role. The prior experiences of the learner can influence the learner's disposition and thereby motivate or demotivate the learner's engagement in the learning task. Hence, elaborating positive learning experiences and expanding learning opportunities with the meaningful use of technology are pivotal to having a learner who is eager to return to class the next day. Similarly, the emotions of the moment and the self-efficacy of the learner derived from their self-perception of their abilities and competency, increase or inhibit the learner's drive to participate in the learning process. Encouraging and boosting the learner's confidence in their own abilities enhance not only the learner's self-perception, but also the teacher-learner relationship and through this, the general learning environment. The social and physical environment of the learner encompasses his/her cultural and social background, environment (together with the possible digital devices used for learning), and context. These are all out of the learner's own control, but they still affect the learner, because they can create an emotional connection to learning, classmates, and school in general. Therefore, exploring and expanding perspectives can create a sensitive, dialogical, and positive learning environment that energizes and empowers learners to achieve their potential and goals, supporting their development into reflective learners. Moreover, affect plays a significant role in learning, impacting how learners maintain their activity, reflect on their experiences, and motivate themselves to carry out tasks. Affect is shaped by learners' cultural, contextual, and environmental issues, extending to their identity and perception. Hence, the created model can extend one's understanding of one's history and how it influences the present, as well as helping learners to locate themselves in time.

5 Conclusion and Future Directions

In this paper, we have shown how the unification of two theories [6, 18] can provide a fruitful foreground for a technology enhanced affective learning approach. The theories were adopted based on four aspects; action and perception, experiences and motivations, emotions and self-efficacy, and culture, environment and context. Affects were thought to impact all of these aspects.

We see that the model of technology enhanced affective learning can extend the existing theoretical frameworks by highlighting the multidimensionality of learning combined with the use of technology. In our opinion, the model can serve as an adaptive theoretical and practical guide at all educational level for students and teachers when discussing and guiding learning. However, we understand that the model has shortfalls that must be addressed when applying the model in practice. First, it is probable that the implementation of the model requires specific guiding questions to be used by students and supervisors. Hence, the model requires practical testing. Second, the model does not provide guidelines as to how to use technology in affective learning. Rather, it remains to be refined for each context. Third, the term *affective learning* remains ambiguous and requires users of the model to understand the basic theoretical elements involved. Therefore, it would be necessary to guide users in how to concretize the model when applying it.

Future research should address the defining of guiding questions and practical testing of the model of technology enhanced affective learning at different educational levels. Through empirical research, it is possible to determine how the model should be further developed and how technology can support the learning process. Further research will also help to clarify the meaning of affect in learning, making this element more visible in the model and to develop a new way of approaching and implementing affective learning.

References

1. Bandura, A.: Social Learning Theory. Prentice-Hall, Englewood Cliffs (1977)
2. Bamidis, P.D.: Affective learning: principles, technologies, practice. BFAL 2017. LNCS (LNAI), vol. 10512, pp. 1–13. Springer, Cham (2017). https://doi.org/10.1007/978-3-319-67615-9_1
3. Blömeke, S., Gustafsson, J., Shavelson, R.J.: Beyond dichotomies: Competence viewed as a continuum. Zeitschrift Für Psychologie **223**(1), 3–13 (2015). https://doi.org/10.1027/2151-2604/a000194
4. Davids, K., Button, C., Bennett, S.: Dynamics of Skill Acquisition: A Constraints-led Approach. Human Kinetics, Champaign (2015)
5. Dewey, J.: How we think: a restatement of the relation of reflective thinking to the educative process. DC Heath and Company, Boston (1933)
6. Frangou, S.M.: Write to recall–An embodied knowledge construction model of affects in writing. Doctoral dissertation. University of Lapland, Rovaniemi (2020)
7. Hayes, J.R.: A new framework for understanding cognition and affect in writing. In: Levy, C.M., Ransdell, S. (eds.) The Science of Writing: Theories, Methods, Individual Differences and Applications, pp. 1–27. Routledge, New York, NY (1996)
8. Headrick, J.J.: Affective learning design: A principled approach to emotion in learning. Doctoral dissertation. Queensland University of Technology, Queensland (2015)
9. Hutto, D.D.: Truly enactive emotion. Emot. Rev. **4**(2), 176–181 (2012). https://doi.org/10.1177/1754073911430134
10. Immordino-Yang, M.H.: Implications of affective and social neuroscience for educational theory. Educ. Phil. Theory **43**(1), 98–103 (2011)
11. Immordino-Yang, M.H., Damasio, A.: We feel, therefore we learn: the relevance of affective and social neuroscience to education. Mind Brain Educ. **1**(1), 3–10 (2007)
12. Järvilehto, T.: Feeling as knowing Part 1: emotion as reorganization of the organism-environment system. Conscious. Emot. **1**, 53–65 (2000)
13. Kelso, J.A.S.: Cognitive coordination dynamics. In: Tshacher, W., Dauwalder, J.P. (eds.) The Dynamical Systems Approach to Cognition: Concepts and Empirical Paradigms Based on Self-Organisation, Embodiment and Coordination Dynamics, pp. 45–71. World Scientific Publishing, Singapore (2003)
14. Kolb, D.A.: Experiential learning: Experience as the source of learning and development. Prentice Hall, Englewood Cliffs (1984)

15. Korthagen, F.A.J.: Teacher education: a problematic enterprise. In: Korthagen, F.A.J., Kessels, J., Koster, B., Lagerwerf, B., Wubbels, T. (eds.) Linking Practice and Theory: The Pedagogy of Realistic Teacher Education, pp. 1–19. Lawrence Erlbaum Associates, Mahwah (2001)
16. Korthagen, F.A.J.: In search of the essence of a good teacher: towards a more holistic approach in teacher education. Teach. Teach. Educ. **20**(1), 77–97 (2004). https://doi.org/10.1016/j.tate.2003.10.002
17. Korthagen, F.A.J.: Inconvenient truths about teacher learning: towards professional development 3.0. Teach. Teach. **23**(4), 387–405 (2017). https://doi.org/10.1080/13540602.2016.1211523
18. Körkkö, M.: Beneath the Surface: Developing video-based reflective practice in the primary school teacher education programme. Doctoral dissertation. University of Lapland, Rovaniemi (2020)
19. LeDoux, J.: Rethinking the emotional brain. Neuron **73**(4), 653–676 (2012)
20. Patience, A.: The art of loving in the classroom: a defence of affective pedagogy. Aust. J. Teach. Educ. (Online) **33**(2), 55–67 (2008)
21. Shen, L., Wang, M., Shen, R.: Affective e-learning: using "emotional" data to improve learning in pervasive learning environment. J. Educ. Technol. Soc. **12**(2), 176–189 (2009)
22. Schön, D.A.: The Reflective Practitioner: How Professionals Think in Action. Temple Smith, London (1983)
23. Solomon, R.C.: The philosophy of emotions. In: Lewis, M., Haviland-ones, J.M., Feldman Barrett, L. (eds.) Handbook of Emotions, 3rd edn, pp. 3–16. The Guilford Press, New York (2008)
24. Vygotsky, L.S.: Mind in Society: The Development of Higher Psychological Processes. Harvard University Press, Cambridge (1978)
25. Wilson, M.: Six views of embodied cognition. Psychon. Bull. Rev. **9**(4), 625–636 (2002)

Outcomes of Problem-Solving Using Constructivist Learning Environment to Enhance Learners' Problem Solving

Sumalee Chaijaroen[1(✉)], Issara Kanjug[1], Charuni Samat[2], and Piyaporn Wonganu[3]

[1] Educational Technology, Faculty of Education, Khon Kaen University, Khon Kaen, Thailand
sumalee@kku.ac.th
[2] Computer Education, Faculty of Education, Khon Kaen University, Khon Kaen, Thailand
[3] Educational Technology and Innovation, Faculty of Education, Loei Rajabhat University, Loei, Thailand

Abstract. This study aims to study and affirm the use of the constructivist learning environment to enhance learners' problem solving. The sample groups consisted of the 40 students of Sanambin school, Khon Kaen, Thailand as the experimental group while the other 40 students in the same school was the control group. The instruments were 1) the learning environment to enhance problem solving in science subject titled Life Relationship 2) achievement tests 3) assessment form of executive functions based on Tower of London and 4) interviewing form of problem solving. The Model Research phrase 3- Model Use was employed by interviewing and protocol analysis based on Jonassen [1] with descriptive analysis and interpreting for percentage, Standard Deviation, and t-test value.

The results revealed that the control group had the difference of problem solving after learning while the experimental group showed the same. In addition, the executive function assessment based on Tower of London by time using in problem solving showed the experimental group spent less time than the control group as 18.60 and 21.15 min that differed significantly at .05 and moving time of those both groups as 4.15 and 7.40 min at .05 significantly. Likewise, the experiment group presented the higher achievement test scores as 34.85 than the control group as 20.72.

Keywords: Constructivist · Learning environment · Problem-solving

1 Introduction

In the rapidly changing of Thai society in the 21st century, the information has been transmitting into a variety of channels and resulted in the information consuming of people both moderately and immoderately [2]. The different uses of ideas checking in simple or complex system could arouse and cause a problem and become more complex problems that happen in the society all the time. In addition, the competitive conditions that occur in both the Association of Southeast Asian Nations (ASEAN) community and the world society requires the characteristics of people that being curious to learn throughout life, have the ability to discover, analyze and process information including apply various kinds of knowledge to solve problems in life effectively. This could help to enrich a national intellectual capital that helps increase the capacity of human resources which is consistent with the research plans and government education policies Including the 12th National Economic and Social Development Plan (2017–2021) [3]. Problem solving is a learning process that students will learn through both at school and throughout our daily lives.

Furthermore, much research has been carried out to study problem solving. For instance, Cornoldi C. et al. [4] examined the feasibility of improving problem-solving skills in primary school students. Yanjie S. [5] explored an innovative pedagogical design to improve upper primary students' collaborative problem solving. Csaba C. and Judit S. [6] aimed to reveal teachers' views and pedagogical content knowledge on teaching elementary students to solve word problems. Robert M., Patricia M. and Sara H. [7] investigating the nature of 'problem-solving' activity in technology classrooms. From above studies, it revealed that the problem solving is the importance skill for students. Moreover, the World Economic Forum envisages that the one importance skill for the future job is problem solving [8].

Therefore, for people to be able to live in society, it is necessary to learn and develop thinking systems as problem solving process. That could help develop both cognitive and physical aspects as increasing cognitive activities or brain cell numbers along with the satisfaction of studying. It also can be a motivation for learners and enhance human efficiency for the readiness of ASEAN community and world society creatively.

The practicing in the study was to have the pedagogy that emphasizes on the cognitive processes that based on cognitive theories in which to promote cognitive processes in depth more than study the behavior that can only be measured and observed. This study also focuses on constructivist learning theory which highlights the cognitive process that help the learner construct their own knowledge by elaborating the prior and new knowledge together.

As mentioned above, the focusing on conducting studies to promote cognitive processes based on the two theoretical foundations mentioned above, processes of data collection and analysis for both quantitative and qualitative for the purpose of empirical data, and the objective of enhancing the learner to be able to construct their own knowledge and improve thinking skills by using technology are all the keys to shift the learning paradigm into learner-centered and lifelong learning. This could be beneficial to national intellectual capital and capability of human resources for the readiness of world competition and cooperation.

2   Research Purpose

To study the problem solving of learners who learned with the constructivist learning environment to enhance learners' problem solving and compare the executive function using Tower of London between the experimental group who learned with the constructivist learning environment to enhance learners' problem solving and the control group who used the normal learning style.

3 Research Methodology

3.1 Research Design

The Model Research (phase 3: model use) [9] was employed in this study.

3.2 The Participations

The sample group was the 80 students of Sanambin school, Mueang, Khon Kaen who studied in science subject in the second semester of 2016 by randomly selecting to be the experimental and control groups by 40 students each.

3.3 Research Instruments

The interviewing form of problem solving were used to study the learners' problem solving. Then, the Tower of London were used to study executive functions. Furthermore, the achievement tests were used to study learners' achievement scores.

3.4 Data Collection

Before learning with learning environment, those two experimental and control groups was assigned to do the executive function form based on Tower of London. They were then allocated to work in groups with 3–5 members each and provided the instructions. Each group studied the problem situations presented in the learning environment and completed the learning tasks. After that, the assessment form of executive functions based on Tower of London was used after learning with the environment. Finally, the learners had an interview towards problem solving.

3.5 Data Analysis

The data of problem solving was analyzed by interviewing and protocol analysis based on Jonassen [1] as interpreting and descriptive analysis. Then, the data collected from the assessment form of executive functions based on Tower of London was used after learning with the environment was analyzed by statistics as mean scores, standard deviation, percentage, and t-test.

4 Results

4.1 Learners' Problem Solving

The outcomes of the study of learners' problem solving in science subject titled Life Relationship which based on Jonassen [1] found that those two groups were unable to identify the solving steps clearly. However, the control group had the difference of problem solving after learning while the experimental group could not show the difference. In addition, the control group could choose the appropriate solutions to be applied in various situations. They could process by the 6 steps of Jonassen's problem solving as the following.

Step 1. They could specify the gap pf the problem which found out that they analyzed the problem and identify the situation they wanted to have after solving it, for instance; 1) if the rice could grow up then the fish could survive and live 2) the fish and rice could grow and 3) the rice provided more productive.

Step 2. The leaners could identify and explain the real problems with causes. For example, the problems of life and environment, they identified many possible factors that could cause the problems such as polluted water or bad plant species but they finally made the real factor that undisturbed fish affected the real problem.

Step 3. They sample group generated various possible solutions for each situation. In this case, they listed possible solutions as reducing amount of frog spawn, getting rid of all frog spawn and buying fish feed, keeping all spawn but moving water plants out, or trying reducing some of spawn and monitoring the grow up rate of fish and other water plants.

Step 4. They could assess the possibility of all proposed alternatives that could be used to solve a problem. For instance, the relationships in this situation that the fish died or unable to grow up because of the fast spreading of frog spawn that affected their fish feed. The learners assessed and selected the possible solution that reducing amount of frog spawn which some still could be the fish feed and provided more air space.

Step 5. They were able to use the solution in real problem situation as selecting a simple, effective, useful, and economize solution. For instance, in the learning topic as "What is the food chain?" which the problem was the decreasing of rice product that affected from the situation that many grasshoppers and insects consume rice. The students chose the possible solution that use bird net because it was simple, effective, and economized by letting it balance the insect amount naturally and making profit since those caught insects could be sold.

Step 6. The students could adjust the solutions for the best of efficiency, usefulness, cost, and appropriateness as in the topic of "What is the food chain?" which presented the problem of low volume in rice product due to the grasshoppers and rice insects. Hence, they adjust the solution by finding animal that eating those type of insect instead of using bird net.

4.2 The Comparison of the Executive Functions Using Tower of London

The comparison results were found that the mean scores of time consuming in solving a problem of plate moving based on Tower of London test of the experimental group and control group were 4.15 and 7.40 with significantly different at .05 level as shown in Table 1.

Table 1. Results presented the executive functions using Tower of London.

	Student number	Experimental group		Control group		T value	Sig.
		$\bar{x}$	S.D.	$\bar{x}$	S.D.		
Average value of time consuming of plate moving solution	40	18.60	6.01	21.15	8.20	−0.737	.033
Average value of frequency of plate moving solution	40	4.15	1.53	7.40	2.85	−2.284	.025

4.3 The Comparison of the Achievement Scores

The results of comparison were found that the mean scores from achievement test of the experimental group were higher than the control group as 34.85 and 20.72 respectively which differed significantly at .05 level as shown in Table 2.

Table 2. Results of the achievement scores.

Students	Student Number	$\bar{x}$	S.D.	T value	Sig.
Experimental group	40	34.85	5.79	−7.820	.000
Control group	40	20.72	9.84		

5 Conclusion and Discussion

The outcomes of problem-solving using constructivist learning environment to enhance learner problem solving was found consistent with the studies of Chaijareon Sumalee, Samat Charuni, and Kanjug Issara [10]; Clover [11]; Samat Charuni [12]; Chaijaroen Sumalee et al. [13] that conducted the researches based on problem solving theory of Jonassen [1]. The theory was fundamentally used in design of learning environment to enhance problem solving as well as pedagogy. To study the problem solving, such pedagogy was used to develop the assessment instruments, for example, an evaluation of problem solving, and an interviewing form. Despite this, this study presented the difference by integrating with neuroscience as the executive function evaluation form based on Tower of London was used to examine the learner outcomes.

The learner solving results revealed that they had all 6 steps of the solving as 1) identify the problem gap 2) identify the real problem and cause with explanation 3) generate possible solutions 4) assess each possible solution 5) choose the most possible solution to and 6) adjust and apply the solution used in various situations. Furthermore, the comparison of the experimental and control groups could present the obvious results. The comparison results were found that the mean scores of time consuming in solving a problem of plate moving based on Tower of London test of the experimental group and control group were 4.15 and 7.40 with significantly different at

.05 level. Whereas, the results of comparison were found that the mean scores from achievement test of the experimental group were higher than the control group as 34.85 and 20.72 respectively which differed significantly at .05 level.

This is consistent with the studies of Khumphai Ariya [14]; Sriphutorn Wichian [15]; E. Hartman, S. Houwen, E. Scherder, C. Visscher [16]; Ramakrishnan, M et al. [17]; Schurink, J. et al. [18]; Abdul Aziz S, Fletcher J, Bayliss DM. [19]; George E., et al. [20]; Rebecca Bull., et al. [21] which found that the evaluation of executive function using Tower of London could help the learners have better planning, decision making, and problem solving. Moreover, children with language Impairment could probably had higher score of Tower of London to self-speaking regulation.

In conclusion, the study presented the obvious results of problem solving enhancing by using the developed constructivist learning environment to enhance learner problem solving. In according to this, all of the instructional design theories were the basis of learning environment design, moreover as well as Model Research method which processed theory and related research review, learning context survey, theoretical and designing framework synthesizing, and innovative components developing were purposive to knowledge construction in 6 steps of problem solving theory based on Jonassen [1]. This empirical evidence can represent that the developed innovation integrating pedagogy and neuroscience can result in problem solving eventually.

Acknowledgement. This work was supported by the Innovation and Cognitive Technology Research Center, Faculty of Education, and the Research and Technology Transfers Affairs Division, Khon Kaen University.

References

1. Jonassen, D.H.: Instructional design models for well-structured and ill-structured problem-solving learning outcomes. Educ. Tech. Res. Dev. **45**(1), 65–97 (1997)
2. Dede, C.: Comparing frameworks for 21st century skills. In: 21st Century Skills: Rethinking. How Students Learn, vol. 20, pp. 51–76 (2010)
3. National Economic and Social Development Plan 12th Edition 2017–2021. https://www.nesdc.go.th/main.php?filename = develop_issue. Accessed 03 June 2020
4. Cornoldi, C., et al.: Improving problem solving in primary school students: the effect of a training programme focusing on metacognition and working memory. Br. J. Educ. Psychol. **85**, 424–439 (2015)
5. Yanjie, S.: Improving primary students' collaborative problem solving competency in project-based science learning with productive failure instructional design in a seamless learning environment. Educ. Tech. Res. Dev. **66**, 979–1008 (2018)
6. Csíkos, C., Szitányi, J.: Teachers' pedagogical content knowledge in teaching word problem solving strategies. ZDM **52**(1), 165–178 (2019). https://doi.org/10.1007/s11858-019-01115-y
7. Robert, M., Patricia, M., Sara, H.: Problem-solving processes in technology education: a pilot study. Int. J. Technol. Des. Educ. **4**, 5–34 (1994)
8. World Economic Forum: The Future of Jobs: Employment, Skills and Workforce Strategy for the Fourth Industrial Revolution. Global Challenge Insight Report (2016)

9. Richey, R.C., Klein, J.: Design and Developmental Research. Lawrence Erlbaum Associates, Hillsdale (2007)
10. Chaijareon, S., Samat, C., Kanjug, I.: Design and develop of constructivist learning environment on learning management system. Procedia – Soc. Behav. Sci. **46**, 3426–3430 (2012)
11. Clover, K.: Becoming a More Creative Person. Prentice-Hall, Englewood Cliffs (1980)
12. Samat, C., Chaijaroen, S., Wattanachai, S.: The designing of constructivist web-based learning environment to enhance problem solving process and transfer of learning for computer education student. In: Rønningsbakk, L., Wu, T.-T., Sandnes, F.E., Huang, Y.-M. (eds.) ICITL 2019. LNCS, vol. 11937, pp. 117–126. Springer, Cham (2019). https://doi.org/10.1007/978-3-030-35343-8_13
13. Chaijaroen, S., et al.: Study the thinking potential of learners learning from learning innovations that enhance thinking potential. Khon Kaen University, Khon Kaen (2007)
14. Koompha, A.: Executive problem solving and planning by tower of London-Drexel University (TOLDXTM) 2nd edition of psychiatric inpatients at Suansaranrom Psychiatric Hospital, Surat Thani. Thai J. Clin. Psychol. **47**(1), 1–13 (2016)
15. Sripootorn, W.: The study of neuropsychological deficits and quality of life in healthy elderly people. R. Thai Navy Med. J. **45**(2), 328–348 (2018)
16. Hartman, E.S., Houwen, E.S., Visscher, C.: On the relationship between motor performance and executive functioning in children with intellectual disabilities. J. Intellect. Disabil. Res. **54**(5), 468–477 (2010)
17. Ramakrishnan, M., Sartory, G., van Beekum, A., Lohrmann, T., Pietrowsky, R.: Sleep-related cognitive function and the K-complex in schizophrenia. Behav. Brain Res. **234**(2), 161–166 (2012)
18. Schurink, J., Hartman, E., Scherder, E.J.A., Houwen, S., Visscher, C.: Relationship between motor and executive functioning in school-age children with pervasive developmental disorder not otherwise specified. Res. Autism Spectr. Disord. **6**(2), 726–732 (2012)
19. Abdul, A.S., Fletcher, J., Bayliss, D.M.: Self-regulatory speech during planning and problem-solving in children with SLI and their typically developing peers. Int. J. Lang. Commun. Disord. **52**(3), 311–322 (2016)
20. George, M.S., et al.: Regional brain activity when selecting a response despite interference: an H2 15O PET study of the Stroop and an emotional Stroop. Hum. Brain Mapp. **1**, 194–209 (1994)
21. Bull, R., et al.: A comparison of performance on the towers of London and Hanoi in young children. J. Child Psychol. Psychiatry **45**(4), 743–754 (1997)

Removing Digital Natives from Technological Illiteracy with the Weblog

Michele Della Ventura[✉]

Department of Music Technology, Music Academy "Studio Musica",
Treviso, Italy
michele.dellaventura@tin.it

Abstract. The terms "Digital Natives" and "Digital Immigrants" were introduced by Prensky to underline how the use of the Information and Communication Technologies is different between young people and their teachers, parents and more generally "adult people". Digital Native is not synonymous with technological literacy or digital literacy. This article aims to reflect on the possible uses of ICT to help students to acquire a heightened critical awareness in the use of technologies. The study investigates the digital literacy of a group of students in the fourth and fifth years of high school, through the development and use of the Weblog. The results show that students can improve their digital skills when they become the protagonists of the learning process through the use of technologies. However, they must be leaded by teachers on this process, making them know the pillars of the digital literacy and offering them the opportunity to use these pillars for significant purposes.

Keywords: Digital skill · ICT · Technological illiteracy · Weblog

1 Introduction

Digital technologies have now become an integral part of the society of the 21st century. APPs (Applications) represent a new way to learn about social reality and make decisions. If we consider the fact that an APP is enough to buy, travel, manage your car or home, we can understand that digital technologies are taking shape a new way of life. Young people are fascinated by this digital world because they are digital natives [1, 2] and feel in their natural habitat [3].

Digital technologies are what writing was for Plato's generation.

Educating through digital systems can be difficult, risky, but it is a fundamental resource for what concerns the free circulation of knowledge [4]. The digital education that is needed today must be based on specific skills that allow a balanced, critical and aware use of technology [5]. As an educator, the teacher must teach these skills to students, because even if they are defined as "digital natives", this does not mean that they know how to use technologies correctly. They have not enough experience and knowledge to use technology safely and consciously [6]. They spend a lot of time on social networks every day, but they are unable to register on a site, write a message and/or send emails correctly, attach a document, install applications or use the main programs productively. They use the APPs mechanically, without associating a meaning to the images (icons) of the various functions, thus finding themselves disoriented when they approach a new APP. They use the APPs without knowing their potential [7]: they use Social Networks to publish photos but are not aware of the fact that these platforms can be used for art or literature projects; record and/or send voice messages (rather than written) without thinking that these APPs could be used for journalism projects or as an aid to studying, especially in the presence of dyslexic students.

Students need to be guided in this new world of theirs [8], to avoid that mistakes and wrong habits, over time, take the place of good habits, they get confused with them and, finally, replace them, because after a little everyone thinks that's right, just because everyone does this or because it has always been like this [9].

Helping students to get out of technological illiteracy becomes a necessity and teachers must work in this direction, looking for tools that are suitable for this purpose and that can help students use them as tools to expand their learning opportunities.

This paper presents a case study referred to a Music Technologies teaching project developed in a Music High School. The goal of the study was to analyse the benefits of using the Weblog (or Blog) as a tool to make know to all students the meaning and the importance of the "digital literacy".

This paper is organized as follows.

Section 2 presents a brief introduction of the use of the weblog in education in the related researches. Section 3 describes the characteristics of the weblog. This is followed by a description of the strengths and opportunity of using the weblog in education. Section 4 shows a case study that illustrate the effectiveness of the proposed method. Finally, in Sect. 5 the paper ends with concluding remarks.

2 Related Researches

In today's society, defined as the information society (to emphasize the centrality of information as the engine of contemporary society), it is very important to know how to read and understand a message in order to be able to actively participate in society. The school has become the ideal environment for developing these skills by identifying the most suitable tools to achieve this goal.

One of these tools is the weblog.

Ranker [10] highlights how the blog can improve learning and writing skills through written social interaction, when the research topic is stimulating for students. The results are better when the interaction takes place between peers [11]. Writing a text allows students, even those who are less confident, to improve their vocabulary [12]. Stover et al. [13, 14] focused their attention on the advantages deriving from the use of the weblog to help students share personal opinions regarding certain readings. The goal of their research was to introduce teachers to new tools and strategies to help students improve reading and understanding of a text. Clark [15] points out that young people enjoy writing texts when they can be read by other people like in the case of the blog.

In all these researches the weblog is used by teachers to help students improve their reading, writing, analysis and argumentation skills. The research presented in this article was developed based on these researches, to introduce students to digital literacy through the weblog. The fact that young people enjoy using digital technologies to share sensations/emotions/opinions, looking for and creating interactions with multiple people (but especially among peers), through tools (from the web) capable of involving a wide audience of readers, can help teachers get students away from digital illiteracy. It is not only important to know how to write a text well in order to share it and make it understood, but it is important that this text respects the multiple rules that underlie netiquette, privacy, copyright.

3 The Weblog

The object of teaching is teaching which creates favorable conditions for student learning [16, 17]. More and more teachers work with heterogeneous classes, from the point of view of learning. The presence of dyslexic students imposes on the teacher some didactic choices which help these students and which are also useful for all the other students (those who are not dyslexic) in order to make didactic practice more efficient, the study method more conscious and the learning more long lasting and more profound [18].

To teach digital literacy, teachers must create learning paths adaptable to the class group, placing students at the center of the learning process to allow each of them to develop their own potential, through meaningful activities (within the field of study) and which sees them creative, critical and collaborative [19, 20].

In this sense, the weblog proves to be a useful tool for teaching.

First of all, the Weblog (or Blog) is a tool that takes technological aspects into consideration: it is a web page where texts, images, sounds, videos and links are published [21].

Considering its content, the Weblog can be classified according to the topic it deals with and the purpose for which it is written [22]. In this case we can speak of: Review weblog, with the aim of signaling (through the link) information available on the net; Comment weblog, which considers a link to information available on the net as a starting point to trigger a broader comment; Storytelling Weblog, which allows the publication of writings in the form of a personal story; Project weblog, which has an informative purpose because it allows the collection and sharing of information on a project; Collaborative weblog, in which the responsibility for inserting contents is shared by a group of people; Experimental weblog, characterized by the desire to test new multimedia languages, which technologies make increasingly accessible.

Finally, the Weblog is a complex system that considers its contents, the people who write them, the social bonds that derive from them and the relationships that exist between all these elements [21].

The Weblog, therefore, is a text that must be written by the student thinking about the content, which must be consistent with the theme of the Blog and must motivate a reader to read. Therefore, it is necessary to avoid a text that cannot be understood independently by a person, excluding people with learning disabilities (such as dyslexic people). The text must respect the ideas of others but also the spelling and punctuation [23].

All this allows the student to develop a critical sense in front of the writing of a text, not only as regards the content and form, but above all as regards the concept of inclusiveness [24]. The student can learn that "diversity" is not a danger or a limit to communication, but an advantage, a resource. The person with learning disabilities should not be considered an obstacle, but a continuous source of enrichment, both humanly and professionally.

In addition to being a text (or set of texts), the Weblog is part of a collective hypertext because, by its very nature, it is related to many other Weblogs (Churchill, D.: Educational applications of Web 2.0: using blogs to support teaching and learning. Br. J. Educ. Technol. 40[22], pp. 179−183 2009; [24].

From the didactic point of view, this means that the student must learn to: know the web by improving research techniques; analyze and select information in order to obtain quality content; develop the ability to generate good connections (links) to give the reader the opportunity to continue on his path and therefore to leave the reading of the Blog to go and read another Blog, creating a virtuous circle in which the shift of attention is functional and not detrimental to interest.

Developing these skills allows the student to learn about the meaning of copyright and plagiarism. The fight against plagiarism is an important part of managing a reliable and credible Weblog. The student must learn that: if he decides to take inspiration from an article found on the web, he must first ascertain whether the author allows its use and which use is allowed; if he wants his copyright to be respected, he must also respect the copyrights of others, making sure to use images, videos or multimedia files that are not protected by copyright.

The weblog is therefore a tool "for and of didactics", which can actively involve students in the learning process and in the process of building new knowledge: developing the ability to participate in the community life of practice by building knowledge in a virtual environment, in a cooperative way. During this practice, individuals create new objects (documents, concepts etc.) and new procedures, which enrich the shared repertoire and the knowledge distributed within the community.

4 Application and Analysis: A Case Study

The case study described in this paper refers to a Music Technologies teaching project developed in a Music High School. The goal of the study was to analyse the benefits of using the weblog as a tool to make know to all students the meaning and the importance of the "digital literacy". The project was conducted for a time period of 20 weeks.

4.1 Participants

The project engaged 43 students in the fourth and fifth years of high school, 22 girls (of which 2 affected by dyslexia) and 21 boys.

Before starting with the project, the teacher asked students to fill in a survey to know:

1. their attitudes towards thinking and learning [25]: in this way it was possible to evaluate if a student was a "connected knower" (that means a person able to find learning enjoyable, to cooperate with other students, to accept the ideas of other students) or a "separate knower" (that means a person who has a critical and argumentative position towards learning);
2. their confidence in using technology (see Table 1): in this way it was possible to know the "affective-motivational" relationship that everyone of them had with the technologies.

The survey supplied important information.

Students showed relatively high value in questions related to "Connected Learning" (Fig. 1). This pattern was repeated in the survey related to "Separate Learning" but with lower value: here the lowest value were the ones of the declaration "Argue with others" (Fig. 2).

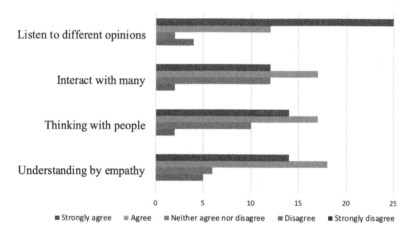

Fig. 1. Attitudes towards thinking and learning survey: connected learning.

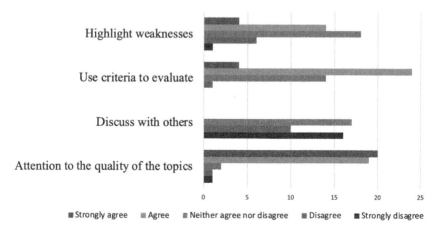

Fig. 2. Attitudes Towards Thinking and Learning Survey: Separated Learning.

The teacher was also interested to capture information about the level of confidence in digital skills among students, in order to know their ability in using the technologies and the relationships that everyone of them had with the digital information (see Table 1).

Table 1. Excerpt from the Use of Technologies Survey.

Item	Very unconfident	Unconfident	Somewhat confident	Confident	Very confident
Browsing, searching, filtering data, information and digital content					
Scanning/skimming a web page to get to the key relevant information quickly					
Keeping track of Websites you have visited so that you can return to them later					
Sharing through digital technologies					
Managing data, information and digital content					
Interacting through digital technologies					
Solving technical problems					
Developing content					
Identifying needs and technological responses					
Collaborating through digital technologies					
Managing digital identity					
...	...	...	...	...	...

The main results emerging from the survey (Fig. 3) can be summarized as follows: it was difficult to state the presence of relevant differences among the answers, because in general students declared to have good skills in managing digital resources (Table 1, questions 1, 2, 3, 4, 5 and 8), good skills in using the digital technologies to communicate with a peer (Table 1, questions 6, 10 and 11), and difficulties in dealing with technical problems (Table 1, questions 7 and 9): for examples, not recognizing the lack of a drive or a software to reproduce an audio/video file, not knowing the possibilities to use an opensource software instead of a commercial software. These are some information provided by the students in the survey.

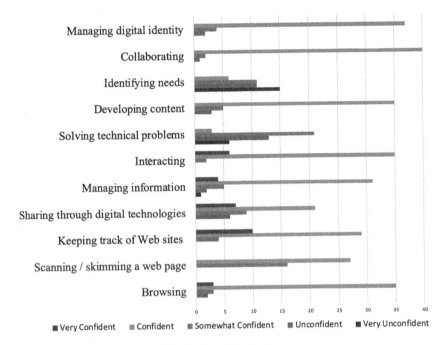

Fig. 3. Use of technology.

From these considerations and based on the classrooms group structure (that included 2 dyslexic students), the teacher decided to start the project: realize a Weblog on the theme "The Spring".

4.2 The Method

During the first period (5 weeks) the lessons took place in the classroom (3 h a week). In the first week the teacher explained the "Filter Bubble" concept and asked students to write a newspaper article about it: the aim was to verify their ability to search for information on the Internet and manage the information in order to realize the assigned work. This work confirmed the teacher's initial hypotheses about the students, namely the lack of knowledge in using a search engine (almost all the students wrote the same references corresponding to the first items on the search engine list), use of unknow technical terms that made it difficult to understand the text, poor reworking skills and lack of knowledge of the concept of plagiarism (many texts were a copy and paste of various sentences found on websites and there were no certain information about the copyright of the images included in the text).

- In the following four weeks students were introduced to the concepts of internet research, in order to learn how to find, manage and use online information more effectively and with less risks. Every week students had to do an online research on a different topic.

In the following period (from the sixth to the fifteenth week) the didactic activity was divided between classroom lesson (where the teacher used the "face-to-face" lessons to focus and check their oral skills) and online lesson: students were invited to start working in a digital classroom set up on Moodle.

The online class was divided in five section: Blog Management and Maintenance (a group of students responsible for identifying the platform that could host the blog for free and for publishing the materials produced by the other sections); Editorial board (a group of students in charge of writing the posts to be published on the blog); Proofreading (a group of students with the task of identifying and correcting grammatical errors, spelling, punctuation, or the presence and typos and oversights in the posts written by Editorial board); Research materials (a group of students who work together with the editorial staff to search for resources on the web); Production: Audio/Video (a group of students with the task of creating multimedia resources to support posts written by the Editorial board).

In addition to these sections, a discussion forum (where students could present a doubt or a problem that could be solved with everyone's participation) and links to online resources (blogs, FAQ) were added.

The students had to work together, exchanging information among the various sections regarding:

- which platform to choose to host the blog, among the ones available on the web; they had to collect information in order to make the best choice based on their needs; the final choice was related to Blogger.com (which is owed by Google) because it could host the blog for free, it was one of the easiest to use and it had some levels of privacy that were important for a class blog;
- the topics of the posts: they had to write one a week; they learned to share and accept ideas and opinions;
- the type of online resources they needed (texts, images, videos, links, ...): this required them to pay attention to the copyright; they had the opportunity to know the Creative Commons License and then they found out a lot of website where it was possible to get images, videos and other resources for free;
- how to exchange information (with reference to the format of the files used to share information or resources); students used different operating systems and software, so they had to identify software that allowed the sharing of resources among all of them. This allowed them to get to know the Open Source World, therefore to learn to evaluate the types of files necessary for their purposes and to search and find suitable software.

Teamwork entailed an individual work for each student based on his role.

Individual work often required online research which allowed the student to apply the concepts acquired during the classroom lessons regarding the web search techniques. In this way, they learned to share their doubts or problems in the discussion forum, but also their findings in order to obtain the approval of the teacher and the other students. Sometimes, the research led the student to find interesting or valuable things by chance (serendipity) that they shared in the discussion forum.

At the beginning there were few conversations in the forum and only by the students with high academic performance; gradually there was an increase of the interventions with the participation (more or less wide) of all students.

Students learned to write a post, taking into account the concepts explained by the teacher during the classroom lessons, such as the link to a web page to avoid copyright and plagiarism problems, the use of an easy and simple language to make the text understandable to everyone (the presence of two dyslexic students helped in this regard), the use of specific layouts and fonts to attract more readers and avoid that readers with reading difficulties bypassed the blog (such as dyslexic readers).

The individual work within the group work allowed students: to improve their creativity, writing original content leads to a continuous creative process; to express both their opinions and their personalities through the writing of posts and responses to the interactions received in the forum (and always respecting the ideas and opinions of others); to improve writing and communication skills (the blog is essentially communication, exchange of thoughts, experiences, knowledge), and become more responsible (creating content, respecting the deadlines, ideas and opinions of others, accepting the differences).

4.3 The Results

The results of project, indicate positive opinion of the students for the integration of the weblog into the process of learning/teaching digital literacy.

Students showed positive attitudes towards working collaboratively with peers throughout the project, even if some students highlighted the little work done by someone.

Students recognized that there were advantages in realizing the weblog with lessons both in the classroom and in the virtual classroom: in terms of effectiveness, when they attempted to solve an information sharing problem, a technical problem or a doubt in general; in terms of efficiency, because through both theoretical and practical examples it was possible to acquire and/or improve individual skills.

At the end of the project, in order to evaluate its effectiveness, the teacher asked the students to fill in the initial survey related to the use of technologies, rethought how they should have answered the various questions based on the knowledge and skills acquired during the project. Figure 4 shows the results of the survey from which it is easy to verify that the students declared that level of confidence in digital skills was lower than the level they thought to have before starting the project.

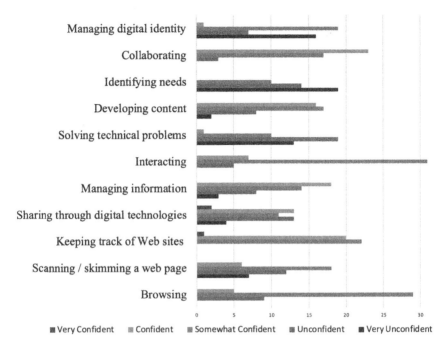

Fig. 4. Use of technology.

5 Discussion and Conclusions

The research presented in this article has focused on the concept of digital (or technological) literacy, highlighting how this is not limited only to the use of the computer or an app, but also to the ability to use a technology to participate in an active way to the Society. In other words, knowing how to access information and therefore develop communication and collaboration skills with others (through digital technologies).

The weblog has proved to be useful for the students, improving learning processes and offering opportunities to carry out collaborative activities even outside the conventional classroom. The social aspect of the weblog and the possibility of working side-by-side with dyslexic classmates helped students to develop a reflective thought, paying attention not only to the contents but also and above all to the form of the messages. The technical aspect of the weblog has allowed students to learn more about the internet and research techniques, to discover the philosophy of open-source and consequently concepts such as copyright and plagiarism (helping them to develop and/or improve the skills of textual reworking).

The weblog offered students the opportunity to think through the information and resources found on the net; having to search and consult more than one source, students learned to select the sources by analysing their content.

In this context (characterized by the intertwining person/communication/society) the teacher must be able to guide the students towards a critical use of digital technologies, teaching to find information, to adequately relate to the virtual community, to build and organize effectively own knowledge and to know how to share it.

In conclusion, the teacher must pay attention to how to avoid teaching students to become passive consumers/users, who ultimately represent digital illiterates.

References

1. Prenksy, M.: Digital natives, digital immigrants. Horizon **9**(5), 1–6 (2001a)
2. Prenksy, M.: Digital natives, digital immigrants, part II. Do they really think differently? Horizon **9**(6), 1–6 (2001b)
3. Muchsini, B., Siswandari, S.: Digital natives' behaviours and preferences: pre-service teachers studying accounting. Int. J. Pedagogy Teach. Educ. **2**(2), 355–366 (2018)
4. Ventura, M.D.: Between research and action: the generative sense of technology. In: Rønningsbakk, L., Wu, T.-T., Sandnes, F.E., Huang, Y.-M. (eds) ICITL 2019. LNCS, vol. 11937, pp. 754–763. Springer, Cham (2019). https://doi.org/10.1007/978-3-030-35343-8_78
5. Bottino, R.: Schools and the digital challenge: evolution and perspectives. Educ. Inf. Technol. **25**(3), 2241–2259 (2019). https://doi.org/10.1007/s10639-019-10061-x
6. Gkioulos, V., Wangen, G., Katsikas, S.K., Kavallieratos, G., Kotzanikolaou, P.: Security awareness of the digital natives. Information **8**, 42 (2017)
7. Lim, J., Newby, T.J.: Preservice teachers' Web 2.0 experiences and perceptions on Web 2.0 as a personal learning environment. J. Comput. High. Educ. **32**(2), 234–260 (2019). https://doi.org/10.1007/s12528-019-09227-w
8. Smith, E.E., Kahlke, R., Judd, T.: From digital natives to digital literacy: anchoring digital practices through learning design. In: Proceedings of the Australasian Society for Computers in Learning in Tertiary Education Conference, pp. 510–515 (2018)
9. Perera, M.U., Gardner, L., Peiris, A.: Investigating the interrelationship between undergraduates' digital literacy and self-regulated learning skills. In: Paper Presented at the 37th International Conference on Information Systems, Dublin, Ireland (2016)
10. Ranker, J.: The affordances of blogs and digital video: new potentials for exploring topics and representing meaning. J. Adolesc. Adult Lit. **58**, 568–578 (2015)
11. Alsamadani, H.A.: The effectiveness of using online blogging for students' individual and group writing. Int. Educ. Stud. **11**(1), 44 (2017)
12. Mills, K.A., Levido, A.: iPed: pedagogy for digital text production. Read. Teach. **65**, 80–91 (2011)
13. Stover, K., Yearta, L.S.: Using blogs as formative assessment of reading comprehension. In: Rasinski, T.V., Pytash, K.E., Ferdig, R. (eds.) Using Technology to Enhance Reading: Innovative Approaches to Literacy Instruction, pp. 223–232 (2015)
14. Stover, K., Yearta, L., Harris, C.: Formative assessment in the digital age: blogging with third graders. Read. Teach. **69**, 377–381 (2016)
15. Clark, C.: Children and young people's writing in 2017/18. National Literacy Trust, London (2018)
16. Della Ventura, M.: Monitoring the learning process to enhance motivation by means of learning by discovery using Facebook. In: Ma, W.W.K., Chan, W.W.L., Cheng, C.M. (eds.) Shaping the Future of Education, Communication and Technology. ECTY, pp. 117–128. Springer, Singapore (2019). https://doi.org/10.1007/978-981-13-6681-9_9
17. Laneve, C.: Elementi di didattica generale. La Scuola, Brescia (1998)

18. Della Ventura, M.: Creating inspiring learning environments by means of digital technologies: a case study of the effectiveness of WhatsApp in music education. EAI Endorsed Trans. e-Learn. (J.) **4**, 1–9 (2017). https://doi.org/10.4108/eai.26-7-2017.152906
19. Martin, A.: The Landscape of Digital Literacy Glasgow. DigEuLit Project (2006a). www.digeulit.ec
20. Della Ventura, M.: Twitter as a music education tool to enhance the learning process: conversation analysis. In: Deng, L., Ma, W.W.K., Fong, C.W.R. (eds.) New Media for Educational Change. ECTY, pp. 81–88. Springer, Singapore (2018). https://doi.org/10.1007/978-981-10-8896-4_7
21. Burgess, J.: Blogging to learn, learning to blog. In Bruns, A., Jacobs, J. (eds.) Uses of Blogs, pp. 105–115 (2006)
22. Churchill, D.: Educational applications of Web 2.0: using blogs to support teaching and learning. Br. J. Educ. Technol. **40**(1), pp. 179–183 (2009)
23. Ducate, L.C., Lomicka, L.L.: Adventureis in the blogosphere: from blog readers to blog writers. Comput. Assist. Lang. Learn. **21**(1), 9–28 (2008)
24. Kerawalla, L., Minocha, S., Kirkup, G., Conole, G.: An empirically grounded framework to guide blogging in higher education. J. Comput. Assist. Learn. **25**(1), 31–42 (2009). https://doi.org/10.1111/j.1365-2729.2008.00286.x
25. Galotti, K.M., Clinchy, B.M., Ainsworth, K.H., et al.: A new way of assessing ways of knowing: the attitudes toward thinking and learning survey (ATTLS). Sex Roles **40**, 745–766 (1999)

The Use of E-learning Tools and Log Data in a Course on Basic Logic

Peter Øhrstrøm[1(✉)], Steinar Thorvaldsen[2], Ulrik Sandborg-Petersen[1], Thomas Ploug[1], and David Jakobsen[1]

[1] Department of Communication and Psychology, Aalborg University, 9000 Aalborg, Denmark
poe@hum.aau.dk
[2] Department of Education, Uit the Arctic University of Norway, 9037 Tromsø, Norway

Abstract. This paper is a study of the use of e-learning tools and log data in evaluating and further developing a course on basic logic. It is a continuation of earlier studies involving practical experiments with students of communication from Aalborg University. Two tools are involved: *Syllog* for training syllogistic reasoning and *Proplog* for training basic propositional logic. The data are logged anonymously during the course, as well as during the individual exam. Using the log data, we have obtained important insights into the effects of the lectures and exercises. We argue that the log data from using the two tools can be transformed into useful learning analytics. Careful studies based on log data can provide useful information on how the quality of the course. On this basis, it can be suggested how the course can be improved using the learning analytics based on the log data. This is evident from studies carried out over seven to eight years using log data from the use of *Syllog* and recent studies based on log data from the use of *Proplog*, also show how insight based on the log data may lead us to improvements of the course. During the present study we have developed a method by which we can determine whether the students will handle one kind of symbolic logic test better than another.

Keywords: Syllogistics · Propositional logic · Validity of arguments · Learning analytics · E-learning tools · Logic teaching

1 Introduction

For more than 20 years, a course on basic logic and argumentation has been offered to students in the area of 'communication and digital media' at Aalborg University. One of the authors of this paper (Peter Øhrstrøm) has been involved as a teacher throughout this whole period, whereas two of the other authors (Thomas Ploug and David Jakobsen) have been involved for some of the years. The topics covered in the course have varied a bit from year to year, but Aristotelian syllogistics [1] and basic propositional logic have been on the agenda throughout the whole period. A joint textbook [2] is used for the course, along with two learning tools, *Syllog* and *Proplog*, which have been developed specifically for this course.

The focus in the present study is on the use of log data that emerged from using the tools to develop and improve the parts of the course on basic logic dealing with Aristotelian syllogistics and basic propositional logic. The students using these tools to further their learning, and the teachers and course developers can improve the quality of the course using insight based on the log data.

In 2010, the *Syllog* tool was designed (cf. [3–5, 10]), and slightly improved versions of it have been used in the course since then. The tool has been employed during logic exercises to make the learning experience game-like and joyful. Furthermore, all the interactions with the tools are logged in a database. Of course, the students have been informed that this is done, but none of them have seen it as problematic because the logging is done anonymously.

Studies of the log data have led to several improvements in the course when it comes to teaching syllogistics (cf. [6, 7]). Since 2018, the ambition has been to do something similar based on the analysis of log data from the use of *Proplog*. In the current paper, we discuss the use of *Syllog* and *Proplog* as teaching tools and as tools for providing valuable learning analytics.

2 Syllog and Proplog

The interface of the present version of the *Syllog* tool is shown in Fig. 1. The user can click on 'New syllogism' to get a new syllogism presented on the screen. Then, the user will have to decide whether the syllogism presented is valid or invalid, that is, whether the conclusion follows necessarily from the premises (in any possible/thinkable scenario). The systems allow for some kind of gamification, since a sound will play when the group obtains 10 right answers in a row. This has worked as a kind of competition (see [7] and [10]). During the exercises, the students were asked to work with *Syllog* in small groups of two to three people each for about 15 min.

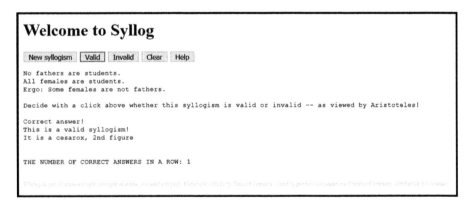

Fig. 1. Interface of the *Syllog* tool. Note that in case of a valid syllogism, the system will give the medieval name of the argument. The student may compare these names with the Aristotelian theory presented during the lectures of the course.

A student's ability to do logic reasoning can be analysed in terms of a score calculated based on the log data from the use of *Syllog*. This score is calculated as follows:

$$Score = correctanswers / answercount \quad (1)$$

The statistical analyses of the scoring data were performed using standard methods from descriptive statistics and statistical testing. Student t-tests and Cohen's d effect size were applied to measure the difference between the responses in two independent samples. The following Cohen's conventions were applied: 0.2 = small effect, 0.5 = medium effect and 0.8 = large effect [10, p. 267]. The quantitative data were analysed with MS Excel (Windows). Data from the groups that answered less than five questions were excluded from the measurements; thus, the value N of each test does not include sessions with very few answers. Furthermore, some student groups apparently took long pauses during their sessions, and groups with an average time of more than two minutes per exercise were not taken into account in the computation of the time statistics in the tables. The aggregated scores and use of time are shown in Tables 1, 2, 3 and 4.

It is well-known that there are 256 possible syllogistic arguments. According to Aristotelian theory, 24 of them are valid, whereas 232 are invalid (cf. [1] and [8]). In *Syllog*, valid and invalid arguments occur with the same frequency. This means that a student who is giving answers at random should end up with a score of about 50%. One interesting result is that the score is significantly higher than 50% even before they have been taught any logic. At this early stage, the score is typically 60–70%, mainly depending on an individual's abilities (cf. [6, 7, 11]).

A very important learning goal is to make the student able to decide on the question of validity/invalidity in a qualified manner. The student should not only be able to raise his or her ability to identify a valid argument (and an invalid argument), but he or she should also be able to understand and explain why a particular argument is valid (or invalid).

The strategy in case of the use of *Proplog* is basically the same as in the *Syllog* case. The user interface of *Proplog* is shown in Fig. 2.

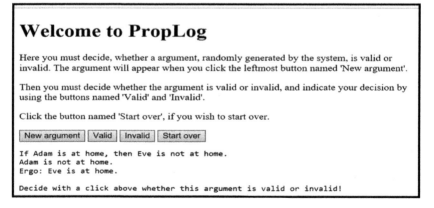

Fig. 2. The user interface of the *Proplog* system. The user can click on 'New argument' to have a new problem presented on the screen, cf. [9].

All the propositions in *Proplog* have to do with 'Adam' and 'Eve' being at home or not being at home. Furthermore, the system uses negation, implication, conjunction and disjunction. The tool uses the below set of simple propositional arguments, where p stands for 'Adam is at home' and q stands for 'Eve is at home'.

For the construction of *Proplog*, we have considered two kinds of basic propositional reasoning:

1. Implicative: $A \rightarrow B, C \models D$
2. Disjunctive: $\sim(A \wedge B), C \models D$ and $(A \vee B), C \models D$

Here, each of the pairs, (A, B) and (C, D), includes both p and q in any order and with each of the two propositions being negated or unnegated. Clearly, this gives us 64 possible arguments for each of the above structures. However, many of these arguments seem rather similar and uninteresting. Furthermore, it will be good to bring the number of arguments down to obtain reliable statistics when calculating scores on the basis of the log data. For this reason, we have chosen to concentrate on the following set of 32 arguments, 16 valid and 16 invalid, which we find representative for basic implicative and disjunctive reasoning (cf. the classical forms mentioned above).

1. $p \rightarrow q, p \models q$
2. $q \rightarrow p, q \models p$
3. $\sim p \rightarrow q, \sim p \models q$
4. $\sim q \rightarrow p, \sim q \models p$
5. $p \rightarrow \sim q, p \models \sim q$
6. $q \rightarrow \sim p, q \models \sim p$
7. $p \rightarrow q, \sim q \models \sim p$
8. $q \rightarrow p, \sim p \models \sim q$
9. $\sim p \rightarrow q, \sim p \models q$
10. $\sim q \rightarrow p, \sim q \models p$
11. $p \rightarrow \sim q, q \models \sim p$
12. $q \rightarrow \sim p, p \models \sim q$
13. $\sim(p \wedge q), p \models \sim q$
14. $\sim(q \wedge p), q \models \sim p$
15. $(p \vee q), \sim q \models p$
16. $(q \vee p), \sim p \models q$

17. $p \rightarrow q, q \models p$
18. $q \rightarrow p, p \models q$
19. $\sim p \rightarrow q, q \models \sim p$
20. $\sim q \rightarrow p, p \models \sim q$
21. $p \rightarrow \sim q, \sim q \models p$
22. $q \rightarrow \sim p, \sim p \models q$
23. $p \rightarrow q, \sim p \models \sim q$
24. $q \rightarrow p, \sim q \models \sim p$
25. $p \rightarrow \sim q, \sim p \models q$
26. $q \rightarrow \sim p, \sim q \models p$
27. $q \rightarrow \sim p, \sim q \models p$
28. $p \rightarrow \sim q, \sim p \models q$
29. $\sim(p \wedge q), \sim q \models p$
30. $\sim(q \wedge p), \sim p \models q$
31. $(p \vee q), p \models \sim q$
32. $(q \vee p), q \models \sim p$

It would, of course, have been possible to base the *Proplog* tool on another selection of propositional arguments. However, some selection of this kind will be needed to build the *Proplog* tool because we need a procedure for picking the new arguments, that is, a scope to the arguments that can occur in the system. The above set has been composed in a rather systematic manner. In the first place, it consists of arguments in which one premise is an implication between p and q (perhaps with one of them negated), and the antecedent and the consequent (or their negations) in any order serve as another premise and as a conclusion, respectively. In addition, a few arguments from disjunctive reasoning (and their invalid counterparts) have been included in the set. It is evident that the set is closed under permutations of p and q.

Proplog is—like *Syllog*—using the same frequency of valid and invalid arguments. Again, the score before any logic teaching will be significantly higher than 50%. As in the *Syllog* case, we have reasons to believe that the score will be 60–70% properly, mainly depending on an individual's abilities (cf. [11]).

The results of a recent study (cf. [11]) indicate that our current lectures and exercises help the student be able to perform significantly better when it comes to *Syllog*. In fact, the score rises from 67% at the pretest (before the teaching) to 80% at the post-test (after the teaching). It should also be mentioned that the students on average take more time for the post-test (70 s) compared with the pretest (47.5 s). This seems to indicate that based on the teaching, they knew how to handle the problem and that they—given a little extra time to ponder—could come up with more precise answers. However, in the same study, something similar did not happen in the *Proplog* case. On average, the students took more time for the post-test (90 s) than the pretest (37.7 s). Nevertheless, the *Proplog* score remained the same (65%).

The difference between the *Syllog* and *Prolog* cases is rather surprising because we have tried to show the students through the lectures and exercises how the questions of validity/invalidity should be handled. It was definitely not the intention that the *Prolog* teaching should be sloppier than the *Syllog* teaching. In the following section, we have tried to explore this surprising difference again using new data and another group of students.

3 A New Experiment

The surprising observation mentioned above has recently been studied empirically using data from new students. Whereas the earlier study (cf. [11]) was based on data from the course offered in the spring of 2019, the current study is based on data from the course offered to second-year students in 'communication and digital media' at Aalborg University in Aalborg and Copenhagen during the spring of 2020. All the lectures on the two topics in question were given before the COVID-19 lockdown in Denmark on March 11, 2020. The same holds true for most of the exercises. We use data from the training sessions (exercises) after the lectures in question and before the COVID-19 lockdown. The results are shown in Table 1.

Table 1. Summarising counts from the 2020 course of how well student groups scored on the training period after the lectures. The training sessions are carried out in groups of two to three people, and the students are encouraged to discuss the question carefully before they agree on an answer.

	Score Mean (*SD*)	Time Mean (*SD*), [sec]
Syllog training (N = 103 groups)	0.73 (0.20)	36.8 (28.8)
Proplog training (N = 138 groups)	0.65 (0.17)	35.9 (24.3)
P-value (Effect size)	0.0009 (0.43)	–

Based on the study of an experiment from 2019 (cf. [11]), it seems likely that many students found the *Proplog* case more difficult to handle than the *Syllog* case. If so, the *Proplog* score should be significantly lower than the *Syllog* score if both scores are measured during the training period. The above results confirm this expectation (p-value = 0.0009 and effect size = 0.43).

Given that many students find propositional logic more difficult than syllogistics and that most students have been unable to improve their *Proplog* score based on lectures, the challenge is to update the lectures to support the students' learning in a more effective manner. For this reason, it would be helpful to know which aspects of propositional logic the students need help with. Actually, the new experiment has also provided information on the *Proplog* scores of each of the arguments—1–32—during the training session. However, it is evident that the differences between the evaluations of the members of the symmetric pairs (1/2, 3/4, 5/6, etc.) are very small. It seems reasonable to ignore these differences as variations within statistically acceptable limits. As a consequence, we may consider the pairs as units in the further discussion (i.e., each pair basically represents the same argument). The results are shown in Table 2.

Table 2. The scores of the arguments based in log data from the use of *Proplog* during the training period after the lectures in propositional logic. The training sessions are carried out in groups of two to three people, and the students are encouraged to discuss the question carefully before they agree on an answer.

Task number	Total number of responses	Score
1/2	216	0.97
3/4	233	0.93
5/6	191	0.93
7/8	198	0.44
9/10	216	0.36
11/12	206	0.54
13/14	226	0.75
15/16	216	0.87
17/18	210	0.49
19/20	202	0.48
21/22	208	0.53
23/24	224	0.62
25/26	204	0.63
27/28	235	0.70
29/30	197	0.58
31/32	225	0.65

The number of responses for each task varies between 191 and 235, as generated by a random number generator in the programme. By the Kolmogorov-Smirnov Uniform Test, the distribution of the numbers of responses is not significantly different from a uniform distribution (p-value = 0.98). Obviously, calculating scores based on just 200 responses may be uncertain. On the other hand, the results are sufficiently clear to show some important tendencies.

The highest score—97%—is obtained for arguments 1 and 2:
If Adam is at home, then Eve is at home.
Adam is at home.
Therefore, Eve is at home.

This is clearly an instance of Modus Ponens, and almost all students found this argument valid. In general, the scores of the Modus Ponens argument are very high.

The lowest *Proplog* score in the experiment—36%—is obtained for the arguments 9/10:
If Eve is not at home, then Adam is at home.
Adam is not at home.
Therefore, Eve is at home.

This is like arguments 7–12 an instance of Modus Tollens, which is known to be significantly more difficult to handle than Modus Ponens. However, 36% is a very low score for somebody who has attended a course dealing with basic propositional logic. It should also be mentioned that the responses are given by groups of two to three students after some discussion.

It should also be mentioned that the *Proplog* score of argument 19/20 is as low as 47%:
If Eve is not at home, then Adam is at home.
Adam is at home.
Therefore, Eve is not at home.
Furthermore, the score of argument 29/30 is just 58%:
Adam and Eve are both not at home.
Eve is not at home.
Therefore, Adam is at home.

In both cases, the score is at the level of random answers. These results suggest that the students' understanding of the properties of implicative and disjunctive reasoning is unsatisfactory.

All this is a very strong indication of the need for rethinking the introduction to propositional logic in the course on basic logic. Apparently, the students need to understand the use of truth values better, and the course should focus more on making the students able to evaluate simple propositional arguments using truth values and techniques based on semantical trees.

We should note one further insight into the students' understanding of basic logic. This has to do with the asymmetry between the evaluation of valid and invalid arguments. The mean value of the scores of the 16 valid arguments in the set is 72%, whereas the mean value of the scores of the 16 valid arguments in the set is 59%. This indicates that it is significantly easier to identify a valid propositional argument than to identify an invalid propositional argument.

4 The Use of *Syllog* and *Proplog* at the Exam

Syllog and *Proplog* have both been used during individual exams at the end of the logic course. For the exam, the students were asked to find 10 syllogistic arguments using *Syllog* and five propositional arguments using *Proplog*. They were supposed to include the arguments found by the tools in their assignments in the form of screenshots from the systems. Their task was to explain carefully why the arguments have the validities suggested by the system. This means that the students should be able to demonstrate that the valid arguments actually are valid and that the invalid arguments actually are invalid. This kind of assignment is quite relevant because the answer given by the student clearly indicates to what extent he or she has understood the validity of the syllogistic and propositional logic. In both cases, it turns out that understanding the notion of validity is rather weak. In particular, it should be noted that although many students have a rather clear understanding of what it takes to demonstrate that a syllogistic argument is valid, the students have a very weak understanding of how it should be shown that a syllogistic argument is invalid. In the analysis of the syllogistic arguments in their assignments for the exam, most of the students failed to explain or demonstrate the invalidity of one or more arguments offered by *Syllog*. Given this weakness in the assignments, it would be a good idea in the lectures to put more emphasis on the use of Venn diagrams to show the invalidity of a syllogistic argument. It might even be possible to create a new tool for analysing invalid syllogistic arguments.

A lot of log data from the use of *Syllog* and *Proplog* have been stored during the exam period. The context of these data is clearly very different from the context of the log data collected during the training sessions. First, the use of the tools during the exam period is not motivated by obtaining a high score or 10 right answers in a row. In this period, the tools are just used to find the number of arguments that the student wants to write about in his or her assignment for the exam. This means that the student is using less time to consider his or her responses. Furthermore, the student is working alone during the exam period (four days), whereas the training sessions are carried out in groups of two to three people, and the students are encouraged to discuss the question carefully before they agree on an answer. All this means that it should be expected that the *Syllog* score is less during the exam period, mainly because of using less time for each response and not being able to discuss the response with a group. The results are shown in Table 3.

Table 3. Summarising the counts from the 2020 course of how well the students in groups and individually scored using *Syllog* in the training period and in the exam period after the lectures.

Syllog	Score Mean (SD)	Time Mean (SD), [sec]
Training ($N = 103$ groups)	0.73 (0.20)	36.8 (28.8)
Exam ($N = 288$ individual sessions)	0.62 (0.19)	17.8 (23.8)
P-value (Effect size)	$<10^{-6}$ (0.56)	–

These results show that the students tended to speed up their interaction with *Syllog* when left alone with the system. The results also show that the *Syllog* score is significantly higher when more time is used to consider the responses and when the responses can be discussed with a group. The individual sessions displayed a strongly significant negative effect of medium size (effect size = 0.56). However, when restricting the mean response time per exercise for the exam sample to be more than 10 s, the score raised to 0.72 (SD = 0.20). Apparently, several students used the program quite hastily and with mistakes.

When it comes to *Proplog*, the situation is different. The results in Table 4 show that the students do not speed up their interaction with *Proplog* when left alone with the system. The results also show that the *Proplog* score is not very diverse compared with the responses that coming from a group. The individual sessions show a significant negative effect of small size (effect size = 0.28).

This indicates a difference in familiarity with the two systems. The students probably felt that they knew *Syllog* better and could use it much easier than *Proplog*. For this reason, they were ready to move faster on the *Syllog* tests when left alone during the individual exam period. Because propositional logic and the *Proplog* tool remained rather unfamiliar to the students, something similar did not happen in this case. This is at least a possible explanation of the difference between the results in Tables 3 and 4.

In the analysis of the propositional arguments, many students have apparently not obtained a clear understanding of how propositional validity and invalidity can be demonstrated. It seems that there is a need for an even stronger emphasis on the analysis of arguments in terms of truth values and semantical trees.

Table 4. Summarising counts from the 2020 course of how well the students in groups and individually scored using *Proplog* in the training period and in the exam period after the lectures.

Proplog	Score Mean (SD)	Time Mean (SD), [sec]
Training (N = 155 groups)	0.65 (0.17)	35.9 (24.3)
Exam (N = 195 individual sessions)	0.60 (0.19)	34.9 (29.1)
P-value (Effect size)	0.015 (0.28)	–

5 Conclusion

It is evident that the two e-learning tools *Syllog* and *Proplog* can be useful for the students during their course in basic logic. The use of the tools can make logic learning much more joyful, and the game-like properties of the systems can stimulate their exploration of the logical structures significantly. Furthermore, the use of *Syllog* and *Proplog* can support teamwork and groupwork in logic learning because they can stimulate cooperation and discussion in the joint exploration of logical structures and problems. It may, in fact, be possible to develop the material further to establish a proper online course in logic and argumentation. For this purpose, we may consider further developments of the tools. One obvious option could be an automatic and online calculation of the score during a session.

It is very welcome that *Syllog* and *Proplog* offer quantitative feedback on the effect of their teaching in terms of the log data. As we have seen, these data can be very helpful when we want to improve our logic course. In fact, an interesting learning analytics can be based on log data. It seems that we in this way can obtain a very detailed account of how much formal logic the students have actually learned during the course. This makes it rather obvious how we can improve our course in basic logic. In the present case, there is no doubt that there should be a stronger emphasis on propositional logic in the next version of the course. In particular, the course should include a better and more precise introduction to the evaluation of propositional arguments with respect to validity.

The results of the present study show that the students handle the *Syllog* test significantly better than the *Proplog* test. It is tempting to conclude that students' performance in logic tests depends on the type of formalism. Maybe the majority of students will simply handle syllogistic logic better than propositional logic. However, it is important to be careful here. In principle, the relation between the *Syllog* and *Proplog* performances may alternatively depend on order in which the topics have been presented during the course. For this reason, it should be investigated whether a new organisation of the topics in the course would provide different learning conditions for the students. Right now, the two topics within basic symbolic logic—syllogistics and propositional logic—are presented at the beginning of the course. Syllogistics is presented first mainly for historical reasons, given that syllogistics goes back to Aristotle, whereas the first propositional logic was formulated by the generation of logicians succeeding Aristotle. For systematic reasons, however, the opposite order might be more natural. In addition, it might be attractive to have more informal material presented between the introductions of the two formal topics. It might be attractive to design and run a new experiment in order to investigate whether another organisation and order to the topics in itself could enable the students to handle the two kinds of symbolic logic in a better manner.

References

1. Aristotle: Prior analytics, Translated by A.J. Jenkinson. The Internet Classics Archive, http://classics.mit.edu/Aristotle/prior.html. Accessed 16 Sep 2020
2. Øhrstrøm, P., Ploug, T., Jakobsen, D.: Logisk set, 2nd edn. Metaphysica, Aalborg (2020)
3. Kabbaj, A., Janta-Polczynski, M.: From PROLOG++ to PROLOG+CG: a CG object-oriented logic programming language. In: Ganter, B., Mineau, Guy W. (eds.) ICCS-ConceptStruct 2000. LNCS (LNAI), vol. 1867, pp. 540–554. Springer, Heidelberg (2000). https://doi.org/10.1007/10722280_37
4. Kabbaj, A., Moulin, B., Gancef, J., Nadeau, D., Rouleau, O.: Uses, improvements, and extensions of Prolog+ CG: case studies. In: Delugach, H.S., Stumme, G. (eds.) ICCS-ConceptStruct 2001. LNCS (LNAI), vol. 2120, pp. 346–359. Springer, Heidelberg (2001). https://doi.org/10.1007/3-540-44583-8_25
5. Sandborg-Petersen, U., Øhrstrøm, P., Ploug, T., Thorvaldsen, S.: Syllog. https://syllog.emergence.dk. Accessed 16 Sep 2020

6. Øhrstrøm, P., Sandborg-Petersen, U., Thorvaldsen, S., Ploug, T.: Classical syllogisms in logic teaching. In: Pfeiffer, Heather D., Ignatov, Dmitry I., Poelmans, J., Gadiraju, N. (eds.) ICCS-ConceptStruct 2013. LNCS (LNAI), vol. 7735, pp. 31–43. Springer, Heidelberg (2013). https://doi.org/10.1007/978-3-642-35786-2_4
7. Øhrstrøm, P., Sandborg-Petersen, U., Thorvaldsen, S., Ploug, T.: Teaching logic through web-based and gamified quizzing of formal arguments. In: Hernández-Leo, D., Ley, T., Klamma, R., Harrer, A. (eds.) Scaling up Learning for Sustained Impact, EC-TEL 2013. LNCS, vol. 8095, pp. 410–423. Springer, Heidelberg (2013). https://doi.org/10.1007/978-3-642-40814-4_32
8. Parry, W., Hacker, E.: Aristotelian Logic. State University of New York Press, Albany (1991)
9. Sandborg-Petersen, U., Øhrstrøm, P., Ploug, T., Thorvaldsen, S.: Proplog. https://proplog.emergence.dk. Accessed 16 Sep 2020
10. King, B.M., Rosopa, P.J., Minium, E.W.: Statistical Reasoning in the Behavioral Sciences, 6th edn. John Wiley & Sons Inc., Hoboken (2011)
11. Øhrstrøm, P., Thorvaldsen, S., Sandborg-Petersen, U., Ploug, T.: Teaching propositional and syllogistic logic using E-learning tools. In: Rønningsbakk, L., Wu, T.-T., Sandnes, F.E., Huang, Y.-M. (eds.) ICITL 2019. LNCS, vol. 11937, pp. 854–864. Springer, Cham (2019). https://doi.org/10.1007/978-3-030-35343-8_89

Towards a Knowledge Conversion Platform to Support Information Systems Analysis and Design Industry Ready Graduates

Marie Hattingh(✉) and Lizette Weilbach

University of Pretoria, Private Bag X20, Hatfield, Pretoria 0028, South Africa
marie.hattingh@up.ac.za

Abstract. The dynamic field of Information Systems Design (ISD) presents several challenges to educators at Higher Education Institutions (HEIs) when being tasked to provide "industry-ready" graduates. An added challenge is the lack of instructional material that not only provides the theoretical content, but also includes appropriate applicable examples and an environment where "lessons learnt" can be integrated into the instructional content. This paper reports on a study undertaken by the authors to develop a web-based knowledge conversion platform that will allow ISD educators to provide theoretical content, case study examples and lessons learnt by lecturers and students from previous years, which could assist current students' understanding of this dynamic environment. The paper presents the BA bot: a chatbot integrated with Google Drive which provides a knowledge conversion platform for students and lecturers. The authors map the BA bot to the knowledge conversion platform to illustrate how knowledge conversion takes place, from the lowest level (data) to the highest level (capability). The paper concludes with a reflection and a summary of future work to be undertaken in order to extend the capabilities of the BA bot.

Keywords: Knowledge conversion model · Chatbot · Technology platform · ISD industry ready graduates

1 Introduction

The field of Information Systems Design (ISD) is dynamic [1, 2] and ISD educators need to ensure that ISD graduates have the capability to meet the needs of industry. A number of researchers have reported on the challenges of ISD education, for example: Tepper [3] reported on the importance of analytical and inter-personal skills for ISD graduates. Saulnier [4] emphasized the need for ISD graduates to have both soft skills and hard skills. Furthermore, Pretorius and Hattingh [5] reported on the contextual environment which influences student performance whilst completing their ISD course modules. These challenges are compounded by the need for good instructional content that will give the students the "real-life" exposure required to be "industry-ready".

The authors are respectively the second year and third year ISD module coordinators at their institution. The way in which their modules are aligned, allows students gradual exposure to ISD concepts until they have to complete their capstone project (for a real-life client) in their final year. Their main challenge is to optimize the transition between the first and second year; the second and third year; and finally completing the third year, while there is no "textbook" that provides an all-encompassing theory explanation with appropriate examples, supported by add-on lessons learnt throughout the years (by both the students and the lecturers). Finding a suitable and all-encompassing textbook to prepare "industry-ready" graduates is problematic.

One way to address this challenge is to create an online platform where the knowledge from lecturers, current and former students can be shared with students preparing for, and those currently busy with, the capstone project. In this context, ISD knowledge refers to the soft- and technical skills of a lecturer facilitating the project implementation, as well as the soft- and technical abilities of a student who needs to operate in a group to deliver such a project. Researchers distinguish between tacit/explicit and implicit knowledge [6] and [7]. Tacit/explicit knowledge refers to knowledge that is contained in books, databases and manuals [6]. It is proposed that the platform includes explicit knowledge for ease of reference in a summarized (abbreviated) form. Implicit knowledge is knowledge contained in organizational practices, which is not necessary documented [5]. Capturing the implicit knowledge of both the lecturers (based on their years of experience in facilitating the capstone project) and that of the students who completed the project is invaluable to students preparing for, and those that are currently completing the capstone project. To this extent, the research question answered by this paper is:

To what extent can an Education Chatbot be developed as a knowledge conversion platform for industry ready ISD students?

In order to answer this question, the authors provide an overview of the knowledge conversion model in Sect. 2, followed by a brief discussion on the use of chatbots in education in Sect. 3. Section 4 provides a summary of the case for which the knowledge conversion platform was developed. Section 5 details the methodology followed and Sect. 6 presents the mapping of the chatbot platform to the knowledge conversion model. The paper concludes in Sect. 7 with a reflection on the applicability of the platform for ISD educators and explanations of future research in Sect. 8.

2 The Knowledge Conversion Model

The knowledge conversion model used as basis to develop the knowledge conversion platform presented in this paper was proposed by Smuts and Hattingh [1] and needs further explanation (see Fig. 1). In their model Smuts and Hattingh describe the four learning process steps of turning data into information; information into knowledge; knowledge into capability; and capability back into knowledge. These steps are important for learning to take place and should be considered from a bottom up approach when developing a platform to cater for knowledge conversion. Smuts and Hattingh link each of the steps to the level of understanding required for the step to take place and they describe the knowledge conversion process which is linked to each step. Furthermore, their model proposes examples of educational program enablers to assist with each of the steps.

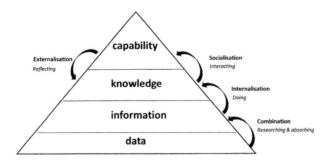

Fig. 1. Knowledge conversion model [1].

Data is found on the lowest level of the model and represents the learning of concepts or facts without context which need to be remembered so that students can recall it when needed. The process of converting data into information is called "combination" and the level of understanding required for this process to take place is described as researching and absorbing. The mechanisms proposed to be used as enablers on this level in Higher Education Institutions (HEI) are email, online message forums, gazettes, lecture notes, textbooks, book marking, learning based on repetition and reading.

The second layer of the knowledge conversion model is information. For data to be converted into information, it has to have added relevance and purpose to make it more usable. This knowledge conversion process is called "internalization" and the required level of understanding needed is described as doing. The mechanisms proposed to be used as enablers on this level in HEIs are lectures, workshops, tutorials, group work, simulations, experiments, virtual reality, e-learning, context-steered learning, blogs, 'fishbowls' and debates.

The knowledge layer is the third layer of the model. On this layer a number of different sources of information merges to form conceptual frameworks that provide perspective. Knowledge is gained through experience and insights and includes the holder's beliefs and expectations. Having knowledge means that you will be able to apply what you understand and have learnt in a new situation.

The fourth layer of the model is capability. Having capability means that you are able to apply your knowledge to solve problems and that you are able to build new meaning from different fundamentals while making use of your own judgement and evaluation capabilities. The knowledge conversion process when moving from knowledge to capability is called "socialization" and the required level of understanding needed, is interacting. The mechanisms proposed to be used on this level in HEIs are social activities, industrial training, apprenticeship, hands-on experience, design labs and incubation centers.

The knowledge conversion process called "externalization" takes place when capability is transformed back into knowledge. This process requires a reflecting level of understanding and entails the articulation of tacit knowledge by transforming capabilities into a graspable or understandable form. It is only when tacit knowledge is made explicit and clear that it could be shared with others and turned back into knowledge. The mechanisms proposed to be used as enablers on this level in HEIs are orals, tests, examination, assignments, peer presentations, tutoring, industry projects, co-operative research, community collaboration, academic spin-offs, mentoring, imitation, observation and practice.

3 The Use of Chatbots in Formal Education

Shawar and Atwell (in: Molnár and Szüts [8]) define chatbots as chat software or computer programs which are supported by artificial intelligence. The functionalities of these bots range from answering simple elementary questions, to acting as fully-fledged participants in complex conversations. Chatbots can take part in both text-based and voice dialogues and can typically provide answers to questions posed by different users. According to Britz [9] chatbots, also known at conversational agents or dialogue systems, are currently a hot topic and well-known companies such as Microsoft, Facebook (M), Apple (Siri), Google, WeChat, and Slack are making big bets on them.

Chatbots range from simple bots that can only handle basic messages and requests to more complex bots that are able to participate in more complex dialogues by being programmed to learn from their previous conversations [9]. A taxonomy of chatbots differentiates between retrieval-based and generative models [8].

Retrieval-based chatbots use repositories and heuristic imitation of human memory to answer questions. This is done by simple pairing, while more complex questions are answered through the incorporation of machine language. Decision tree structures are created which are used to direct users to pre-determined conversations.

Generative models on the other hand are smarter and they might mislead you into thinking that you are talking to a real human. They imitate a human conversation and are not 'taught' to provide predetermined human answers. They rely on machine-based translation and generate the responses they provide from scratch. One disadvantage of these type of chatbots are that they might make some grammatical errors in their responses and training them is a lot more time consuming as they require quite a lot of training data to perform well.

According to Cunningham-Nelson et al. [10] chatbots could be used to improve student interaction as they are able to provide standardized information to hundreds of students in a prompt way. This information can include assessment criteria, assessment due dates, and the location of suggested resources. In doing so they can reduce the administrative burden of lecturers and increase the support offered to students. Lecturers could consequently have more time at hand to do course development and needed research. The current methods to engage with students, which include email and face-to-face conversations, lack prompt and personalized communication at more suitable times.

Another common use for chatbots in education is to provide answers on common questions [10]. Answering FAQs on behalf of the lecturer could mean that the bot is available 24/7 and able to answer students' questions in a timeous way. The knowledge base of multiple FAQ could also be kept for several years and could easily be transferred between lecturers who might be presenting the same subject. The chatbot also offers the potential to identify problematic communication between the lecturer and the learners should many students ask the same question.

Chatbots could also play a significant role in answering online short response questions [10]. The advantage offered by this is that the bot could confirm the wording or understanding of a student and if misconceptions are discovered, the student could be directed to the sources relevant for clarifying the misconception. The statistics of the feedback provided could furthermore also highlight the areas that most students struggle with.

4 The Case for Which the Knowledge Conversion Platform Was Developed

In a second year ISD module students are expected to follow a structured systems development methodology to analyze and design an end-to-end software solution for a given mini business case. Students choose their own teams of five members each and are given a detailed case study. They are then required to complete four project deliverables which include: (1) a software solution proposal (i.e. a written-up business case with a complete set of functional (use cases) and non-functional requirements); (2) a functional specification (i.e. a detailed logical analysis including logical models that represent the various functional requirements (use cases) and the data needed to fulfill the requirements as set out in the solution proposal – in doing this they could either follow the structured analysis or the object oriented route (UML models)); (3) a technical specification (i.e. a detailed technical design including technical models that add the technology required to implement the different functional requirements); and (4) a complete prototype (i.e. detailed screen designs for each requirement).

When students reach their third and final year, they again get exposed to the complete development of an end-to-end software solution, but this time around they don't get given a written-up mini business case as in their second year. They now have to find their own real-life client for which they can develop a solution and use the knowledge gained from their second year, to write up the business case themselves.

By completing the mini case in their second year and the real-life project in their third year, students are inter alia exposed to data and facts on the following topics: (1) Information Systems Development methodologies; (2) Problem Solving Techniques; (3) Project Management aspects; (4) Project Management tools (MS Project and ASANA), (5) Process Modelling (logical and technical); (6) Relational Database Modelling (logical and technical); (7) Object Oriented modeling (UML); (8) Modelling tools (Systems Architect and PowerDesigner); (9) Interface design; and (10) Output design.

5 The Research Methodology Used

In order to design and develop the knowledge conversion platform to support the learning of ISD industry ready students, the authors followed a design-based research approach [11]. According to van den Akker [12] this approach is also known as design research, development research or design experiments. It can be defined as a: "systematic but flexible methodology aimed to improve educational practices through iterative analysis, design, development, and implementation, based on collaboration among researchers and practitioners in real-world settings, and leading to contextually-sensitive design principles and theories" [13] (p. 6). This approach typically consists of four cycles which include [14]: (1) Analysis of practical problems by researchers and practitioners in collaboration; (2) Development of solutions informed by existing design principles and technological innovations; (3) Iterative cycles of testing and refinement of solutions in practice; and (4) Reflection to produce design principles and enhance solution implementation.

During the first phase of the research, the practical problem of representing the required content on ISD to both second and third year students were investigated. Furthermore, the problem of third year students not having a platform on which they could share their tacit knowledge, knowhow, tips, and lessons learnt, with forthcoming third year students, were analyzed. In the same way, the problem of finding a way in which the tacit knowledge and knowhow of the third year lecturer could be captured to assist newly assigned lecturers in facilitating the third year projects and in preparing the second year students for their final year, were also analyzed and discussed.

In the second phase of the research, the knowledge conversion model, as proposed by Smuts and Hattingh [1], as well as the characteristics and possibilities offered by chatbots to assist with formal education, were studied and used to inform the design and structure of the knowledge conversion platform proposed in this paper.

In anticipation of formal testing, a feedback link has been included in the chatbot connected to a Google Form to allow students to provide feedback. The intention is to use this feedback to adjust, enhance and refine the proposed platform, after which the researchers will aim at reflecting on the platform in an attempt to come up with the design principles of a typical knowledge conversion platform to support ISD learning on undergraduate level.

6 The Proposed Knowledge Conversion Platform

The first iteration of the knowledge conversion platform was developed as a web-based chat bot using free online Chabot software - Snatchbot.me. As the bot provides a platform to share content on ISD topics, it was named the Business Analysis bot, or in short, the BA bot. The following sections will discuss the structure of the BA Bot and the tools used to support the structure of the BA Bot.

Towards a Knowledge Conversion Platform 627

6.1 The Structure of the Platform

On determining the content of the platform, it became evident that the bot had to contain both tacit and explicit knowledge to produce industry-ready students. Figure 2 represents how the BA Bot was structured. Each topic included a theoretical overview of the most important concepts of that topic, with additional examples and case studies (from past tests, examinations and assignments) which allow students to practice the concepts in different scenarios, Frequently Asked Questions (FAQs)/Common mistakes, and videos and notes explaining how to execute the modelling concepts within the modelling tool.

The current structure of the bot is represented in Fig. 2 below.

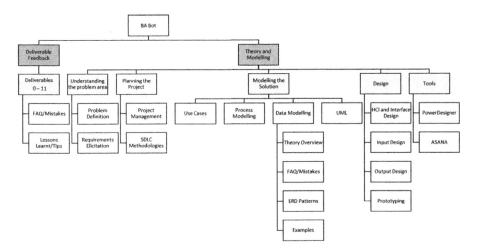

Fig. 2. The current structure of the BA bot.

Finding a textbook which ticks all the necessary boxes on the content required by the second and third year curriculums, is a tedious and almost impossible task, especially when one considers the extent to which the IT industry evolves and changes. Extending the bot to include changes or new topics is easy and much less cumbersome. For each of the topics presented in Sect. 5, the bot provides content which can be related to all four levels of the knowledge conversion model as presented by Smuts and Hattingh and as presented in Fig. 3 [1]:

6.1.1 Converting Data into Information

On the data level the platform presents discreet building blocks in the format of theoretical overviews, and FAQs, populated by the second and third year lecturers and assistant lecturers. Students have to move upwards through the levels of the knowledge conversion model to use the data or facts they learnt in their first and second years, to combined it with relevance and purpose, and to consequently turn it into information. Figure 3 below is a snapshot of theoretical concepts covered in the BA Bot.

All the principles for logical data modelling (entities, relationships, keys and attributes) also apply to technical data modelling. The only difference is that a technical data model expands on details that are not shown on a logical data model.

Jul 20, 2020, 4:12:13 PM

To create a technical data model, start with the logical model. Then, the following is added:
- Referential integrity on relationships
- Data type for each attribute

Jul 20, 2020, 4:12:13 PM

An important role of a technical data model is to **ensure data integrity.** This can be done in the following ways:
- Key integrity: every entity must have a unique primary key for each record.
- Domain integrity: no field in an entity should be able to have a value outside the domain range.
- Referential integrity: relationships between tables are established via foreign keys. A referential integrity error indicates that a foreign key value in one entity does not have a matching primary key value in the related table.

You can reference Whitten & Bentley (2007) page 535-537 for more information.

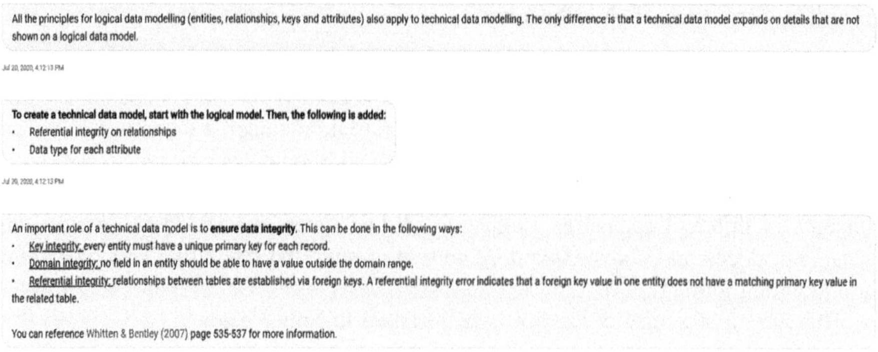

Fig. 3. Applying the knowledge conversion model to the knowledge conversion platform.

Figure 4 presents a snapshot from the Google Doc for Logical data modelling FAQ and common mistakes.

Please do not request edit access to this document. The document can be downloaded by navigating to File > Download As > PDF Document.

Logical Data Modelling (ERDs)

Frequently asked questions

How do I identify relationships?
- Always ask the question *"How many instances of one entity (Entity X) can be related to one instance of the other entity (Entity Y)?"* Ask the question for both entities in the relationship (swap X and Y).
- **Example 1: Order and customer**
  - **1** customer can have **many** orders over time.
  - **1** order can belong to **only 1** customer over time.
- **Example 2: Product and order**
  - **1** product can form part of **1 or many** orders.
  - **1** order can contain **1 or many** products.
  - This is a **many-to-many relationship** and should be resolved with an associative entity in-between product and order. In this example, it could be called OrderProduct.

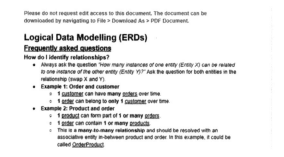

Fig. 4. Applying the knowledge conversion model to the knowledge conversion platform.

6.1.2 Converting Information into Knowledge

Internalization happens by doing. As experience and insight are needed to turn information into knowledge, students on the second-year level tend to struggle with applying their knowledge to the context of the given case studies. The platform presents integrated examples, case studies and "know how" videos which could assist them in this regard (Fig. 5).

Additionally, lecturers developed integrated notes that integrate the Commerce subject content within the ISD environment. Figure 6 provides an excerpt where lecturer notes within Google Docs explain how the VAT component needs to be integrated within an IS.

6.1.3 Converting Knowledge into Capability and Capability into Knowledge

These two processes happen firstly through socialization and then through externalization. For the former, students get to turn their knowledge into capabilities to solve

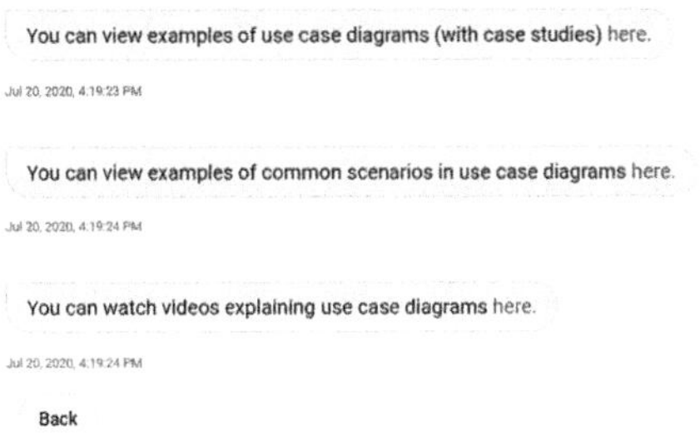

Fig. 5. Options in the BA Bot to learn from contextualized case studies.

Point of Sale / Point of Service / Point of Purchase System

Retail transactions (buying/selling products and services) are typically called Point Of Sale **or** Point Of Service (POS) **or** Point Of Purchase (POP) systems. When a customer buys a product or service, the **merchant** has to produce an **invoice** which shows the following:

- the **order number** and **date** of transaction {each invoice needs to have an **unique consecutive number** and no number may be skipped for auditing purposes}
- for customers that have an **account** with the merchant, their **personal details** such as name, surname, telephone number and address details (for cash sales the customer's details are not required)

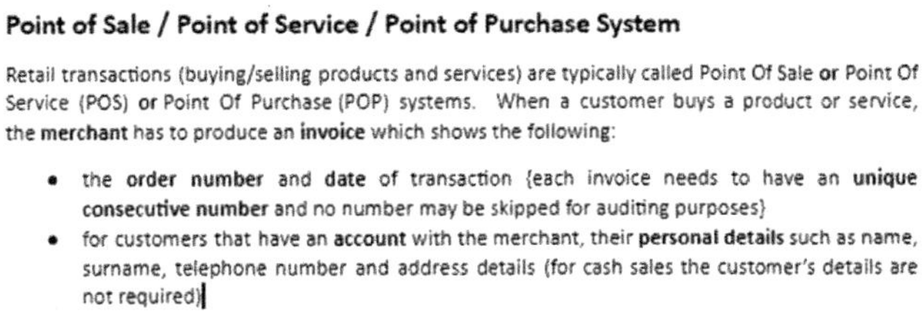

Fig. 6. Integrating commerce knowledge within the ISD environment.

real world problems when they attempt the capstone project in their third year. For the latter, students and lecturers can capture their learnt lessons and knowhow using Google Forms. In this way they can provide feedback and add to the content of the bot. In the same way third year students can share their tips, knowhow and lessons learnt with the bot, making it available and accessible to second (and future third year) students. Figure 7 shows a screenshot of the Google Form used for feedback that is accessible through the BA Bot.

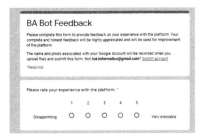

Fig. 7. BA bot feedback form.

6.2 The Tools Utilized in Conjunction with the Platform

The tools associated with creating the BA Bot environment in which knowledge conversion takes place, is free, which makes it an attractive approach for HEIs. The following tools were used: (1) Snatchbot.me used for the bot environment; (2) Google

Drive which provides flexibility in updating content; (3) Google Forms used for student feedback; (4) Google Docs used for FAQs, summary feedback on assignments/tutorial and lessons learnt. This dynamic environment makes it very easy for lectures to add to their content, as opposed to only having a static textbook with set case studies; and (5) A YouTube video channel used to post recordings of practical lessons and tutorials using the document camera, as well as student recordings (to instigate a learning community/culture).

7 Conclusion

The proof of concept of the knowledge conversion platform proposed in this paper was implemented as a Chabot, better known as the BA bot. The aim of the bot was to develop a platform that could support knowledge conversion between the different levels of the knowledge conversion model as presented by Smuts and Hattingh [1], in an attempt to support industry-ready ISD graduates. Finding an appropriate textbook that stays up to date and covers all aspects as required by the IS curriculum is a tedious and almost impossible task. The flexibility and adjustability of the BA bot provides for the timeous and constant adjustment of its content. The bot therefore contains the necessary discreet building blocks and theoretical overviews required by ISD students and students can turn these facts into information by combining it with relevance and purpose, but the biggest advantage of the bot is that it provides a platform on which students and lecturers could share their tacit knowledge in the form of lessons learnt, knowhow and best practices. This provides for the externalization of ISD knowledge and offers a way in which both the tacit an explicit knowledge apparent in the second and third year ISD modules could be cultivated and preserved for the future.

8 Future Work

For future work we intend to enhance the current bot by integrating it with Slack – a collaboration platform. The success of the bot will be measured through experimental research to determine the continuous intention of second year ISD students to use the platform for their capstone project.

Acknowledgement. Publication funded by NRF UID/127494.

References

1. Smuts, H., Hattingh, M.J.: Towards a knowledge conversion model enabling programme design in higher education for shaping industry-ready graduates. In: Kabanda, S., Suleman, H., Gruner, S. (eds.) SACLA 2018. CCIS, vol. 963, pp. 124–139. Springer, Cham (2019). https://doi.org/10.1007/978-3-030-05813-5_9
2. Abdullah, S., Fatima, S.: Improving teaching methodology in system analysis and design using problem based learning for ABET. Int. J. Mod. Educ. Comput. Sci. **5**, 60–68 (2013)

3. Tepper, J.: Assessment for learning Systems Analysis and Design using constructivist techniques. In: STEM Annual Conference (2014)
4. Saulnier, B.M.: Towards a 21st century information systems education. High impact practices and essential learning outcomes. Issues Inf. Syst. **17**, 168–177 (2016)
5. Pretorius, H.W., Hattingh, M.J.: Factors influencing poor performance in systems analysis and design: student reflections. In: Liebenberg, J., Gruner, S. (eds.) SACLA 2017. CCIS, vol. 730, pp. 251–264. Springer, Cham (2017). https://doi.org/10.1007/978-3-319-69670-6_18
6. Howells, J.: Tacit knowledge. Technol. Anal. Strateg. Manag. **8**, 91–106 (1996)
7. Polanyi, M.: II.—knowing and being. Mind **LXX**, 458–470 (1961)
8. Molnár, G., Szüts, Z.: The role of chatbots in formal education. In: 2018 IEEE 16th International Symposium on Intelligent Systems and Informatics (SISY), pp. 000197–000202 (2018)
9. Deep Learning for Chatbots. Part 1. WILDML. Artificial Intelligence, Deep Learning, and NLP. http://www.wildml.com/2016/04/deep-learning-for-chatbots-part-1-introduction/. Accessed 08 Mar 2020
10. Cunningham-Nelson, S., Boles, W., Trouton, L., Margerison, E.: A review of chatbots in education: practical steps forward. In: Proceedings of the AAEE 2019 Conference, Brisbane, Australia (2019)
11. Sandoval, W.A., Bell, P.: Design-based research methods for studying learning in context: introduction. Educ. Psychol. **39**, 199–201 (2004)
12. Van den Akker, J.: Principles and methods of development research. In: van den Akker, J., Gravemeijer, K., McKenney, S., Nieveen, N. (eds.) Educational Design Research. Routledge, Abingdon, Oxon (2006)
13. Wang, F., Hannafin, M.J.: Design-based research and technology-enhanced learning environments. Education Tech. Research Dev. **53**, 5–23 (2005). https://doi.org/10.1007/BF02504682
14. Reeves, T.C.: Design research from a technology perspective. In: van den Akker, J., Gravemeijer, K., McKenney, S., Nieveen, N. (eds.) Design Methodology and Developmental Research in Education and Training. Kluwer, Deventer (2006)

Author Index

Asmara, Andik 59
Attane, Poramin 361

Bardone, Emanuele 349
Barroso, João 409
Black, Emily 514

Chaijaroen, Nat 475
Chaijaroen, Sumalee 189, 328, 385, 391, 399, 442, 475, 483, 591
Chang, Chi-Cheng 567
Chang, Jen-Chia 172, 182
Chang, Kuang-Ling 182
Chang, Li-Yun 289
Chang, Pei-Yu 100
Chang, Rong-Chi 137
Chang, Yu-mei 109
Chao, Wen-Hung 137
Chen, Chia-Chen 33
Chen, Dyi-Cheng 172
Chen, Hong-Ren 33
Chen, Judy F. 167, 453
Chen, Su-Chang 172
Chen, Ying Ling 128
Chen, You-Ren 263
Cheng, Shu-Chen 227
Cheng, Wai Khuen 40
Cheng, Yuh-Ming 84
Cheng, Yu-Ping 227
Chiang, I. Robert 227
Chien, Pei-ling 77
Chien, Yu-Cheng 100
Chou, Pao-Nan 71
Chung, Chih-Chao 84

Dai, Zhicheng 317
de H. Basoeki, Olivia 23
Della Ventura, Michele 598

Fayziev, Mirzaali 576
Figliolia, Amanda Coelho 557
Fodor, Szabina 147
Frangou, Satu-Maarit 582

Gao, Yu-Chen 172
Guo, Jia-Yue 172

Haider, Imran 536
Halubitskaya, Yuliya 576
Hattingh, M. J. 504
Hattingh, Marie 514, 621
Hooshyar, Danial 349
Hsiao, Hsi-Chi 172
Hsu, Jane Lu 263
Huang, Chih-Wei 33
Huang, Tai-Yi 100
Huang, Tien-Chi 77
Huang, Yu-Che 93
Huang, Yueh-Min 13, 23, 100, 227, 268
Huang, Yueh-Ming 93

Jackpeng, Sarawut 475
Jakobsen, David 610
Javed, Fahad 536
Junruang, Chinnaphat 219

Kanjug, Issara 219, 338, 361, 493, 591
Kiyani, Midhat Noor 536
Komany, Kan 189
Körkkö, Minna 582
Kwan, Christopher Chung Lim 196

Lai, ChinLun 109
Lai, Hui-Min 77
le Roux, Petra 373
Lee, Hsin-Yu 100
Lee, Tony Szu-Hsien 289
Li, Shuijing 296
Li, Zhe 296, 419
Lin, Chen-Yu 40
Lin, Jim-Min 40
Lisboa, Isolda 409
Liu, Feng 317
Liu, Shiang-Yao 289
Lou, Shi-Jer 84
Lu, Yi-Chen 50

Maneeratana, Autsanee Seenonlee 391
Mawas, Nour El 349
Medola, Fausto Orsi 557
Mîndruț, Bogdan M. 119
Murti, Astrid Tiara 13

Øhrstrøm, Peter 610
Oprea, Claudiu A. 119

Pilkington, Colin 306
Pimdee, Paitoon 158
Pimsook, Pitchaya 483
Ploug, Thomas 610
Puratep, Pasatorn 385

Rocha, Tânia 409
Rønningsbakk, Lisbet 547

Saengrith, Waristha 158
Samat, Charuni 338, 465, 493, 591
Sandborg-Petersen, Ulrik 610
Sandnes, Frode Eika 206, 557
Sari, Noviati Aning Rizki Mustika 3
Sathanarugsawait, Benjaporn 465
Shadiev, Narzikul 576
Shadiev, Rustam 576
Shen, Wei-Wei 40
Shih, Hsiao-Fang 182
Shih, Ru-Chu 71
Singkaew, Chan 399
Sirimathep, Kanyarat 493
Smith, C. 504
Smuts, Corlia 428
Smuts, Hanlie 428
Stanworth, James O. 524
Starcic, Andreja Istenic 93
Steynberg, Johanna 306
Su, Yi-Lun 33
Szabó, Ildikó 147

Tang, Jih-Hsin 245
Ternai, Katalin 147
Thammabut, Thawach 328
Thorvaldsen, Steinar 255, 610
Tsai, Ming-Hsiu Michelle 40
Tung, Chun-Chun 84

van Biljon, Judy 306
van Staden, Corné 373
Viriyavejakul, Chantana 158

Wang, Hei Chia 367
Wang, Mengting 317
Wang, Yi-Jin 77
Wannapipat, Wanwisa 442
Warden, Clyde A. 167, 453
Wattanachai, Suchat 328, 338, 465, 493
Wei, Chih-Fen 245
Wei, Yin-Ling 289
Weilbach, Lizette 621
Wen, Kuo-Cheng 172
Wonganu, Piyaporn 591
Wongchiranuwat, Sathaporn 338
Wu, Chih-Hung 268
Wu, Ting-Ting 3, 13, 23, 50, 59

Yan, Ming 296, 419
Yang, Fu-Rung 245
Yang, Yeongwook 349
Yen, Wan-Hsuan 567
Yordanova, Zornitsa 236, 277
Yu, Sen-Chi 33
Yuan, Huimin 419

Zhang, Xin 296
Zhao, Ya Lan 367